ENGLISH
MADRIGAL VERSE
1588-1632

E. H. FELLOWES

ENGLISH
MADRIGAL VERSE
1588–1632

Revised and Enlarged by

FREDERICK W. STERNFELD

and

DAVID GREER

THIRD EDITION

OXFORD
AT THE CLARENDON PRESS
1967

Oxford University Press, Ely House, London W. 1

GLASGOW NEW YORK TORONTO MELBOURNE WELLINGTON
CAPE TOWN SALISBURY IBADAN NAIROBI LUSAKA ADDIS ABABA
BOMBAY CALCUTTA MADRAS KARACHI LAHORE DACCA
KUALA LUMPUR HONG KONG TOKYO

FIRST EDITION 1920
SECOND EDITION 1929
THIRD EDITION 1967

PRINTED IN GREAT BRITAIN

FOREWORD TO THIRD EDITION

SOME ten years ago editors of Sidney, Shakespeare, and other Elizabethan and Jacobean authors were discussing the possibility of a new edition of *English Madrigal Verse* to facilitate brief, yet effective, cross-references. I took this question up with the Clarendon Press, pointing out the desirability of summarizing the research on these matters since 1929, enlarging the scope of the Collection, and combining footnotes and indexes at the end of the volume. The Press readily agreed to these suggestions and invited me to be the editor, with the consent of the estate of the late E. H. Fellowes.

Commitments which had been previously entered into unfortunately prevented me from attending to this important task with the single devotion it deserved, and I was gratified when, in 1960, David Greer, one of my pupils, embarked on a study of Poetry and Music in the English Lute Song. I suggested to him that he should become my co-editor. The quality of Mr. Greer's work, and the dispatch with which he carried it out, were such that I soon retired from active editorship, and passed on to him the notes and material I had so far collected. As a result, the work now completed might more accurately be termed his, and my role characterized as that of an instigator and supervisor. For various reasons, however, it seemed best to call this third edition a joint effort. For one thing, Mr. Greer and I have collaborated before and may well do so again, and the precise delimitation of this team-work between two persons who have been teacher and pupil and become colleagues is always difficult to determine. Moreover, it seems only just that I should shoulder any criticism, both of the general plan and of individual shortcomings. But to make quite clear that the credit for the painstaking work contained in the bulk of this edition belongs to my collaborator, I am signing this foreword singly.

Finally, it is my pleasant duty to acknowledge the kindness of several persons who have assisted the work. The Delegates of the Clarendon Press agreed to an expansion of the second edition, which has, alas, increased the bulk considerably. The compilation of the index, and countless editorial and clerical chores, have been graciously shouldered by Mrs. Greer, whose skill in administering the quaint hybrid of domestic and academic responsibilities has been a pleasure to witness.

F. W. STERNFELD

Faculty of Music
University of Oxford
February 1966

PREFACE TO THIRD EDITION

THIS new, revised, and enlarged edition of *English Madrigal Verse* contains the poetic texts of most of the madrigal collections and song-books printed in England between 1588 and 1632. It is in two parts, Part I containing poems set as madrigals and Part II those set as lute songs. In each part the various collections are arranged in the alphabetical order of the composers' or compilers' names, and, within this arrangement, in chronological order of publication.

From the outset the title of the book was a little misleading since about half of it comprises verse set to music by the composers of lute songs. Moreover, the application of the term 'madrigal' to some of the items in Part I, such as the compositions in Ravenscroft's *A Briefe Discovrse*, was questionable, as Dr. Fellowes was aware. Since the book's first appearance in 1920 further research has given us a much clearer insight into the nature of the true madrigal, and in the light of this it must be accepted that to class many of the part-songs of such composers as Alison, Byrd, Peerson, and Mundy (not to mention Ravenscroft) as 'madrigals' is strictly inaccurate; the work of these men was hardly touched by the spirit of the real Italianate madrigal. But although Dr. Fellowes's use of the term 'madrigal' was more comprehensive than would normally be acceptable today, the division of the book into two parts is a convenient one, so long as it is understood that the term madrigal as applied to Part I embraces all types of part-song, as distinguished from the solo songs with lute accompaniment represented in Part II.[1]

Two collections, Michael Cavendish's *14. Ayres in Tabletorie* and Thomas Greaves's *Songes of sundrie kindes*, pose a special problem in that they contain both madrigals and solo songs. Dr. Fellowes included them in Part II on the ground that each contains a majority of solo songs, and we have seen no reason to alter this arrangement. As for Walter Porter's *Madrigales And Ayres*, Dr. Fellowes admitted in the Preface to the first edition (p. xxi) that he was stretching a point in

---

[1] Many of these were also printed in alternative part-song form, but that is another matter.

including it at all, since it contains neither madrigals nor lute songs, but songs with consort accompaniment. In our view the obvious usefulness of having the poems set by Porter available for reading and study outweighs any question of consistency; hence they can still be found in their appropriate place in Part II.

Serviceability, rather than a strict regard for consistency, has indeed been our own criterion in deciding which poems to add to this new edition of *English Madrigal Verse*. The items not hitherto included are as follows:

Part I: Thomas Ravenscroft, *Pammelia* (1609), *Deuteromelia* (1609), and *Melismata* (1611).
         Thomas Watson, *Italian Madrigalls Englished* (1590).
         Nicholas Yonge, *Mvsica Transalpina* (1588).
Part II: Thomas Campian, *The Discription Of A Maske* (1607) and *The Description of a Maske* (1614).
         Robert Dowland, the French, Spanish, and Italian songs, Nos. xi–xx, in *A Musicall Banquet* (1610).
         George Handford, *Ayres* (1609).
         Thomas Morley, *The First Booke of Ayres* (1600).

The addition of the three Ravenscroft items, together with *A Briefe Discovrse*, which Dr. Fellowes included in the first and second editions, means that the complete texts of this composer's secular publications are now available in a modern edition: an obvious advantage to the literary student, since they contain material that is relevant to Elizabethan and Jacobean drama. The inclusion of the first two anthologies of Italian madrigals printed in England, Watson's *Italian Madrigalls Englished* and Yonge's *Mvsica Transalpina*, was also considered desirable, since they were so important in fostering the vogue of the native English madrigal. As for the items in Part II, Morley's *The First Booke of Ayres* qualified automatically, as it was only because the sole surviving copy was not available for inspection that it was omitted from the earlier editions. The lyrics printed with musical settings in Campian's two *Descriptions* and the foreign lyrics in Robert Dowland's *A Musicall Banquet* were also obvious candidates: hitherto the poetic contents of the Dowland anthology have only been partially represented. Handford's *Ayres*, a manuscript collection of lute songs dedicated to Henry, Prince of Wales, and preserved in the library of Trinity College, Cambridge, is the sole item in this volume that was not printed. But it closely resembles the printed song-books in character and presentation and may have been intended for publication.

Apart from the addition of these new items, the existing text of *English Madrigal Verse* has been completely checked with the original copies, and, where necessary, corrections and alterations have been made. In some respects our editorial procedure differs from that which Dr. Fellowes outlined in his Prefaces to the previous editions. Such differences are indicated in the Editorial Commentary to the Third Edition on p. xxix. Line numbers have been inserted and new notes on the poems have been provided at the end of the book. These incorporate most of Dr. Fellowes's material, but much new information as well, including the identification of some more authors of the poems. Even so, they are not comprehensive, for reasons of space, and the manuscript references in particular only scratch the surface. New indexes have been prepared. As it is not practicable to distinguish between the work of the original editor and that of the present revisers, either in the text or the notes, we must assume responsibility for the book in its present form.

It is our pleasant duty to acknowledge the information and assistance we have received from a number of scholars. Dr. Edward Doughtie, with whom we have had a fruitful exchange of information, provided us with a number of references that we have included in the Notes. Mrs. Elsie Duncan-Jones gave us further material for the Notes, and Dr. J. N. Birdsall helped us to identify some of the Vulgate quotations in Ravenscroft's *Pammelia*. Dr. William Ringler made available material on Sidney and other authors, Dr. Helen Gardner on Donne and related lyrics. Mr. R. E. Hallmark, Miss Gillian Weston, and Mr. D. G. Rees helped us with the French, Spanish, and Italian poems respectively. Mrs. J. M. Mason assisted with the proofs.

Acknowledgement is due to the governing bodies or librarians of the following institutions for permission to publish material in their possession: The Bodleian Library, Oxford; The British Museum, London; Cambridge University Library; Huntington Library, California; The Library of Congress, Washington, D.C.; Manchester Public Library; Trinity College, Cambridge.

FREDERICK W. STERNFELD
DAVID GREER

PREFACE TO SECOND EDITION

THE publication of the first edition of *English Madrigal Verse* in 1920 was received with a degree of approval very gratifying to the Editor. He now welcomes the opportunity, provided by the publication of a second edition, for correcting such errors that have come to his notice after a further careful collation of the text with the original editions of the song-books. Some additional notes are now inserted, and revised readings of certain passages are substituted, some as a result of suggestions communicated to the Editor, and some which he himself has thought well to make. The authorship of about a dozen more poems has been identified, and a list of all the identified poems, classified under the names of the poets, is now printed.

With reference to the first edition of this work, it should be stated that it was prepared and printed at a period of exceptional difficulty during the war and immediately after it. The complete manuscript was submitted to the Press in the summer of 1917. At that time many of the original part-books had been removed from the shelves of the British Museum and the Royal College of Music to places of greater security, and the task of transcription and revision became a difficult one. In the case of two unique books, those of Cavendish and Porter, the words, if they were to be included at all, had to be copied against time and without any chance of revision, the former in a sale-room and the latter in a private house. Both these books have since been acquired by the British Museum, but it was not until long after the Editor had made his transcription that they were again made available for reference.

It may be well to direct further attention to the Editor's observations on pages xix–xxv of his former Preface. His purpose was not to give the best possible readings of those poems the text of which is available apart from the song-books, but to reproduce the text of the song-books themselves, although emending obvious misprints and restoring the words to metrical form where the composer has disregarded the metre. This is by no means a mere matter of accurate copying. In dealing with many of the madrigals a good deal of discretion is called for, and the reconstruction of the poems is often a subject of personal opinion, for, as stated in the former Preface, the madrigal composers sometimes treated the text with much freedom, transposing and interpolating words on their own initiative; there are, moreover, many variants and inconsistencies in the actual text of the several part-books. There is also in the original editions great variety in the spelling, not to mention misprints, and occasionally either the composer or the printer substituted different words of similar meaning. It must be understood that the frequent repetition of a verbal phrase is one of the leading features of the madrigal as a musical form; also that in a madrigal there are several voice-parts, woven together quite independently as regards details of phrasing, but seldom coinciding in rhythm. Thus, for example, if a single phrase is repeated three times in each voice-part in, say, a six-part madrigal, it will be printed eighteen times altogether in six separately bound part-books. In these circumstances it cannot cause surprise that there are variant readings in the original text.

The Editor's method of dealing with such matters was explained in the former Preface, but one or two further observations may be made here. Except in a few instances the Editor has avoided elisions; an intelligent reader will always be guided by his eye and ear in reading these poems, and the Editor's decision in reference to this detail is consistent with his decision to adopt modern spelling. His reasons for this were set out on page xxv of the Preface. But with reference to elisions, the original song-books are far from being consistent in the use, for example, of such words as *even*, or *e'en*, and *spirit*, or *sprite*; the longer form is frequently found printed under a single note of music. And as regards the elision of the *e* in a final *ed*, an editor would often have to make arbitrary choice, for instance, where the composer for the purposes of musical construction has treated the syllable both with and without the elision alternately in a single passage. Thus in Dowland's *Lady, if you so spite me* (p. 507) the word *overjoyed* is fitted in three syllables to three notes as *overjoy'd*, and repeated immediately in the same voice-part fitted to four notes as *overjoyéd*. Many more such examples could be quoted. As regards variety of spelling, another example may be added to that given in the former preface. In Jones's *My love bound me with a kiss* (p. 560) the last line of each of the four verses is the same: *Kisses makes men loth to go*; and, the poem being set out in full apart from the music, as was customary in the lutenists' books, the word *loth* is spelt alternately *loath* and *loth*; but to suppose that any difference of meaning is intended here is a mistake, not only because it is unnecessary, but because in the first verse, which alone is set out with the music, the word is printed *loth* in the Bassus part whereas the Cantus has *loath*, and the two would be contradictory. The variants here are quite fortuitous.

The Editor much regrets that he is still unable to print the poems in Morley's *First Booke of Ayres* (1600); Mr. Folger, who owns the only known copy of this book, is intending shortly to build a library in Washington D.C. and the Morley volume will then be available for transcription. It is intended to print this book in full in the Editor's *English School of Lutenist Song-writers* as soon as it may be available. It should be stated that another copy of Morley's book perished in the disastrous fire at the Birmingham Public Library in 1878.

Since the publication of the first edition of *English Madrigal Verse* the Editor's *English Madrigal School*[1] has been completed and published in thirty-six volumes. In that work the words and music of practically all the English madrigals are printed in score, and reference to them may be made more particularly in the case of those madrigals in which the composers dealt freely with the text of the poem. The Editor's *English School of Lutenist Song-writers*[2] is now also completed and issued in thirty-one separate publications; this work gives the words and music of the 'Ayres' in song-form, and includes among other sets, the four books of Dowland and the five of both Campian and Jones.

The Editor wishes to express his warm appreciation of the valuable advice as well as encouragement which he has received from Mr. Percy Simpson, and he also gratefully acknowledges the courteous assistance and information which has been given to him by numerous correspondents, among whom he would particularly mention Mr. Norman Ault, the Revd. J. R. Milne, Mr. Philip Heseltine, and Mr. G. Woledge.

[1] London, 1913–24. This series, renamed *The English Madrigalists*, is currently being revised and enlarged by Thurston Dart.—Revisers.
[2] London, 1920–32. This series, renamed *The English Lute-Songs*, is currently being revised and enlarged by Thurston Dart.—Revisers.

PREFACE TO FIRST EDITION

IT has for many years been recognized that the song-books of the great English musical composers who flourished for a brief but brilliant period at the close of the sixteenth and beginning of the seventeenth century contain a splendid collection of lyric poetry written in the golden age of English literature, some of it available from other sources and well known to lovers of poetry, but much of it forgotten and undiscovered except by the rare students of the song-books themselves. Several volumes of poems selected from these song-books have been published from time to time. A certain number of lyrics appeared in Beloe's *Anecdotes of Literature,* in Brydges's *Censura Literaria,* and in the *British Bibliographer;* while Rimbault mentions a proposal made in 1816, but never carried out, for publishing a more complete collection of madrigal poetry. Another collection was that of Thomas Oliphant, the enthusiastic secretary of the Madrigal Society, whose *La Musa Madrigalesca* was published in 1837; and John Payne Collier's *Lyrical Poems selected from musical publications between the years 1589 and 1600* was printed for the Percy Society in 1844. Professor Arber did much more comprehensive work in this direction, though it was very far from covering the whole field; but among the shorter Elizabethan poems of *An English Garner* he included the complete words of Byrd's three sets, Wilbye's first set, *The Triumphes of Oriana,* Yonge's first collection of *Mvsica Transalpina,* together with the whole of the sets of Campian and John Dowland, and that of Alison. In more recent times Mr. A. H. Bullen's *Lyrics from the Elizabethan Song-books* has done much to draw further public attention to this rich store of verse. Among other books of the same kind may be mentioned Mr. F. A. Cox's *Madrigals in the time of Shakespeare,* although Mr. Cox does not always appear to have consulted the original editions, and has rather rashly printed several known poems by Elizabethan writers as being those employed by the madrigalists on no more evidence than the similarity of the first two or three words. Mr. Barclay Squire has printed in their entirety the lyrics of Robert Jones's *Muses Gardin for Delights;* and Campian's works have somewhat tardily been published in complete form both by Mr. A. H. Bullen and Mr. Percival Vivian. A comprehensive work by Herr Wilhelm Bolle entitled *Die gedruckten englischen Liederbücher bis 1600* was published in Berlin in 1903, and is the nearest approach to a complete edition of the English madrigal lyrics that has hitherto been achieved. But since it stops short at the year 1600 it leaves more than half the field untouched; and the fact that the notes and all other comment on the text are in German lessens its practical use for a section, at any rate, of English readers.

Apart from the purely literary interest which a complete collection of these poems should arouse, a definite need of such an edition is being felt by those, and they are no inconsiderable number, who are first brought into contact with the lyrics through musical channels. The names of the authors of the words were never given in the Elizabethan song-books, and, although the authorship of some few of the poems is definitely known, the identification of the greater number is a task beyond those who may become familiar with the words only through the medium of the music; for it must be remembered that only a small fraction of the madrigal music has as yet been reprinted in modern and accessible form,[1] and that in modern editions of the music the authorship of the words is not always recorded even when known. The complete edition of the lyrics now issued, which is based solely upon the original part-books, will, it is hoped, fill all these needs.

For neglecting to produce such an edition in the past the musicians of this country are far more blameworthy than are the students of literature; for it is due to their neglect of these song-books that only such of the lyrics are familiar as have come down to us from other and purely literary sources. Meanwhile it is a fact too little known to the ordinary man of letters or to people of average education, that English music at the close of the Elizabethan era stood in the forefront of the music of Europe. This indisputable truth not only deserves to be recognized as a matter of general interest, but ought to be inseparable from the ordinary course of general education. To those who take a reasonable pride in the past achievements of their own countrymen, the names of Byrd, Morley, Wilbye, Dowland, and many another ought to be at least as well known as are the names of

---

[1] The works of the English madrigalists were reprinted by Dr. Fellowes in *The English Madrigal School*, 36 vols., London, 1913–24. Renamed *The English Madrigalists*, this series is currently being revised and enlarged.—Revisers.

the great national leaders in poetry and painting. Yet many people of wide culture would confess unashamed to ignorance of such English composers, although they would be covered with confusion if they had to admit unfamiliarity with the achievements of, say, Marlowe or Dryden, of Reynolds or Turner.

The Elizabethan song-books belong to two entirely separate classes, each with its own distinctive features, namely, those of the madrigal-composers proper, and those of the lutenists; and in the present edition the lyrics are arranged under these two headings. It is not proposed here to consider in much detail the subject of madrigals from a technical point of view, since it has been fully treated by the present Editor in his *English Madrigal Composers*.[1] It will be sufficient to say that the madrigal took the form of unaccompanied song for at least three, and rarely for more than six, voice-parts. It was constructed mainly upon short musical phrases treated contrapuntally, while each voice-part had an equal share of melodic interest, the musical phrases being taken up consecutively rather than simultaneously by the various voice-parts, the verbal phrases being several times reiterated. Occasionally this method was varied by short periods in which all the voices moved together in blocks of harmony. The true madrigal was seldom set to more than one stanza of poetry; and indeed these composers studied their words so closely, and expressed themselves with such intimate regard for the particular meaning of each word and each phrase, that the exact repetition of their music to a fresh stanza of words was scarcely ever possible. Every kind of device was employed by the composers both to secure variety and to sustain interest; and, above all other considerations, they strove to add meaning and point to the words which they had chosen to set. It is especially in this last detail that they proved themselves supreme. The poetry of the period is admittedly of the first rank, but the fine imagination of the greatest of the English madrigal-composers may be said without exaggeration to have been equal to that of the poets, with the result that the music added new beauty to the 'golden-vowelled' lyrics, and intensified their meaning, so that Elizabethan music was indeed 'married to immortal verse' in equal partnership.

Of the various kinds of madrigal it need only be said here in a general way that the canzonet and other such alternative terms, as

---

[1] *The English Madrigal Composers*, by E. H. Fellowes, London, 1921.

used by the composers, do not imply any very material difference of constructive principles. The ballet is an exception; it is founded upon much more regular rhythmic outlines, having originally been an art-form in which singing and dancing were combined; and a distinctive feature of the ballet in the hands of the madrigalists was the introduction, at certain well-defined closes of the words, of a passage of music sung to no regular words but to the syllables *fa la la*. In music of a later date these passages have their counterpart in interludes for the pianoforte or orchestra, while the voices are silent. It is for this reason that the *fa la* refrains, which, with rare exceptions, have nothing to do with the poem, are omitted in the present edition, which purports to deal with the words alone; but in the Notes reference will be given to each individual poem in which the *fa la* or any other similar refrain is to be found in the musical setting.

The music of the madrigals was printed in separate part-books, each of these books containing the music for one voice-part alone, and not simultaneously showing the music of the composition as a whole, as in modern vocal score. The music was printed without bars of any kind; and the singer, unhampered by any such obstacle as that of bar-lines placed at regular intervals, was allowed to sing his music with the true *ictus* of the words, in exact accordance with the design of the composer. A false tradition in this matter, which has its origin in the introduction of bars at regular intervals in all reprints of music of this class since the middle of the seventeenth century, has unfortunately led to the serious error of supposing that the Elizabethan musicians wantonly disregarded the laws of true accent as employed in speech, whereas the reverse was actually the case. When the madrigal music is properly rendered the *ictus* should fall exactly as it would do when the words are well spoken.

We turn now to the lute-song composers, who expressed themselves in a different type of musical composition. They commonly gave to their song the title of Air,[1] a term which was occasionally used by the madrigalists also for distinctively madrigalian compositions. The Airs of the lutenists usually took the form of solo-songs with several stanzas of words, for each of which, as a general rule, the same music was repeated; the first stanza being set up with the music in the song-

---

[1] There is no special virtue in retaining the Elizabethan spelling of this word when dealing with the lute-songs, especially as the modern word *Air* retains the old meaning of *tune* or song. It was the common practice to use *y* in place of *i*, and final *e* was in general use.

books, while the subsequent stanzas were printed in metrical form on another part of the page. When performed as solo-songs they were accompanied with the lute, reinforced by a bass viol or some such instrument, to add support and body to the general effect; while occasionally, as in three of the songs of Dowland in *A Pilgrimes Solace*, more elaborate instrumental accompaniment was added. All the composers who published volumes of this kind were themselves eminent performers on the lute, and lute accompaniments form an invariable feature in their songs as contrasted with those of the madrigal writers. As an alternative method of performance the lutenists frequently harmonized their melodies for four voices so that they could be sung without accompaniment, as were the madrigals; but the style of treatment was very much simpler and lacked many of the essential features of the true madrigal. Sometimes again the lutenists' Airs were in the form of vocal duet; and sometimes, too, the composer would arrange the music so as to admit of several different ways of performance. Thus, for instance, John Dowland's *First Booke of Songes* in 1597 was 'So made that all the partes together, or either of them seuerally may be song to the Lute, Orpherian or Viol de gambo'. Another distinctive feature of the lutenists' song-books was their shape and size. The madrigal part-books were in quarto, the lute-song books almost invariably folio. When the solo-songs were adapted by the composer for alternative performance as part-songs, all the voice-parts were printed in one book, but were so arranged on the open page that the four performers could sing from the one book placed in the centre of the group.

The details of the composers' works to be treated under these two headings must next be discussed. We are fortunate in knowing with some degree of completeness what sets of compositions were published by these composers; several of these sets are now represented by only one known exemplar, but very few seem to have perished entirely. One of the sets, for instance, that cannot be traced is Nathaniel Patrick's *Songs of sundrye Natures*, 1597, the full title of which is given in Mr. Robert Steele's catalogue. The present editor would for various reasons take 1588, the year which saw the publication of William Byrd's first set, as the date when the English madrigal school may be said to have come into being. This leads to the exclusion of Thomas Whythorne's work from the present volume; for his first publication was as many as seventeen years earlier, and contains nothing of quite first-rate interest, either as poetry or music, while his second set, published in 1590, is one of those music-books in which nothing more than the opening words are printed except of the compositions set to sacred words. The great bulk of the wonderful output of madrigals was issued in the very short period covered by the subsequent twenty-five years, Bateson's second set in 1618 and that of Tomkins in 1622 being among the few really first-rate publications of a later date. The series actually closes with the younger Hilton's somewhat feeble volume of *Fa Las*; but in a book dealing with the lyrics rather than with the music, it may be thought permissible to include the poems in the two volumes of Peerson's compositions, although the second volume was published as late as 1630, and in spite of the fact that Peerson's music cannot strictly be described as of madrigalian design. Furthermore, within this range of years, 1588 to 1630, such sets as John Amner's *Sacred Hymns of 3, 4, 5, and 6 Parts*, 1615, which deal solely with sacred music, are excluded; and Sir William Leighton's *Teares or Lamentacions of a Sorrowfull Soule*, 1614, consisting almost entirely of biblical or semi-religious words, appeared to be out of place in a collection of lyric verse. On the other hand, it was though desirable, for the sake of completeness, not to omit the sacred words that are found interspersed among the secular compositions of Byrd, John Mundy, and others; and for the same reason translations from Italian madrigals, and even a few examples of Italian words, are not excluded when they form part of a genuine English madrigal set. Complete sets of adaptations, even though of contemporary work, have been omitted. Thus such volumes as Thomas Watson's *Italian Madrigalls Englished*, Yonge's two sets of *Mvsica Transalpina*, and Morley's volumes of Italian madrigals with English words, fall outside the scope of the present volume. Ravenscroft's *Pammelia*, *Deuteromelia*, and *Melismata* are excluded because they consist almost entirely of rounds and folk-songs, and neither from a literary nor a musical point of view come under the heading of madrigals. On the other hand, the same composer's examples in his *Brief Discourse of the True Use of Charact'ring the Degrees . . . in Measurable Music* have been admitted, without, it may be hoped, undue inconsistency. Very few of the songs in this last-mentioned book of Ravenscroft's are really madrigalian; but some of the lyrics are quite in keeping with the scheme of the present volume, and, though others in the set are in the nature of tavern songs, the sporting numbers are characteristic and full of interest, and some even of beauty. Greaves's *Songes of sundrie kindes*, which concludes with six madrigals, contains, for the most part, music with lute accompaniment; and as it seemed advisable not to divide the set, it is included in its entirety among the compositions of the lutenists. Cavendish's book is similar in design to that of Greaves.

The lute-song series begins with Dowland's *First Book* in 1597, and, strictly speaking, ends with Attey's book in 1622. But a point has, perhaps pardonably, been stretched in order to include Walter Porter's volume of 1632. This is certainly not accurately described by the composer as a set of 'madrigals', nor can it really be said to belong to the lute-song series; but the lute is actually named as one of the accompanying instruments, and this fact must serve as an excuse for including this volume, which certainly contains several beautiful lyrics. The incidental songs in the masques of the period are entirely outside the scope of the present collection; and Edward Filmer's *French Court Airs with their Ditties Englished*, 1629, is passed over for reasons already stated.

No biographical details of the composers are given here, as the reader is referred to the Editor's *English Madrigal Composers* and elsewhere, for information of that kind. But mention must be made here of the spelling of Thomas Campian's name, which has been deliberately adopted by the Editor in spite of the usual custom. There is authority both for *Campian* and *Campion* in books printed in his own time, but the title-pages of his books of airs give *Campian*; and in a Latin epigram addressed to John Dowland and printed in the latter's first book of airs (1597) he adopted the Latin form THO. CAMPIANI Epigramma, etc. The weight of contemporary evidence is certainly in favour of *Campian*.

The sets of lyrics are arranged under the names of the musical composers in alphabetical order. Any attempt to follow an exact chronological order would have involved some insurmountable difficulties, and would, moreover, necessitate the separation of individual composers' sets. But little, if any, advantage would be gained by a chronological arrangement, since the composers drew from literary sources which cover a comparatively wide period, while the poems have no actual relation to the dates of the musical publications.

The reconstruction of the poems from the words as given in the

part-books can be carried out with no great difficulty in the large
majority of cases. As regards the lutenists' song-books the task is but
slight, because almost invariably one stanza or more of each poem is
set up in metrical form apart from the music; so that in any case of
doubt in dealing with those words that are fitted to the musical
notation, the subsequent stanzas form a guide to metre and other
details. Yet it must be mentioned that for economy of space, or for
other reasons, the verses were seldom so well arranged metrically as in
the contemporary editions of the works of the poets, and the arrangement of the song-books has been freely handled in the present edition.

But in dealing with the madrigal part-books, with some few
exceptions, each lyric has to be separated from the music, and then
arranged in metrical form, without any such indication as is provided
in the lute-song books. That the scope of an editor's work in this
connexion may be fully understood, it is necessary to explain how the
musician usually dealt with his words in composing a madrigal.
These compositions consisted largely of brief musical phrases, often
requiring no more than half a line of verse at a time; and such a
fragment of verse was repeated more than once by all the voice-
parts before the introduction of a new musical phrase with further
words. Very often the musical requirements of one or more of the
voice-parts could not be exactly met by the verbal phrase as it
stood in the poem, and this difficulty was sometimes overcome by the
addition of fresh material, taking perhaps the form of some inter-
jection—such as 'alas!' or 'ay me!'; while occasionally some fresh
epithet or other unimportant word was introduced by the composer
to satisfy his needs. The elimination of words was also an obvious
device when circumstances required the shortening of a phrase; and
it is not unusual to find a word of one syllable substituted for another
of two syllables. Again, when a fragment of a line of verse was
separated from its context for contrapuntal treatment, the real
meaning of the words was sometimes rendered uncertain, and in such
circumstances the composers did not hesitate to transpose words to
make the meaning clear in its musical setting. Such methods of
dealing with the text may be termed musical licences, and, although
such licences were very much more the exception than the rule, it
will be recognized that an editor's task of reconstructing even the
simplest texts from the madrigal part-books involves much more
than simple transcription.

Examples may here be quoted to illustrate the preceding statement: The following are the opening lines of Morley's three-part canzonet 'What ails my darling' (1593 Canzonets, No. 18) as they actually stand in the part-books with the music:

Cantus. What ails my darling, say what ails my darling, what ails my sweet pretty darling, what ails my sweet, what ails mine own sweet darling? What ails my darling dear thus sitting all alone, sitting all alone, all alone so weary? Say, why is my dear now not merry?

Altus. What ails my darling, say what ails my darling, what ails my darling dear, what ails mine only sweet, mine only sweet darling? What ails my darling, what ails my darling dear, sitting all alone, sitting all alone so weary? Say what grieves my dear that she is not merry?

Bassus. What ails my darling, say what ails my darling, what ails my darling, say what ails my dainty dainty darling, what ails mine own sweet darling? What ails my dainty darling, my dainty darling so to sit alone, so to sit alone so weary, and is not merry?

The problem of reconstructing the metrical form of these words is of course capable of several different solutions (that of the Editor will be found on p. 137). But this is an unusually difficult case, and similar examples are rare, and almost entirely confined to the earlier work of Thomas Morley. In madrigals of this type the words and music are really in a sense inseparable, forming together one artistic whole, and when the music is taken away an integral part of the whole has been removed; therefore, what is left—an incomplete thing in itself—must be rearranged to give it the semblance of a whole. And this rearrangement should attempt to trace backwards the several steps taken by the musician in the course of evolving his composition. The reconstruction of the poem must in just a few such cases be a little speculative; yet even in these it is well worth attempting; for if the words were literally transcribed as above, poetic feeling would be wholly eliminated. One other example may be quoted to show the kind of material upon which an editor has to work. The following is from Peerson's *Private Music* (No. 24), the unique complete exemplar of which is in the Bodleian Library.

Cantus. See, see, O see, who is here, who comes a-maying. . . . And his sweet beauteous Orian. Why left we off our playing to gaze on them that gods as well as men amaze? Jug, jug, jug, lark raise thy note and wing. All birds, all birds, their music bring . . . Record on every bush . . . whose like was never seen, for good and fair. Nor can be though fresh May should every day invite a several pair.

Altus. See, see, who is here come a-maying. The master of the Ocean. Why left we off our playing. To gaze on them that gods as men amaze? Jug, jug, jug, thy note (*words missing here*) . . . Robin, Linnet, Thrush, the welcome of the king and queen whose like we (*sic*) never seen for good and fair, nor can be though fresh May should every day invite a several pair.

Cantus secundus. See O see, who is here come a-maying . . . Why left we off our playing . . . On them that gods as men amaze. Up Nightingale and sing jug, jug, jug. All birds their music bring. . . . The welcome of the King and Queen whose like were never seen for good and fair. Nor can be though fresh May should every day invite a several pair.

The Editor had the satisfaction of reconstructing this poem exactly as it stands in the present volume (see p. 183) before finding it among Ben Jonson's works.

And here it may be remarked that the text of poems of which the authorship has been ascertained, as given in the song-books, usually shows many small variations from the accepted version. The textual differences are of two kinds, namely, those that are due to careless transcription or faulty memory on the part of the composer himself or of whoever gave him the copy of the words to set, and those that have been deliberately made by the composer for musical reasons. Moreover, it is possible that such variations sometimes had the sanction of the poet. Most of the song-books were contemporary with the lyrics, and it is probable that the poets themselves may sometimes have offered the musicians words on which to exercise their skill. A copy of his own verses written down by an author from memory may well show small variations from the accepted and considered text. The preservation of such textual differences as are exhibited in the music-books is therefore of no small literary importance. On the other hand, obvious transpositions made for musical reasons, as well as the variants that are clearly due to scribal error, may reasonably be rectified in a modern edition such as this; and this applies especially to rhyming words, which not infrequently are replaced in the song-books by words of similar meaning.

An illustration may be given here which will suffice to show one sort of mistake that sometimes finds its way into the composer's text. One of Robert Jones's madrigals begins with the line 'Stay, wandering thoughts, O whither do you haste?' (see p. 123), but the text of the cantus part-book is 'O whither do you fly', and, as no pair of words in the opening lines showed any semblance of a rhyme, the difficulty of reconstructing the lyric seemed insuperable until the Editor noticed that the bassus part-book had the variant 'haste' for 'fly', and this obviously supplied the necessary rhyming word for matching the line 'Joy is at hand and sorrows past'. Again, in Corkine's setting of Sidney's 'The fire to see my woes' an obvious misprint occurs at the end of line 4 in the repetition of the word *turneth* with which line 3 also ends. The second line ends with the word *weepeth*; and there would have been no difficulty in conjecturing that *keepeth* is the correct reading in the fourth line, even if the text of the *Arcadia* had never survived to provide corroborative evidence. It will be readily understood that slips of this kind would have more easily escaped detection in the music-books than when the words are set out in metrical form. The existence of errors of this kind which can be corrected with certainty from other versions is a reasonable ground for correcting similar errors which can be mended only by conjecture. Accordingly the Editor has, for instance, substituted 'grieving' for 'groaning' (Dowland's *Second Book*, No. 15); 'true' for 'fair' (Jones's *Second Book of Songs*, No. 14); 'seek' for 'find' (Gibbons's Madrigals, No. 2). Corrections of this nature have been suggested throughout the present edition in a strictly conservative spirit, and textual alterations of any consequence are always made the subject of a note. It is important to state that, though small problems abound, it has been possible to reconstruct the great majority of the madrigal poems with absolute certainty.

After much careful consideration of the subject, modern spelling and punctuation have been adopted in this edition. It must be remembered by those who would prefer Elizabethan spelling for all reprints of the poetry of that period that the words of these song-books were often repeated several times in each of the voice-parts, so that individual words were sometimes spelt in every possible variety of ways in one single passage. In one madrigal by Robert Jones, for example, the word *old* is spelt in the same sentence of the bassus-part alone, *old*, *olde*, and *auld*, and it could not be claimed that the selection of any one of these variants would really represent the original text in preference to another; and, in dealing with the text as a whole, an editor would often have to make an arbitrary choice. As regards punctuation, it will be obvious that where short phrases and fragments of lines were constantly repeated by the composers, the punctuation that had to be employed in the part-books would be quite unsuitable to the text without the music. On these grounds alone, apart from other reasons, modern spelling and punctuation appeared to be a matter of necessity. At the same time, of course, obsolete words and curious variants of modern words have been retained, as well as certain Elizabethan forms, such as, for instance, the form of the genitive in names such as *Orianaes*, *Dianaes*, etc., or again, the singular in place of the plural of the verb in such phrases as 'mine eyes presents me with a double doubting', wherever they occur in the original.

The Editor desires to express his sincerest thanks to Miss Evelyn Heaton-Smith for much valuable help in preparing this edition.

An expression of gratitude is also due to Mr. Percy Simpson for his helpful suggestions and criticisms; and to Lord Ellesmere and Mr. S. R. Christie-Miller for their kindness in enabling the Editor to transcribe the text of the unique exemplars in their possession; namely, Robert Jones's *The Muses Gardin for Delights* at Bridgewater House, and Walter Porter's *Madrigales And Ayres* at Britwell Court, Burnham. Lord Ellesmere's book has since passed into the hands of Mr. Edward Huntington of New York, and Mr. Christie-Miller's copy of Porter's *Madrigales And Ayres* is now in the British Museum, The unique exemplar of Morley's *First Booke of Ayres*, 1600, is in the possession of Mr. Henry Clay Folger of New York, who has kindly promised to give the Editor an opportunity of making a transcription at some future date so that it may be added in a later edition of these poems.

In conclusion, the Editor will warmly welcome any information as to the authorship of any poems in these song-books that have not yet been identified by him, so that it may be added in any future edition; he is fully conscious that in this difficult matter his work must inevitably be far from complete.

EDMUND H. FELLOWES

The Cloisters, Windsor Castle
July 8, 1917

PS.—The delay in the publication of this volume has been necessitated by the abnormal conditions resulting from the Great War.

E. H. F.

December 31, 1919

CONTENTS

EDITORIAL COMMENTARY TO THIRD EDITION

SPELLING, PUNCTUATION, AND CAPITALIZATION. With the two exceptions listed below, the spelling, punctuation, and capitalization have been modernized throughout. Contrary to Dr. Fellowes's practice (see p. xxvi), the old genitive form in names such as *Orianaes* and *Dianaes* has been modernized to *Oriana's* and *Diana's*.

(*a*) In the title-pages, printed on pp. 3 and 339, and at the beginning of each collection, the original spelling, punctuation, and capitalization have been preserved, including the old forms of *i*, *j*, *u*, and *v*. The long *s*, however, has not been reproduced.

(*b*) In the few foreign and dialect poems the original spelling has been preserved, but not the original punctuation, capitalization, and old letter-forms. Accents have been supplied.

ELISION. Elisions have been made where they occur in the original texts. This is contrary to Dr. Fellowes's practice (see p. xii) of expanding elisions.

STANZA FORM AND INDENTATION. Where the poem is set out metrically in the original editions we have adhered to the original line-formation (Dr. Fellowes frequently rearranged the text), but not necessarily to the original indentation.

'FA LA' REFRAINS. Dr. Fellowes omitted these on the ground that they do not form an integral part of the poem (see p. xviii), but we have indicated their presence by the syllables 'Fa la'.

VARIANT READINGS. The Prefaces to the first and second editions explain the difficulties that sometimes arise in attempting to reconstruct a poem from the texts printed under the music in the part-books, particularly when the several parts contain variant readings.

In this edition our general practice has been to adopt whatever reading occurs in a majority of parts, and to record other readings in the Notes if they are found in more than one other part, or if they seem to be of any importance or interest. Minor variants that occur only in one part and are of no significance are not recorded in the Notes. When a minority reading has been adopted the majority reading is automatically recorded in the Notes.

EDITIONS. Where a publication passed through more than one edition the editions have been collated and any variants recorded in the Notes.

PART I
MADRIGALS

LIST OF PUBLICATIONS

Concerning the letters [*a*] and [*b*] printed after some dates see p. 677.

PAGE

THE POEMS

RICHARD ALISON

An Howres Recreation in Musicke, apt for Instrumentes and Voyces. Framed for the delight of Gentlemen and others which are wel affected to that qualitie, All for the most part with two trebles, necessarie for such as teach in priuate families, with a prayer for the long preseruation of the King and his posteritie, and a thankesgiuing for the deliuerance of the whole estate from the late conspiracie. 1606

I–II

THE man upright of life,
   Whose guiltless heart is free
From all dishonest deeds
   Or thought of vanity:

That man whose silent days   5
   In harmless joys are spent,
Whom hopes cannot delude
   Nor sorrows discontent:

That man needs neither towers
   Nor armour for defence,   10
Nor secret vaults to fly
   From thunder's violence.

He only can behold
   With unaffrighted eyes
The horrors of the deep   15
   And terrors of the skies.

Thus scorning all the cares
   That fate or fortune brings,
He makes his heaven his book,
   His wisdom heavenly things.   20

Good thoughts his only friends,
    His wealth a well-spent age,
The earth his sober inn
    And quiet pilgrimage.

                            [*Thomas Campian*]

III–VII

O HEAVY heart whose harms are hid,
    Thy help is hurt, thy hap is hard;
If thou shouldst break, as God forbid,
    Then should desert want his reward.
Hope well to have, hate not sweet thought;   5
Foul cruel storms fairer calms have brought.
    After sharp showers the sun shines fair,
    Hope comes likewise after despair.

In hope a king doth go to war,
    In hope a lover lives full long,   10
In hope a merchant sails full far,
    In hope just men do suffer wrong,
In hope the ploughman sows his seed;
Thus hope helps thousands at their need.
    Then faint not, heart, among the rest,   15
    Whatever chance, hope thou the best.

Though Wit bids Will to blow retreat,
    Will cannot work as Wit would wish;
When that the roach doth taste the bait,
    Too late to warn the hungry fish.   20
When cities burn on fiery flame,
Great rivers scarce may quench the same.
    If Will and Fancy be agreed,
    Too late for Wit to bid take heed.

But yet it seems a foolish drift   25
    To follow Will and leave the Wit.
The wanton horse that runs too swift
    May well be stayed upon the bit;
But check a horse amid his race,
And out of doubt you mar his pace.   30
    Though Wit and Reason doth men teach
    Never to climb above their reach.

I can no more but hope, good heart,
   For though the worst doth chance to fall,
I know a wile shall ease thy smart,   35
   And turn to sweet thy sugared gall.
When thy good will and painful suit
Hath shaked the tree and wants the fruit,
   Then keep thou Patience well in store,
   That sovereign salve shall heal thy sore.   40

VIII

WHO loves this life, from love his love doth err,
   And choosing dross rich treasure doth deny,
Leaving the pearl, Christ's counsel to prefer
   With selling all we have the same to buy.
O happy soul that doth disburse a sum   5
To gain a kingdom in the life to come.

IX–X

MY prime of youth is but a frost of cares;
   My feast of joy is but a dish of pain;
My crop of corn is but a field of tares;
   And all my good is but vain hope of gain.
My life is fled, and yet I saw no sun;   5
And now I live, and now my life is done.

The Spring is past, and yet it hath not sprung;
   The fruit is dead, and yet the leaves be green;
My youth is gone, and yet I am but young;
   I saw the world, and yet I was not seen.   10
My thread is cut, and yet it is not spun;
And now I live, and now my life is done.
                          [*Chidiock Tichborne*]

XI–XII

REST with yourselves, you vain and idle brains,
   Which youth and age in lewdest lust bestow;
And find out frauds and use ten thousand trains
   To win the soil where nought but sin doth grow.
And live with me, you chaste and honest minds,   5
   Which do your lives in lawful love employ,
And know no sleights but friends for virtue finds,
   And loathe the lust which doth the soul destroy.

For lust is frail, where love is ever sound,
 Lust outward sweet, but inward bitter gall, 10
A shop of shows where no good ware is found,
 Not like to love where honest faith is all.
So that is lust where fancy ebbs and flows,
And hates and loves as beauty dies and grows;
And this is love where friendship firmly stands 15
On virtue's rock and not on sinful sands.

XIII–XIV

SHALL I abide this jesting?
I weep, and she's a-feasting.
O cruel fancy that so doth blind thee
 To love one doth not mind thee.

Can I abide this prancing? 5
I weep, and she's a-dancing.
O cruel fancy so to betray me,
 Thou goest about to slay me.

XV–XVI

THE sturdy rock for all his strength
 By raging seas is rent in twain;
The marble stone is pierced at length
 With little drops of drizzling rain;
The ox doth yield unto the yoke; 5
The steel obeyeth the hammer stroke.

The stately stag that seems so stout
 By yelping hounds at bay is set;
The swiftest bird that flies about
 At length is caught in fowler's net; 10
The greatest fish in deepest brook
Is soon deceived with subtle hook.

       [*John Thorn*]

XVII–XVIII

WHAT if a day, or a month, or a year
 Crown thy delights with a thousand sweet contentings;
Cannot a chance of a night or an hour
 Cross thy desires with as many sad tormentings?

Fortune, honour, beauty, youth 5
  Are but blossoms dying;
Wanton pleasure, doting love
  Are but shadows flying.
    All our joys
    Are but toys, 10
  Idle thoughts deceiving.
    None have power
    Of an hour
  In their lives bereaving.

Earth's but a point to the world; and a man 15
  Is but a point to the world's compared centre.
Shall then a point of a point be so vain
  As to triumph in a seely point's adventure?
All is hazard that we have,
    There is nothing biding; 20
Days of pleasure are like streams
  Through fair meadows gliding.
    Weal and woe,
    Time doth go,
  Time is never turning. 25
    Secret fates
    Guide our states
  Both in mirth and mourning.

                              [*Thomas Campian*]

XIX–XXI

T H E R E is a garden in her face
  Where roses and white lilies grow;
A heavenly paradise is that place,
  Wherein all pleasant fruits do flow.
There cherries grow that none may buy, 5
Till 'cherry ripe' themselves do cry.

Those cherries fairly do enclose
  Of orient pearl a double row,
Which when her lovely laughter shows,
  They look like rosebuds filled with snow. 10
Yet them no peer nor prince may buy
Till 'cherry ripe' themselves do cry.

Her eyes like angels watch them still;
　　Her brows like bended bows do stand,
Threat'ning with piercing frowns to kill   15
　　All that approach with eye or hand
These sacred cherries to come nigh,
　　Till 'cherry ripe' themselves do cry.
　　　　　　　　　　　　　　[*Thomas Campian*]

XXII

BEHOLD, now praise the Lord, all ye servants of the Lord;
Ye that by night stand in the house of the Lord, even in the
courts of the house of our God.
　Lift up your hands in the sanctuary, and praise the Lord.
　The Lord that made both heaven and earth give thee blessing　5
out of Sion.　Amen.
　　　　　　　　　　　　　　[*Psalm cxxxiv*]

XXIII

O LORD, bow down thine ear unto our prayers, which we make to
thee in thy Son's name. And for his sake preserve our gracious King
and Queen from all their enemies. Continue, O Lord, their deliverance
from the conspiracies of all such as rise up against them. Preserve also
his royal progeny, prince Henry and the rest, even through the　5
same our Lord Jesus Christ, who liveth and reigneth with thee and
the Holy Ghost, both now and ever.　Amen.

XXIV

THE sacred choir of Angels sings
　　The praises of the living Lord,
That is the God and King of kings,
　　Protecting those that keep his word.
O well of grace, O spring of life,   5
　　To those that thirst thy truth to taste,
But unto them that live in strife
　　A terror that will ever last.
Chorus. 'Tis thou, O Lord, through strength of thy right hand alone,
That Satan's secrets hast revealed and bloody treasons overthrown.

We'll tune our voices to the lute
　　And instruments of sweetest sound;
No tongue shall in thy praise be mute,
　　That doth thy foes and ours confound,

Who hath preserved our king and state   15
    From ruin that was near at hand;
    While all good men rejoice thereat,
    Thy will no power can withstand.
Chorus. 'Tis thou, O Lord, through strength of thy right hand alone,
That Satan's secrets hast revealed and bloody treasons over-
    thrown.   20

THOMAS BATESON

The first set of English Madrigales: to 3. 4. 5. and 6. voices.
1604

WHEN Oriana walked to take the air,
The world did strive to entertain so fair:
By Flora fair and sweetest flowers were strone
Along the way for her to tread upon;
The trees did blossom, silver rivers ran,   5
The wind did gently play upon her fan;
And then for to delight her grace's ear,
The woods a temple seemed, the birds a choir.
    Then sang the shepherds and nymphs of Diana:
        Long live fair Oriana.   10

I

    BEAUTY is a lovely sweet
    Where pure white and crimson meet,
    Joined with favour of the face,
    Chiefest flower of female race.
    But if Virtue might be seen,   5
    It would more delight the eyne.

II

LOVE would discharge the duty of his heart
  In Beauty's praise, whose greatness doth deny
Words to his thoughts, and thoughts to his desert;
  Which high conceit since nothing can supply,
Love, here constrained through conquest to confess,   5
Bids silence sigh that tongue cannot express.

III

THE nightingale, so soon as April bringeth
  Unto her rested sense a perfect waking,
While late bare earth, proud of new clothing, springeth,
  Sings out her woes, a thorn her song-book making.
    And mournfully bewailing,   5
    Her throat in tunes expresseth
    What grief her breast oppresseth.

                                        [*Sir Philip Sidney*]

IV

    AY me, my mistress scorns my love,
    I fear she will most cruel prove.
    I weep, I sigh, I grieve and groan,
    Yet she regardeth not my moan.
    Then Love, adieu, it fits not me   5
    To weep for her that laughs at thee.

V

    COME, follow me, fair nymphs; hie! run apace;
    Diana hunting honoureth this chase;
    Softly, for fear her game we rouse,
    Lodged in this grove of briars and boughs.
    Hark how the huntsmen winds their horns,   5
    See how the deer mounts o'er the thorns.
    The *White*, the *Black*, oho, he pinched thee there,
    Gowen ran well, but *I Love* killed the deer.

VI

    YOUR shining eyes and golden hair,
    Your lily-rosed lips most fair,
    Your other beauties that excel,
    Men cannot choose but like them well;
    But when for them they say they'll die,   5
    Believe them not, they do but lie.

VII

WHITHER so fast? See how the kindly flowers
  Perfume the air, and all to make thee stay.
The climbing woodbind, clipping all these bowers,
  Clips thee likewise for fear thou pass away.
  Fortune our friend, our foe will not gainsay.   5

Stay but awhile; Phoebe no tell-tale is;
She her Endymion, I'll my Phoebe kiss.

VIII

DAME VENUS, hence to Paphos go,
  For Mars is gone to th' field;
He cannot tend sweet love's embrace
  In hand with spear and shield.
The roaring cannons thunder out   5
  Such terrors as not fit
A tender imp of your regard,
  Which dallying still doth sit.

IX

DOWN from above falls Jove in rain
Into fair Danäe's lap amain.
She starts thereat, yet lamblike still
At last performeth all his will.
Both high and low such golden gifts   5
Will put their conscience to the shift.

X

ADIEU, sweet love! O thus to part
  Kills my bleeding heart,
Yet fates, alas, will have it so.
Cruel their doom so to decree,
At once to part two lovers true.   5
  But since we needs must part,
  Once again, adieu, sweet heart.

XI

IF Love be blind, how hath he then the sight
  With beauty's beams my careless heart to wound?
Or, if a boy, how hath he then the might
  The mightiest conquerors to bring to ground?
O no, he is not blind, but I, that leese   5
  My thoughts the ways that bring to restless fears;
Nor yet a boy, but I, that live in dread
  Mixed with hope, and seek for joy in tears.

XII

PHYLLIS, farewell, I may no longer live;
Yet if I die, fair Phyllis, I forgive.
I live too long; come, gentle death, and end
My endless torment, or my grief amend.

XIII

THOSE sweet delightful lilies
Which nature gave my Phyllis,
Ay me, each hour makes me to languish,
So grievous is my pain and anguish.

XIV

AND must I needs depart, then?
Can pity none come nigh her?
Farewell, alas, desert, then.
    O break asunder, heart, to satisfy her.

XV–XVI

SWEET Gemma, when I first beheld thy beauty,
I vowed thee service, honour, love, and duty.
        Oh then, I said, the best
        Is hither come to make me blest.
        But thou, alas, sweet, thou   5
        Dost not regard my vow.
        Go, go, let me not see
        Cruel, though fairest, thee.
Yet stay alway, be chained to my heart
With links of love, that we do never part.   10
Then I'll not call thee serpent, tiger cruel,
But my sweet Gemma, and my dearest jewel.

XVII

STRANGE were the life that every man would like;
    More strange the state that should mislike each one.
Rare were the gem that everyone would seek,
    And little worth that all would let alone.
Sweet were the meat that every one would choose,   5
And sour the sauce that all men would refuse.

XVIII

ALAS, where is my love, where is my sweeting
That hath stol'n away my heart? God send us meeting!
That renewing my lament with friendly greeting,
She may release my smart and all my weeping.
      But if my sight she fly   5
      Till heartless I die,
My grieved ghost with shrikes and dreadful crying,
      Always about her flying,
      Shall murmur out complaining,
To be revenged of all her deep disdaining.   10

XIX

O FLY not, love, O fly not me;
Stay but awhile, O stay thee,
And hear a wretch complaining
His grief through thy disdaining.
O do not thus unfriendly use me,   5
To kiss me once, and so refuse me.

XX

WHO prostrate lies at women's feet,
And calls them darlings dear and sweet,
Protesting love, and craving grace,
And praising oft a foolish face,
Are oftentimes deceived at last,   5
Then catch at nought and hold it fast.

XXI

SISTER, awake, close not your eyes,
    The day her light discloses;
And the bright morning doth arise
    Out of her bed of roses.
See the clear sun, the world's bright eye,   5
    In at our window peeping;
Lo, how he blusheth to espy
    Us idle wenches sleeping.
Therefore awake, make haste I say,
    And let us without staying   10
All in our gowns of green so gay
    Into the park a-maying.

XXII

Oriana's Farewell

HARK! hear you not a heavenly harmony?
  Is't Jove, think you, that plays upon the spheres?
Heavens! is not this a heavenly melody,
  Where Jove himself a part in music bears?

Now comes in a choir of nightingales.   5
Mark how the nymphs and shepherds of the dales,
How all do join together in the praise
Of Oriana's life and happy days.

Then sing ye shepherds and nymphs of Diana:
In heaven lives Oriana.   10

XXIII

DEAR, if you wish my dying,
In vain your wish redounds, in vain your prayer,
For can he die that breathes not vital air?
  Then with those eyes that slew me,
  New life infusing, renew me.   5
So shall we both obtain our wished pleasure,
You my death joying, and I my life's sweet treasure.

XXIV

FAIR Hebe when dame Flora meets,
  She trips and leaps as gallants do,
Up to the hills and down again
  To the valleys runs she to and fro.
But out alas, when frosty locks   5
  Begirds the head with cark and care,
Peace! laugh no more, let pranks go by,
  Slow crawling age forbids such ware.

XXV

[*The words are the same as those of No. 12 in this set.*]

XXVI

THYRSIS on his fair Phyllis' breast reposing
 Sweetly did languish.
 When she in love's sweet anguish
Him kissing gently said thus with sugared glosing:
Thyrsis, O tell me, thy true love best approved,   5
 Art not thou my best beloved?
Then he, which to her heart was ever nearest,
Kissed her again and said: Yes, lady dearest.

XXVII

MERRILY my love and I
 Upon the plains were sporting;
Cheerfully the nymphs and fauns
 Oft-times to us resorting.
Sorrow did not us assail,   5
 We tasted of each pleasure.
Happy those that may with us
 Have part of love's rich treasure.

XXVIII

MUSIC some think no music is
Unless she sing of clip and kiss,
And bring to wanton tunes *fie fie*,
Or *ti-ha*, *ta-ha*, or *I'll* cry.
But let such rhymes no more disgrace   5
Music sprung of heavenly race.

ɔɕɔɕɔɕɔɕɔɕɔɕɔɕɔɕ

The Second Set Of Madrigales to 3. 4. 5. *and* 6. *Parts:*
Apt for Viols and Voyces. 1618.

I

LOVE is the fire that burns me;
 The smokes are thoughts confused
Which dims my soul and hath my sense abused.
 Though fire to ashes turn me,
 Yet doth the smoke more grieve me   5
That dims my mind, whose light should still relieve me.

II

MY mistress after service due
Demanded if indeed my love were true.
  I said it was. Then she replied
  That I must hate whom she defied,
  And so myself above the rest,   5
Whom she, she swore, did most of all detest.
In sooth, said I, you see I hate myself,
Who sets my love on such a peevish elf.

III

ONE woman scarce of twenty
But hath of tears great plenty,
Which they pour out like fountains
That run down from the mountains.
Yet all is but beguiling,   5
Their tears and eke their smiling.
I'll therefore never trust them,
Since Nature hath so cursed them
That they can weep in smiling,
Poor fools thereby beguiling.   10

IV

IF I seek to enjoy the fruits of my pain,
She careless denies me with endless disdain.
  Yet so much I love her
That nothing can either remove me or move her.
Alas! why contend I? why strive I in vain   5
  The water to mingle
With oil that is air, and loves to be single?
'Tis not Love, but Fate, whose doom I abide.
You powers and you planets, which destinies guide,
  Change you opposition;   10
It fits heavenly powers to be mild of condition.

V

PLEASURE is a wanton thing,
When old and young do dance and spring.
Pleasure it is that most desire,
And yet 'tis but a fool's hire.

VI

SWEET, those trammels of your hair
Golden locks more truly are,
   My thoughts locking to your beauty.
Thus you do my captive mind
From my dying body bind   5
   Only to you to do duty.

O, my dear, let it go free,
Or my body take to thee,
   So your captive you shall cherish;
For if parted thus they lie,   10
Or my thoughts, or I, must die.
   'Twill grieve thee if either perish.

VII

LIVE not, poor bloom, but perish,
   Whose Spring frosty Winter blasteth.
Other buds fresh Mays do cherish,
   Hyems o'er thee his snow casteth,
   And in withered arms thee graspeth.   5

Tyrants, nothing worse you can.
   Now my lively body's yoked
To the dead corpse of a man,
   Thus, with loathed burden choked,
   Lingering death with tears invoked.   10

VIII

THE nightingale in silent night
Doth sing as well as in the light.
To lull Love's watchful eyes asleep
She doth such nightly sonnets keep.
Hey ho, hey ho, sing we withal   5
What fortune us so e'er befall.

IX–X

O WHAT is she whose looks like lightnings pierce
   Thus suddenly my breast, scorching no skin?
Yet O my heart burns with a fire fierce,
   The flames ascending in my face are seen.
Yet courage, man, her speaking eye doth show   5
Some fire remains from whence those lightnings flew.

See, forth her eyes her startled spirit peeps,
Which now she on me, straight she off me, keeps;
Not able long, looks off, looks on, doth blush, doth tremble;
Sweet wretch, she would, but cannot, love dissemble.   10
Happy event, what's lingering is but slight;
Who ever loved that loved not at first sight?

XI

WHEN to the gloomy woods,
  When to the barren plain,
When to the stony rocks and sullen floods
I wailing often go, and of my love complain,
  How senseless then, think I, by love I grow   5
    To senseless things that tell my woe.
    Yet these my piercing moans
      Have touched oft so nigh,
      That they to me reply;
But cruel she, more senseless than hard stones,   10
    Quite senseless of my pains
No answer gives, unmoved still remains.

XII

IF floods of tears could cleanse my follies past,
  Or smokes of sighs might sacrifice for sin;
If groaning cries might salve my faults at last,
  Or endless moan for error pardon win,
Then would I cry, weep, sigh, and ever moan,   5
Mine errors, faults, sins, follies, past and gone.

XIII

HAVE I found her, (O rich finding!)
  Goddess-like for to behold,
Her fair tresses seemly binding
  In a chain of pearl and gold?
Chain me, chain me, O most fair,   5
Chain me to thee with that hair.

XIV

DOWN the hills Corinna trips,
Fetching many wanton skips.
To the groves she doth go,
Where thousand birds in a row,

Sitting all upon a tree,   5
Came two by two and three by three,
Corinna coveting to see,
Tuning notes of her praise,
Do welcome her with roundelays.

XV

CAMILLA fair tripped o'er the plain.
    I followed quickly after.
Have overtaken her I would fain,
    And kissed her when I caught her.
But hope being past her to obtain,   5
    Camilla loud I call.
She answered me with great disdain:
    I will not kiss at all.

XVI

SADNESS, sit down, on my soul feed;
    Tear up thought's tomb, a numbed heart;
Make wounds to speak and scars to bleed;
    On withered strings tune springing smart,
And leave this farewell for posterity: 5
Life is a death where sorrow cannot die.

XVII

LIFE of my life, how should I live alas,
    Since thou art thus resolved for to depart?
    Or how should I disguise my secret smart,
Wanting the sweet fruition of thy face,
Where Beauty, Love, with Majesty and Grace   5
(Things seld or never meeting in one place)
    Have all conspired to plague a plagued heart,
All always careless of my careful case?
Then if thou wilt not have thy love to mourn,
    Dear to my soul, I pray thee make no stay. 10
Go not at all, or else with speed return;
    Nay, rather far, my dear, go not away.
But thou must go? Then, sweet, while I thee see,
Farewell, farewell, but bide or let me die.

XVIII

I HEARD a noise and wished for a sight.
  I looked aside and did a shadow see,
Whose substance was the sum of my delight;
  It came unseen, and so it went from me.
But yet conceit persuaded my intent   5
There was a substance where the shadow went.
I did not play Narcissus in conceit,
  I did not see my shadow in a spring;
I knew my eyes were dimmed with no deceit,
  I saw the shadow of some worthy thing;   10
For as I saw the shadow passing by,
I had a glance of something in my eye.
Shadow, or she, or both, or choose you whether,
Blest be the thing that brought the shadow hither.

XIX

WITH bitter sighs I heard Amyntas plaining,
For his chaste love he found but deep disdaining.
As thus he sat, and in his grief did tremble,
To cheer his spirits the aerial choir assemble.
They sweetly sing, in doleful tunes he cries: 5
Griefs are long-lived and Sorrow seldom dies.

XX

WHY do I, dying, live and see my life bereft me?
Why do I doubt to die and see death only left me?
Th' enlargement of my better self by Nature's foe
Confines my hapless life to never-dying woe.
Immured in sorrow's hold, I only see the light   5
Of all my joys wrapped up in horror's blackest night.
    Then like Meander swans before my death
    In fatal notes I'll sigh my latest breath.

XXI

IN depth of grief and sorrow great
  Oft have I myself bewailed
Of that same love, that late had seat
  In my heart, but now is failed.
And, Sorrow, thou hast done the worst   5
That thou canst do to make me cursed.

XXII–XXIII

ALL the day I waste in weeping,
   Grieved with my love's disdaining.
   All the night I lie complaining,
Sighs and sobs me watchful keeping
   For thy loss, my life's bright jewel,   5
   Once too kind, but now too cruel.

Why dost thou fly in such disdain?
Stay, or I die with endless pain.
       Pity my plaint.
       Alas, I faint,   10
       Unhappy me!
       Will 't never be?
Then yet at last glance back thy eye,
And see thy wretched lover die.

XXIV

COME, Sorrow, help me to lament,
   For plaining now must ease my heart.
No pleasure can give me content,
   For all delights doth breed my smart.
Only my love can yield relief,   5
Whose absence causeth all my grief.

XXV–XXVI

CUPID, in a bed of roses
   Sleeping, chanced to be stung
   Of a bee that lay among
The flowers where he himself reposes.

And thus to his mother, weeping,
   Told that he this wound did take
   Of a little winged snake,
As he lay securely sleeping.

Cytherea, smiling, said
   That if so great sorrow spring   10
   From a silly bee's weak sting,
As should make thee thus dismayed,
What anguish feel they, think'st thou, and what pain,
Whom thy empoisoned arrows cause complain?

XXVII

HER hair the net of golden wire,
    Wherein my heart, led by my wandering eyes,
    So fast entangled is that in no wise
It can nor will again retire;
    But rather will in that sweet bondage die,   5
    Than break one hair to gain her liberty.

XXVIII–XXIX

FOND Love is blind, blind therefore lovers be;
But I more blind, who ne'er my love did see.
Pygmalion loved an image, I a name,
I laughed at him, but now deserve like blame.
Thus foolishly I leap before I look,   5
Seeing no bait, I swallowed have the hook.

Ah, Cupid, grant that I may never see
Her through mine ear, that thus hath wounded me.
If through mine eyes another wound she give,
Cupid, alas, then I no longer live   10
But die, poor wretch, shot through and through the liver
With those sharp arrows she stole from thy quiver.

XXX

SHE with a cruel frown
Oppressed my trembling heart with deadly swoon.
    Yet pitying my pain,
Restored with a kiss my life again.
Thus let me daily be of life deprived,   5
So I be daily thus again revived.

JOHN BENNET

Madrigalls To Fovre Voyces. *1599*

I

I WANDER up and down and fain would rest me,
Yet cannot rest, such cares do still molest me.
All things conspire, I see, and this consent in,
To find a place for me fit to lament in.

II

WEEP, silly soul disdained,
    Thy hapless hap lamenting,
That Love, whose passion pained,
    Wrought never thy contenting.
And since thou art disdained   5
    By them thou most affected,
    Let them be now rejected.

III

SO gracious is thy sweet self, so fair, so framed,
That whoso sees thee without a heart enflamed,
Either he lives not, or love's delight he knows not.

IV

LET go, let go! why do you stay me?
I will for spite go run and slay me.
O new-found tormenting, O strange disdaining,
I die for love, yet feigned is my complaining.
    But you that say I feigned,   5
    Now see what you have gained.
I will for spite go run and slay me,
Let go, let go! why do you stay me?

V

COME, shepherds, follow me,
    Run up apace the mountain.
    See, lo, besides the fountain
Love laid to rest, how sweetly sleepeth he.

O take heed, come not nigh him,   5
But haste we hence and fly him;
And, lovers, dance with gladness,
For while Love sleeps is truce with care and sadness.

VI

I LANGUISH to complain me with ghastly grief tormented;
I stand amazed to see you discontented.
Better I hold my peace and stop my breath,
Than cause my sorrows to increase and work my death.

VII

SING out, ye nymphs and shepherds of Parnassus,
    With sweet delight your merry notes consenting,
    Sith time affords to banish love relenting,
Fortune she smiles sweetly still to grace us.

VIII

THYRSIS, sleepest thou? Holla! Let not sorrow stay us.
Hold up thy head, man, said the gentle Meliboeus.
See Summer comes again, the country's pride adorning,
Hark how the cuckoo singeth this fair April morning.
O, said the shepherd, and sighed as one all undone,   5
Let me alone, alas, and drive him back to London.

IX

YE restless thoughts, that harbour discontent,
Cease your assaults, and let my heart lament,
And let my tongue have leave to tell my grief,
That she may pity, though not grant relief.
Pity would help what Love hath almost slain,   5
And salve the wound that festered this disdain.

X

WHENAS I glance on my lovely Phyllis,
Whose cheeks are decked with roses and lilies,
I me complained that she me nought regarded,
And that my love with envy was rewarded.
        Then wantonly she smileth,   5
        And grief from me exileth.

XI

CRUEL, unkind, my heart thou hast bereft me,
And will not leave while any life is left me,
And yet still will I love thee.

XII

O SLEEP, fond Fancy, sleep, my head, alas, thou tirest
With false delight of that which thou desirest.
Sleep, sleep, I say, and leave my thoughts molesting,
Thy master's head hath need of sleep and resting.

XIII

WEEP, O mine eyes, and cease not,
Alas, these your springtides, methinks, increase not.
O when, O when begin you
To swell so high that I may drown me in you?

XIV

SINCE neither tunes of joy nor notes of sadness,
Cruel unkind, can move thee;
I will go run away for rage and madness
Because I will not love thee.
O come again, thy fruitless labour waste not.   5
How wilt thou run, fool, when thy heart thou hast not?

XV

O GRIEF, where shall poor grief find patient hearing?
Footsteps of men I fly, my paths each creature baulking.
Wild and unhaunted woods seem tired with my walking.
Earth with my tears are drunk, air with my sighs tormented.
Heavens with my crying grown deaf and discontented.   5
Infernal ears affrighted with my doleful accenting,
Only my Love loves my lamenting.

XVI

O SWEET grief, O sweet sighs, O sweet disdaining,
O sweet repulses, sweet wrongs, sweet lamenting.
Words sharply sweet, and sweetly sharp consenting;
O sweet unkindness, sweet fears, sweet complaining.
Grieve then no more, my soul, those deep groans straining; 5
Your bitter anguish now shall have relenting,
And sharp disdains receive their full contenting.

XVII

REST now, Amphion, rest thy charming lyre,
    For Daphne's love, sweet love, makes melody.
Her love's concord with mine doth well conspire,
    No discord jars in our love's sympathy.
Our concords have some discords mixed among;   5
Discording concords makes the sweetest song.

WILLIAM BYRD

Psalmes, Sonets, & songs of sadnes and pietie, made into Musicke of fiue parts:
whereof, some of them going abroad among diuers, in vntrue coppies, are heere
truely corrected, and th'other being Songs very rare and newly composed,
are heere published, for the recreation of all such as delight in Musick.   1588

I. *Psalm 55*

O GOD, give ear and do apply
    To hear me when I pray:
And when to thee I call and cry
    Hide not thyself away.

Take heed to me, grant my request,   5
    And answer me again:
With plaints I pray full sore oppressed,
    Great grief doth me constrain.

Because my foes with threats and cries
    Oppress me through despite,   10
And so the wicked sort likewise
    To vex me have delight.

For they in council do conspire
    To charge me with some ill:
So in their hasty wrath and ire   15
    They do pursue me still.

                     [*John Hopkins*]

II. *Psalm 123*

MINE eyes with fervency of sprite
  I do lift up on high
To thee, O Lord, that dwell'st in light,
  Which no man may come nigh.

Behold, e'en as the servants' eyes   5
  Upon their master wait,
And as the maid her mistress' hand
  With careful eye and straight

Attends, so we, O Lord our God,
  Thy throne with hope and grief   10
Behold, until thou mercy send
  And give us some relief.

O Lord, though we deserve it not,
  Yet mercy let us find,
A people that despised are,   15
  Thrown down in soul and mind.

The mighty proud men of the world,
  That seeks us to oppress,
Have filled our souls with all contempts
  And left us in distress.   20

III. *Psalm 119*

MY soul, oppressed with care and grief,
  Doth cleave unto the dust;
O quicken me after thy word,
  For therein do I trust.

My ways unto thee have I showed,   5
  Thou answerest me again.
Teach me thy law and so I shall
  Be eased of my pain.

The way of thy commandments, Lord,
  Make me to understand;   10
And I will muse upon the power
  And wonders of thy hand.

My heart doth melt and pine away
   For very pain and grief;
O raise me up after thy word   15
   And send me some relief.

All falsehood and false ways, O Lord,
   Do thou from me remove;
And grant me grace to know thy law,
   And only that to love.   20

The way of truth I choose to tread,
   To keep my life in awe;
And set before me as a mark
   Thy sacred word and law.

I cleave, O Lord, unto all things   25
   Witnessed by thy speech,
Whereof that I repent me not
   I humbly thee beseech.

When that my heart thou shalt enlarge,
   To seek and run the ways   30
Of thy precepts, I will not fail
   The length of all my days.

IV. 2. *Pars Psalm 119*

How shall a young man prone to ill
   Cleanse his unbridled heart?
If that thy law, O Lord, he do,
   All frailty set apart,

Embrace with settled mind and learn   5
   Thy word with care to keep,
And seek to find with humble sprite
   Thy judgements that are deep.

With my whole heart I have thee sought,
   And searched out thy way;   10
O suffer not that from thy word
   I swerve and go astray.

Thy word, O Lord, within my heart,
   Lest I should thee offend,
I have laid up as treasure great,   15
   For that shall me defend.

The Lord is blest, he shall me teach
   The judgements of his mouth,
Thereby to rule and dress the ways
   Of mine untamed youth.   20

Thy laws therefore in open place
   My lips shall ever sound,
And never fail to show forth that
   To which thou hast me bound.

For in the way of thy precepts   25
   I set my whole delight,
No wealth, no treasure of the world
   So precious in my sight.

What thou command'st I will think on
   With diligent respect,   30
And to thy laws have due regard,
   For they shall me protect.

In thy precepts, O Lord, my soul
   Her whole delight hath set.
Thy words therefore more pure than gold   35
   I never will forget.

v. *Psalm 13*

O LORD, how long wilt thou forget
   To send me some relief?
For ever wilt thou hide thy face
   And so increase my grief?

How long shall I with vexed heart   5
   Seek counsel in my sprite?
How long shall my malicious foes
   Triumph, and me despite?

O Lord my God, hear my complaint,
   Uttered with woeful breath;   10
Lighten mine eyes, defend my life,
   That I sleep not in death.

Lest that mine enemy say: I have
   Against him, lo, prevailed.
At my downfall they will rejoice   15
   That thus have me assailed.

But in thy mercy, Lord, I trust,
    For that shall me defend;
My heart doth joy to see the help
    Which thou to me wilt send.   20

Unto the Lord therefore I sing,
    And do lift up my voice;
And for his goodness showed to me
    I will alway rejoice.

VI. *Psalm 15*

O LORD, who in thy sacred tent
    And holy hill shall dwell?
E'en he that both in heart and mind
    Doth study to do well;

In life upright, in dealing just,   5
    And he that from his heart
The truth doth speak with singleness,
    All falsehood set apart;

With tongue besides that hurts no man
    By false and ill report,   10
Nor friend nor neighbour harm will do
    Wherever he resort;

That hates the bad and loves the good,
    And faith that never breaks,
But keeps always, though to his loss,   15
    The word that once he speaks;

Nor filthy gain by love that seeks,
    Nor wealth so to possess,
Nor that for bribes the guiltless soul
    Doth labour to oppress.   20

Like as a mount so shall he stand;
    Nothing shall him remove
That thus shall do, the Lord hath said.
    No man can it disprove.

VII. *Psalm 12*

HELP, Lord, for wasted are those men
  Which righteousness embrace,
And rarely found that faithful are
  But all the truth deface.

Each to his neighbour falsehood speaks,   5
  And them seeks to beguile
With flattering lips and double heart
  When the smoothest he doth smile.

All flattering lips the Lord our God
  In justice will confound;   10
And all proud tongues that vaunt great things
  He will bring to the ground.

Our tongues, say they, shall lift us up,
  By them we shall prevail;
Who should us let, or stop our course,   15
  That thereof we should fail?

For the destruction of the just,
  And such as be oppressed,
And for the mournings of the poor
  That likewise be distressed,   20

I will rise up now, saith the Lord,
  And ease their grief and care
Of those which he full craftily
  Hath drawn into his snare.

Like silver fine that tried is   25
  Seven times by heat of fire,
So are thy words, Lord, pure and clean
  To such as them desire.

Thou, Lord, wilt keep and wilt defend
  All such as in thee trust,   30
And from that cursed race of men
  Save all such as be just.

When evil men exalted be,
  The wicked gad about
Far from all fear of pain; but thou,   35
  O Lord, wilt root them out.

VIII. *Psalm 112*

BLESSED is he that fears the Lord,
 He walketh in his ways,
And sets his great delight therein
 The length of all his days.

His seed and those which of him come 5
 Mighty on earth shall be,
The race of such as faithful are
 Men blessed shall them see.

Plenteousness within his house,
 And want there shall be never; 10
His righteous and upright dealing
 Endure shall for ever.

In misty clouds of troubles dark
 Which do the just oppress,
The Lord in mercy sends them light, 15
 And easeth their distress.

The righteous man is merciful,
 And lendeth where is need;
He guides with judgement all his things,
 Be it in word or deed. 20

Though storms do fall and tempests rise
 The righteous shall stand fast,
A good remembrance of the just
 For ever that shall last.

None evil tidings shall him fear, 25
 His heart is fully set,
He trusteth and believes the Lord,
 That will him not forget.

A stablished heart within his breast,
 No fear where so he goes. 30
The Lord in justice will revenge
 The malice of his foes.

A hand that doth relieve the poor,
 For which he may be sure
A good report will follow him 35
 That always shall endure.

This shall the wicked see and fret
  And waste away with ire,
Perish shall and consume to nought
  All that he doth desire.   40

IX. *Psalm 6*

LORD, in thy wrath·reprove me not,
  Though I deserve thine ire,
Ne yet correct me in thy rage,
  O Lord, I thee desire.

For I am weak; therefore, O Lord,   5
  Of mercy me forbear,
And heal me, Lord; forwhy thou know'st
  My bones do quake for fear.

                            [*Thomas Sternhold*]

X. *Psalm 130*

E'EN from the depth unto thee, Lord,
  With heart and voice I cry;
Give ear, O God, unto my plaint,
  And help my misery.

Here endeth the psalms, and beginneth the sonnets and pastorals

XI

I JOY not in no earthly bliss;
  I force not Croesus' wealth a straw;
For care I know not what it is;
  I fear not Fortune's fatal law.
My mind is such as may not move   5
For beauty bright, nor force of love.

I wish but what I have at will;
  I wander not to seek for more;
I like the plain, I climb no hill;
  In greatest storms I sit on shore,   10
And laugh at them that toil in vain
To get what must be lost again.

I kiss not where I wish to kill;
    I feign not love where most I hate;
I break no sleep to win my will;   15
    I wait not at the mighty's gate.
I scorn no poor, nor fear no rich,
I feel no want, nor have too much.

The court and cart I like nor loathe;
    Extremes are counted worst of all;   20
The golden mean between them both
    Doth surest sit and fear no fall.
This is my choice; forwhy I find
No wealth is like the quiet mind.

XII

THOUGH Amaryllis dance in green
        Like fairy queen;
        And sing full clear
Corinna can, with smiling cheer.
Yet since their eyes make heart so sore,   5
Heigh ho, 'chill love no more.

My sheep are lost for want of food,
        And I so wood,
        That all the day
I sit and watch a herdmaid gay,   10
Who laughs to see me sigh so sore,
Heigh ho, 'chill love no more.

Her loving looks, her beauty bright
        Is such delight,
        That all in vain   15
I love to like and lose my gain,
For her that thanks me not therefor,
Heigh ho, 'chill love no more.

Ah, wanton eyes, my friendly foes,
        And cause of woes,   20
        Your sweet desire
Breeds flames of ice and freeze in fire.
Ye scorn to see me weep so sore,
Heigh ho, 'chill love no more.

Love ye who list, I force him not,   25
    Sith, God it wot,
    The more I wail,
The less my sighs and tears prevail.
What shall I do but say therefore,
Heigh ho, 'chill love no more.   30

XIII

WHO likes to love, let him take heed.
    And wot you why?
Among the gods it is decreed
    That Love shall die.
And every wight that takes his part   5
Shall forfeit each a mourning heart.

The cause is this, as I have heard,
    A sort of dames,
Whose beauty he did not regard
    Nor secret flames,   10
Complained before the gods above
That gold corrupts the god of love.

The gods did storm to hear this news,
    And there they swore
That sith he did such dames abuse   15
    He should no more
Be god of love, but that he should
Both die and forfeit all his gold.

His bow and shafts they took away
    Before their eyes,   20
And gave these dames a longer day
    For to devise
Who should them keep, and they be bound
That love for gold should not be found.

These ladies, striving long, at last   25
    They did agree
To give them to a maiden chaste,
    Whom I did see,
Who with the same did pierce my breast.
Her beauty's rare, and so I rest.   30

XIV

MY mind to me a kingdom is;
  Such perfect joy therein I find,
That it excels all other bliss
  Which God or Nature hath assigned.
Though much I want that most would have   5
Yet still my mind forbids to crave.

No princely port, nor wealthy store,
  No force to win a victory,
No wily wit to salve a sore,
  No shape to win a loving eye;   10
To none of these I yield as thrall,
Forwhy my mind despise them all.

I see that plenty surfeits oft,
  And hasty climbers soonest fall.
I see that such as are aloft   15
  Mishap doth threaten most of all.
These get with toil, and keep with fear,
Such cares my mind can never bear.

I press to bear no haughty sway.
  I wish no more than may suffice.   20
I do no more than well I may.
  Look what I want my mind supplies.
Lo, thus I triumph like a king,
My mind content with anything.

I laugh not at another's loss,   25
  Nor grudge not at another's gain.
No worldly waves my mind can toss;
  I brook that is another's bane.
I fear no foe, nor fawn on friend.
I loathe not life, nor dread mine end.   30

My wealth is health and perfect ease,
  And conscience clear my chief defence.
I never seek by bribes to please,
  Nor by desert to give offence.
Thus do I live, thus will I die;   35
Would all did so as well as I.

[*Sir Edward Dyer*]

XV

WHERE Fancy fond for Pleasure pleads,
   And Reason keeps poor Hope in jail,
There time it is to take my beads
   And pray that Beauty may prevail;
Or else Despair will win the field   5
Where Reason, Hope, and Pleasure yield.

My eyes presume to judge this case,
   Whose judgement Reason doth disdain.
But Beauty with her wanton face
   Stands to defend, the case is plain;   10
And at the bar of sweet Delight,
She pleads that Fancy must be right.

But Shame will not have Reason yield,
   Though Grief do swear it shall be so,
As though it were a perfect shield   15
   To blush and fear to tell my woe.
Where silence force Will at the last
To wish for Wit when Hope is past.

So far hath fond Desire outrun
   The bond which Reason set out first,   20
That where Delight the fray begun
   I would now say, if that I durst,
That in her stead ten thousand woes
Have sprung in field where Pleasure grows.

O that I might declare the rest   25
   Of all the toys which Fancy turns,
Like towers of wind within my breast,
   Where fire is hid that never burns.
Then should I try one of the twain
Either to love, or to disdain.   30

But since Conceit dares not declare
   The strange conflict of Hope and Fear,
Lest Reason should be left so bare,
   That Love durst whisper in mine ear
And tell me how my Fancy shall   35
Bring Reason to be Beauty's thrall.

I must therefore with silence build
   The labyrinth of my delight,
Till Love have tried in open field
   Which of the twain shall win the fight.   40
I fear me Reason must give place,
If Fancy fond win Beauty's grace.

XVI

   O YOU that hear this voice,
     O you that see this face,
   Say whether of the choice
     May have the former place.
   Who dare judge this debate,   5
   That it be void of hate?

   This side doth Beauty take,
     For that doth Music speak,
   Fit orators to make
     The strongest judgements weak.   10
   The bar to plead their right
   Is only true delight.

   Thus doth the voice and face,
     These gentle lawyers, wage,
   Like loving brothers' case   15
     For father's heritage,
   That each, while each contends,
   Itself to other lends.

   For Beauty beautifies,
     With heavenly hue and grace,   20
   The heavenly harmonies;
     And in that faultless face
   The perfect beauties be
   A perfect harmony.

   Music more lofty swells   25
     In phrases finely placed.
   Beauty as far excels
     In action aptly graced.
   A friend each party draws
   To countenance his cause.   30

Love more affected seems
 To Beauty's lovely light,
And Wonder more esteems
 Of Music wondrous might.
But both to both so bent   35
As both in both are spent.

Music doth witness call
 The ear his truth doth try.
Beauty brings to the hall
 Eye witness of the eye.   40
Each in his object such
As none exceptions touch.

The Commonsense, which might
 Be arbiter of this,
To be forsooth upright   45
 To both sides partial is.
He lays on this chief praise,
Chief praise on that he lays.

Then Reason, princess high,
 Which sits in throne of mind,   50
And Music can in sky
 With hidden beauties find,
Say whether thou wilt crown
With limitless renown.

        [*Sir Philip Sidney*]

XVII

IF women could be fair and never fond,
 Or that their beauty might continue still,
I would not marvel though they made men bond
 By service long to purchase their goodwill;
But when I see how frail these creatures are 5
I laugh that men forget themselves so far.

To mark what choice they make, and how they change;
 How, leaving best, the worst they choose out still;
And how, like haggards wild, about they range,
 Scorning after reason to follow will: 10
Who would not shake such buzzards from the fist,
And let them fly (fair fools) which way they list?

Yet for our sport we fawn and flatter both,
   To pass the time when nothing else can please,
And train them on to yield by subtle oath   15
   The sweet content that gives such humour ease.
And then we say, when we their follies try,
To play with fools, O what a fool was I.
               [*Edward de Vere, Earl of Oxford*]

XVIII

AMBITIOUS Love hath forced me to aspire
   The beauties rare which do adorn thy face.
Thy modest life yet bridles my desire,
   Whose severe law doth promise me no grace.
But what? may Love live under any law?   5
   No, no, his power exceedeth man's conceit,
Of which the gods themselves do stand in awe,
   For on his frown a thousand torments wait.
Proceed then in this desperate enterprise
   With good advice, and follow Love thy guide,   10
That leads thee to thy wished paradise.
   Thy climbing thoughts this comfort take withal,
That if it be thy foul disgrace to slide,
   Thy brave attempt shall yet excuse thy fall.

XIX

WHAT pleasure have great princes
   More dainty to their choice,
Than herdmen wild, who careless
   In quiet life rejoice,
And Fortune's fate not fearing   5
Sing sweet in Summer morning.

Their dealings plain and rightful
   Are void of all deceit;
They never know how spiteful
   It is to kneel and wait   10
On favourite presumptuous
   Whose pride is vain and sumptuous.

All day their flocks each tendeth,
  At night they take their rest,
More quiet than who sendeth   15
  His ship into the East,
Where gold and pearl are plenty,
But getting very dainty.

For lawyers and their pleading
  They 'steem it not a straw;   20
They think that honest meaning
  Is of itself a law;
Where conscience judgeth plainly
They spend no money vainly.

O happy who thus liveth,   25
  Not caring much for gold,
With clothing which sufficeth
  To keep him from the cold.
Though poor and plain his diet,
Yet merry it is and quiet.   30

XX

As I beheld I saw a herdman wild
  With his sheep-hook a picture fine deface,
Which he sometime, his fancy to beguild,
  Had carved on bark of beech in secret place;
And with despite of most afflicted mind   5
  Through deep despair of heart, for love dismayed,
He pulled e'en from the tree the carved rind;
  And weeping sore these woeful words he said:
Ah, Phillida, would God thy picture fair
  I could as lightly blot out of my breast,   10
Then should I not thus rage with great despite,
  And tear the thing sometime I liked best.
But all in vain! It booteth not, God wot,
What printed is in heart on tree to blot.

XXI

Although the heathen poets did
  Apollo famous praise,
As one who for his music sweet
  No peer had in his days.

XXII

IN fields abroad, where trumpets shrill do sound,
  Where glaives and shields do give and take the knocks,
Where bodies dead do overspread the ground,
  And friends to foes are common butchers' blocks,
A gallant shot, well managing his piece,   5
In my conceit deserves a Golden Fleece.

Amid the seas a gallant ship set out,
  Wherein nor men nor yet munitions lacks,
In greatest winds that spareth not a clout,
  But cuts the waves in spite of weather's wracks,   10
Would force a swain that comes of coward's kind
To change himself and be of noble mind.

Who makes his seat a stately stamping steed,
  Whose neighs and plays are princely to behold,
Whose courage stout, whose eyes are fiery red,   15
  Whose joints well knit, whose harness all of gold,
Doth well deserve to be no meaner thing
Than Persian knight whose horse made him a king.

By that bedside where sits a gallant dame,
  Who casteth off her brave and rich attire,   20
Whose petticoat sets forth as fair a frame
  As mortal men or gods can well desire,
Who sits and sees her petticoat unlaced,
I say no more, the rest are all disgraced.

XXIII

CONSTANT Penelope sends to thee, careless Ulysses.
Write not again, but come, sweet mate, thyself to revive me.
Troy we do much envy, we desolate lost ladies of Greece,
Not Priamus, nor yet all Troy can us recompense make.
Oh, that he had, when he first took shipping to Lacedaemon,   5
That adulter I mean, had been o'erwhelmed with waters.
Then had I not lain now all alone, thus quivering for cold,
Nor used this complaint, nor have thought the day to be so long.

XXIV

LA virginella è simil' alla rosa
  Ch' in bel giardin sulla nativa spina,
Mentre sola è, sicura si riposa.
  Nè gregge, nè pastor, se le avvicina.
L'aura soave e l'alba rugiadosa,   5
  L'acqua, la terra, al suo favor s'inchina:
Giovani vaghi e donn' innamorate
  Amano haverne e seni e tempie ornate.

                         [*Ludovico Ariosto*]

XXV

FAREWELL false Love, the oracle of lies,
  A mortal foe and enemy to rest,
An envious boy, from whom all cares arise,
  A bastard vile, a beast with rage possessed,
A way of error, a temple full of treason,   5
In all effects contrary unto reason.

A poisoned serpent covered all with flowers,
  Mother of sighs, and murtherer of repose,
A sea of sorrows from whence are drawn such showers
  As moisture lend to every grief that grows;   10
A school of guile, a net of deep deceit,
A gilded hook that holds a poisoned bait.

A fortress foiled, which reason did defend,
  A Syren song, a fever of the mind,
A maze wherein affection finds no end,   15
  A raging cloud that runs before the wind,
A substance like the shadow of the sun,
A goal of grief for which the wisest run.

A quenchless fire, a nurse of trembling fear,
  A path that leads to peril and mishap,   20
A true retreat of sorrow and despair,
  An idle boy that sleeps in pleasure's lap.
A deep mistrust of that which certain seems,
A hope of that which reason doubtful deems.

                         [*Sir Walter Raleigh*]

XXVI

THE match that's made for just and true respects,
  With e'enness both of years and parentage,
Of force must bring forth many good effects.
    Pari jugo dulcis tractus.

For where chaste love and liking sets the plant,   5
  And concord waters with a firm good will,
Of no good thing there can be any want.
    Pari jugo dulcis tractus.

Sound is the knot that chastity hath tied,
  Sweet is the music unity doth make,   10
Sure is the store that plenty doth provide.
    Pari jugo dulcis tractus.

Where chasteness fails, there concord will decay;
  Where concord fleets, there plenty will decrease;
Where plenty wants, there love will wear away.   15
    Pari jugo dulcis tractus.

I, Chastity, restrain all strange desires.
  I, Concord, keep the course of sound consent.
I, Plenty, spare and spend as cause requires.
    Pari jugo dulcis tractus.   20

Make much of us, all ye that married be;
  Speak well of us, all ye that mind to be;
The time may come to want and wish all three.
    Pari jugo dulcis tractus.

Here endeth the sonnets and pastorals, and beginneth songs of sadness and piety

XXVII

PROSTRATE, O Lord, I lie,
  Behold me, Lord, with pity;
Stop not thine ears against my cry,
  My sad and mourning ditty,
Breathed from an inward soul,   5
  From heart heart'ly contrite,
An offering sweet, a sacrifice
  In thy high heavenly sight.

Observe not sins, O Lord,
    For who may then abide it?   10
But let thy mercy cancel them,
    Thou hast not man denied it.
Man melting with remorse and thoughts
    Thought past repenting,
O lighten, Lord; O hear our songs,   15
    Our sins full sore lamenting.

The wonders of thy works
    Above all reason reacheth,
And yet thy mercy above all
    This us thy spirit teacheth.   20
Then let no sinner fall
    In depth of foul despair,
Since never soul so foul there was
    But mercy made it fair.

XXVIII

ALL as a sea the world no other is,
   Ourselves are ships still tossed to and fro.
And lo, each man his love to that or this
   Is like a storm that drives the ship to go.
That thus our life in doubt of shipwrack stands,   5
Our wills the rocks, our want of skill the sands.

Our passions be the pirates still that spoil,
   And overboard casts out our reason's freight,
The mariners, that day and night do toil,
   Be our conceits that do on pleasure wait.   10
Pleasure, master, doth tyrannize the ship,
And giveth virtue secretly the nip.

The compass is a mind to compass all,
   Both pleasure, profit, place, and fame for nought.
The winds that blow, men overweening call,   15
   The merchandize is wit full dearly bought.
Trial th' anchor, cast upon experience,
For labour, life and all ado the recompense.

XXIX

Susanna fair some time assaulted was
   By two old men desiring their delight,
Whose false intent they thought to bring to pass,
   If not by tender love, by force and might.
To whom she said: If I your suit deny,   5
You will me falsely accuse and make me die.

And if I grant to that which you request,
   My chastity shall then deflowered be,
Which is so dear to me that I detest
   My life, if it berefted be from me.   10
And rather would I die of mine accord
Ten thousand times, than once offend the Lord.

XXX

If that a sinner's sighs be angels' food,
   Or that repentant tears be angels' wine,
Accept, O Lord, in this most pensive mood
   These hearty sighs and faithful tears of mine,
That went with Peter forth most sinfully,   5
But not with Peter wept most bitterly.

If I had David's crown to me betide,
   Or all his purple robes that he did wear,
I would lay then such honour all aside
   And only seek a sackcloth weed to bear.   10
His palace would I leave that I might show,
And mourn in cell for such offence, my woe.

There should these hands beat on my pensive breast,
   And, sad to death, for sorrow rend my hair;
My voice to call on thee should never rest,   15
   Whose grace I seek, whose judgement I do fear.
Upon the ground all grovelling on my face
I would beseech thy favour and good grace.

But since I have not means to make the show
   Of my repentant mind, and yet I see   20
My sin to greater heap than Peter's grow,
   Whereby the danger more it is to me,
I put my trust in his most precious blood
Whose life was paid to purchase all our good.

Thy mercy greater is than any sin;   25
  Thy greatness none can ever comprehend;
Wherefore, O Lord, let me thy mercy win,
  Whose glorious name no time can ever end.
Wherefore, I say, all praise belongs to thee,
Whom I beseech be merciful to me.   30

XXXI

CARE for thy soul as thing of greatest price,
  Made to the end to taste of power divine,
Devoid of guilt, abhorring sin and vice,
  Apt by God's grace to virtue to incline.
Care for it so as by thy retchless train   5
It be not brought to taste eternal pain.

Care for thy corpse, but chiefly for soul's sake;
  Cut off excess, sustaining food is best;
To vanquish pride but comely clothing take;
  Seek after skill, deep ignorance detest.   10
Care so, I say, the flesh to feed and clothe
That thou harm not thy soul and body both.

Care for the world to do thy body right;
  Rack not thy wit to win by wicked ways;
Seek not t'oppress the weak by wrongful might;   15
  To pay thy due do banish all delays.
Care to dispend according to thy store,
And in like sort be mindful of the poor.

Care for thy soul, as for thy chiefest stay;
  Care for thy body for thy soul's avail;   20
Care for the world for body's help alway;
  Care yet but so as virtue may prevail.
Care in such sort that thou be sure of this:
Care keep thee not from heaven and heavenly bliss.

XXXII

LULLA la, lulla lulla lullaby.
  My sweet little baby, what meanest thou to cry?
Be still, my blessed babe, though cause thou hast to mourn,
Whose blood most innocent to shed the cruel king hath sworn.

And lo, alas, behold, what slaughter he doth make, 5
Shedding the blood of infants all, sweet Saviour, for thy sake.
A King is born, they say, which King this king would kill.
O woe, and woeful heavy day, when wretches have their will.

Lulla la, lulla lulla lullaby.
My sweet little baby, what meanest thou to cry? 10
Three kings this King of kings to see are come from far,
To each unknown, with offerings great, by guiding of a star.
And shepherds heard the song which angels bright did sing,
Giving all glory unto God for coming of this King,
Which must be made away, king Herod would him kill. 15
O woe, and woeful heavy day, when wretches have their will.

Lulla la, lulla lulla lullaby.
My sweet little baby, what meanest thou to cry?
Lo, lo, my little babe, be still, lament no more.
From fury shalt thou step aside, help have we still in store. 20
We heavenly warning have some other soil to seek,
From death must fly the Lord of life, as lamb both mild and meek.
Thus must my babe obey the king that would him kill.
O woe, and woeful heavy day, when wretches have their will.

Lulla la, lulla lulla lullaby. 25
My sweet little baby, what meanest thou to cry?
But thou shalt live and reign as Sibyls have foresaid,
As all the Prophets prophesy, whose mother, yet a maid
And perfect virgin pure, with her breasts shall upbreed
Both God and man, that all hath made, the Son of heavenly seed, 30
Whom caitiffs none can 'tray, whom tyrants none can kill.
O joy, and joyful happy day, when wretches want their will.

XXXIII

WHY do I use my paper, ink, and pen,
    And call my wits to counsel what to say?
Such memories were made for mortal men,
    I speak of saints whose names cannot decay.
An angel's trump were fitter for to sound 5
Their glorious death, if such on earth were found.

That store of such were once on earth pursued
    The histories of ancient times record,
Whose constancy great tyrants' rage subdued,
    Through patient death professing Christ their Lord. 10

As his Apostles perfect witness bare,
With many more that blessed martyrs were.

Whose patience rare and most courageous mind
  With fame renomed perpetual shall endure,
By whose examples we may rightly find   15
  Of holy life and death a pattern pure.
That we therefore their virtues may embrace,
Pray we to Christ to guide us with his grace.

                        [*attrib. to Henry Walpole*]

The funeral songs of that honourable gent[leman] Sir Philip Sidney, knight.

XXXIV

    COME to me, grief, for ever;
    Come to me, tears, day and night;
    Come to me, plaint, ah, helpless;
    Just grief, heart, tears, plaint worthy.

    Go fro me, dread to die now;   5
    Go fro me, care to live more;
    Go fro me, joys all on earth;
    Sidney, O Sidney is dead.

    He whom the court adorned,
    He whom the country courtes'd,   10
    He who made happy his friends,
    He that did good to all men.

    Sidney, the hope of land strange,
    Sidney, the flower of England,
    Sidney, the spirit heroic,   15
    Sidney is dead, O dead, dead.

    Dead? no, no, but renomed,
    With the Anointed oned;
    Honour on earth at his feet,
    Bliss everlasting his seat.   20

    Come to me, grief, for ever;
    Come to me, tears, day and night;
    Come to me, plaint, ah, helpless;
    Just grief, heart, tears, plaint worthy.

XXXV

O THAT most rare breast, crystalline, sincere,
Through which like gold thy princely heart did shine.
O sprite heroic, O valiant worthy knight,
O Sidney, prince of fame and men's good will,
For thee both kings and princesses do mourn.   5
Thy noble tomb three cities strange desired;
Foes to the cause thy prowess did defend
Bewail the day that crossed thy famous race.
The doleful debt due to thy hearse I pay,
Tears from the soul that aye thy want shall moan,   10
And by my will my life itself would yield,
If heathen blame ne might my faith disdain.
O heavy time that my days draw behind thee.
Thou dead dost live, thy friend here living dieth.

Songs of sundrie natures, some of grauitie, and others of myrth, fit for all companies and voyces. Lately made and composed into Musicke of 3. 4. 5. and 6. parts: and published for the delight of all such as take pleasure in the exercise of that Art.   1589

I

Domine in furore. Psalm 6

LORD, in thy rage rebuke me not
    For my most grievous sin,
Nor in thine anger chasten me,
    But let me favour win.
Have mercy, Lord, on me because   5
    My state is weak to see,
Heal me, O Lord, for that my bones
    Are troubled sore in me.

II

Beati quorum. Psalm 32

RIGHT blest are they whose wicked sins
    By God remitted be,
And whose defaults are covered
    Through his great clemency.

The man is blest to whom our Lord   5
    Hath not imputed sin,
Nor in his sprite deceit is found,
    Nor takes delight therein.

III

Domine ne. Psalm 38

LORD, in thy wrath correct me not,
    Nor in thy fury vex.
Give tears, give grace, give penitence
    Unto my sinful sex.
For that the arrows of thy wrath   5
    Are fixed in my heart,
And thou hast laid thine hand on me
    For my most just desert.

IV

Miserere mei Deus. Psalm 51

O GOD, which art most merciful,
    Have mercy, Lord, on me;
According to thy mercy great
    Let me relieved be.
And put away my wickedness   5
    Which sundry ways hath been,
According to the multitude
    Of thy compassions seen.

V

Domine exaudi. Psalm 102

LORD, hear my prayer instantly
    Which I before thee make;
And let my cry come unto thee,
    Do not the same forsake.
Turn not away thy face from me,   5
    When troubles me oppress,
Each day incline thine ear to me,
    And succour my distress.

VI

De profundis. Psalm 130

FROM depth of sin, O Lord, to thee
    I have made humble cry.
Lord, hear my voice, make it ascend
    Unto thy throne so high.
Unto the voice of my request   5
    Poured out before thy sight,
Lord, let thine ears attentive be
    To hear me day and night.

VII

Domine exaudi. Psalm 143

ATTEND mine humble prayer, Lord,
    With thine attentive ear;
E'en in thy truth and justice, Lord,
    Vouchsafe my suit to hear.
And into judgement enter not   5
    With thy poor servant here,
Because none shall be justified
    And stand before thee clear.

Here endeth the seven psalms

VIII

SUSANNA fair some time assaulted was
    By two old men desiring their delight,
Which lewd intent they thought to bring to pass,
    If not by tender love, by force and might.
To whom she said: If I your suit deny   5
You will me falsely accuse and make me die.

And if I grant to that which you request,
    My chastity shall then deflowered be,
Which is so dear to me that I detest
    My life, if it berefted be from me.   10
And rather would I die of mine accord
Ten thousand times, than once offend our Lord.

IX

THE nightingale so pleasant and so gay
    In greenwood groves delights to make his dwelling,
In fields to fly, chanting his roundelay
    At liberty, against the cage rebelling.
    But my poor heart, with sorrows over-swelling,   5
Through bondage vile binding my freedom short,
    No pleasure takes in these his sports excelling,
Nor in his song receiveth no comfort.

X–XI

WHEN younglings first on Cupid fix their sight,
    And see him naked, blindfold, and a boy,
Though bow and shafts and firebrand be his might,
    Yet ween they he can work them none annoy.
And therefore with his purple wings they play,   5
    For glorious seemeth Love, though light as feather,
And when they have done, they ween to 'scape away,
    For blind men, say they, shoot they know not whither.
But when by proof they find that he did see,
    And that his wound did rather dim their sight,   10
They wonder more how such a lad as he
    Should be of such surpassing power and might.
But ants have galls, so hath the bee his sting.
Then shield me, heavens, from such a subtle thing.

XII–XIII

UPON a summer's day Love went to swim,
    And cast himself into a sea of tears.
The clouds called in their light, and heaven waxed dim,
    And sighs did raise a tempest causing fears.
The naked boy could not so wield his arms,   5
    But that the waves were masters of his might,
And threatened him to work far greater harms,
    If he devised not to 'scape by flight.
Then for a boat his quiver stood instead,
    His bow unbent did serve him for a mast,   10
Whereby to sail his cloth of vail he spread,
    His shafts for oars on either board he cast.
From shipwrack safe, this wag got thus to shore,
And sware to bathe in lovers' tears no more.

XIV

THE greedy hawk with sudden sight of lure
  Doth stoop in hope to have her wished prey.
So many men do stoop to sights unsure,
  And courteous speech doth keep them at the bay.
Let them beware lest friendly looks be like   5
  The lure, whereat the soaring hawk did strike.

                                        [*Geoffrey Whitney*]

XV–XVI

Is Love a boy? What means he then to strike?
  Or is he blind? Why will he be a guide?
Is he a man? Why doth he hurt his like?
  Is he a god? Why doth he men deride?
No one of these, but one compact of all.   5
  A wilful boy, a man still dealing blows,
Of purpose blind to lead men to their thrall,
  A god that rules unruly, God He knows!
Boy, pity me that am a child again.
  Blind, be no more my guide to make me stray.   10
Man, use thy might to force away my pain.
  God, do me good and lead me to my way.
And if thou beest a power to me unknown,
Power of my life, let here thy grace be shown.

XVII–XVIII

WOUNDED I am, and dare not seek relief
  For this new stroke, unseen but not unfelt;
No blood nor bruise is witness of my grief,
  But sighs and tears wherewith I mourn and melt.
If I complain, my witness is suspect;   5
  If I contain, with cares I am undone;
Sit still and die, tell truth and be reject;
  O hateful choice, that sorrow cannot shun.
Yet of us twain, whose loss shall be the less?
  Mine of my life, or you of your good name?   10
Light is my death, regarding my distress,
  But your offence cries out to your defame.
A virgin fair hath slain for lack of grace
The man that made an idol of her face.

XIX–XXI

FROM Cytheron the warlike boy is fled,
   And smiling sits upon a virgin's lap,
   Thereby to train poor misers to the trap,
Whom beauty draws with fancy to be fed.
And when desire with eager looks is led,   5
      Then from her eyes
      The arrow flies,
Feathered with flame, armed with a golden head.

There careless thoughts are freed of that flame,
   Wherewith her thralls are scorched to the heart.   10
   If Love would so, would God th' enchanting dart
Might once return and burn from whence it came,
Not to deface of beauty's work the frame,
      But by rebound
      It might be found   15
What secret smart I suffer by the same.

If Love be just, then just is my desire.
  And if unjust, why is he called a god?
  O god, O good, O just, reserve thy rod
To chasten those that from thy laws retire.   20
But choose aright, good Love, I thee require,
      The golden head,
      Not that of lead;
Her heart is frost and must dissolve by fire.

XXII

O LORD my God, let flesh and blood thy servant not subdue;
Nor let the world deceive me with his glory most untrue.
Let not, O Lord, O mighty God, let not thy mortal foe,
Let not the fiend with all his craft thy servant overthrow.
But to resist give fortitude, give patience to endure,   5
Give constancy, that always thine I may persever sure.

XXIII

WHILE that the sun with his beams hot
   Scorched the fruits in vale and mountain,
Philon the shepherd, late forgot,
   Sitting besides a crystal fountain

In shadow of a green oak tree,   5
Upon his pipe this song played he:
  Adieu love, adieu love, untrue love,
  You mind is light, soon lost for new love.

So long as I was in your sight
  I was as your heart, your soul, your treasure;   10
And evermore you sobbed, you sighed,
  Burning in flames beyond all measure.
Three days endured your love to me,
And it was lost in other three.
    Adieu love, adieu love, untrue love,   15
    Your mind is light, soon lost for new love.

Another shepherd you did see,
  To whom your heart was soon enchained.
Full soon your love was leapt from me,
  Full soon my place he had obtained.   20
Soon came a third your love to win,
And we were out, and he was in.
    Adieu love, adieu love, untrue love,
    Your mind is light, soon lost for new love.

Sure you have made me passing glad   25
  That you your mind so soon removed,
Before that I the leisure had
  To choose you for my best beloved.
For all my love was past and done
Two days before it was begun.   30
    Adieu love, adieu love, untrue love,
    Your mind is light, soon lost for new love.

XXIV

[Chorus only (ll. 7–8) of the Christmas Carol, No. xxxv]

XXV

[Chorus only (ll. 7–10) of the Christmas Carol, No. xl]

XXVI

WEEPING full sore, with face as fair as silver,
  Not wanting rose, nor lily white to paint it,
I saw a lady walk fast by a river,
  Upon whose banks Diana's nymphs all danced.

Her beauty great had divers gods enchanted,   5
　Among the which Love was the first transformed,
Who unto her his bow and shafts had granted,
　And by her sight to adamant was turned.
Alas, quoth I, what meaneth this demeanour,
　So fair a dame to be so full of sorrow?   10
No wonder, quoth a nymph, she wanteth pleasure,
　Her tears and sighs ne cease from eve to morrow.
This lady rich is of the gifts of beauty,
But unto her are gifts of fortune dainty.

XXVII

PENELOPE, that longed for the sight
　Of her Ulysses, wandering all too long,
Felt never joy wherein she took delight,
　Although she lived in greatest joys among.
So I, poor wretch, possessing that I crave,   5
Both live and lack by wrong of that I have.
Then blame me not, although to heavens I cry,
And pray the gods that shortly I might die.

XXVIII

COMPEL the hawk to sit that is unmanned,
　Or make the hound, untaught, to draw the deer,
Or bring the free against his will in band,
　Or move the sad a pleasant tale to hear;
　　Your time is lost, and you are ne'er the near.   5
So Love ne learns by force the knot to knit,
He serves but those that feel sweet Fancy's fit.
                                        [*Thomas Churchyard*]

XXIX & XXXIV

SEE those sweet eyes, those more than sweetest eyes,
　Eyes whom the stars exceed not in their grace.
See Love at gaze, Love that would fain devise,
　But cannot speak to plead his wondrous case.
Love would discharge the duty of his heart   5
　In Beauty's praise, whose greatness doth deny
Words to his thoughts, and thoughts to her desert;
　Which high conceits since nothing can supply,

Love, here constrained through conquest to confess,
Bids silence sigh that tongue cannot express.   10

XXX

WHEN I was otherwise than now I am,
   I loved more, but skilled not so much;
Fair words and smiles could have contented then,
   My simple age and ignorance was such.
But at the length experience made me wonder   5
That hearts and tongues did lodge so far asunder.

As watermen which on the Thames do row
   Look to the east, but west keeps on the way,
My sovereign sweet her countenance settled so
   To feed my hope, while she her snares might lay.   10
And when she saw that I was in her danger,
Good God, how soon she proved then a ranger.

I could not choose but laugh, although too late,
   To see great craft deciphered in a toy.
I love her still, but such conditions hate   15
   Which so profanes my paradise of joy.
Love whets the wits, whose pain is but a pleasure,
A toy by fits to play withal at leisure.

XXXI

WHEN first by force of fatal destiny
   From Carthage town the Trojan knight did sail,
Queen Dido fair with woeful weeping eye
   His strange depart did grievously bewail.
And when no sighs nor tears could ease her smart,   5
With sword full sharp she pierced her tender heart.

XXXII

I THOUGHT that Love had been a boy
    With blinded eyes;
Or else some other wanton toy
    That men devise,
Like tales of fairies often told   5
By doting age that dies for cold.

XXXIII

O DEAR life, when may it be
That mine eyes thine eyes may see,
   And in them my mind discover
Whether absence hath had force
Thy remembrance to divorce   5
   From the image of thy lover?

O if I myself find not
Through my parting aught forgot,
   Nor debarred from beauty's treasure,
Let no tongue aspire to tell   10
In what high joys I shall dwell,
   Only thought aims at the pleasure.

Thought therefore I will send thee,
To take up the place for me,
   Long I will not after tarry.   15
There unseen thou may'st be bold
These fair wonders to behold,
   Which in them my hopes do carry.
                  [*Sir Philip Sidney*]

XXXIV
[*See No. xxix*]

XXXV & XXIV
A Carol for Christmas Day

FROM Virgin's womb this day did spring
   The precious seed that saved man.
This day let man rejoice and sweetly sing,
   Since on this day salvation first began.
This day did Christ man's soul from death remove   5
With glorious saints to dwell in Heaven above.
   Rejoice, rejoice, with heart and voice,
   In Christ his birth this day rejoice.

This day to man came pledge of perfect peace,
   This day to man came love and unity,   10
This day man's grief began for to surcease,
   This day did man receive a remedy

For each offence and every deadly sin
With guilty heart that erst he wandered in.
    Rejoice, rejoice, with heart and voice,   15
    In Christ his birth this day rejoice.

In Christ his flock let love be surely placed,
   From Christ his flock let concord hate expel,
Of Christ his flock let love be so embraced,
   As we in Christ and Christ in us may dwell.   20
Christ is the author of sweet unity
From whence proceedeth all felicity.
    Rejoice, rejoice, with heart and voice,
    In Christ his birth this day rejoice.

O sing unto this glittering glorious King;   25
   O praise his name let every living thing.
Let heart and voice like bells of silver ring
   The comfort that this day to man doth bring.
Let lute, let shalm with sound of sweet delight
These joys of Christ his birth this day recite.   30
    Rejoice, rejoice, with heart and voice,
    In Christ his birth this day rejoice.

                                [*Francis Kindlemarsh*]

XXXVI–XXXVII

OF gold all burnished and brighter than sunbeams
   Were those curled locks upon her noble head,
   From whose deep conceits my true deservings fled.
Wherefore these mine eyes such store of tears outstreams.
Her eyes are fair stars; her red, like damask rose;   5
   Her white, silver shine of moon on crystal stream;
   Her beauty perfect, whereon my fancies dream.
Her lips are rubies; her teeth, of pearl two rows.
Her breath is more sweet than perfect amber is;
   Her years are in prime; and nothing doth she want   10
That might draw angels from heaven to further bliss.
   Of all things perfect this do I most complain,
   Her heart is a rock, made all of adamant.
Which gifts all delight, this last doth only pain.

XXXVIII–XXXIX

BEHOLD how good a thing it is
    For brethren to agree,
When men amongst them do no strife
    But peace and concord see.
Full like unto the precious balm   5
    From Aaron's head that fell,
And did descend upon his beard
    His garment skirts until.
And as the pleasant morning dew
    The mountains doth relieve,   10
So God will bless where concord is
    And life eternal give.

                         [*Psalm cxxxiii*]

XL & XXV

A Carol for Christmas Day

AN earthly tree a heavenly fruit it bare;
    A case of clay contained a crown immortal,
A crown of crowns, a King, whose cost and care
    Redeemed poor man, whose race before was thrall
To death, to doom, to pains of everlasting,   5
By his sweet death, scorns, stripes, and often fasting.
        Cast off all doubtful care,
           Exile and banish tears,
        To joyful news divine
           Lend us your listening ears.   10

A Star above the stars, a Sun of light,
    Whose blessed beams this wretched earth bespread
With hope of heaven and of God's Son the sight,
    Which in our flesh and sinful soul lay dead.
O faith, O hope, O joys renowned for ever,   15
O lively life, that deathless shall persever.
        Cast off all doubtful care,
           Exile and banish tears,
        To joyful news divine
           Lend us your listening ears.   20

Then let us sing the lullabies of sleep
    To this sweet Babe, born to awake us all
From drowsy sin, that made old Adam weep,
    And by his fault gave to mankind the fall.
For lo, this day, the birth day, day of days,   25
Summons our songs to give him laud and praise.
        Cast off all doubtful care,
        Exile and banish tears,
        To joyful news divine
        Lend us your listening ears.   30

XLI

A Dialogue between two Shepherds

[*1st Shepherd.*]   W HO made thee, Hob, forsake the plough
                                And fall in love?
[*2nd Shepherd.*]   Sweet Beauty, which hath power to bow
                                The gods above.
[*1st Shepherd.*]   What, dost thou serve a shepherdess?   5
[*2nd Shepherd.*]   Aye, such as hath no peer, I guess.
[*1st Shepherd.*]   What is her name who bears thy heart
                                Within her breast?
[*2nd Shepherd.*]   Sylvana fair, of high desert,
                                Whom I love best.   10
[*1st Shepherd.*]   O Hob, I fear she looks too high.
[*Both.*]   Yet love I must, or else I die.

XLII–XLIII

A N D think ye, nymphs, to scorn at Love,
    As if his fire were but of straws?
He made the mighty gods above
    To stoop and bow unto his laws;
And with his shaft of beauty bright   5
He slays the hearts that scorn his might.

        Love is a fit of pleasure
            Bred out of idle brains.
        His fancies have no measure,
            No more than have his pains.   10
    His vain affections, like the weather,
    Precise or fond, we wot not whether.

XLIV

IF in thine heart thou nourish will,
    And give all to thy lust,
Then sorrows sharp and griefs at length
    Endure of force thou must.
But if that reason rule thy will,   5
    And govern all thy mind,
A blessed life then shalt thou lead
    And fewest dangers find.

XLV

UNTO the hills mine eyes I lift,
    My hope shall never fade;
But from the Lord I look for help,
    That heaven and earth hath made.

Thy foot he will from slipping save,   5
    And he that doth thee keep
With watchful eye will thee preserve
    Without slumber or sleep.

The Lord thy keeper and shade is
    And stands at thy right arm;   10
The sun by day shall not thee burn,
    Nor moon by night thee harm.

The Lord shall keep thee from all ill,
    Thy soul he shall preserve,
And all thy ways both in and out   15
    For ever shall conserve.

                      [*Psalm cxxi*]

XLVI–XLVII

CHRIST rising again from the dead now dieth not. Death from henceforth hath no power upon him. For in that he died, he died but once
to put away sin, but in that he liveth he liveth unto God. And so
likewise count yourselves dead unto sin, but living unto God in
Christ Jesus our Lord. [*Romans* vi. 9.]

Christ is risen again, the first fruits of them that sleep. For seeing that by man came death, by man also cometh the resurrection of the dead. For as by Adam all men do die, so by Christ all men shall be restored to life. Amen. [1 *Corinthians* xv. 20.]

ᴐᴐᴐᴐᴐᴐᴐᴐᴐᴐᴐᴐᴐ

Psalmes, Songs, and Sonnets: some solemne, others ioyfull, framed to the life of the Words: Fit for Voyces or Viols of 3. 4. 5. and 6. Parts.   1611

I

THE eagle's force subdues each bird that flies.
    What metal may resist the flaming fire?
Doth not the sun dazzle the clearest eyes,
    And melt the ice, and make the frost retire?
    Who can withstand a puissant king's desire?   5
The stiffest stones are pierced through with tools.
The wisest are with princes made but fools.

[*Thomas Churchyard*]

II

OF flattering speech with sugared words beware;
    Suspect the heart whose face doth fawn and smile;
With trusting these the world is clogged with care,
    And few there be can 'scape these vipers vile.
With pleasing speech they promise and protest,   5
When hateful hearts lie hid within their breast.

[*Geoffrey Whitney*]

III–IV

IN Winter cold when tree and bush was bare,
    And frost had nipped the roots of tender grass,
The ants with joy did feed upon their fare,
    Which they had stored while Summer season was.
To whom for food a grasshopper did cry,   5
And said she starved if they did help deny.

Whereat an ant with long experience wise,
    And frost and snow had many Winters seen,
Inquired what in Summer was her guise.
    Quoth she, I sung and hopped in meadows green.   10

Then quoth the ant: Content thee with thy chance,
For to thy song now art thou like to dance.

V

WHO looks may leap and save his shins from knocks.
  Who tries, may trust, else flattering friends shall find.
He saves the steed that keeps him under locks.
  Who speaks with heed may boldly speak his mind.
But he whose tongue before his wit doth run,   5
Oft speaks too soon, and grieves when he hath done.

[*Geoffrey Whitney*]

VI

SING ye to our Lord a new song, His praise in the church of saints.
  Let Israel be joyful in Him that made him, and let the daughters
of Sion rejoice in their King.

[*Psalm cxlix.* 1–2]

VII

I HAVE been young, but now am old, yet did I never see the righteous
forsaken, nor his seed begging their bread.

[*Psalm xxxvii.* 25]

VIII

IN crystal towers and turrets richly set
  With glittering gems that shine against the sun,
In regal rooms of jasper and of jet
  Content of mind not always likes to woon.
But often times it pleaseth her to stay   5
In simple cotes enclosed with walls of clay.

[*Geoffrey Whitney*]

IX

THIS sweet and merry month of May,
  While Nature wantons in her prime,
And birds do sing, and beasts do play
  For pleasure of the joyful time,

I choose the first for holiday,   5
  And greet Eliza with a rhyme:
O beauteous Queen of second Troy,
Take well in worth a simple toy.
               [*Attributed to Thomas Watson*]

X

LET not the sluggish sleep
  Close up thy waking eye,
Until with judgement deep
  Thy daily deeds thou try.

He that one sin in conscience keeps,   5
  When he to quiet goes,
More vent'rous is than he that sleeps
  With twenty mortal foes.

XI

A FEIGNED friend by proof I find
  To be a greater foe
Than he that with a spiteful mind
  Doth seek my overthrow;
For of the one I can beware,   5
With craft the other breeds my care.

Such men are like the hidden rocks
  Which in the seas do lie,
Against the which each ship that knocks
  Is drowned suddenly.   10
No greater fraud, nor more unjust,
Than false deceit hid under trust.

XII

AWAKE, mine eyes, see Phoebus bright arising,
  And lesser lights to shades obscure descending.
Glad Philomela sits, tunes of joy devising,
      Whilst in sweet notes
      From warbling throats   5
      The sylvan choir
      With like desire
To her are echoes sending.

XIII

COME, jolly swains, come, let us sit around,
And with blithe carols sullen cares confound.
    The shepherd's life
    Is void of strife.
    No worldly treasures   5
    Distastes our pleasures;
    With free consenting
    Our minds contenting,
We smiling laugh, while others sigh repenting.

XIV

WHAT is life or worldly pleasure?
    Seeming shadows quickly sliding.
What is wealth or golden treasure?
    Borrowed fortune never biding.
What is grace or princes' smiling?   5
    Hoped honour, time beguiling.
What are all in one combined, which divided so displease?
Apish toys and vain delights, mind's unrest and soul's disease.

XV. *Fantasia* [*for strings alone*]

XVI

COME let us rejoice unto our Lord; let us make joy to God our
Saviour.
    Let us approach to his presence in confession, and in psalms let us
make joy to him.   [*Psalm xcv.* 1–2]

XVII

RETIRE, my soul, consider thine estate,
    And justly sum thy lavish sin's account;
Time's dear expense, and costly pleasure's rate,
    How follies grow, how vanities amount.
Write all these down in pale Death's reckoning tables,   5
Thy days will seem but dreams, thy hopes but fables.

XVIII

ARISE, Lord, into thy rest, thou and the Ark of thy sanctification.
Let the Priests be clothed with justice, and let the Saints rejoice.
[*Psalm cxxxii*. 8–9]

XIX

COME, woeful Orpheus, with thy charming lyre,
And tune my voice unto thy skilful wire;
Some strange chromatic notes do you devise,
That best with mournful accents sympathise;
Of sourest sharps and uncouth flats make choice,   5
And I'll thereto compassionate my voice.

XX–XXI

SING we merrily unto God our Strength, make a cheerful noise unto
the God of Jacob.

    Take the shawm, bring hither the tabret, the merry harp with the
lute.

    Blow up the trumpet in the new moon, even in the time   5
appointed, and upon our solemn feast-day.

    For this was made a statute for Israel and a law of the God of
Jacob.   [*Psalm lxxxi*. 1–4]

XXII

CROWNED with flowers I saw fair Amaryllis
    By Thyrsis sit, hard by a fount of crystal,
And with her hand, more white than snow or lilies,
    On sand she wrote 'My faith shall be immortal'.
And suddenly a storm of wind and weather   5
Blew all her faith and sand away together.

XXIII

WEDDED to Will is Witless,
    And seldom he is skilful
That bears the name of wise and yet is wilful.
    To govern he is fitless
        That deals not by election,   5
        But by his fond affection.
    O that it might be treason
For men to rule by Will and not by Reason.

XXIV

MAKE ye joy to God, all the earth, serve ye our Lord in gladness.
Enter ye in before his sight in jollity.

Know ye that our Lord he is God, He made us and not we ourselves. [*Psalm c.* 1–2]

XXV

HAVE mercy upon me, O God, after thy great goodness, and according to the multitude of thy mercies wipe away mine offences.

Wash me clean from my wickedness, and purge me from my sins.
Amen. [*Psalm li.* 1–2]

XXVI

Fantasia [for strings alone]

XXVII

A Carol for Christmas Day

THIS day Christ was born.
This day our Saviour did appear.
This day the Angels sing in earth,
The Archangels are glad.
This day the just rejoice, saying: 5
Glory be to God on high. Alleluia.

XXVIII

A Carol for New Year's Day

O GOD, that guides the cheerful sun
   By motions strange the year to frame,
Which, now returned whence it begun,
   From heaven extols thy glorious name;
This New Year's season sanctify 5
   With double blessings of thy store,
That graces new may multiply,
   And former follies reign no more.
      So shall our hearts with heaven agree,
      And both give laud and praise to thee. 10

Th'old year by course is past and gone,
  Old Adam, Lord, from us expel;
New creatures make us every one,
  New life becomes the New Year well;
As new-born babes from malice keep;   15
  New wedding garments, O Christ, we crave,
That we thy face in heaven may see,
  With angels bright our souls to save.
      So shall our hearts with heaven agree,
      And both give laud and praise to thee. Amen. 20

XXIX

PRAISE our Lord, all ye Gentiles, praise him, all ye people;
Because his mercy is confirmed upon us, and his truth remaineth
for ever. Amen.   [*Psalm cxvii*]

XXX

TURN our captivity, O Lord, as a brook in the south.
They that sow in tears shall reap in joyfulness.
Going they went, and wept, casting their seeds; but coming they
shall come with jollity, carrying their sheaves with them.
                                [*Psalm cxxvi.* 5–7]

XXXI

AH, silly soul, how are thy thoughts confounded
  Betwixt two loves that far unlikely are.
Lust's love is blind, and by no reason bounded,
  Heaven's love is clear and fair beyond compare.
No wonder though this love light not thy mind,   5
Whilst looking through false love thine eyes are blind.

XXXII

HOW vain the toils that mortal men do take
  To hoard up gold, that time doth turn to dross,
Forgetting him, who only for their sake
  His precious blood did shed upon the Cross,
And taught us all in heaven to hoard our treasure,   5
Where true increase doth grow above all measure.

RICHARD CARLTON

Madrigals To Fiue voyces. 1601

I

THE love of change hath changed the world throughout;
   And what is counted good but that is strange?
New things wax old, old new, all turns about,
   And all things change except the love of change.
Yet find I not that love of change in me,   5
But as I am so will I always be.

II

CONTENT thyself with thy estate;
   Seek not to climb above the skies;
For often love is mixed with hate,
   And 'twixt the flowers the serpent lies.
Where fortune sends her greatest joys,   5
There, once possessed, they are but toys.

What thing can earthly pleasure give
   That breeds delight when it is past?
Or who so quietly doth live
   But storms of cares do drown at last?   10
This is the loan of worldly hire,
The more we have, the more desire.

Wherefore I hold him best at ease
   That lives content with his estate,
And doth not sail in worldly seas   15
   Where *mine* and *thine* do breed debate.
This noble mind e'en in a clown
Is more than to possess a crown.

III

THE self-same thing that gives me cause to die
   Is only means for which I life desire;
The self-same cold by which as dead I lie,
   Is only means to kindle greater fire;
The less I feel myself in hope to speed,   5
The more desire this want of hope doth breed.

IV–V

WHEN Flora fair the pleasant tidings bringeth
   Of Summer sweet with herbs and flowers adorned,
The nightingale upon the hawthorn singeth,
   And Boreas' blasts the birds and beasts have scorned.
When fresh Aurora with her colours painted,   5
   Mingled with spears of gold, the sun appearing,
Delights the hearts that are with love acquainted,
   And maying maids have then their time of cheering.
All creatures then with Summer are delighted,
   The beasts, the birds, the fish with scale of silver;   10
Then stately dames by lovers are invited
   To walk in meads, or row upon the river.
I all alone am from these joys exiled;
No Summer grows where love yet never smiled.

VI–VII

FROM stately tower King David sat beholding
   Fair Bathshebe, who in a fountain, naked,
Her golden locks against the sun unfolding,
   In crystal waves the same did wash and shaked.
Not Cynthia pale, though she be clad in lilies,   5
   Nor whitest snow that lies upon the mountain,
Nor Venus bright, nor dainty Amaryllis,
   Did show more fair than she did in the fountain.
With her sweet locks this king was so inflamed,
   That he to wed this lady most desired,   10
By whose great might the matter so was framed,
   That he possessed her beauty most admired.
Yet afterward that he to love consented
Ten thousand tears he wept when he repented.

VIII

LIKE as the gentle heart itself bewrays
   In doing gentle deeds with frank delight,
E'en so the baser mind itself displays
   In cankered malice and revengeful spite.

IX–X

NOUGHT under heaven so strongly doth allure
  The sense of man, and all his mind possess,
As beauty's lovely bait that doth procure
  Great warriors oft their rigour to repress.
  And mighty hands forget their manliness   5
Drawn with the power of an heart-robbing eye,
  And wrapped in fetters of a golden tress,
That can with melting pleasance mollify
Their hardened hearts, inured to blood and cruelty.

  So whilom learned that mighty Jewish swain,   10
    Each of whose locks did match a man of might,
  To lay his spoils before his leman's train.
    So also did that great Œtean knight
    For his love's sake his lion's skin undight.
  And so did warlike Antony neglect   15
    The world's whole rule for Cleopatra's sight.
  Such wondrous power hath women's fair aspect
  To captive men, and make them all the world reject.
                                    [*Edmund Spenser*]

XI–XII

An elegy in memorial of the death of that honourable knight
Sir John Shelton

  SOUND saddest notes with rueful moaning;
    Tune every strain with tears and weeping;
  Conclude each close with sighs and groaning;
    Sing, but your song no music keeping
  Save direful sound of dismal word: 5
  Shelton is slain with fatal sword.

  Let every sharp in sharp tune figure
    The too sharp death he hath endured;
  Let every flat show flat the rigour
    Of Fortune's spite to all inured.   10
  And in his death and fortune tell
  That neither Death nor Fates did well.

Say Death hath lost, by him devouring,
  The chief of all his kingdom's glory.
Say Fortune, by her sudden lowering,   15
  Hath hid her honour in Death's story.
Yet say, for all that they can do,
He lives where neither have to do.

He lives, although his loss lamented
  Of prince and country (to both precious).   20
He lives, whose honour is imprinted
  In Virtue's roll (foe to the vicious).
He lives at rest in heaven's high throne,
Whom here on earth his friends bemoan.

XIII

IF women can be courteous when they list,
  And, when they list, disdainful and unkind;
If they can bear affection in their fist,
  And sell their love as they the market find,
'Twere not amiss, while Smithfield Fair doth hold,   5
That jades and drabs together all were sold.

XIV

NOUGHT is on earth more sacred or divine,
  That gods and men do equally adore,
Than this same virtue that doth right define;
For the heavens themselves, whence mortal men implore
  Right in their wrongs, are ruled by righteous lore   5
Of highest Jove, who doth true justice deal
  To his inferior gods, and evermore
Therewith contains his heavenly commonweal,
The skill whereof to princes' hearts he doth reveal.
                                        [*Edmund Spenser*]

XV

YE gentle ladies, in whose sovereign power
  Love hath the glory of his kingdom left,
And the hearts of men as your eternal dower,
  In iron chains of liberty bereft,

Delivered hath into your hands by gift;   5
Be well aware how you the same do use,
   That pride do not to tyranny you lift;
Lest if men you of cruelty accuse,
He from you take that chiefdom which you do abuse.
                                          [*Edmund Spenser*]

XVI

THE witless Boy, that blind is to behold,
   Yet blinded sees what in our fancy lies,
With smiling looks and hairs of curled gold
   Hath oft entrapped and oft deceived the wise.
No wit can serve his fancy to remove,   5
For finest wits are soonest thralled to love.

XVII

WHO seeks to captivate the freest minds
   By prayers, sighs, deep oaths, by vows and tears,
Showing affection in the truest kinds,
   Swearing to free their loves from any fears,
Yet under show of these have them beguiled,   5
Let such be far from God and man exiled.

XVIII

WHO vows devotion to fair beauty's shrine,
   And leads a lover's life in pilgrimage;
Or, that his constant faith may brighter shine,
   Dwells days and nights in fancy's hermitage,
Shall find his truth's reward but loss of labour,   5
Although he merit never so much favour.

XIX

THE heathen gods for love forsook their state,
   And changed themselves to shape of earthly kind.
But my desire is of another rate,
   That into heavenly grace transforms my mind.
      Their often change by new desire   5
         Declared they loved not that was best,
      For they that to the best aspire
         Do never change in hope of rest.

XX

O VAIN desire, wherewith the world bewitches
  To covet still for more, the more is gotten;
Sith when we die, we leave behind our riches,
  And all we reap is but to be forgotten.
The virtuous life is only that which lasteth,   5
And all the rest with Time or Fortune blasteth.

XXI

E'EN as the flowers do wither
That maidens fair do gather,
So doth their beauty blazing,
Whereon there is such gazing.

As day is dimmed with the night,   5
So age doth vade the red and white;
And death consumes e'en in an hour
The virgin's weed, that dainty flower.

And unto them it may be told,
Who clothe most rich in silk and gold,   10
Ye dames, for all your pride and mirth
Your beauty shall be turned to earth.

MICHAEL EAST

Madrigales To 3. 4. and 5. parts: apt for Viols and voices.   1604

I

O COME again, my lovely jewel,
  That we may kindly kiss and play,
  And sweetly pass the time away;
O go not, sweet, you are too cruel.
What now, ye run away disdaining,   5
And leave me here alone complaining?

II–III

IN the merry month of May,
In a morn by break of day,

Forth I walked by the woodside,
Whenas May was in her pride.
There I spied all alone   5
Phillida and Corydon.
Much ado there was, God wot,
He would love and she would not.
She said, never man was true.
He said, none was false to you.   10
He said, he had loved her long.
She said, love should have no wrong.
Corydon would kiss her then;
She said, maids must kiss no men
Till they did for good and all.   15
Then she made the shepherd call
All the heavens to witness truth,
Never loved a truer youth.
Thus with many a pretty oath,
Yea and nay, and faith and troth,   20
Such as seely shepherds use,
When they will not love abuse,
Love which had been long deluded
Was with kisses sweet concluded.
And Phillida with garlands gay   25
Was made the Lady of the May.

                                      [*Nicholas Breton*]

IV

YOUNG Cupid hath proclaimed a bloody war,
    And vows revenge on all the maiden crew.
O yield, fair Cloris, lest in that foul jar
    Thine after-penance make thy folly rue.
And yet I fear her wondrous beauty's such,   5
A thousand Cupids dare not Cloris touch.

V

TO bed, to bed, she calls, and never ceaseth;
    Which words do pierce and grieve my heart full sore.
To bed, to bed, I say; my pain increaseth,
    Yet I'll to bed and trouble you no more.
Good night, sweet heart, good night, my dear, to bed I must be
                                              gone,   5
And being there I'll muse on thee alone.

VI

O DO not run away from me, my jewel.
Thou hast cast me down to the ground, unkind and cruel.
Wilt thou away? Then well I may repent the day I loved,
Since so suddenly I feel all thy love from me removed.

VII

IN an evening late as I was walking,
Fair Phillida I saw where she was talking
With her love Corydon, who stood all sadly,
And ever he sighed but looked full badly.

VIII

ALAS, must I run away from her that loves me,
And running curse the causers of my flight?
Yet Wisdom saith it now behoves me
To depart from my heart and yield unto their spite.

IX

O STAY, fair cruel, do not still torment me
With frowns, disgraces, and disdainful deeds,
When every eye with pity doth lament me
That views my face and my misfortune reads.
O be not so hard-hearted still,   5
Your glory's greater for to spare than spill.

X

MY Hope a counsel with my Love
Hath long desired to be,
And marvels much so dear a friend
Is not retained by me.

She doth condemn my foolish haste   5
In passing the estate
Of my whole life into your hands
Who nought pays for't but hate.

And not sufficed with this, she says
    I did release the right   10
Of my enjoyed liberties
    Unto your beauteous sight.

XI

PITY, dear love, my pity-moving words,
    Fetched from the depth of grief and sad lament,
Whose thoughts before they speak no hope affords,
    Saving that thus you know my discontent.

XII

MOPSIE, leave off to love, thy hopes are vain.
    I have another that doth much excel thee,
Whose meanest graces thy perfections stain.
    Yet Love himself to love cannot compel me.
Yet she is modest, virtuous, wise and chaste,   5
Of all which parts no little part thou hast.

XIII

SWEET love, I err, and do my error know.
    As he that burns and nourisheth the fire,
My grief doth wax, and reason less doth grow;
    Yet want I power to bridle my desire.
Content is dead; my joys are all distressed.   5
Ay, thus it is to be with love oppressed.

XIV

IN vain, my tongue, thou begg'st to ease my care;
    In vain, mine eyes, you gaze or look for aid;
In vain, mine ears, you listen after air;
    In vain, my thoughts, you think what hath been said.
In vain my faith serves where 'tis not regarded;   5
In vain my hope when truth is not rewarded.

XV

WHEN on my dear I do demand the due
   That to affection and firm faith belongeth;
A friend to me, she saith, she will be true;
   And with this answer still my joys prolongeth.
But, dear, tell me what friendship is in this,   5
Thus for to wrong me and delay my bliss?

XVI

JOY of my life, that hath my love in hold,
   Vouchsafe to read these lines my heart doth send;
And having read, some pity, dear, unfold
   To these sad abstracts drawing to their end.
Let those sweet eyes that stellafy the light   5
Show equal power and dayify my night.

XVII

   ALL ye that joy in wailing,
Come, seat yourselves a-row and weep besides me,
   That, while my life is failing,
The world may see in love what ill betide me.
And after death do this in my behove,   5
Tell Cressid Troilus is dead for love.

XVIII–XIX

MY prime of youth is but a frost of cares;
   My feast of joy is but a dish of pain;
My crop of corn is but a field of tares;
   And all my good is but vain hope of gain.
The day is fled, and yet I saw no sun;   5
And now I live, and now my life is done.

The Spring is past, and yet it hath not sprung;
   The fruit is dead, and yet the leaves be green;
My youth is gone, and yet I am but young;
   I saw the world, and yet I was not seen.   10
My thread is cut, and yet it is not spun;
And now I live, and now my life is done.
                      [*Chidiock Tichborne*]

XX

FAIR is my love, my dear and only jewel;
Mild are her looks, but yet her heart is cruel.
O that her heart were, as her looks are, mild;
Then should I not from comfort be exiled.

XXI–XXII

SLY thief, if so you will believe
It nought or little did me grieve
That my true heart you had bereft
Till that unkindly you it left.
Leaving, you lose; losing, you kill   5
That which I may forgo so ill.

What thing more cruel can you do
Than rob a man, and kill him too?
Wherefore of Love I ask this meed—
To bring you where you did this deed,   10
That there you may for your amisses
Be damaged in a thousand kisses.

XXIII

YE restless cares, companions of the night,
    That wrap my joys in folds of endless woes,
Tire on my heart, and wound it with your spite,
    Since Love and Fortune proves my equal foes.
Farewell, my hopes, farewell, my happy days,   5
Welcome, sweet grief, the subject of my lays.
                                            [*Robert Greene*]

XXIV

YOU mournful gods and goddesses, descend
    And aid my soul with sadness, and my sprite.
Sadness is fittest now for me t'intend;
    Let heaviness and grief be my delight,
    And pensive sorrow always in my sight.   5
I pray thee stand, and help me sing lamenting,
The powers divine to it are all assenting.

The Second set of Madrigales to 3. 4. and 5. parts: apt for Viols and voices.
1606

I

I DO not love my Phyllis for her beauty,
   Yet is it such as praise of all it gaineth;
It is her love that stole my heart from me.
   Sweet is the cause of love that still remaineth.

II

  SEE Amaryllis shamed
  When Phyllis is but named,
Who, though her heart be now untamed,
Her like on earth was never framed.

III

WHY smilest thou, sweet jewel,
   And art so full of gladness,
When thou, to me most cruel,
   Dost cause me pine in sadness?
But since you joy to see me thus tormented,   5
E'en for thy love I am with grief contented.

IV

HOW merrily we live that shepherds be;
Roundelays still we sing with merry glee
On the pleasant downs whereas our flocks we see.
  We feel no cares, we fear not Fortune's frowns,
  We have no envy which sweet mirth confounds.   5

V

FOLLOW me, sweet love and soul's delight,
Or else by my exile my soul is severed quite.
My hand, my heart, my faith, my love, my life is thine.
O save thine own, if thou wilt not do mine.

VI

ROUND about I follow thee,
Yet thou fliest still from me,
    My jewel.

O sweet heart now return,
  Or else in flames of love I burn.   5
      Most cruel!
O cease my grief by turning unto me,
So shalt thou heal me of my misery.

VII–VIII

IN dolorous complaining
  I sat with tears bedewed
To see her deep disdaining,
  Whom I with love pursued;
And though I found no comfort of obtaining,   5
Yet left I weeping, but my love still remaining.

Since tears could not obtain
  Of her some small compassion,
Despair bid me refrain
  Sad tears and lamentation;   10
And though I still did see her deep disdaining,
Yet left I weeping, but my love still remaining.

IX–X

WHY runs away my love from me disdaining,
And too too cruel leaves me here complaining?
Yet O ne'er think by flight me to remove,
Men are not where they live, but where they love.

Why do you seek by flight me to eschew,   5
Whom to yourself you with your beauty drew?
If I did seek your love by subtle feigning,
Then might you run away from me disdaining.

XI

FAREWELL, false love, for so I find;
  Farewell, my hope mistaken;
Farewell, the friend that proves unkind;
  Farewell, I end forsaken.

XII

So much to give, and be so small regarded,
    Is fault in you or folly great in me.
And when the richest gifts are not rewarded,
    What then for meaner can expected be?

XIII–XIV

Sound out, my voice, with pleasant tunes recording
    The new delight that love to me inspireth,
    Pleased and content with that my mind desireth,
Thanked be love so heavenly joys affording.

She that my plaints with rigour long rejected,   5
    Binding my heart with those her golding tresses,
    In recompense of all my long distresses
Said with a sigh: Thy grief hath me infected.

XV

[*The words are the same as those of No. iii in this Set*]

XVI

Dear, why do you joy and take such pleasure,
    And still delight to see me lie and languish?
O pity me, my joy and only treasure,
    And cure my grief and bitter anguish.
And now at last regard me,   5
And with thy love for my true love reward me.

XVII–XVIII

Now Cloris laughs and swears how she affects me;
And now she weeps, and now, e'en now rejects me.
By sad experience now at length I find
Women can weep and laugh both with a wind.

Forsaken Thyrsis, sighing, sings: Alas,   5
Unconstant Cloris is not as she was.
Their fading face shows their unconstant mind.
Women can weep and laugh both with a wind.

XIX

I FALL, and then I rise again aloft;
　I sing and sigh, and all within a stound;
I sleep on stones although my bed be soft;
　I climb full high, then tumble to the ground.
Thus my poor heart with Cupid's dart sore wounded　　5
Doth tire itself, and thus sweet love is founded.

XX

　　WHAT doth my pretty darling?
　　What doth my song and chanting
That they sing not of her the praise and vaunting?
　　To her I give my violets,
　　And garlands sweetly smelling　　　　　　5
For to crown her sweet locks, pure gold excelling.

XXI

　　HENCE stars! too dim of light,
　　You dazzle but the sight,
　　You teach to grope by night.
　　See here the shepherds' star,
　　Excelling you so far.　　　　　　　　5

　　　Then Phoebus wiped his eyes,
　　　And Zephyr cleared the skies;
　　　In sweet accented cries
　Then sang the shepherds and nymphs of Diana:
　　　Long live fair Oriana.　　　　　　10

XXII

　O METAPHYSICAL tobacco,
　Fetched as far as from Morocco,
　　　Thy searching fume
　　　Exhales the rheum,
　O metaphysical tobacco.　　　　　　5

*The Third Set Of Bookes: Wherein are Pastorals, Anthemes, Neopolitanes,
Fancies, and Madrigales, to 5. and 6. parts: Apt both for Viols and Voyces.*
1610

I–III. *Pastorals*

Versus.   SWEET Muses, nymphs, and shepherds sporting,
              Sound your shrillest notes of joy consorting.
                   Fauns and satyrs all, and thou, Echo,
                   Sing after me: Ta na na no.
Chorus.   Now join we altogether   5
                   To welcome Sylvia hither,
                   And sweetly sing: Ta na na no.

Versus.   Ay me! wherefore sighs the fair Sylvia?
              Alas, for her Syrenio.
              But why Rodanthe fairest?   10
              For her sweet Sylvio dearest.
                   Ay me, Echo, sweetly sing,
                   Nymphs and swains reporting
Chorus.   Ay me.

Versus.   My peace and my pleasure,   15
                   Love and chiefest treasure,
                   Lady, thou goddess Pallas,
                        And all thy satyrs,
              Sweet Muses, nymphs, and shepherds sporting,
              Sound your shrillest notes of joy consorting.   20
                   Fauns and satyrs all, and thou, Echo,
                   Sing after me: Ta na na no.
Chorus.   Now join we altogether
                   To welcome Sylvia hither,
                   And sweetly sing: Ta na na no.   25

IV–V. *Anthem*

WHEN Israel came out of Egypt; and the house of Jacob from
among the strange children.
    Judah was his sanctuary, and Israel his dominion.
    The sea saw that, and fled; Jordan was driven back.
    The mountains skipped like rams, and the little hills like young   5
sheep.

What aileth thee, O thou sea, that thou fleddest, and thou Jordan,
that thou wert driven back?

Ye mountains, that ye skipped like rams, and ye little hills like the
young sheep?   10

Tremble, thou earth, at the presence of the Lord, at the presence of
the God of Jacob. Amen.   [*Psalm cxiv.* 1–7]

VI. *Neapolitan*

COME life, come death, I care not,
If I may only see my lovely fere.
But further, ah, I dare not!
When she but spies me,
    She flies me,   5
    She fools me,
    She cools my desire.

VII–XIV

[*These numbers are 'Fancies' for instruments alone*]

XV. *Neapolitan*

POOR is the life that misses
    The lover's greatest treasure,
Innumerable kisses,
    Which end in endless pleasure.
    O, then, if this be so   5
    Shall I a virgin die? Fie no!

XVI–XVII. *Anthem*

TURN thy face from my wickedness, O Lord, and put out all my
misdeeds.

Make me a clean heart, O God, and renew a right spirit within
me.

Cast me not away from thy presence, and take not thy holy   5
spirit from me.

O give me the comfort of thy help again, and stablish me with thy
free spirit.

Then shall I teach thy ways unto the wicked, and sinners shall be
converted unto the Lord. Amen.   [*Psalm li.* 9–13]   10

XVIIII. *Neapolitan*

DAINTY white pearl, and you fresh-smiling roses,
   The nectar sweet distilling,
   Oh, why are you unwilling
   Of my sighs inly firing?
Ah yet my soul herself in them discloses,   5
   Some relief thence desiring.

XIX. *Madrigal*

SAY, dear, when will your frowning leave,
Which doth my heart of joy bereave?
To sing and play becomes you better,
Such pleasures makes my heart your debtor;
But if you frown you wound my heart,   5
And kill my soul with double smart.

XX. *Madrigal*

LO, here I leave my heart in keeping
With her that laughs to see me weeping.
   O what comfort or treasure
   Is life with her displeasure?
Break, heart, and die, that she which still doth pain me   5
May live the more content, when grief hath slain me.

XXI. *Madrigal*

LIFE, tell me, what is the cause of each man's dying?
   Careful grief mixed with crying.
   No no, heart stay thee,
Let no such thought or care of mind dismay thee.
Tell me, life, how grief killeth, or how it woundeth?   5
   When it so sore aboundeth.
   Sweet heart, content thee,
Thy cares are so great I can but lament thee.

XXII. *Madrigal*

NOW must I part, my darling,
   Of life and soul deceased.
   And love therewith is pleased.
   O, what a death is parting!

But if the fates ordain it   5
Who can refrain it?
O what grief is now lacking,
Yet needs I must be packing.
Farewell, sweet heart unfeigned,
I die, to part constrained.   10

ɔɑɔɔɑɔɔɑɔɔɑɔɔɑ

*The Fovrth Set Of Bookes, Wherein Are Anthemes for Versus and Chorus,
Madrigals, and Songs of other kindes, To 4. 5. and 6. Parts: Apt for Viols and
Voyces. 1618*

I

THYRSIS, sleepest thou? Holla! Let not sorrow stay us.
Hold up thy head, man, said the gentle Meliboeus.
See Summer comes again, the country's pride adorning,
Hark how the cuckoo singeth this fair April morning.
O, said the shepherd, and sigh'th as one all undone,   5
Let me alone alas, and drive him back to London.

II

I DID woo her with my looks,
Courting verses, and with books.
Yet found I not myself neglected
Till I saw my books rejected.

III

WHY are our summer sports so brittle?
    The leaves already fall,
    The meads are drowned all;
Alas, that Summer lasts so little.
No, no. No pleasure could be tasted   5
If flowery Summer always lasted.

IV

DEAR love, be not unkind to thy beloved,
    Who lies a-dying,
    In mournful crying.
With a kiss revive me, O be thou moved.

V

WHENAS I glance on my lovely sweet Phyllis,
Whose cheeks are decked with roses, pinks and lilies,
I me complained that she me nought regarded,
And that my love with envy was rewarded.
       Then wantonly she smileth,   5
       And grief from me exileth.

VI

YOUR shining eyes and golden hair,
Your lily-rosed lips most fair,
Your other beauties that excel,
Men cannot choose but like them well.
But when for them they say they'll die,   5
Believe them not, they do but lie.

VII

WHEN I lament, my light o' love she smileth;
   Yet must I love, though she my love disdaineth.
For such is love, and so the heart beguileth,
   That 'tis most sweet when most the heart it paineth.

VIII

FAREWELL, sweet woods and mountains,
Green boughs and silver fountains,
     Roses and cherries,
     Grapes and strawberries,
     Nymphs and shepherdesses,   5
     Your garlands and your tresses,
Farewell, for Winter now returning
Turns all your sweets to black sad mourning.

IX

TO hear men sing I care not,
   By them I fear no leasing.
Hear women sing I dare not,
   Their voices are so pleasing.
For she that better singeth,   5
The greater danger bringeth.

X–XI

O CLAP your hands together, all ye people, O sing unto God with
the voice of melody.

For the Lord is high and to be feared; He is the greatest King upon
all the earth.

He shall subdue the people under us, and the nations under our
feet.

He shall choose out an heritage for us, even the worship of Jacob
whom he loved.

God is gone up with a merry noise, and the Lord with the sound
of the trumpet.   10

O sing praises, sing praises unto God: O sing praises, sing praises
to our King.

For God is the King of all the earth. Sing praises with under-
standing. Amen.   [*Psalm xlvii.* 1–7]

XII–XIII

I HEARD three virgins sweetly singing,
　　And for the Muses them reputed,
Such sweetness from their lips was springing;
　　But straight their number that confuted.
Then looking better on their faces,   5
I found they were the lovely Graces.

What heart such doubled force resisteth,
　　Or to be won by them refuses,
In whom such excellence consisteth,
　　For beauty, Graces, for singing, Muses?   10
Where Music looks and Beauty soundeth,
What heart so stony but it woundeth?

XIV

Versus.　FAIR Daphne, gentle shepherdess, sat weeping
　　　　　Good Thyrsis' loss. The swains their flocks left keeping,
Chorus.　Attending all on Daphne's mournful lays,
　　　　　Whose ditties were her griefs and Thyrsis' praise.
Versus.　　　　Thus she sat singing,   5
　　　　　　　　Her poor hands wringing:
　　　　　　　　Ah, Death hath slain
　　　　　　　　The gentlest swain.

Thyrsis is dead,
And wrapped in lead.   10
Chorus.   O heavy hearse,
O mournful verse.

XV

O LORD, of whom I do depend,
Behold my careful heart.
And when thy will and pleasure is,
Release me of my smart.

[*John Marckant*]

XVI

Versus.   COME, shepherd swains, and on this cypress tree
Hang all your pipes.
Sing not a note of mirth, but sigh with me:
Adieu delights!
Chorus.   For she is dead, who while she lived was such   5
As in her praises none could sing too much.
Versus.   But now her body lies full low,
The more her joy, [*Chorus:*] the more our woe.

XVII–XVIII

*A song made upon the marriage of the right worshipful, and my very good
friend Edward Oldisworth of Lincoln's Inn Esquire.*

QUICK, quick, away, dispatch!
Be nimble, quick, away!
Bells are a-ringing,
Maids are singing,
The priest for you doth stay.   5

An holiday, a happy day, a merry day!
The last of nothing,
The first of something.
Be nimble, quick, away!

No haste but good, yet stay!   10
A while of free
I bound must be,
But bound to him that's bound to me;
Such bondage makes me free.

An holiday, a happy day, a merry day!   15
          The last of nothing,
          The first of something.
    With joy I come away!

XIX

FLY away, Care, for Venus goes a-maying.
So, by her happy aid, we here together playing
May sweetly kiss, and fear no fraying.

XX

WHEN David heard that Absalom was slain he went up to his
chamber over the gate and wept; and thus he said: O my son Absalom,
my son, my son! Would God I had died for thee, O Absalom, my
son, my son!

                                              [2 *Samuel xviii.* 33]

XXI–XXII

HASTE thee, O God, to deliver me; make haste to help me, O Lord.
    Let them be ashamed and confounded that seek after my soul; let
them be turned backward and put to confusion that wish me evil.
    Let them for their reward be soon brought to shame that cry over
me: There, there.   5
    But let all those that seek thee be joyful and glad in thee; and let
all such as delight in thy salvation say alway: The Lord be praised.
    As for me I am poor and in misery; make haste to help me, O Lord.
    Thou art my helper and redeemer. O Lord, make no long tarrying.
Amen.   [*Psalm lxx*]   10

XXIII

WEEP not, dear love, but joy, I am a-dying.
          O cease this crying.
       For tears and sighs and moaning
No ways can help; but quickly Death will end my groaning.

XXIV

[*The words are the same as those of No. 6*]

ᗙᑕᗞᑕᗞᑕᗞᑕᗞᑕᗞᑕᗞ

The Sixt Set of Bookes, Wherein Are Anthemes for Versus and Chorus, of
5. and 6. Parts; Apt for Violls and Voyces. 1624

Y O U meaner beauties of the night
   Which poorly satisfy men's eyes
More with your number than your light;
   You common people of the skies,
   What are you when moon doth rise?   5

You violets, which first appear
   By those your purple mantles known,
Much like proud virgins of the year,
   As if the Spring were all your own;
   What are you when rose is blown?   10

You wandering chanters of the wood
   Who fill the ears with Nature's lays
Thinking your passions understood
   By weaker accents; what's your praise
   When Philomel her voice doth raise?   15

So when my Princess shall be seen
   In sweetness of her looks and mind
By virtue first, then choice a Queen;
   O tell if she were not designed
   Th'eclipse and glory of her kind?   20

                             [*Sir Henry Wotton*]

JOHN FARMER

The First Set Of English Madrigals: To Foure Voices. 1599

I

YOU pretty flowers, that smile for Summer's sake,
   Pull in your heads before my watery eyes
Do turn the meadows to a standing lake,
   By whose untimely floods your glory dies.
For lo, my heart resolved to moistening air,   5
Feeding mine eyes, which doubles tear for tear.
                                  [*Henry Constable*]

II

NOW each creature joys the other,
   Passing happy days and hours;
One bird reports unto another
   By the fall of silver showers;
Whilst the earth, our common mother,   5
   Hath her bosom decked with flowers.
                                  [*Samuel Daniel*]

III

YOU'LL never leave still tossing to and fro,
   Till at the last you catch a fall;
For wavering minds doth always harbour woe,
   Losing true friendship, love and all.
Be constant then, and thou shalt find it best   5
To scorn the world in hope to live at rest.

IV–V

LADY, my flame still burning and my consuming anguish
   Doth grow so great that life I feel to languish.
      O let your heart be moved
   To end your grief and mine, so long time proved;
And quench the heat that my chief part so fireth,   5
Yielding the fruit that faithful love requireth.

Sweet lord, your flame still burning and your continual anguish
   Cannot be more than mine in which I languish.
         Nor more your heart is moved
To end my grief and yours, so long time proved.   10
But if I yield, and so your flame decreaseth,
I then lose my life, and so our love ceaseth.

VI

SOON as the hungry lion seeks his prey
   In solitary range of pathless mountains;
Soon as the passenger sets on his way;
   So soon as beasts resort unto the fountains;
So soon mine eyes their office are discharging,   5
And I my griefs with greater griefs enlarging.

                                             [*B. Griffin*]

VII–VIII

O STAY, sweet love, see here the place of sporting.
   These gentle flowers smiles sweetly to invite us,
And chirping birds are hitherwards resorting,
   Warbling sweet notes only to delight us.
Then stay, dear love, for though thou run from me,   5
Run ne'er so fast, yet I will follow thee.

I thought, my love, that I should overtake you.
   Sweet heart, sit down under this shadowed tree,
And I will promise never to forsake you,
   So you will grant to me a lover's fee.   10
Whereat she smiled, and kindly to me said:
I never meant to live and die a maid.

IX

COMPARE me to the child that plays with fire,
   Or to the fly that dieth in the flame,
Or to the foolish boy that did aspire
   To touch the glory of high heaven's frame.
No man to these me fitly can compare;   5
These live to die, I die to live in care.

                                             [*B. Griffin*]

X

WHO would have thought that face of thine
  Had been so full of doubleness?
Or that within those crystal eyne
  Had been so much unstableness?
Thy face so fair, thy look so strange,   5
Who would have thought of such a change?

                                    [*Thomas Howell*]

XI

For the love of his most dear friend Edmund Keate

SWEET friend, thy absence grieves my bleeding heart;
  Yet do I joy to hear of thy good health.
Ah, woe is me, that now I shall depart
  From thee, more dear to me than Croesus' wealth.
But if on earth I may not see thy face,   5
I'll fly to heaven to seek thee in that place.

XII

THE flattering words, sharp glosses that men use
  To trap poor silly women in their snares,
With feigned looks their gentle sex abuse,
  Which yields nought else but grief and endless cares.
    Sometimes they smile, and sometimes frown,   5
        But never pleased indeed,
  Till time and place where they may watch
        Their sorrows for to breed.

XIII

CEASE now thy mourning and thy sad lamenting,
  For fair Aurora's lovely face doth light thee.
Thy mistress' heart is now upon relenting,
  Vowing henceforth never more to spite thee.
Then harbour not those thoughts that still may grieve
                                            thee,   5
Since that thy mistress swears she will relieve thee.

XIV

A LITTLE pretty bonny lass was walking
  In midst of May before the sun 'gan rise.
I took her by the hand and fell to talking
  Of this and that, as best I could devise.
I swore I would, yet still she said I should not   5
Do what I would, and yet for all I could not.

XV

FAIR Phyllis I saw sitting all alone,
  Feeding her flock near to the mountain side.
The shepherds knew not whither she was gone,
  But after her lover Amyntas hied.
Up and down he wandered whilst she was missing;   5
When he found her, O, then they fell a-kissing.

XVI

TAKE time while Time doth last;
Mark how Fair fadeth fast;
Beware if Envy reign;
Take heed of proud Disdain.
Hold fast now in thy youth;   5
Regard thy vowed Truth;
Lest when thou waxeth old
Friends fail and Love grow cold.

XVII

YOU blessed bowers, whose green leaves now are spreading,
  Shadow the sunshine from my mistress' face.
And you, sweet roses, only for her bedding
  When weary she doth take her resting-place.
Your fair white lilies, and pretty flowers all,   5
Give your attendance at my mistress' call.

GILES FARNABY

Canzonets To Fowre Voyces, With a Song of eight parts.   *1598*

I

MY lady's coloured cheeks were like the damask roses,
  Which clad in damask mantles spread the arbours.
But thrice more pleasant were her sweet supposes,
  Proceeding from her lips where sweet love harbours.
For viewing those her cheeks and roses sprouting,   5
The judgement of the sweetest breeds a doubting.

II

CARTERS now cast down your whips,
And shepherds put off your scrips,
  Whilst that your sheep are grazing,
  Behold fair stars blazing;
Ambrosia talking with Amaryllis,   5
And Corydon walking with fair Phyllis,
  To set your eyes a-gazing.

III

PHILLIDA bewailed the want of Corydon;
  And Herpulus of Phillida complained;
For Corin often would she sigh and groan,
  But Herpulus that loved her she disdained.
Poor Herpulus, why should not rigour move thee   5
To hate her thrice that once disdained to love thee?

IV

DAPHNE on the rainbow riding
When all the gods were chiding,
  Fell suddenly amazed,
  Full ghastly then she gazed,
And presently the god of anger   5
Frowned, and in his fury down he flang her.

V

BLIND Love was shooting,
  And loosing off his arrow
  He killed his mother's sparrow.
And tracing forth his footing,
  His mother Venus spied it,   5
  Before the boy could hide it.

VI

PEARCE did love fair Petronel,
Because she sang and danced well,
  And gallantly could prank it.
He pulled her and he hauled her,
And oftentimes he called her   5
  Primrose peerless, pricked in a blanket.

VII

PEARCE did dance with Petronella
La Siamise and La Duncella,
Pretty almans that were new;
Such he danced and nothing true.
But when Parnel danced without him,   5
All the maids began to flout him.

VIII

THE wavering planet most unstable,
  Goddess of the waters flowing,
  That bears a sway in each thing growing
And makes my lady variable.
  Oft I seek to undermind her,   5
  Yet I know not where to find her.

IX

LADY, the silly flea of all disdained
  Because it hath complained,
  I pity that poor creature,
  Both black and small of stature.
Were I a flea in bed I would not bite you,   5
But search some other way for to delight you.

X

THRICE blessed be the giver
That gave sweet Love that golden quiver.
And live he long among the gods anointed
That made the arrow heads sharp pointed.
If either of them both had quailed,   5
She of my love, and I of hers had failed.

XI

THE curtain drawn, I saw my love lie sleeping;
Thrice happy was that peeping.
For viewing her sweet lying
Preserves my life and keeps my soul from dying.
Of thousand joys, missing her, I had missed all,   5
Whose sight revives me more than ruby, pearl, or crystal.

XII

SUSANNA fair, sometime of love requested
By two old men, whom her sweet looks allured,
Was in her heart full sad and sore molested,
Seeing the force her chastity endured.
To them she said: If I, by craft procured,   5
Do yield to you my body to abuse it,
I lose my soul; and if I shall refuse it
You will me judge to death reproachfully.
But better it is in innocence to choose it,
Than by my fault to offend my God on high.   10

XIII–XIV

LOVE, shooting among many,
By chance he hit not any
Because the shaft rebounded
And Love himself was wounded.
When Psyche saw the dart had missed her,   5
She smiled and said that all the gods had blessed her.
Love, shooting at another,
He missed that mark and chanced to hit his mother;
But as the lady fainted,
God Mars did start, and therewith was attainted.   10
When Vulcan saw the shoot did fret him,
He cursed the boy and sware that he would beat him.

XV

AY me, poor heart!
Since Love hath played his part,
My senses all are lost,
    My mind eke tossed,
    Like waves that swell.   5
    Sweet god of Love,
    Thou dost excel!
    Thy passions move
    My mind to prove.
    That turtle dove   10
        She flies,
        My love
        She tries.
Help, gods that sit on high!
O, send me remedy.   15

XVI

SOMETIME she would, and sometime not;
    The more request, the more disdained.
Each woman hath her gift, God wot,
    And ever had since Venus reigned.
Though Vulcan did to Venus yield,   5
I would have men to win the field.

XVII

AMONG the daffadillies
And fair white splendent lilies
The god of Love came creeping,
Where Dian's nymphs lay sleeping.
He bent his bow but missed his footing,   5
And loosing, lost both labour, shaft, and shooting.

XVIII

SIMKIN said that Sis was fair
    And that he meant to love her;
He set her on his ambling mare;
    All this he did to prove her.

When they came home Sis floted cream,   5
   And poured it through a strainer;
But sware that Simkin should have none
   Because he did disdain her.

XIX

LADY, when I behold your passions,
   So divers and so oft constrained
Upon such slight or no occasions,
   As though you were with grief sore pained,
I enter into these persuasions: 5
A man might sail from Trent unto Danuby
And yet not find so strange a piece as you be.

XX

CONSTURE my meaning, wrest not my method;
Good will craves favour, witness the high God.
If I have meant well, good will reward me;
When I deserve ill, no man regard me.
What shall I say more? speech is but blasting.   5
Still will I hope for life everlasting.

XXI

WITNESS, ye heavens, I vow to love the fairest.
   To love, but how? For virtue, not for lust.
For virtue, why? Because she is the rarest;
   Come life, come death, in her I only trust.
Hap death, hap life, I force not which betide me,   5
By her I live, from death I cannot hide me.

ORLANDO GIBBONS

The First Set Of Madrigals And Mottets of 5. Parts: apt for Viols and Voyces. 1612

I

THE silver swan, who living had no note,
When death approached unlocked her silent throat;
Leaning her breast against the reedy shore,
Thus sung her first and last, and sung no more:
Farewell, all joys; O death, come close mine eyes;   5
More geese than swans now live, more fools than wise.

II

O THAT the learned poets of this time,
   Who in a love-sick line so well can speak,
Would not consume good wit in hateful rhyme,
   But with deep care some better subject find.
For if their music please in earthly things,   5
How would it sound if strung with heavenly strings?
                    [attrib. to Nicholas Breton]

III–VI

I WEIGH not fortune's frown nor smile,
   I joy not much in earthly joys,
I seek not state, I reck not style,
   I am not fond of fancy's toys.
I rest so pleased with what I have,   5
I wish no more, no more I crave.

I tremble not at noise of war,
   I quake not at the thunder's crack,
I shrink not at a blazing star,
   I sound not at the news of wrack.   10
I fear no loss, I hope no gain,
I envy none, I none disdain.

I see ambition never pleased,
   I see some Tantals starve in store,
I see gold's dropsy seldom eased,   15
   I see each Midas gape for more.
I neither want nor yet abound,
Enough's a feast, content is crowned.

I feign not friendship where I hate,
   I fawn not on the great for grace,   20
I prize, I praise a mean estate,
   Ne yet too lofty nor too base.
This, this is all my choice, my cheer,
A mind content, and conscience clear.
                     [*Joshua Sylvester*]

VII–VIII

HOW art thou thralled, O poor despised creature,
   Sith by creation Nature made thee free.
O traitorous eyes to gaze so on her feature,
   That quits with scorn thy dear lost liberty.
        Farewell all joys. O hell!   5
          Now restless care's my pillow.
      Sweet myrtle shades farewell,
Now come, sad cypress, and forlorn love's willow.
   She smiles, she laughs, she joys at my tormenting.
Break then, poor heart, tossed on despair's black billow. 10
        O let me die lamenting.

IX

DAINTY fine bird that art encaged there,
Alas, how like thine and my fortunes are.
Both prisoners be; and both singing, thus
Strive to please her that hath imprisoned us.
Only thus we differ, thou and I,   5
Thou liv'st singing, but I sing and die.

X–XI

FAIR ladies, that to love captived are,
   And chaste desires do nourish in your mind,
Let not her fault your sweet affections mar;
   Ne blot the bounty of all womankind,
     'Mongst thousands good one wanton dame to find. 5

Amongst the roses grow some wicked weeds.
For this was not to love, but lust inclined.
For love doth always bring forth bounteous deeds,
And in each gentle heart desire of honour breeds.

[*Edmund Spenser*]

XII

NOW each flowery bank of May
Woos the streams that glides away;
Mountains fanned by a sweet gale
Loves the humble-looking dale;
Winds the loved leaves do kiss;   5
Each thing tasteth of love's bliss.
Only I, though blest I be
To be loved by destiny,
Love confessed by her sweet breath,
Whose love is life, whose hate is death.   10

XIII

LAIS now old, that erst attempting lass,
To goddess Venus consecrates her glass;
For she herself hath now no use of one,
No dimpled cheeks hath she to gaze upon.
She cannot see her springtime damask grace,   5
Nor dare she look upon her winter face.

XIV

WHAT is our life? a play of passion.
Our mirth the music of division.
Our mothers' wombs the tiring-houses be,
Where we are dressed for this short comedy.
Heaven the judicious sharp spectator is,   5
That sits and marks still who doth act amiss.
Our graves that hide us from the searching sun
Are like drawn curtains when the play is done.
Thus march we, playing, to our latest rest,
Only we die in earnest, that's no jest.   10

XV

AH, dear heart, why do you rise?
The light that shines comes from your eyes.
The day breaks not, it is my heart,
To think that you and I must part.
O stay, or else my joys will die   5
And perish in their infancy.

XVI

FAIR is the rose, yet fades with heat or cold.
Sweet are the violets, yet soon grow old.
The lily's white, yet in one day 'tis done.
White is the snow, yet melts against the sun.
So white, so sweet was my fair mistress' face,   5
Yet altered quite in one short hour's space.
So short-lived beauty a vain gloss doth borrow,
Breathing delight today, but none tomorrow.

XVII–XIX

NAY, let me weep, though others' tears be spent;
    Though all eyes dried be, let mine be wet.
Unto thy grave I'll pay this yearly rent,
    Thy lifeless corse demands of me this debt.
I owe more tears than ever corse did crave;   5
I'll pay more tears than e'er was paid to grave.

Ne'er let the sun with his deceiving light
    Seek to make glad these watery eyes of mine.
My sorrow suits with melancholy night;
    I joy in dole, in languishment I pine.   10
My dearest friend is set, he was my sun,
With whom my mirth, my joy, and all is done.

Yet if that age had frosted o'er his head,
    Or if his face had furrowed been with years,
I would not so bemoan that he is dead,   15
    I might have been more niggard of my tears.
But O the sun new-rose is gone to bed,
And lilies in their springtime hang their head.

XX

TRUST not too much, fair Youth, unto thy feature;
  Be not enamoured of thy blushing hue.
Be gamesome whilst thou art a goodly creature;
  The flowers will fade that in thy garden grew.
Sweet violets are gathered in their spring,   5
White primit falls withouten pitying.

JOHN HILTON

Ayres, Or, Fa Las For Three Voyces. 1627

I

TO sport our merry meeting
We sing our pleasant greeting. Fa la.
If consort will agree,
Then everyone sing ye. Fa la.

II–III

MY mistress frowns when she should play;
I'll please her with a Fa la la.
Sometimes she chides, but I straightway
Present her with a Fa la la.

You lovers that have loves astray   5
May win them with a Fa la la.
Quick music's best, for still they say
None pleaseth like your Fa la la.

IV

PHOEBE tells me when I woo,
Fortune's blind, and Cupid too. Fa la.
And that's the cause she's coy by light,
Yet starts not from a kiss by night. Fa la.

V

CELIA'S wound and mine were one,
When Celia had blasphemed alone. Fa la.
I accused the god; he said: In time
Still loyal be, and Celia's thine. Fa la.

VI

DEAR, may some other, since not I,
Pull that flower ere it die. Fa la.
Flora would not have it kept;
The time once come it should be reaped. Fa la.

VII

THOUGH me you do disdain to view,
Yet give me leave to gaze on you. Fa la.
The sun as yet did never hide him
When a Moor or Tartar eyed him. Fa la.

VIII

LOVE wounded me but did not touch
Cloris, that deserved as much. Fa la.
Can a blind judge partial be?
But he hath hands and those wronged me. Fa la.

IX

THE woodbine, Flora, doth decay
If near it be not stuck a stay. Fa la.
So maidens droop that live alone.
To cheer thee up choose therefore one. Fa la.

X

I HEARD a withered maid complain,
Who wished that she were young again. Fa la.
She would not then man's love despise.
In time be therefore, young ones, wise. Fa la.

XI

LEAVE off, sad Philomel, to sing
Such doleful notes in merry spring.
The Winter's fittest for thy turn,
When every bird and tree doth mourn. Fa la.

XII

O HAD not Venus been beguiled,
To lovers she had been more mild. Fa la.
She now doth suitors' vows disdain
Because that she sued once in vain. Fa la.

XIII

Quest[ion].   TELL me, dear, fain would I know,
             Mean ye Nay when ye say No?
Answ[er].   Turn but No, and you'll discover
             'Tis On we mean unto a lover! Fa la.

XIV

FAINT not, lovers, for denials;
Women's Nays are but your trials. Fa la.
From one to two or three they'll move
To try which is the constant love. Fa la.

XV

GIFTS of feature and of mind
Are in Flora both combined. Fa la.
Though Fate through time the first deface
Nor Fate nor Time can th'other rase. Fa la.

XVI

As Flora slept and I lay waking,
I smiled to see a bird's mistaking. Fa la.
For from a bough it down did skip
And for a cherry pecked her lip. Fa la.

XVII

WHEN Flora frowns I hope for peace,
Which, having got, my woes increase;
For then I fear her frowns again,
And so 'twixt hope and fear remain.

XVIII

LOVE laid his yoke upon me,
Thinking to have undone me. Fa la.
I shook it off and did reply,
That none but fools for love will die. Fa la.

XIX

Now is the Summer springing
And merry lads are singing. Fa la.
Harken how the May comes home
Cheerfully with pipe and drum. Fa la.

XX

Come, sprightly Mirth, like birds i' th' Spring
We'll teach you lively notes to sing. Fa la.
No care nor grief shall you molest
Whilst thus your music is expressed. Fa la.

XXI

Come, let's crown this famous night
With sportings and delight. Fa la.
The heavenly powers invite
Thereto each mortal wight. Fa la.
And they with curious art   5
Herein will bear a part. Fa la.

XXII–XXIII

Hero, kiss me or I die.
On thy lips my soul doth lie. Fa la.
There I left it, for in kissing
Thee, I found my soul was missing. Fa la.

Quickly send it then unto me   5
By a kiss, or you undo me. Fa la.
If to send it you deny,
        I needs must die,
And all the world shall know thy cruelty.

XXIV

If it be love to sit and mourn,
To grieve and sigh and be forlorn, fa la,
I love. But if in't joy there be
I do not, for there's none in me. Fa la.

XXV

FLY, Philomel, to deserts fly,
They'll better suit thy misery.
Leave Flora's garden to sweet joys,
Thy sighing her delight annoys;
Or if thou wilt thy mansion keep,   5
Sing not but when she is asleep. Fa la.

XXVI

WHO master is in music's art,
In this song come bear a part. Fa la.
The best are set before, yet you shall find
This here is not the worst, though 't comes behind. Fa la.

WILLIAM HOLBORNE

The Cittharn Schoole, by Antony Holborne. . . . Hereunto are added six
short Aers Neapolitan like to three voyces, without the Instrument: done
by his brother William Holborne. 1597

I

CHANGE then, for lo she changeth, fa la,
And after new loves rangeth. Fa la.
    Ay, change and 'quite her;
    No! love and spite her. Fa la.

II

SINCE Bonny-boots was dead, that so divinely
Could toot and foot it, (O he did it finely!)
    We ne'er went more a-Maying
    Nor had that sweet fa-laing. Fa la.

III

HERE rest, my thoughts. What needeth all this hasting
To fry in pangs and torments everlasting?
And yet my heart is e'en to you as cruel,
Her eye the flame, but my heart lends the fuel.

IV

SWEET, I grant that I am as black and homely
As thou art fair and comely.
But ah! why dost thou fly me?
Were I a Moor thou couldst no less set by me.

V

GUSH forth, my tears, and stay the burning either
Of my poor heart or her eyes, choose you whether.
O peevish fond desire,
For, out alas, my sighs still blow the fire.

VI

SIT still and stir not, lady,
Here it is cool and shady. Fa la.
O no! away! I dare not.
Let me then kiss and spare not. Fa la.

ROBERT JONES

*The First Set Of Madrigals of 3. 4. 5. 6. 7. 8. Parts, for Viols and Voices,
or for Voices alone; or as you please.   1607*

I

THINE eyes so bright
Bereft my sight,
When first I viewed thy face.
So now my light
Is turned to night,   5
I stray from place to place.
Then guide me of thy kindness,
So shall I bless my blindness.

II

SHE only is the pride of Nature's skill;
In none but her all graces friendly meet.
In all save her may Cupid have his will;
By none but her is Fancy under feet.
Most strange of all, her praise is in her want;   5
Her heart that should be flesh is adamant.

III–IV

WHEN I behold her eyes,
Methinks I see where wanton Cupid lies.
But when I look more near,
'Tis but my shadow in her eyes so clear.
Which with a wink she, like a peevish elf,   5
Takes great delight to rob me of myself.

But let her look in mine,
And she shall seem to see a nymph divine;
Until she take more heed,
When she would swear that she were there indeed,   10
Where she may gaze her fill, and never doubt
That any wink should rase her image out.

V

LOVE, if a god thou art,
Then evermore thou must
Be merciful and just.
If thou be just O wherefore doth thy dart
Wound me alone, and not my lady's heart?   5
[*Francis Davison*]

VI

O I do love, then kiss me;
And after I'll not miss thee
With bodies' lovely meeting
To dally, pretty sweeting.
Though I am somewhat aged,   5
Yet is not love assuaged;
But with sweet ardent clips,
I'll lay thee on the lips,
And make thee ever swear:
Farewell, old bachelor.   10

VII

SING, merry birds, your cheerful notes,
For Progne you have seen
To come from Summer's queen.
O tune your throats.

When Progne comes we then are warm,   5
Forgetting all cold Winter's harm.
Now may we perch on branches green,
And singing sit and not be seen.

VIII

I COME, sweet birds, with swiftest flight,
Who never knew what was delight.
      Still am I pressed
      To take no rest,
        Still must be flying.   5
      Which I ever
      Must endeavour
        Till my dying.
It was assigned me by hard lot,
And all you see I break it not.   10

IX

COCK-A-DOODLE-DOO, thus I begin,
And loudly crow when none doth sing.
     All cocks that are abed,
     Look well your hens you tread,
     Forwhy the morning grey   5
     Calls up the cheerful day.

X–XI

SHRILL-sounding bird, call up the drowsy morn;
   Proclaim black Morpheus thrice to loathsome cell;
That Phoebus' face may the fair skies adorn,
   Whose beams unwholesome vapours doth expel;
That I may mount up to the clearest sky   5
And bear a part in heavenly harmony.

And when day's fled, with slow pace I'll return
   To meet dark Night attired in sable weed,
And dress myself in black with him to mourn,
   For from like cause the like effects proceed.   10
He mourns because the sun doth shun his sight;
I mourn 'cause darkness cuts off my delight.

XII

HERE is an end of all the songs
  That are in number but four parts;
And he loves music well, we say,
  That sings all five before he starts.

XIII

COME, doleful owl, the messenger of woe,
  Melancholy's bird, companion of despair,
Sorrow's best friend, and mirth's professed foe,
  The chief discourser that delights sad care.
O come, poor owl, and tell thy woes to me,   5
Which having heard, I'll do the like for thee.

XIV–XV

SWEET, when thou sing'st I leave my careful nest.
  Thou giv'st me warning that my foes do sleep.
The silent night befits our sorrows best,
  The chattering day-birds can no counsel keep.

Thou tell'st thy sorrows in a soft sweet note,   5
But I proclaim them with the loudest throat.
But we, poor fools, when the fair morn doth come,
Would fainest speak, but sorrow strikes us dumb.

XVI–XVII

WHEN to her lute Corinna sings,
Her voice revives the leaden strings,
And doth in highest notes appear
As any challenged echo clear;
But when she doth of mourning speak,   5
E'en with her sighs the strings do break.

And as her lute doth live or die,
Led by her passions, so must I;
For when of pleasure she doth sing,
My thoughts enjoy a sudden spring;   10
But if she do of sorrow speak,
E'en from my heart the strings do break.
                              [*Thomas Campian*]

XVIII

IF I behold your eyes,
Love is a paradise;
But if I view my heart,
'Tis an infernal smart.

[*Francis Davison*]

XIX–XX

SINCE your sweet cherry lips I kissed,
No want of food I once have missed;
My stomach now no meat requires,
My throat no drink at all desires;
For by your breath, which then I gained,   5
Chameleon-like my life's maintained.

Then grant me, dear, those cherries still,
O let me feed on them my fill;
If by a surfeit death I get,
Upon my tomb let this be set: 10
Here lieth he whom cherries two
Made both to live and life forgo.

[*Francis Davison*]

XXI

STAY, wandering thoughts, O whither do you haste?
      Leave off your mourning,
      Rest is returning,
Joy is at hand and heavy sorrows past.
      Down fall your fears,   5
      Hope highly rears.
Ah, then rejoice, and never cease to sing.

XXII–XXIV

YOUR presence breeds my anguish,
Your absence makes me languish,
Your sight with woe doth fill me,
And want of your sweet sight, alas, doth kill me.

If those dear eyes that burn me,   5
With mild aspect you turn me,
For life my weak heart panteth;
If frowningly, my spirit and life-blood fainteth.

If you speak kindly to me,
Alas, kind words undo me;   10
Yet silence doth dislike me,
And one unkind ill word stark dead will strike me.

                     [*Francis Davison*]

XXV–XXVI

A R E lovers full of fire?
How comes it then my verses are so cold?
     And how, when I am nigh her
And fit occasion wills me to be bold,
The more I burn, the more I do desire,   5
     The less I dare require?
Ah, Love, this is thy wondrous art,
To freeze the tongue and fire the heart.

                     [*Francis Davison*]

GEORGE KIRBYE

The first set Of English Madrigalls, to 4. 5. & 6. voyces. 1597

I

L O, here my heart I leave with her remaining,
    That never yet did deign to do me pleasure.
And when I seek to move her with complaining,
    She scorns my sighs and tears, alas, past measure.
Sweet Love, O turn her heart at last and joy me,   5
Or else her deep disdain will soon destroy me.

II

A L A S, what hope of speeding,
Where Hope beguiled lies bleeding?
She bade come when she spied me;
And when I came she flied me.
Thus when I was beguiled,   5
She at my sighing smiled.

But if you take such pleasure
Of Hope and Joy, my treasure,
By deceit to bereave me,
Love me, and so deceive me.   10

III

WHAT can I do, my dearest, of the sweet help deprived
Of those thy fair eyes, by which I still have lived?
How can my soul endure, thus charged with sadness,
Exile from thy dear sight, so full of gladness?

IV

WOE am I! my heart dies,
    As that which on thy will relies.
Since then I die, only in hope to please thee,
No grief of death, though cruel, shall disease me.
    Yet, shall I be tormented,   5
Cruel, to see thee pleased and contented.

V

FAREWELL, my love, I part contented,
    Since 'tis ordained that I must leave thee.
O might I stay, although tormented,
    The pain next death would little grieve me.
No greater torment can be proved   5
Than thus to part from my beloved.

VI

SLEEP now, my Muse, and henceforth take thy rest,
    Which all too long thyself in vain had wasted.
Let it suffice, I still must live oppressed,
    And of my pains the fruit must ne'er be tasted.
Then sleep, my Muse, Fate cannot be withstood;   5
It's better sleep, than wake and do no good.

VII

AH sweet, alas, when first I saw those eyes,
    Those eyes so rich with crystal majesty,
Their wounding beauty 'gan to tyrannize,
    And made mine eyes bleed tears full piteously.
I felt the wound, yet feared I not the deed,   5
Till ah! I found my tears did inward bleed.

VIII

MOURN now, my soul, with anguish of my pain;
    Crossed are my joys which hope did ever give;
Dry are mine eyes with shedding tears in vain;
    Dead is my heart which never more can live.
Hard are my torments, living thus in grief,   5
Harder yet her heart, that yieldeth no relief.

IX–X

SOUND out, my voice, with pleasant tunes recording
    The new delight that love to me inspireth,
    Pleased and content with that my mind desireth,
Thanked be love, so heavenly joys affording.

She that my plaints with rigour long rejected,   5
    Binding my heart with those her golden tresses,
    In recompense of all my long distresses
Said with a sigh: Thy love hath me infected.

XI

WHAT? shall I part thus unregarded
    From you, whom death could not dissever?
Is faithful service thus cruelly rewarded?
    Why then, vain hope, adieu for ever!

XII–XIII

SORROW consumes me, and instead of rest
With folded arms I sadly sit and weep,
And if I wink, it is but for fear to see
The fearful dreams' effects that trouble me.

O heavens, what shall I do?   5
Alas, must I be murderer of myself?
Must I myself be forced to ope the way
Whereat my soul in wounds may sally forth?
Hard is my hap! and thus in grief I die.

XIV

WHY should I love since she doth prove ungrateful,
    Since for reward I reap nought but disdain?
Love thus to be requited it is hateful;
    And Reason would I should not love in vain.

Yet all in vain when all is out of season,   5
For Love hath no society with Reason.

XV

SWEET love, O cease thy flying,
And pity me now dying;
   To ease my heart distressed
With haste make thy returning,
And quench my restless burning,   5
   That I by you redressed
May be revived and honour you as blessed.

XVI

THAT Muse, which sung the beauty of thy face
   In sweet well-tuned songs
     And harmony that pleased,
     If still I be diseased
   Can carol of thy wrongs   5
And blaze these faults that will thy worth disgrace.
     Yet if thou dost repent thee,
I will forgive; that mends shall well content me.

XVII

  SEE what a maze of error,
And labyrinth of terror,
   My love hath traced.
Wretched I, whom love paineth,
And true faith only gaineth,   5
   Hope utterly disgraced,
   And by disdain defaced.

XVIII

IF Pity reign with Beauty,
   Then may I be assured
   That what my harm procured
Will yield me help of duty;
For wrongful she was never.   5
Then why should I still in despair persever?

XIX

AH, cruel hateful fortune!
Now must I death importune,
Since that I am of all my hope deprived,
Nor but for sorrow had my soul survived.
Only this hope doth rest for my contentment,   5
That fortune tired will yield me some amendment.

XX

I LOVE, alas, yet am I not beloved.
    My suits are all rejected,
    And all my looks suspected.
Experience now too late hath proved,
That 'twas in vain that erst I loved.   5

XXI

MUST I part, O my jewel,
Hapless from my fair sun whose beams me nourish?
Alas who now comforteth or doth me cherish,
    Pained with grief so cruel?
    O if it so must needs be   5
My wicked fortune, how can she further harm me?

XXII–XXIII

UP then, Melpomene! the mournfull'st Muse of nine
    Such cause of mourning never hadst afore.
Up grisly ghosts! and up, my rueful rhyme!
    Matter of mirth now shalt thou have no more,
    For dead she is that mirth thee made of yore.   5
        Dido, my dear, alas, is dead,
        Dead, and lieth wrapped in lead.
            O heavy hearse!
    Let streaming tears be poured out in store,
        O careful verse!   10

Why wail we thus? why weary we the gods with plaints,
    As if some evil were to her betight?
She reigns a goddess now among the saints,
    That whilom was the saint of shepherds' light,
    And is installed now in heaven's height   15

I see thee, blessed soul, I see,
Walk in Elysian fields so free.
O happy hearse!
Might I once come to thee (O that I might)
O joyful verse!   20

[*Edmund Spenser*]

XXIV

[*The words are the same as those of No. vi*]

༄ᨏᨏᨏᨏᨏᨏᨏᨏᨏᨏᨏᨏᨏᨏᨏᨏᨏᨏᨏᨏᨏᨏᨏᨏᨏᨏᨏᨏ

HENRY LICHFILD

The First Set Of Madrigals of 5. Parts: apt both for Viols and Voyces. 1613

I

ALL ye that sleep in pleasure,
Awake, awake, and lose not Time's fair treasure,
For Time doth never cease his restless turning.
O I repent
The time I spent   5
In love's sweet burning.

II

SHALL I seek to ease my grief?
No, my sight is lost with eyeing.
Shall I speak and beg relief?
No, my voice is hoarse with crying.
What remains but only dying?   5

III–IV

THE shepherd Claius, seeing
His lovely Daphne flying,
He wept with deep lamenting,
His poor poor heart tormenting.
But O the shepherd, when they met together,   5
To live or die for joy he knew not whether.

First with looks he lived and died,
Then with sighs her faith he tried;
After sighs he sent his tears,
And all to show his trembling fears.   10
At last he said: a truer heart was never;
Pity, pity, Daphne, disdain me not for ever.

V

AY me, that life should yet remain,
When heart and living spirits are bereft me.
    Ay me, than thus to live in pain,
It better were no life at all were left me.
    Then die betimes, that when my heart return   5
    That may die too, and so I cease to mourn.

VI

O MY grief, were it disclosed
    To her, alas, that scorns my plaining,
Or were she but disposed
    To turn her eyes disdaining
From me that sit in sadness,   5
My grief would turn to gladness.

VII

I ALWAYS loved to call my lady Rose,
For in her cheeks roses do sweetly glose;
And from her lips she such sweet odours threw,
As roses do 'gainst Phoebus' morning view.
But when I thought to pull't, hope was bereft me,   5
My Rose was gone, and nought but prickles left me.

VIII

O COME, shepherds, all together,
To meet fair Daphne coming hither.
Tell her poor Claius for her sake
Many woes did undertake.

IX

SWEET Daphne, stay thy flying,
And hark to my complaining.
Fly not, my dear, so fast away,
But suffer me with thee to play.
 Which if thou shalt deny me,   5
 Of life thou dost deprive me.

X

ALAS, my Daphne, stay but and hear my moaning,
 O stay, or I faint with groaning.
Nay, you run away as if you meant to leave me,
I'll set me down and die if thus you grieve me.
 Adieu, my Daphne, adieu for ever,   5
I'll tell Apollo how cruel you persever.
But if you by returning do revive me,
 I'll sing again of Daphne.

XI

AY me, when to the air I breath my plaining,
To merry fountains my disdaining;
When to rude rocks and pleasant groves
I tell all my unhappy loves;
They hear me whilst I thus condole,   5
But with their echo call me fool.

XII

ARISE, sweetheart, and come away to play.
See, see, with flowery garlands all the meads are gay.
  The pretty birds are singing,
  And echo sweetly ringing.
Then, Daphne, pity me, or else I die,   5
If with hard heart 'No, no, no, no,' you cry.

XIII–XIV

WHEN first I saw those cruel eyes,
Those eyes the authors of my cries,
Adoring them for saints divine,
Placed in such a heavenly shrine,
  You told me then to prove me,   5
  You would for ever love me.

If this be love to scorn my crying,
To laugh at me when I lie dying,
To kill my heart with too much grieving,
To fly, and yield me no relieving,   10
    If love be thus to prove me,
    O then I know you love me.

XV

CRUEL, let my heart be blessed;
No life is sweet with a heart oppressed.
For though my greater grief be flying,
My smile is turned to sighing.
And when I would thy praise be singing,   5
I change my note and say:
Alas, my heart is sore with stinging.
Yet, cruel love, for this woe if thou dost languish,
O then I die with anguish.

XVI–XVII

A SEELY sylvan kissing heaven-born fire,
Scorched his lips for his so fond desire.
I, not so fond, but gazed whilst such fire burned,
And all my heart straight into flames was turned.

The sylvan justly suffered for his kiss,   5
His fire was stol'n, and stol'n things go amiss.
But I alas unjustly, for to have her,
Her heavenly fire the Gods and Graces gave her.

XVIII

INJURIOUS hours, whilst any joy doth bless me,
With speedy wings you fly, and so release me.
But if some sorrow do oppress my heart,
You creep as if you never meant to part.

XIX

WHILST that my lovely Daphne down from the hills came walking
The nymphs of Diana in a shade sat talking.
    This shepherds' queen,
    That there was unseen,

All suddenly inrushed.   5
Lord, how the nymphs then blushed!
And all danced round about her with this sweet cry:
Long live my lovely Daphne.

XX

MY heart, oppressed by your disdaining,
Doth flow in tears by just complaining.
All joys from me are quite exiled,
Since of your love I am beguiled.

THOMAS MORLEY

Canzonets. Or Little Short Songs To Three Voyces. 1593

I

SEE, see, mine own sweet jewel, what I have for my darling,
A robin redbreast and a starling;
These I give, both, in hope to move thee,
And yet thou say'st I do not love thee.

II

JOY, joy doth so arise and so content me,
When I but see thee, O my life's fair treasure,
That seeing makes me blind through too great pleasure.
But if such blinding, sweet Love, doth so delight thee,
Come, Love, and more thus blind me still and spite me.   5

III

CRUEL, you pull away too soon your lips whenas you kiss me;
But you should hold them still, and then should you bliss me.
        Now or ere I taste them,
        Straight away they haste them.
        But you perhaps retire them   5
To move my thoughts thereby the more to fire them.
Alas, such baits you need to find out never;
If you would but let me, I would kiss you ever.

IV

LADY, those fair eyes of yours, that shine so clearly,
Why do you hide from me that bought their beams so dearly?
Think not when thou exilest me,
Less heat in me sojourneth.
O no, then thou beguilest thee,   5
Love doth but shine in thee, but O in me he burneth.

V

HOLD out, my heart, with joy's delights accloyed,
Hold out, my heart, and show it,
That all the world may know it,
What sweet content thou lately hast enjoyed.
She that 'Come, dear' would say   5
Then laugh and run away,
And if I stayed her, cry:
Nay fie, for shame, fie!
My true love not regarding,
Hath given my love at length his full rewarding.   10
So that, unless I may tell the joys that overfill me,
My joys kept in I know in time will kill me.

VI

GOOD morrow, fair ladies of the May!
Where is fair Cloris, my sweet cruel?
See lo where she comes, a Queen
All in green,
All in gaudy green arraying!   5
O how gaily goes my jewel!
Was never such a maying,
Since May delights decaying!
So was my Cloris sheen
Brought home for the May Queen.   10

VII

WHITHER away, so fast
From your true love approved?
What haste, I say, what haste,
Tell me, my darling dear beloved?
Then will we try   5
Who best runs, thou or I.

Then lo, I come! dispatch thee!
Hence I say, or else I catch thee.
No, think not thus away to 'scape without me.
    But run! You need not doubt me.   10
What! faint you? Of your sweet feet forsaken?
O well I see you mean to mock me.
Run, I say, or else I catch you.
What? You halt? O do you so?
Alack the while! what! are you down?   15
Pretty maid, well overtaken!

VIII

BLOW, shepherds, blow your pipes with gladsome glee resounding.
See where the fair Eliza comes with love and grace abounding.
    Run nymphs, apace, go meet her,
    With flowers and garlands greet her.
All hail Eliza fair, the country's pride and goddess!   5
Long may'st thou live the shepherds' Queen and lovely mistress!

IX

    DEEP lamenting, grief bewraying,
    Poor Amyntas thus sat saying:
    Glut now thine eyes while I lie dying,
    Killed with disdain, and pity crying.
    Now may'st thou laugh full merrily,   5
    For dead is thy mortal enemy.
    O no, weep not, I cannot bide this blindness,
All too late now, God wot, comes this your kindness.
But if you would that death should of life deprive me,
Weep not, alas, lest you thereby revive me.   10
    Ah, cease to bewail me,
    My life now doth fail me.

X

FAREWELL, disdainful, since love no love avails me.
    O sharp and bitter anguish!
    What discord grief assails me!
Needs must I part, yet parting makes me languish.
    But yet it pleaseth thee,   5
Therefore, unkind, adieu, there is no remedy.

O come again, return thee.
No, no, false love, thy flames no more shall burn me.
Be still, content thee.
When I am gone, perhaps thou wilt repent thee.   10

XI

O FLY not! O take some pity! I faint, O stay her!
See how she flies. O stay, and hear my prayer!
    With one sweet look you may of torment ease me.
I am no tiger fierce that seeks to spill thee.
No, no, I see thou dost but this to kill me;   5
    Lo then I die, I die, and all to please thee.

XII

THYRSIS, O let some pity move thee.
Thou knowest thy Cloris too too well doth love thee.
Then why O dost thou fly me?
I faint, alas. Here must I lie me.
Cry alas now for grief, since he is bereft thee.   5
Up the hills and down the dales thou seest I have not left thee.
Ah, can these trickling tears no whit procure love?
What shepherd ever killed a nymph for pure love?
See, cruel, see the beasts their tears reward me,
    Yet thou dost not regard me.   10

XIII

NOW must I die recureless, when faith is thus regarded,
And poor love, alas, unkindly is thus rewarded.
    O grief! who may abide it!
    Hold out, O break not, heart, O hide it!
    O Nature, cruel, witty,   5
    Beauty so to make sans pity!
Farewell! Adieu! With this your love unfeigned
I die, alas, through your disdain constrained.

XIV

LADY, if I through grief and your disdaining,
Judged be to live in hell eternally remaining,
Of those my burning flames well shall I rest contented,
    But you I wail, who there must be tormented.

For when I shall behold you, your eyes alone will so delight me,   5
    That no great pain can once affright me.
But this, alas, would quite have killed me, do not doubt you,
    There to have been alone without you.

XV

CEASE, mine eyes, cease your lamenting.
In vain you hope of her hard heart's relenting.
      O cease your flowing!
    O drop not where no grace is growing!
See, she laughs, she smiles, she plays with joy and gladness   5
      To see your grief and sadness.
      O love, thou art abused!
Was ne'er true love so scornfully thus used!

XVI

DO you not know how Love lost first his seeing?
      Because with me once gazing
On those fair eyes, where all powers have their being,
      She with her beauty blazing,
      Which death might have revived,   5
Him of his sight, and me of heart deprived.

XVII

WHERE art thou, wanton? and I so long have sought thee.
See where thy true love his heart to keep hath brought thee.
    Nay, why then dost thou hide thee?
      Still I follow thee,
      But thou fliest me,   5
    Say, unkind, and do no more deride me.
Where art thou, wanton? and I so long have sought thee.
See where thy love his heart to keep hath brought thee.

XVIII

WHAT ails my darling thus sitting all alone so weary?
    Say why is my dear now not merry?
      O cease, alas, to grieve thee,
    And here a kiss take to relieve thee.
Up now! arise!—how can my love lie sleeping?—   5
    And see yon lusty leaping.

XIX

SAY, dear, will you not have me?
Here, take your kiss you gave me.
　You elsewhere perhaps think to bestow it,
　And I as loth again would be to owe it.
Or if you will not so take the thing once given,   5
Let me kiss you, and so we shall be even.

XX

ARISE, get up, my dear, make haste, begone thee!
Lo, where the bride, fair Daphne, tarries on thee!
　　Hark! yon merry maidens squealing:
　　Spice-cake, sops in wine, are now a-dealing!
　　　Run then, run apace,   5
　　　And get a bride-lace,
And a gilt rosemary branch the while yet there is catching,
　　And then hold fast for fear of old snatching.
　　　Alas, my dear, why weep ye?
　　O fear not that, dear love, the next day keep we.   10
List! Hark yon minstrels! how fine they firk it!
　　And see how the maids jerk it!
　　　With Kate and Will,
　　　Tom and Jill.
　　　Now a skip,   15
　　　Then a trip,
　　　Finely set aloft,
　　　There again as oft.
　　Hey ho, blessed holiday!
　　All for fair Daphne's wedding day!   20

XXI

LOVE learns by laughing first to speak,
Then slyly gains cares passing great. Fa la.
But I will laugh without that care,
And bid Love touch me if he dare. Fa la.

XXII

THIS Love is but a wanton fit,
Deluding every youngling's wit. Fa la.
The winged boy doth never light
But where he finds an idle wight. Fa la.

XXIII

THOUGH Philomela lost her love,
    Fresh notes she warbleth yet again. Fa la.
He is a fool that lovers prove,
    And leaves to sing to live in pain. Fa la.

XXIV

SPRING-TIME mantleth every bough,
    And bowers make for shepherds' sport.
    Birds and beasts are of consort. Fa la.
Our hearts in true love we do vow
    Unto that fairy shepherd's maid.   5
    We with true love are repaid. Fa la.

Madrigalls To Fovre Voyces. . . . The First Booke. 1594

I

APRIL is in my mistress' face,
And July in her eyes hath place,
Within her bosom is September,
But in her heart a cold December.

II

CLORINDA false, adieu, thy love torments me.
Let Thyrsis have thy heart since he contents thee.
    O grief and bitter anguish!
    For thee, unkind, I languish!
    Fain I, alas, would hide it,   5
O but who can abide it? I cannot, I, abide it.
Adieu, then, farewell. Leave me, death now desiring.
    Thou hast, lo, thy requiring.
Thus spake Philistus on his hook relying,
    And sweetly fell a-dying.   10

III

WHY sit I here, alas, complaining
With sobs and groanings my unjust disdaining?
    O this mirth contenteth
    Whom grief of mind tormenteth.

Ah, cease this weeping, fool, she does but this to prove thee.   5
Away, false comfort! no, thou canst not move me!
You that saw too much, mine eyes, shall dearly buy it,
That made my heart believe I did espy it.
Hence, false comfort, in vain thou seek'st to ease me.
Away, I say, then away! thou canst not please me.   10

IV

SINCE my tears and lamenting,
False love, bred thy contenting,
Still thus to weep for ever
These fountains shall persever,
Till my heart grief brim-filled,   5
Out alas, be distilled.

V

HELP! I fall! Lady, my hope, lo, doth betray me,
O help, alas, I fall, but you vouchsafe to stay me.
See a nymph unkind and cruel
To scorn her only jewel!

VI

LADY, why grieve you still me?
O no, you love me, if this be love to kill me.
O strange tormenting!
Break heart! alas, her heart contenting.
And you that now disdain me,   5
Say then that grief hath slain me.

VII

IN dew of roses steeping
Her lovely cheeks, Lycoris thus sat weeping:
Ah, Dorus false, that hast my heart bereft me,
And now, unkind, hast left me.
Hear, alas, O hear me! Cannot my beauty move thee?   5
Pity me then, because I love thee.
Thou scorn'st the more I pray thee,
And this thou dost to slay me.
Ah, then kill me and vaunt thee,
Yet my ghost still shall haunt thee.   10

VIII

IN every place fierce love, alas, assails me,
  And grief doth so torment me,
  That how can joy content me,
When hope and faith and all no whit avails me?
O gentle love, O grant me less to grieve me,   5
Or grieve me more, and grief will soon relieve me.

IX–X

NOW is the gentle season freshly flowering,
To sing and play and dance, while May endureth,
And woo and wed, that sweet delight procureth.

The fields abroad with spangled flowers are gilded,
 The meads are mantled, and closes,   5
In may each bush arrayed and sweet wild roses.
The nightingale her bower hath gaily builded,
And full of kindly lust and love's inspiring,
'I love, I love', she sings, hark, her mate desiring.

XI

COME, lovers, follow me, and leave this weeping.
See where the lovely little god lies sleeping.
   Softly! for fear we wake him,
   And to his bow he take him.
   O then if he but spy us,   5
   Whither shall we then fly us?
   And if he come upon us,
Out! well away! then are we woe-begone us.
Hence, follow me, away! begone! dispatch us!
And that apace, ere he wake, for fear he catch us. 10

XII

  NO, no, thou dost but flout me!
    Fie away, I say,
  Nay, thou canst live without me!
  Since for me then you care not,
   Spite me, and spare not!   5
    O heavy parting!
   O turn and cure this smarting.
  Come then with comfort, pity my crying.
  O help, alas, for now I lie a-dying.

XIII

I will no more come to thee,
That flout'st me when I woo thee.
Still 'tie hie hie' thou criest,
And all my rings and pins and gloves deniest.
O say, alas, what moves thee,   5
To grieve him so that loves thee?
Ah, leave alas tormenting,
And give my burning yet some small relenting.

XIV

Besides a fountain of sweet briar and roses
Heard I two lovers talk in sweet and wanton gloses.
Say, dainty dear, quoth he, to whom is thy liking tied?
To whom but thee, my bonny love? the gentle nymph replied.
I die, I die, quoth he.   5
And I, and I, and I, said she.
Ah give me then, quoth he, but durst not say, some token.
And with his hands the rest he would have spoken.
Nay fie, away, then cried the nymph, alas, you well do know it!
Quoth he, sweetly come kiss me then and show it.   10

XV–XVI

Sport we, my lovely treasure!
Forwhy long love long serving
Asketh equal deserving.
Let be our sportful pleasure
To kiss the while we may now, and that love's other token   5
Joy more than can be spoken.

O sweet, alas, what say you? Ay me, that face discloses
The scarlet blush of sweet vermilion roses.
And yet, alas, I know not
If such a crimson staining   10
Be for love, or disdaining!
But if of love it grow not,
Be it disdain conceived,
To see us of love's fruits so long bereaved.

XVII

HARK! jolly shepherds, hark! Hark you yon lusty ringing!
How cheerfully the bells dance the whilst the lads are springing.
  Go then, why sit we here delaying,
 And all yon merry lads and lasses playing?
   How gaily Flora leads it,   5
   And how she sweetly treads it!
The woods and groves they ring, loudly resounding,
   With echo sweet rebounding!

XVIII

HO! who comes here all along with bagpiping and drumming?
O 'tis the morris dance I see a-coming.
  Come ladies out, come quickly!
 And see about how trim they dance and trickly.
  Hey! there again! how the bells they shake it! 5
  Hey ho! now for our town! and take it!
Soft awhile, not away so fast! They melt them.
Piper, be hanged, knave! see'st thou not the dancers how they swelt
   them?
  Stand out awhile! you come too far, I say, in.
  There give the hobby-horse more room to play in! 10

XIX

  DIE now, my heart, from thy delight exiled,
  Thy love is dead, and all our hope beguiled.
    O Death, unkind and cruel
  To rob the world so of that her fairest jewel!
  Now shoot at me and spare not,   5
    Kill me, I care not!
  O think not, Death, alas, thy dart will pain me.
  Why shouldst thou here against my will retain me?
    O hear a doleful wretch's crying,
    Or I die for want of dying.   10

XX

  SAY, gentle nymphs that tread these mountains,
   Whilst sweetly you sit playing,
   Saw you my Daphne straying
   Along your crystal fountains?

If so you chance to meet her,   5
Kiss her and kindly greet her.
Then these sweet garlands take her,
And say from me, I never will forsake her.

XXI

ROUND, around, about a wood as I walked,
   Late in the evening, so fair, so fresh, and gay,
Under a hawthorn tree I heard a pretty maid that talked,
A pretty merry maid that long before had walked:
   Hey ho! trolly lo! heavy heart! quoth she,   5
      My lovely lover hath disdained me!

XXII

ON a fair morning as I came by the way,
Met I with a merry maid in the merry month of May,
   When a sweet love sings his lovely lay,
And every bird upon the bush bechirps it up so gay.
      With an heave and ho,   5
   Thy wife will be thy master, I trow!
      Hey, lustily, all in a row!
      Sing care away, let the world go!

The First Booke Of Canzonets To Two Voyces. 1595

I

GO ye, my canzonets, to my dear darling,
And with your gentle, dainty, sweet accentings
Desire her to vouchsafe these my lamentings,
And with a crownet of her rays supernal
T'adorn your locks and make your name eternal.   5

II

WHEN, lo, by break of morning
My love herself adorning
Doth walk the woods so dainty,
Gath'ring sweet violets and cowslips plenty,
The birds enamoured sing and praise my Flora: 5
   Lo, here a new Aurora!

III

SWEET nymph, come to thy lover.
Lo here, alone, our loves we may discover,
Where the sweet nightingale with wanton gloses,
    Hark! her love too discloses.

IV

Fantasy: Il Doloroso

V

I GO before, my darling.
Follow thou to the bower in the close alley.
    There we will together
    Sweetly kiss each other,
    And like two wantons dally.   5

VI

Fantasy: La Girandola

VII

MIRACULOUS love's wounding!
E'en those darts my sweet Phyllis
So fiercely shot against my heart rebounding,
Are turned to roses, violets and lilies,
    With odour sweet abounding.   5

VIII

Lo, here another love from heaven descended,
That with forces anew and with new darting
Doth wound the heart and yet doth breed no smarting.

IX

Fantasy: La Rondinella

X

LEAVE now, mine eyes, lamenting;
Your tears do but augment this my tormenting.
    Death, Death, come thou relieve me.
Alas! to live forsaken thus doth grieve me.
    Ah! see now where he lieth!   5
Then farewell, false unkind, thy Flora dieth!

XI

FIRE and lightning from heaven fall!
And sweetly enflame that heart with love arightful
Of Flora my delightful,
So fair, but yet so spiteful.

XII

Fantasy: Il Grillo

XIII

FLORA, wilt thou torment me
And yet must I content me?
And shall I have no pleasure
Of that thy beauty's treasure?
Lo, then I die, and dying thus complain me: 5
Flora gentle and fair, alas, hath slain me.

XIV

Fantasy: Il Lamento

XV

IN nets of golden wires,
With pearl and ruby spangled,
    My heart entangled
Cries and help requires.
Sweet love, from out those briars   5
But thou vouchsafe to free me,
E're long, alive, alas, thou shalt not see me.

XVI

Fantasy: La Caccia

XVII

O THOU that art so cruel,
My dainty lovely jewel,
Why thus in my tormenting
Dost thou still use relenting?
Alas, right out come slay me,   5
Do not thus still from time to time delay me.

XVIII

Fantasy: La Sampogna

XIX

I SHOULD for grief and anguish die recureless,
That day I missed my Flora fair and sightly,
Clearer than is the sun that shines so brightly.

XX

Fantasy: La Sirena

XXI

Fantasy: La Torello

༄༅༄༅༄༅༄༅༄༅

The First Booke Of Balletts To Five Voyces. 1595

I

DAINTY fine sweet nymph delightful,
  While the sun aloft is mounting,
    Sit we here our loves recounting, fa la,
      With sugared gloses
      Among those roses. Fa la.   5

Why, alas, are you so spiteful,
  Dainty nymph, but O too cruel?
    Wilt thou kill thy dearest jewel? Fa la.
      Kill then, and bliss me,
      But first come, kiss me. Fa la.   10

II

SHOOT, false Love, I care not.
Spend thy shafts and spare not. Fa la.
I fear not, I, thy might;
And less I weigh thy spite.
All naked I unarm me,   5
If thou canst, now shoot and harm me.
So lightly I esteem thee,
As now a child I deem thee. Fa la.

Long thy bow did fear me,
While thy pomp did blear me. Fa la.   10
But now I do perceive
Thy art is to deceive;
And every simple lover
All thy falsehood can discover.
Then weep, Love, and be sorry,   15
For thou hast lost thy glory. Fa la.

III

Now is the month of maying,
When merry lads are playing, fa la,
Each with his bonny lass
Upon the greeny grass. Fa la.

The Spring, clad in all gladness,   5
Doth laugh at Winter's sadness, fa la,
And to the bagpipe's sound
The nymphs tread out their ground. Fa la.

Fie then! why sit we musing,
Youth's sweet delight refusing? Fa la.   10
Say, dainty nymphs, and speak,
Shall we play barley-break? Fa la.

IV

Sing we and chant it
While love doth grant it. Fa la.
Not long youth lasteth,
And old age hasteth.
Now is best leisure   5
To take our pleasure. Fa la.

All things invite us
Now to delight us. Fa la.
Hence, care, be packing!
No mirth be lacking!   10
Let spare no treasure
To live in pleasure. Fa la.

V

Singing alone sat my sweet Amaryllis, fa la,
The satyrs danced, all with joy surprised.
Was never yet such dainty sport devised. Fa la.

Come, love, again, sung she, to thy beloved. Fa la.
Alas! what fear'st thou? Will I not persever?   5
Yes, thou art mine, and I am thine for ever. Fa la.

VI

No, no, no, no, Nigella!
Let who list prove thee,
I cannot love thee. Fa la.
Have I deserved
Thus to be served?   5
Well then, content thee,
If thou repent thee. Fa la.

No, no, no, no, Nigella!
In sign I spite thee,
Lo, I requite thee. Fa la.   10
Henceforth complaining
Thy love's disdaining,
Sit, thy hands wringing,
Whilst I go singing. Fa la.

VII

My bonny lass she smileth
When she my heart beguileth. Fa la.
Smile less, dear love, therefore,
And you shall love me more. Fa la.

When she her sweet eye turneth,   5
O how my heart it burneth! Fa la.
Dear love, call in their light,
O else you burn me quite! Fa la.

VIII

I saw my lovely Phyllis
Laid on a bank of lilies. Fa la.
But when herself alone she there espieth,
On me she smileth, and home away she flieth. Fa la.

Why flies my best beloved   5
From me her love approved? Fa la.
See, see what I have here: fine sweet musk roses,
To deck that bosom where Love herself reposes. Fa la.

IX

WHAT saith my dainty darling?
Shall I now your love obtain? Fa la.
Long time I sued for grace,
   And grace you granted me,
When time should serve and place.   5
   Can any fitter be? Fa la.

This crystal running fountain
In his language saith: Come, love! Fa la.
The birds, the trees, the fields,
   Else none can us behold.   10
This bank soft lying yields,
   And saith: Nice fools, be bold. Fa la.

X

THUS saith my Galatea:
Love long hath been deluded,
When shall it be concluded? Fa la.

The young nymphs all are wedded.
O then why do I tarry?   5
Or let me die, or marry. Fa la.

XI

ABOUT the maypole new, with glee and merriment,
   While as the bagpipe tooted it,
Thyrsis and Cloris fine together footed it. Fa la.
   And to the wanton instrument
Still they went to and fro and finely flaunted it,   5
And then both met again, and thus they chanted it:
     Fa la la!

The shepherds and the nymphs them round enclosed had,
   Wond'ring with what facility
About they turned them in such strange agility. Fa la.   10
   And still, when they unloosened had,
With words full of delight they gently kissed them,
And thus sweetly to sing they never missed them:
     Fa la la!

XII

MY lovely wanton jewel,
To me at once both kind, alas, and cruel, fa la,
    By hopeless words torments me,
And with her lips again straightway contents me. Fa la.

    If this you do to kill me,   5
Say, cruel nymph, why kiss not you then still me? Fa la.
    So shall you ease my crying,
And I could never wish a sweeter dying. Fa la.

XIII

YOU that wont to my pipe's sound
Daintily to tread your ground,
Jolly shepherds and nymphs sweet, lirum lirum,
    Here met together
    Under the weather,   5
Hand in hand uniting, the lovely god come greet. Lirum lirum.

Lo, triumphing brave comes he,
All in pomp and majesty,
Monarch of the world and king! Lirum lirum.
    Let whoso list him   10
    Dare to resist him,
We, our voice uniting, of his high acts will sing. Lirum lirum.

XIV

    FIRE! fire! my heart! Fa la.
O help! Alas! Ay me! I sit and cry me,
And call for help, alas, but none comes nigh me! Fa la.

    O, I burn me! alas! Fa la.
I burn! Alas! Ay me! will none come quench me?   5
O cast, cast water on, alas, and drench me. Fa la.

XV

    THOSE dainty daffadillies,
    Which gave to me sweet Phyllis, fa la,
To me, alas, of life and soul deprived,
    My spirits they have revived. Fa la.

As their fair hue excelleth,   5
In her so beauty dwelleth. Fa la.
And ever to behold them they invite me,
So sweetly they delight me. Fa la.

XVI

LADY, those cherries plenty,
Which grow on your lips dainty,
  Ere long will fade and languish.
Then now, while yet they last them,
O let me pull and taste them.   5

XVII

I LOVE, alas, I love thee, my dainty darling.
Come kiss me then, come kiss me, Amaryllis,
  More lovely than sweet Phyllis.

XVIII

LO, she flies when I woo her.
Nor can I get unto her.
But why do I complain me?
Say, if I die, she hath unkindly slain me.

XIX

LEAVE, alas, this tormenting and strange anguish,
Or kill my heart oppressed. Alas, it skill not!
  For thus I will not,
    Now contented,
    Then tormented,   5
  Live in love and languish.

XX

WHY weeps, alas, my lady love and mistress?
Sweet heart, O fear not, what though while I leave thee?
My life may fail, but I will not deceive thee.

XXI. *A Dialogue*

[*Amyntas*.] PHYLLIS, I fain would die now.
[*Phyllis*.]   O to die what should move thee?

[*Amyntas.*] For that you do not love me.
[*Phyllis.*]   I love thee! but plain to make it,
                Ask what thou wilt and take it.   5
[*Amyntas.*] O sweet, then this I crave thee,
                Since you to love will have me,
                Give me in my tormenting,
                One kiss for my contenting.
[*Phyllis.*]   This unawares doth daunt me.   10
                Else what thou wilt I grant thee.
[*Amyntas.*] Ah Phyllis! well I see then
                My death thy joy will be then.
[*Phyllis.*]   O no, no, no, I request thee
                To tarry but some fitter time and leisure.   15
[*Amyntas.*]   Alas, death will arrest me
                You know before I shall possess this treasure.
[*Both.*]   No, no, dear, do not languish,
                    Temper this sadness,
                    For time and love with gladness   20
                Once ere long will provide for this our anguish.

ᖌᖍᖌᖍᖌᖍᖌᖍᖌᖍᖌᖍ

Canzonets Or Little Short Aers To Five And Sixe Voices. 1597

I

FLY, Love, that art so sprightly,
To Bonny-boots uprightly,
And when in heaven thou meet him,
Say that I kindly greet him,
And that his Oriana,   5
True widow maid, still followeth Diana.

II

FALSE love did me inveigle,
And she, like to the eagle,
Upon my breast ay tiring,
Permits me no respiring.

Then would she once but bill me   5
By the lips, and so kill me!
O but Calisto teareth
My heart out, like the bear whose name she beareth!

III

ADIEU, you kind and cruel.
And you mine own sweet jewel.
Thus said these lovers, and as they hands were shaking,
The groom his heart fell quaking,
And then fell down a-dying;   5
And she sat by him crying.

IV

LOVE's folk in green arraying,
At barley-break were playing.
Laura in hell was caught then.
But, Lord, how Dorus laughed then,
And said: Good mistress, sith you   5
Will needs thither have with you!

V

LOVE took his bow and arrow,
And slew his mother's sparrow.
I know not how it chanced,
Perhaps his arrow glanced.
Away the wag him hied,   5
And then his mother cried:
Lord! how am I a-paid!
My bird is dead, and now my boy is strayed!

VI

LO! where with flowery head and hair all brightsome,
Rosy cheeked, crystal eyed, e'en weeping lightsome,
The fresh Aurora springeth!
And wanton Flora flingeth
Amorous odours unto the winds delightsome!   5
Ah! for pity and anguish
Only my heart doth languish!

VII

O GRIEF! e'en on the bud that fairly flowered
The sun hath lowered.
And, ah, that breast which Love durst never venture,
Bold Death did enter.

Pity, O heavens, that have my love in keeping,   5
        My cries and weeping.

VIII

SOVEREIGN of my delight, hear my complaining.
Fly to her, my sad thoughts, my cares containing.
        Beauty by pleasure only crowned
        Now in herself lies drowned
            By her unkind disdaining.   5

IX

OUR Bonny-boots could toot it, yea and foot it.
Say, lusty lads, who now shall bonny-boot it?
Who but the jolly shepherd, bonny Dorus?
He now must lead the morris dance before us.

X

AY me! the fatal arrow,
That drives e'en to the marrow,
Cupid from out his quiver
Hath plucked and pierced my liver.
The blood, through which the fell venom close creepeth,   5
Alas, e'en through mine eyes my heart out weepeth.

XI

MY nymph the deer, and her my dear I follow.
Trussed is her hair in gold, than gold more yollow.
Say, did you see her, the divinest creature
        That ever was of feature?
        O love, the world's sweet-maker,   5
Change her mood, and more humane minded make her.

XII

    CRUEL, wilt thou persever
        Peace to leave ever?
    Peace shalt thou have, and gladness.
        But when in sadness?
    When thou the morn seest even   5
        To fall from heaven.

XIII

SAID I that Amaryllis
Was fairer than is Phyllis?
Upon my death I take it,
Sweet Phyll, I never spake it.
But if you think I did, then take me and hang me.   5
Yet let more and more love and beauty pang me.

XIV

DAMON and Phyllis squared,
And to point her the place the nymph him dared.
Her glove she down did cast him,
And to meet her alone she bade him haste him.
Alike their weapons were, alike their smiting,   5
And little Love came running to the fighting.

XV

LADY, you think you spite me,
When by the lip you bite me.
But if you think it trouble,
Then let my pain be double,
Ay triple, but you bliss me,   5
For though you bite, you kiss me,
And with sour sweet delight me.

XVI

YOU black bright stars, that shine while daylight lasteth,
Ah! why haste you away when night time hasteth?
In darker nights the stars still seem the lighter.
On me shine then a-nights with your beams brighter.
Beams that are cause my heart hath so aspired,   5
Fire mounts aloft, and they my heart have fired.

XVII

I FOLLOW, lo, the footing
Still of my lovely cruel,
Proud of herself that she is beauty's jewel.

And fast away she flieth,
Love's sweet delight deriding,   5
In woods and groves sweet Nature's treasure hiding.
Yet cease I not pursuing,
But since I thus have sought her,
Will run me out of breath till I have caught her.

XVIII

STAY, heart, run not so fast from him that loves thee
To her that deadly hates thee.
Her sharp disdain reproves thee,
And worse than ill still rates thee.
Then let her go and spare not.   5
Hold thou thyself contented, and I care not.
Up, gentle swains, we'll have a round this morrow.
My love is gone, and with her go my sorrow!
O vile wretch, that so base a mind dost carry.
Thou lovedst her once, and why now dost thou vary?   10
Then straight away I haste me,
And after her will run while life shall last me.
Ah! Death his force now trieth.
Flora, farewell, for lo, thy shepherd dieth!

XIX

GOOD love, then fly thou to her,
And see if thou canst woo her.
Go, sweet, and turn about her,
For sure I die without her.
But if she still abhor me,   5
And will do nothing for me,
Sweet love, this favour do me,
Return thou never to me.

XX

LADIES, you see time flieth,
And beauty too, it dieth.
Then take your pleasure,
While you have leisure.
Nor be so dainty   5
Of that which you have plenty.

XXI

A reverend memorial of that honourable true gentleman
Henry Noel Esquire

HARK! Alleluia cheerly
    With angels now he singeth,
That here loved music dearly,
    Whose echo heaven ringeth,
Where thousand cherubs hover   5
About th' eternal Mover.

ເວຄວເຄວເຄວເຄວ

Madrigales The Triumphes of Oriana, to 5. and 6. voices: composed by diuers
seuerall aucthors. 1601

MICHAEL EAST

HENCE stars! too dim of light,
You dazzle but the sight,
You teach to grope by night.
See here the shepherds' star,
Excelling you so far.   5
Then Phoebus wiped his eyes,
And Zephyr cleared the skies;
In sweet accented cries
Then sang the shepherds and nymphs of Diana:
    Long live fair Oriana.   10
                I. L.

I

DANIEL NORCOME

WITH angel's face and brightness
And orient hue fair Oriana shining,
With nimble foot she tripped o'er hills and mountains.
    At last in dale she rested
    Hard by Diana's fountains.   5
This is that maiden Queen of the fairyland
    With sceptre in her hand.
    The fauns and satyrs dancing
    Did show their nimble lightness.

Fair Nais and the nymphs did leave their bowers,   10
And brought their baskets full of herbs and flowers.
    Then sang the shepherds and nymphs of Diana:
      Long live fair Oriana.

II

JOHN MUNDY

LIGHTLY she whipped o'er the dales,
  Making the woods proud with her presence;
    Gently she trod the flowers,
And they as gently kissed her tender feet.
The birds in their best language bade her welcome,   5
Being proud that Oriana heard their song.
    The clove-foot satyrs singing
    Made music to the fauns a-dancing,
    And both together with an emphasis
      Sang Oriana's praises,   10
Whilst the adjoining woods with melody
Did entertain their sweet sweet harmony.
Then sang the shepherds and nymphs of Diana:
    Long live fair Oriana.

III

ELLIS GIBBONS

    LONG live fair Oriana!
Hark! did you ever hear so sweet a singing?
    They sing young Love to waken.
The nymphs unto the woods their Queen are bringing.
    There was a note well taken!   5
O good! Hark, how joyfully 'tis dittied,
A Queen and song most excellently fitted!
      I never heard a rarer,
      I never saw a fairer.
    Then sing ye shepherds and nymphs of Diana: 10
      Long live fair Oriana.

IV

JOHN BENNET

ALL creatures now are merry, merry-minded.
    The shepherds' daughters playing,
    The nymphs are fa-la-laing,
  Yond bugle was well winded.

At Oriana's presence each thing smileth.
   The flowers themselves discover;
     Birds over her do hover;
    Music the time beguileth.
See where she comes with flowery garlands crowned,
   Queen of all queens renowned.
Then sang the shepherds and nymphs of Diana:
   Long live fair Oriana.

V

JOHN HILTON

FAIR Oriana, beauty's queen,
Tripped along the verdant green.
The fauns and satyrs running out
Skipped and danced round about.
Flora forsook her painted bowers,
And made a coronet of flowers.
Then sang the nymphs of chaste Diana:
   Long live fair Oriana.

VI

GEORGE MARSON

THE nymphs and shepherds danced
Lavoltos in a daisy-tapstred valley.
   Love from their face-lamps glanced,
   Till wantonly they dally.
   Then in a rose-banked alley
   Bright Majesty advanced,
A crown-graced Virgin, whom all people honour.
   They leave their sport amazed,
   Run all to look upon her.
   A moment scarce they gazed
Ere beauty's splendour all their eyes had dazed,
Desire to see yet ever fixed on her.
   Then sang the shepherds and nymphs of Diana:
    Long live fair Oriana.

VII

RICHARD CARLTON

CALM was the air and clear the sky,
Fair Oriana passing by
Over the downs to Ida plains,
Where heaven-born sisters with their trains
Did all attend her sacred beauty,   5
Striving to excel in duty.
Satyrs and nymphs dancing together,
Shepherds triumphing flocking thither,
Seeing their sovereign mistress there,
That kept their flocks and them from fear,   10
    With high-strained voice
    And hearts rejoice.
Thus sang the shepherds and nymphs of Diana:
    Long live fair Oriana.

VIII

JOHN HOLMES

THUS Bonny-boots the birthday celebrated
    Of her his lady dearest,
Fair Oriana, which to his heart was nearest:
    The nymphs and shepherds feasted
With clowted cream were, and to sing requested.   5
    Lo here the fair created,
    Quoth he, the world's chief goddess.
Sing then, for she is Bonny-boots' sweet mistress.
    Then sang the shepherds and nymphs of Diana:
      Long live fair Oriana.   10

IX

RICHARD NICOLSON

SING, shepherds all, and in your roundelays
Sing only of fair Oriana's praise.
The gods above will help to bear a part,
And men below will try their greatest art.
Though neither gods nor men can well apply   5
Fit song or tune to praise her worthily.
    Then sang the shepherds and nymphs of Diana:
      Long live fair Oriana.

M

X

THOMAS TOMKINS

THE fauns and satyrs tripping
With lively nymphs of fresh cool brooks and fountains,
And those of woods and mountains,
Like roes came nimbly skipping,
By signs their mirth unripping.   5
My fair Queen they presented
In peace's arms with amaltheias twenty,
Brimful of wealthy plenty;
And still to give frequented,
With bare gifts not contented.   10
The demi-gods pray to the gods supernal,
Her life, her wealth, her fame may be eternal.
Then sang the shepherds and nymphs of Diana:
Long live fair Oriana.

XI

MICHAEL CAVENDISH

COME, gentle swains, and shepherds' dainty daughters,
Adorned with courtesy and comely duties,
Come, sing and joy and grace with lovely laughters
The birthday of the beautiest of beauties.
Then sang the shepherds and nymphs of Diana: 5
Long live fair Oriana.

XII

WILLIAM COBBOLD

WITH wreaths of rose and laurel
Withdraw yourselves, ye shepherds, from your bowers,
And strew the path with flowers.
The nymphs are coming;
Sweetly the birds are chirping, the swift beasts running.   5
As all amazed they stand still gazing
To see such bright stars blazing,
Lo, Dian bravely treading,
Her dainty daughter leading,
The powers divine to her do veil their bonnets.   10
Prepare yourselves to sound your pastoral sonnets.
Then sang the shepherds and nymphs of Diana:
Long live fair Oriana.

XIII
THOMAS MORLEY

ARISE, awake, awake, awake,
    You silly shepherds sleeping;
Devise some honour for her sake
    By mirth to banish weeping.
Lo where she comes in gaudy green arraying,   5
    A prince of beauty rich and rare
For her delighting pretends to go a maying.
    You stately nymphs draw near
    And strew your paths with roses;
    In you her trust reposes.   10
Then sang the shepherds and nymphs of Diana:
    Long live fair Oriana.

XIV
JOHN FARMER

FAIR nymphs, I heard one telling,
Diana's train are hunting in this chase.
    To beautify the place
    The fawns are running,
    The shepherds their pipes tuning   5
    To show their cunning.
The lambs amazed leave off their grazing,
    And blind their eyes with gazing,
Whilst the earth's goddess doth draw near your places,
Attended by the Muses and the Graces.   10
    Then sang the shepherds and nymphs of Diana:
    Long live fair Oriana.

XV
JOHN WILBYE

THE Lady Oriana
Was dight all in the treasures of Guiana.
And on her Grace a thousand Graces tended.
And thus sang they: Fair Queen of peace and plenty,
    The fairest Queen of twenty.   5
Then with an olive wreath for peace renowned
    Her virgin head they crowned.

Which ceremony ended
Unto her Grace the thousand Graces bended.
　Then sang the shepherds and nymphs of Diana:　　　10
　　Long live fair Oriana.

XVI

THOMAS HUNT

HARK! did ye ever hear so sweet a singing?
　They sing young Love to waken.
The nymphs unto the woods their Queen are bringing.
　There was a note well taken!
Hark, hark! O good! O most divinely dittied!　　　5
A Queen and song most excellently fitted.
　　　I never saw a fairer,
　　　I never heard a rarer.
　Then sung the nymphs and shepherds of Diana:
　　Long live fair Oriana.　　　10

XVII

THOMAS WEELKES

As Vesta was from Latmos hill descending,
She spied a maiden Queen the same ascending,
Attended on by all the shepherds' swain,
To whom Diana's darlings came running down amain,
First two by two, then three by three together,　　　5
Leaving their goddess all alone, hasted thither;
And mingling with the shepherds of her train,
With mirthful tunes her presence entertain.
　Then sang the shepherds and nymphs of Diana:
　　Long live fair Oriana.　　　10

XVIII

JOHN MILTON

　FAIR Orian in the morn,
　Before the day was born,
　With velvet steps on ground,
　Which made nor print nor sound,
　Would see her nymphs abed,　　　5
　What lives those ladies led.

The roses blushing said:
O stay, thou shepherds' maid.
And on a sudden all
They rose and heard her call.   10
Then sang those shepherds and nymphs of Diana:
Long live fair Oriana.

XIX

ELLIS GIBBONS

ROUND about her charret with all-admiring strains
The Hyades and Dryades give sweetest entertains.
Lo! how the gods in revels do accord,
Whilst doth each goddess melodies afford.
Now Bacchus is consorting,   5
Sylvanus falls to sporting,
Amphion's harp's reporting.
To the shepherds' pipes sing the nymphs of Diana:
Long live fair Oriana.

XX

GEORGE KIRBYE

BRIGHT Phoebus greets most clearly
With radiant beams fair Oriana sitting.
Her apple Venus yields as best befitting
A Queen beloved most dearly.
Rich Pluto leaves his treasures,   5
And Proserpine glad runs in her best array.
Nymphs deck her crown with bay.
Her feet are lions kissing.
No joy can there be missing.
Now Thetis leaves the mermaids' tunes admired,   10
And swells with pride to see this Queen desired.
Then sang the shepherds and nymphs of Diana:
Long live fair Oriana.

XXI

ROBERT JONES

FAIR Oriana, seeming to wink at folly,
Lay softly down to sleeping.
But hearing that the world was grown unholy,
Her rest was turned to weeping.

So waked, she sighed, and with crossed arms   5
Sat drinking tears for others' harms.
   Then sang the nymphs and shepherds of Diana:
   Long live fair Oriana.

XXII

JOHN LISLEY

FAIR Cytherea presents her doves, Minerva sweetly singeth,
Jove gives a crown, a garland Juno bringeth.
   Fame summons each celestial power
   To bring their gifts to Oriana's bower,
     Then sang the shepherds and nymphs of Diana: 5
     Long live fair Oriana.

XXIII

THOMAS MORLEY

HARD by a crystal fountain
   Oriana the bright lay down a-sleeping.
The birds they finely chirped, the winds were stilled,
Sweetly with these accenting the air was filled.
   This is that fair whose head a crown deserveth   5
     Which Heaven for her reserveth.
     Leave, shepherds, your lambs keeping
     Upon the barren mountain,
And, nymphs, attend on her and leave your bowers,
For she the shepherds' life maintains and yours.   10
   Then sang the shepherds and nymphs of Diana:
   Long live fair Oriana.

XXIV

EDWARD JOHNSON

COME, blessed bird, and with thy sugared relish
Help our declining choir now to embellish,
For Bonny-boots, that so aloft would fetch it,
O he is dead, and none of us can reach it.
   Then tune to us, sweet bird, thy shrill recorder,   5
     Elpin and I and Dorus
For fault of better will serve in the chorus.
Begin and we will follow thee in order.
   Then sang the wood-born minstrel of Diana:
     Long live fair Oriana.   10

JOHN MUNDY

Songs And Psalmes composed into 3. 4. and 5. parts, for the vse and delight of all such as either loue or learne Mvsicke. 1594

I

PRAISE the Lord, O my soul; while I live will I praise the Lord; yea as long as I have any being, I will sing praises unto my God.

[*Psalm cxlvi.* 1]

Every day will I give thanks to thee, and praise thy name for evermore. [*Psalm cxlv.* 2]

II

SAVE me, O God, and that with speed,
    The waters flow full fast;
So nigh my soul do they proceed
    That I am sore aghast.
I stick full deep in filth and clay,   5
    Whereas I feel no ground;
I fall into such floods I say
    That I am like be drowned.

[*Psalm lxix.* 1–2]

III

O ALL ye nations of the Lord,
    Praise ye the Lord always;
And all ye people everywhere
    Set forth his noble praise.
For great his kindness is to his,   5
    His truth endures for aye;
Wherefore praise ye the Lord our God,
    Praise ye the Lord I say.

[*Thomas Norton*]

IV–V

BLESSED art thou that fearest God,
    And walkest in his way,
For of thy labour thou shalt eat,
    Happy art thou I say.

Like fruitful vines on thy house side   5
     So doth thy wife spring out,
Thy children stand like olive plants
     Thy table round about.

Thus art thou blest that fearest God,
     And he shall let thee see   10
The promised Jerusalem
     And his felicity.
Thou shalt thy children's children see
     To thy great joy's increase;
And likewise grace on Israel,   15
     Prosperity and peace.

[*Thomas Sternhold*]

VI

HEAR my prayer, O Lord, and consider my desire; hearken unto me, and enter not into judgement with thy servant, for in thy sight shall no man living be justified.   [*Psalm cxliii.* 1–2]

VII

YE people all in one accord
     Clap hands and eke rejoice;
Be glad and sing unto the Lord
     With sweet and pleasant voice.

Sing praises to our God, sing praise,   5
     Sing praises to our King,
For God is king of all the earth,
     All thankful praises sing.

[*John Hopkins*]

VIII

O LORD, turn not away thy face
     From him that lies prostrate,
Lamenting sore his sinful life,
     Before thy mercy gate;
Which gate thou openest wide to those
     That do lament their sin,
Shut not that gate against me, Lord,
     But let me enter in.

[*John Marckant*]

IX

O COME, let us lift up our voice
  And sing unto the Lord,
In him, our Rock of health, rejoice
  Let us with one accord.
Yea, let us come before his face   5
  To give him thanks and praise;
In singing psalms unto his grace
  Let us be glad always.

                    [*John Hopkins*]

X

OF all the birds that I have heard,
  The nightingale doth bear the bell,
Whose pretty fine sweet pleasing tunes
  All other birds doth far excel.
But if such voices were not dear,   5
I would my mistress sung so clear.

XI

As I went a-walking
  In the month of May,
Merrily talking,
  I thus began to say:
Where dwelleth Love, that lively boy,   5
  How might I see his face,
That breedeth pain and bringeth joy,
  That altereth every case?
Then with a sigh I did refrain,
And to the world let it remain.   10

XII

TURN about and see me,
  How lustily I spring,
As joyfully as may be,
  As glad as anything.
If you will ask the cause and why,   5
I mean to tell you by and by.

She lives that I do honour most,
   Far passing all the rest,
A mighty Prince and excellent,
   Sweet Eglantine the best.   10
Then joy with me, both great and small,
Her life brings joy unto us all.

XIII

LORD, to thee I make my moan
   When dangers me oppress;
I call, I sigh, I plain and groan,
   Trusting to find release.
Hear now, O Lord, hear my request,   5
   For it is full due time,
And let thine ears be ever prest
   Unto this prayer mine.

                                [William Whittingham]

XIV

O LORD of whom I do depend,
   Behold my careful heart,
And when thy will and pleasure is
   Release me of my smart.
Thou seest my sorrows what they are,   5
   My grief is known to thee;
And there is none that can remove
   Or take the same from me.

                                 [John Marckant]

XV

SING ye unto the Lord our God
   A new rejoicing song;
And let the praise of him be heard
   His holy saints among.
Let Israel rejoice in him   5
   That made him of nothing,
And let the seed of Sion eke
   Be joyful of their king.

                                 [Thomas Norton]

XVI

I LIFT my heart to thee
   My God and guide most just,
Now suffer me to take no shame
   For in thee do I trust.
Let not my foes rejoice,   5
   Nor make a scorn of me,
And let them not be overthrown
   That put their trust in thee.

                                 [*Thomas Sternhold*]

XVII

MY prime of youth is but a frost of cares;
   My feast of joy is but a dish of pain;
My crop of corn is but a field of tares;
   And all my goods is but vain hope of gain.
The day is past, and yet I saw no sun;   5
And now I live, and now my life is done.

                         [*Chidiock Tichborne*]

XVIII

IN deep distress to live without delight,
   Were such a life as few I think would crave.
In pangs and pains to languish day and night,
   Were too too much for one poor soul to have.
If weal and woe will thus continue strife,   5
A gentle death were good to cut off such a life.

XIX

THE longer that I live,
   The more offence doth flow.
The more offence I give,
   The more account I owe.
The more account I make,   5
   The harder it will be;
Wherefore to live my heart doth shake,
   Death is a gain to me.

XX–XXI

THE shepherd Strephon loved fair Dorida,
   The finest shepherdess in all our field;
Whose loyal love when she would not obey,
   Ne by entreaties forced once to yield,
All on his knees unto that seemly saint,   5
In woeful wise thus 'gan he make his plaint:

Witness ye heavens, the palace of the gods,
   Witness ye gods, which hold your seats therein,
Witness hell furies with revengeful rods,
   Witness fond love, and all that love can win,   10
Witness the air, fire, water, earth and all,
How I have lived a vassal at thy call.

XXII

HEY ho! 'chill go to plough no more.
   Sit down and take thy rest.
Of golden groats I have good store
   To flaunt it with the best.
But I love and I love,—and who think you?   5
The finest lass that e'er you knew,
Which makes me sing when I should cry,
   Hey ho, for love I die.

XXIII

LORD, arise and help thy servant, which only trusteth in thee, for I am in misery.

XXIV

HAVE mercy on me, O Lord, and grant me my desire. Let truth and righteousness dwell with me for ever.   [*Psalm cxliii.* 1]
So shall I always praise thy name, and sing to thee O my God.
                      [*Psalm cxlv.* 1–2]

XXV

UNTO thee lift I up mine eyes, thou that dwellest in the heavens.
                      [*Psalm cxxiii.* 1]
Do well, O Lord, to those that are true of heart, for only in thee do I trust.   [*Psalm cxxv.* 4]

XXVI

WERE I a king I might command content.
    Were I obscure, unknown should be my cares.
And were I dead, no thoughts should me torment,
    Nor words, nor wrongs, nor loves, nor hopes, nor fears.
A doubtful choice, of three things one to crave,   5
A kingdom, or a cottage, or a grave.

                     [*William Gager*]

XXVII–XXVIII

IN midst of woods or pleasant grove
    Where all sweet birds do sing,
Methought I heard so rare a sound,
    Which made the heavens to ring.
The charm was good, the noise full sweet,   5
    Each bird did play his part;
And I admired to hear the same;
    Joy sprung into my heart.

The blackbird made the sweetest sound,
    Whose tunes did far excel,   10
Full pleasantly and most profound
    Was all things placed well.
Thy pretty tunes, mine own sweet bird,
    Done with so good a grace,
Extols thy name, prefers the same   15
    Abroad in every place.

Thy music grave, bedecked well
    With sundry points of skill,
Bewrays thy knowledge excellent,
    Engrafted in thy will.   20
My tongue shall speak, my pen shall write,
    In praise of thee to tell.
The sweetest bird that ever was,
    In friendly sort, farewell.

XXIX

PENELOPE that longed for the sight
    Of her Ulysses, wandering all too long,
Felt never joy wherein she took delight,
    Although she lived in greatest joys among,

So I, poor wretch, possessing that I crave,   5
Both live and lack by wrong of that I have.
Then blame me not although to heavens I cry,
And pray the gods that shortly I might die.

XXX

WHO loves a life devoid of quiet rest,
  And seeks content in dens of cruel care:
Who most triumphs when most he is oppressed,
  And weens him free when fast he is in snare:
Who in the sweet doth find the sourest taste,   5
His life is love, his food is vain repast.

MARTIN PEERSON

Priuate Musicke. Or The First Booke of Ayres and Dialogues: Contayning Songs of 4. 5. and 6. parts, of seuerall sorts, and being Verse and Chorus, is fit for Voyces and Viols. And for want of Viols, they may be performed to either the Virginall or Lute, where the Proficient can play vpon the Ground, or for a shift to the Base Viol alone. 1620

I

OPEN the door, who's there within?
The fairest of thy mother's kin.
   O come, come, come abroad,
   And hear the shrill birds sing,
   The air with tunes that load.   5
It is too soon to go to rest,
The sun not midway yet to west.
   The day doth miss thee,
     And will not part
   Until it kiss thee.   10

Were I as fair as you pretend,
Yet to an unknown sild-seen friend
   I dare not ope the door.
   To hear the sweet birds sing
   Oft proves a dangerous thing.   15

The sun may run his wonted race,
And yet not gaze on my poor face.
    The day may miss me;
      Therefore depart,
    You shall not kiss me.   20

II

RESOLVED to love, unworthy to obtain,
    I do no favour crave; but humble-wise
    To thee my sighs in verse I sacrifice,
Only some pity and no help to gain.

Much sorrow in myself my love doth move;   5
    More my despair to love a hopeless bliss;
    My folly most to love when sure to miss.
O help me but this last grief to remove.

All pain, if you command it, joy shall prove
    And wisdom to seek joy. Then say but this: 10
    Because my pleasure in thy torment is,
I do command thee without hope to love.
                    [*Henry Constable*]

III

AH, were she pitiful as she is fair,
    Or but so mild as she is seeming so,
Then were my hopes greater than my despair,
    Then all the world were heaven and nothing woe.

But beauty being pitiless and stern,   5
    Cruel in deed though mild in outward show,
Will neither hopes or my despairs discern,
    But leads me to a hell of endless woe.

IV

    DISDAIN that so doth fill me,
    Hath surely sworn to kill me,
        And I must die.
    Desire that still doth burn me,
    To life again will turn me,   5
        And live must I.
    O kill me then, Disdain,
    That I may live again.

Thy looks are life unto me,
And yet those looks undo me,   10
   O death and life!
Thy smile some rest doth show me,
Thy frown with war o'erthrow me,
   O peace and strife!
Nor life nor death is either;   15
Then give me both, or neither.

Life only cannot please me;
Death only cannot ease me,
   Change is delight.
I live that death may kill me,   20
I die that life may fill me,
   Both day and night.
   If once despair decay,
   Desire will wear away.

V

   O PRECIOUS Time,
  Created by the might
   Of his blest word,
That made all comely features,
And wisely parted into day and night   5
For the best use and service of the creatures.
O woe is me, that have mis-spent this treasure
In vain delight and fond and wicked pleasure.

VI

CAN a maid that is well bred,
Hath a blush so lovely red,
Modest looks, wise, mild, discreet,
And a nature passing sweet,

Break her promise, untrue prove,   5
On a sudden change her love,
Or be won ere to neglect
Him to whom she vowed respect?

Such a maid, alas, I know.
O that weeds 'mongst corn should grow,   10
Or a rose should prickles have,
Wounding where she ought to save!

I that did her parts extol,
Will my lavish tongue control.
Outward parts do blind the eyes,   15
Gall in golden pills oft lies.

Reason, wake and sleep no more;
Land upon some safer shore;
Think of her and be afraid
Of a faithless fickle maid.   20

Of a faithless fickle maid
Thus true love is still betrayed.
Yet it is some ease to sing
That a maid is light of wing.

VII

O I DO love, then kiss me,
And after I'll not miss thee
With bodies' loving meeting
To dally, pretty sweeting.
Though I am somewhat aged,   5
Yet is not love assuaged;
But with sweet ardent clips,
I'll lay thee on the lips,
And make thee ever swear:
Farewell old bachelor.   10

VIII

SINCE just disdain began to rise,
    And cry revenge for spiteful wrong,
What erst I praised I now despise,
    And think my love was all too long.
I tread in dirt that scornful pride   5
Which in thy looks I have descried.
Thy beauty is a painted skin
For fools to see their faces in.

Thine eyes that some as stars esteem,
    From whence themselves, they say, take light,   10
Like to the foolish fire I deem,
    That leads men to their death by night.

Thy words and oaths are light as wind,
And yet far lighter is thy mind.
Thy friendship is a broken reed   15
That fails thy friend in greatest need.

IX

AT her fair hands how have I grace entreated
        With prayers oft repeated;
        Yet still my love is thwarted.
Heart, let her go, for she'll not be converted.
        Say, shall she go?   5
        O no, no, no, no, no!
She is most fair, though she be marble-hearted.

How often have my sighs declared mine anguish,
        Wherein I daily languish!
        Yet doth she still procure it.   10
Heart, let her go, for I cannot endure it.
        Say, shall she go?
        O no, no, no, no, no!
She gave the wound, and she alone must cure it.
                                        [*Walter Davison*]

X

        NOW, Robin, laugh and sing,
        Thy master's sheep-shearing,
        When pies and custards smoke
        Then Robin plies his poke,
        And plays the merry cater,   5
        My teeth doth run a-water.
        And when the bagpipes play
        For this the merry day,
        Then comes in little Joan
        And bids strike up the drone.   10

        And while the drone doth play
        Upon this merry day,
        The country lasses throng
        With timbrels to their song
        In praise of lusty Bobin,   15
        The town's chief jolly Robin,

Who foots it o'er the downs,
Not caring for such clowns
As scorn his little Joan;
Then strike up still the drone!   20

XI

HEY, the horn, the horn-a
  To Vulcan doth belong.
And Venus, for she gave it,
  Is mistress of my song.
If Vulcan should not have it,   5
  Then Vulcan should have wrong.
The horn, the horn, the horn-a.

If Vulcan have the horn-a,
  Then Venus is to blame,
And Mars that did entice her   10
  Unto that wanton game.
Yet Vulcan needs must keep it,
  To set all well in frame.
The horn, the horn, the horn-a.

XII

UPON my lap my sovereign sits
  And sucks upon my breast.
Meantime his love maintains my life,
  And gives my sense her rest.
    Sing lullaby, my little boy,   5
    Sing lullaby, mine only joy.

When thou hast taken thy repast,
  Repose, my babe, on me;
So may thy mother and thy nurse
  Thy cradle also be.   10
    Sing lullaby, my little boy,
    Sing lullaby, mine only joy.

I grieve that duty doth not work
  All what my wishing would,
Because I would not be to thee   15
  But in the best I should.
    Sing lullaby, my little boy,
    Sing lullaby, mine only joy.

    Yet as I am, and as I may,
      I must and will be thine,   20
    Though all too little for thyself,
      Vouchsafing to be mine.
        Sing lullaby, my little boy,
        Sing lullaby, mine only joy.
                [*Richard Verstegan*]

XIII

LOCK up, fair lids, the treasure of my heart;
  Preserve those beams, this age's only light.
To her sweet sense, sweet sleep, some ease impart,
  Her sense too weak to bear her spirit's might.
  And while, O sleep, thou closest up her sight,   5
Her light where Love did forge his fairest dart,
  O harbour all her parts in easeful plight,
Let no strange dream make her fair body start.
But yet, O dream, if thou wilt not depart
  In this rare subject from thy common right   10
  But wilt thyself in such a seat delight,
Then take my shape, and play a lover's part;
  Kiss her from me, and say unto her sprite,
  Till her eyes shine I live in darkest night.
                [*Sir Philip Sidney*]

XIV

    LOVE her no more,
    Herself she doth not love.
    Shame and the blackest clouds of night
    Hide her for ever from thy light.
O day, why do thy beams in her eyes move?   5

Fly her, dear honoured friend, do so;
She'll be the cause of much much woe.
    Alas, she will undo thee,
    Her love is fatal to thee.
    Curse her then, and go!   10

XV–XVI

    COME, pretty wag, and sing;
    The sun's all-ripening wing
    Fans up the wanton spring.

O let us both go chant it,
Dainty, dainty flowers   5
Sprout up with April showers
And deck the summer bowers;
    O how fresh May doth flaunt it.

Then with reports most sprightly
Trip with thy voice most lightly.   10
O sing so prettily, so wittily, for now
The cuckoo sings cuckoo, cuckoo,
        That echo doth rebound,
        And dally with the sound.

XVII

PRETTY wantons, sweetly sing
In honour of the smiling Spring.
Look how the light-winged chirping choir
With nimble skips the Spring admire.
But O, hark how the birds sing, O mark that note,   5
        Jug, jug, tereu, tereu,
O prett'ly warbled from a sweet sweet throat.

XVIII

SING, Love is blind.
So now is Love's lady. Yet in the dark
    Love light can find.
    Love's a good clerk,
        Reads perfectly and puts together.   5
        Then tell me whether
He's not a fool that cries to hit the mark?
    Cupid wants eyes, and is a baby.
O no, though Cupid's young and blind withal,
    Yet he can make the strongest fall.   10
        With a hey nonny nonny no.

XIX

WHAT need the morning rise,
Seeing a sun in both thine eyes?
    What need a sun to shine,
Seeing a clearer light in thine?
    { O, 'tis on thee to gaze.   5
    { No, 'tis on thee to gaze.

Strike them into amaze
By thy more golden rays.
Let no eye dare to see
{ How thus I challenge thee. }
{ How thus I yield to thee. }   10
O let no hate never
Our white hands sever.

XX–XXI

GAZE not on Youth; let Age contain
Thy wandering eye from objects vain.

No, I must look about and see
In love what heavenly objects be.
But when the eye is on the face,   5
The mind is in another place.

True pleasure is in chastity.
I only seek to please mine eye.
I may be chaste, yet gaze my fill.

No, learn of me, and sing this still: 10
She, only she, is ever chaste,
That is with every look outfaced.

XXII

THE spring of joy is dry
That ran into my heart;
And all my comforts fly.
My love and I must part.
Farewell, my love, I go,   5
If fate will have it so.
Yet to content us both
Return again, as doth
The shadow to the hour,
The bee unto the flower,   10
The fish unto the hook,
The cattle to the brook,
That we may sport our fill,
And love continue still.

XXIII

Is not that my fancy's queen,
  In the brightness of her rays
  Passing Summer's cheerest days,
That comes tripping o'er the green?

Is not that my shepherd's swain,   5
  Sprightly clad in lovely blue,
  Fairest of the fairest crew
That comes gliding o'er the plain?

'Tis my love, and thus we meet.
'Tis my love, and thus we greet.   10
Happier than the gods above,
Meeting, may we ever love.
Meeting, may we love for ever,
And never, never, never sever.

XXIV

*This song was made for the King and Queen's entertainment at Highgate
on May-day, 1604*

SEE, O see, who is here come a-maying?
  The Master of the Ocean
  And his sweet beauteous Orian.
  Why left we off our playing?
    To gaze on them   5
That gods as well as men amaze.
  Up, nightingale, and sing
  Jug, jug, jug, jug.
  Lark, raise thy note and wing,
  All birds their music bring.   10
  Robin, linnet, thrush,
  Record from every bush
The welcome of the King and Queen,
  Whose like were never seen
    For good and fair;   15
Nor can be; though fresh May
  Should every day
Invite a several pair.

                                 [*Ben Jonson*]

Mottects Or Grave Chamber Mvsiqve. Containing Songs of fiue parts of seuerall sorts, some ful, and some Verse and Chorus. But all fit for Voyces and Vials, with an Organ Part; which for want of Organs, may be performed on Virginals, Base-Lvte, Bandora, or Irish Harpe. Also, A Mourning Song of sixe parts for the Death of the late Right Honorable Sir Fvlke Grevil, Knight of the Honourable order of the Bath, Lord Brooke, Baron Brooke of Beauchamps-Court in the Countie of Warwicke, and of his Maiesties most honourable priuie Councell, &c. Composed according to the Rules of Art. 1630

I–III

L O V E, the delight of all well-thinking minds;
   Delight the fruit of Virtue dearly loved;
Virtue, the highest good that Reason finds;
   Reason, the fire wherein men's thoughts be proved,
Are from the world by Nature's power bereft,   5
And in one creature for her glory left.

Beauty her cover is, the eye's true pleasure;
   In Honour's fame she lives, the ear's sweet music;
Excess of wonder grows from her true measure;
   Her worth is passion's wound and passion's physic.   10
From her true heart clear springs of wisdom flow,
Which, imaged in her words and deeds, men know.

Time fain would stay, that she might never leave her;
   Place doth rejoice that she must needs contain her;
Death craves of Heaven that she may not bereave her;   15
   The heavens know their own and do maintain her.
Delight, Love, Reason, Virtue, let it be
To set all women light but only she.
                  [*Fulke Greville, Lord Brooke*]

I V – V

M O R E than most fair, full of all heavenly fire
   Kindled above to show the maker's glory.
Beauty's first-born, in whom all powers conspire
   To write the Graces' life, and Muses' story,
If in my heart all nymphs else be defaced,   5
Honour the shrine where you alone are placed.

Thou window of the sky, and pride of spirits,
   True character of honour in perfection,
Thou heavenly creature, judge of earthly merits,
   And glorious prison of men's pure affection,   10

If in my heart all nymphs else be defaced,
Honour the shrine where you alone are placed.
[Fulke Greville, Lord Brooke]

VI–VII

Y O U little stars that live in skies,
    And glory in Apollo's glory,
In whose aspect conjoined lies
    The heavens' will and Nature's story,
Joy to be likened to those eyes,   5
    Which eyes makes all eyes glad or sorry.
For when you force thoughts from above,
Those over-rule your force by love.

And thou, O Love, which in those eyes
    Hast married Reason with Affection,   10
And made them saints of beauty's skies,
    Where joys are shadows of perfection,
Lend me thy wings, that I may rise
    Up, not by worth but thy election.
For I have vowed in strangest fashion   15
To love, and never seek compassion.
[Fulke Greville, Lord Brooke]

VIII–IX

O L O V E, thou mortal sphere of powers divine,
    The paradise of Nature in perfection,
What makes thee thus thy kingdom undermine,
    Veiling thy glories under woe's reflection?
Tyranny counsel out of fear doth borrow   5
To think her kingdom safe in fear and sorrow.

If I by nature, wonder and delight,
    Had not sworn all my powers to worship thee,
Justly mine own revenge receive I might,
    And see thee, tyrant, suffer tyranny.   10
See thee thyself despair and sorrow breeding,
Under the wounds of woe and sorrow bleeding.
[Fulke Greville, Lord Brooke]

X

CUPID, my pretty boy, leave off thy crying,
  Thou shalt have bells or apples, be not peevish.
Kiss me, sweet lad. Beshrew her for denying!
  Such rude denials do make children thievish.
Did Reason say that boys must be restrained?   5
  What was it, tell, hath cruel Honour chidden?
Or would they have thee from sweet Myra weaned?
  Are her fair breasts made dainty to be hidden?
Tell me, sweet boy, doth Myra's beauty threaten?
  Must you say grace when you should be a playing?   10
Doth she make thee make faults to make thee beaten?
  Is Beauty's pride in Innocence betraying?
Give me a bow, let me thy quiver borrow,
And she shall play the child with love, or sorrow.
                    [*Fulke Greville, Lord Brooke*]

XI

LOVE is the peace whereto all thoughts do strive,
  Done and begun with all our powers in one;
The first and last in us that is alive,
  End of the good, and therewith pleased alone.
Perfection's spirit, goddess of the mind,   5
  Passed through hope, desire, grief and fear,
A simple goodness in the flesh refined,
  Which of the joys to come doth witness bear.
                    [*Fulke Greville, Lord Brooke*]

XII

SELF-PITY'S tears, wherein my hope lies drowned,
  Sighs from thought's fire, where my desires languish,
Despair by humble love of beauty crowned,
  Furrows not worn by Time, but wheels of anguish,
Dry up, smile, joy, make smooth and see   5
Furrows, despairs, sighs, tears in beauty be.
                    [*Fulke Greville, Lord Brooke*]

XIII

WAS ever man so matched with boy?
  When I am thinking how to keep him under,
He plays and dallies me with every toy,
  With pretty stealths he makes me laugh and wonder.

When with the child, the child-thoughts of wisdom   5
   Do long to play and toy as well as he,
The boy is sad and melancholy grown
   And with one humour cannot long agree,
Straight do I scorn and bid the child away.
   The boy knows fury, and soon showeth me   10
Caelica's sweet eyes, where love and beauty play;
   Fury turns into love of that I see.
If these mad changes do make children gods,
Women and children are not far at odds.
                    [*Fulke Greville, Lord Brooke*]

XIV

O FALSE and treacherous Probability,
   Enemy of Truth and friend to Wickedness,
With blear-eyed opinion learn to see
   Truth's feeble pity here and barrenness.
When thou hast thus misled humanity,   5
   And lost obedience in the pride of wit,
With reason dar'st thou judge the Deity,
   And in thy flesh make bold to fashion it.
Vain thought! the word of power a riddle is,
   And till the veils be rent, the flesh new-born,   10
Reveals no wonders of that inward bliss,
   Which, but where faith is, everywhere finds scorn.
Who therefore censures God with fleshly sprite,
As well in Time may wrap up infinite.
                    [*Fulke Greville, Lord Brooke*]

XV–XVI

MAN, dream no more of curious mysteries;
   As what was here before the world was made,
The first man's life, the state of Paradise,
   Where heaven is, or hell's eternal shade;
For God's works are, like him, all infinite,   5
And curious search but crafty Sin's delight.

The flood that did, and dreadful fire that shall
   Drown and burn up the malice of the earth;
The divers tongues, or Babylon's downfall,
   Are nothing to the man's renewed birth.   10
First let the Law plough up thy wicked heart,
That Christ may come, and all those types depart.

When thou hast swept the house that all is clear,
 When thou the dust hast shaken from thy feet,
When God's Almight doth in thy flesh appear,   15
 Then seas with streams above the sky do meet;
For God doth only goodness comprehend,
Knows what was first, and what shall be the end.
       [*Fulke Greville, Lord Brooke*]

XVII–XVIII

WHO trusts for trust, or hopes of love for love;
 Or who, beloved, in Cupid's laws doth glory;
Who joys in vows, or vows not to remove;
 Who, by this light god hath not been made sorry:
Let him see me eclipsed from my sun   5
With shadows of an earth quite over-run.

Who thinks that sorrows felt, desires hidden,
 Or humble faith with constant honour armed,
Can keep love from the fruit that is forbidden.
 Change I do mean by no faith to be charmed: 10
Looking on me let him know love's delights
Are treasures hid in caves but kept with sprites.
       [*Fulke Greville, Lord Brooke*]

XIX

[*The words are the same as those of No. xv, 1st stanza*]

XX

FAREWELL, sweet Boy, complain not of my truth,
 Thy mother loved thee not with more devotion;
For to thy boy's play I gave all my youth.
 Young master, I did hope for your promotion.
While some sought honours, princes' thoughts observing, 5
 Many wooed Fame, the child of Pain and Anguish,
Others judged inward good a chief deserving,
 I in thy wanton visions joyed to languish.
I bowed not to thy image for succession,
 Nor bound thy bow to shoot reformed kindness; 10
The plays of hope and fear were my confession;
 The spectacles to my life was thy blindness.
But, Cupid, now farewell, I will go play me
With thoughts that please me less, and less betray me.
       [*Fulke Greville, Lord Brooke*]

XXI

UNDER a throne I saw a virgin sit,
  The red and white rose quartered in her face;
Star of the North, and for true guards to it,
  Church, Princes, States, all pointing out her grace.
The homage done her was not born of wit,   5
  Fear did admire, Zeal took Ambition's place,
State in her eyes taught Order how to fit
  And fix Conclusion's unobserving race.
Fortune can here claim nothing truly great
But that this princely creature is her seat.   10
              [Fulke Greville, Lord Brooke]

XXII–XXIII

WHERE shall a sorrow great enough be sought
For this sad ruin which the Fates have wrought,
Unless the Fates themselves should weep and wish
Their curbless power had been controlled in this?
For thy loss, worthiest lord, no mourning eye   5
Has flood enough; no Muse nor elegy
Enough expression to thy worth can lend;
No, though thy Sidney had survived his friend.
Dead, noble Brooke shall be to us a name
Of grief and honour still, whose deathless fame   10
And virtue purchased as makes us to be
Unjust to Nature in lamenting thee,
Wailing an old man's fate, as if in pride
And heat of youth he had untimely died.

XXIV–XXV

[The words are the same as in the preceding numbers, xxii–xxiii]

FRANCIS PILKINGTON

The First Set Of Madrigals And Pastorals of 3. 4. and 5. Parts. 1613

I

SEE where my love a-maying goes, with sweet Dame Flora sporting,
She most alone with nightingales in woods' delights consorting.
Turn again, my dearest, the pleasant'st air's in meadows,
    Else by the rivers let us breathe, and kiss amongst the willows.

II

I FOLLOW, lo, the footing
Still of my lovely cruel,
Proud of herself that she is beauty's jewel;
And fast away she flieth,
Love's sweet delight deriding,   5
In woods and groves sweet Nature's treasure hiding.
Yet cease I not pursuing,
But since I thus have sought her,
Will run me out of breath till I have caught her.

III

POUR forth, mine eyes, the fountains of your tears;
Break, heart, and die, for now no hope appears.
Hope, upon which before my thoughts were fed,
Hath left me quite forlorn and from me fled.
Yet see, she smiles; O see, some hope appears.   5
Hold, heart, and live; mine eyes, cease off your tears.

IV

STAY, nymph, the ground seeks but to kiss thy feet.
    Hark, hark, how Philomela sweetly sings;
Whilst water-wanton fishes, as they meet,
    Strike crotchet-time amidst these crystal springs,
    And Zephyrus 'mongst the leaves sweet murmur rings.   5
Stay but a while, Phoebe no tell-tale is,
She her Endymion, I'll my Phoebe kiss.

V

DORUS, a seely shepherd's swain,
  Whilst he his flock was keeping
Upon the vast Arcadian plain,
  Found Amoretta sleeping,
And fearing lest she had been slain   5
  His eyes burst forth a-weeping.
Yet feeling her pure pulses beat,
  Not minding to molest her,
He viewed her most admired parts,
  And so most kindly kissed her.   10

VI

IS this thy doom, and shall thy shepherd die,
Wounded with love, stabbed with affection's eye?
Say then, sweet saint, what breast shall be thy shrine,
When thou hast slain the heart that erst was thine?
Pity, O pity, O life for love me give,   5
And sweetly say to me: Kind shepherd, live.

VII

AMYNTAS with his Phyllis fair in height of Summer's sun
Grazed arm in arm their snowy flock; and scorching heat to shun
Under a spreading elm sat down, where love's delightments done,
Down-dillie-down, thus did they sing, there is no life like ours,
No heaven on earth to shepherds' cells, no hell to princely bowers. 5

VIII

HERE rest, my thoughts. What meaneth all this hasting
To fry in pangs and torments everlasting?
And yet her heart is even to me as cruel,
Her eye's the flame, but my heart lends the fuel.

IX

WHY should I grieve that she disdains my love,
  Or seek for love, since love's a grief?
A noble mind his tortures ill behove.
  He spoils, thralls, murthers like a thief,
  Debarring beauty's bar all loved relief.   5

X

THE messenger of the delightful Spring,
    The cuckoo, proud bird mocking man,
On lofty oaks and every under-spring
    To chant out cuckoo scarce began,
    Whenas Menalcas, soote as swan   5
His Winter cloak cast off, did nimbly spring;
And as the cuckoo, cuck did sing,
    The shepherd's down a down was farra diddle dan.

XI

HAVE I found her, (O rich finding!)
    Goddess-like for to behold,
Her fair tresses seemly binding
    In a chain of pearl and gold?
Chain me, chain me, O most fair,   5
Chain me to thee with that hair.

XII

WHAT though her frowns and hard entreaties kill,
I will not cease to love, affect her still.
Still will I love her beauty, hate her scorn,
Love her for beauty at her beauty's morn.

XIII

LOVE is a secret feeding fire that gives all creatures being,
Life to the dead, speech to the dumb, and to the blind man seeing.
And yet in me he contradicts all these his sacred graces,
Sears up my lips, my eyes, my life, and from me ever flying,
Leads me in paths untracked, ungone, and many uncouth places, 5
Where in despair I beauty curse, curse love and all fair faces.

XIV

WHY do I fret and grieve,
Since she denies and will no comfort give?
    O fatal foul decree.
She stops her ears and smiles at my complaint;
        Whilst wounded with disdain,   5
I seek all means I can to set me free.
        And yet it will not be.
            O bitter pain!

XV

ALL in a cave a shepherd's lad met wanton Thestalis.
Where he, unskilled in better sports, begged only for a kiss.
Alas, quoth she, and take thee this, and this, and this, and this.
But knowest thou not, fair boy, in love a more contented sweet?
Oh no, he said, for in a kiss our souls together meet.   5

XVI

SING we, dance we on the green,
    And fill these valleys with our melodious strains,
        For joy that our Summer's queen,
    Environed with all the country swains,
        Fairly trips it o'er the plains.   5
    Let us about these daffadillies sweet
        Tread a ring-dance with our feet.

XVII

UNDER the tops of Helicon,
    Not far from Parnasse' stately towers,
Springs forth the fountain Hippocrene
    With banks beset with fragrant flowers.
The hill is it my Muses use,   5
The fountain which my heart doth choose.

XVIII

SWEET Phillida, my flocks as white and pure as snowy down
        Sit mourning for thy sake.
    Come when thou wilt, I never mean to frown.
        Thy love I will partake.
    Come, quickly come, I sigh for thee my dearest sweet.   5
        I'll turn my flocks away,
        And with them I'll not stay,
So thee and I most lovingly in love each other meet.

XIX

    MY heart is dead within me,
    For that my love forsakes me.
Yet why should I shed tears in vain?
She will not once respect my pain.
I therefore will joy, sing, and dance,   5
    In hope to cast a better chance.

XX

No, no, no, it will not be,
Your labour is in vain.
I stay you not, but set you free;
Why do you then complain
And wail conceited wrongs as done to me?   5
No, no, I tell you once again
You have your travail for your pain.
No, no, no, it will not be.

XXI

WHEN Oriana walked to take the air,
The world did strive to entertain so fair.
By Flora fair and sweetest flowers were strone
Along the way for her to tread upon.
The trees did blossom, the silver rivers ran,   5
The wind did gently play upon her fan.
And then for to delight her Grace's ear,
The woods a temple seemed, the birds a choir.
    Then sang the shepherds and nymphs of Diana:
    In heaven lives Oriana.   10

XXII

NOW I see thou floutest me,
And disdains the gifts I offer thee.
Then since thou scorns to accept it
On Cloris' head I'll set it.
For her I'll gather dainty posies.   5
Of gillyflowers and purple roses.
    With her on each holiday
    I'll dance the merry roundelay.
    And this I know will move thee,
    To say, I do not love thee.   10

*The Second Set of Madrigals and Pastorals, of 3. 4. 5. and 6. Parts; Apt for
Violls and Voyces. 1624*

I

SOVEREIGN of my delight, hear my complaining.
Fly to her my sad thoughts containing.
    Beauty by pleasure only crowned
    Now in herself lies drowned
    By her unkind disdaining.   5

II

YOND hill-tops Phoebus kissed
    At his last night's farewell.
This morn the same he blissed
    In homage to her cell.
The nymphs and wood-gods cried: 5
    Lord Phoebus, go your way;
We her, she us, will have,
    You are too hot to play.

III

WAKE, sleepy Thyrsis, wake
For Love and Venus' sake.
Come, let us mount the hills,
Which Zephyrus' cool breath fills;
Or let us tread new alleys   5
In yonder shady valleys.
Rise, rise, rise,
Lighten thy heavy eyes;
See how the streams do glide,
And the green meads divide.   10
But stream nor fire shall part
This and this joined heart.

IV

STAY, heart, run not so fast from him that loves thee
    To her that deadly hates thee.
    Her sharp disdain reproves thee,
    And worse than ill still rates thee.
    Then let her go and spare not.   5
Hold thou thyself contented and I care not.
My love is gone, and with her go my sorrow.

O vile wretch, thou lovedst once, and why now dost thou vary?
    Then straight away I haste me,
And after thee will run while life shall last me.   10
    Ah, Death his force now trieth;
Flora farewell, for lo, thy shepherd dieth.

V

YE bubbling springs that gentle music makes
    To lovers' plaints, with heart-sore throbs immixed,
Whenas my dear this way her pleasure takes,
    To tell her with tears how firm my love is fixed;

And Philomel report my timorous fears,   5
And Echo sound my 'heigh-hos' in her ears;
But if she ask if I for love will die,
Tell her, good faith, not I.

VI

YOUR fond preferments are but children's toys,
    And as a shadow all your pleasures pass;
As years increase, so waning are your joys;
    Your bliss is brittle like a broken glass.
Death is the salve that ceaseth all annoy.   5
Death is the port by which we sail to joy.

VII

MENALCAS in an evening walking was
With Daphne his beloved lovely lass.
She weeps, and doth of Cupid oft complain;
But, 'Comfort, Daphne', said the jolly swain,
'Come kiss me, sweet, and let us merry be.   5
The gods are crossed in love as well as we.'

VIII–IX

COY Daphne fled from Phoebus' hot pursuit,
    Careless of passion, senseless of remorse.
Whilst he complained his griefs, she rested mute;
    He begged her stay, she still kept on her course.
But what reward she had for this you see,   5
She rests transformed, a winter-beaten tree.

Chaste Daphne fled from Phoebus' hot pursuit,
    Knowing men's passions idle and of course.
And though he plained, 'twas fit she should be mute;
    And honour would she should keep on her course.   10
For which fair deed her glory still we see;
She rest still green. And so wish I to be.

X

IF she neglect me,
    I do wail and cry.
If she affect me,
    Straight for grief I die.

For though our sorrow, joy, and death one be,   5
Yet we in one shall ne'er be joined, I see.
    So that I cry:
    I die, I die.
    O dismal fate!
Whether she love, affect, neglect, or hate.   10

XI

PALAEMON and his Sylvia forth must walk,
Of passions past and divers things to talk.
He sighs, she weeps, they kiss, and both complain,
And both of them would something utter fain.
But voice and words were to them both denied,   5
For they had nought to say that was not said.

XII

YOU gentle nymphs that on these meadows play,
   And oft relate the loves of shepherds young,
Come sit you down, for if you please to stay,
   Now may you hear an uncouth passion sung!
A lad there is, and I am that poor groom,   5
That's fall'n in love, and cannot tell with whom.

                                [*George Wither*]

XIII

CHASTE Syrinx fled, fear hasting on her pace,
With loosed hair and tear-bedewed face,
Weary, God wot, and Pan behind her nigh;
She fills the woods with many a dreary cry.
The gods did see, and seem her case to mourn,   5
And into reeds her dainty limbs transform.
So now she makes most joyous melody
For joy she kept her loved virginity.

XIV

COME, shepherds' weeds, attend my woeful cries;
   Disuse yourselves from sweet Menalcas' voice;
For other be those tunes which sorrow ties
   From those clear notes which freely may rejoice.
Then pour out plaint, and in one word say this: 5
Helpless his plaint who spoils himself of bliss.

                                [*Sir Philip Sidney*]

XV

CROWNED with flowers I saw fair Amaryllis
   By Thyrsis sit, hard by a fount of crystal.
And with her hand, more white than snow or lilies,
   On sand she wrote 'My faith shall be immortal'.
But suddenly a storm of wind and weather   5
Blew all her faith and sand away together.

XVI

An elegy on the death of his worshipful friend, Master Thomas Purcell of
Dinthill, Esquire, in Salop

WEEP, sad Urania, weep, for thou hast lost thy dear,
And now must fix thy sacred love elsewhere.
For he that lately made thy numbers e'en,
Forsaking earth, is now possessed of heaven.
Where he, though dead, still lives with God on high.   5
He found, we lost; he sings, we sigh and die.

XVII

O GRACIOUS God, pardon my great offence,
   Increase my faith, renew thy spirit of grace;
Invest me with thy Christ his innocence,
   And from me, Lord, turn not away thy face;
Let not my sins, full many though they be,   5
Make a divorce between thy grace and me.

XVIII

   GO, you skipping kids and fawns,
      Exercise your swift career
   Over pleasant fields and lawns,
      Rousing up the fearful deer.
   Greet them all with what I sing,   5
   Endless love eternizing.

XIX

CARE for thy soul as thing of greatest price,
   Made to the end to taste of power divine,
Devoid of guilt, abhorring sin and vice,
   Apt by God's grace to virtue to incline.
Care for it so as by thy retchless train   5
It be not brought to taste eternal pain.

XX

DROWN not with tears, my dearest love,
Those eyes, which my affections move.
Do not with weeping those lights blind
Which me in thy subjection bind.
Time, that hath made us two of one,   5
And forced thee now to live alone,
Will once again us reunite,
To show how she can Fortune spite.

XXI–XXII

DEAR shepherdess, thou art more lovely fair
    Than the both roses in the prime of May.
Thou art more tender sweet without compare
    Than the bright morning at the break of day.
But unto me, that do thy praise declare,   5
    More cold and dead than the most cold dismay.
Cruel Pabrilla, with thine angry look
    Thou ever holdst my soul in alteration.
And of the pleasure that I whilome took
    In my fair flocks, thy threats are deprivation.   10
Thee I more love than hill or valley-brook,
    Or thrifty shadow, my flock's delectation.
But yet my sight more hateful is to thee
Than thorns or nettles to thy white feet be.

XXIII

[*A Fancy for the viols*]

XXIV

O SOFTLY singing Lute,
See with my tears thou time do keep.
    Yet softly, gentle strings,
Agree with Love that cannot sleep.
    Sorrow hist whenas it sings.   5
When tears do fall then sighs arise.
So grief oft shines in most sad eyes,
    Yea love through heart it dies.

XXV

O PRAISE the Lord, all ye heathen; praise him all ye nations.
For his merciful kindness is ever more and more towards us, and
the truth of the Lord endureth for ever. O praised be the Lord.

[*Psalm cxvii.* 1–2]

XXVI

A Dialogue for the Viols and Voices, and the Lute

SURCEASE, you youthful shepherdesses all,
Fond folly breeding love so sensual.

2 verse. Peace, Malediction, stop thy yawning jaws,
Love's gods, though partial, will protect his laws.

3 verse. Stint then our strife, contention be content.   5
Love in itself maintains an argument.

4 verse. See Summer's lady, savour-scenting May,
Ties Terra's temples in a garland gay;
And we that erst with Hyems did condole,
Now dance about Sylvanus' summer-pole.   10

Chorus. Love, be propitious. Shepherdesses, sing.
Olympus likes and loves our carolling.

XXVII

A Pavan made for the Orpharion

THOMAS RAVENSCROFT

Pammelia. Mvsicks Miscellanie. Or, Mixed Varietie of Pleasant Roundelayes, and delightfull Catches, of 3. 4. 5. 6. 7. 8. 9. 10. Parts in one. 1609

I

HEY ho!
To the greenwood now let us go;
  Sing heave and ho.
And there shall we find both buck and doe;
  Sing heave and ho.
The hart, the hind, and the little pretty roe;   5
  Sing heave and ho.

II

O MY fearful dreams never forget shall I;
Methought I heard a maiden child condemned to die,
  Whose name was Jesus.

III

JOLLY shepherd and upon a hill as he sate,
So loud he blew his little horn, and kept right well his gate.
    Early in a morning,
    Late in an evening,
And ever blew this little boy, so merrily piping: 5
    Tere liter lo.

IV

ALL into service let us ring, merrily together.
  Ding dong ding dong bell.

V

NEW oysters, new oysters new.
Have you any wood to cleave?
What kitchen stuff have you, maids?

VI

OAKEN leaves in the merry wood so wild,
    When will you grow green-a?
Fairest maid and thou be with child,
    Lullaby may'st thou sing-a.

VII

Now God be with old Simeon,
For he made cans for many a one,
    And a good old man was he.
And Jinkin was his journeyman,
And he could tipple of every can,   5
    And thus he said to me:
        To whom drink you?
        Sir knave, to you!
Then hey ho, jolly Jinkin,
I spy a knave in drinking,   10
    Come troll the bowl to me.

VIII

WELL fare the nightingale,
Fare fall the thrush-cock too;
But foul fare the filthy bird that singeth 'cuckoo'.

IX

        FOLLOW me quickly,
    Jack is a pretty boy;
        Round about,
        Standing stout,
    Singing ale in a bowl: 5
        Fa, la, sol, la, mi,
        Dirry come dandy.

X

Now kiss the cup, cousin, with courtesy,
And drink your part with a heart willingly,
Then so shall we all agree merrily.

XI

NEW oysters, new oysters, new Walfleet oysters!
At a groat a peck, each oyster worth twopence.
   Fetch us bread and wine, that we may eat;
   Let us lose no time with such good meat.
      A banquet for a prince!   5

XII

   ALL into service, the bells toll;
All into service now ring they, all into service,
   Ding, dong, bell.

XIII

         HEY down a down!
         Behold and see,
         What song is this,
         Or how may this be?
         Three parts in one,   5
         Sing all after me,
         With hey down a down,
         Troll the berry,
         Drink and be merry.

XIV

MISERERE nostri Domine, secundum misericordiam tuam.

XV

PIETAS omnium virtutum parens et fundamentum.

XVI

INTENDE voci orationis meae, rex meus et Deus meus quoniam ad
te orabo.

XVII

HAEC est vita aeterna: ut cognoscant te, solum Deum verum, et
quem misisti Jesum Christum. Amen.

XVIII

MISERERE nostri Domine viventium et mortuorum.

XIX

O PRAISE the Lord, ye that fear Him; magnify Him, all ye seed of
Jacob, and praise Him, all ye seed of Israel.

XX

THE merry nightingale she sweetly sits and sings;
    The pretty nimble doe
    Doth trip it to and fro;
    The stond horse kicks and flings;
  The cuckoo he doth fly from tree to tree,   5
And merrily through the woods 'cuckoo' rings.

XXI

THE jolly old dog as he lay in his den-a;
    Huffa, buffa, trolilo,
    As he lay in his den-a.

XXII

JOAN, come kiss me now,
    Once again for my love,
Gentle Joan, come kiss me now.

XXIII

MY dame has in her hutch at home
    A little dog
    With a clog.
    Hey, dog, hey!

XXIV

GO no more to Brainford unless you love a punk,
For that wicked sinful town hath made me drunk.
    Come, follow me!

XXV

DAME, lend me a loaf
    From Saturday to Saturday,
    And longer if you longer may.

XXVI

I AM a-thirst, what should I say?
Alas, I have no money to pay.
Fill the pot, butler, fill, fill,
For I will drink with a good will.

XXVII

THERE lies a pudding in the fire,
    And my part lies therein-a,
Whom should I call in?
    O thy good fellows and mine-a.

XXVIII

HEY down a down, behold and see,
Good hostess, fill the pot for me,
This is the best ale, believe me,
And yet it is the first of three.
If ye will drink more, then call me.   5
Take and fill this pot yet once again,
We will for this time thus remain.
When this is spent fill pot again.

XXIX

WHAT hap had I to marry a shrow,
For she hath give me many a blow,
And how to please her, alack, I do not know.

From morn to even her tongue ne'er lies,
Sometimes she brawls, sometime she cries,   5
Yet can I scarce keep her tallants from my eyes.

If I go abroad, and late come in,
Sir knave (saith she), where have you been?
And do I well or ill, she claps me on the skin.

XXX

HEY down a down, heave and ho, Rumbelo!
Follow me my sweet heart, follow me where I go.
    Shall I go walk the woods so wild,
        Wandering here and there,

As I was once full sore beguiled?   5
  What remedy though,
Alas, for love I die with woe.
Oft have I ridden upon my grey nag,
And with his cut tail he played the wag,
And down he fell upon his crag.   10
  Fa, la, re, la, lari dan dino.

XXXI

UT, re, mi, fa, sol, la,
La, sol, fa, mi, re, ut.
  Hey down a down a!

My heart of gold, as true as steel,
  As I me leant unto the bowers,   5
But if my lady love me well,
  Lord, so Robin lowers.

    Heave and ho,
    Rumbelo.
    Hey trolo, troly lo!   10

My lady's gone to Canterbury,
  Saint Thomas, be her boot!
She met with Kate of Malmesbury,
  Why weep'st thou, maple root?

O sleep'st thou or wak'st thou, Jeffery Cook?   15
The roast it burns; turn round about.

    O Friar, how fares thy bandelow?
    Friar, how fares thy sandelow?

XXXII

MISERERE mei Deus, secundum magnam misericordiam tuam.

XXXIII

CONDITOR Kyrie omnium qui vivunt, Kyrie [e]leison.

XXXIV

IN te Domine speravi; non confundar in aeternum.

XXXV

EXAUDI Domine orationem meam.

XXXVI

ORA et labora.

XXXVII

QUICQUID petieritis Patrem in nomine meo, dabit vobis.

XXXVIII

CANTATE Domino canticum novum.

XXXIX

MANE nobiscum Christe, quoniam advesperascit, et dies inclinata est.

XL

EMITTE lucem tuam et veritatem: ipsa me deducant et adducant in montem sanctum tuum et in tabernacula.

XLI

FIDES est animae vita sicut anima est vita corporis.

XLII

DESCENDIT Christus de coelo.

XLIII

ASCENDIT Christus in coelum.

XLIV

ADIUVA nos Deus.

XLV

O LORD of whom I do depend,
    Behold my careful heart,
And when Thy will and pleasure is,
    Release me of my smart.

Thou seest my sorrows what they are,   5
　　My grief is known to Thee;
And there is none that can remove
　　Or take the same from me,

But only Thou, whose aid I crave,
　　Whose mercy still is pressed   10
To ease all those that come to Thee
　　For succour and for rest.

[John Marckant]

XLVI

ATTEND, my people, and give ear,
　　Of ferly things I shall thee tell;
See that my words in mind thou bear
　　And to my precepts listen well.

I am thy sovereign Lord and God,   5
　　Which have thee brought from careful thrall
And eke reclaimed from Pharaoh's rod.
　　Make thee no gods on them to call,

Nor fashioned form of any thing
　　In heaven or earth to worship it.   10
For I thy God by revenging
　　With grievous plagues this sin will smite.

[William Whittingham]

XLVII

O LORD, in Thee is all my trust,
　　Give ear unto my woeful cry;
Refuse me not that am unjust,
　　But, bowing down Thy heavenly eye,

Behold how I do still lament   5
　　My sins wherein I do offend.
O Lord, for them shall I be shent
　　Sith Thee to please I do intend.

No, no, not so, Thy will is bent
　　To deal with sinners in Thine ire;   10
But when in heart they shall repent,
　　Thou grant'st with speed their just desire.

[John Marckant]

XLVIII

O LORD, turn not away Thy face
  From him that lieth prostrate,
Lamenting sore his sinful life
  Before Thy mercy's gate.
Which gate Thou openest wide to those   5
  That do lament their sin.
Shut not that gate against me, Lord,
  But let me enter in.

And call me not to mine accounts,
  How I have lived here,   10
For then I know right well, O Lord,
  How vile I shall appear.
I need not to confess my life,
  I am sure Thou canst tell,
What I have been, and what I am,   15
  I know Thou knowest it well.

                      [*John Marckant*]

XLIX

A DIEU seul soit honneur et gloire.

L

CELEBRONS sans cesse de Dieu ces bontés.

LI

SANCT' escriture te propose,
  Si tu veux acompler la loy,
D'amer ton Dieu sour toute chose,
  Et ton prochain autant que toy.

LII

DONEZ à boire; allé[z] bon companion. Alleluia.

LIII

As I me walked
In a May morning
I heard a bird sing
Cuckoo.

She nodded up and down,   5
And swore all by her crown
She had friends in the town.
    Cuckoo.

All you that married be
Learn this song of me,   10
So shall we not agree:
    Cuckoo.

All young men in this throng
To marry that think it long,
Come learn of me this song: 15
    Cuckoo.

LIV

THE white hen she cackles
    And lays in the puddles;
Sing hey, cock without a comb,
    Cock-a-dle luddle.

LV

THE wind blows out of the west, thou gentle mariner-a;
    Look to the luff well, beware the lee still,
For deadly rocks do now appear-a.
        Look to thy tack!
        Let bowling go slack!   5
So shall we 'scape them and go clear.
        Tarra tan tarra!
        Steer well thy course, sirra!
The wind waxeth large, the sheets do thou veer,
    Go fill the can, give us some beer;   10
            I'll drink thee,
            I'll brinks thee,
        My mates, what cheer!

LVI

JACK, boy, ho boy, news!
    The cat is in the well;
Let us ring now for her knell,
    Ding, dong, ding, dong, bell.

LVII

Blow thy horn, thou jolly hunter,
   Thy hounds for to revive-a;
Show thyself a good huntsman
   Whilst that thou art alive-a,
That men may say and sing with thee,   5
   Thou hast a merry life-a;
In pleasure all the day,
   And Venus mate to wife-a.

LVIII

Banbury Ale! where, where, where?
At the blacksmith's house, I would I were there!

LIX

A miller, a miller would I be,
To learn his craft as well as he.
By art to steal, by cunning to lie,
To get a poling penny thereby.

LX

Birch and green holly, birch and green holly,
If thou beest beaten, boy, thank thine own folly.

LXI

The lark, linnet and nightingale
   To sing, some say, are best;
Yet merrily sings little robin,
   Pretty robin with the red breast.

LXII

   Troll the bowl to me,
And I will troll the same again to thee.
Begin now! Hold in now, for we must merry be.
      As you see,
      Be lusty   5
      So must we.

O it is a brave thing
For to pass away the Spring,
With mirth and joy to sing,
    Tan tan tan tara!   10
All aflant brave boys!
What joy is this to see,
When friends so well agree.

LXIII

NOW, Robin, lend to me thy bow,
Sweet Robin, lend to me thy bow,
For I must now a-hunting with my lady go,
    With my sweet lady go.

And whither will thy lady go?   5
Sweet Wilkin, tell it unto me,
And thou shalt have my hawk, my hound, and eke my bow,
    To wait on thy lady.

My lady will to Uppingham,
To Uppingham forsooth will she,   10
And I myself appointed for to be the man
    To wait on my lady.

Adieu, good Wilkin all beshrewed,
Thy hunting nothing pleaseth me,
But yet beware thy babbling hounds stray not abroad   15
    For ang'ring of thy lady.

My hounds shall be led in the line,
So well I can assure it thee,
Unless by view of strain some pursue I may find,
    To please my sweet lady.   20

With that, the lady she came in,
And willed them all for to agree;
For honest hunting never was accounted sin,
    Nor never shall for me.

LXIV

FAREWELL, mine own sweet heart,
    Farewell, whom I love best;
Since I must from my love depart,
    Adieu, my joy and rest.

LXV

FA, mi, fa, re, la, mi,
Begin, my son, and follow me;
   Sing flat, fa mi,
So shall we well agree.
   Hey tro loly lo.   5
   Hold fast, good son,
With hey tro lily lo.
O sing this once again, lustily.

LXVI

MUSING mine own self all alone,
I heard a maid making great moan,
With sobs and sighs, and many a grievous groan,
For that her maidenhead was gone.

LXVII

O PORTSMOUTH it is a gallant town,
And there we will have a quart of wine with a nutmeg brown.
   Diddle down.
The gallant ship the Mermaid, the Lion hanging stout,
Did make us to spend there our sixteen pence all out.   5

LXVIII

COME, drink to me, and I will drink to thee,
And then shall we full well agree.
I have loved the jolly tankard full seven winters and more;
I loved it so long till that I went upon the score.
He that loves not the tankard is no honest man,   5
And he is no right soldier that loves not the can.
   Tap the canakin,
   Toss the canakin,
   Troll the canakin,
   Turn the canakin.   10
Hold, good son, and fill us a fresh can,
That we may quaff it round about from man to man.

LXIX

LET's have a peal for John Cook's soul,
   For he was an honest man;
   With bells all in an order,
   The cruse with the black bowl,

The tankard likewise with the can,   5
And I mine own self will ring the treble bell,
    And drink to you everyone.
        Stand fast now, my mates,
        Ring merrily and well
    Till all this good ale is gone.   10

LXX

SING we this roundelay merrily, my mate,
Ill may he thrive that doth us hate;
Sing we this roundelay merrily, each one,
Take care who will, for I'll take none.

LXXI

    UT, re, mi, fa, mi, re, ut.
        Hey derry derry,
        Sing and be merry,
            Quando veni,
            Quando coeli,   5
    Whip little David's bum.

LXXII

        LADY, come down and see,
        The cat sits in the plumtree.

LXXIII

LOVE, sweet love, for evermore farewell to thee,
For fortune hath deceived me.
Fortune my foe, most contrary,
Hath wrought me this misery.
But yet, my love, farewell to thee.   5

LXXIV

A Round of Three Country Dances in One

Bass or Ground. SING after, fellows, as you hear me,
        A toy that seldom is seen-a.
    Three country dances in one to be,
        A pretty conceit as I ween-a.

Cantus.   Now foot it as I do, Tom boy, Tom,   5
              Now foot it as I do, Swithen-a;
              And Hick, thou must trick it all alone,
              Till Robin come leaping in between-a.

Medius.   The cramp is in my purse full sore,
              No money will bide therein-a;   10
              And if I had some salve therefore,
              O lightly then would I sing-a,
              Hey ho, the cramp-a!

Tenor.   Robin Hood, said Little John,
              Come dance before the Queen-a,   15
              In a red petticoat, and a green jacket,
              A white hose and a green-a.

                              LXXV

              COME, follow me merrily, my mates,
              Let's all agree and make no faults;
              Take heed of time, tune and ear,
              And then, without all doubt,
              We need not fear   5
              To sing this catch throughout.

                 Malkin was a country maid,
                 Trick and trim as she might be;
                 She would need to the court, she said,
                 To sell milk and firmenty.   10
                    Hey ho!

              Have with you now to Westminster,
              But before you come there,
              Because the way is far,
              Some pretty talk let's hear.   15

                 Adieu, you dainty dames,
                 Go whither you will for me,
                 You are the very same
                 I took you for to be.

LXXVI

WHITE wine and sugar is good drink for me,
  For so said Parson Brat;
  But Gough said 'nay' to that,
  For he loved Malmesey.

LXXVII

LIBERA me Domine a persequentibus me: quia comfortati sunt super me.

LXXVIII

UNIVERSA transeunt.

LXXIX

VIAS tuas Domine demonstra mihi: et semitas tuas edoce me.

LXXX

FIDES est animae vita sicut anima est vita corporis.

LXXXI

SI non pavisti occidisti.

LXXXII

VERBUM Domini manet in aeternum.

LXXXIII

SING you now after me,
  And as I sing, sing ye;
  So shall we well agree,
  Five parts in unity.
    Ding, dong, bell.   5

LXXXIV

JINKIN the jester was wont to make glee
With Jarvis the juggler till angry was he;
Then Wilkin the wiseman did wisely foreseee
That juggler and jester should gently agree.
  Hey down derry down.   5

LXXXV

HEY ho! nobody at home;
Meat, nor drink, nor money have I none.
Fill the pot, Eadie!

LXXXVI

UT, re, mi, fa, sol, la,
La, sol, fa, mi, re, ut.
Hey down a down a dising.
You three, after me, and follow me, my lads,
And we will merry be. Fa la la!   5
  Well sung before! Hold fast betime!
  Take heed you miss not nor break the time;
  For if thou miss the bass a note
  There's ne'er a man can sing a jot.

LXXXVII

LET Lobcock leave his wife at home
With lusty Jinkin, that clownish groom.
With tig-hee, with two alone,
With ta-ha, farewell, my kind mome.
Yet must we look kindly when Lobcock comes home.   5

LXXXVIII

UT, re, mi, fa, sol, la,
La, sol, fa, mi, re, ut.
Hey down! Sing you now after me,
La, mi, sol, re, fa,
So shall we well agree.   5
Take heed to your time, and rest as you find,
The round and the square must be tuned in their kind.
  O well sung, my lads, I say,
  We are as good by night as by day.
    La, mi, sol, re, fa,   10
    Let us be merry
  Here so long time as you may,
  For time truly passeth away.
    Hey ho!

LXXXIX

KEEP well your ray, my lads,
    And show yourselves like men;
This day our foes shall feel
    Our forces once again.
Now let the trumpets sound their deadly blast,   5
Tantara tan! Stand to it, first and last!
With tantara ra! See, hey, they fly full fast!

XC

HOW should I sing well, and not be weary,
Since we lack money to make us merry.

XCI

JOY in the gates of Jerusalem; peace be in Sion.

XCII

LAUDATE nomen Domini, laudate servi Dominum qui statis in
domo Domini.

XCIII

DOMINE Fili Dei vivi miserere nostri, qui tollis peccata mundi.

XCIV

BENEDIC, Domine, nobis his donis tuis quae de tua largitate sumus
sumpturi.

XCV

NOW thanked be the great god Pan,
    Which thus preserves my loved life,
And thanked be I that keep a man
    Who ended hath this bloody strife.
For if my man must praises have,   5
What then must I, that keep the knave?
                                        [*Sir Philip Sidney*]

XCVI

LAUDATE nomen Domini super omnes gentes.

XCVII

LET'S have a peal for John Cook's soul,
For he was a very honest man.

XCVIII

DELICTA quis intelligit? Ab occultis meis munda me.

XCIX

HEY ho, what shall I say?
Sir John hath carried my wife away.
 They were gone ere I wist,
 She will come when she list.
  Hey trolly lolly,   5
  Come again, ho!

C

SING we now merrily,
Our purses be empty.
 Hey ho!
Let them take care
That list to spare,   5
For I will not do so.
Who can sing so merry a note
As he that cannot change a groat?
 Hey ho! trolly lolly lo!

*Deuteromelia: Or The Second part of Musicks melodie, or melodius Musicke.
Of Pleasant Roundelaies; K. H. mirth, or Freemens Songs. And such delightfull Catches. 1609*

I

As it fell on a holy day,
 And upon a holy tide-a,
John Dory bought him an ambling nag,
 To Paris for to ride-a.

And when John Dory to Paris was come,   5
 A little before the gate-a,
John Dory was fitted, the porter was witted
 To let him in thereat-a.

The first man that John Dory did meet
 Was good King John of France-a;   10
John Dory could well of his courtesy,
 But fell down in a trance-a.

A pardon, a pardon my liege and my king,
 For my merry men and for me-a,
And all the churls in merry England   15
 I'll bring them all bound to thee-a.

And Nichol was then a Cornishman,
 A little beside Bohide-a,
And he mand forth a good black barque
 With fifty good oars on a side-a.   20

Run up, my boy, unto the main top,
 And look what thou canst spy-a;
Who ho! who ho! a goodly ship I do see,
 I trow it be John Dory.

They hoist their sails both top and top, 25
 The mizzen and all was tried-a,
And every man stood to his lot,
 Whatever should betide-a.

The roaring cannons then were plied,
 And dub-a-dub went the drum-a;   30
The braying trumpets loud they cried
 To courage both all and some-a.

The grappling hooks were brought at length,
 The brown bill and the sword-a;
John Dory at length, for all his strength, 35
 Was clapped fast under board-a.

II

THE fly she sat in Shamble Row,
 And shambled with her heels, I trow,
And then came in Sir Cranion,
 With legs so long and many a one,

And said: Jove speed, Dame Fly, Dame Fly; 5
 Marry, you be welcome, good Sir, quoth she.
The Master Humble Bee hath sent me to thee
 To wit and if you will his true love be.

But she said: nay, that may not be,
   For I must have the butterfly,   10
For and a greater lord there may not be.
   But at the last consent did she.

And there was bid to this wedding
   All flies in the field and worms creeping;
The snail she came crawling all over the plain,   15
   With all her jolly trinkets at her train.

Ten bees there came all clad in gold,
   And all the rest did them behold;
But the thonbud refused this sight to see,
   And to a cow-plat away flies she.   20

But where now shall this wedding be?
   For and hey nonino in an old Ive tree.
And where now shall we bake our bread?
   For and hey nonino in an old horse head.

And where now shall we brew our ale?   25
   But even within one walnut shale.
And also where shall we our dinner make?
   But even upon a galde horse back.

For there we shall have good company,
   With humbling and bumbling and much melody.   30
When ended was this wedding day
   The bee he took his fly away,

And laid her down upon the marsh,
   Between one marigold and one long grass,
And there they begot good Master Gnat,   35
   And made him the heir of all, that's flat!

III

   WE be soldiers three,
      Pardonnez-moi je vous en prie,
   Lately come forth of the Low Country
      With never a penny of money.
   Fa la la la lantido dilly.   5

Here, good fellow, I drink to thee,
    Pardonnez-moi je vous en prie,
To all good fellows wherever they be,
    With never a penny of money.
Fa la la la lantido dilly.   10

And he that will not pledge me this,
    Pardonnez-moi je vous en prie,
Pays for the shot, whatever it is,
    With never a penny of money.
Fa la la la lantido dilly.   15

Charge it again, boy, charge it again,
    Pardonnez-moi je vous en prie,
As long as there is any ink in thy pen,
    With never a penny of money.
Fa la la la lantido dilly.   20

IV

BY merry Landsdale, hey ho,
There dwelt a jolly miller,
And a very good old man was he, was he, hey ho.

He had, he had and a son-a,
Men called him Reynold,   5
And mickle of his might was he, was he, hey ho.

And from his father a wode-a,
His fortune for to seek-a;
From merry Landsdale wode he, wode he, hey ho.

His father would him seek-a,   10
And found him fast asleep;
Among the leaves green was he, was he, hey ho.

He took, he took him up-a,
All by the lily-white hand,
And set him on his feet, and bade him stand, hey ho.   15

He gave to him a benbow
Made all of a trusty tree,
And arrows in his hand, and bade him let them flee.

And shoot was that that a did-a,
Some say he shot a mile,   20
But half a mile and more was it, was it, hey ho.

And at the half-mile's end
There stood an armed man,
This child he shot him through, and through, and through,
  hey ho.

His beard was all on a white-a,   25
As white as whale is bone,
His eyes they were as clear as crystal stone, hey ho.

And there of him they made
Good yeoman Robin Hood,
Scarlet, and Little John, and Little John, hey ho.   30

V

[The words are the same as those of No. iv]

VI

WE be three poor mariners,
  Newly come from the seas.
We spend our lives in jeopardy
  Whiles others live at ease.

Shall we go dance the round, the round?   5
  And shall we go dance the round?
And he that is a bully boy
  Come pledge me on the ground.

We care not for those martial men
  That do our states disdain;   10
But we care for those merchantmen
  Which do our states maintain.

To them we dance this round, a round,
  To them we dance this round.
And he that is a bully boy   15
  Come pledge me on the ground.

VII

OF all the birds that ever I see
The owl is the fairest in her degree,
For all the day long she sits in a tree,
And when the night comes away flies she.
  Te whit, te whoo.   5
  To whom drinks thou?
  Sir knave, to you!

This song is well sung I make you a vow,
And he is a knave that drinketh now.
   Nose, nose, nose, nose!
And who gave { thee that / me this } jolly red nose?
Cinnamon and ginger, nutmegs and cloves,
And that gave { thee thy / me my } jolly red nose!

VIII

   LORD, hear the poor that cry,
The which do live in pain and misery.
   Son of God, show some pity.

IX

BROWNING madam! browning madam!
So merrily we sing 'browning madam'.
   The fairest flower in garden green
   Is in my love's breast full comely seen,
And with all others compare she can,   5
Therefore now let us sing 'browning madam'.

X

   HOLD thy peace!
And I prithee, hold thy peace, thou knave, thou knave!
   Hold thy peace, thou knave!

XI

   GLAD am I, glad am I
   My mother is gone to Henley.
     Shut the door and spare not,
     Do thy worst, I care not;
   If I die upon the same   5
     Bury me a God's name.

XII

MARGERY, serve well the black sow
All in a misty morning.
Come to thy dinner, sow, come, come, come,
Or else thou shalt have never a crumb.

XIII

THREE blind mice, three blind mice,
  Dame Julian, Dame Julian,
The miller and his merry old wife,
She scraped her tripe, lick thou the knife.

XIV

THE great bells of Osney they ring, they jing;
The tenor of them goeth merrily.

XV

MALT's come down! malt's come down!
From an old angel to a French crown.
There's never a maid in all this town
But well she knows that malt's come down.
The greatest drunkards in this town   5
Are very glad that malt's come down.

XVI

MARTIN said to his man
  Fie man, fie!
O Martin said to his man
  Who's the fool now?
Martin said to his man   5
Fill thou the cup and I the can,
Thou hast well drunken, man,
  Who's the fool now?

I see a sheep shearing corn.
  Fie man, fie!   10
I see a sheep shearing corn.
  Who's the fool now?
I see a sheep shearing corn,
And a cuckold blow his horn.
Thou hast well drunken, man,   15
  Who's the fool now?

I see a man in the moon.
  Fie man, fie!
I see a man in the moon.
  Who's the fool now?   20

I see a man in the moon
Clouting of Saint Peter's shoon.
Thou hast well drunken, man,
   Who's the fool now?

I see a hare chase a hound.   25
   Fie man, fie!
I see a hare chase a hound.
   Who's the fool now?
I see a hare chase a hound
Twenty mile above the ground.   30
Thou hast well drunken, man,
   Who's the fool now?

I see a goose ring a hog.
   Fie man, fie!
I see a goose ring a hog.   35
   Who's the fool now?
I see a goose ring a hog,
And a snail that did bite a dog.
Thou hast well drunken, man,
   Who's the fool now?   40

I see a mouse catch the cat.
   Fie man, fie!
I see a mouse catch the cat.
   Who's the fool now?
I see a mouse catch the cat   45
And the cheese to eat the rat.
Thou hast well drunken, man,
   Who's the fool now?

XVII

Chorus.   GIVE us once a drink for and the black bowl,
      Sing gentle butler, balla moy.

Give us once a drink for and the pint pot,
      Sing gentle butler, balla moy;
        The pint pot,   5
Chorus.   For and the black bowl,
      Sing gentle butler, balla moy.

Give us once a drink for and the quart pot,
   Sing gentle butler, balla moy;
   The quart pot, the pint pot,   10
Chorus.   For and the black bowl,
   Sing gentle butler, balla moy.

Give us once a drink for and the pottle pot,
   Sing gentle butler, balla moy;
   The pottle pot, the quart pot, the pint pot,   15
Chorus.   For and the black bowl,
   Sing gentle butler, balla moy.

Give us once a drink for and the gallon pot,
   Sing gentle butler, balla moy;
The gallon pot, the pottle pot, the quart pot, the pint pot, 20
Chorus.   For and the black bowl,
   Sing gentle butler, balla moy.

Give us once a drink for and the firkin,
   Sing gentle butler, balla moy;
   The firkin, the gallon pot, the pottle pot, the quart pot, the
      pint pot,   25
Chorus.   For and the black bowl,
   Sing gentle butler, balla moy.

[In subsequent stanzas add: kilderkin, barrel, hogshead, pipe, butt,
tun.]

XVIII

Who liveth so merry in all this land
As doth the poor widow that selleth sand?
Chorus.   And ever she singeth, as I can guess,
    Will you buy any sand, any sand, mistress?

The broom-man maketh his living most sweet   5
With carrying of brooms from street to street.
Chorus.   Who would desire a pleasanter thing
    Than all the day long to do nothing but sing?

The chimney sweeper all the day long
He singeth and sweepeth the soot away.   10
Chorus.   Yet when he comes home, although he be weary,
    With his sweet wife he maketh full merry.

The cobbler he sits cobbling till noon,
And cobbleth his shoes till they be done.
Chorus.   Yet doth he not fear, and so doth say,   15
For he knows his work will soon decay.

The merchantman doth sail on the seas,
And lie on the ship-board with little ease.
Chorus.   Always in doubt the rock is near,
How can he be merry and make good cheer?   20

The husbandman all day goeth to plough,
And when he comes home he serveth his sow.
Chorus.   He moileth and toileth all the long year,
How can he be merry and make good cheer?

The serving man waiteth from street to street,   25
With blowing his nails and beating his feet,
Chorus.   And serveth for forty shillings a year,
That 'tis impossible to make good cheer.

Who liveth so merry and maketh such sport
As those that be of thy poorest sort?   30
Chorus.   The poorest sort wheresoever they be,
They gather together by one, two and three.

And every man will spend his penny,
What makes such a shot among a great many.
Chorus.   And every man will spend his penny,   35
What makes such a shot among a great many.

XIX

By a bank as I lay,
Musing on a thing that was past and gone, hey ho,
In the merry month of May,
O somewhat before the day,
Methought I heard at the last   5

O the gentle nightingale,
The lady and mistress of all music, hey ho.
She sits down ever in the dale
Singing with her notes small,
Quavering them wonderful thick.   10

O for joy my spirits were quick
To hear the sweet bird how merrily she could sing, hey ho,
  And said: Good Lord, defend
  England with Thy most holy hand,
  And save noble James our King.   15

XX

  TOMORROW the fox will come to town,
    Keep, keep, keep, keep, keep!
  Tomorrow the fox will come to town,
    O keep you all well there.
      I must desire you neighbours all   5
      To halloo the fox out of the hall,
      And cry as loud as you can call:
      Whoop! whoop! whoop! whoop! whoop!
      And cry as loud as you can call,
      O keep you all well there.   10

He'll steal the cock out from his flock,
  Keep, keep, keep, keep, keep!
He'll steal the cock even from his flock,
  O keep you all well there.
    I must desire *etc.*   15

He'll steal the hen out of the pen,
  Keep, keep, keep, keep, keep!
He'll steal the hen out of the pen,
  O keep you all well there.
    I must desire *etc.*   20

He'll steal the duck out of the brook,
  Keep, keep, keep, keep, keep!
He'll steal the duck out of the brook,
  O keep we all well there.
    I must desire *etc.*   25

He'll steal the lamb even from his dam,
  Keep, keep, keep, keep, keep!
He'll steal the lamb even from his dam,
  O keep we all well there.
    I must desire *etc.*   30

XXI

WILLY, prithee go to bed,
For thou wilt have a drowsy head.
Tomorrow we must a-hunting,
And betimes be stirring.
Chorus.   With a hey troliloli.   5

It is like to be fair weather,
Couple up all thy hounds together.
Couple Jolly with little Jolly,
Couple Trole with old Trolly.
Chorus.   With a hey troliloli.   10

Couple Finch with black Trole,
Couple Chaunter with Jumbole.
Let Beauty go at liberty,
For she doth know her duty.
Chorus.   With a hey troliloli.   15

Let Merry go loose, it makes no matter,
For Cleanly sometimes she will clatter,
And yet I am sure she will not stray,
But keep with us still, all the day.
Chorus.   With a hey troliloli.   20

With, O masters, and wot you where,
This other day I start a hare,
On what-call hill, upon the knoll,
And there she started before troll.
Chorus.   With a hey troliloli.   25

And down she went the common dale
With all the hounds at her tail.
With yeaffe a yaffe! yeaffe a yaffe!
Hey Trole! hey Chaunter! hey Jumbole!
Chorus.   With a hey troliloli.   30

See how Chooper chops it in,
And so doth Gallant now begin.
Look how Trole begins to tattle,
Tarry awhile, ye shall hear him prattle.
Chorus.   With a hey troliloli.   35

For Beauty begins to wag her tail,
Of Cleanly's help we shall not fail;
And Chaunter opens very well,
But Merry she doth bear the bell.
Chorus.   With a hey trololi.   40

Go prick the path and down the lane,
She useth still her old train.
She is gone to what-call wood,
Where we are like to do no good.
Chorus.   With a hey trololi.   45

XXII

YONDER comes a courteous knight,
    Lustily raking over the lay;
He was well 'ware of a bonny lass
    As she came wand'ring over the way.
Chorus.   Then she sang down a down, hey down derry.   5

Jove you speed, fair lady, he said,
    Among the leaves that be so green;
If I were a king and wore a crown
    Full soon, fair lady, shouldst thou be a queen.
Chorus.   Then she sang down a down, hey down derry.   10

Also Jove save you, fair lady,
    Among the roses that be so red;
If I have not my will of you,
    Full soon, fair lady, shall I be dead.
Chorus.   Then she sang down a down, hey down derry.   15

Then he looked east then he looked west,
    He looked north, so did he south;
He could not find a privy place,
    For all lay in the Devil's mouth.
Chorus.   Then she sang down a down, hey down derry.   20

If you will carry me, gentle sir,
    A maid unto my father's hall,
Then you shall have your will of me
    Under purple and under pall.
Chorus.   Then she sang down a down, hey down derry.   25

He set her up upon a steed,
　　And himself upon another,
And all the day he rode her by
　　As though they had been sister and brother.
Chorus. Then she sang down a down, hey down derry.   30

When she came to her father's hall,
　　It was well walled round about,
She yode in at the wicket gate
　　And shut the four-eared fool without.
Chorus. Then she sang down a down, hey down derry.   35

You had me, quoth she, abroad in the field,
　　Among the corn, amidst the hay,
Where you might had your will of me,
　　For, in good faith sir, I never said nay.
Chorus. Then she sang down a down, hey down derry.   40

Ye had me also amid the field,
　　Among the rushes that were so brown,
Where you might had your will of me,
　　But you had not the face to lay me down.
Chorus. Then she sang down a down, hey down derry.   45

He pulled out his nut-brown sword,
　　And wiped the rust off with his sleeve,
And said: Jove's curse come to his heart,
　　That any woman would believe.
Chorus. Then she sang down a down, hey down derry.   50

When you have your own true love
　　A mile or twain out of the town,
Spare not for her gay clothing,
　　But lay her body flat on the ground.
Chorus. Then she sang down a down, hey down derry.   55

XXIII

Ut, re, mi, fa, sol, la,
La, sol, fa, mi, re, ut.
Hey down down down!

　Farewell, my heart of gold,
　　Farewell, my pigsny,
　Farewell the flower of all the world,   5
　　The like may no man see.

Hey down down down!
  Her lips they were as soft as any silk,
    Her breath as sweet as spice;   10
  Her legs, her thighs, as white as milk,
    She is a bird of price.

Hey down down down!
  Adieu, farewell, my pretty Nell,
  Thou bearest the bell. But you do well   15
  If you not tell where I do dwell.
    And so farewell!

XXIV

My love, lov'st thou me?
Then quickly come and save him that dies for thee.

XXV

Go to Joan Glover,
And tell her I love her,
And at the mid of the moon I will come to her.

XXVI

The maid she went a-milking,
All in a misty morning.
Down fell her milking pail,
Up went her diddle diddle tail.

XXVII

I C U B A K,
  And evermore will be;
  Though John Cook he saith nay,
    O what a knave is he!

XXVIII

Sing with thy mouth, sing with thy heart,
Like faithful friends sing 'loth to depart'.
Though friends together may not always remain,
  Yet 'loth to depart' sing once again.

XXIX

By hills and dales she rode,
   And followed still the game;
She rode so fast that down she fell
   And then appeared her shame.

      Hey down!   5
  In a May morning betimes
I heard an old swad say to a young drab:
   This gear is thine and mine.
Thorough the woods this trull full swiftly springs,
   With a merry note chanting,   10
   Where a knave was haunting,
   And so lost her apern-strings.

     Hey down down derry!
It is a light heart and a heavy purse which makes a man so merry.

XXX

The pigeon is never woe
Till absenting she go.
With heave and ho,
So let the wind blow.

XXXI

   Hey down down a down!
Sing you three, after me, and follow me, my lads,
And we will merry be. Fa la la!
  Well sung before! hold fast betime!
  Take heed you miss not nor break the time;   5
  For if thou miss the bass a note
  There's ne'er a man can sing a jot.

Melismata. Mvsicall Phansies. Fitting The Covrt, Citie, and Covntrey
Hvmovrs. To 3, 4, and 5. Voyces. 1611

COURT VARIETIES

I

The Courtier's Goodmorrow to his Mistress

CANST thou love and lie alone?
    Love is so disgraced.
Pleasure is best wherein is rest
    In a heart embraced.

Chorus.   Rise, rise, rise,   5
        Daylight do not burn out.
        Bells do ring
        And birds do sing,
        Only I that mourn out.

Morning star doth now appear,   10
    Wind is hushed, and skies clear.
Come, come away, come, come away,
    Canst thou love and burn out day?

Chorus.   Rise, rise, rise,
        Daylight do not burn out.   15
        Bells do ring,
        Birds do sing,
        Only I that mourn out.

II

The Crowning of Belphoebe

Chorus.   NOW flowers your odours breathe,
        And all the air perfume;
    Grow in this honoured wreath,
        And with no storms consume.

Verse.   Hail, hail and welcome her,   5
        Thou glory of our green,
    Receive this flowery sphere,
        And be the shepherds' queen.
    O kneel and do her homage now,
    O now, that calls our hearts like fate;   10
    Now rise, your humble bosoms bow,
    O bow, and lead her to her state.

Chorus.   [Now flowers *etc.*]

III

Mercury's Song: the Messengers of the Gods

HASTE, haste, post haste, make haste and away,
The tide tarrieth no man, it makes no delay.
Trudge, trudge for thy life, for virtue must fly;
These journeys are rife with thee, with the poor Mercury.

IV

The Courtier's Courtship to his Mistress

Courtier. WILL ye love me, lady sweet?
Mistress. Fie away, fie away, fie, fie, fie!
Courtier. You are young and love is meet.
Mistress. No, no, not I! I'll live a maid till I be forty.
Courtier. Out alas, out alas! who then will sport thee?   5
      Wanton, yet in the spring love is a pretty thing.
Mistress. Fie away, fie away, fie, fie, fie!
Courtier. Kiss, sweet, as lovers do; prove kind to them that woo.
Mistress. No, no, no, not I!

V

A Song of Pages, Cashiered from their Masters

LONG have we bin perplexed and vexed
    With a life that I loathed.
Now may we sing hey ding a ding a ding,
    And leave to lament any longer.
Glad to the heart to depart,   5
    That I must bid adieu to my master.
Thanks to the heavens will I give while I live
    For joy that I leave him.
Gone may he be, ne'er more that we see,
    Nor again to come at us.   10
Troll we the bowls! let's in, pretty souls,
    To carouse with the wenches!

VI

Servants out of Service are going to the City to look for New

Chorus.   HEY ho! away the mare!
             Let us set aside all care.

If any man be disposed to try,
Lo, here comes a lusty crew
That are enforced to cry   5
'A new master' anew.

    Hey now!
We neither mind to beg nor starve,
We'll take small pains and yet will thrive,
We will have more than we deserve,   10
We'll cut their throats that are alive.

Chorus.   [Hey ho! away the mare! *etc.*]

CITY ROUNDS

VII

BROOMS for old shoes, pouch-rings, boots and buskings!
Will ye buy any new broom? New oysters, new oysters new!
New cockles, cockles nigh, fresh herrings!
Will ye buy any straw? Ha'y'any kitchen stuff, maids?
Pippins fine, cherry ripe, ripe, ripe! Ha'y'any wood to cleave?   5
    Give ear to the clock,
    Beware your lock,
    Your fire and your light,
    And God give you goodnight.
    One o'clock!   10

VIII

I PRAY you, good mother, give me leave to play with little John,
To make his bed and comb his head, and come again anon.
Or else beat me as you think good, for I love John alone.

IX

    MY mistress will not be content
    To take a jest as Chaucer meant,
    But following still the woman's fashion
    Allows it for the new translation.
    For with the word she would not dispense,   5
    And yet I know she loves the sense.

X

    I LAY with an old man all the night
      I turned to him and he to me.
    He could not do so well as he might,
      But he would fain, but it would not be.

CITY CONCEITS

XI

The Painter's Song of London

WHERE are you, fair maids,
    That have need of our trades?
I'll sell you a rare confection.
    Will ye have your faces spread
Either with white or red?   5
    Will ye buy any fair complexion?

My drugs are no dregs,
    For I have whites of eggs
Made in a rare confection.
    Red leather and surflet water,   10
Scarlet colour or stavesacre;
    Will ye buy any fair complexion?

XII

The Scrivener's Servant's Song of Holborn

MY master is so wise, so wise, that he's proceeded wittall.
My mistress is a fool, a fool, and yet 'tis the most get-all.
    Let the usurer cram him
    In interest that excel,
    Their pit's enough to damn him   5
    Before he goes to hell.
    In Holborn some, in Fleet Street some,
    Where e'er he come there's some, there's some.

XIII

A Bellman's Song

MAIDS to bed and cover coal,
Let the mouse out of her hole;
Crickets in the chimney sing
Whilst the little bell doth ring.
If fast asleep, who then can tell   5
When the clapper hits the bell?

XIV

The Crier's Song of Cheapside

OYEZ! Oyez! Oyez!
If anyone at fifteen hath taken up and found
A pretty thing that hath her maidenhead unbound;
  If any gallant have with catertray
  Played the wiseacre, and made all away;   5
    Let him come to the crier.
  There will be laid a thousand pound to ten
  That none of these will e'er be had again.
    Oyez! Oyez!
  If note or line or word be here let fall   10
  That gives to any man the taste of gall,
    Let him come to the crier.
  I will lay my lips to a fat shroving hen
  That none of these will be had again.
For this I say, and likewise I protest,   15
No arrow's hereat shot at any breast,
But all are welcome to my music feast.

COUNTRY ROUNDS

XV

HE that will an alehouse keep must have three things in store:
A chamber and a feather bed, a chimney and a hey nonino.

XVI

  AND seest thou my cow today, Fowler?
    The bells ring into matins:
  Bim bome, bim bome-a-bome bome.

XVII

    KIT and Tom chid-a,
    Tom and Kit chid;
    Kit chid Tom,
    Tom chid Kit,
    Kit and Tom chid-a.   5

XVIII

  DERRY ding ding ding dasson,
    I am John Cheston.
  We weeddon we wodden,
    Bim bom bim bom.

XIX

As I went by the way, holum trolum,
There met I by the way, hazom gazom,
And I had my little companion.
I would a catch'd, hazom gazom,
And hung him upon holum trolum.   5

XX

THERE were three ravens sat on a tree,
   Down a down hey down;
There were three ravens sat on a tree,
   With a down;
There were three ravens sat on a tree,   5
They were as black as they might be,
   With a down derry down.

The one of them said to his mate,
   Down a down hey down;
The one of them said to his mate,   10
   With a down;
The one of them said to his mate:
Where shall we our breakfast take?
   With a down derry down.

Down in yonder green field,   15
   Down a down hey down;
Down in yonder green field,
   With a down;
Down in yonder green field
There lies a knight slain under his shield,   20
   With a down derry down.

His hounds they lie down at his feet,
   Down a down hey down;
His hounds they lie down at his feet,
   With a down;   25
His hounds they lie down at his feet,
So well they can their master keep,
   With a down derry down.

His hawks they fly so eagerly,
   Down a down hey down;   30
His hawks they fly so eagerly,
   With a down;

His hawks they fly so eagerly
There's no fowl dare him come nigh,
   With a down derry down.   35

Down there comes a fallow doe,
   Down a down hey down;
Down there comes a fallow doe,
   With a down;
Down there comes a fallow doe   40
As great with young as she might go,
   With a down derry down.

She lift up his bloody head,
   Down a down hey down;
She lift up his bloody head,   45
   With a down;
She lift up his bloody head
And kissed his wounds that were so red,
   With a down derry down.

She got him up upon her back,   50
   Down a down hey down;
She got him up upon her back,
   With a down;
She got him up upon her back
And carried him to earthen lake,   55
   With a down derry down.

She buried him before the prime,
   Down a down hey down;
She buried him before the prime,
   With a down;   60
She buried him before the prime,
She was dead herself ere evensong time,
   With a down derry down.

God send every gentleman,
   Down a down hey down;   65
God send every gentleman,
   With a down;
God send every gentleman
Such hawks, such hounds and such a leman,
   With a down derry down.   70

XXI

The Marriage of the Frog and the Mouse

IT was the frog in the well,
    Humble dum humble dum,
And the merry mouse in the mill,
    Tweedle tweedle twino.

The frog would a-wooing ride,   5
    Humble dum humble dum,
Sword and buckler by his side,
    Tweedle tweedle twino.

When he was upon his high horse set,
    Humble dum humble dum,   10
His boots they shone as black as jet,
    Tweedle tweedle twino.

When he came to the merry mill pin,
    Humble dum humble dum,
Lady mouse, been you within?   15
    Tweedle tweedle twino.

Then came out the dusty mouse,
    Humble dum humble dum,
I am lady of this house,
    Tweedle tweedle twino.   20

Hast thou any mind of me?
    Humble dum humble dum.
I have e'en great mind of thee,
    Tweedle tweedle twino.

Who shall this marriage make?   25
    Humble dum humble dum.
Our lord which is the rat,
    Tweedle tweedle twino.

What shall we have to our supper?
    Humble dum humble dum.   30
Three beans in a pound of butter,
    Tweedle tweedle twino.

When supper they were at,
    Humble dum humble dum,
The frog, the mouse and even the rat,   35
    Tweedle tweedle twino.

Then came in Gib our cat,
   Humble dum humble dum,
And catched the mouse even by the back,
   Tweedle tweedle twino.   40

Then did they separate,
   Humble dum humble dum,
And the frog leapt on the floor so flat,
   Tweedle tweedle twino.

Then came in Dick our drake,   45
   Humble dum humble dum,
And drew the frog even to the lake,
   Tweedle tweedle twino.

The rat run up the wall,
   Humble dum humble dum.   50
A goodly company, the devil go with all!
   Tweedle tweedle twino.

XXII

A Wooing Song of a Yeoman of Kent's Son

I HAVE house and land in Kent,
And if you'll love me, love me now.
Twopence halfpenny is my rent,
I cannot come every day to woo.
Chorus.   Twopence halfpenny is his rent,   5
       He cannot come every day to woo.

Ich am my vather's eldest zon,
My mother eke doth love me well,
For ich can bravely clout my shoon
And ich full well can ring a bell.   10
Chorus.   For he can bravely clout his shoon
       And he full well can ring a bell.

My vather he gave me a hog,
My mother she gave me a zow,
I have a Godvather dwells thereby   15
And he on me bestowed a plough.
Chorus.   He has a Godvather dwells thereby
       And he on him bestowed a plough.

Once time I gave thee a paper of pins,
Anoder time a tawdry lace,   20
And if thou wilt not grant me love
In truth ich die bevore thy vace.
Chorus.   And if thou wilt not grant him love
In truth he'll die bevore thy vace.

Ich have been twice our Whitson Lord,   25
Ich have had ladies many rare,
And eke thou hast my heart in hold
And in my mind zeems passing rare.
Chorus.   And eke thou hast his heart in hold
And in his mind seems passing rare.   30

Ich will put on my best white slop,
And ich will wear my yellow hose,
And on my head a good grey hat,
And in't ich stick a lovely rose.
Chorus.   And on his head a good grey hat,   35
And in't he'll stick a lovely rose.

Wherefore cease off, make no delay,
And if you'll love me, love me now,
Or else ich zeek zome oder where,
For I cannot come every day to woo.   40
Chorus.   Or else he'll zeek zome oder where,
For he cannot come every day to woo.

XXIII

A Christmas Carol

REMEMBER, O thou man,
O thou man, O thou man,
Remember, O thou man,
Thy time is spent.
Remember, O thou man,   5
How thou art dead and gone,
And I did what I can:
Therefore repent.

Remember Adam's fall
O thou man, O thou man,   10
Remember Adam's fall
From heaven to hell.

Remember Adam's fall,
How we were condemned all
In hell perpetual   15
   Therefore to dwell.

Remember God's goodness
   O thou man, O thou man,
Remember God's goodness
   And his promise made.   20
Remember God's goodness,
How He sent His Son doubtless
Our sins for to redress.
   Be not afraid.

The angels all did sing,   25
   O thou man, O thou man,
The angels all did sing
   Upon the shepherds' hill.
The angels all did sing
Praises to our heavenly King,   30
And peace to man living,
   With a goodwill.

The shepherds amazed was,
   O thou man, O thou man,
The shepherds amazed was   35
   To hear the angels sing.
The shepherds amazed was
How it should come to pass
That Christ our Messias
   Should be our King.   40

To Bethlem did they go,
   O thou man, O thou man,
To Bethlem did they go,
   The shepherds three.
To Bethlem did they go   45
To see where it were so or no,
Whether Christ were born or no
   To set man free.

As the angels before did say,
   O thou man, O thou man,   50
As the angels before did say,
   So it came to pass.

As the angels before did say
They found a babe whereas it lay
In a manger, wrapped in hay,   55
    So poor He was.

In Bethlem He was born,
    O thou man, O thou man,
In Bethlem He was born
    For mankind's sake.   60
In Bethlem He was born
For us that were forlorn,
And therefore took no scorn
    Our flesh to take.

Give thanks to God alway,   65
    O thou man, O thou man,
Give thanks to God alway
    With heart most joyfully.
Give thanks to God alway
For this our happy day.   70
Let all men sing and say:
    Holy, holy.

ᴃᴐᴃᴐᴃᴐᴃᴐᴃᴐ

A Briefe Discovrse Of the true (but neglected) vse of Charact'ring the Degrees, by their Perfection, Imperfection, and Diminution in Measurable Musicke, against the Common Practise and Custome of these Times. Examples whereof are exprest in the Harmony of 4. Voyces, Concerning the Pleasure of 5. vsuall Recreations. 1. Hunting, 2. Hawking, 3. Daucing, 4. Drinking, 5. Enamouring. 1614

HUNTING AND HAWKING

I

A Hunt's Up.—John Bennet

Chorus.   THE hunt is up, the hunt is up!
                   Sing merrily we, the hunt is up!

                       The birds they sing;
                       The deer they fling;
                           Hey nonny, nonny no!   5

The hounds they cry;
The hunters they fly.
 Hey trolilo, trololilo!
The hunt is up, etc.

 The woods resounds   10
 To hear the hounds,
  Hey nonny nonny no!
 The rocks report
 This merry sport,
  Hey trolilo, trololilo!   15
The hunt is up, etc.

 Then hie apace
 Unto the chase.
  Hey nonny nonny no!
 Whilst everything   20
 Doth sweetly sing
  Hey trolilo, trololilo!

The hunt is up, the hunt is up!
Sing merrily we, the hunt is up!

II

The Hunting of the Hare.—Edward Peirs

HEY trola, trola!
There boys, there!
Hoicka, hoick, whoop!
Cry there they go.
They are at fault.   5
Boy, wind the horn!
Sing tive tive tive now in full cry
With yeeble yabble, gibble gabble, hey!
The hounds do knock it lustily
With open mouth and lusty cry.   10

III

A Hawk's Up, for a Hunt's Up.—Thomas Ravenscroft

AWAKE, awake,
The day doth break.
 Our spaniels couple them.

Our hawks shall fly
Low, mean or high,   5
  And truss it if you can.
Chorus.   Hey troly loly lo!
  And truss it if you can.

Then rise, arise,
For Phoebus dyes   10
  In gold the dawn of day,
And coveys lie
In fields hard by.
  Then sing we care away:
Chorus.   Hey troly loly lo!   15
  Then sing we care away!

IV

Hawking for the Partridge.—Thomas Ravenscroft

SITH sickles and the shearing scythe
  Hath shorn the fields of late,
Now shall our hawks and we be blithe.
  Dame Partridge ware your pate!
    Our murdering kites   5
    In all their flights
    Will seld or never miss
To truss you ever and make your bale our bliss.

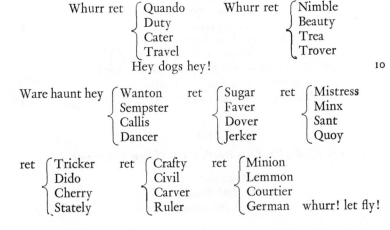

Whurr ret { Quando / Duty / Cater / Travel }   Whurr ret { Nimble / Beauty / Trea / Trover }

Hey dogs hey!   10

Ware haunt hey { Wanton / Sempster / Callis / Dancer } ret { Sugar / Faver / Dover / Jerker } ret { Mistress / Minx / Sant / Quoy }

ret { Tricker / Dido / Cherry / Stately } ret { Crafty / Civil / Carver / Ruler } ret { Minion / Lemmon / Courtier / German } whurr! let fly!

O well flown, eager kite, mark!
We falconers thus make sullen kites
    Yield pleasure fit for kings,   15
And sport with them in those delights,
    And oft in other things.

V

For the Hern and Duck.—*John Bennet*

LURE, Falconers, lure! give warning to the field!
Let fly! let fly! make mounting herns to yield.
Die, fearful ducks, and climb no more so high;
The nyas-hawk will kiss the azure sky.
But when our soar-hawks fly and stiff winds blow,   5
Then long too late we Falconers cry hey lo!

DANCING

VI

The Fairies' Dance.—*Thomas Ravenscroft*

DARE you haunt our hallowed green?
None but fairies here are seen.
    Down and sleep!
    Wake and weep!
    Pinch him black   5
    And pinch him blue
That seeks to steal a lover true.
When you come to hear us sing
Or to tread our fairy ring,
    Pinch him black   10
    And pinch him blue!
O thus our nails shall handle you!

VII

The Satyrs' Dance.—*Thomas Ravenscroft*

ROUND, around a, keep your ring,
To the glorious sun we sing.
    Ho, ho!

He that wears the flaming rays
And the imperial crown of bays,
Him with shouts and songs we praise,
　　Ho, ho!
That in his bounty would vouchsafe to grace
The humble sylvans and their shaggy race.

VIII

The Urchins' Dance.—Thomas Ravenscroft

By the moon we sport and play,
With the night begins our day.
As we frisk the dew doth fall.
Trip it, little urchins all,
Lightly as the little bee,
Two by two, and three by three,
And about, about go we.

IX

The Elves' Dance.—John Bennet

Round about, round about
　　In a fair ring-a,
Thus we dance, thus we dance
　　And thus we sing-a,
Trip and go, to and fro
　　Over this green-a,
All about, in and out
　　Over this green-a.

DRINKING

X

Of Beer.—Thomas Ravenscroft

Chorus. Trudge away quickly, and fill the black bowl
　　Devoutly as long as we bide.
Now welcome, good fellows, both strangers and all,
　　Let madness and mirth set sadness aside.

Of all reckonings I love good cheer
　　With honest folks in company;
And when drink comes my part for to bear,
　　For still methinks one tooth is dry.
　　　　Trudge away quickly, etc.

Love is a pastime for a king, 10
   If one be seen in phisnomie.
But I love well this pot to wring,
   For still methinks one tooth is dry.
      Trudge away quickly, etc.

Masters, this is all my desire, 15
   I would no drink should pass us by.
Let us now sing and mend the fire,
   For still methinks one tooth is dry.
      Trudge away quickly, etc.

Master Butler, give us a taste 20
   Of your best drink so gently;
A jug or twain to make no waste,
   For still methinks one tooth is dry.
      Trudge away quickly, etc.

Master Butler, of this take part, 25
   Ye love good drink as well as I;
And drink to me with all your heart,
   For still methinks one tooth is dry.
      Trudge away quickly, etc.

XI

Of Ale.—Thomas Ravenscroft

Chorus. Toss the pot, toss the pot, let us be merry,
   And drink till our cheeks be as red as a cherry.
     We take no thought, we have no care,
     For still we spend and never spare
     Till of all money our purse is bare, 5
       We ever toss the pot.
         Toss the pot, etc.

We drink, carouse with heart most free,
A hearty draught I drink to thee,
Then fill the pot again to me, 10
     And ever toss the pot.
       Toss the pot, etc.

And when our money is all spent,
Then sell our goods and spend our rent,
Or drink it up with one consent, 15
     And ever toss the pot.
       Toss the pot, etc.

When all is gone, we have no more,
Then let us set it on the score,
Or chalk it up behind the door,   20
    And ever toss the pot.
       Toss the pot, etc.

And when our credit is all lost,
Then may we go and kiss the post,
And eat brown bread instead of roast,   25
    And ever toss the pot.
       Toss the pot, etc.

Let us conclude as we began,
And toss the pot from man to man,
And drink as much now as we can,   30
    And ever toss the pot.

Toss the pot, toss the pot, let us be merry,
And drink till our cheeks be as red as a cherry!

XII

Ale and Tobacco.—Thomas Ravenscroft

    TOBACCO fumes
    Away all nasty rheums;
But health away it never lightly frets.
    And nappy ale makes mirth,
    As April rain doth earth,   5
Spring like the pleasant Spring where'er it soaking wets.

Chorus.   But in that spring of mirth
      Such madness high doth grow
    As fills a fool by birth
      With crotchets, with ale and tobacco.   10

    One clears the brain,
      The other glads the heart,
    Which they retain
      By nature and by art.
    The first by nature cleareth;   15
      By art makes giddy will.
    The last by nature cheereth,
      By art makes heady still.

Chorus.   So we whose brains else low
          Swell high with crotchet rules,   20
      Feed on these two as fat
      As heady giddy fools.

ENAMOURING

XIII

Three Fools.—John Bennet

W H A T seek'st thou, fool, what seek'st thou in this place?
      A woman's stubborn will?
What seek'st thou, fool, what seek'st thou in this place?
      The bable of a fool?
What seek'st thou, fool, what seek'st thou in this place?   5
      Gay clothes and a purse of gold?
Fool! fool! fool! whom a woman sets to school!

XIV

The Servant of his Mistress.—John Bennet

M Y mistress is as fair as fine,
      Milk-white fingers, cherry nose.
Like twinkling day-stars looks her eyne,
      Lightening all things where she goes.
   Fair as Phoebe, though not so fickle,   5
   Smooth as glass, though not so brickle.

My heart is like a ball of snow
      Melting at her lukewarm sight;
Her fiery lips like night-worms glow,
      Shining clear as candle-light.   10
   Neat she is, no feather lighter;
   Bright she is, no daisy whiter.

XV

The Mistress of her Servant.—Edw: Peirs

L O V E for such a cherry lip
      Would be glad to pawn his arrows.
Venus here to take a sip
      Would sell her doves and team of sparrows.

But she shall not so,   5
Hey nonny, nonny, no!
None but I this lip must owe,
Hey nonny, nonny, no!

Did Jove see this wanton eye,
    Ganymede should wait no longer.   10
Phoebe here one night to lie
    Would change her face and look much younger.
        But she shall not so,
        Hey nonny, nonny, no!
        None but I this lip must owe,   15
        Hey nonny, nonny, no!

XVI

Their Marriage Solemnized.—Thomas Ravenscroft

Chorus. LEAVE off, Hymen, and let us borrow
        To bid the sun good morrow!

    See the sun cannot refrain
    But doth rise and give again
        That which you of Hymen borrow,   5
        And with smiling bid'st good morrow
    To the sun and to our brides.
    Good night to your sweet beauties,
    Sweet beauties touch your side.

Chorus.   Leave off, Hymen, and let us borrow   10
            To bid the sun good morrow.

XVII

Hodge Trillindle to his Zweet hort Malkyn.—Thomas Ravenscroft

COAME, Malkyn, hurle thine oyz at Hodge Trillindle,
And zet azide thy Distave and thy Zpindle.
A little tyny let a ma brast my minde
To thee which I have vownd as ghurst as ghinde.
Yet loave ma, Zweet, a little tyny vit,   5
And wee a little tyny Wedelocke wooll gommit.
    Y vaith wooll wee, that wee wooll y vaith lo!

XVIII

Malkinz anzwer to Hodge Trillindle.—*Thomas Ravenscroft*

Yo tell ma zo; but, Roger, I cha vound
Your words but wynde; thon not for vorty bound
Wooll I beeleave yo vurther thon Ich zee
Your words and deeds loyke beeans and bacoan gree.
But if yol loave ma long a little vit   5
Thon wedlocke Ich a little wool gommit.
     Y vayth wooll I, thot ich wooll, i vayth lo!

XIX

Their Goncluzion.—*Thomas Ravenscroft*

Roger.   ICH con but zweare, ond thot I chill,
         Unbonably to loave a tha ztill.
         Thot wool I lo!
Malkyn.   Thon, Roger, zweare
         Yo wooll be virmer thon yo weare.
         Zo, Roger, zweare an oape; hold Hodge,   5
         O hold, oie to wyd yo gape,
         O hold, thowlt byte I zweare my wozen.
Roger.   By thease ten Boans, by Jaby,
         Whay thou beleave ma whon ich zweare.
         Zo do thou.
Malkyn.   Ich do, good Hodge, thon zweare no more,   10
         Ich wooll bee thoyne and God a bee vore.
Chorus. Thon geat wee Growdes and Boagbipes, Harbes ond Dabors,
         To leead us on to eand ower loaves great labors.

XX

Their Wedlocke.—*John Bennet*

Chorus.   A BORGENS a borgen, cha hord long agoe.
         Be merry, be merry, ond a vig vor woe.

         Zing gleare, zing zweet and zure, ower zong zhall bee but
           zhort,
         Muzicke, foice and daunzing, O tis faliant zport!
             Then let this burden zweetly zung be ztill: 5
             A borgens a borgen, bee't good, be it ill.

Chorus.   A borgens a borgen, vor weale or vor woe,
         So ever led dis bleasing borden goe.

THOMAS TOMKINS

Songs Of 3. 4. 5. and 6. parts. 1622

I

OUR hasty life away doth post
Before we know what we have lost.
Hours into days, days into years are gone,
Years make a life, which straight is none.
Thus soon is Man's short story told,   5
We scarce are young, when we are waxed old.

II

NO more I will thy love importune,
    Or curse my fortune.
No more I will thy hate accuse,
    Or pity use.
Only thus much of love I will require: 5
Since I can never hope, I never may desire.

III

SURE, there is no god of Love,
    Cupid's but an idle name;
Only men his forces prove;
    Women never feel his flame.
Is he then of gods' descent   5
Whose power is not omnipotent?

IV

FOND men that do so highly prize
A woman's forehead, lips, and eyes,
And look not to the better part,
What virtues dwelleth in the heart;
Such kind of loving showeth plain,   5
You please the sense and not the brain.

V

How great delight from those sweet lips I taste,
  Whether I hear them speak or feel them kiss.
Only this want I have, that being graced
  With one of them, the other straight I miss.
Love, since thou canst do wonders, heap my blisses,   5
And grant her kissing words, or speaking kisses.

VI

  Love, cease tormenting,
  My lady is relenting.
How can it be so precious a jewel
Should harbour thoughts so pitiless and cruel?
  O no, that breast so dainty   5
Doth not enclose a heart of stone or flinty.

VII–VIII

  O let me live for true love! Fa la.
  Yet let me live no longer
Than that my life may make my love the stronger.
  O let me die for true love! Fa la.
Let not Hope or old Time come to end my woe.   5

IX

  Oyez! Oyez! Oyez!
    Has any found a lad
      With purple wings fair painted,
    In naked beauty clad
      With bow and arrows tainted?   5
Here, alas! here close he lieth;
Take him quick before he flieth.

X–XI

Weep no more, thou sorry boy,
Love's pleased and angered with a toy.
Love a thousand passions brings,
Laughs and weeps, and sighs and sings.
If she smiles, he dancing goes,   5
Not thinking on his future woes;
If she chide with angry eye,
Sits down and sighs, 'Ay me, I die'.

Yet again, as soon revived,
Joys as much as late he grieved.   10
Change there is of joy and sadness,
Sorrow much, but more of gladness.
Then weep no more, thou sorry boy,
Turn thy tears to weeping joy;
Sigh no more, 'Ay me, I die'.   15
But dance and sing, and 'ty hy' cry.

XII

W AS ever wretch tormented
   In midst of heaven retiring?
Was ever soul contented
   In midst of hellish firing?
Yet I with flames requited   5
Am in my hell delighted;
And in my heavens languish
With pining grief and anguish.

XIII

T O the shady woods now wend we,
And there the mid-day spend we. Fa la.
There Phoebus' self is colder,
And we may be the bolder. Fa la.

XIV

T OO much I once lamented,
   While Love my heart tormented. Fa la.
Alas, and Ay me, sat I wringing;
Now chanting go, and singing. Fa la.

XV

C OME, shepherds, sing with me.
Thrice happy might we be
If we should never see
Love and his misery. Fa la.
Love, now we hate thy lore,   5
More than we loved before.
From hence we all have swore
To love false love no more. Fa la.

XVI

CLORIS, whenas I woo,
Why still repliest thou No?
If as a maid you use it,
Say No, and ne'er refuse it.

XVII

SEE, see the shepherds' queen,
Fair Phyllis all in green, fa la,
The shepherds home her bringing
With piping and with singing. Fa la.
Then dance we on a row,   5
And chant it as we go. Fa la.

XVIII

PHYLLIS, now cease to move me,
For I shall never love thee. Fa la.
Content thee, I have swore
To love false love no more. Fa la.

XIX

WHEN David heard that Absalom was slain, he went up to his chamber
over the gate and wept; and thus he said: O my son Absalom, my son,
my son! Would God I had died for thee, O Absalom, my son, my son!
[2 *Samuel xviii.* 33]

XX

PHYLLIS, yet see him dying,
Who by thy oft denying
Love, life, and thee is flying,
His life too wretched hateful,
Phyllis and love ungrateful.   5
Yet when thine eyes have slain,
Thine eyes can raise again.

XXI

FUSCA, in thy starry eyes
Love, in black still mourning, dies, fa la,
That among so many slain,
Thou hast loved none again. Fa la.

XXII

ADIEU, ye city-prisoning towers;
Better are the country bowers.
Winter is gone, the trees are springing;
Birds on every hedge sit singing.
Hark, how they chirp, come, love, delay not,   5
Come, sweet love, O come and stay not.

XXIII

WHEN I observe those beauty's wonderments,
        Mine eyes, how do you burn!
But when those ears, so deaf at my laments,
        Mine eyes, how do you mourn!
Then for my torment, Love, this help devise,   5
Or open her deaf ears, or close mine eyes.

XXIV

MUSIC divine, proceeding from above,
Whose sacred subject oftentimes is love,
In this appears her heavenly harmony,
Where tuneful concords sweetly do agree.
And yet in this her slander is unjust,   5
To call that love which is indeed but lust.

XXV

OFT did I marle how in thine eyes
    Water and fire did dwell together,
Seeing 'tis known in contraries
    Each seeks the hurt and spoil of either;
But fire and water there may mell   5
Where love and hate together dwell.

XXVI

WOE is me that I am constrained to dwell with Mesech, and to
have my habitation among the tents of Kedar.   [*Psalm cxx.* 5]

XXVII

IT is my well-beloved's voice
    That soundeth in my ear.
My heart hereat doth much rejoice
    To see him draw so near.

See, see, on yonder mountain top,   5
  On yon same hill so tall,
How hitherward my Love doth hop,
  My heart doth skip withal.

           [*Canticles ii.* 8]

XXVIII

T URN unto the Lord our God.   [*Joel ii.* 13]
 For the Lord is gracious, his mercy is everlasting, and his truth
endureth from generation to generation.   [*Psalm c.* 5]

THOMAS VAUTOR

*The First Set: Beeing Songs of diuers Ayres and Natures, of Fiue and Sixe
parts: Apt for Vyols and Voyces. 1619*

I

CO ME forth, sweet nymph, and play thee;
Thy true love here doth stay thee;
Dallida make me sing, fa la.
Come, lull thee in mine arms,
I'll keep thee safe from harms. Fa la.   5

II

SING on, sister, and well met,
Lovely Mabel and fair Bet. Fa la.
Younglings must have a beginning;
Virtues they are hard of winning. Fa la.

But we will spare for no pains,   5
If we win contents or gains, fa la,
Which if we attain unto
We shall do that few can do. Fa la.

III

A H sweet, whose beauty passeth all my telling,
To thee my love all others are excelling. Fa la.
By thee I live and have mine only pleasure,
Thou art my life and eke my whole heart's treasure. Fa la.
Let not unkindness then eclipse my gladness,   5
But let sweet smiles expel the clouds of sadness. Fa la.
For if my love sweet looks and liking reapeth,
O happy I, my heart for joy it leapeth. Fa la.

IV

MOTHER, I will have a husband,
And I will have him out of hand.
    Mother, I will sure have one,
    In spite of her that will have none.

John a Dun should have had me long ere this,   5
He said I had good lips to kiss.
    Mother, I will sure have one,
    In spite of her that will have none.

For I have heard 'tis trim when folks do love,
By good Sir John I swear now I will prove.   10
    For, mother, I will sure have one,
    In spite of her that will have none.

To the town therefore will I gad,
To get me a husband good or bad.
    Mother, I will have a husband,   15
    And I will have him out of hand.
    Mother, I will sure have one,
    In spite of her that will have none.

V

FAIR'ST are the words that cover deep'st deceit,
    As next sweet honey lie the poisoned stings.
The crooked hook is hid in pleasant'st bait,
    Which unforeseen too late repentance brings.
Sinon's sweet speech, the outside of untruth,   5
Thick laid with art, procured the Trojan's ruth.

VI

CRUEL madam, my heart you have bereft me,
And to myself no part have you left me,
For yours all wholly Love hath fast infeoffed me.
    Wherefore thus plain I must for ever.

My woeful heart both night and day bewaileth;   5
My death draws on, and my poor life it faileth;
I sue for mercy where no tears availeth.
    Wherefore thus plain I must for ever.

Yet if your eyes did see how you torment me,
Alas, poor man, it would the more content thee,   10
But now in absence, ah, do I lament me.
   Wherefore thus plain I must for ever.

VII

NEVER did any more delight to see his enemy,
Than I, more fool, finding no remedy.
It was because I loved her in my heart,
Although, alas, she loved to make it smart.
What shall I say then but bid her adieu,   5
Because unkind to him that is most true.

VIII–IX

LOCK up, fair lids, the treasures of my heart;
   Preserve those beams, this age's only light.
To her sweet sense, sweet sleep, some ease impart,
   Her sense too weak to bear the spirit's might.
   And while, O sleep, thou closest up her sight,   5
Where Love doth forge his fairest dart,
   O harbour all her parts in easeful plight,
Let no strange dream make her fair body start.
And yet, O dream, if thou wilt not depart
   From this rare subject of thy common right,   10
   But wilt thyself in such a seat delight,
Then take my shape and play a lover's part;
   Kiss her from me, and say unto her sprite,
   Till her eyes shine I live in darkest night.
                         [*Sir Philip Sidney*]

X

O MERRY world, when every lover with his mate
Might walk from mead to mead and cheerfully relate
Sour pleasures and sweet griefs, following a wanton state.
Those days knew no suspect, each one might freely prate,
And dance and sing and play with his consociate.   5
   Then lovers used like turtles to kiss full lovingly,
     O honey days and customs of antiquity.
   But the world now is so full of so fond jealousy,
     That we count charity wanton iniquity.

XI

SWEET thief, when me of heart you reft,
You did a murther and a theft.
And could you ought more cruel do
Than rob a man and kill him too?
Wherefore of Love I crave this meed—   5
To bring you where you did the deed,
That there you may for him disgracing,
Suffer in chains in my embracing.

XII

SWEET Suffolk owl, so trimly dight
With feathers like a lady bright,
Thou sing'st alone, sitting by night,
    Te whit, te whoo, te whit, te whoo.
Thy note, that forth so freely rolls,   5
With shrill command the mouse controls,
And sings a dirge for dying souls,
    Te whit, te whoo, te whit, te whoo.

XIII–XIV

THOU art not fair for all thy red and white,
  For all those rosy ornaments in thee.
Thou art not sweet though made of mere delight,
  Nor fair nor sweet unless thou pity me.
I will not sooth thy fancies. Thou shalt prove   5
That beauty is no beauty without love.

Yet love not me, nor seek not to allure
  My thoughts with beauty, were it more divine.
Thy smiles and kisses I cannot endure,
  I'll not be wrapped up in those arms of thine.   10
Now show it, if thou be a woman right,
Embrace, and kiss, and love me in despite.
                    [*Thomas Campian*]

XV

MIRA cano: sol occubuit, nox nulla secuta est.

XVI

*An elegy on the death of his right worshipful master, Sir Thomas Beaumont,
Knight, of Stoughton in Leicestershire*

WEEP, weep, mine eyes; salt tears, due honour give;
  With sighs deplore my grief and mourning state,

Since he is dead by whom I still do live;
　　Beaumont is dead, O cursed, cruel fate.
Beaumont, farewell! the earth doth sweetly sleep　　　5
To hold thy corpse, though heaven thy soul doth keep.

XVII

BLUSH, my rude present, blushing yet say this,
　　That he that sent thee meant a better thing.
Best meaners oft of their best purpose miss,
　　Best runners sometime fail to hit the ring.
Tell my sweet mistress, saint of womankind,　　　5
What wants in show, he doth supply in mind.

XVIII

DAINTY sweet bird, who art encaged there,
Alas, how like thine and my fortunes are.
Both prisoners, both sing, and both singing thus
Strive to please her, who hath imprisoned us.
Only in this we differ, thou and I,　　　5
Thou liv'st singing, but I singing die.

XIX

UNKIND, is this the meed of lover's pain?
Doth loyal faith no better guerdon gain?
Adieu, thy looks are coy, thy fancy strange.
O stay, my heart relents and will not change,
But rather die than from my saint once swerve.　　　5
My life she gave, my love she doth deserve.

XX–XXI

MELPOMENE, bewail thy sisters' loss,
　　In tragic dumps their dolours deep display.
Curse cruel death, that so their bliss did cross,
　　And music's peerless patron took away.
Though they do sleep, yet thou alone mayest sing:　　　5
Prince Henry's dead, farewell the Muses' king.

Whilst fatal sisters held the bloody knife,
　　A peerless prince on earth he did remain.
Too soon sad death ensued his blissful life,
　　And now he with the King of kings doth reign.　　　10
No earthly music doth he more desire,
Such joy he hath to hear the heavenly choir.

XXII

SHEPHERDS and nymphs, that trooping
 Were wont to fetch home May with hey and whooping,
  Why sit you dead and drooping?
 Up, up, for shame, and leave this heavy mourning,
  For Orian is not dead, but lives renowned   5
Beyond all human honour, base earth scorning.
 Orian now a saint in heaven is crowned.
   Both bonfires and bell-ringers
   She left us, and good singers.
 Sing then, ye shepherds and nymphs of Diana: 10
  Farewell, fair Oriana.

JOHN WARD

*The First Set of English Madrigals To 3. 4. 5. and 6. parts apt both for Viols
and Voyces. With a Mourning Song in memory of Prince Henry. 1613*

I–II

MY true love hath my heart, and I have his,
 By just exchange one for the other given.
I hold his dear, and mine he cannot miss;
 There never was a better bargain driven.
His heart in me keeps me and him in one,   5
 My heart in him his thoughts and senses guides;
He loves my heart, for once it was his own;
 I cherish his because in me it bides.
His heart his wound received from my sight,
 My heart was wounded with his wounded heart;   10
For as from me on him his heart did light,
 So still methought in me his heart did smart.
Both equal hurt, in this change sought our bliss,
My true love hath my heart, and I have his.
         [Sir Philip Sidney]

III

O SAY, dear life, when shall these twin-born berries,
 So lovely ripe, by my rude lips be tasted?
Shall I not pluck (sweet, say not nay,) those cherries?
 O let them not with Summer's heat be blasted.

Nature, thou know'st, bestowed them free on thee,   5
Then be thou kind, bestow them free on me.

IV

In health and ease am I;
Yet, as I senseless were, it nought contents me.
     You sick in pain do lie;
And, ah, your pain exceedingly torments me.
     Whereof I can this only reason give,   5
     That, dead unto myself, in you I live.

[*Francis Davison*]

V

     Go, wailing accents, go
     To the author of my woe.
Say, dear, why hide you so from him your blessed eyes,
Where he beholds his earthly Paradise,
     Since he hides not from you   5
His heart, wherein love's heaven you may view?

[*Francis Davison*]

VI

Fly not so fast, my only joy and jewel;
Pity at last my tears, O be not cruel.
Ay me, alas, ay me, she's gone and left me;
Die, die, my heart, all joy is now bereft me.

VII

A satyr once did run away for dread
     At sound of horn which he himself did blow;
Fearing and feared, thus from himself he fled,
     Deeming strange evil in that he did not know.

[*Sir Philip Sidney*]

VIII

O my thoughts, my thoughts, surcease;
Thy delights my woes increase;
My life melts with too much thinking,
     Think no more, but die in me,
     Till thou shalt revived be,   5
At her lips my nectar drinking.

[*Sir Philip Sidney*]

IX

SWEET pity, wake, and tell my cruel sweet
  That if my death her honour might increase,
I would lay down my life at her proud feet,
  And willing die and, dying, hold my peace;
And only live and, living, mercy cry,   5
Because her glory in my death will die.
                               [*Francis Davison*]

X

    LOVE is a dainty, mild and sweet.
A gentle power, a feeling fine and tender.
    So that those harms and pains unmeet
Which I do pass, thou only dost engender.
Only to him his torments Love deviseth   5
That scorns his laws, his rites, and Love despiseth.
                           [*Bartholomew Yong*]

XI

    FREE from love's bonds I lived long.
But now to love I change my song
With discords sweet in every strain,
And of my joy and pleasing pain.
But, out alas, my wounded heart   5
Can neither rest nor end my smart.

XII

HOW long shall I with mournful music stain
  The cheerful notes these pleasant valleys yields,
Where all good haps a perfect state maintain.
  O cursed hap! and cursed be these fields
Where first mine eyes were causers of my pain!   5
                             [*Sir Philip Sidney*]

XIII–XIV

SWEET Philomel, cease thou thy songs awhile,
  And will thy mates their melodies to leave.
And all at once attend my mournful style,
  Which will of mirth your sugared notes bereave.
If you desire the burthen of my song,   5
I sigh and sob, for Phyllis I did wrong.

Ye sylvan nymphs, that in these woods do shroud,
  To you my mournful sorrows I declare.
You savage satyrs, let your ears be bowed,
  To hear my woe your sacred selves prepare.   10
Trees, herbs and flowers, in rural fields that grow,
While thus I mourn, do you some silence show.

XV

FLORA, fair nymph, whilst silly lambs are feeding,
    Grant my request in speeding.
For your sweet love my silly heart doth languish,
And die I shall, except you quench the anguish.

XVI

PHYLLIS the bright, when frankly she desired
Thyrsis, her sweet heart, to have expired;
    Sweet, thus fell she a-crying,
    Die, for I am a-dying.

XVII

    HOPE of my heart,
O wherefore do the words,
Which your sweet tongue affords,
    No hope impart?
But, cruel without measure,   5
    To my eternal pain
    Still thunder forth disdain
On him whose life depends upon your pleasure.
                   [*Francis Davison*]

XVIII

UPON a bank with roses set about,
  Where pretty turtles, joining bill to bill,
And gentle springs steal softly murmuring out,
  Washing the foot of pleasure's sacred hill
    There little Love sore wounded lies,   5
    His bow and arrows broken,
    Bedewed with tears from Venus' eyes;
    O grievous to be spoken!
                   [*Michael Drayton*]

XIX

RETIRE, my troubled soul; rest and behold
Thy days of dolour, dangers manifold.
See Life is but a dream, whose best contenting,
Begun with hope, pursued with doubt, enjoyed with fear, ends in
repenting.

XX

OFT have I tendered tributary tears,
Mixed with grief and melancholy fears;
And sometime frolic Hope, sad woes beguiling,
Hath shined on my desires. O but from smiling
Of late she changed, my sorrow not resenting,   5
Bade me despair, sigh, groan, and die lamenting.

XXI

OUT from the vale of deep despair
With mournful tunes I fill the air,
To satisfy my restless ghost,
Which Daphne's cruelty hath lost.
O'er hills and dales in her dull ears   5
I'll send my notes with bitter tears.

XXII

O DIVINE Love, which so aloft can raise
    And lift the mind out of this earthly mire,
And doth inspire us with so glorious praise
    As with the heavens doth equal man's desire;
Who doth not help to deck thy holy shrine   5
    With Venus' myrtle and Apollo's tree?
Who will not say that thou art most divine,
    At least confess a deity in thee?
                                        [*Michael Drayton*]

XXIII–XXIV

IF the deep sighs of an afflicted breast
    O'erwhelmed with sorrow, or the rected eyes
Of a poor wretch with miseries oppressed,
    For whose complaints tears never could suffice,

Have not the power your deities to move,   5
Who shall e'er look for succour from above?
From whom too long I tarried for relief,
Now ask but death, that only ends my grief.

There's not a grove that wonders not my woe,
   Nor not a river weeps not at my tale,   10
I hear the echoes wandering to and fro
   Resound my grief through every hill and dale.
The birds and beasts, yet in their simple kind,
Lament for me; no pity else I find.
And tears I find do bring no other good,   15
But as new showers increase the rising flood.

                        [*Michael Drayton*]

XXV

   DIE not, fond man, before thy day.
      Love's cold December
      Will surrender
   To succeeding jocund May.
   And then, O then, sorrow shall cease;   5
      Comforts abounding
      Cares confounding
   Shall conclude a happy peace.

XXVI

I HAVE entreated, and I have complained,
  I have dispraised, and praise I likewise gave.
  All means to win her grace I tried have,
And still I love, and still I am disdained.
O could my sighs once purchase me relief,   5
Or in her heart my tears imprint my grief!
But cease vain sighs! cease, cease, ye fruitless tears!
Tears cannot pierce her heart, nor sighs her ears.

                        [*Walter Davison*]

XXVII

COME, sable night, put on thy mourning stole,
And help Amyntas sadly to condole.
Behold, the sun hath shut his golden eye,
The day is spent, and shades fair lights supply.

All things in sweet repose   5
Their labours close;
Only Amyntas wastes his hours in wailing,
Whilst all his hopes do faint, and life is failing.

XXVIII

In memory of Prince Henry
WEEP forth your tears, and do lament. He's dead
  Who living was of all the world beloved.
Let dolorous lamenting still be spread
    Through all the earth, that all hearts may be moved
      To sigh and plain,   5
  Since death hath slain Prince Henery.
O, had he lived, our hopes had still increased;
But he is dead, and all our joys deceased.

THOMAS WATSON

The first sett, Of Italian Madrigalls Englished, Not to the sense of the originall dittie, but after the affection of the Noate. By Thomas Watson Gentleman. There are also heere inserted two excellent Madrigalls of Master William Byrds, composed after the Italian vaine, at the request of the sayd Thomas Watson. 1590

I. *Luca Marenzio*

WHEN first my heedless eyes beheld with pleasure,
Both of nature and beauty all the treasure
In Astrophel, whose worth exceeds all measure,
My fawning heart, with hot desire surprised,
Willed me entreat I might not be despised.   5
But gentle Astrophel, with looks unfeigned,
Before I spake, my prayer entertained,
And smiling said: unless Stella dissembleth,
Her look so passionate my love resembleth.

II. *Luca Marenzio*

O MERRY world, when every lover with his mate
Might walk from mead to mead, and cheerfully relate

Sour pleasures and sweet griefs, following a wanton state;
Those days knew no suspect, each one might freely prate,
And dance, or sing, or play with his consociate.   5
Then lovers used like turtles to kiss full lovingly;
O honey days, and customs of antiquity.
But the world now is full of so fond jealousy,
That we term charity wanton iniquity.

III. *Luca Marenzio*

FAREWELL, cruel and unkind,
    Alone will I wail me,
    Till breath fail me,
And till my life-thread be untwined.
Then my poor ghost, still weeping,   5
    Shall thus disturb thee sleeping:
O Amaryllis, O Amaryllis,
Why art thou prouder than sweet Phyllis?
    In whose fair face are placed
Two heavenly stars, wherewith heaven is disgraced.   10

IV. *Luca Marenzio*

ZEPHYRUS breathing, now calls nymphs from out their bowers,
To play and wanton, in robes of sundry flowers.
Progne chirpeth, and sweet Philomel recordeth,
And Flora, seeing what the spring affordeth,
Smileth so sweetly, that heaven, itself enflamed,   5
Greatly rejoiceth to but hear her named.
The welkin, water and earth, all are full of pleasure,
All creatures joy in love, as nature's treasure.

V. *Luca Marenzio*

FAIR shepherds' queen, let us hand in hand enchained,
Dance up and down the green like friends unfeigned,
And merrily recount our happy days,
While my tender flock climbs up the mount, and there stays.
And shepherds all, come and follow me, praising Amaryllis;   5
All but Amyntas, whose only joy is Phyllis.

VI. *Luca Marenzio*

EVERY singing bird, that in the wood rejoices,
Come and assist me with your charming voices;
Zephyrus, come too, and make the leaves and the fountains
Gently to send a whispering sound unto the mountains;

And from thence pleasant Echo, sweetly replying,   5
Stay here playing, where my Phyllis now is lying;
And lovely Graces, with wanton satyrs come and play,
Dancing and singing, a hornpipe or a roundelay.

VII. *Luca Marenzio*

ALAS, what a wretched life is this! Nay, what a death,
    Where the tyrant Love commandeth.
My flowering days are in their prime declining,
All my proud hope quite fall'n, and life untwining;
    My joys each after other   5
In haste are flying, and leave my heart dying
    For her that scorns my crying.
O she from hence departs, my love refraining,
From whom, all heartless, alas, I die complaining.

VIII. *Byrd*

THIS sweet and merry month of May,
    While Nature wantons in her prime,
    And birds do sing, and beasts do play,
    For pleasure of the joyful time,
    I choose the first for holiday   5
    And greet Eliza with a rhyme.
    O beauteous queen of second Troy,
    Take well in worth a simple toy.

IX. *Luca Marenzio*

THOUGH faint and wasted with overlong desiring
    Of my beloved but cruel foe,
    Whose delights are in my woe,
Yet fancy frameth no retiring, but dies admiring.
O Love, O help at last, let her feel thy dart,   5
    That so unkindly kills my heart.

X. *Luca Marenzio*

SINCE my heedless eyes began to be ranging,
I, thrice accursed, always have been changing.
First was I made a hart, and deadly wounded
By Phyllis, in whom yet all my hope was grounded;
Then to a dying swan my alt'ring state was turned,   5
For though I sung, yet my fainting heart still mourned;
And now to a salamander changed, with flames surrounded,
O what a life is this, to live still wounded.

XI. *Girolamo Conversi*

WHEN all alone my bonny love was playing,
And I saw Phoebus stand at a gaze staying,
Alas, I feared there would be some betraying.

XII. *Luca Marenzio*

WHEN I beheld the fair face of Phyllis sleeping
  I showed my joy by weeping,
And kissing oft her cheeks with roses stained,
  To myself I thus complained:
Now feed yourselves, my feeble eyes, with gazing,   5
While her eyes with a cloud of sleep are kept from blazing;
And thou, my heart, whom she hath fired,
  Despair not of thy desired.
  As now mine eyes are pleased,
So, haply when she wakes, thou shalt be eased.   10

XIII. *Luca Marenzio*

ALAS, where is my love, where is my sweeting,
That hath stol'n away my heart? God send us meeting,
That, rueing my lament, with friendly greeting
She may release my smart, and all my weeping.
  But if my sight she fly,   5
  Till heartless I die,
My grieved ghost, with shrieks and dreadful crying,
  Always about her flying,
  Shall murmur out complaining,
To be revenged of all her deep disdaining.   10

XIV–XV. *Luca Marenzio*

SWEET heart, arise, that we may take our pleasure,
With pretty pastimes, lovers' only treasure,
Dancing among fair nymphs and lovely Graces,
Where a chaste kiss is mixed with sweet embraces.
O to the woods wend we without delaying,   5
Where sweetly singing birds on boughs are playing,
And beasts in wanton order, from every mountain,
Each after other come to wait on Flora's train.

But if the country gods seek to surround thee,
Fly then, my sweet Phyllis, trust not their smiling; 10
False wanton satyrs do use much beguiling.
Alas, if they but catch thee the sight will wound me,
And my poor heart, though now it live in pleasure,
Will die with only fear, to leese his treasure.

XVI. *Luca Marenzio*

WHEN from myself sweet Cupid first bereft me,
   In Phyllis' hands he left me,
   Where, in a sun of gladness
   That sees no clouds of sadness,
Mine eye beholds the beams of beauty's treasure, 5
   Adoring Love, for god of pleasure.

XVII. *Luca Marenzio*

SWEET singing Amaryllis
   My listening ear encharmed;
And my heedless eye it was deadly harmed,
When I there beheld the wanton looks of Phyllis.
Alas, wherefore have not heavenly Fates provided, 5
   By whom all things are guided,
That either Phyllis' face were not so brightsome,
Or Amaryllis' singing were less delightsome.

XVIII. *Luca Marenzio*

FANCY, retire thee!
   Alas, my heart will fire thee,
   And bonny love, now friendless,
Depart away, that life may remain,
   Released of pain. 5
   Alas, thy hopes are endless,
   Yielding much grief, but no gain.
And thou that wert my jewel,
   But always cruel,
   Yet because I loved thee,
When love and fancy moved me, 10
   O Amaryllis, farewell.

XIX. *Luca Marenzio*

How long with vain complaining,
How long with dreary tears, and joys refraining,
  Shall we renew his dying,
  Whose happy soul is flying,
  Not in a place of sadness,   5
  But of eternal gladness.
Sweet Sidney lives in heaven, therefore let our weeping
Be turned to hymns and songs of pleasant greeting.

XX. *Giovanni Maria Nanino*

All ye that joy in wailing,
Come, seat yourselves a-row, and weep beside me,
  That while my life is failing,
The world may see in love what ill betide me;
  And after death do this in my behove,   5
  Tell Cressid Troilus is dead for love.

XXI. *Luca Marenzio*

O hear me, heavenly powers, all at one calling,
While you see my chiefest pleasure down falling;
Stay Phyllis now departing, and inspire her,
That only my desert and love may fire her.
And thou, for whom, alas, I feel so deep smart,   5
Unless thou wish my death, come again, sweet heart.

XXII. *Luca Marenzio*

In chains of hope and fear, singing and crying,
I climb and fall, I live, but ever dying.
O tyrant Love, O come at once and slay me,
That, flying hence down, where Charon's boat doth stay me,
From cruel Amaryllis to convey me,   5
Whose proud aspiring heart doth but delay me,
I may dance in Elysium, there resounding
With joy the pains of love, and the deep wounding.

XXIII–XXIV. *Luca Marenzio*

When Meliboeus' soul, flying hence, departed,
Astrophel, whom not long before death darted,
Rising up fro the star with him late graced,
Down along the heavens he swiftly traced,

Where, meeting with his friend, they both embraced,　　5
And both together joyfully were placed.
O thrice happy pair of friends, O Arcady's treasure,
Whose virtues drew them up to heavenly pleasure.

Now twinkling stars do smile, and dance, and play them,
Their lights increased; and heavens all new array them　　10
To honour Meliboeus, that did obey them.
Tityrus, leave lamenting, and to bewail him
That is placed in heaven, where joy shall never fail him;
And Death, go pack thee, for nothing now can quail him.

XXV. *Luca Marenzio*

UNKIND, O stay thy flying,
And if I needs must die, pity me dying;
　　But in thee my heart is lying,
　　And no death can assail me,
　　Alas, till life do fail thee.　　5
O therefore, if the Fates bid thee be fleeting,
Stay for me, whose poor heart thou hast in keeping.

XXVI. *Alessandro Striggio*

LOVE hath proclaimed war by trumpet sounded,
And made a vow that beauty shall be wounded.
Diana, see thy nymphs be strongly guarded,
For his strokes will amaze them, if not well warded.
And Amaryllis, hide thy beauty's treasure,　　5
Lest in thy looks Love take too great a pleasure;
If he assault thee, being thus enraged,
His wrath in thee, alas, must be assuaged.

XXVII. *Luca Marenzio*

THE fates, alas, too cruel,
Have slain, before his day, Diana's chiefest jewel;
But worthy Meliboeus, even in a moment,
With Astrophel was placed above the firmament.
　　O they live both in pleasure,　　5
　　Where joys excel all measure.

XXVIII. *William Byrd*

[*The words are the same as those of No. viii*]

THOMAS WEELKES

Madrigals To 3. 4. 5. & 6. voyces. 1597

I

SIT down and sing.
Amyntas joys, his little lambs rejoice
  To see the Spring.
Each chirping bird records a piping voice.

Sweet be the fruits that Nature first do yield,   5
Where Winter's cold not long before hath killed.
Pan with his pipe resounds his roundelays,
And Flora's name adorns with worthy praise.
Each living thing full gladly takes the Spring,
Both nymphs and shepherds pleasantly do sing.   10

II–IV

  MY flocks feed not,
  My ewes breed not,
  My rams speed not,
   All is amiss.
  Love is dying,   5
  Faith's defying,
  Heart's denying,
   Causer of this.

All our merry jigs are quite forgot;
All my lady's love is lost, God wot;   10
Where our faith was firmly fixed in love,
There annoy is placed without remove.

  One seely cross
  Wrought all my loss,
O frowning Fortune, cursed fickle dame!   15
  For now I see
  Inconstancy
More in women than in many men to be.

  In black mourn I,
  All fear scorn I,   20
  Love hath forlorn me,
   Living in thrall.

    Heart is bleeding,
    All help needing,
    O cruel speeding   25
     Fraught with gall!

My shepherd's pipe will sound no deal;
My wether's bell rings doleful knell;
My curtall dog that wont to have played,
Plays not at all, but seems afraid.   30

    My sighs so deep
    Procures to weep
With howling noise to see my doleful plight.
    How sighs resound
    Through harkless ground,   35
Like a thousand vanquished men in bloody fight.

    Clear wells spring not,
    Sweet birds sing not,
    Loud bells ring not
     Cheerfully.   40
    Herds stand weeping,
    Flocks all sleeping,
    Nymphs back creeping
     Fearfully.

All our pleasures known to us poor swains, 45
All our merry meetings on the plains,
All our evening sports from us are fled,
All our loves are lost, for Love is dead.

    Farewell, sweet lass,
    The like ne'er was   50
For a sweet content, the cause of all my woe.
    Poor Corydon
    Must live alone,
Other help for him I know there's none.

       v

A COUNTRY pair were walking all alone
And wantonly were talking to each one.
  Quoth she: I will not hate nor love thee.
   Ay me, said he, what wilt thou do?
   Take time and thou shalt prove me. 5
  Quoth he: Alas, I know not how.

What though I wed, I am thy friend.
Then kiss me, Kate, and so an end.

VI

CEASE, sorrows, now, for you have done the deed.
   Lo, Care hath now consumed my carcase quite.
No hope is left, nor help can stand instead,
   For doleful Death doth cut off pleasure quite.
Yet whilst I hear the knolling of the bell,   5
Before I die, I'll sing my faint farewell.

VII

NOW every tree renews his Summer's green,
   Why is your heart in Winter's garments clad?
Your beauty, says my love, is Summer's queen,
   But your cold love like Winter makes me sad.
Then either spring with buds of love again,   5
Or else congeal my thoughts with your disdain.

VIII

YOUNG Cupid hath proclaimed a bloody war,
   And vows revenge on all the maiden crew.
O yield, fair Cloris, lest in that foul jar
   Thine after-penance makes thy folly rue.
And yet I fear her wondrous beauty's such,   5
A thousand Cupids dare not Cloris touch.

IX

AY me, my wonted joys forsake me,
And deep despair doth overtake me.
I whilom sung, but now I weep;
Thus sorrows run when joy doth creep.
I wish to live, and yet I die,   5
For love hath wrought my misery.

X

THREE virgin nymphs were walking all alone,
   Till rude Sylvanus chanced to meet them.
Ravished with joy, he leapt and snatched at one,
   But missing her, thus rudely greets them:
Nymphs of the woods, come back again and kiss me;   5
Sylvanus calls, come back again and bliss me.

XI

OUR country swains in the morris dance
   Thus woo and win their brides:
Will for our town! For Kate the next prance!
   The hobby horse at pleasure frolic rides.
I woo with tears, and ne'er the near.   5
I die in grief, and live in fear.

XII

LO, country sports that seldom fades,
   A garland of the Spring,
A prize for dancing, country maids,
   With merry pipes we bring.
Then all at once 'For our town' cries,   5
'Pipe on, for we will have the prize.'

XIII

YOUR beauty it allureth,
And wanton love procureth,
Which makes me wait on you,
Though tired with grief I know not how.

XIV

IF thy deceitful looks have enchained my heart,
O be not cruel to procure my smart.
     Rather love,
     Pretty dove,
   Thy true and loving friend,   5
   Than so to hasten mine end.
For if by thee I suffer pain
Right reason would thou help my heart again.

XV

THOSE sweet delightful lilies
Which Nature gave my Phyllis,
Ay me, each hour makes me to languish,
So grievous is my pain and anguish.

XVI

LADY, your spotless feature
Noteth a heavenly creature;
And heavenly things by course of kind
Both live and love desire to find.

XVII

MAKE haste, ye lovers plaining,
To see my sighs and her disdaining.
My heart his grief espying,
Comfortless is dying.

XVIII

WHAT haste, fair lady? leave me not behind thee.
   I faint, alas, O stay thee,
   Or else return and kill me.
   For thus will I complain me,
   O heavens, she doth disdain me.   5

XIX

RETIRE, my thoughts, unto your rest again,
Your proffered service may incur disdain.
The dice are cast, and if the gamesters please,
I'll take my chance and rest myself at ease.

XX

SAY, dear, when will your frowning leave,
Which doth my heart of joy bereave?
To sing and play becomes you better,
Such pleasures makes my heart your debtor.
But when you frown, you wound my heart,   5
And kill my soul with double smart.

XXI

THOSE spots upon my lady's face appearing,
   The one of black, the other bright carnation,
Are like the mulberries in dainty gardens growing,
   Where grows delight and pleasures of each fashion.
They grow too high, and warely kept from me,   5
Which makes me sing: Ay me 'twill never be.

XXII

IF beauty be a treasure,
Sweet heart, enjoy your pleasure.
You need not fear the wasting
Of beauty everlasting,
For yours exceeds the measure   5
Of any earthly treasure.

XXIII

MY tears do not avail me,
And hope doth ever fail me.
Wherefore my comfort's treasure
Shall be to live in pleasure.
The more I spend, the more I may;   5
Then welcome, pleasure, every day.

XXIV

MY Phyllis bids me pack away,
And yet she holds me in delay.
I, weeping, cry my heart will break;
She tells me, no, I need not speak.
Then if my fortune fall not wrong   5
I need not sing another song.

Balletts and Madrigals To fiue voyces, with one to 6. voyces. 1598

I

ALL at once well met, fair ladies,
Sing we now: our love repaid is. Fa la.
    Sweet hearts, do not forsake us
    Till night to sleep betake us. Fa la.

Cytherea shall requite you   5
With delight, lest sorrow fright you. Fa la.
    Then help, ye dainty ladies,
    To sing: our love repaid is. Fa la.

II

TO shorten Winter's sadness,
See where the nymphs with gladness, fa la,
Disguised all are coming
Right wantonly a-mumming. Fa la.

Though masks encloud their beauty,
Yet give the eye her duty. Fa la.   5
When heaven is dark it shineth,
And unto love inclineth. Fa la.

III

SWEET love, I will no more abuse thee;
Nor with my voice accuse thee;
But tune my notes unto thy praise,
And tell the world love ne'er decays.
Sweet love doth concord ever cherish,   5
What wanteth concord soon doth perish.

IV

WHILST youthful sports are lasting,
To feasting turn our fasting. Fa la.
With revels and with wassails
Make grief and care our vassals. Fa la.

For youth it well beseemeth   5
That pleasure he esteemeth. Fa la.
And sullen age is hated
That mirth would have abated. Fa la.

V

ON the plains
Fairy trains
Were a-treading measures;
Satyrs played,
Fairies stayed,   5
At the stops set leisures. Fa la.

Nymphs begin
To come in,
Quickly, thick and threefold;
Now they dance,   10
Now they prance,
Present there to behold. Fa la.

[*Barnabe Barnes*]

VI

SWEET heart, arise, why do you sleep,
When lovers wanton sports do keep?
The sun doth shine, the birds do sing,
And May delight and joy doth bring.
Then join we hands and dance till night,   5
'Tis pity Love should want his right.

VII

GIVE me my heart, and I will go,
Or else forsake your wonted 'no'.
   But since my dear doth doubt me,
   With 'no' I mean to flout thee.

Now is there hope we shall agree,   5
When double 'no' imparteth 'yea'.
   If that be so, my dearest,
   With 'no' my heart thou cheerest.

VIII

HARK, all ye lovely saints above,
Diana hath agreed with Love
His fiery weapon to remove. Fa la.
   Do you not see
   How they agree?   5
Then cease, fair ladies; why weep ye? Fa la.

See, see, your mistress bids you cease,
And welcome Love, with love's increase;
Diana hath procured your peace. Fa la.
   Cupid hath sworn   10
   His bow forlorn
To break and burn, ere ladies mourn. Fa la.

IX

SAY, dainty dames, shall we go play,
And run among the flowers gay,
About the valleys and high hills,
Which Flora with her glory fills? Fa la.
The gentle heart will soon be won   5
To dance and sport till day be done. Fa la.

X

PHYLLIS, go take thy pleasure!
  My heart thou now hast broken,
Go frolic there sans measure;
  Those wounds thy looks laid open.
Engraven there Phyllis may find: 5
Phyllis is fair, but too unkind!

XI

IN pride of May
  The fields are gay,
The birds do sweetly sing. Fa la.
  So Nature would
  That all things should   5
With joy begin the Spring. Fa la.

Then, lady dear,
  Do you appear
In beauty like the Spring. Fa la.
  I well dare say   10
  The birds that day
More cheerfully will sing. Fa la.

XII

SING we at pleasure,
Content is our treasure. Fa la.
Sweet Love shall keep the ground,
Whilst we his praises sound.
All shepherds in a ring   5
Shall, dancing, ever sing: Fa la.

XIII

NOW is the bridals of fair Choralis,
  Where every shepherd tunes his roundelays;
And I in honour of my Thoralis
  Will not forget to sing her gentle praise.
For ere the sun his journey doth renew   5
Sweet love shall act that now I wish were true.

XIV

SING, shepherds, after me,
    Our hearts do never disagree. Fa la.
No war can spoil us of our store,
Our wealth is ease, we wish no more;
Black are our looks, we go not brave,   5
A merry heart is all we have. Fa la.

XV

WELCOME, sweet pleasure, my wealth and treasure;
    To haste our playing
    There's no delaying. No, no, no.
This mirth delights me, when sorrows frights me.
    Then sing we all Fa la la.   5

Sorrow, content thee; mirth must prevent thee;
    Though much thou grievest,
    Thou none relievest. No, no, no.
Joy, come delight me, though sorrow spite me.
    Then sing we all Fa la la.   10

Grief is disdainful, sottish and painful.
    Then wait on pleasure,
    And lose no leisure. No, no, no.
Heart's ease it lendeth, and comfort sendeth.
    Then sing we all Fa la la.   15

XVI

LADY, your eye my love enforced,
And your proud look my heart divorced. Fa la.
That now I laugh and now I cry,
And thus I sing before I die: Fa la.

XVII

WE shepherds sing, we pipe, we play,
With pretty sport we pass the day. Fa la.
    We care for no gold,
    But with our fold
        We dance   5
        And prance
    As pleasure would. Fa la.

XVIII

I LOVE, and have my love regarded,
And sport with sport as well rewarded. Fa la.
Which makes me laugh when others weep,
And play with love when others sleep. Fa la.

My love with love hath me requited,   5
With twenty kisses me delighted. Fa la.
Which makes me laugh when others weep,
And play with love when others sleep. Fa la.

Sweet heart, thou hast my love for ever,
That sweetly didst my heart deliver. Fa la.   10
Which makes me laugh when others weep,
And play with love when others sleep. Fa la.

XIX–XX

COME, clap thy hands, thou shepherd's swain,
Phyllis doth love thee once again.
If thou agree, then sing with me:
Phyllis my choice of choice shall be.

Phyllis hath sworn she loves the man   5
That knows what's love, and love her can.
Philemon then must needs agree
Phyllis my choice of choice shall be.

XXI

FAREWELL, my joy;
Adieu, my love and pleasure!
To sport and toy
We have no longer leisure. Fa la.
Farewell! adieu!   5
Until our next consorting
Sweet love be true.
And thus we end our sporting. Fa la.

XXII

NOW is my Cloris fresh as May,
All clad in green and flowers gay. Fa la.
O might I think August were near,
That harvest joy might soon appear. Fa la.

But she keeps May throughout the year,   5
And August never comes the near. Fa la.
Yet will I hope, though she be May,
August will come another day. Fa la.

XXIII

UNTO our flocks, sweet Corolus,
Our bagpipe song now carol thus: Fa la.
   Whilst flocks and herds be grazing,
   Let us our rest be praising. Fa la.

To teach our flocks their wonted bounds,   5
Our bagpipes play the shepherds' grounds. Fa la.
   The tender lambs with bleating
   Will help our joyful meeting. Fa la.

XXIV

An elegy in remembrance of the Ho: the Lord Borough

CEASE now, Delight; give Sorrow leave to speak
   In floods of tears bewailing his decease,
Whose timeless death a stony heart would break.
   Sweet Borough's life was music's life's increase.
Borough is dead. Great Lord of greater fame   5
Live still on earth by virtue of thy name.

ɔɑɒɔɑɒɔɑɒɔɑɒɔɑ

Madrigals Of 5. and 6. parts, apt for the Viols and voices. 1600
[Part I: five part madrigals]

I

COLD Winter's ice is fled and gone,
   And Summer brags on every tree;
The redbreast peeps amidst the throng
   Of wood-born birds that wanton be.
Each one forgets what they have been,   5
And so doth Phyllis, Summer's queen.

II

NOW let us make a merry greeting,
And thank god Cupid for our meeting.

My heart is full of joy and pleasure
Since thou art here, mine only treasure.
Now will we dance and sport and play,   5
And sing a merry roundelay.

III

TAKE here my heart, I give it thee for ever;
No better pledge can love to love deliver.
Fear not, my dear, it will not fly away,
For hope and love command my heart to stay;
But if thou doubt, desire will make it range.   5
Love but my heart, my heart will never change.

IV–V

O CARE, thou wilt despatch me,
If music do not match thee. Fa la.
So deadly dost thou sting me,
Mirth only help can bring me. Fa la.

Hence, Care, thou art too cruel,   5
Come, music, sick man's jewel. Fa la.
His force had well nigh slain me,
But thou must now sustain me. Fa la.

VI

SEE where the maids are singing,
Their lovers garlands bringing.
Yet my love, my tormenter,
To grieve me doth absent her.
Ah, would she but delight me,   5
I care not who would spite me.

VII–VIII

WHY are you ladies staying,
And your lords gone a-maying?
Run, run apace and meet them,
And with your garlands greet them.
'Twere pity they should miss you,   5
For they will sweetly kiss you.

Hark! hark! I hear some dancing
And a nimble morris prancing.
The bagpipe and the morris bells
That they are not far hence us tells.   10
Come let us all go thither,
And dance like friends together.

IX

LADY, the birds right fairly
Are singing ever early.
The lark, the thrush, the nightingale,
The make-sport cuckoo and the quail:
These sing of love, then why sleep ye?   5
To love your sleep it may not be.

X

AS wanton birds, when day begins to peep,
   With chirping notes salute the sun's arise,
So I, whom love had lately lulled asleep,
   Do now with joy pay tribute to her eyes,
Whose sane bright beams presage a happy day.   5
Long may he live that honours Phillida!

[*Part II: six part madrigals*]

I

LIKE two proud armies marching in the field,
Joining a thund'ring fight, each scorns to yield;
So in my heart your Beauty and my Reason,
The one claims the crown, the other says 'tis treason.
But O your Beauty shineth as the sun,   5
And dazzled Reason yields as quite undone.

II

WHEN Thoralis delights to walk,
   The fairies do attend her.
They sweetly sing, and sweetly talk,
   And sweetly do commend her.

The satyrs leap and dance the round,   5
And make their congés to the ground;
And evermore their song it is:
Long mayst thou live, fair Thoralis!

III–IV

WHAT, have the gods their consort sent from heaven,
  To charm my senses with heaven's harmony?
Care they for me, of all my joys bereaven?
  Send they heaven's choir to make me melody,
  Blessing me with music's felicity?   5
If it be so, great may your godheads be,
And greater still to ease my misery.

Methinks I hear Amphion's warbling strings,
  Arion's harp distilling silv'ring sound,
Orpheus' mean lute, which all in order brings,   10
  And with soul-pleasing music doth abound,
  Whilst that old Phemius softly plays the ground.
O sweet consort, great may your comfort be,
And greater still to ease my misery.

V

THREE times a day my prayer is,
To gaze my fill on Thoralis.
And three times thrice I daily pray
Not to offend that sacred may.
But all the year my suit must be   5
That I may please, and she love me.

VI

MARS in a fury 'gainst love's brightest queen
  Put on his helm and took him to his lance;
And marching to the mount this warrior was seen,
  And there his ensigns did the god advance;
And by heaven's greatest gates he stoutly swore   5
Venus should die, for she had wronged him sore.
                                        [*Robert Greene*]

VII–VIII

THULE, the period of cosmography,
  Doth vaunt of Hecla, whose sulphurious fire

Doth melt the frozen clime and thaw the sky;
  Trinacrian Ætna's flames ascend not higher.
These things seem wondrous, yet more wondrous I,   5
Whose heart with fear doth freeze, with love doth fry.

The Andalusian merchant, that returns
  Laden with cochineal and China dishes,
Reports in Spain how strangely Fogo burns
  Amidst an ocean full of flying fishes.   10
These things seem wondrous, yet more wondrous I,
Whose heart with fear doth freeze, with love doth fry.

IX

A SPARROW-HAWK proud did hold in wicked jail
Music's sweet chorister, the nightingale;
To whom with sighs she said: O set me free,
And in my song I'll praise no bird but thee.
The hawk replied: I will not lose my diet   5
To let a thousand such enjoy their quiet.

X

NOEL, adieu, adieu, thou Court's delight,
  Upon whose locks the Graces sweetly played;
Now thou art dead our pleasures dies outright,
  For who can joy when thou in dust art laid?
Bedew, my notes, his death-bed with your tears.   5
Time helps some grief, no time your grief outwears.

ɷɔɿɔɕɔɿɔɕɔɿɔɕɔɿɔɕ

Ayeres Or Phantasticke Spirites for three voices. 1608

I

COME, let's begin to revel 't out,
And tread the hills and dales about,
That hills and dales and woods may sound
An echo to this warbling round.

Lads merry be with music sweet,   5
And fairies trip it with your feet.
Pan's pipe is dull, a better strain
Doth stretch itself to please your vein.

II

JOCKIE, thine horn pipes dull;
Give wind, man, at full.
Fie upon such a sad gull,
Like an hoody doody, all too moody.
    Toodle, toodle.   5
    Pipe it up thicker,
    I'll tread it the quicker.
Why then about it roundly,
And I will foot it soundly;
I'll take my steps the shorter,   10
As if I trampled mortar.

Darité grows so grave,
I may not her have
In a round, when I do crave.
With a hoop, sir, hoy day! O you do hurt me!   15
    Toodle, toodle.
    Set me thy work by,
    And come to me smirkly.
Then if she chance to glance in,
Give us two room to dance in.   20
Though my green jerkin bare is,
Us two to all the parish!

III

SOME men desire spouses
That come of noble houses.
And some would have in marriage
Ladies of courtly carriage. Fa la.
    But few desire, as I do,   5
    The maidenhead of a widow. Fa la.

Some think fair youth will cherish
Strength that begins to perish.
I'll have no colts to taming,
Let me be young'st at gaming. Fa la.   10
    I'll get or I'll go nigh to
    The maidenhead of a widow. Fa la.

IV

TOMORROW is the marriage day
Of Mopsus and fair Phillida.
Come, shepherds, bring your garlands gay.

If Love lie in so foul a nest,
And foulness on so fair a breast,   5
What lover may not hope the best?

O do not weep, fair Bellamoure,
Though he be gone there's many more,
For Love hath many loves in store.

V

UPON a hill the bonny boy,
    Sweet Thyrsis, sweetly played;
And called his lambs their master's joy,
    And more he would have said;
But Love, that gives the lovers wings,   5
Withdrew his mind from other things.

His pipe and he could not agree,
    For Milla was his note.
This silly pipe could never get
    This lovely name by rote.   10
With that they both fell in a sound,
He fell asleep, his pipe to ground.

VI

COME, sirrah Jack, ho!
Fill some tobacco.
    Bring a wire
    And some fire!   .
    Haste away,   5
    Quick I say!
    Do not stay!
    Shun delay!
For I drank none good to-day.
I swear that this tobacco   10
It's perfect Trinidado.
By the very very Mass
Never never never was
Better gear than is here. By the rood, for the blood,
    It is very very good.   15

Fill the pipe once more,
My brains dance Trenchmore.
    It is heady,
    I am giddy.
    My head and brains,   20
    Back and reins,
    Joints and veins
    From all pains
It doth well purge and make clean.
Then those that do condemn it,   25
Or such as not commend it,
Never were so wise to learn
Good tobacco to discern;
Let them go pluck a crow, and not know as I do
The sweet of Trinidado.   30

VII

TAN ta ra: cries Mars on bloody rampier.
Fa la la: cries Venus in a chamber.
    Toodle loodle loo!
    Cries Pan, that cuckoo,
    With bells at his shoe,   5
    And a fiddle too.
Ay me, but I, alas, lie weeping,
For Death hath slain my sweeting,
Which hath my heart in keeping.

VIII

THE gods have heard my vows,
Fond Lyce, whose fair brows
Wont scorn with such disdain
My love, my tears, my pain. Fa la.

But now those Springtide roses   5
Are turned to Winter posies,
To rue and thyme and sage,
Fitting that shrivelled age. Fa la.

Now, youths with hot desire,
See, see that flameless fire,   10
Which erst your hearts so burned,
Quick into ashes turned. Fa la.

IX

THOUGH my carriage be but careless,
  Though my looks be of the sternest,
Yet my passions are compareless;
  When I love, I love in earnest.

No, my wits are not so wild,   5
  But a gentle soul may yoke me.
Nor my heart so hard compiled,
  But it melts if Love provoke me.

X

THE Ape, the Monkey and Baboon did meet,
And breaking of their fast in Friday Street,
Two of them sware together solemnly
In their three natures was a sympathy.
Nay, quoth Baboon, I do deny that strain,   5
I have more knavery in me than you twain.

Why, quoth the Ape, I have a horse at will
In Paris Garden for to ride on still,
And there show tricks. Tush, quoth the Monkey, I
For better tricks in great men's houses lie.   10
Tush, quoth Baboon, when men do know I come,
For sport, from city, country, they will run.

XI

No, No!
    Though I shrink still,
    Yet I think still
    That a wink will
Do what lovers best know. Fa la.   5
Till then I will be glad,
And then I will be mad.
Hang up all love that is sad. Fa la.

What, what?
    If she fain so,   10
    Then I plain go
    In a vein to
Overthrow her, that's flat! Fa la.
O but she loved me well.
No, but I cannot tell.   15
Who dares trust women or hell? Fa la.

XII

Ay me, alas, heigh ho, heigh ho!
Thus doth Messalina go
Up and down the house a-crying,
For her monkey lies a-dying.
Death, thou art too cruel   5
To bereave her jewel,
Or to make a seizure
Of her only treasure.
If her monkey die,
She will sit and cry,   10
Fie fie fie fie fie!

XIII

Late in my rash accounting
My fortune was amounting. Fa la.
And now all is undone,
All courses backwards run. Fa la.

Hearts greedy in desiring,   5
Are speedy in aspiring. Fa la.
But this female sex
Make stout hearts break their necks. Fa la.

You ladies fair and fickle,
Whose climbing thoughts do tickle, fa la,   10
Shall most deeply repent,
And find a base descent. Fa la.

XIV

Four arms, two necks, one wreathing,
Two pair of lips, one breathing. Fa la.
Two hearts that multiply
Sighs interchangeably. Fa la.

The thought of this confounds me,   5
And as I speak it wounds me. Fa la.
It cannot be expressed.
Good help me, whilst I rest. Fa la.

Bad stomachs have their loathing,
And, O, this all is nothing. Fa la.   10
This No with griefs doth prove
Report oft turns in love. Fa la.

XV

LORD, when I think
What a paltry thing
Is a glove or a ring,
Or a top of a fan to brag of;
And how much a noddy   5
Will triumph in a busk-point,
Snatch with the tag off;
    Then I say:
Well fare him that hath ever used close play.

And when I see   10
What a pitiful grace
Hath a frown in the face,
Or a no in the lips of a lady;
And when I had wist
She would be kissed   15
When she away did go
    With hey ho;
    I end so:
Never trust any woman more than you know.

XVI

SAY, wanton, will you love me?
    I love no long delaying.
Whilst that you strive to prove me,
    I fear your love's decaying.

Fear not my love's decaying,   5
    Whilst that you strive to prove me.
I love no long delaying,
    Come, wanton, then and love me.

XVII

I BEI ligustri e rose
Ch'in voi natura pose,
Donna gentil, mi fanno ogn' hor morire,
Sì grave è la mia pena e 'l mio martire.

XVIII

STRIKE it up, Tabor,
And pipe us a favour!
Thou shalt be well paid for thy labour.
  I mean to spend my shoe sole
  To dance about the maypole!   5
    I will be blithe and brisk,
      Leap and skip,
      Hop and trip,
      Turn about
      In the rout,   10
Until weary joints can scarce frisk.

    Lusty Dick Hopkin,
    Lay on with thy napkin,
The stitching cost me but a dodkin.
      The morris were half undone   15
      Were't not for Martin of Compton.
      O well said, jigging Al'ce!
        Pretty Jill
        Stand you still!
        Dapper Jack   20
        Means to smack.
How now? fie! fie! fie! you dance false.

XIX

HA ha! ha ha! This world doth pass
  Most merrily I'll be sworn,
For many an honest Indian ass
  Goes for a unicorn.
          Fara diddle dyno,   5
          This is idle fyno.

Tie hie! tie hie! O sweet delight!
  He tickles this age that can
Call Tullia's ape a marmasyte
  And Leda's goose a swan.   10
          Fara diddle dyno,
          This is idle fyno.

So, so! so so! Fine English days!
   For false play is no reproach,
For he that doth the coachman praise   15
   May safely use the coach.
               Fara diddle dyno,
               This is idle fyno.

XX

SINCE Robin Hood, Maid Marian,
   And Little John are gone-a,
The hobby horse was quite forgot,
   When Kemp did dance alone-a,
      He did labour   5
      After the tabor.
      For to dance
      Then into France.
      He took pains
To skip it in hope of gains.   10
He will trip it on the toe,
Diddle diddle diddle doe.

XXI

   FA la la la.
   O now weep, now sing! Fa la.
For this is love: in frost to fry,
   In tears to sing,
   In life to die,   5
And never to have ending.

   Fa la la la,
   I die willingly, fa la.
And yet I live in spite of love,
   In hope of gain,   10
   And think to prove
Some pleasure mingled with pain.

XXII

ALAS! O tarry but one half hour,
Until an opportunity fit my power,
Then will I look and sigh out all my sorrow.
   Now everybody looketh on,
   And you know I must be gone   5
      To-morrow.

Adieu! Why did I aspire high,
When I see my ruinous end so nigh?
Yet will I now prolong my last farewell.
Else in sudden sort to part   10
Will go near to break my heart,
    That doth swell.

XXIII

As deadly serpents lurking,
So envy lieth working
    Still to disgrace those men
Which do strive by virtue's fame
To augment their height of name   5
    By labour, art and pen.

But let all carping Momi,
And idle foolish Zoili,
    Whatsoe'er they will, report;
I put myself in venture   10
To judgement's learned censure
    And men of better sort.

XXIV

DONNA, il vostro bel viso
Apr'a chi mir'ogn'hor il paradiso,
    Ma 'l mio misero core
Sen viv'ogn'hor in lagrim'e dolore.

XXV

THE nightingale, the organ of delight,
    The nimble lark, the blackbird, and the thrush,
And all the pretty quiristers of flight,
    That chant their music notes in every bush,
Let them no more contend who shall excel;   5
The cuckoo is the bird that bears the bell.

XXVI

A remembrance of my friend Mr. Thomas Morley

DEATH hath deprived me of my dearest friend;
    My dearest friend is dead and laid in grave.

In grave he rests until the world shall end.
  The world shall end, as end all things must have.
All things must have an end that Nature wrought;   5
That Nature wrought must unto dust be brought.

                                    [*John Davies of Hereford*]

JOHN WILBYE

The First Set Of English Madrigals To 3. 4. 5. and 6. voices. 1598

I

FLY, Love, aloft to heaven and look out Fortune;
      Then sweetly her importune
That I from my Calisto best beloved,
As you and she set down, be never moved.
And, Love, to Carimel see you commend me,   5
Fortune for his sweet sake may chance befriend me.

II

AWAY, thou shalt not love me.
So shall my love seem greater,
And I shall love the better.
Shall it be so? what say you?
Why speak you not, I pray you?   5
Nay, then I know you love me,
That so you may disprove me.

III

AY me, can every rumour
Thus start my lady's humour?
Name ye some gallant to her,
Why straight forsooth I woo her!
Then burst she forth in passion: 5
You men love but for fashion.
Yet sure I am that no man
Ever so loved woman.
Yet, alas, Love, be wary,
For women be contrary.   10

IV

WEEP, O mine eyes, and cease not;
Your spring-tides, out alas, methinks increase not.
    O when, O when begin you
To swell so high that I may drown me in you?

V

DEAR Pity, how, ah how wouldst thou become her,
    That best becometh Beauty's best attiring?
Shall my desert deserve no favour from her,
    But still to waste myself in deep admiring?
Like him that calls to Echo to relieve him   5
Still tells and hears the tale, O tale that grieves him.

VI

YE restless thoughts, that harbour discontent,
Cease your assaults and let my heart lament;
And let my tongue have leave to tell my grief,
That she may pity, though not grant relief.
Pity would help what Love hath almost slain,   5
And salve the wound that festered this disdain.

VII–VIII

WHAT needeth all this travail and turmoiling,
        Shortening the life's sweet pleasure
        To seek this far-fetched treasure
In those hot climates under Phoebus broiling?
O fools, can you not see a traffic nearer   5
In my sweet lady's face, where Nature showeth
Whatever treasure eye sees or heart knoweth?
        Rubies and diamonds dainty,
        And orient pearls such plenty,
Coral and ambergris sweeter and dearer   10
Than which the South Seas or Moluccas lend us,
Or either Indies, East or West, do send us.

IX

        ALAS, what hope of speeding
        Where Hope beguiled lies bleeding?
        She bade come when she spied me;
        And when I came she flied me.

Thus when I was beguiled,   5
She at my sighing smiled.
But if you take such pleasure
Of Hope and Joy, my treasure,
By deceit to bereave me,
Love me, and so deceive me.   10

                          X

LADY, when I behold the roses sprouting,
   Which clad in damask mantles deck the arbours,
   And then behold your lips where sweet Love harbours,
My eyes presents me with a double doubting.
For, viewing both alike, hardly my mind supposes   5
Whether the roses be your lips, or your lips the roses.

                         XI

         THUS saith my Cloris bright
When we of love sit down and talk together:
Beware of Love, Love is a walking sprite,
         And Love is this and that,
         And O I wot not what,   5
And comes and goes again, I wot not whither.
No, no, these are but bugs to breed amazing,
For in her eyes I saw his torchlight blazing.

                        XII

         ADIEU, sweet Amaryllis,
         For since to part your will is,
         O heavy tiding,
         Here is for me no biding.
Yet once again, ere that I part with you,   5
         Amaryllis, sweet, adieu.

                       XIII

DIE, hapless man, since she denies thee grace;
   Die and despair, sith she doth scorn to love thee.
Farewell, most fair, though thou dost fair deface
   Sith for my duteous love thou dost reprove me.
Those smiling eyes that sometimes me revived,   5
Clouded with frowns, have me of life deprived.

XIV–XV

I FALL, I fall, O stay me!
Dear love, with joys ye slay me;
Of life your lips deprive me;
Sweet, let your lips revive me.
O whither are you hasting,   5
And leave my life thus wasting?
My health on you relying,
'Twere sin to leave me dying.
And though my love abounding
Did make me fall a-sounding,   10
Yet am I well contented
Still so to be tormented.
And Death can never fear me
As long as you are near me.

XVI–XVII

I ALWAYS beg, yet never am relieved;
I grieve because my griefs are not believed.
I cry aloud in vain, my voice outstretched,
And get but this: mine Echo calls me wretched.

Thus Love commands that I in vain complain me,   5
And Sorrow will that she shall still disdain me.
Yet did I hope, which hope my life prolonged,
To hear her say: Alas, his love was wronged.

XVIII

LADY, your words do spite me;
Yet your sweet lips so soft kiss and delight me;
Your deeds my heart surcharged with over-joying,
    Your taunts my life destroying.
    Since both have force to spill me,   5
    Let kisses sweet, Sweet, kill me.
    Knights fight with swords and lances,
    Fight you with smiling glances.
    So like swans of Leander
Singing and dying my ghost from hence shall wander.   10

XIX

ALAS, what a wretched life is this! Nay, what a death,
    Where the tyrant Love commandeth.

My flowering days are in their prime declining,
All my proud hope quite fall'n and life untwining.
My joys each after other in haste are flying,   5
And leave me dying for her that scorns my crying.
O she from hence departs, my love refraining,
For whom all heartless, alas, I die complaining.

XX

UNKIND, O stay thy flying;
And if I needs must die, pity me dying.
But in thee my heart is lying;
And no death can assail me
Alas, till life doth fail thee.   5
O therefore, if the Fates bid thee be fleeting,
Stay for me, whose poor heart thou hast in keeping.

XXI

I SUNG sometimes my thoughts and fancy's pleasure
Where then I list, or time served best and leisure;
While Daphne did invite me
To supper once, and drank to me to spite me.
I smiled; yet still did doubt her,   5
And drank where she had drank before, to flout her.
But O while I did eye her,
Mine eyes drank love, my lips drank burning fire.

XXII

FLORA gave me fairest flowers,
None so fair in Flora's treasure.
These I placed on Phyllis' bowers,
She was pleased, and she my pleasure.
Smiling meadows seem to say: 5
Come, ye wantons, here to play.

XXIII

SWEET Love, if thou wilt gain a monarch's glory,
Subdue her heart, who makes me glad and sorry.
Out of thy golden quiver
Take thou thy strongest arrow,
That will through bone and marrow,   5
And me and thee of grief and fear deliver.

But come behind, for if she look upon thee,
Alas, poor Love, then thou art woebegone thee.

XXIV

[The words are the same as those of No. x]

XXV

WHEN shall my wretched life give place to death,
 That my sad cares may be enforced to leave me?
Come, saddest shadow, stop my vital breath,
 For I am thine. Then let not Care bereave thee
Of thy sad thrall, but with thy fatal dart   5
Kill Care and me, while Care lies at my heart.

XXVI–XXVII

OF joys and pleasing pains I late went singing,
 O joys with pains, O pains with joys consenting;
 And little thought as then of now repenting,
But now think of my then sweet bitter stinging.
All day long I my hands, alas, go wringing,   5
 The baleful notes of which my sad tormenting
 Are ruth and moan, frights, sobs and loud lamenting,
From hills and dales in my dull ears still ringing.
My throat is sore, my voice is hoarse with skriking,
 My rests are sighs deep from the heart-root fetched; 10
My song runs all on sharps, and with oft striking
 Time on my breast I shrink with hands outstretched.
Thus still and still I sing, and ne'er am linning,
For still the close points to my first beginning.

XXVIII

CRUEL, behold my heavy ending.
 See what you wrought by your disdaining.
Causeless I die, love still attending
 Your hopeless pity of my complaining.

Suffer those eyes, which thus have slain me,   5
 With speed to end their killing power;
So shall you prove how love doth pain me,
 And see me die still yower.

XXIX

THOU art but young, thou say'st,
  And Love's delight thou weigh'st not.
O take time while thou may'st,
  Lest when thou would'st, thou may'st not.

If Love shall then assail thee,   5
  A double double anguish will torment thee;
And thou wilt wish—but wishes all will fail thee—
  O me, that I were young again! and so repent thee.

XXX

WHY dost thou shoot, and I seek not to shield me?
  I yield, sweet Love, spare then my wounded liver,
  And do not make my heart thy arrow's quiver.
O hold! What needs this shooting, when I yield me?

*The Second Set Of Madrigales To 3. 4. 5. and 6. parts, apt both for Voyals
and Voyces. 1609*

I

COME, shepherd swains, that wont to hear me sing,
      Now sigh and groan.
Dead is my love, my hope, my joy, my spring,
      Dead, dead and gone.

O she that was your Summer's Queen,   5
      Your day's delight,
Is gone and will no more be seen;
      O cruel spite!

Break all your pipes that wont to sound
      With pleasant cheer,   10
And cast yourselves upon the ground
      To wail my dear.

Come, shepherd swains, come, nymphs, and all a-row,
      To help me cry:
Dead is my love. And, seeing she is so,   15
      Lo now I die.

II

FLOURISH, ye hillocks, set with fragrant flowers,
    So graced with her deity,
Whose eyes bedew you with their pearled showers,
    Bewailing Love's impiety.
Happy ye are, be prodigal disposed,   5
    Disdain not Love's lamenting;
Let me but kiss those steps where she reposed
    To ease my heart's tormenting.
Then while she flies me, here I lie and languish,
Sounding my sorrows tuned in notes of anguish.   10

III

AH, cruel Amaryllis, since thou tak'st delight
    To hear the accents of a doleful ditty,
    To triumph still without remorse or pity,
I loathe this life; Death must my sorrows right.
And, lest vain Hope my miseries renew,   5
    Come quickly, Death,
    Reave me of breath.
Ah cruel Amaryllis, adieu, adieu.

IV

So light is Love in matchless beauty shining,
    When she revisits Cypris' hallowed bowers,
Two feeble doves, harnessed in silken twining,
    Can draw her chariot midst the Paphian flowers.
       Lightness to Love, how ill it fitteth,   5
       So heavy on my heart she sitteth!

V

As fair as morn, as fresh as May,
A pretty grace in saying Nay,
Smil'st thou sweet heart? Then sing and say
       Ta na na no.
But O that love-enchanting eye!   5
Lo here my doubtful doom I try:
Tell me, my sweet, live I or die?
She smiles. Ah, she frowns. Ay me, I die.

VI

O WHAT shall I do, or whither shall I turn me?
Shall I make unto her eyes? O no, they'll burn me.
  Shall I seal up my eyes and speak my part?
Then in a flood of tears I drown my heart.
    For tears being stopped will swell for scope,   5
    Though they o'erflow love, life and hope.
        By Beauty's eye
        I'll choose to die.

At thy feet I fall, fair creature rich in beauty;
And for pity call; O kill not love and duty.   10
  Let thy smooth tongue fan on my sense thy breath,
  To stay thine eyes from burning me to death.
    But if mercy be exiled
    From a thing so fair compiled,
      Then patiently   15
      By thee I'll die.

VII–VIII

I LIVE, and yet methinks I do not breathe.
I thirst and drink; I drink and thirst again.
I sleep, and yet I dream I am awake.
I hope for that I have; I have and want.
I sing and sigh; I love and hate at once.   5
  O tell me, restless soul, what uncouth jar
  Doth cause such want in store, in peace such war?

Riposta

There is a jewel which no Indian mines
Can buy, no chimic art can counterfeit.
It makes men rich in greatest poverty;   10
Makes water wine, turns wooden cups to gold,
The homely whistle to sweet music's strain.
  Seldom it comes, to few from Heaven sent,
  That much in little, all in nought, Content.

IX

WHEN Cloris heard of her Amyntas dying,
She grieved then for her unkind denying.
Oft sighing sore, and with a heart unfeigned,
I die, I die, I die, she thus complained.

Whom when Amyntas spied,   5
Then both for joy out-cried:
I love, I love sweet Cloris' eye,
And I Amyntas till I die.

X

HAPPY streams, whose trembling fall
    With still murmur softly gliding,
Happy birds, whose chirping call
    With sweet melody delighting
Hath moved her flinty and relentless heart   5
    To listen to your harmony,
And sit securely in these downs apart,
    Enchanted with your melody.
    Sing on and carol forth your glee,
    She grants you leave her rays to see.   10
Happy were I, could Love but so delight her,
But, ay alas, my love doth still depite her.

XI

CHANGE me, O heavens, into the ruby stone
    That on my love's fair locks doth hang in gold.
Yet leave me speech to her to make my moan,
    And give me eyes her beauties to behold.
Or if you will not make my flesh a stone,   5
Make her hard heart seem flesh that now seems none.

XII

LOVE me not for comely grace,
For my pleasing eye or face,
Nor for any outward part,
No nor for my constant heart;
For those may fail or turn to ill,   5
        So thou and I shall sever.
    Keep therefore a true woman's eye,
        And love me still, but know not why,
So hast thou the same reason still
        To dote upon me ever.   10

XIII

FLY not so swift, my dear, behold me dying.
If not a smiling glance for all my crying,
    Yet kill me with thy frowns.
The satyrs o'er the lawns full nimbly dancing
Frisk it apace to view thy beauty's glancing.   5
    See how they coast the downs.
Fain wouldst thou turn and yield them their delight,
But that thou fear'st lest I should steal a sight.

XIV

I LOVE, alas, alas, yet am not loved,
For cruel she to pity is not moved.
My constant love with scorn she ill rewardeth,
Only my sighs a little she regardeth;
Yet more and more the quenchless fire increaseth,   5
Which to my greater torment never ceaseth.

XV

AS matchless beauty thee a Phoenix proves,
Fair Leonilla, so thy sour-sweet loves.
For when young Acon's eye thy proud heart tames,
Thou diest in him, and livest in my flames.

XVI

HAPPY, O happy he, who not affecting
    The endless toils attending worldly cares,
With mind reposed, all discontents rejecting,
    In silent peace his way to heaven prepares,
Deeming his life a scene, the world a stage   5
Whereon man acts his weary pilgrimage.

XVII–XVIII

SWEET honey-sucking bees, why do you still
    Surfeit on roses, pinks and violets,
As if the choicest nectar lay in them
    Wherewith you store your curious cabinets?
Ah, make your flight to Melisuavia's lips;   5
    There may you revel in ambrosian cheer,
Where smiling roses and sweet lilies sit,
    Keeping their Spring-tide graces all the year.

Yet, sweet, take heed, all sweets are hard to get.
Sting not her soft lips, O beware of that;   10
For if one flaming dart come from her eye,
Was never dart so sharp, ah, then you die!

XIX

ALL pleasure is of this condition,
It pricks men forward to fruition;
But if enjoyed, then, like the humming bee
The honey being shed, away doth flee,
But leaves a sting that wounds the inward heart   5
With gnawing grief and never-ending smart.

XX

OFT have I vowed how dearly I did love thee,
    And oft observed thee with all willing duty.
Sighs I have sent, still hoping to remove thee,
    Millions of tears I tendered to thy beauty.

Yet thou, of sighs and silly tears regardless,   5
    Suff'rest my feeble heart to pine with anguish,
Whilst all my barren hopes return rewardless,
    My bitter days do waste and I do languish.

XXI–XXII

DOWN in a valley as Alexis trips,
    Daphne sat sweetly sleeping.
Soon as the wanton touched her ruddy lips,
    She nicely falls a-weeping.
        The wag full softly lifts her,   5
        And to and fro he sifts her.
But when nor sighs nor tears could move her pity,
With plaints he warbles forth this mournful ditty:
Hard destinies, are Love and Beauty parted,
        Fair Daphne so disdainful?   10
Cupid, thy shafts are too unjustly darted;
        Fond Love, thy wounds be painful.
        But sith my lovely jewel
        Is proved so coy and cruel,
I'll live and frolic in her beauty's treasure,   15
But languish, faint and die in her displeasure.

XXIII

WEEP, weep, mine eyes, my heart can take no rest.
Weep, weep, my heart, mine eyes shall ne'er be blest.
Weep eyes, weep heart, and both this accent cry:
A thousand deaths, Flamminia, I die.

Ay me, ah cruel Fortune! Now, Leander, to die I fear not.   5
      Death, do thy worst! I care not!
I hope when I am dead in Elysian plain
To meet, and there with joy we'll love again.

XXIV

THERE, where I saw her lovely beauty painted,
   Where Venus-like my sacred goddess shineth,
There with precellent object mine eyes fainted,
   That fair but fatal star my dole divineth.
As soon as morning in her light appeareth,   5
Her sweet salute my mind o'erclouded cleareth.
When night again the day's delight bereaveth,
My heart's true sacrifice she quick receiveth.
But night and day she craftily forsakes me,
To tedious day, to loathsome night betakes me.   10

XXV

YE that do live in pleasures plenty,
   And dwell in Music's sweetest airs,
Whose eyes are quick, whose ears are dainty,
   Not clogged with earth or worldly cares,
Come sing this song made in Amphion's praise,   5
Who now is dead, yet you his fame can raise.

Call him again, let him not die,
   But live in Music's sweetest breath.
Place him in fairest memory,
   And let him triumph over death.   10
O sweetly sung, his living wish attend ye.
These were his words: The mirth of heaven God send ye.

XXVI

A SILLY sylvan, kissing heaven-born fire,
Scorched his lips for his so fond desire.
I, not so fond, but gazed whilst such fire burned,
And all my heart straight into flames was turned.

The sylvan justly suffered for his kiss,   5
His fire was stol'n, and stol'n things go amiss.
But I, alas, unjustly, for to have her,
Her heavenly fire the Gods and Graces gave her.

XXVII

O WRETCHED man, why lov'st thou earthly life,
   Which nought enjoys but cares and endless trouble?
What pleasure here but breeds a world of grief?
   What hour's ease that anguish doth not double?
No earthly joys but have their discontents;   5
Then loathe that life which causeth such laments.

XXVIII–XXIX

WHERE most my thoughts, there least my eye is striking;
   Where least I come, there most my heart abideth;
Where most I love, I never show my liking;
   From what my mind doth hold, my body slideth.
I careless seem where most my care dependeth,   5
A coy regard, where most my soul attendeth.

Despiteful thus unto myself, I languish;
   And in disdain myself from joy I banish.
These secret thoughts enwraps me so in anguish,
   That life I hope will soon from body vanish,   10
And to some rest will quickly be conveyed,
That on no joy, while so I lived, hath stayed.

XXX

AH, cannot sighs, nor tears, nor aught else move thee
To pity me, who more than life do love thee?
O cruel fates, see now away she's flying;
And fly she will, alas, and leave me dying.
Farewell, most fair, farewell, yet more disdainful,   5
Was never grief like mine, nor death more painful.

XXXI

DRAW on, sweet Night, best friend unto those cares
   That do arise from painful melancholy.
My life so ill through want of comfort fares,
   That unto thee I consecrate it wholly.

Sweet Night, draw on! My griefs when they be told   5
  To shades and darkness, find some ease from paining.
And while thou all in silence dost enfold,
  I then shall have best time for my complaining.

XXXII

    STAY, Corydon, thou swain,
  Talk not so soon of dying.
    What though thy heart be slain?
  What though thy love be flying?
  She threatens thee but dares not strike.   5
    Thy nymph is light and shadow-like;
For if thou follow her, she'll fly from thee,
But if thou fly from her, she'll follow thee.

XXXIII

SOFTLY, O softly drop, my eyes, lest you be dry;
And make my heart with grief to melt and die.
      Now pour out tears apace;
      Now stay! O heavy case,
        O sour-sweet woe!   5
Alas, O grief, O joy, why strive you so?
Can pains and joys at once in one poor heart consent?
  Then sigh and sing, rejoice, lament.
Ay me, O passions strange and violent!
  Was never poor wretch so sore tormented.   10
Nor joy nor grief can make my heart contented;
  For while with joy I look on high,
  Down, down I fall with grief, and die.

XXXIV

LONG have I made these hills and valleys weary
With noise of these my shrieks and cries that fill the air.
  She only who should make me merry,
      Hears not my prayer,
That I, alas, Misfortune's son and heir,   5
Hope in none other hope but in despair.
  O unkind and cruel, if thus my death may please thee,
    Then die I will to ease thee.
Yet if I die the world will thee control,
And write upon my tomb: O sweet departure.   10
    Lo here lies one, alas poor soul,
        A true love's martyr.

NICHOLAS YONGE

Mvsica Transalpina. Madrigales translated of foure, fiue and sixe parts, chosen out of diuers excellent Authors, with the first and second part of La Verginella, made by Maister Byrd, vpon two Stanz's of Ariosto, and brought to speake English with the rest. Published by N. Yonge, in fauour of such as take pleasure in Musick of voices. 1588

I. *Noel Faignient*

THESE that be certain signs of my tormenting,
No sighs be they, nor any sigh so showeth;
Those have their truce sometime, these no relenting,
Not so exhales the heat that in me gloweth;
Fierce Love that burns my heart makes all this venting,   5
While with his wings the raging fire he bloweth.
Say Love, with what device thou canst for ever
Keep it in flames and yet consume it never.

II. *Giovanni de Macque*

THE fair Diana never more revived
Her lover's heart, that spied her in the fountain,
While she her naked limbs in water dived,
Than me the country wench set by the mountain,
Washing a veil to clothe the locks refined,   5
That on fair Laura's head the gold resemble,
Which made me quake, although the sun then shined,
And every joint with loving frost to tremble.

III. *G. P. A. Palestrina*

JOY so delights my heart, and so relieves me,
When I behold the face of my beloved,
That any hard mischance or pang that grieves me
Is quite exiled, and presently removed;
And if I might, to perfite up my pleasure,   5
Without controlment bestow mine eyes
    Where I repose my treasure,
For a crown and a kingdom sure possessed
I would not change my state so sweet and blessed.

IV. *G. P. A. Palestrina*

FALSE Love, now shoot and spare not,
Now do thy worst, I care not; and to dispatch me,
Use all thine art and all thy craft to catch me.
  For youth amiss bestowed
I now repent me, and for my faults I languish,   5
That brought me nothing else but grief and anguish,
  And now at length have vowed
At liberty to live, since to assail me
Both thy bow and thy brand nought doth avail thee.
For from thee good nor ill, comfort nor sorrow,   10
I will not hope nor fear, now nor tomorrow.

V. *Baldissera Donato*

O GRIEF, if yet my grief be not believed,
  Cry with thy voice outstretched,
That her despiteful heart, and ears disdaining,
  May hear my just complaining.
And when thou hast her told my state most wretched,   5
Tell her, that though my heart be thus tormented,
  I could be well contented,
  If she that now doth grieve me
Had but the least desire once to relieve me.

VI. *Baldissera Donato*

AS in the night we see the sparks revived,
And quite extinct so soon as day appeareth,
So when I am of my sweet sun deprived,
New fears approach, and joy my heart forbeareth.
But not so soon, she is again arrived,   5
As fear retires and present hope me cheereth.
O sacred light, O turn again to bless me,
And drive away this fear that doth oppress me.

VII. *Philippe de Monte*

IN vain he seeks for beauty that excelleth,
That hath not seen her eyes where Love sojourneth,
How sweetly here and there the same she turneth.
He knows not how Love heals and how he quelleth,
That knows not how she sighs and sweet beguileth,   5
And how she sweetly speaks and sweetly smileth.

VIII. *G. P. A. Palestrina*

WHAT meaneth Love to nest him
  In the fair eyes admired,
With lovely grace and heavenly sprite inspired,
  Of my mistress delightful?
Envious dames, confess and be not spiteful.   5
  Ah, fools, do you not mind it
That Love hath sought, and never yet could find it,
From sun arising, till where he goes to rest him,
A braver place, than in her eyes to nest him.

IX. *G. P. A. Palestrina*

SWEET Love, when hope was flowering
With fruits of recompense for my deserving,
Rest was the price of all my faithful serving.
O spiteful Death accursed, O Life most cruel.
  The first by wrong doth pain me,   5
And all my hope hath turned to lamenting;
The last against my will here doth detain me.
  Fain would I find my Jewel,
But Death, to spite me more, is not consenting.
  Yet with a mild relenting,   10
Methinks within my heart her place she holdeth,
And what my torment is plainly beholdeth.

X. *Marc' Antonio Pordenone*

LADY, that hand of plenty,
  That gave unto the needful,
  Did steal my heart unheedful.
Sweet thief of love so dainty,
  What will you do by thieving,   5
  That rob when you are giving?
But you do give so surely
That you may rob and steal the more securely.
  If you sometime be pleased
  That my poor heart be eased,   10
  You do it not to joy me,
But still by fresh assaults quite to destroy me.

XI. *Giaches de Wert*

WHO will ascend to heaven, and there obtain me
My wits forlorn and silly sense decayed?
For since I took my wound, that sore doth pain me,
From your fair eyes, my sprites are all dismayed.
Nor of so great a loss I do complain me,   5
If it increase not, but in some bounds be stayed;
But if I still grow worse, I shall be lotted
To wander through the world, fond and assotted.

XII. *Cornelio Verdonck*

LADY, your look so gentle
So to my heart deep sinketh,
That of none other, nor of myself, it thinketh.
Why then do you constrain me,
Cruel, to live in plaint, in pain and sadness?   5
When one sweet word may gain me
Peace to my thoughts, and everlasting gladness.

XIII–XIV. *Philippe de Monte*

FROM what part of the heaven, from what example
Brought was the mould, whence Nature hath derived
That sweet face full of beauty, in which she strived
To prove in earth her power above was ample.
Was never nymph nor silvan queen adored,   5
That so dainty fine locks in air displayed;
Nor heart divine with so great virtue stored.
Yet by her looks my life is all betrayed.

In vain he seeks for beauty that excelleth,
That hath not seen her eyes where Love sojourneth,   10
How sweetly here and there the same she turneth.
He knows not how Love heals and how he quelleth,
That knows not how she sighs and sweet beguileth,
And how she sweetly speaks and sweetly smileth.

XV. [*Palestrina*]

IN every place I find my grief and anguish,
Save where I see those beams that me have burned,
And eke mine eyes to floods of tears have turned.
Thus in extremest pangs each hour I languish:

O me! My shining star so sweet and sacred,   5
Cause of all comfort, of this world the jewel,
For want of thee my life I have in hatred;
Was never grief so great, nor death so cruel.

XVI–XVIII. *Luca Marenzio*

THYRSIS to die desired,
Marking her eyes that to his heart was nearest;
And she that with his flame no less was fired,
    Said to him: O heart's love, dearest,
    Alas, forbear to die now;   5
By thee I live, with thee I wish to die too.

    Thyrsis that heat refrained,
Wherewith in haste to die he did betake him,
Thinking it death that life would not forsake him;
And while his look full fixed he retained   10
    On her eyes full of pleasure,
And lovely nectar sweet from them he tasted,
His dainty nymph, that now at hand espied
    The harvest of love's treasure,
Said thus, with eyes all trembling, faint and wasted: 15
    Die now, sweet heart, I die now.
    The shepherd then replied:
    And I, sweet life, do die too.

Thus these two lovers fortunately died,
Of death so sweet, so happy and so desired,   20
That to die so again, their life retired.

XIX. *Orlando di Lasso*

SUSANNA fair, sometime of love requested
By two old men, whom her sweet looks allur'd,
Was in her heart full sad and sore molested,
Seeing the force her chastity endur'd,
To them she said: If I, by craft procur'd,   5
Do yield to you my body to abuse it,
I kill my soul; and if I shall refuse it,
You will me judge to death reproachfully.
But better it is in innocence to choose it,
Than by my fault t'offend my God on high.   10

XX. *Alfonso Ferrabosco*

[*The words are the same as those of No. xix*]

XXI. *Noel Faignient*

WHEN shall I cease lamenting?
When shall my plaint and moaning
To tunes of joy be turned?
Good Love, leave thy tormenting;
Too long thy flames within my heart have burned.   5
   O grant, alas, with quickness,
Some little comfort for so long a sickness.

XXII. *Luca Marenzio*

I MUST depart all hapless,
But leave to you my careful heart oppressed,
   So that if I live heartless,
Love doth a work miraculous and blessed.
   But so great pains assail me,   5
That sure ere it be long my life will fail me.

XXIII–XXIV. *Alfonso Ferrabosco*

I SAW my lady weeping, and Love did languish,
And of their plaint ensued so rare consenting
That never yet was heard more sweet lamenting,
Made all of tender pity and mournful anguish.
The floods, forsaking their delightful swelling,   5
Stayed to attend their plaint. The winds enraged,
Still and content to quiet calm assuaged
Their wonted storms, and every blast rebelling.

Like as from heaven the dew, full softly showering,
Doth fall, and so refresh both fields and closes,   10
Filling the parched flowers with sap and savour,
So while she bathed, the violets and the roses
Upon her lovely cheeks so freshly flowering,
The spring renewed his force with her sweet favour.

XXV. *Giovanni Ferretti*

SO gracious is thy self, so fair, so framed,
That whoso sees thee without a heart inflamed,
Either he lives not, or love's delight he knows not.

XXVI. *Giovanni Ferretti*

CRUEL, unkind, my heart thou hast bereft me,
And wilt not leave while any life is left me,
    And yet still will I love thee.

XXVII. *Luca Marenzio*

WHAT doth my pretty dearling?
What doth my song and chanting,
That they sing not of her the praise and vaunting?
    To her I give my violets
    And garland sweetly smelling,   5
For to crown her sweet locks, pure gold excelling.

XXVIII–XXIX. *Stefano Felis*

SLEEP, sleep, mine only jewel,
Much more thou didst delight me
Than my belov'd too cruel,
That hid her face to spite me.

    Thou bringst her home full nigh me,   5
    While she so fast did fly me;
By thy means I behold those eyes so shining,
Long time absented, that look so mild appeased.
    Thus is my grief declining;
Thou, in thy dreams, dost make desire well pleased. 10
Sleep, if thou be like death as thou art fained,
A happy life by such a death were gained.

XXX. *Gianetto Palestrina*

SOUND out, my voice, with pleasant tunes recording,
The new delight that Love to me inspireth,
Pleased and content with that my mind desireth.
Thanked be Love, so heavenly joys affording.
She, that my plaints with rigour long rejected,   5
Binding my heart with those her golden tresses,
In recompense of all my long distresses,
Said with a sigh: Thy grief hath me infected.

XXXI. *Luca Marenzio*

LIQUID and wat'ry pearls Love wept full kindly,
  To quench my heart inflamed.
  But he, alas, unfriendly,
  So great a fire had framed,
  As were enough to burn me   5
Without recomfort, and into ashes turn me.

XXXII. *Orlando di Lasso*

THE nightingale, so pleasant and so gay,
In greenwood groves delights to make his dwelling.
In fields to fly, chanting his roundelay,
At liberty, against the cage rebelling.
But my poor heart, with sorrows over-swelling,   5
Through bondage vile, binding my freedom short,
No pleasure takes in these his sports excelling,
Nor of his song receiveth no comfort.

XXXIII. *Giovanni Ferretti*

WITHIN a greenwood sweet of myrtle savour,
Whenas the earth was with fair flowers revested,
I saw a shepherd with his nymph that rested.
Thus spake the nymph with sugared words of favour:
Say (sweet love) to thy love, tell me my darling,   5
Where is thy heart bestowed? Where is thy liking?
The shepherd answered then with a deep sighing,
All full of sweetness and of sorrow mixed:
On thee, dainty dear life, my love is fixed.
With that the gentle nymph, full sweetly smiling,   10
With kind words of delight and flattering glozes,
She kindly kissed his cheek with lips of roses.

XXXIV. *Rinaldo del Mel*

SOMETIME, when hope relieved me, I was contented
  To see my star so sightly,
  That shines so clear and brightly.
  O, since she first consented
To leave the world, all earthly joy defying,   5
Clouds of care all about my heart are flying;
In vain lament I, since a veil now hideth
The rarest beauty that on earth abideth.

XXXV. *Alfonso Ferrabosco*

RUBIES and pearls and treasure,
    Kingdom's renown and glory,
Please the delightful mind, and cheer the sorry.
    But much the greater measure
    Of true delight he gaineth,   5
That for the fruits of love sues and obtaineth.

XXXVI. *Alfonso Ferrabosco*

O SWEET kiss, full of comfort,
    O joy to me envied,
So often sought, so oft to me denièd,
    For thee my life is wasted,
    Yet thee I never tasted.   5
    O lips, so false and wily,
That me to kiss provoked, and shrunk so slyly;
O looks empoisoned, O face, well may I fear thee,
That killst who thee beholds, and comes not near thee.
    I die a death most painful,   10
Killed with unkindness. Farewell, sweet lips disdainful.

XXXVII. *Alfonso Ferrabosco*

SOMETIME my hope full weakly
    Went on by line and leisure;
But now it grows to do my heart some pleasure.
    Yet, that my hope decay not
    By over-much contenting,   5
Love will not give my joys their full augmenting;
    But still with some disaster
Allays my bliss, that hope may be the faster.

XXXVIII. *Lelio Bertani*

[*The words are the same as those of No. x*]

XXXIX. *Girolamo Conversi*

MY heart, alas, why dost thou love thine enemy?
Laughing so merrily, she goes with gladness
    To see thy grief and sadness.
Cruel disdain, lasting pain no remedy,
Save most singular beauty, and little pity.   5

XL. *Alfonso Ferrabosco*

LADY, if you so spite me,
Wherefore do you so oft kiss and delight me?
Sure that my heart, oppressed and overjoyed,
    May break and be destroyed.
    If you seek so to spill me,   5
    Come, kiss me sweet and kill me.
    So shall your heart be eased,
And I shall rest content, and die well pleased.

XLI. *Giovanni Battista Pinello*

Cantio Rustica

WHEN I would thee embrace
    Thou dost but mock me,
And when I lament my case
    Thou criest 'tee hee',
And 'no' still saith my pigsny.   5

XLII. *Alfonso Ferrabosco*

THYRSIS enjoyed the graces
Of Cloris' sweet embraces,
Yet both their joys were scanted,
For dark it was, and candlelight they wanted.
Wherewith kind Cynthia in the heaven that shined,   5
    Her nightly veil resigned
    And that fair face disclosed,
Where love and joy were met, and both reposed.
Then each from other's looks such joy derived
That both of mere delight died and revived.   10

XLIII. *Alfonso Ferrabosco*

[*The words are the same as those of No. xxxii*]

XLIV–XLV. *William Byrd*

THE fair young virgin is like the rose untainted
In garden fair, while tender stalk doth bear it.
Sole and untouched, with no resort acquainted,
No shepherd nor his flock doth once come near it.

Th'air full of sweetness, the morning fresh depainted,   5
The earth, the water, with all their favours cheer it.
Dainty young gallants, and ladies most desired,
Delight to have, therewith, their heads and breasts attired.

But not so soon; from green stock where it growed
The same is plucked, and from the branch removed,   10
As lost is all from heaven and earth that flowed,
Both favour, grace, and beauty best beloved.
The virgin fair, that hath the flower bestowed
Which more than life to guard, it her behoved,
Loseth her praise, and is not more desired   15
Of those that late unto her love aspired.

XLVI. *Luca Marenzio*

I WILL go die for pure love,
Except rage and disdain come to recure love,
Since in reward of all my faithful serving,
My lady gives disgrace for well deserving,
    And in my flames sans measure   5
    Takes her disport and pleasure.
Unless some frost assuage this heat and cure love,
    I will go die for pure love.

XLVII. *Alfonso Ferrabosco*

[*The words are the same as those of No. i*]

XLVIII–XLIX. *Alfonso Ferrabosco*

So far from my delight, what cares torment me;
Fields do record it, and valleys, and woods and mountains,
And running rivers and reposed fountains.
Where I cry out, and to the heavens lament me,
None other sounds but tunes of my complaining,   5
Nymph of the groves or pleasant bird once heareth.
Still recount I my grief, and her disdaining,
To every plant that groweth, or blossom beareth.

She only doth not feel it. O fields, O mountains,
O woods, O valleys, O floods and fountains,   10

O stay no more to hear a wretch appealing.
O that someone this life and soul would sever,
And these mine eyes oppressed would close for ever,
For best were me to die, my love concealing.

L

LO, here my heart in keeping
I leave with her, that laughs to see me weeping.
　O what comfort or treasure
　Is life with her displeasure.
Break, heart, and die, then that she which still doth pain me,　5
May live the more content, when grief hath slain me.

LI. *Luca Marenzio*

NOW must I part, my darling,
Of life and soul diseased,
And Love therewith is pleased.
O what a death is parting.
But if the fates ordain it,　5
Who can refrain it?
O what grief is now lacking?
Yet must I needs be packing.
Farewell, sweet heart unfeigned,
I die to part constrained.　10

LII–LIII. *Girolamo Conversi*

ZEPHYRUS brings the time that sweetly scenteth
With flowers and herbs, and Winter's frost exileth.
Progne now chirpeth, and Philomel lamenteth,
Flora the garlands white and red compileth;
Fields do rejoice, the frowning sky relenteth,　5
Love to behold his dearest daughter smileth;
Th'air, the water, the earth to joy consenteth,
Each creature now to love him reconcileth.

But with me, wretch, the storms of woe persever,
And heavy sighs, which from my heart she straineth,　10
That took the key thereof to heaven for ever,
So that singing of birds, and springtime flowering,
And ladies' love that men's affection gaineth,
Are like a desert and cruel beast's devouring.

LIV–LV. *Alfonso Ferrabosco*

I WAS full near my fall, and hardly 'scaped,
Through fond desire that headlong me transported;
And with the darts and with the nets I sported,
That Love himself for me devised and shaped.
And if my reason but awhile had stayed   5
To rule my sense, misled and unadvised,
To my mishap I had no doubt assayed
What a death is to live by Love surprised.

But as the bird that, in due time espying
The secret snares and deadly bush enlimed,   10
Quick to the heaven doth mount with song and pleasure,
Trains of false looks and faithless words defying,
Mounting the hill so hard for to be climbed,
I sing for joy of liberty the treasure.

LVI–LVII. *Luca Marenzio*

I SUNG sometime the freedom of my fancy,
The fire extinct, the yoke and bonds subdued;
With heart congealed, I quenched the burning franzy,
And with disdain the harmful bait eschewed.
But now I wail my bonds and my enchaining,   5
Naked, unarmed, in lovely nets engaged;
Nor by tears can I find, nor by complaining,
Mercy, nor comfort, nor my grief assuaged.

Because my love, too lofty and despiteful,
While I with sighs resound her name delightful,   10
Doth smile whenas the flame my life depriveth.
If I seek to break off the strings that bind me,
The more I fly, the faster I do find me,
Like the bird in the snare in vain that striveth.

HENRY YOULL

Canzonets To Three Voyces. 1608

I

EACH day of thine, sweet month of May,
Love makes a solemn holiday;
   I will perform like duty,
Since thou resemblest every way
    Astræa, Queen of Beauty.   5

                        [Sir John Davies]

II–IV

COME, love, let's walk into the spring,
Where we may hear the blackbird sing,
The robin redbreast and the thrush,
The nightingale in thorny bush,
The mavis sweetly carolling,   5
These to my love content will bring.

In yonder dale there are fine flowers,
And many pleasant shady bowers,
A purling brook whose silver streams
Are beautified by Phoebus' beams,   10
Which stealing through the trees for fear,
Because Diana bathes her there.

See where this nymph with all her train
Comes tripping o'er the park amain,
And in this grove here will she stay,   15
At barley-break to sport and play;
Where we may sit us down and see
Fair beauty mixed with chastity.

V

PIPE, shepherds, pipe full merrily,
Let sweetest music sound on high,
   Till all the valleys ring.
This is the joyful bridal day
Of Corydon and Phillida,   5
   Sing, shepherds, sweetly sing.

VI

ONLY joy, now here you are,
Fit to hear and ease my care.
Let my whispering voice obtain
Sweet reward for sharpest pain.
Take me to thee and thee to me.   5
No, no, no, no, my dear, let be.

[*Sir Philip Sidney*]

VII

OF sweet and dainty flowers
    A garland I have dight;
And many pleasant shady bowers
    For my true love's delight,
Adorned with roses and lilies,   5
Sweet violets and daffadillies;
    Where she may sit and sing,
    Like Flora in her pride,
    And welcome in the Spring,
    By her thus beautified.   10

VIII

SLOW, slow, fresh fount; keep time with my salt tears.
    Yet slower yet. O faintly, gentle springs,
List to the heavy part the music bears;
    Woe weeps out her division when she sings.
        Droop, herbs and flowers.   5
        Fall, grief, in showers.
        Our beauties are not ours.
        O I could still,
Like melting snow upon some craggy hill,
        Drop, drop, O drop,   10
Since Nature's pride is now a withered daffodil.

[*Ben Jonson*]

IX

IN pleasant Summer's morning,
    Close shrouded in a grove,
Amyntas thus sat mourning
    For Scylla, his fair love:

O cruel fates and spiteful,   5
    Her absence I lament,
Whose presence so delightful
    Did yield such sweet content.

X

ONCE I thought to die for love,
Till I found that women prove
    Traitors in their smiling.
They say men unconstant be,
But they themselves love change we see,   5
Till new grows old, and old grows stale, and all is but beguiling.

XI

AWAKE, sweet love, 'tis time to rise;
    Phoebus is risen in the East,
Spreading his beams on those fair eyes,
    Which are enclosed with Nature's rest.
Awake, awake from heavy sleep,   5
Which all thy thoughts in silence keep.

XII

PITY me, mine own sweet jewel,
Be not still unkind and too too cruel.
Come, sit by me, let us together sing,
And thou shalt be my bonny sweet darling.

XIII

CEASE, restless thoughts, to vex my careful mind,
    And bid adieu to vain delights of love,
Since Phyllis, she, alas, is proved unkind,
    Whom my complaints could not to pity move.
Farewell, unkind, my silly sheep and I   5
Henceforth will join in equal sympathy.

XIV

SWEET Phyllis, stay, let pity move thee;
O come again, and take me with thee.
Be not still unkind and too too cruel,
    My only best beloved jewel.

XV–XVI

THE shepherds' daughters are all gone,
Leaving their flocks to feed alone,
From the greenwood fresh May to bring.
    So sweetly they play,
    And sing all the way,   5
That fields and groves with heavenly music ring.
    But behold where they return along
    With Daphne fair their virgin troops among,
    Upon whose golden locks they all have set
    Of fragrant flowers a seemly coronet,   10
        Sounding on high in Daphne's praise
        Pleasant songs and roundelays.

XVII–XVIII

SAY, shepherd, say, where is fair Phyllis gone,
    Thus carelessly to leave her flock distressed?
See how they wander up and down alone,
    And mourn her absence whom they loved best;
While she forgetful of her silly sheep,   5
Love stole her heart and all her thoughts doth keep.

But though poor sheep fair Phyllis thus do mourn,
    Yet willingly help thou their weak estate;
For she though careless may again return,
    And love neglected may convert to hate;   10
When she rejoicing in her freedom's gain,
That wanton boy despised shall remain.

XIX

IN the merry month of May
The fields are decked with flowers gay. Fa la.
The woods and groves, where birds do sing,
Redoubling echoes, sweetly ring. Fa la.

XX

COME, merry lads, let us away,
    For Philliday, our shepherds' queen, fa la,
About the maypole there doth stay,
    With all her virgins clad in green. Fa la.
Hark, hark, I heard the bagpipe sound,   5
While they dance lightly on the ground. Lirum, lirum.

XXI

WHILES joyful Springtime lasteth,
Each thing of pleasure tasteth,
   And with delights abound. Fa la.
The birds so sweetly singing,
The flowers so freshly springing,   5
   With Nature's beauty crowned. Fa la.

XXII

EARLY, before the day doth spring,
Let us awake, my Muse, and sing,
   It is no time to slumber. Fa la.
So many joys this time doth bring,
   As time will fail to number. Fa la.   5
                       [*Sir John Davies*]

XXIII–XXIV

WHERE are now those jolly swains,
That were wont to grace these plains,
And in their merry, merry veins,
     Sing fa la?
   Now they have time and leisure,   5
   They're gone to take their pleasure,
   Each one to dance his measure,
     And sing fa la.

Now the country lasses hie them,
And these merry lads they spy them,   10
And still as they come nigh them,
     Sing fa la.
   This is a merry greeting,
   Each one doth kiss his sweeting,
   And this is their first meeting.   15
     Sing fa la!

PART II
LUTE SONGS

LIST OF PUBLICATIONS

Concerning the letters [*a*] and [*b*] printed after some dates see p. 677.

tunde the Lute way. The Second Are Pauens, Galiards, Almaines, Toies, Iigges, Thumpes and such like, for two Basse-Viols, the Liera way, so made as the greatest number may serue to play alone, very easie to be performde. . . . Imprinted at London by Iohn Windet at the Assignes of William Barley and are to be sold by Iohn Browne in Saint Dunstons churchyard in Fleet-street. 1607   521

THOMAS GREAVES. Songes of sundrie kindes: First, Aires To Be Svng To the Lute, and Base Violl. Next, Songes of sadnesse, for the Viols and Voyce. Lastly, Madrigalles, for fiue voyces. . . . Imprinted by Iohn Windet dwelling at Powles wharfe, at the Signe of the Crosse Keyes, and are there to be solde. 1604   527

GEORGE HANDFORD. Ayres To be sunge to ye Lute, and Base Vyole, Newly composed by George Handford. [1609]   533

TOBIAS HUME. The First Part of Ayres, French, Pollish, and others together, some in Tabliture, and some in Pricke-Song: With Pauines, Galliards, and Almaines for the Viole De Gambo alone, and other Musicall Conceits for two Base Viols, expressing fiue partes, with pleasant reportes one from the other, and for two Leero Viols, and also for the Leero Viole with two Treble Viols, or two with one Treble. Lastly for the Leero Viole to play alone, and some Songes to bee sung to the Viole, with the Lute, or better with the Viole alone. Also an Inuention for two to play vpon one Viole. . . . Printed by Iohn Windet, dwelling at the Signe of the Crosse Keyes at Powles Wharfe. 1605   540

Captaine Hvmes Poeticall Musicke. Principally made for two Basse-Viols, yet so contriued, that it may be plaied 8. seuerall waies vpon sundry Instruments with much facilitie. 1. The first way or musicke is for one Bass-Viole to play alone in parts, which standeth alwaies on the right side of this Booke. 2. The second musicke is for two Basse-Viols to play together. 3. The third musicke, for three Basse-Viols to play together. 4. The fourth musicke, for two Tenor Viols and a Basse-Viole. 5. The fift musicke, for two Lutes and a Basse-Viole. 6. The sixt musicke, for two Orpherions and a Basse-Viole. 7. The seuenth musicke, to vse the voyce to some of these musicks, but especially to the three Basse-Viols, or to the two Orpherions with one Basse-Viole to play the ground. 8. The eight and last musicke, is consorting all these Instruments together with the Virginals, or rather with a winde Instrument and the voice. . . . Printed by Iohn Windet. 1607   543

ROBERT JONES. The First Booke Of Songes & Ayres Of foure parts with Tableture for the Lute. So made that all the parts together, or either of them seuerally may be song to the Lute, Orpherian or Viol de Gambo. . . . Printed by Peter Short with the assent of Thomas Morley, and are to be sold at the signe of the Starre on Bredstreet hill. 1600   545

The Second Booke of Songs and Ayres, Set out to the Lute, the base Violl the playne way, or the Base by tableture after the leero fashion. . . . Printed by P. S. for Mathew Selman by the assent of Thomas Morley, and are to be sold at the Inner temple gate. 1601   559

Vltimvm Vale, with a triplicity of Musicke, Whereof The first part is for the Lute, the Voyce, and the Viole Degambo, The 2. part is for the Lute,

THE POEMS

JOHN ATTEY

The First Booke Of Ayres Of Foure Parts, With Tableture for the Lute: So made, that all the parts may be plaide together with the Lute, or one voyce with the Lute and Base-Vyoll. 1622

I

On a time the amorous Silvy
Said to her shepherd: Sweet, how do you?
Kiss me this once and then God be wi' you,
    My sweetest dear;
Kiss me this once and then God be wi' you,   5
For now the morning draweth near.

With that, her fairest bosom showing,
Opening her lips, rich perfumes blowing,
She said: Now kiss me and be going,
    My sweetest dear;   10
Kiss me this once and then be going,
For now the morning draweth near.

With that the shepherd waked from sleeping,
And spying where the day was peeping,
He said: Now take my soul in keeping,   15
    My sweetest dear;
Kiss me and take my soul in keeping,
Since I must go now day is near.

II

The Gordian knot, which Alexander great
  Did whilom cut with his all-conquering sword,
Was nothing like thy busk-point, pretty peat,
  Nor could so fair an augury afford;

Which if I chance to cut or else untie,   5
Thy little world I'll conquer presently.
                                        [*Ascribed to Thomas Tomkis*]

III

WHAT is all this world but vain?
What are all our joys but pain?
What our pleasures but a dream
Passing swiftly like a stream?

Like a flower now we grow,   5
Like the sea we ebb and flow,
Still uncertain is our change;
Like the wind so do we range.

No contented joy we have
Till within the silent grave   10
Our frail flesh be laid to sleep;
Then we cease to mourn, to weep.

Who would trust to worldly things,
Which beguile the greatest kings?
I will set my heart on high,   15
And contented so will die.

IV

IN a grove of trees of myrtle
    Venus met fair Myrrha's child.
Kiss, quoth she, my pretty turtle!
    But her hopes he did beguile
        With no, no, no, no, no.   5

Come, O come, my dearest treasure,
    And look babies in my eyes;
Cull and kiss, enjoy thy pleasure
    But her kindness he denies
        With no, no, no, no, no.   10

Loutish lad, come learn to venture
    On the ivory breast of love;
I dare stay thy worst encounter,
    But her words as wind did prove
        With no, no, no, no, no.   15

Shall then love be thus abused
   By the beauty of a boy?
Shall my temple be refused?
   Will Adonis still be coy
      With no, no, no, no, no?   20

Then I vow that beauty ever
   Shall neglected be of love;
Let the foolish boy persever;
   He the folly now shall prove
      Of no, no, no, no, no.   25

V

SHALL I tell you whom I love?
   Hearken then awhile to me,
And, if such a woman move
   As I now shall versify,
Be assured 'tis she or none   5
That I love, and love alone.

Nature did her so much right
   As she scorns the help of art,
In as many virtues dight
   As e'er yet embraced a heart.   10
So much good so truly tried,
Some for less were deified.

Wit she hath without desire
   To make known how much she hath;
And her anger flames no higher   15
   Than may fitly sweeten wrath;
Full of pity as may be,
Though perhaps not so to me.

Reason masters every sense,
   And her virtues grace her birth;   20
Lovely as all excellence,
   Modest in her most of mirth;
Likelihood enough to prove
Only worth could kindle love.

Such she is, and if you know   25
   Such a one as I have sung,
Be she brown, or fair, or so
   That she be but somewhat young,

      Be assured 'tis she or none
      That I love, and love alone.   30

                [*William Browne*]

VI

  MY dearest and divinest love,
    Imagine my distress
When thou retir'st from my desires
    And sorrows me oppress;
For my sense sees no other sun   5
    But that which in thine eyes,
That in another sphere doth run,
    And clouds thy native skies.
Then come again, then come again,
    Display thy pleasing beams,   10
Else all my pleasures are but pain,
    My comforts are but dreams.

VII

BRIGHT star of beauty, on whose temples sit
Apollo's wisdom and Dame Pallas' wit;
O what fair garland worthy is to fit
Thy fair blest brows, that compass in all merit?

Thou shalt not crowned be with vulgar bays,   5
Because for thee it is a crown too base.
Apollo's tree can yield thee but small praise,
It is too stale a vesture for that place.

The birds, the beasts their goddess do thee call;
Thou art their keeper, thou preserv'st them all.   10
Thy skill doth equal Pallas, not thy birth,
She to the heavens yields music, thou to the earth.

VIII

  THINK not 'tis I alone that sing her praise.
    No, all regard her whom my Muse respects;
Each sweetly singing Syren in her lays
    Deserved trophies of her worth erects;
And Philomela on her thorny perch   5
Her neatest notes to note her praise doth search.

IX

JOY, my Muse, since there is one
Deserves best admiration
   Of all that e'er did heed her.
Let all the deities yield their places
To her still well-deserving graces, 5
   Since none of them exceeds her.

X

MY days, my months, my years I spend
   About a moment's gain,
A joy that in th' enjoying ends,
   A fury quickly slain.

A frail delight, like that wasp's life, 5
   Which now both frisks and flies
And in a moment's wanton strife
   It faints, it pants, it dies.

And when I charge my lance in rest,
   I triumph in delight, 10
And when I have the ring transpierced,
   I languish in despite.

Or like one in a lukewarm bath
   Light-wounded in a vein,
Spurts out the spirits of his life, 15
   And fainteth without pain.

XI

MADAM, for you I little grieve to die,
   In and to whom I live because I love.
For if my ill do please your dainty eye,
   It cannot me displease nor greatly move,
Unless a mind in you so cruel be 5
To kill yourself to make an end of me.

Only I grieve that all my life is you,
   Who by my death must needs in danger be;
For if I die it cannot be but true,
   The sweetest of my life must die with me, 10
If that a mind in you so cruel be
To kill yourself to make an end of me.

Wherefore, if of my life you have no care,
    Which I esteem but only for your sake,
Yet of your own, which death itself would spare,   15
    I am in hope you will some pity take,
Unless a mind in you so cruel be
To kill yourself to make an end of me.

XII

R ESOUND my voice, ye woods that hear me plain,
    Both hills and dales causing reflection;
And rivers eke, record ye of my pain
    That oft hath forced you to compassion;
'Mongst whom pity I find doth yet remain,   5
But where I seek, alas, there is disdain.

Ye wandering rivers oft to hear me sound
    Have stopped your course, and plainly to express
Your griefs have cast tears on the wailing ground;
    The earth hath mourned to hear my heaviness,   10
Whose dull and senseless nature I do find
Far more relenting than a woman's mind.

When that my woes I do reiterate,
    The mighty oaks have roared in the wind;
And in the view of this my wretched state   15
    Each living thing bemoans me in their kind,
Save only she, that most my plaints should rue,
Upon my o'ercharged heart doth griefs renew.
                                    [*Sir Thomas Wyatt*]

XIII

V AIN Hope, adieu! thou life-consuming moth,
    Which frets my soul in pieces with delay;
My well-spun threads will make no cloth
    To shroud me from the tempest of decay;
For storms of fortune drench me like a flood,   5
Whilst rancour's frost nips merit in her bud.

XIV

S WEET was the song the Virgin sung,
    When she to Bethelem was come
And was delivered of her Son,
    That blessed Jesus hath to name.

Lullaby, sweet Babe, quoth she,   5
  My Son and eke a Saviour born,
Who hath vouchsafed from on high
  To visit us that were forlorn.
Lullaby, sweet Babe, sang she
And sweetly rocked him on her knee.   10

WILLIAM BARLEY

A new Booke of Tabliture, Containing sundrie easie and familiar
Instructions. 1596

I

THOUGHTS make men sigh, sighs make men sick at heart;
  Sickness consumes, consumption kills at last;
Death is the end of every deadly smart,
  And sweet the joy where every pain is past.
But O the time of death too long delayed,   5
Where tried patience is too ill apaid!

Hope harps on heaven but lives in half a hell;
  Heart thinks of life but finds a deadly hate;
Ears hark for bliss but hears a doleful bell;
  Eyes look for joy but see a woeful state.   10
But eyes and ears and heart and hope deceived,
Tongue tells a truth how is the mind conceived.

Conceited thus to think but say no more,
  To sigh and sob till sorrow have an end,
And so to die till death may life restore,   15
  Or careful faith may find a constant friend,
That patience may yet in her passion prove
Just at my death I found my life of love.

II

LOVE is a spirit high presuming,
  That falleth oft ere he sit fast.
Care is a sorrow long consuming,
  Which yet doth kill the heart at last.
Death is a wrong to life and love,   5
And I the pains of all must prove.

Words are but trifles in regarding
   And pass away as puffs of wind.
Deeds are too long in their rewarding
   And out of sight are out of mind,   10
And though so little favour feed
As finds no fruit in word or deed.

Truth is a thought too long in trial
   And known but coldly entertained.
Love is too long in his denial   15
   And in the end but hardly gained,
And in the gain the sweet so small,
That I must taste the sour of all.

But O the death too long enduring,
   Where nothing can my pain appease;   20
And O the care too long in curing,
   Where patient hurt hath never ease;
And O that ever love should know
The ground whereof a grief doth grow.
But heavens, release me from this hell,   25
Or let me die and I am well.

III

YOUR face, your tongue, your wit,
  So fair, so sweet, so sharp,
First bent, then drew, so hit
   Mine eye, mine ear, my heart.

Mine eye, mine ear, my heart   5
   To like, to learn, to love,
Your face, your tongue, your wit
   Doth lead, doth teach, doth move.

Your face, your tongue, your wit,
   With beams, with sound, with art   10
Doth blind, doth charm, doth rule
   Mine eye, mine ear, my heart.

Mine eye, mine ear, my heart,
   With life, with hope, with skill
Your face, your tongue, your wit   15
   Doth feed, doth feast, doth fill.

O face, O tongue, O wit,
    With frowns, with checks, with smart
Wrong not, vex not, wound not
    Mine eye, mine ear, my heart.   20

    This eye, this ear, this heart
        Shall joy, shall bend, shall swear
    Your face, your tongue, your wit
        To serve, to trust, to fear.

                                    [*Sir Arthur Gorges*]

                    IV

FLOW forth, abundant tears, bedew this doleful face,
Disorder now thy hairs, that lives in such disgrace.
Ah, death exceedeth far this life which I endure,
That still keeps me in war who can no peace procure.
I love whom I should hate. She flies, I follow fast.   5
Such is my bitter state, I wish no life to last.
Alas, affection strong, to whom I must obey,
My reason so doth wrong as it can bear no sway.
My field of flint I find, my harvest vain desire;
For he that sowed wind now reapeth storm for hire.   10
Alas, like flowers of spine thy graces rosy be;
I prick these hands of mine for haste to gather thee.
But now shall sorrow slack; I yield to mortal strife,
To die; this for thy sake shall honour all my life.

                    V

THOSE eyes that set my fancy on a fire;
    Those crisped hairs which hold my heart in chains;
Those dainty hands which conquered my desire;
    That wit which of my thought doth hold the reins.
Those eyes for clearness doth the stars surpass;   5
    Those hairs obscure the brightness of the sun;
Those hands more white than ever ivory was;
    That wit even to the skies hath glory won.
O eyes that pierce our hearts without remorse;
    O hairs of right that wears a royal crown;   10
O hands that conquer more than Caesar's force;
    O wit that turns huge kingdoms upside-down.
Then Love be judge what heart may there withstand
Such eyes, such head, such wit and such a hand.

VI

SHORT is my rest, whose toil is over long;
  My joys are dark, but clear is seen my woe;
In safety small, great wracks I bide through wrong;
  Whose time is swift, and yet my hope but slow.
Each grief and wound in my poor soul appears   5
That laugheth hours and weepeth many years.

Deeds of the day are fables for the night;
  Sighs of desire are smokes of thoughtful tears;
My steps are false although my path is right;
  Disgrace is bold, my favour full of fears.   10
Disquiet sleep keeps audit of my life,
Where rare content doth make displeasure rife.

The doleful clock, which is the voice of Time,
  Calls on my end before my hap is seen;
Thus falls my hopes, whose harms have power to climb, 15
  Not come to have which long in wish have been.
I trust your love, and fear not others' hate;
Be you with me and I have Caesar's fate.

VII

HOW can the tree but waste and wither away
  That hath not sometime comfort of the sun?
How can the flower but fade and soon decay
  That always is with dark clouds over-run?
Is this a life? Nay, death I may it call   5
That feels each pain and knows no joy at all.

What foodless beast can live long in good plight?
  Or is it life where senses there be none?
Or what availeth eyes without their sight?
  Or else a tongue to him that is alone?   10
Is this a life? Nay, death I may it call
That feels each pain and knows no joy at all.

Whereto serves ears if that there be no sound?
  Or such a head where no device doth grow
But all of plaints, since sorrow is the ground   15
  Whereby the heart doth pine in deadly woe?
Is this a life? Nay, death I may it call
That feels each pain and knows no joy at all.
                                [*Thomas, Lord Vaux*]

JOHN BARTLET

A Booke Of Ayres With a Triplicitie of Musicke, Whereof The First Part is for the Lute or Orpharion, and the Viole de Gambo, and 4. Partes to sing, The second part is for 2. Trebles to sing to the Lute and Viole, the third part is for the Lute and one Voyce, and the Viole de Gambo. 1606

I

O LORD, thy faithfulness and praise
  I will with viol sing,
My harp shall sound thy laud and praise,
  O Israel's holy King.
My mouth will joy with pleasant voice   5
  When I shall sing to thee,
And eke my soul will much rejoice,
  For thou hast made me free.

II

IF ever hapless woman had a cause
  To breathe her plaints into the open air,
And never suffer inward grief to pause,
  Or seek her sorrow-shaken soul's repair:
Then I, for I have lost my only brother,   5
Whose like this age can scarcely yield another.

Come therefore, mournful Muses, and lament;
  Forsake all wanton pleasing motions;
Bedew your cheeks. Still shall my tears be spent,
  Yet still increased with inundations.   10
For I must weep, since I have lost my brother,
Whose like this age can scarcely yield another.

The cruel hand of murther cloyed with blood
  Lewdly deprived him of his mortal life.
Woe the death-attended blades that stood   15
  In opposition 'gainst him in the strife
Wherein he fell, and where I lost a brother,
Whose like this age can scarcely yield another.

Then unto Grief let me a temple make,
 And, mourning, daily enter Sorrow's ports,   20
Knock on my breast, sweet brother, for thy sake.
 Nature and love will both be my consorts,
And help me aye to wail my only brother,
Whose like this age can scarcely yield another.

III

WHEN from my love I looked for love and kind affection's due,
Too well I found her vows to prove most faithless and untrue.
  For when I did ask her why,
  Most sharply she did reply
  That she with me did ne'er agree   5
  To love but jestingly.

Mark but the subtle policies that female lovers find,
Who loves to fix their constancies like feathers in the wind.
  Though they swear, vow and protest
  That they love you chiefly best,   10
  Yet by and by they'll all deny,
  And say 'twas but in jest.

IV

WHO doth behold my mistress' face
 And seeth not, good hap hath he.
Who hears her speak and marks her grace,
 Shall think none ever spake but she.
In short for to resound her praise,   5
She is the fairest of her days.

Who knows her wit, and not admires,
 Shall show himself devoid of skill.
Her virtues kindle strange desires
 In those that think upon her still.   10
In short for to resound her praise,
She is the fairest of her days.

Her red is like unto the rose
 When from a bud unto the sun
Her tender leaves she doth disclose,   15
 The first degree of ripeness won.
In short for to resound her praise,
She is the fairest of her days.

And with her red mixed is a white,
    Like to that same of fair moonshine   20
That doth upon the water light
    And makes the colour seem divine.
In short for to resound her praise,
She is the fairest of her days.

V

IF there be any one whom love hath wounded
    And of the hurt is near his death;
If there be any one in grief confounded
    And still with sighs doth fetch his breath,
Such is my case. Let him come sit with me and mourn   5
Whom grief doth grip, and Cupid blind doth overturn.

If there be any one which hath been racked,
    And joint from joint is all too torn;
If there be any one these pangs have smacked,
    And in his heart with love doth burn,   10
Such is my case. Come, let him sit with me and mourn,
For I am racked and scorched with love, and left forlorn.

If there be any one in ship oppressed
    At pinch of wrack to drowned be;
If there be any one with waves betossed,   15
    Or blinded that he cannot see,
Such is my case. Let him come sit with me and mourn,
Whom shipwrack spoils, and eyes put out as lovers' scorn.

If there be any one that fraud hath perplexed,
    Or burst his heart at love's command;   20
If there be any one whom all griefs have vexed,
    Or in hell's pains do daily stand,
Such is my case. Let him come sit with me and mourn,
That feels hell's pain and lover's grief with love's great scorn.

VI

I HEARD of late that Love was fall'n asleep;
    Too late, alas, I find it was not so.
Methought I saw the little villain weep;
    But, thief, he laughs at them that wail in woe.
I dreamt his bow was broke and he was slain;   5
But, lo, awaked, I see all whole again.

His blinking eyes will ever be awake;
  His idle head is full of laughing toys;
His bow and shafts are tickle things to take;
  It is no meddling with such apish boys,   10
For they shall find that in his fetters fall,
Love is a deadly thing to deal withal.

Yet where the wretch doth take a happy vein,
  It is the kindest worm that ever was;
But let him catch a coy conceit again,   15
  In frantic fits he doth a fury pass.
So that, in sum, who hopes of happy joy,
Take heed of Love, it is a parlous boy!

VII

ALL my wits hath will enwrapped;
All my sense desire entrapped;
All my faith to fancy fixed;
All my joys to love a-mixed.
All my love I offer thee,   5
Once for all yet look on me.

Let me see thy heavenly feature.
O heavens! what a heavenly creature!
All the powers of heaven preserve thee;
Love himself is sworn to serve thee.   10
Princess in a goddess' place,
Blessed be that angel's face.

Look how Love, thy servant, dieth;
Hark how Hope for comfort crieth.
Take some pity on poor Fancy;   15
Let not Fancy prove a franzy.
Comfort this poor heart of mine;
Love and I and all are thine.

VIII

GO, wailing verse, the issue of thy sire,
  Begot on sighs which vent from my torn heart.
Tell thou thy parent's never quenched desire;
  Tell of his griefs and of his endless smart;
Tell of his passions and his sad laments,   5
How still he sues hard, she yet ne'er relents.

Deep sobs, the silent orators of Love;
   Sad sighs, the muttering echoes of my pain;
Heart-renting groans, the agent which would move
   Compassion with that cheek-bedewed rain;   10
Rain which doth trickle from my watery eyes,
Hoping at length she'll hear my doleful cries.

But O, would that sweet fair had been the butt
   For Cupid to have aimed at with his shafts!
Then had not these my passions bolted out,   15
   Blazing my follies unto wise men's hates;
Then could not I, deciphering my harms,
Sought to have gained that fair with my rude charms.

But why wish I to Cupid so much good,
   When he hath broke his shafts and silver bow,   20
And finds a flame enkindled in my blood,
   Which neither ice can quench nor mountain snow?
And sure no marvel if he conquer men,
When gods so fair a saint have never seen.

Her eyes like globes contain a thousand orbs,   25
   Her ruby lips, her pearled teeth, in number
With that sweet tongue such harmony affords,
   As with applause makes all the world to wonder,
To wonder at her only, and no other,
Since Cupid did mistake her for his mother.   30

IX

   A PRETTY duck there was that said:
      To whom shall I make moan?
   I have been long a pretty maid,
      And yet I lie alone.

   Alone I lie in deep despair,   5
      Which kills my lovely heart,
   For none will my sweet joys repair,
      Or play a lover's part.

   A tickling part that maidens love,
      But I can never get;   10
   Yet long have sought, and still do crave,
      At rest my heart to set.

X

OF all the birds that I do know,
  Philip my sparrow hath no peer;
For sit she high, or sit she low,
  Be she far off, or be she near,
There is no bird so fair, so fine,   5
Nor yet so fresh as this of mine;
For when she once hath felt a fit,
Philip will cry still: yet, yet, yet.

Come in a morning merrily
  When Philip hath been lately fed;   10
Or in an evening soberly
  When Philip list to go to bed;
It is a heaven to hear my Phipp,
How she can chirp with merry lip,
For when she once hath felt a fit,   15
Philip will cry still: yet, yet, yet.

She never wanders far abroad,
  But is at home when I do call.
If I command she lays on load
  With lips, with teeth, with tongue and all.   20
She chants, she chirps, she makes such cheer,
That I believe she hath no peer.
For when she once hath felt a fit,
Philip will cry still: yet, yet, yet.

And yet besides all this good sport   25
  My Philip can both sing and dance,
With new found toys of sundry sort
  My Philip can both prick and prance.
And if you say but: fend cut, Phipp!
Lord, how the peat will turn and skip!   30
For when she once hath felt a fit,
Philip will cry still: yet, yet, yet.

And to tell truth he were to blame,
  Having so fine a bird as she
To make him all this goodly game   35
  Without suspect or jealousy;

He were a churl and knew no good,
Would see her faint for lack of food,
For when she once hath felt a fit,
Philip will cry still: yet, yet, yet.   40

[*George Gascoigne*]

XI

THE Queen of Paphos, Ericine,
   In heart did rose-cheeked Adone love.
He mortal was, but she divine,
   And oft with kisses did him move.
With great gifts still she did him woo   5
But he would never yield thereto.

Then since the Queen of Love by love
   To Love was once a subject made,
And could thereof no pleasure prove
   By day, by night, by light or shade.   10
Why, being mortal, should I grieve,
Since she herself could not relieve?

She was a goddess heavenly
   And loved a fair-faced earthly boy,
Who did contemn her deity   15
   And would not grant her hope of joy;
For Love doth govern by a fate
That here plants Will, and there leaves Hate.

But I a hapless mortal wight
   To an immortal beauty sue.   20
No marvel then she loathes my sight,
   Since Adone Venus would not woo.
Hence, groaning sighs! Mirth, be my friend!
Before my life my love shall end.

XII

I WOULD thou wert not fair, or I were wise.
I would thou hadst no face, or I no eyes.
I would thou wert not wise, or I not fond,
Or thou not free, or I not so in bond.

But thou art fair, and I cannot be wise.   5
Thy sun-like face hath blinded both mine eyes.
Thou canst not but be wise, nor I but fond,
Nor thou but free, nor I but still in bond.

Yet am I wise to think that thou art fair.
Mine eyes their pureness in thy face repair.   10
Nor am I fond that do thy wisdom see,
Nor yet in bond because that thou art free.

Then in thy beauty only make me wise,
And in thy face the grace guide both mine eyes;
And in thy wisdom only see me fond,   15
And in thy freedom keep me still in bond.

So shalt thou still be fair, and I be wise.
Thy face shine still upon my cleared eyes.
Thy wisdom only see how I am fond,
Thy freedom only keep me still in bond.   20

So would I thou were fair, and I were wise.
So would I thou hadst thy face, and I mine eyes.
So would I thou wert wise, and I were fond,
And thou wert free and I were still in bond.

                          [*attrib. to Nicholas Breton*]

XIII

UNTO a fly transformed from human kind,
    Methought I ranged on a sunshine day;
When, for to ease my sad afflicted mind,
    Upon my mistress' robe I 'gan to play.
At length I mounted up her dainty breast,   5
From whence I sought my solace and my rest.

Yet, not content with these aspiring toys,
    Changing my seat into her curled hair,
By seeking to increase my new-found joys
    I turned my sweet applause to sudden fear,   10
For, chancing on her eyes of flame and fire,
I burnt my wings whereby I did aspire.

Thus falling to the ground in my decay,
  With mournful buzzings craving her relief,
Methought she mourned with ruth my heavy lay   15
  And crushed me with her foot to end my grief,
And said: Lo, where the silly wretch doth lie,
Whose end was such because he flew so high.

XIV

WHAT thing is love, I pray thee tell?
  It is a prickle, it is a sting,
  It is a pretty, pretty thing,
  It is a fire, it is a coal
  Whose flame creeps in at every hole;   5
  And as my wits can best devise,
  Love's darling lies in ladies' eyes.
                                   [*George Peele*]

XV

FORTUNE, Love and Time hath made me happy;
  Happy I was by Fortune, Love, and Time.
My hap at highest the gods began to vary
  And threw me down that caused me first to climb.
They proved their wings, and took their flight in rage,   5
Fortune to fools, Love to youth, Time to age.

XVI

POETS to love such power ascribe,
As no power else can circumscribe;
True love by true desire refined
Can never be by bounds confined.

It first did kindle in mine eye,   5
And thence stole inward presently,
Possessed my breast, my heart and soul,
And doth my better parts control.

The more I seek it to expel,
The more it doth my thoughts compel.   10
Since then it hath such power within,
To let it burn still were a sin.

XVII–XVIII

WHITHER runneth my sweet heart?
    Stay, and take me with thee;
Merrily I'll play my part;
    Stay, and thou shalt see me.
O, have I ketched thee, hey ding a ding!   5
This ketching is a pretty thing!

    Tarry! are you gone again?
      What, no longer liking?
    I will ketch thee once again;
      Stay, while I am rising.   10
Do you tarry then, pretty little one? I thought
I should please thee ere we did part.

XIX–XXI

SURCHARGED with discontent,
    To Sylvane's bower I went
To ease my heavy grief-oppressed heart,
    And try what comfort winged creatures
Could yield unto my inward troubled smart,   5
    By modulating their delightful measures
      To my ears pleasing ever.
Of strains so sweet, sweet birds deprive us never.

    The thrush did pipe full clear,
      And eke with very merry cheer   10
The linnet lifted up her pleasant voice.
    The goldfinch chirped and the pie did chatter,
The blackbird whistled and bade me rejoice,
    The stockdove murmured with a solemn flatter.
      The little daw, ka-ka he cried;   15
      The hic-quail he beside
Tickled his part in a parti-coloured coat.
    The jay did blow his hautboy gallantly.

The wren did treble many a pretty note.
    The woodpecker did hammer melody.   20
      The kite, tiw-whiw, full oft
      Cried, soaring up aloft,
And down again returned presently.

To whom the herald of cornutos all sung cuckoo
Ever, whilst poor Margery cried: Who   25
    Did ring night's 'larum bell?
    Withal all did do well.
    O might I hear them ever.
Of strains so sweet, sweet birds deprive us never.

    Then Hesperus on high   30
    Brought cloudy night in sky,
When lo, the thicket-keeping company
  Of feathered singers left their madrigals,
Sonnets and elegies, and presently
  Shut them within their mossy severals.   35
And I came home and vowed to love them ever.
Of strains so sweet, sweet birds deprive us never.

THOMAS CAMPIAN

The Discription Of A Maske, Presented before the Kinges Maiestie at White-Hall, on Twelfth Night last, in honour of the Lord Hayes, and his Bride, Daughter and Heire to the Honourable the Lord Dennye, their Marriage hauing been the same Day at Court solemnized. 1607

1. [*Thomas Campian*]

Now hath Flora robbed her bowers
To befriend this place with flowers;
    Strow about, strow about,
The sky rained never kindlier showers.
Flowers with bridals well agree,   5
Fresh as brides and bridegrooms be,
    Strow about, strow about,
And mix them with fit melody.
    Earth hath no princelier flowers
Than roses white and roses red,   10
    But they must still be mingled;
And as a rose new-plucked from Venus' thorn,
So doth a bride her bridegroom's bed adorn.

    Divers divers flowers affect
    For some private dear respect;   15
      Strow about, strow about,
    Let every one his own protect;
    But he's none of Flora's friend
    That will not the rose commend;
      Strow about, strow about,   20
    Let princes princely flowers defend.
      Roses, the garden's pride,
      Are flowers for love and flowers for kings,
      In courts desired and weddings;
    And as a rose in Venus' bosom worn,   25
    So doth a bridegroom his bride's bed adorn.

II. [*Thomas Campian*]

MOVE now with measured sound,
    You charmed grove of gold,
    Trace forth the sacred ground
      That shall your forms unfold.
Diana and the starry night for your Apollo's sake   5
Endue your silvan shapes with power this strange delight to make.
Much joy must needs the place betide, where trees for gladness move;
A fairer sight was ne'er beheld, or more expressing love.

    Yet nearer Phoebus' throne
      Meet on your winding ways,   10
    Your bridal mirth make known
      In your high-graced Hayes.
Let Hymen lead your sliding rounds, and guide them with his light,
While we do 'Io Hymen' sing in honour of this night.
Join three by three, for so the night by triple spell decrees,   15
Now to release Apollo's knights from these enchanted trees.

III. [*Lupo*]

    SHOWS and nightly revels, signs of joy and peace,
    Fill royal Britain's court, while cruel war far off doth rage,
      for ever hence exiled.
    Fair and princely branches with strong arms increase,
    From that deep-rooted tree whose sacred strength and glory
      foreign malice hath beguiled.

Our divided kingdoms now in friendly kindred meet,   5
And old debate to love and kindness turns, our power with
  double force uniting.
Truly reconciled, grief appears at last more sweet
Both to ourselves and faithful friends, our undermining
  foes affrighting.

IV. [*Thomas Giles*]

TRIUMPH now with joy and mirth,
The God of Peace hath blessed our land;
 We enjoy the fruits of earth
Through favour of his bounteous hand.
 We through his most loving grace   5
A king and kingly seed behold,
 Like a sun with lesser stars
Or careful shepsherd to his fold.
 Triumph then, and yield him praise
 That gives us blessed and joyful days.   10

V. [*Lupo*]

TIME, that leads the fatal round,
Hath made his centre in our ground,
 With swelling seas embraced;
And there at one stay he rests,
And with the Fates keeps holy feasts,   5
 With pomp and pastime graced.
Light Cupids there do dance, and Venus sweetly sings
With heavenly notes tuned to sound of silver strings.
Their songs are all of joy, no sign of sorrow there,
But all as stars glist'ring fair and blithe appear.   10

Two Bookes Of Ayres. The First Contayning Diuine and Morall Songs: The Second, Light Conceits of Louers. To be sung to the Lute and Viols, in two, three, and foure Parts: or by one Voyce to an Instrument. [*c. 1613*]

I

AUTHOR of light, revive my dying sprite;
Redeem it from the snares of all-confounding night.
     Lord, light me to thy blessed way,
For blind with worldly vain desires I wander as a stray.
     Sun and moon, stars and underlights I see,   5
But all their glorious beams are mists and darkness being compared
     to thee.

Fountain of health, my soul's deep wounds recure.
Sweet showers of pity rain, wash my uncleanness pure.
     One drop of thy desired grace
The faint and fading heart can raise, and in joy's bosom place.   10
     Sin and death, hell and tempting fiends may rage;
But God his own will guard, and their sharp pains and grief in time
     assuage.

II

     THE man of life upright,
       Whose cheerful mind is free
     From weight of impious deeds
       And yoke of vanity:

     The man whose silent days   5
       In harmless joys are spent,
     Whom hopes cannot delude
       Nor sorrows discontent:

     That man needs neither towers
       Nor armour for defence,   10
     Nor vaults his guilt to shroud
       From thunder's violence.

     He only can behold
       With unaffrighted eyes
     The horrors of the deep   15
       And terrors of the skies.

Thus scorning all the cares
    That fate or fortune brings,
His book the heavens he makes,
    His wisdom heavenly things.   20

Good thoughts his surest friends,
    His wealth a well-spent age,
The earth his sober inn
    And quiet pilgrimage.

III

WHERE are all thy beauties now, all hearts enchaining?
Whither are thy flatterers gone with all their feigning?
All fled; and thou alone still here remaining.

Thy rich state of twisted gold to bays is turned.
Cold as thou art are thy loves that so much burned.   5
Who die in flatterers' arms are seldom mourned.

Yet in spite of envy this be still proclaimed,
That none worthier than thyself thy worth hath blamed;
When their poor names are lost, thou shalt live famed.

When thy story long time hence shall be perused,   10
Let the blemish of thy rule be thus excused:
None ever lived more just, none more abused.

IV

OUT of my soul's depth to thee my cries have sounded.
Let thine ears my plaints receive on just fear grounded.
Lord, should'st thou weigh our faults, who's not confounded?

But with grace thou censur'st thine when they have erred;
Therefore shall thy blessed name be loved and feared.   5
E'en to thy throne my thoughts and eyes are reared.

Thee alone my hopes attend, on thee relying;
In thy sacred word I'll trust, to thee fast flying,
Long ere the watch shall break the morn descrying.

In the mercies of our God who live secured,   10
May of full redemption rest in him assured,
Their sin-sick souls by him shall be recured.

V

VIEW me, Lord, a work of thine;
   Shall I then lie drowned in night?
Might thy grace in me but shine,
   I should seem made all of light.

But my soul still surfeits so   5
   On the poisoned baits of sin,
That I strange and ugly grow,
   All is dark and foul within.

Cleanse me, Lord, that I may kneel
   At thine altar pure and white;   10
They that once thy mercies feel,
   Gaze no more on earth's delight.

Worldly joys like shadows fade
   When the heavenly light appears;
But the cov'nants thou hast made,   15
   Endless, know nor days nor years.

In thy word, Lord, is my trust.
   To thy mercies fast I fly.
Though I am but clay and dust,
   Yet thy grace can lift me high.   20

VI

BRAVELY decked, come forth, bright day,
Thine hours with roses strew thy way
   As they well remember.
Thou received shalt be with feasts,
Come, chiefest of the British guests,   5
   Thou fift of November.
Thou with triumph shalt exceed
   In the strictest ember;
For by thy return the Lord records his blessed deed.

Britons, frolic at your board,   10
But first sing praises to the Lord
   In your congregations.
He preserved your State alone;
His loving grace hath made you one
   Of his chosen nations.   15
But this light must hallowed be
   With your best oblations.
Praise the Lord, for only great and merciful is he.

Death had entered in the gate,
And ruin was crept near the State,   20
   But heaven all revealed.
Fiery powder hell did make,
Which ready long the flame to take
   Lay in shade concealed.
God us helped of his free grace;   25
   None to him appealed.
For none was so bad to fear the treason or the place.

God his peaceful monarch chose,
To him the mist he did disclose,
   To him and none other.   30
This he did, O king, for thee,
That thou thine own renown might'st see,
   Which no time can smother.
May blest Charles thy comfort be,
   Firmer than his brother.   35
May his heart the love of peace and wisdom learn from thee.

VII

To music bent is my retired mind,
   And fain would I some song of pleasure sing.
But in vain joys no comfort now I find;
   From heavenly thoughts all true delight doth spring.
Thy power, O God, thy mercies to record   5
Will sweeten every note and every word.

All earthly pomp or beauty to express
   Is but to carve in snow, on waves to write.
Celestial things, though men conceive them less,
   Yet fullest are they in themselves of light.   10
Such beams they yield as know no means to die;
Such heat they cast as lifts the spirit high.

VIII

TUNE thy music to thy heart;
　Sing thy joy with thanks, and so thy sorrow.
　　Though devotion needs not art,
　Sometime of the poor the rich may borrow.

　　Strive not yet for curious ways;　　　　　　　5
　Concord pleaseth more the less 'tis strained.
　　Zeal affects not outward praise,
　Only strives to show a love unfeigned.

　　Love can wondrous things effect,
　Sweetest sacrifice all wrath appeasing.　　　　　10
　　Love the highest doth respect;
　Love alone to him is ever pleasing.

IX

MOST sweet and pleasing are thy ways, O God,
　Like meadows decked with crystal streams and flowers.
Thy paths no foot profane hath ever trod,
　Nor hath the proud man rested in thy bowers.
There lives no vulture, no devouring bear,　　　　5
But only doves and lambs are harboured there.

The wolf his young ones to their prey doth guide;
　The fox his cubs with false deceit endues;
The lion's whelp sucks from his dam his pride;
　In hers the serpent malice doth infuse.　　　　　10
The darksome desert all such beasts contains,
Not one of them in Paradise remains.

X

WISE men patience never want,
　　Good men pity cannot hide.
Feeble spirits only vaunt
　　Of revenge, the poorest pride.
He alone forgive that can　　　　　　　　　　　5
Bears the true soul of a man.

Some there are debate that seek,
　　Making trouble their content;
Happy if they wrong the meek,
　　Vex them that to peace are bent.　　　　　　　10

Such undo the common tie
Of mankind, society.

Kindness grown is lately cold.
   Conscience hath forgot her part.
Blessed times were known of old, 15
   Long ere Law became an art.
Shame deterred, not statutes, then.
Honest love was law to men.

Deeds from love and words that flow
   Foster like kind April showers; 20
In the warm sun all things grow,
   Wholesome fruits and pleasant flowers.
All so thrives his gentle rays
Whereon human love displays.

XI

NEVER weather-beaten sail more willing bent to shore,
Never tired pilgrim's limbs affected slumber more,
Than my weary sprite now longs to fly out of my troubled breast.
O come quickly, sweetest Lord, and take my soul to rest.

Ever blooming are the joys of Heaven's high Paradise. 5
Cold age deafs not there our ears, nor vapour dims our eyes;
Glory there the sun outshines, whose beams the blessed only see.
O come quickly, glorious Lord, and raise my sprite to thee.

XII

LIFT up to heaven, sad wretch, thy heavy sprite.
   What though thy sins thy due destruction threat?
The Lord exceeds in mercy as in might.
   His ruth is greater, though thy crimes be great.
Repentance needs not fear the heaven's just rod. 5
It stays e'en thunder in the hand of God.

With cheerful voice to him then cry for grace.
   Thy faith and fainting hope with prayer revive.
Remorse for all that truly mourn hath place.
   Not God, but men of him themselves deprive. 10
Strive then and he will help. Call him, he'll hear.
The son needs not the Father's fury fear.

XIII

LO, when back mine eye
    Pilgrim-like I cast,
What fearful ways I spy,
Which blinded I securely passed.

But now heaven hath drawn   5
    From my brows that night;
As when the day doth dawn,
So clears my long-imprisoned sight.

Straight the caves of hell
    Dressed with flowers I see,   10
Wherein false pleasures dwell,
That winning most, most deadly be.

Throngs of masked fiends
    Winged like angels fly;
E'en in the gates of friends   15
In fair disguise black dangers lie.

Straight to heaven I raised
    My restored sight;
And with loud voice I praised
The Lord of ever-during light.   20

And since I had strayed
    From his ways so wide,
His grace I humbly prayed
Henceforth to be my guard and guide.

XIV

AS by the streams of Babylon
    Far from our native soil we sat,
Sweet Sion thee we thought upon,
    And every thought a tear begat.

Aloft the trees that spring up there   5
    Our silent harps we pensive hung.
Said they that captived us: Let's hear
    Some song which you in Sion sung.

Is then the song of our God fit
  To be profaned in foreign land? 10
O Salem, thee when I forget,
  Forget his skill may my right hand.

Fast to the roof cleave may my tongue,
  If mindless I of thee be found;
Or if when all my joys are sung, 15
  Jerusalem be not the ground.

Remember, Lord, how Edom's race
  Cried in Jerusalem's sad day:
Hurl down her walls, her towers deface,
  And stone by stone all level lay. 20

Cursed Babel's seed, for Salem's sake
  Just ruin yet for thee remains.
Blest shall they be thy babes that take
  And 'gainst the stones dash out their brains.

XV

  SING a song of joy,
    Praise our God with mirth.
  His flock who can destroy?
  Is he not Lord of heaven and earth?

  Sing we then secure, 5
    Tuning well our strings,
  With voice as echo pure
  Let us renown the King of kings.

  First who taught the day
    From the East to rise; 10
  Whom doth the sun obey
  When in the seas his glory dies.

  He the stars directs
    That in order stand.
  Who heaven and earth protects 15
  But he that framed them with his hand?

Angels round attend,
    Waiting on his will.
Armed millions he doth send
To aid the good or plague the ill.   20

All that dread his name,
    And his hests observe,
His arm will shield from shame,
Their steps from truth shall never swerve.

Let us then rejoice,   25
    Sounding loud his praise,
So will he hear our voice,
And bless on earth our peaceful days.

XVI

AWAKE, awake, thou heavy sprite,
    That sleep'st the deadly sleep of sin.
Rise now and walk the ways of light,
    'Tis not too late yet to begin.
Seek heaven early, seek it late;   5
True faith still finds an open gate.

Get up, get up, thou leaden man,
    Thy tracks to endless joy or pain
Yields but the model of a span,
    Yet burns out thy life's lamp in vain.   10
One minute bounds thy bane or bliss;
Then watch and labour while time is.

XVII

COME, cheerful day, part of my life, to me;
    For while thou view'st me with thy fading light,
Part of my life doth still depart with thee,
    And I still onward haste to my last night.
Time's fatal wings do ever forward fly,   5
So every day we live a day we die.

But, O ye nights, ordained for barren rest,
    How are my days deprived of life in you;
When heavy sleep my soul hath dispossessed
    By feigned death life sweetly to renew.   10
Part of my life in that you life deny;
So every day we live a day we die.

XVIII

SEEK the Lord and in his ways persever.
　O faint not, but as eagles fly,
　　For his steep hill is high,
Then striving, gain the top and triumph ever.

When with glory there thy brows are crowned　　5
　New joys so shall abound in thee,
　　Such sights thy soul shall see,
That worldly thoughts shall by their beams be drowned.

Farewell world, thou mass of mere confusion,
　False light with many shadows dimmed,　　10
　　Old witch with new foils trimmed,
Thou deadly sleep of soul and charmed illusion.

I the King will seek, of kings adored,
　Spring of light, tree of grace and bliss,
　　Whose fruit so sovereign is　　15
That all who taste it are from death restored.

XIX

　LIGHTEN, heavy heart, thy sprite,
　　The joys recall that thence are fled;
　Yield thy breast some living light;
　　The man that nothing doth is dead.
　Tune thy temper to these sounds,　　5
　　And quicken so thy joyless mind;
　Sloth the worst and best confounds,
　　It is the ruin of mankind.

　From her cave rise all distastes,
　　Which unresolved despair pursues,　　10
　Whom soon after violence hastes
　　Herself ungrateful to abuse.
　Skies are cleared with stirring winds,
　　Th'unmoved water moorish grows.
　Every eye much pleasure finds　　15
　　To view a stream that brightly flows.

XX

JACK and Joan they think no ill,
But loving live, and merry still;
Do their weekdays' work, and pray
Devoutly on the holy day:
Skip and trip it on the green,   5
And help to choose the Summer Queen.
Lash out at a country feast
Their silver penny with the best.

Well can they judge of nappy ale,
And tell at large a winter tale.   10
Climb up to the apple loft,
And turn the crabs till they be soft.
Tib is all the father's joy,
And little Tom the mother's boy,
All their pleasure is content,   15
And care to pay their yearly rent.

Joan can call by name her cows,
And deck her windows with green boughs.
She can wreaths and tutties make,
And trim with plums a bridal cake.   20
Jack knows what brings gain or loss,
And his long flail can stoutly toss;
Make the hedge which others break,
And ever thinks what he doth speak.

Now you courtly dames and knights,   25
That study only strange delights,
Though you scorn the home-spun grey
And revel in your rich array,
Though your tongues dissemble deep
And can your heads from danger keep,   30
Yet for all your pomp and train,
Securer lives the silly swain.

XXI

ALL looks be pale, hearts cold as stone,
For Hally now is dead and gone.
　　Hally in whose sight,
　　　　Most sweet sight,
All the earth late took delight.   5

Every eye weep with me,
Joys drowned in tears must be.

His ivory skin, his comely hair,
His rosy cheeks so clear and fair,
   Eyes that once did grace   10
     His bright face,
Now in him all want their place.
   Eyes and hearts weep with me,
   For who so kind as he?

His youth was like an April flower,   15
Adorned with beauty, love, and power.
   Glory strowed his way,
     Whose wreaths gay
Now are all turned to decay.
   Then again weep with me,   20
   None feel more cause than we.

No more may his wished sight return
His golden lamp no more can burn.
   Quenched is all his flame,
     His hoped fame   25
Now hath left him nought but name.
   For him all weep with me,
   Since more him none shall see.

*The Second Booke of Ayres. Containing Light Conceits of Louers. To be sung
to the Lute and Viols, in two, and three Parts: or by one Voyce to an Instrv-
ment.* [c. 1613]

I

VAIN men, whose follies make a god of Love,
   Whose blindness beauty doth immortal deem,
Praise not what you desire but what you prove;
   Count those things good that are, not those that seem.
I cannot call her true that's false to me,   5
Nor make of women more than women be.

How fair an entrance breaks the way to love,
　How rich of golden hope and gay delight.
What heart cannot a modest beauty move?
　Who seeing clear day once will dream of night?　10
She seemed a saint that brake her faith with me,
But proved a woman, as all other be.

So bitter is their sweet that true content
　Unhappy men in them may never find.
Ah! but without them none! Both must consent,　15
　Else uncouth are the joys of either kind.
Let us then praise their good, forget their ill.
Men must be men, and women women still.

11

　HOW eas'ly wert thou chained,
　Fond heart, by favours feigned.
　Why lived thy hopes in grace
　Straight to die disdained?
　But since thou'rt now beguiled　5
　By Love that falsely smiled,
　In some less happy place
　Mourn alone exiled.
　My love still here increaseth,
　And with my love my grief;　10
　While her sweet bounty ceaseth
　That gave my woes relief.
　Yet 'tis no woman leaves me,
　For such may prove unjust.
　A goddess thus deceives me,　15
　Whose faith who could mistrust?

　A goddess so much graced,
　That Paradise is placed
　In her most heavenly breast,
　Once by love embraced.　20
　But love that so kind proved
　Is now from her removed,
　Nor will he longer rest,
　Where no faith is loved.

If powers celestial wound us, 25
And will not yield relief,
Woe then must needs confound us,
For none can cure our grief.
No wonder if I languish
Through burden of my smart, 30
It is no common anguish
From Paradise to part.

III

HARDEN now thy tired heart with more than flinty rage;
Ne'er let her false tears henceforth thy constant grief assuage.
Once true happy days thou saw'st, when she stood firm and kind;
Both as one then lived, and held one ear, one tongue, one mind.
But now those bright hours be fled, and never may return. 5
  What then remains but her untruths to mourn?

Silly traitress, who shall now thy careless tresses place?
Who thy pretty talk supply? Whose ear thy music grace?
Who shall thy bright eyes admire? What lips triumph with thine?
Day by day who'll visit thee, and say: thou'rt only mine? 10
Such a time there was, God wot, but such shall never be.
  Too oft, I fear, thou wilt remember me.

IV

O WHAT unhoped-for sweet supply!
 O what joys exceeding!
What an affecting charm feel I
 From delight proceeding!
That which I long despaired to be, 5
To her I am, and she to me.

She that alone in cloudy grief
 Long to me appeared,
She now alone with bright relief
 All those clouds hath cleared. 10
Both are immortal and divine,
Since I am hers, and she is mine.

V

WHERE she her sacred bower adorns
   The rivers clearly flow,
The groves and meadows swell with flowers,
   The winds all gently blow.
Her sun-like beauty shines so fair,   5
   Her Spring can never fade;
Who then can blame the life that strives
   To harbour in her shade?

Her grace I sought, her love I wooed.
   Her love though I obtain,   10
No time, no toil, no vow, no faith
   Her wished grace can gain.
Yet truth can tell my heart is hers,
   And her will I adore;
And from that love when I depart,   15
   Let heaven view me no more.

Her roses with my prayers shall spring,
   And when her trees I praise,
Their boughs shall blossom; mellow fruit
   Shall straw her pleasant ways.   20
The words of hearty zeal have power
   High wonders to effect.
O why should then her princely ear
   My words or zeal neglect?

If she my faith misdeems, or worth,   25
   Woe-worth my hapless fate.
For though time can my truth reveal,
   That time will come too late.
And who can glory in the worth
   That cannot yield him grace?   30
Content in everything is not,
   Nor joy in every place.

But from her bower of joy since I
   Must now excluded be,
And she will not relieve my cares,   35
   Which none can help but she:

My comfort in her love shall dwell,
   Her love lodge in my breast,
And though not in her bower, yet I
   Shall in her temple rest.   40

VI

FAIN would I my love disclose,
   Ask what honour might deny;
But both love and her I lose
   From my motion if she fly.
Worse than pain is fear to me,   5
   Then hold in fancy though it burn.
If not happy, safe I'll be,
   And to my cloistered cares return.

Yet, O yet in vain I strive
   To repress my schooled desire.   10
More and more the flames revive,
   I consume in mine own fire.
She would pity, might she know
   The harms that I for her endure.
Speak then and get comfort so,   15
   A wound long hid grows past recure.

Wise she is, and needs must know
   All th' attempts that beauty moves.
Fair she is and honoured so
   That she sure hath tried some loves.   20
If with love I tempt her then,
   'Tis but her due to be desired;
What would women think of men
   If their deserts were not admired?

Women courted have the hand   25
   To discard what they distaste.
But those dames whom none demand
   Want oft what their wills embraced.
Could their firmness iron excel,
   As they are fair, they should be sought.   30
When true thieves use falsehood well,
   As they are wise they will be caught.

VII

GIVE beauty all her right.
    She's not to one form tied.
Each shape yields fair delight,
    Where her perfections bide.
Helen I grant might pleasing be,   5
And Ros'mund was as sweet as she.

Some the quick eye commends,
    Some swelling lips and red;
Pale looks have many friends,
    Through sacred sweetness bred.   10
Meadows have flowers that pleasure move,
Though roses are the flowers of love.

Free beauty is not bound
    To one unmoved clime.
She visits every ground,   15
    And favours every time.
Let the old loves with mine compare,
My sovereign is as sweet and fair.

VIII

O, DEAR, that I with thee might live
    From human trace removed;
Where jealous care might neither grieve,
    Yet each dote on their loved.
While fond fear may colour find, love's seldom pleased,   5
But much like a sick man's rest, it's soon diseased.

Why should our minds not mingle so,
    When love and faith is plighted,
That either might the other's know,
    Alike in all delighted?   10
Why should frailty breed suspect when hearts are fixed?
Must all human joys of force with grief be mixed?

How oft have we ev'n smiled in tears,
    Our fond mistrust repenting!
As snow when heavenly fire appears,   15
    So melts love's hate relenting.
Vexed kindness soon falls off and soon returneth:
Such a flame the more you quench, the more it burneth.

IX

GOOD men, show if you can tell,
Where doth human pity dwell.
Far and near her would I seek,
   So vexed with sorrow is my breast.
She, they say, to all is meek,   5
   And only makes th' unhappy blest.

O if such a saint there be,
Some hope yet remains for me.
Prayer or sacrifice may gain
   From her implored grace relief   10
To release me of my pain,
   Or at the least to ease my grief.

Young am I, and far from guile,
The more is my woe the while.
Falsehood with a smooth disguise   15
   My simple meaning hath abused,
Casting mists before mine eyes,
   By which my senses are confused.

Fair he is, who vowed to me
That he only mine would be.   20
But, alas, his mind is caught
   With every gaudy bait he sees;
And too late my flame is taught
   That too much kindness makes men freeze.

From me all my friends are gone,   25
While I pine for him alone.
And not one will rue my case,
   But rather my distress deride,
That I think there is no place
   Where pity ever yet did bide.   30

X

WHAT harvest half so sweet is
As still to reap the kisses
   Grown ripe in sowing;
And straight to be receiver
Of that which thou art giver,   5
   Rich in bestowing?

Kiss then, my harvest Queen,
   Full garners heaping.
Kisses, ripest when they're green,
   Want only reaping.   10

The dove alone expresses
Her fervency in kisses.
   Of all most loving,
A creature as offenceless
As those things that are senseless   15
   And void of moving.
Let us so love and kiss,
   Though all envy us;
That which kind and harmless is,
   None can deny us.   20

XI

SWEET, exclude me not, nor be divided
   From him that ere long must bed thee.
All thy maiden doubts law hath decided;
   Sure we are, and I must wed thee.
Presume then yet a little more,   5
Here's the way, bar not the door.

Tenants to fulfil their landlord's pleasure
   Pay their rent before the quarter.
'Tis my case, if you it rightly measure.
   Put me not then off with laughter.   10
Consider then a little more.
Here's the way to all my store.

Why were doors in love's despite devised?
   Are not laws enough restraining?
Women are most apt to be surprised   15
   Sleeping, or sleep wisely feigning.
Then grace me yet a little more.
Here's the way, bar not the door.

XII

THE peaceful western wind
   The winter storms hath tamed;
And Nature in each kind
   The kind heat hath inflamed.

The forward buds so sweetly breathe   5
  Out of their earthy bowers,
That heaven, which views their pomp beneath,
  Would fain be decked with flowers.

    See how the morning smiles
      On her bright eastern hill;   10
    And with soft steps beguiles
      Them that lie slumbering still.
The music-loving birds are come
  From cliffs and rocks unknown
To see the trees and briars bloom,   15
  That late were over-flown.

    What Saturn did destroy,
      Love's queen revives again;
    And now her naked boy
      Doth in the fields remain,   20
Where he such pleasing change doth view
  In every living thing,
As if the world were born anew
  To gratify the Spring.

    If all things life present,   25
      Why die my comforts then?
    Why suffers my content?
      Am I the worst of men?
O Beauty, be not thou accused
  Too justly in this case;   30
Unkindly if true love be used,
  'Twill yield thee little grace.

              XIII

THERE is none, O none but you,
  That from me estrange your sight,
Whom mine eyes affect to view,
  Or chained ears hear with delight.

Other beauties others move,   5
  In you I all graces find.
Such is the effect of love
  To make them happy that are kind.

Women in frail beauty trust.
　Only seem you fair to me;　　　　　　　　　　10
Yet prove truly kind and just,
　For that may not dissembled be.

Sweet, afford me then your sight;
　That, surveying all your looks,
Endless volumes I may write,　　　　　　　　　15
　And fill the world with envied books.

Which when after ages view,
　All shall wonder and despair:
Woman to find man so true,
　Or man a woman half so fair.　　　　　　　　20

XIV

PINED I am, and like to die,
And all for lack of that which I
　Do every day refuse.
If I musing sit, or stand,
Some puts it daily in my hand　　　　　　　　　5
　To interrupt my muse.
The same thing I seek and fly,
And want that which none would deny.

In my bed, when I should rest,
It breeds such trouble in my breast　　　　　　10
　That scarce mine eyes will close.
If I sleep, it seems to be
Oft playing in the bed with me,
　But, waked, away it goes.
'Tis some spirit sure I ween,　　　　　　　　　15
And yet it may be felt and seen.

Would I had the heart and wit
To make it stand, and conjure it
　That haunts me thus with fear.
Doubtless 'tis some harmless sprite,　　　　　　20
For it by day as well as night
　Is ready to appear.
Be it friend or be it foe,
Ere long I'll try what it will do.

XV

So many loves have I neglected,
  Whose good parts might move me,
That now I live of all rejected,
  There is none will love me.
Why is maiden heat so coy?   5
  It freezeth when it burneth,
Loseth what it might enjoy,
  And having lost it, mourneth.

Should I then woo, that have been wooed,
  Seeking them that fly me?   10
When I my faith with tears have vowed,
  And when all deny me?
Who will pity my disgrace
  Which love might have prevented?
There is no submission base,   15
  Where error is repented.

O happy men, whose hopes are licensed
  To discourse their passion,
While women are confined to silence,
  Losing wished occasion.   20
Yet our tongues than theirs, men say,
  Are apter to be moving.
Women are more dumb than they,
  But in their thoughts more roving.

When I compare my former strangeness   25
  With my present doting,
I pity men that speak in plainness,
  Their true hearts devoting.
While we with repentance jest
  At their submissive passion,   30
Maids, I see, are never blest
  That strange be but for fashion.

XVI

THOUGH your strangeness frets my heart,
  Yet may not I complain.
You persuade me 'tis but art
  That secret love must feign.

　　　If another you affect,　　　　　　　　　　　5
　　　'Tis but a show t' avoid suspect.
　Is this fair excusing? O no, all is abusing.

　　　Your wished sight if I desire,
　　　　Suspicions you pretend.
　　　Causeless you yourself retire,　　　　　　10
　　　　While I in vain attend.
　　　This a lover whets, you say,
　　　Still made more eager by delay.
　Is this fair excusing? O no, all is abusing.

　　　When another holds your hand,　　　　　15
　　　　You swear I hold your heart.
　　　When my rivals close do stand,
　　　　And I sit far apart,
　　　I am nearer yet than they,
　　　Hid in your bosom, as you say.　　　　　20
　Is this fair excusing? O no, all is abusing.

　　　Would my rival then I were,
　　　　Some else your secret friend.
　　　So much lesser should I fear,
　　　　And not so much attend.　　　　　　　25
　　　They enjoy you every one,
　　　Yet I must seem your friend alone.
　Is this fair excusing? O no, all is abusing.

XVII

　COME away, armed with love's delights,
　Thy spriteful graces bring with thee;
　　　When Love and Longing fights
　　　They must the sticklers be.
Come quickly, come! The promised hour is well nigh spent,　　5
And pleasure being too much deferred, loseth her best content.

　　Is she come? O how near is she?
　How far yet from this friendly place?
　　　How many steps from me?
　　　When shall I her embrace?　　　　　　10
These arms I'll spread, which only at her sight shall close,
Attending as the starry flower that the sun's noontide knows.

XVIII

CO ME, you pretty false-eyed wanton,
   Leave your crafty smiling.
Think you to escape me now
   With slipp'ry words beguiling?
No, you mocked me th' other day,   5
When you got loose, you fled away.
But since I have caught you now,
   I'll clip your wings for flying;
Smoth'ring kisses fast I'll heap,
   And keep you so from crying.   10

Sooner may you count the stars,
   And number hail down-pouring,
Tell the osiers of the Thames,
   Or Goodwin's Sands devouring,
Than the thick-showered kisses here,   15
Which now thy tired lips must bear.
Such a harvest never was,
   So rich and full of pleasure.
But 'tis spent as soon as reaped,
   So trustless is love's treasure.   20

Would it were dumb midnight now,
   When all the world lies sleeping.
Would this place some desert were,
   Which no man hath in keeping.
My desires should then be safe,   25
And when you cried, then would I laugh.
But if ought might breed offence,
   Love only should be blamed.
I would live your servant still,
   And you my saint unnamed.   30

XIX

A SECRET love or two, I must confess,
   I kindly welcome for change in close playing.
Yet my dear husband I love ne'er the less,
   His desires, whole or half, quickly allaying,
At all times ready to offer redress.   5
     His own he never wants but hath it duly,
     Yet twits me I keep not touch with him truly.

The more a spring is drawn, the more it flows.
　No lamp less light retains by lightening others.
Is he a loser his loss that ne'er knows?　　　　　　　　10
　Or is he wealthy that waste treasure smothers?
My churl vows no man shall scent his sweet rose.
　　His own enough and more I give him duly,
　　Yet still he twits me I keep not touch truly.

Wise archers bear more than one shaft to field.　　　15
　The venturer loads not with one ware his shipping.
Should warriors learn but one weapon to wield?
　Or thrive fair plants e'er the worse for the slipping?
One dish cloys, many fresh appetite yield.
　　Mine own I'll use, and his he shall have duly.　　20
　　Judge then what debtor can keep touch more truly.

XX

Her rosy cheeks, her ever-smiling eyes,
Are spheres and beds where love in triumph lies.
Her rubine lips, when they their pearl unlock,
　　Make them seem as they did rise
　　　All out of one smooth coral rock.　　　　　　5
O that of other creatures' store I knew
　　More worthy and more rare;
　　For these are old, and she so new,
　　　That her to them none should compare.

O could she love, would she but hear a friend,　　10
Or that she only knew what sighs pretend!
Her looks inflame, yet cold as ice is she.
　　Do or speak, all's to one end;
　　　For what she is, that will she be.
Yet will I never cease her praise to sing,　　　　15
　　Though she gives no regard;
　　For they that grace a worthless thing
　　　Are only greedy of reward.

XXI

Where shall I refuge seek, if you refuse me?
　In you my hope, in you my fortune lies,
In you my life; though you unjust accuse me,
　My service scorn, and merit underprise.

O bitter grief, that exile is become   5
Reward for faith, and pity deaf and dumb!

Why should my firmness find a fear so wavering?
   My simple vows, my love you entertained,
Without desert the same again disfavouring;
   Yet I my word and passion hold unstained.   10
O wretched me, that my chief joy should breed
My only grief, and kindness pity need!

ຕຕຕຕຕຕຕຕຕ

The Description of a Maske: Presented in the Banqueting roome at White-
hall, on Saint Stephens night last, At the Mariage of the Right Honourable the
Earle of Somerset: And the right noble the Lady Frances Howard. 1614

I

Made and expressed by Mr. Nicholas Lanier

BRING away this sacred tree,
The tree of grace and bounty,
   Set it in Bel-Anna's eye,
For she, she, only she
   Can all knotted spells untie.   5
Pulled from this stock, let her blessed hand convey
   To any suppliant hand a bough,
   And let that hand advance it now
Against a charm, that charm shall fade away.

These three songs following were composed by Mr. Coprario, and sung by Mr.
John Allen and Mr. Lanier

II

GO, happy man, like th' evening star
Whose beams to bridegrooms welcome are;
May neither hag nor fiend withstand
The power of thy victorious hand.
   Th' uncharmed knights surrender now,   5
   By virtue of thy raised bough.

Away, enchantments, vanish quite,
No more delay our longing sight;

'Tis fruitless to contend with Fate,
Who gives us power against your hate.   10
  Brave knights, in courtly pomp appear,
  For now are you long looked-for here.

III

WHILE dancing rests, fit place to music granting,
Good spells the Fates shall breathe, all envy daunting,
  Kind ears with joy enchanting.
    Io, Io Hymen.

Like looks, like hearts, like loves are linked together;   5
So must the Fates be pleased, so come they hither,
  To make this joy persever.
    Io, Io Hymen.

Love decks the Spring, her buds to th'air exposing
Such fire here in these bridal breasts reposing,   10
  We leave with charms enclosing,
    Io, Io Hymen.

IV

COME ashore, come merry mates,
With your nimble heels and pates,
Summon every man his knight,
Enough honoured is this night.
Now, let your sea-born goddess come,   5
Quench these lights and make all dumb;
Some sleep, others let her call,
And so goodnight to all, goodnight to all.

Haste aboard, haste now away,
Hymen frowns at your delay.   10
Hymen doth long nights affect,
Yield him then his due respect.
The sea-born goddess straight will come,
Quench these lights and make all dumb;
Some sleep, others she will call,   15
And so goodnight to all, goodnight to all.

V

Song, made by Thos. Campian, and sung in the Lords Masque at the Count
Palatine's marriage, we have here added, to fill up these empty pages.

> Woo her and win her, he that can,
>   Each woman hath two lovers,
> So she must take and leave a man,
>   Till time more grace discovers.
> This doth Jove to show that want   5
>   Makes beauty more respected.
> If fair women were more scant
>   They would be more affected.
>
> Courtship and music suit with love,
>   They both are works of passion;   10
> Happy is he whose words can move,
>   Yet sweet notes help persuasion.
> Mix your words with music then,
>   That they the more may enter;
> Bold assaults are fit for men   15
>   That on strange beauties venter.

The Third . . . Booke Of Ayres: Composed. . . . So as they may be expressed
by one Voyce, with a Violl, Lute, or Orpharion. [*c. 1618*]

I

> Oft have I sighed for him that hears me not,
> Who, absent, hath both love and me forgot.
> O yet I languish still through his delay.
> Days seem as years when wished friends break their day.
>
> Had he but loved as common lovers use,   5
> His faithless stay some kindness would excuse.
> O yet I languish still, still constant mourn
> For him that can break vows but not return.

II

> Now let her change and spare not.
> Since she proves strange, I care not.

Feigned love charmed so my delight,
That still I doted on her sight.
But she is gone, new joys embracing,   5
    And my desires disgracing.

When did I err in blindness,
Or vex her with unkindness?
If my cares served her alone,
Why is she thus untimely gone?   10
True love abides to th' hour of dying.
    False love is ever flying.

False, then farewell for ever.
Once false proves faithful never.
He that boasts now of thy love   15
Shall soon my present fortunes prove.
Were he as fair as bright Adonis,
    Faith is not had where none is.

III

WERE my heart as some men's are thy errors would not move me;
But thy faults I curious find, and speak because I love thee.
Patience is a thing divine, and far, I grant, above me.

Foes sometimes befriend us more, our blacker deeds objecting,
Than th' obsequious bosom guest with false respect affecting.   5
Friendship is the glass of Truth, our hidden stains detecting.

While I use of eyes enjoy and inward light of reason,
Thy observer will I be, and censor, but in season.
Hidden mischief to conceal in State and Love is treason.

IV

MAIDS are simple, some men say.
    They forsooth will trust no men.
But should they men's wills obey,
    Maids were very simple then.

Truth a rare flower now is grown,   5
    Few men wear it in their hearts.
Lovers are more easily known
    By their follies than deserts.

Safer may we credit give
   To a faithless wandering Jew,   10
Than a young man's vows believe,
   When he swears his love is true.

Love they make a poor blind child,
   But let none trust such as he.
Rather than to be beguiled   15
   Ever let me simple be.

V

So tired are all my thoughts that sense and spirits fail.
   Mourning I pine, and know not what I ail.
      O what can yield ease to a mind,
      Joy in nothing that can find?

How are my powers forespoke? What strange distaste is this? 5
   Hence cruel hate of that which sweetest is!
      Come, come, delight, make my dull brain
      Feel once heat of joy again.

The lover's tears are sweet, their mover makes them so.
   Proud of a wound the bleeding soldiers grow.   10
      Poor I alone, dreaming, endure
      Grief that knows nor cause nor cure.

And whence can all this grow? Even from an idle mind
   That no delight in any good can find.
      Action alone makes the soul blest.   15
      Virtue dies with too much rest.

VI

Why presumes thy pride on that that must so private be,
Scarce that it can good be called, though it seems best to thee,
Best of all that Nature framed, or curious eye can see?

'Tis thy beauty, foolish maid, that like a blossom grows,
Which who views no more enjoys than on a bush a rose,   5
That by many's handling fades, and thou art one of those.

If to one thou shalt prove true and all beside reject,
Then art thou but one man's good, which yields a poor effect,
For the common'st good by far deserves the best respect.

But if for this goodness thou thyself wilt common make,   10
Thou art then not good at all. So thou canst no way take
But to prove the meanest good, or else all good forsake.

Be not then of beauty proud, but so her colours bear
That they prove not stains to her that them for grace should wear;
So shalt thou to all more fair than thou wert born appear.   15

VII

KIND are her answers,
But her performance keeps no day;
Breaks time, as dancers
From their own music when they stray.
All her free favours   5
And smooth words wing my hopes in vain.
O did ever voice so sweet but only feign?
Can true love yield such delay,
Converting joy to pain?

Lost is our freedom   10
When we submit to women so.
Why do we need them
When in their best they work our woe?
There is no wisdom
Can alter ends by Fate prefixed.   15
O why is the good of man with evil mixed?
Never were days yet called two,
But one night went betwixt.

VIII

O GRIEF, O spite, to see poor Virtue scorned,
Truth far exiled, false Art loved, Vice adored,
Free Justice sold, worst causes best adorned,
Right cast by Power, Pity in vain implored.
O who in such an age could wish to live,   5
When none can have or hold but such as give?

O times, O men, to Nature rebels grown,
Poor in desert, in name rich, proud of shame;
Wise but in ill, your styles are not your own;
Though dearly bought, honour is honest fame.   10
Old stories only goodness now contain,
And the true wisdom that is just and plain.

IX

O NEVER to be moved,
    O beauty unrelenting!
Hard heart, too dearly loved,
    Fond love, too late repenting!
Why did I dream of too much bliss?   5
Deceitful hope was cause of this.
O hear me speak this and no more:
Live you in joy, while I my woes deplore.

    All comforts despaired,
        Distaste your bitter scorning.   10
    Great sorrows unrepaired
        Admit no mean in mourning.
Die, wretch, since hope from thee is fled.
He that must die is better dead.
O dear delight, yet ere I die   15
Some pity show, though you relief deny.

X

BREAK now, my heart, and die. O no, she may relent.
Let my despair prevail. O stay, hope is not spent.
Should she now fix one smile on thee, where were despair?
    The loss is but easy which smiles can repair;
    A stranger would please thee if she were as fair.   5

Her must I love or none, so sweet none breathes as she.
The more is my despair, alas, she loves not me.
But cannot Time make way for Love through ribs of steel?
    The Grecian, enchanted all parts but the heel,
    At last a shaft daunted which his heart did feel.   10

XI

IF Love loves Truth, then women do not love.
    Their passions all are but dissembled shows.
Now kind and free of favour if they prove,
    Their kindness straight a tempest overthrows.
Then as a seaman the poor lover fares;   5
The storm drowns him ere he can drown his cares.

But why accuse I women that deceive?
  Blame then the foxes for their subtle wile.
They first from Nature did their craft receive;
  It is a woman's nature to beguile.   10
Yet some I grant in loving steadfast grow;
But such by Use are made, not Nature, so.

O why had Nature power at once to frame
  Deceit and Beauty, traitors both to Love!
O would Deceit had died when Beauty came   15
  With her divineness every heart to move!
Yet do we rather wish, whate'er befall,
To have fair women false than none at all.

XII

N O W winter nights enlarge
  The number of their hours,
And clouds their storms discharge
  Upon the airy towers.
Let now the chimneys blaze,   5
  And cups o'erflow with wine.
Let well-tuned words amaze
  With harmony divine.
Now yellow waxen lights
  Shall wait on honey love,   10
While youthful revels, masks, and courtly sights
  Sleep's leaden spells remove.

This time doth well dispense
  With lovers' long discourse.
Much speech hath some defence   15
  Though beauty no remorse.
All do not all things well:
  Some measures comely tread,
Some knotted riddles tell,
  Some poems smoothly read.   20
The Summer hath his joys,
  And Winter his delights.
Though Love and all his pleasures are but toys,
  They shorten tedious nights.

XIII

AWAKE, thou spring of speaking grace, mute rest becomes not thee.
The fairest women, while they sleep, and pictures, equal be.
    O come and dwell in love's discourses,
        Old renewing, new creating.
    The words which thy rich tongue discourses   5
        Are not of the common rating.

Thy voice is as an echo clear, which music doth beget;
Thy speech is as an oracle which none can counterfeit.
    For thou alone, without offending,
        Hast obtained power of enchanting;   10
    And I could hear thee without ending,
        Other comfort never wanting.

Some little reason brutish lives with human glory share;
But language is our proper grace, from which they severed are.
    As brutes in reason man surpasses,   15
        Men in speech excel each other.
    If speech be then the best of graces,
        Do it not in slumber smother.

XIV

WHAT is it all that men possess, among themselves conversing?
Wealth or Fame or some such boast scarce worthy the rehearsing.
Women only are men's good, with them in love conversing.

If weary, they prepare us rest; if sick, their hand attends us.
When with grief our hearts are pressed, their comfort best befriends
    us.   5
Sweet or sour, they willing go to share what Fortune sends us.

What pretty babes with pain they bear, our name and form present-
    ing.
What we get, how wise they keep; by sparing, wants preventing.
Sorting all their household cares to our observed contenting.

All this of whose large use I sing in two words is expressed: 10
'Good wife' is the good I praise, if by good men possessed.
Bad with bad in ill suit well, but good with good live blessed.

XV

FIRE that must flame is with apt fuel fed.
Flowers that will thrive in sunny soil are bred.
How can a heart feel heat that no hope finds?
Or can he love on whom no comfort shines?

Fair, I confess there's pleasure in your sight.   5
Sweet, you have power, I grant, of all delight.
But what is all to me if I have none?
Churl that you are t' enjoy such wealth alone.

Prayers move the heavens but find no grace with you,
Yet in your looks a heavenly form I view.   10
Then will I pray again, hoping to find,
As well as in your looks, heaven in your mind.

Saint of my heart, Queen of my life and love,
O let my vows thy loving spirit move!
Let me no longer mourn through thy disdain,   15
But with one touch of grace cure all my pain.

XVI

IF thou long'st so much to learn, sweet boy, what 'tis to love,
Do but fix thy thought on me, and thou shalt quickly prove.
          Little suit at first shall win
          Way to thy abashed desire;
          But then will I hedge thee in,   5
          Salamander-like, with fire.

With thee dance I will and sing, and thy fond dalliance bear;
We the grovy hills will climb and play the wantons there.
          Otherwhiles we'll gather flowers,
          Lying dallying on the grass,   10
          And thus our delightful hours
          Full of waking dreams shall pass.

When thy joys were thus at height my love should turn from thee;
Old acquaintance then should grow as strange as strange might be;
          Twenty rivals thou should'st find   15
          Breaking all their hearts for me;
          When to all I'll prove more kind
          And more forward than to thee.

Thus thy silly youth enraged would soon my love defy.
But alas, poor soul, too late; clipped wings can never fly.　　20
    Those sweet hours which we had passed,
      Called to mind thy heart would burn;
    And could'st thou fly ne'er so fast,
      They would make thee straight return.

XVII

    SHALL I come, sweet love, to thee
      When the evening beams are set?
    Shall I not excluded be?
      Will you find no feigned let?
    Let me not, for pity, more　　5
    Tell the long hours at your door.

    Who can tell what thief or foe
      In the covert of the night
    For his prey will work my woe,
      Or through wicked foul despite?　　10
    So may I die unredressed,
    Ere my long love be possessed.

    But to let such dangers pass,
      Which a lover's thoughts disdain,
    'Tis enough in such a place　　15
      To attend Love's joys in vain.
    Do not mock me in thy bed,
    While these cold nights freeze me dead.

XVIII

THRICE toss these oaken ashes in the air.
Thrice sit thou mute in this enchanted chair.
Then thrice three times tie up this true love's knot,
And murmur soft: She will, or she will not.

Go burn these pois'nous weeds in yon blue fire,　　5
These screech-owl's feathers and this prickling briar,
This cypress gathered at a dead man's grave,
That all thy fears and cares an end may have.

Then come, you fairies, dance with me a round;
Melt her hard heart with your melodious sound.　　10
In vain are all the charms I can devise;
She hath an art to break them with her eyes.

XIX

Be thou then my beauty named,
  Since thy will is to be mine.
For by that am I inflamed,
  Which on all alike doth shine.
Others may the light admire,   5
I only truly feel the fire.

But if lofty titles move thee,
  Challenge then a sovereign's place.
Say I honour when I love thee,
  Let me call thy kindness grace.   10
State and Love things diverse be,
Yet will we teach them to agree.

Or if this be not sufficing,
  Be thou styled my goddess then;
I will love thee, sacrificing,   15
  In thine honour hymns I'll pen.
To be thine, what canst thou more?
I'll love thee, serve thee, and adore.

XX

Fire! Fire! Fire! Fire!
Lo, here I burn in such desire,
That all the tears that I can strain
Out of mine idle empty brain
Cannot allay my scorching pain.   5
Come Trent and Humber and fair Thames,
Dread Ocean haste with all thy streams,
And if you cannot quench my fire,
O drown both me and my desire!

Fire! Fire! Fire! Fire!   10
There is no hell to my desire.
See all the rivers backward fly,
And th' Ocean doth his waves deny,
For fear my heat should drink them dry.
Come heavenly showers then pouring down,   15
Come you that once the world did drown.

Some then you spared, but now save all
That else must burn and with me fall.

XXI

O SWEET delight, O more than human bliss,
With her to live that ever loving is!
To hear her speak whose words so well are placed,
That she by them, as they in her, are graced;
Those looks to view that feast the viewer's eye,   5
How blest is he that may so live and die!

Such love as this the golden times did know,
When all did reap, yet none took care to sow.
Such love as this an endless summer makes,
And all distaste from frail affection takes.   10
So loved, so blest in my beloved am I,
Which till their eyes ache, let iron men envy.

XXII

THUS I resolve, and time hath taught me so,
   Since she is fair and ever kind to me,
Though she be wild and wanton-like in show,
   Those little stains in youth I will not see.
That she be constant, heaven I oft implore.   5
If prayers prevail not, I can do no more.

Palm-tree the more you press, the more it grows;
   Leave it alone, it will not much exceed.
Free beauty if you strive to yoke, you lose,
   And for affection strange distaste you breed.   10
What Nature hath not taught, no art can frame.
Wild-born be wild still, though by force made tame.

XXIII

COME, O come, my life's delight,
   Let me not in languor pine.
Love loves no delay; thy sight
   The more enjoyed the more divine.
O come, and take from me   5
The pain of being deprived of thee.

Thou all sweetness dost enclose
   Like a little world of bliss.
Beauty guards thy looks. The rose
   In them pure and eternal is.   10
Come then and make thy flight
As swift to me as heavenly light.

XXIV

COULD my heart more tongues employ
   Than it harbours thoughts of grief;
It is now so far from joy
   That it scarce could ask relief.
Truest hearts by deeds unkind   5
To despair are most inclined.

Happy minds that can redeem
   Their engagements how they please,
That no joys or hopes esteem
   Half so precious as their ease.   10
Wisdom should prepare men so
As if they did all foreknow.

Yet no art or caution can
   Grown affections easily change.
Use is such a lord of man   15
   That he brooks worst what is strange.
Better never to be blest
Than to lose all at the best.

XXV

SLEEP, angry Beauty, sleep, and fear not me.
   For who a sleeping lion dares provoke?
It shall suffice me here to sit and see
   Those lips shut up that never kindly spoke.
What sight can more content a lover's mind   5
Than beauty seeming harmless, if not kind?

My words have charmed her, for secure she sleeps,
   Though guilty much of wrong done to my love.
And in her slumber, see, she close-eyed weeps.
   Dreams often more than waking passions move.   10
Plead, Sleep, my cause, and make her soft like thee,
That she in peace may wake, and pity me.

XXVI

SILLY boy, 'tis full moon yet, thy night as day shines clearly.
Had thy youth but wit to fear, thou couldst not love so dearly.
Shortly wilt thou mourn when all thy pleasures are bereaved;
Little knows he how to love that never was deceived.

This is thy first maiden flame that triumphs yet unstained.   5
All is artless now you speak, not one word yet is feigned.
All is heaven that you behold, and all your thoughts are blessed.
But no Spring can want his Fall, each Troilus hath his Cressid.

Thy well-ordered locks ere long shall rudely hang neglected;
And thy lively pleasant cheer read grief on earth dejected.   10
Much then wilt thou blame thy Saint, that made thy heart so holy;
And with sighs confess in love that too much faith is folly.

Yet be just and constant still, Love may beget a wonder,
Not unlike a Summer's frost, or Winter's fatal thunder.
He that holds his sweetheart true unto his day of dying,   15
Lives of all that ever breathed most worthy the envying.

XXVII

NEVER love unless you can
Bear with all the faults of man.
Men sometimes will jealous be,
Though but little cause they see,
And hang the head as discontent,   5
And speak what straight they will repent.

Men that but one saint adore
Make a show of love to more.
Beauty must be scorned in none,
Though but truly served in one.   10
For what is courtship but disguise?
True hearts may have dissembling eyes.

Men when their affairs require
Must awhile themselves retire;
Sometimes hunt, and sometimes hawk,   15
And not ever sit and talk.
If these and such like you can bear,
Then like and love and never fear.

XXVIII

So quick, so hot, so mad is thy fond suit,
   So rude, so tedious grown in urging me,
That fain I would with loss make thy tongue mute,
   And yield some little grace to quiet thee.
An hour with thee I care not to converse,   5
For I would not be counted too perverse.

But roofs too hot would prove for men all fire;
   And hills too high for my unused pace.
The grove is charged with thorns and the bold briar;
   Gray snakes the meadows shroud in every place.   10
A yellow frog, alas, will fright me so
As I should start and tremble as I go.

Since then I can on earth no fit room find,
   In heaven I am resolved with you to meet.
Till then for hope's sweet sake rest your tired mind,   15
   And not so much as see me in the street.
A heavenly meeting one day we shall have,
But never, as you dream, in bed or grave.

XXIX

Shall I then hope when faith is fled?
   Can I seek love when hope is gone?
Or can I live when love is dead?
   Poorly he lives that can love none.
Her vows are broke, and I am free,   5
She lost her faith in losing me.

When I compare mine own events,
   When I weigh others' like annoy,
All do but heap up discontents
   That on a beauty build their joy.   10
Thus I of all complain, since she
All faith hath lost in losing me.

So my dear freedom have I gained
   Through her unkindness and disgrace.
Yet could I ever live enchained,   15
   As she my service did embrace.
But she is changed, and I am free.
Faith failing her, love died in me.

The . . . Fovrth Booke Of Ayres: Composed. . . . So as they may be expressed
by one Voyce, with a Violl, Lute, or Orpharion. [*c. 1618*]

I

LEAVE prolonging thy distress;
All delays afflict the dying.
Many lost sighs long I spent, to her for mercy crying.
    But now, vain mourning, cease,
      I'll die, and mine own griefs release.   5

Thus departing from this light
To those shades that end all sorrow,
Yet a small time of complaint, a little breath I'll borrow,
    To tell my once delight
      I die alone through her despite.   10

II

RESPECT my faith, regard my service past;
The hope you winged, call home to you at last.
Great prize it is that I in you shall gain,
So great for you hath been my loss and pain.
My wits I spent, and time, for you alone,   5
Observing you and losing all for one.

Some raised to rich estates in this time are,
That held their hopes to mine inferior far.
Such scoffing me or pitying me say thus:
Had he not loved, he might have lived like us.   10
O then, dear sweet, for love and pity's sake
My faith reward, and from me scandal take.

III

THOU joyest, fond boy, to be by many loved,
To have thy beauty of most dames approved.
For this dost thou thy native worth disguise,
And play'st the sycophant t' observe their eyes.
    Thy glass thou counsel'st more t' adorn thy skin,   5
    That first should school thee to be fair within.

'Tis childish to be caught with pearl or amber,
And woman-like too much to cloy the chamber.

Youths should the field affect, heat their rough steeds,
Their hardened nerves to fit for better deeds.   10
   Is't not more joy strongholds to force with swords
   Than women's weakness take with looks or words?

Men that do noble things all purchase glory.
One man for one brave act hath proved a story.
But if that one ten thousand dames o'ercame,   15
Who would record it if not to his shame?
   'Tis far more conquest with one to live true,
   Than every hour to triumph, lord of new.

IV

VEIL, Love, mine eyes. O hide from me
   The plagues that charge the curious mind.
If beauty private will not be,
   Suffice it yet that she proves kind.
Who can usurp heaven's light alone?   5
Stars were not made to shine on one.

Griefs past recure fools try to heal,
   That greater harms on less inflict.
The pure offend by too much zeal;
   Affection should not be too strict.   10
He that a true embrace will find,
To beauty's faults must still be blind.

V

EVERY dame affects good fame, whate'er her doings be;
But true praise is Virtue's bays, which none may wear but she.
Borrowed guise fits not the wise; a simple look is best;
Native grace becomes a face, though ne'er so rudely dressed.
   Now such new-found toys are sold these women to disguise,   5
   That before the year grows old the newest fashion dies.

Dames of yore contended more in goodness to exceed,
Than in pride to be envied for that which least they need.
Little lawn then served the Pawn, if pawn at all there were.
Homespun thread and household bread then held out all the year.   10
   But th' attires of women now wear out both house and land,
   That the wives in silks may flow, at ebb the good men stand.

Once again, Astraea, then from heaven to earth descend,
And vouchsafe in their behalf these errors to amend.
Aid from heaven must make all ev'n, things are so out of frame;   15
For let man strive all he can, he needs must please his dame.
  Happy man content that gives, and what he gives enjoys.
  Happy dame content that lives, and breaks no sleep for toys.

VI

So sweet is thy discourse to me,
  And so delightful is thy sight,
As I taste nothing right but thee.
  O why invented Nature light?
Was it alone for beauty's sake,   5
That her graced words might better take?

No more can I old joys recall,
  They now to me become unknown,
Not seeming to have been at all.
  Alas, how soon is this love grown   10
To such a spreading height in me,
As with it all must shadowed be.

VII

THERE is a garden in her face,
  Where roses and white lilies grow;
A heavenly paradise is that place,
  Wherein all pleasant fruits do flow.
There cherries grow which none may buy,   5
Till 'cherry-ripe' themselves do cry.

Those cherries fairly do enclose
  Of orient pearl a double row,
Which when her lovely laughter shows,
  They look like rosebuds filled with snow.   10
Yet them nor peer nor prince can buy,
Till 'cherry-ripe' themselves do cry.

Her eyes like angels watch them still;
  Her brows like bended bows do stand,
Threatening with piercing frowns to kill   15
  All that attempt with eye or hand
Those sacred cherries to come nigh,
Till 'cherry-ripe' themselves do cry.

VIII

To his sweet lute Apollo sung the motions of the spheres,
The wondrous order of the stars whose course divides the years,
  And all the mysteries above.
  But none of this could Midas move,
  Which purchased him his ass's ears.   5

Then Pan with his rude pipe began the country-wealth t' advance,
To boast of cattle, flocks of sheep, and goats on hills that dance,
  With much more of this churlish kind,
  That quite transported Midas' mind,
  And held him rapt as in a trance.   10

This wrong the God of Music scorned from such a sottish judge,
And bent his angry bow at Pan, which made the piper trudge.
  Then Midas' head he so did trim,
  That every age yet talks of him
  And Phoebus' right-revenged grudge.   15

IX

  Young and simple though I am,
  I have heard of Cupid's name.
  Guess I can what thing it is,
  Men desire when they do kiss.
  Smoke can never burn they say,   5
  But the flames that follow may.

  I am not so foul or fair
  To be proud, nor to despair.
  Yet my lips have oft observed
  Men that kiss them press them hard,   10
  As glad lovers use to do,
  When their new-met loves they woo.

  Faith, 'tis but a foolish mind.
  Yet methinks a heat I find,
  Like thirst longing that doth bide   15
  Ever on my weaker side,
  Where they say my heart doth move.
  Venus, grant it be not love!

If it be, alas, what then?
Were not women made for men?   20
As good 'twere a thing were past,
That must needs be done at last.
Roses that are overblown
Grow less sweet, then fall alone.

Yet nor churl nor silken gull   25
Shall my maiden blossom pull.
Who shall not, I soon can tell;
Who shall, would I could as well!
This I know, whoe'er he be,
Love he must or flatter me.   30

X

LOVE me or not, love her I must, or die.
Leave me or not, follow her needs must I.
O that her grace would my wished comforts give!
How rich in her, how happy should I live.

All my desire, all my delight should be   5
Her to enjoy, her to unite to me.
Envy should cease, her would I love alone;
Who loves by looks is seldom true to one.

Could I enchant, and that it lawful were,
Her would I charm softly that none should hear.   10
But love enforced rarely yields firm content,
So would I love that neither should repent.

XI

WHAT means this folly now to brave it so,
    And then to use submission?
Is that a friend that straight can play the foe?
    Who loves on such condition?

Though briars breed roses, none the briar affect,   5
    But with the flower are pleased.
Love only loves delight and soft respect,
    He must not be diseased.

These thorny passions spring from barren breasts,
   Or such as need much weeding.   10
Love only loves delight and soft respect
   But sends them not home bleeding.

Command thy humour, strive to give content,
   And shame not love's profession.
Of kindness never any could repent,   15
   That made choice with discretion.

XII

DEAR, if I with guile would gild a true intent,
Heaping flatt'ries that in heart were never meant,
   Easily could I then obtain
     What now in vain I force;
   Falsehood much doth gain,   5
     Truth yet holds the better course.

Love forbid that through dissembling I should thrive,
Or in praising you myself of truth deprive.
   Let not your high thoughts debase
     A simple truth in me.   10
   Great is beauty's grace,
     Truth is yet as fair as she.

Praise is but the wind of pride if it exceeds.
Wealth prized in itself no outward value needs.
   Fair you are and passing fair,   15
     You know it, and 'tis true.
   Yet let none despair,
     But to find as fair as you.

XIII

O LOVE, where are thy shafts, thy quiver and thy bow?
Shall my wounds only weep, and he ungaged go?
Be just and strike him too that dares contemn thee so.

No eyes are like to thine, though men suppose thee blind;
So fair they level when the mark they list to find.   5
Then strike, O strike the heart that bears the cruel mind.

Is my fond sight deceived, or do I Cupid spy
Close aiming at his breast, by whom despised I die?
Shoot home, sweet Love, and wound him that he may not fly.

O then we both will sit in some unhaunted shade,   10
And heal each other's wound, which Love hath justly made.
O hope! O thought too vain! how quickly dost thou fade!

At large he wanders still, his heart is free from pain;
While secret sighs I spend and tears, but all in vain.
Yet, Love, thou know'st by right I should not thus complain.   15

XIV

BEAUTY is but a painted hell.
  Aye me! aye me!
 She wounds them that admire it;
 She kills them that desire it.
 Give her pride but fuel,   5
 No fire is more cruel.

Pity from every heart is fled.
  Aye me! aye me!
 Since false desire could borrow
 Tears of dissembled sorrow,   10
 Constant vows turn truthless;
 Love cruel, Beauty ruthless.

Sorrow can laugh and Fury sing.
  Aye me! aye me!
 My raving griefs discover   15
 I lived too true a lover.
 The first step to madness
 Is the excess of sadness.

XV

ARE you what your fair looks express?
  O then be kind!
From law of nature they digress,
  Whose form suits not their mind.
Fairness seen in th' outward shape   5
Is but th' inward beauty's ape.

Eyes that of earth are mortal made,
    What can they view?
All's but a colour or a shade,
    And neither always true.   10
Reason's sight that is eterne
Ev'n the substance can discern.

Soul is the man: for who will so
    The body name?
And to that power all grace we owe   15
    That decks our living frame.
What or how had housen been
But for them that dwell therein?

Love in the bosom is begot,
    Not in the eyes.   20
No beauty makes the eye more hot,
    Her flames the sprite surprise.
Let our loving minds then meet,
For pure meetings are most sweet.

XVI

SINCE she, ev'n she for whom I lived,
    Sweet she, by fate from me is torn,
Why am not I of sense deprived,
    Forgetting I was ever born?
Why should I languish, hating light?   5
Better to sleep an endless night.

Be 't either true or aptly feigned
    That some of Lethe's water write,
'Tis their best medicine that are pained,
    All thought to lose of past delight.   10
O would my anguish vanish so!
Happy are they that neither know.

XVII

I MUST complain, yet do enjoy my love.
    She is too fair, too rich in lovely parts.
Thence is my grief; for Nature, while she strove
    With all her graces and divinest arts
To form her too too beautiful of hue,   5
She had no leisure left to make her true.

Should I, aggrieved, then wish she were less fair?
    That were repugnant to mine own desires.
She is admired, new lovers still repair
    That kindles daily love's forgetful fires.   10
Rest, jealous thoughts, and thus resolve at last:
She hath more beauty than becomes the chaste.

XVIII

THINK'ST thou to seduce me then with words that have no
    meaning?
Parrots so can learn to prate, our speech by pieces gleaning.
Nurses teach their children so about the time of weaning.

Learn to speak first, then to woo; to wooing much pertaineth.
He that courts us, wanting art, soon falters when he feigneth;   5
Looks asquint on his discourse, and smiles when he complaineth.

Skilful anglers hide their hooks, fit baits for every season.
But with crooked pins fish thou, as babes do that want reason.
Gudgeons only can be caught with such poor tricks of treason.

Ruth, forgive me if I erred from human hearts' compassion   10
When I laughed sometimes too much to see thy foolish fashion.
But, alas, who less could do, that found so good occasion?

XIX

HER fair inflaming eyes,
    Chief authors of my cares,
I prayed in humblest wise
    With grace to view my tears.
They beheld me broad awake,   5
But, alas, no ruth would take.

Her lips with kisses rich,
    And words of fair delight,
I fairly did beseech
    To pity my sad plight.   10
But a voice from them brake forth,
As a whirlwind from the North.

Then to her hands I fled,
  That can give heart and all;
To them I long did plead,   15
  And loud for pity call.
But, alas, they put me off
With a touch worse than a scoff.

So back I straight returned,
  And at her breast I knocked,   20
Where long in vain I mourned,
  Her heart so fast was locked.
Not a word could passage find,
For a rock enclosed her mind.

Then down my prayers made way   25
  To those most comely parts,
That make her fly or stay,
  As they affect deserts.
But her angry feet, thus moved,
Fled with all the parts I loved.   30

Yet fled they not so fast
  As her enraged mind.
Still did I after haste,
  Still was I left behind.
Till I found 'twas to no end   35
With a spirit to contend.

XX

TURN all thy thoughts to eyes;
  Turn all thy hairs to ears;
Change all thy friends to spies,
  And all thy joys to fears;
True love will yet be free   5
In spite of jealousy.

Turn darkness into day,
  Conjectures into truth;
Believe what th' envious say;
  Let age interpret youth;   10
True love will yet be free
In spite of jealousy.

Wrest every word and look;
   Rack every hidden thought;
Or fish with golden hook;   15
   True love cannot be caught;
For that will still be free
In spite of jealousy.

XXI

IF any hath the heart to kill,
   Come rid me of this woeful pain.
For while I live I suffer still
   This cruel torment all in vain.
Yet none alive but one can guess   5
What is the cause of my distress.

Thanks be to heaven, no grievous smart,
   No maladies my limbs annoy;
I bear a sound and sprightful heart;
   Yet live I quite deprived of joy,   10
Since what I had in vain I crave,
And what I had not now I have.

A love I had, so fair, so sweet,
   As ever wanton eye did see.
Once by appointment we did meet.   15
   She would, but ah! it would not be.
She gave her heart, her hand she gave.
All did I give, she nought could have.

What hag did then my powers forespeak,
   That never yet such taint did feel?   20
Now she rejects me as one weak,
   Yet am I all composed of steel.
Ah! this is it my heart doth grieve.
Now though she sees she'll not believe.

XXII

BEAUTY, since you so much desire
To know the place of Cupid's fire,
About you somewhere doth it rest,
Yet never harboured in your breast,

Nor gout-like in your heel or toe.   5
What fool would seek Love's flame so low?
   But a little higher,
There, there, O there lies Cupid's fire.

Think not, when Cupid most you scorn,
Men judge that you of ice were born.   10
For though you cast Love at your heel,
His fury yet sometime you feel.
And whereabouts, if you would know,
I tell you still, not in your toe,
   But a little higher,   15
There, there, O there lies Cupid's fire.

XXIII

YOUR fair looks urge my desire.
   Calm it, sweet, with love.
Stay, O why will you retire?
   Can you churlish prove?
If love may persuade,   5
   Love's pleasures, dear, deny not.
Here is a grove secured with shade.
   O then be wise and fly not.

Hark, the birds delighted sing,
   Yet our pleasure sleeps.   10
Wealth to none can profit bring,
   Which the miser keeps.
O come while we may,
   Let's chain love with embraces.
We have not all times time to stay,   15
   Nor safety in all places.

What ill find you now in this,
   Or who can complain?
There is nothing done amiss
   That breeds no man pain.   20
'Tis now flowery May,
   But ev'n in cold December,
When all these leaves are blown away,
   This place shall I remember.

XXIV

FAIN would I wed a fair young man, that day and night could please
  me,
When my mind or body grieved that had the power to ease me.
Maids are full of longing thoughts that breed a bloodless sickness,
And that, oft I hear men say, is only cured by quickness.

Oft I have been wooed and prayed, but never could be moved.　　5
Many for a day or so I have most dearly loved.
But this foolish mind of mine straight loathes the thing resolved.
If to love be sin in me, that sin is soon absolved.

Sure, I think I shall at last fly to some holy Order;
When I once am settled there then can I fly no farther.　　10
Yet I would not die a maid, because I had a mother;
As I was by one brought forth, I would bring forth another.

MICHAEL CAVENDISH

*14. Ayres in Tabletorie to the Lute expressed with two voyces and the base
Violl or the voice & Lute only. 6. more to 4. voyces and in Tabletorie. And 8.
Madrigalles to 5. voyces. 1598*

I

STAY! Glycia stay!
And carry not my heart away.
I will not leave that jewel
To one unkind and cruel,
But if thereto thou have a mind　　5
Buy it of me by being kind.

II

WHY should my muse, thus restless in her woes,
  Summon records of never-dying fears,
And still revive, fresh springing in my thoughts,
  The true memorial of my sad despairs,
Who, forced to love, to those fair eyes am thrall,　　5
Where eyes nor thoughts grant one respect at all?

Endless my griefs, since endless is her course
　Still to inflict more torments on my griefs
Without remorse of poor hearts' scalding sighs,
　When heaven in tears bewails my no reliefs.　　　10
A hard regard where true devoted love
Can merit nought but still these crosses prove.

Cease, world's bright sun, from henceforth once to shine,
　But in my death now suffer springs to perish;
Forbear to grace earth's glory with thy beams,　　　15
　Her richest treasure now forbid to flourish,
Since that her eyes, the sunshine of my life,
Affords no grace but torments, death, and strife.

III

MOURN, Marcus, mourn! and mourning wish to die,
Since she is gone on whom my hopes rely,
Though Marcus' faith deserved with the best,
Yet of her love another is possessed.
Who doth forbid fair Cleopatra smiling　　　5
On his poor soul, for her sweet sake still dying?

IV

　HAVE I vowed and must not break it?
　　Fondly wooed is wisely broken.
　Do I love and dare not speak it?
　　Silence doth no love betoken.
Thus I bind in this my breaking,　　　5
And I am in silence speaking.

Love is bound though I seem free,
　Wrapped in deep affections' snare.
Love I must how so e'er it be.
　Too late, men say, doth come Beware.　　　10
Then vow no more sith vows are vain,
Wrapped in deep affections' chain.

V

　FINETTA, fair and feat,
　　Star of our town a;
　Her beauty, bright as jet,
　　Makes me sing down a;

Grief and I both are one,   5
Love pulls me down a.

VI

LOVE is not blind, but I myself am so;
  With free consent blind-folded by desire,
That guides my will along the paths of woe
  To seek refreshing for a needless fire.

Love is no boy, as fools in fancies feign;   5
  It is myself that play the child so right;
I hope and fear, I weep and laugh again,
  And use no fence against so weak a might.

Love hath no fire, it is mine only lust
  Doth raise the flame which makes my thoughts to
    fry;   10
Vain hope and fond conceits, in which I trust,
  Are th' only wings that bear him up so high.

Love hath no bow nor shafts to shoot withal;
  He hath no bands wherewith to tie us fast;
He hath no power, those that be free to thrall,   15
  More than we give, nor can no longer last.

Love is a poet's lie, a beggar's store,
  A madman's dream, an ignorant's idol great.
In brief, this god whom we so much adore
  Of manners strange doth find as strange a seat. 20

VII

LOVE, the delight of all well-thinking minds,
  Delight, the fruit of virtue dearly loved,
Virtue, the highest good that reason finds,
  Reason, the forge on which men's thoughts are proved,
Are from the world by Nature's power bereft,   5
And in one creature for her glory left.

Beauty her cover is, the eye's true pleasure;
  In honour's fame she lives, the ear's true music.
Excess of wonder grows from her just measure;
  Her inward parts are passion's only physic.   10
From her clear heart the springs of virtue flow,
Which, imaged in her words and deeds, men know.

Time fain would stay that he might never leave her,
  Place doth rejoice that he must needs contain her,
Death craves of heaven that he may not bereave her,   15
  The heavens know their own and do maintain her.
Delight, Love, Reason, Virtue, let it be
To hold all women light but only she.

                              [*Fulke Greville, Lord Brooke*]

                    VIII

THE heart to rue the pleasure of the eye,
  The eye to wound the heart with his delight;
What may be said that owe them both hereby
  But both two serve unto his own despite.
O save and win them both by one desert: 5
Please still the eye, but pity on the heart.

The eye beholds as much as much may be
  In beauty, grace, and honour to require;
The heart conceives more than the eye can see,
  And slays himself to feed his wound's desire.   10
O save and win them both by one desert:
Please still the eye, but pity on the heart.

                    IX

SYLVIA is fair, yet scorning love unseemly,
Plaguing my soul with torments too untimely;
Sylvia, Nature's perfection, bids me love her,
But for love's merit she forbids me move her.
Sweet Sylvia, yet commandress of my thought,   5
Reward me so I may not love for nought.

                    X

CURSED be the time when first mine eyes beheld
  Those rare perfections all men's thoughts admire;
And justly may a shepherd's swain bewail
  Those fatal hours which caused him first desire
Love's sweet consent, that makes so deep impression,   5
As heart and soul will witness in confession.

Why should those eyes, born traitors to my rest,
   Command my thoughts to yield to this presumption—
To love a nymph whose beauty all surpassing
   To all men's thoughts breeds still a strange confusion? 10
Heavens forbid that I should dare to move
A face that gods solicit still in love.

Phyllis, sweet Phyllis, the shepherds' only Queen,
   Scorns to admit a swain into her love;
He pipes and sings and pleads to her for grace,   15
   His sons and sonnets her can nothing move.
He sighs and vows and prays with true devotion,
But vows and prayers work in her no motion.

Then Corydon must yield to this his curse
   Sith that his love cannot her love importune,   20
For fear despairs convert this ill to worse,
   And by disgrace add more plagues to fortune.
Poor man, sit down, pour out thy plaints amain,
Phyllis thee scorns and holds in high disdain.

XI

FAIR are those eyes, whose shine must give me light;
   Sweet is that grace commands my heart to love;
Heavens her thoughts, if they once yield consent
   To that reward affection's truth doth move.
But if my faith cannot his merit gain,   5
Weep, eyes! break, heart! and end this restless pain.

XII

WANDERING in this place, as in a wilderness,
No comfort have I nor yet assurance,
Desolate of joy, replete with sadness.
   Wherefore I may say: O deus, deus,
   Non est dolor sicut dolor meus.   5

XIII

   EVERY bush new springing,
   Every bird now singing,

Merrily sat poor Nicho,
Chanting troli lo loli lo.
Till her he had espied   5
On whom his hope relied,
Down a down, with a frown,
O she pulled him down.

XIV

DOWN in a valley
Shady vales are pleasant ports,
For merry lads' meet resorts.
Such was our hap to catch a swain,
   O happy the valley!   5
With flowers to spangle Flora's train,
   Nor did we dally;
His flowers we took all dyed in grain,
   O dyed was the valley!
Shady vales are pleasant ports,   10
For merry lads' meet resorts.
Of them we made a garland green,
   O green was the valley!
To crown fair Lelia shepherds' Queen,
   Fair as a lily,   15
She sitting in a shade unseen.
   O shady the valley!
Shady vales are pleasant ports,
For merry lads' meet resorts.

XV

WANTON, come hither!
O stay, why do you fly me?
My suit though you deny me,
Yet let us walk together.
Sweet nymph, such haste why make you?   5
Well could I overtake you.
But since words will not move thee,
Farewell! I did but this to prove thee.
   With that the nymph she stayed,
   And, deeply sighing, said: 10
Sweet shepherd, how I love thee!

XVI

SAY, shepherds, say, where is your jolly swain?
    Or what hath bred his anguish?
On idle bank he restless doth remain
    For love doth make him languish.
        Idle lad,   5
        His wit is bad
        There, alone,
        To make such moan,
        To the weeping fountains,
          Whilst she plays   10
        Sweet roundelays
    Up and down the mountains.

XVII

[*The words are the same as those of No. xi*]

XVIII

FAREWELL, despair! sith love hath reconciled
    Those strange delays fond modesty commanded,
And banished now those idle superstitions
    Fear of offence caused her to be enstranged.
Prescribing time this privilege affords;   5
Sweet trespasses love pardons, not vain words.

XIX–XX

SLY thief, if so you will believe
It nought or little did me grieve
That my true heart you had bereft,
Till that unkindly you it left.
Leaving, you lose; losing, you kill   5
That which I may forgo so ill.

What thing more cruel can you do
Than rob a man and kill him too?
Wherefore of Love I ask this meed—
To bring you where you did the deed,   10
That there you may for your amisses
Be damaged in a thousand kisses.

XXI

IN flower of April springing,
　　When pleasant birds to sport them
　　Among the woods consort them,
Warbling with cheerful notes, and sweetly singing
For joy that Clore the fair her song was chanting,　　5
Of her and her Elpin the sweet loves vaunting.

XXII

ZEPHYRUS brings the time that sweetly scenteth
　　With flowers and herbs, and winter's frosts exileth;
Progne now chirpeth and Philomel lamenteth,
　　Flora the garlands white and red compileth.
Fields do rejoice, the frowning sky relenteth;　　5
　　Jove, to behold his dearest daughter, smileth.
The air, the water, the earth to joy consenteth,
　　Each creature now to love him reconcileth.

XXIII

MUCH it delighted
　　To see Phyllis smiling;
　　But it was her beguiling.
Ah! she my faith new-plighted
　　Scorned with disdain reviling.　　5
But sith thy feigned looks faithful I proved not,
　　False, adieu! for I loved not.

XXIV

COME, gentle swains, and shepherds' dainty daughters
　　Adorned with courtesy and comely duties;
Come, sing, and joy, and grace with lovely laughters
　　The birthday of the beautiest of beauties.
Then sang the shepherds and nymphs of Diana:　　5
　　Long live fair Oriana.

XXV

TO former joy now turns the grove, the fountain,
　　The jolly fresh April now loden with flowers;
The seas are calm, hoar-frost falls from the mountain,
　　Shepherds and nymphs walk to their wanton bowers.

But I, all night in tears my pillow steeping,   5
Soon as the sun appears renew my weeping.

XXVI

FAUSTINA hath the fairer face,
And Phillida the feater grace;
   Both have mine eye enriched.
This sings full sweetly with her voice,
Her fingers make as sweet a noise;   5
   Both have mine ear bewitched.
Ay me! sith Fates have so provided,
My heart, alas, must be divided.

XXVII

[*The words are the same as those of No. xiii*]

XXVIII

[*The words are the same as those of No. xii*]

GIOVANNI COPRARIO

Fvneral Teares. For the death of the Right Honorable the Earle of Deuonshire. Figvred In seauen songes, whereof sixe are so set forth that the wordes may be exprest by a treble voice alone to the Lute and Base Viole, or else that the meane part may bee added, if any shall affect more fulnesse of parts. The Seaventh Is made in forme of a Dialogue, and can not be sung without two voyces.   1606

I

OFT thou hast with greedy ear
   Drunk my notes and words of pleasure;
   In affection's equal measure
Now my songs of sorrow hear,
   Since from thee my griefs do grow,   5
Whom alive I prized so dear.
   The more my joy, the more my woe.

Music, though it sweetens pain,
   Yet no whit impairs lamenting,
   But in passions like consenting   10
Makes them constant that complain,
   And enchants their fancies so
That all comforts they disdain,
   And fly from joy to dwell with woe.

II

O SWEET flower, too quickly fading,
   Like a winter sunshine day.
   Poor pilgrim tired in the midway,
Like the earth itself half shading.
So thy picture shows to me   5
But only the one half of thee.

O dear joy, too swiftly flying
   From thy love's enchanted eyes,
   Proud glory spread through the vast skies
Earth of more than earth envying.   10
O how wondrous hadst thou been,
Had but the world thy whole life seen!

III

O TH'UNSURE hopes of men, the brittle state,
   The vain contentions that unluckily
Oft in midst of the race fall ruinate,
   And in their course long overwhelmed be,
   And swallowed up ere they the port could see.   5

O women's fruitless love, unquiet state,
   Too dear affections that despitefully
Ev'n in their height of bliss prove desolate,
   And often fall far from all hope of joy
   Ere they have time to dream on their annoy.   10

IV

IN darkness let me dwell, the ground shall sorrow be,
The roof despair to bar all cheerful light from me;
The walls of marble black that moistened still shall weep;
My music hellish jarring sounds to banish friendly sleep.
   Thus wedded to my woes and bedded in my tomb,   5
   O let me dying live till death doth come.

My dainties grief shall be, and tears my poisoned wine;
My sighs the air through which my panting heart shall pine;
My robes my mind shall suit exceeding blackest night;
My study shall be tragic thoughts sad fancy to delight.   10
 Pale ghosts and frightful shades shall my acquaintance be.
 O thus, my hapless joy, I haste to thee.

V

M Y joy is dead and cannot be revived;
    Fled is my joy and never may return;
Both of my joy and of myself deprived,
    Far from all joy I sing, and singing mourn.
O let no tender heart or gentle ear   5
Partake my passions or my plainings hear.

Rude flinty breasts that never felt remorse;
    Hard craggy rocks that death and ruin love;
Those, only those, my passions shall enforce
    Beyond their kind and to compassion move.   10
My grief shall wonders work, for he did so
That caused my sorrows, and these tears doth owe.

VI

D ECEITFUL Fancy, why delud'st thou me,
    The dead alive presenting?
My joy's fair image carved in shades I see.
    O false, yet sweet, contenting!
Why art not thou a substance like to me,   5
Or I a shade to vanish hence with thee?

Stay, gentle object, my sense still deceive
    With this thy kind illusion.
I die through madness if my thoughts you leave.
    O strange, yet sweet, confusion!   10
Poor blissless heart, that feels such deep annoy
Only to lose the shadow of thy joy!

VII. *A Dialogue*

[*1st Voice.*]   F OE of mankind, why murderest thou my love?
[*2nd Voice.*]   Forbear, he lives!

[*1st Voice.*]   O where?
[*2nd Voice.*]   In heaven above.
[*1st Voice.*]   Poor wretched life, that only lives in name.
[*2nd Voice.*]   Man is not flesh but soul; all life is fame.
[*1st Voice.*]   That is true fame which living men enjoy.   5
[*2nd Voice.*]   That is true life which death cannot destroy.

   [*Both.*]   Live ever through thy merited renown,
                         Fair spirit, shining in thy starry crown.

꙳꙳꙳꙳꙳꙳꙳꙳꙳꙳

*Songs of Mourning: Bewailing the vntimely death of Prince Henry. Worded
by Tho. Campion. And set forth to bee sung with one voyce to the Lute, or
Violl.   1613*

I

To the most sacred King James

O GRIEF, how divers are thy shapes, wherein men languish!
    The face sometime with tears thou fill'st,
      Sometime the heart thou kill'st
        With unseen anguish.
    Sometime thou smil'st to view how Fate   5
      Plays with our human state.
      So far from surety here
      Are all our earthly joys,
   That what our strong hope builds when least we fear,
      A stronger power destroys.   10

O Fate, why shouldst thou take from kings their joy and
    treasure?
    Their image if men should deface
      'Twere death, which thou dost race
      Even at thy pleasure.
    Wisdom of holy kings yet knows   15
      Both what it hath and owes.
      Heaven's hostage which you bred
      And nursed with such choice care,
   Is ravished now, great King, and from us led
      When we were least aware.   20

II

To the most sacred Queen Anne

'TIS now dead night, and not a light on earth
    Or star in heaven doth shine.
Let now a mother mourn the noblest birth
    That ever was both mortal and divine.
    O sweetness peerless! More than human grace!   5
    O flowery beauty! O untimely death!
        Now Music fill this place
        With thy most doleful breath;
    O singing wail a fate more truly funeral
    Than when with all his sons the sire of Troy did fall. 10

Sleep joy, die mirth, and not a smile be seen,
    Or show of hearts content;
For never sorrow nearer touched a queen,
    Nor were there ever tears more duly spent.
    O dear remembrance, full of rueful woe,   15
    O ceaseless passion, O unhuman hour!
        No pleasure now can grow,
        For withered is her flower.
    O anguish! do thy worst and fury tragical,
    Since fate in taking one, hath thus disordered all.   20

III

To the most high and mighty Prince Charles

FORTUNE and glory may be lost and won,
But when the work of Nature is undone
    That loss flies past returning.
    No help is left but mourning.
What can to kind youth more despiteful prove   5
    Than to be robbed of one sole brother?
        Father and mother
Ask reverence, a brother only love.
Like age and birth, like thoughts and pleasures move.
What gain can he heap up, though showers of crowns
    descend,   10
Who for that good must change a brother and a friend?

Follow, O follow yet thy brother's fame;
But not his fate. Let's only change the name,
 And find his worth presented
 In thee, by him prevented.   15
Or past example of the dead be great
 Out of thyself begin thy story.
  Virtue and glory
Are eminent being placed in princely seat.
O heaven, his age prolong with sacred heat,   20
And on his honoured head let all the blessings light
Which to his brother's life men wished, and wished them right.

IV

To the most princely and virtuous the Lady Elizabeth

So parted you, as if the world for ever
 Had lost with him her light.
 Nor could your tears hard flint to ruth excite.
 Yet may you never
 Your loves again partake in human sight.   5
O why should Fate such two kind hearts dissever
As Nature never knit more fair or firm together?

So loved you as sister should a brother,
 Not in a common strain,
 For princely blood doth vulgar fire disdain, 10
 But you each other
On earth embraced in a celestial chain.
Alas, for love! that heavenly-born affection
To change should subject be and suffer earth's infection.

V

To the most illustrious and mighty Frederick the fift, Count Palatine of the Rhine

How like a golden dream you met and parted,
 That pleasing, straight doth vanish.
 O who can ever banish
The thought of one so princely and free-hearted?
But he was pulled up in his prime by Fate,   5
And love for him must mourn, though all too late.
Tears to the dead are due. Let none forbid
Sad hearts to sigh. True grief cannot be hid.

Yet the most bitter storm to height increased
   By heaven again is ceased.   10
   O Time, that all things movest,
In grief and joy thou equal measure lovest.
Such the condition is of human life,
Care must with pleasure mix, and peace with strife.
Thoughts with the days must change; as tapers waste,   15
So must our griefs. Day breaks when night is past.

VI

To the most disconsolate Great Britain

WHEN pale Famine fed on thee
   With her unsatiate jaws;
  When civil broils set murder free,
   Contemning all thy laws;
When heaven enraged consumed thee so   5
With plagues that none thy face could know,
Yet in thy looks affliction then showed less
Than now for one's fate all thy parts express.

  Now thy highest states lament
   A son and brother's loss;   10
  Thy nobles mourn in discontent
   And rue this fatal cross;
Thy Commons are with passion sad
To think how brave a prince they had.
If all thy rocks from white to black should turn,   15
Yet couldst thou not in show more amply mourn.

VII

To the World

O POOR distracted world, partly a slave
   To pagans' sinful rage, partly obscured
With ignorance of all the means that save,
   And ev'n those parts of thee that live assured
Of heavenly grace, O how they are divided   5
With doubts late by a kingly pen decided!
   O happy world, if what the sire begun
   Had been closed up by his religious son.

F f

Mourn all you souls oppressed under the yoke
   Of Christian-hating Thrace! Never appeared   10
More likelihood to have that black league broke,
   For such a heavenly prince might well be feared
Of earthly fiends. O how is zeal inflamed
With power, when Truth wanting defence is shamed.
   O princely soul, rest thou in peace while we   15
   In thine expect the hopes were ripe in thee.

WILLIAM CORKINE

*Ayres, To Sing And Play To The Lvte And Basse Violl. With Pauins,
Galliards, Almaines, and Corantos for the Lyra Violl.* 1610

I

SINK down, proud thoughts, your mounting hopes must now
   descend.
Come grief and care. Hence joys! your triumph now must end.
   Heavens now will smile no more, my light is shaded.
I pine without redress; my life, my spirits like flowers are faded.

O Time, conceal my woe, in mine own tears drown my distress.   5
Griefs none should know, when none their anguish can redress.
   Pale Death hath pierced my blood, and forth it streameth.
I sleep, and in my trance my head, my heart, of sorrow dreameth.

II

SOME can flatter, some can feign;
   Simple truth shall plead for me.
Let not beauty truth disdain,
   Truth is even as fair as she.

But since pairs must equal prove,   5
   Let my strength her youth oppose,
Love her beauty, faith her love,
   On even terms so may we close.

Cork or lead in equal weight
   Both one just proportion yield.   10
So may breadth be paysed with height,
   Steepest mount with plainest field.

Virtues have not all one kind,
   Yet all virtues merits be.
Divers virtues are combined,   15
   Differing so deserts agree.

Let then love and beauty meet,
   Making one divine consent,
Constant as the sounds, and sweet,
   That enchant the firmament.   20
                  [? *Thomas Campian*]

III

SWEET, restrain these showers of kindness
   From distrust proceeding.
Nurse not wrong-conceived blindness
   By too much sigh breeding.
Love by error seems astray,   5
   But dies if once suspected.
Women most believe when they
   Most by men are neglected.

Some forged flatteries only venture,
   Yet return true favours.   10
Just affection, like a centre
   Once fixed, never wavers.
Easily as the day from night
   May women's eyes discover,
If they frame their minds aright,   15
   From the false the true lover.

IV

IF streams of tears could lessen extreme grief,
   Or cause a minute's truce to woe;
If deepest sighs, sad plaints, might yield relief,
   These sorrows to forgo,
Mine eyes, my heart, my tongue should ne'er refrain   5
   To weep, to sigh, and to complain.

But sorrow such impression left,
Of sight, of speech it me bereft.
Only to sigh is left to me
    In this my greatest misery.   10

V

SWEET, let me go! Sweet, let me go!
What do you mean to vex me so?
Cease, cease, cease your pleading force.
Do you think thus to extort remorse?
Now no more; alas, you overbear me;   5
And I would cry, but some would hear, I fear me.

VI

HE that hath no mistress must not wear a favour.
He that woos a mistress must serve before he have her.
He that hath no bed-fellow must lie alone,
And he that hath no lady must be content with Joan.
And so must I, for why? alas! my love and I are parted.   5
False Cupid, I will have thee whipped, and have thy mother carted.

VII

SWEET Cupid, ripen her desire,
    Thy joyful harvest may begin;
If age approach a little nigher,
    'Twill be too late to get it in.

Cold winter storms lay standing corn,   5
    Which once too ripe will never rise,
And lovers wish themselves unborn
    When all their joys lie in their eyes.

Then, sweet, let us embrace and kiss.
    Shall beauty shale upon the ground?   10
If age bereave us of this bliss,
    Then will no more such sport be found.

VIII

VAIN is all this world's contention,
    Fortunes frail and hopes deceiving.
Chance lays ambush of prevention,
    Our attempts of end bereaving.

Future things are placed   5
Beyond our weak conceiving;
Minds in every age
New thoughts engender,
Till all to Fate we render.

IX

BEAUTY sat bathing by a spring,
  Where fairest shades did hide her.
The winds blew calm, the birds did sing,
  The cool streams ran beside her.
My wanton thoughts enticed mine eye   5
  To see what was forbidden;
But better memory said fie,
  So vain desire was chidden.

Into a slumber then I fell;
  But fond imagination   10
Seemed to see, but could not tell
  Her feature or her fashion.
But even as babes in dreams do smile,
  And sometime fall a-weeping,
So I awaked as wise the while   15
  As when I fell a-sleeping.

[Anthony Munday]

X

NOW would chwore hong'd, zis, but thou most ma wrong.
  Gods bors, I crie God mercy to zweare.
  Hast not my rings and things and geare
    With vaith and troth among,
    And wout vorzake ma now?   5
  Nay, masse, ware that, vor if thou doo,
Chil take a knife and honge my zelfe vor one of thow.
  Yea I woll, so I woll, that I woll, I vaith la!

Hadds voote, zweete zis, what aild tha woo ma now?
  I cham as like to zarve thy turne   10
  As yer I wos zince chos I borne,
    And sha not I have thow?

    Lets zee who dare,
    I chould but zee.
    Huds lid, I zweare   15
  Chill take a zweard, and make a yend of I or hee.
    Yea I would, so I would, that I would, I vaith la!

Ha not I bought my kerzie wedding briche,
    Hudds hate, cham angrie, thou makes ma vret.
    And is not my bond redie zet,   20
     Woold zarve ma zucha twich?
     Chill break his brow,
      I vaith I chill,
    That shall love thou.
  Then take a rop and drown thyzelf vor mere good will. 25
    Yea I would, so I would, that I would, I vaith la!

XI

THINK you to seduce me so with words that have no meaning?
Parrots can learn so to speak, our voice by pieces gleaning;
Nurses teach their children so about the time of weaning.

Learn to speak first, then to woo. To wooing much pertaineth.
He that hath not art to hide soon falters when he feigneth, 5
And, as one that wants his wits, he smiles when he complaineth.

If with wit we be deceived, our falls may be excused.
Seeming good with flattery graced is but of few refused.
But of all accursed are they that are by fools abused.
            [*Thomas Campian*]

XII

   SHALL a frown or angry eye,
    Shall a word unfitly placed,
   Shall a shadow make me fly,
    As I were with tigers chased?
    Love must not be so disgraced.   5

   Shall I woo her in despite?
    Shall I turn her from her flying?
   Shall I tempt her with delight?
    Shall I laugh out her denying?
    No! Beware of lovers' crying.   10

Shall I then with patient mind
    Still attend her wayward pleasure?
Time will make her prove more kind.
    Let her coyness then take leisure.
    Pains are worthy such a treasure.   15

ıcıɔcıɔcıɔcıɔcıɔcı

*The Second Booke Of Ayres, Some, to Sing and Play to the Base-Violl alone:
Others, to be sung to the Lute and Base Violl. With new Corantoes, Pauins,
Almaines; as also diuers new Descants vpon old Grounds, set to the Lyra-Violl.*
1612

I

EACH lovely grace my lady doth possess
    Let all men view, and in their view admire;
In whose sweet breast all virtuous thoughts do rest,
    Zealous to pity, chaste in her own desire;
        And to make up a rare and worthy creature,   5
        Both wise and chaste and fair in form and feature.
    Enter but into thought of her perfection;
    Thou wilt confess, and in confessing prove
    How none deserves like praise nor yet like love.

II

TRUTH-TRYING Time shall cause my mistress say,
My love was perfect, constant as the day.
And as the day when evening doth appear
Doth suffer doom to be or foul or clear,
So shall my last bequest make known to all   5
My love in her did rise, did live, did fall.

You gods of love who oft heard my desires,
Prepare her heart by your love-charming fires
To think on those sweet revels, peaceful fights,
Ne'er-changing custom taught at nuptial rites.   10
O guerdonize my prayers but with this,
That I may taste of that long wished-for bliss.

III

    TWO lovers sat lamenting
        Hard by a crystal brook,
    Each other's heart tormenting,
        Exchanging look for look.

With sighs and tears bewraying   5
Their silent thoughts delaying.
> At last quoth one:
> Shall we alone
Sit here our thoughts bewraying?
> Fie, fie, O fie!   10
> O fie, it may not be.
> Set looking by,
Let speaking set us free.

Then thus their silence breaking,
> Their thoughts too long estranged   15
They do bewray by speaking,
> And words with words exchanged.
Then one of them replied:
Great pity we had died
> Thus all alone   20
> In silent moan,
And not our thoughts descried.
> Fie, fie, O fie!
> O fie, that had been ill,
> That inwardly   25
Silence the heart should kill.

From looks and words to kisses
> They made their next proceeding
And as their only blisses
> They therein were exceeding.   30
O what a joy is this,
To look, to talk, to kiss!
> But thus begun
> Is all now done?
Ah! all then nothing is!   35
> Fie, fie, O fie!
> O fie, it is a hell;
> And better die
Than kiss and not end well.

IV

'Tis true 'tis day. What though it be?
And will you therefore rise from me?
What? will you rise because 'tis light?
Did we lie down because 'twas night?

Love, that in spite of darkness brought us hither,   5
In spite of light should keep us still together.

    Light hath no tongue, but is all eye.
    If it could speak as well as spy,
    This were the worst that it could say,
    That being well I fain would stay;   10
And that I love my heart and honour so
That I would not from him that hath them go.

    Is't business that doth you remove?
    O that's the worst disease of Love.
    The poor, the foul, the false, Love can   15
    Admit, but not the busied man.
He that hath business and makes love, doth do
Such wrong as if a married man should woo.

                      [*John Donne*]

V

DEAR, though your mind stand so averse
That no assaulting words can pierce,
Your swift and angry flight forbear.
What need you doubt? what need you fear?
In vain I strive your thoughts to move,   5
But stay and hear me yet, sweet love.

Words may entreat you, not enforce,
Speak though I might till I were hoarse.
Already you resolve, I know,
No gentle look or grace to show.   10
My passions all must hapless rove.
But stay and hear me yet, sweet love.

Sith here no help nor hope remains
To ease my grief or end my pains;
I'll seek in lowest shades to find   15
Rest for my heart, peace for my mind.
Go thou, more cruel far than fair,
And now leave me to my despair.

VI

SHALL I be with joys deceived?
    Can Love's bands be sealed with kisses?
Cupid, of his eyes bereaved,
    Yet in darkness seldom misses.
    Let not dallying lose these blisses.   5

Sleep hath sealed their eyes and ears
    That our loves so long have guarded.
Hymen hides your maiden fears.
    Now my love may be rewarded.
    Let my suit be now regarded.   10

VII

DOWN, down, proud mind! thou soarest far above thy might.
    Aspiring heart, wilt thou not cease to breed my woe?
High thoughts meet with disdain; Peace and Love fight.
    Peace, thou hast won the field, and Love shall hence in bondage go.

This fall from pride my rising is from grief's great deep   5
    That bottom wants, up to the top of happy bliss.
In peace and rest I shall securely sleep
    Where neither scorn, disdain, Love's torment, grief or anguish is.

[*Alternative words for the music of this song*]

STOOP, stoop, proud heart! and mounting hopes down, down
        descend!
Rise, spleen, and burst! hence joys! for grief must now ascend.
My stars conspire my spoil, which is effected.
I die, yet live in death, of love and life at once rejected.

Then O descend, and from the height of hope come down.   5
My love and fates on me, aye me! do jointly frown.
Then Death (if ever) now come, do thy duty
And martyr him, alas, that martyred is by love and beauty.

VIII

BEWARE, fair maids, of musky courtiers' oaths.
    Take heed what gifts and favours you receive.
Let not the fading glose of silken clothes
    Dazzle your virtues, or your fame bereave.

For lose but once the hold you have of grace,   5
Who will regard your fortune or your face?

Each greedy hand will strive to catch the flower,
    When none regards the stalk it grows upon.
Each creature seeks the fruit still to devour
    And leave the tree to fall or stand alone.   10
Yet this advice, fair creatures, take of me:
Let none take fruit, unless he take the tree.

Believe no oaths nor much-protesting men;
    Credit no vows nor their bewailing songs.
Let courtiers swear, forswear, and swear again;   15
    Their hearts do live ten regions from their tongues.
For when with oaths they make thy heart to tremble,
Believe them least, for then they most dissemble.

Beware lest Caesar do corrupt thy mind,
    And fond Ambition sell thy modesty.   20
Say though a king thou ever courteous find,
    He cannot pardon thine impurity.
Begin with king; to subject thou wilt fall;
From lord to lackey, and at last to all.

                                    [*Joshua Sylvester*]

                        IX

    THE fire to see my woes for anger burneth.
        The air in rain for my affliction weepeth.
    The sea to ebb for grief his flowing turneth.
        The earth with pity dull his centre keepeth.
            Fame is with wonder blased.   5
                Time runs away for sorrow.
            Place standeth still amazed
    To see my night of ills which hath no morrow.
        Alas, all only she no pity taketh
    To know my miseries, but, chaste and cruel,   10
                My fall her glory maketh.
    Yet still her eyes give to my flames their fuel.

    Fire, burn me quite till sense of burning leave me.
        Air, let me draw thy breath no more in anguish.
    Sea, drowned in thee, of tedious life bereave me.   15
        Earth, take this earth wherein my spirits languish.

Fame, say I was not born.
   Time, haste my dying hour.
  Place, see my grave uptorn.
Fire, Air, Sea, Earth, Fame, Time, Place, show your power.
  Alas, from all their helps I am exiled,   21
For hers am I, and Death fears her displeasure.
    Fie, Death, thou art beguiled,
Though I be hers, she sets by me no treasure.

                         [*Sir Philip Sidney*]

X

Go, heavy thoughts, down to the place of woe,
  Tell grief, tell pain, and torments how they used me.
Say unto sorrow, who is now my foe,
  And fretfulness, which long time hath abused me,
  Maugre them all in time they shall excuse me.   5
Till then my heart shall bear my wrongs so high,
Until the strings do burst, and then I die.

For, being dead, what grief can me offend?
All pains do cease, all sorrows have their end.
Vexation cannot vex my flesh no more,   10
Nor any torments wrong my soul so sore.
All living will my lifeless corse abhor.
Yet thus I'll say, that Death doth make conclusion,
But yet with righteous souls there's no confusion.

XI

My dearest mistress, let us live and love,
And care not what old doting fools reprove.
Let us not fear their censures nor esteem,
What they of us and of our loves shall deem.
Old Age's critic and censorious brow   5
Cannot of youthful dalliance allow,
Nor never could endure that we should taste
Of those delights which they themselves are past.

XII

Man, like a prophet of ensuing years,
  Begins his life with cries; he ends with pain.
The rest is so distract 'twixt hopes and fears,
  That life seems but a loss and death a gain.

My hopeless love is like my hapless life,   5
Begun in pain and ends itself in grief.

Yet death in one's an end of pain and fears;
    But cruel love, though ever-living, dies;
And she that gives me death, when death appears,
    Revives my dying hopes and death denies.   10
My hopeless love is like my hapless life,
Begun in pain and ends itself in grief.

XIII

As by a fountain chaste Diana sat,
    Viewing of Nature's pride, her beauteous face,
The waters boiled with love, she boils with hate,
    Chastening their pride with exile from their place.
They, murmuring, ran to sea, and being there   5
Each liquid drop turned to a brinish tear.

XIV

Away, away! Call back what you have said
When you did vow to live and die a maid.
O if you knew what shame to them befell
That dance about with bobtail apes in hell,
You'd break your oath, and for a world of gain   5
From Hymen's pleasing sports no more abstain.

Yourself your virgin girdle would divide,
And put aside the maiden veil that hides
The chiefest gem of Nature, and would lie
Prostrate to every peasant that goes by,   10
Rather than undergo such shame. No tongue can tell
What injury is done to maids in hell.

XV

When I was born Lucina cross-legged sat.
    The angry stars with ominous aspects
Frowned on my birth, and the fore-dooming Fate
    Ordained to brand me with their dire effects.
The sun did hide his face, and left the night   5
To bring me to this world's accursed light.

XVI

SHALL a smile or guileful glance,
   Or a sigh that is but feigned,
Shall but tears that come by chance
   Make me dote that was disdained?
   No, I will no more be chained.   5

Shall I sell my freedom so,
   Being now from love remised?
Shall I learn (what I do know
   To my cost) that love's disguised?
   No, I will be more advised.   10

Must she fall? And must I stand?
   Must she fly and I pursue her?
Must I give her heart and land,
   And for nought with them endue her?
   No, first I will find her truer!   15

XVII

WE yet agree, but shall be straightways out.
   Thy passions are so harsh and strange to me
That, when the concord's perfect, I may doubt
   The time is lost which I have spent for thee.
Yet one the ground must be, which you shall prove   5
Can bear all parts that descant on my love.

XVIII

FLY swift, my thoughts, possess my mistress' heart,
And as you find her love, plead my desert.
If she be somewhat wayward, happy my desires;
A little coyness doth but blow men's fires.
But will she needs forbid the baines I crave,   5
Retire and be buried in your master's grave.

JOHN DANYEL

Songs For The Lvte Viol and Voice. 1606

I

COY Daphne fled from Phoebus' hot pursuit,
  Careless of passion, senseless of remorse.
Whilst he complained his griefs, she rested mute.
  He begged her stay, she still kept on her course.
But what reward she had for this you see,   5
She rests transformed, a winter-beaten tree.

The Answer

Chaste Daphne fled from Phoebus' hot pursuit,
  Knowing men's passions idle and of course.
And though he plained, 'twas fit she should be mute,
  And honour would she should keep on her course.   10
For which fair deed her glory still we see:
She rests still *Green*; and so wish I to be.

II

THOU pretty bird, how do I see
Thy silly state and mine agree.
    For thou a prisoner art.
    So is my heart!
Thou sing'st to her; and so do I address   5
My music to her ear that's merciless.
    But herein doth the difference lie,
    That thou art graced, so am not I.
Thou singing liv'st, and I must singing die.

III

HE, whose desires are still abroad, I see
  Hath never any peace at home the while;
And therefore now come back my heart to me.
  It is but for superfluous things we toil.
Rest alone with thyself, be all within;   5
For what without thou gett'st, thou dost not win.

Honour, wealth, glory, fame are no such things
But that which from imagination springs.
High-reaching power, that seems to overgrow,
Doth creep but on the earth, lies base and low.   10

IV

LIKE as the lute delights, or else dislikes,
 As is his art that plays upon the same,
So sounds my Muse according as she strikes
 On my heart strings, high tuned unto her fame.
Her touch doth cause the warble of the sound,   5
 Which here I yield in lamentable wise,
A wailing descant on the sweetest ground,
 Whose due reports gives honour to her eyes.
If any pleasing relish here I use,
 Then judge the world her beauty gives the same;   10
Else harsh my style, untuneable my Muse.
 Hoarse sounds the voice that praiseth not her name,
For no ground else could make the music such,
Nor other hand could give so sweet a touch.
[Samuel Daniel]

V

DOST thou withdraw thy grace
 For that I should not love?
 And think'st thou to remove
M' affections with thy face?
As if that Love did hold no part   5
 But where thy beauty lies,
And were not in my heart
 Greater than in thy fair eyes.
Ah yes! 'tis more; more is Desire,
 There where it wounds and pines,   10
As fire is far more fire
 Where it burns than where it shines.

VI

WHY canst thou not, as others do,
 Look on me with unwounding eyes,
And yet look sweet, but yet not so,
 Smile, but not in killing wise?
Arm not thy graces to confound;   5
Only look, but do not wound.

Why should mine eyes see more in you
  Than they can see in all the rest?
For I can others' beauties view
  And not find my heart oppressed.   10
O be as others are to me,
Or let me be more to thee.

VII

STAY, cruel, stay!
  Pity mine anguish!
  And if I languish
For that which you do bear away,
  Ah! how can you be so unkind   5
As not to grieve for that you leave behind?
And if you'll go, yet let your pity stay.
But will you go and show that you neglect me?
Yet say farewell, and seem but to respect me.

VIII

TIME, cruel Time, canst thou subdue that brow
  That conquers all but thee, and thee too stays,
As if she were exempt from scythe or bow,
  From love and years, unsubject to decays?
Or art thou grown in league with those fair eyes,   5
  That they might help thee to consume our days?
Or dost thou love her for her cruelties,
  Being merciless like thee that no man weighs?
Then do so still, although she makes no 'steem
  Of days nor years, but lets them run in vain.   10
Hold still thy swift-winged hours, that wond'ring seem
  To gaze on her, even to turn back again;
And do so still, although she nothing cares.
  Do as I do, love her although unkind.
Hold still. Yet, O I fear, at unawares   15
  Thou wilt beguile her though thou seem'st so kind.
                              [*Samuel Daniel*]

IX–XI

Mrs. M. E. her funeral tears for the death of her husband.

GRIEF, keep within and scorn to show but tears,
  Since joy can weep as well as thou.
Disdain to sigh, for so can slender cares,
  Which but from idle causes grow.

Do not look forth, unless thou didst know how   5
To look with thine own face and as thou art,
    And only let my heart,
    That knows more reason why,
Pine, fret, consume, swell, burst, and die.

Drop not, mine eyes, nor trickle down so fast,   10
   For so you could do oft before
In our sad farewells and sweet meetings past;
   And shall his death now have no more?
   Can niggard sorrow yield no other store
To show the plenty of affliction's smart?   15
    Then only thou, poor heart,
    That know'st more reason why,
Pine, fret, consume, swell, burst, and die.

Have all our passions certain proper vents,
   And sorrow none that is her own,   20
But she must borrow others' complements
   To make her inward feelings known?
   Are joy's delights and death's compassion shown
With one like face and one lamenting part?
    Then only thou, poor heart,   25
    That know'st more reason why,
Pine, fret, consume, swell, burst, and die.

XII

    LET not Cloris think because
      She hath envassalled me,
    That her beauty can give laws
      To others that are free.
I was made to be the prey   5
      And booty of her eyes;
    In my bosom she may say
      Her greatest kingdom lies.

    Though others may her brow adore,
Yet more must I, that therein see far more   10
Than any others' eyes have power to see.
    She is to me
More than to any others she can be.

I can discern more secret notes,
That in the margin of her cheeks love quotes,   15
Than any else besides have art to read.
          No looks proceed
From those fair eyes but to me wonder breed.

          O then why
          Should she fly   20
     From him to whom her sight
     Doth add so much above her might?
          Why should not she
          Still joy to reign in me?

XIII–XV

CAN doleful notes to measured accents set
Express unmeasured griefs that time forget?
No, let chromatic tunes, harsh without ground,
     Be sullen music for a tuneless heart;
Chromatic tunes most like my passions sound,   5
     As if combined to bear their falling part.
Uncertain certain turns, of thoughts forecast
Bring back the same, then die, and, dying, last.

XVI

EYES, look no more, for what hath all the earth that's worth the
          sight?
Ears, hear no more, for what can breathe the voice of true delight?
Clothe thee, my heart, with dark black thoughts, and think but of
          despair.
Silence, lock up my words and scorn these idle sounds of air.
          Think glory, honour, joys, delights, contents   5
               Are but the empty reports
          Of unappropried terms that breath invents,
               Not knowing what it imports.
          But sorrow, grief, affliction, and despair,
               These are the things that are sure;   10
          And these we feel not as conceits in th' air,
               But as the same we endure.

Joys, delights, and pleasures in us hold such a doubtful part
          As if they were but thrall,
          And those were all in all.   15
For griefs, distrusts, remorse, I see, must domineer the heart.

Joys, delights, and pleasures makes grief to tyrannize us worse.
    Our mirth brings but distastes,
    For nought delights and lasts.
Grief, then take all my heart, for where none strive there needs
    less force.   20

XVII

If I could shut the gate against my thoughts,
    And keep out sorrow from this room within,
Or memory could cancel all the notes
    Of my misdeeds, and I unthink my sin,
How free, how clear, how clean my soul should lie,   5
Discharged of such a loathsome company.

Or were there other rooms without my heart,
    That did not to my conscience join so near,
Where I might lodge the thoughts of sin apart,
    That I might not their clam'rous crying hear,   10
What peace, what joy, what ease should I possess,
Freed from their horrors that my soul oppress.

But, O my Saviour, who my refuge art,
    Let thy dear mercies stand 'twixt them and me,
And be the wall to separate my heart,   15
    So that I may at length repose me free,
That peace and joy and rest may be within,
And I remain divided from my sin.

XVIII

I die whenas I do not see
Her that is life and all to me;
And when I see her, yet I die
In seeing of her cruelty.
So that to me like misery is wrought   5
Both when I see and when I see her not.

Or shall I speak or silent grieve?
Yet who will silency relieve?
And if I speak, I may offend;
    And speaking not, my heart will rend.   10
So that I see to me it is all one,
Speak I or speak I not, I am undone.

XIX

WHAT delight can they enjoy
  Whose hearts are not their own,
But are gone abroad, astray,
  And to others' bosoms flown?
Seely comforts, seely joy,   5
  Which fall and rise as others move,
Who seldom use to turn our way.
    And therefore Cloris will not love.
    For well I see
    How false men be,   10
And let them pine that lovers prove.

XX

NOW the earth, the skies, the air,
  And all things fair,
Seems new-born thoughts t' infuse;
Whilst the returning Spring
  Joys each thing,   5
And blasted hopes renews.
When I, when only I, alone
  Left to moan,
Find no times born for me.
No flowers, no meadow springs,   10
  No bird sings
But notes of misery.

JOHN DOWLAND

The First Booke of Songes or Ayres of fowre partes with Tableture for the Lute: So made that all the partes together, or either of them seuerally may be song to the Lute, Orpherian or Viol de gambo. . . . Also an inuention by the sayd Author for two to playe vpon one Lute. 1597

I

UNQUIET thoughts, your civil slaughter stint
  And wrap your wrongs within a pensive heart;
And you, my tongue, that makes my mouth a mint
  And stamps my thoughts to coin them words by art,
Be still, for if you ever do the like   5
I'll cut the string that makes the hammer strike.

But what can stay my thoughts they may not start,
  Or put my tongue in durance for to die,
Whenas these eyes, the keys of mouth and heart,
  Open the lock where all my love doth lie?   10
I'll seal them up within their lids for ever,
So thoughts and words and looks shall die together.

How shall I then gaze on my mistress' eyes?
  My thoughts must have some vent, else heart will break.
My tongue would rust as in my mouth it lies,   15
  If eyes and thoughts were free, and that not speak.
Speak then, and tell the passions of desire,
Which turns mine eyes to floods, my thoughts to fire.

II

WHO ever thinks or hopes of love for love,
  Or who, beloved, in Cupid's laws doth glory,
Who joys in vows, or vows not to remove,
  Who by this light god hath not been made sorry,
Let him see me eclipsed from my sun   5
With dark clouds of an earth quite overrun.

Who thinks that sorrows felt, desires hidden,
　　Or humble faith in constant honour armed
Can keep love from the fruit that is forbidden,
　　Who thinks that change is by entreaty charmed,　　10
Looking on me let him know love's delights
Are treasures hid in caves but kept by sprites.
　　　　　　　　　　　　　[*Fulke Greville, Lord Brooke*]

III

MY thoughts are winged with hopes, my hopes with love.
　　Mount, Love, unto the moon in clearest night,
And say, as she doth in the heavens move,
　　In earth so wanes and waxeth my delight.
And whisper this but softly in her ears:　　　　　　　　5
Hope oft doth hang the head, and Trust shed tears.

And you, my thoughts, that some mistrust do carry,
　　If for mistrust my mistress do you blame,
Say, though you alter, yet you do not vary,
　　As she doth change and yet remain the same.　　10
Distrust doth enter hearts but not infect,
And love is sweetest seasoned with suspect.

If she for this with clouds do mask her eyes,
　　And make the heavens dark with her disdain,
With windy sighs disperse them in the skies,　　　　15
　　Or with thy tears dissolve them into rain,
Thoughts, hopes, and love return to me no more
Till Cynthia shine as she hath done before.
　　　　　　　　　　[*Ascribed to George, Earl of Cumberland*]

IV

IF my complaints could passions move,
Or make Love see wherein I suffer wrong,
　　My passions were enough to prove
That my despairs had governed me too long.
　　　　O Love, I live and die in thee;　　　　　　5
　　　　　Thy grief in my deep sighs still speaks;
　　　　Thy wounds do freshly bleed in me;
　　　　　My heart for thy unkindness breaks.

Yet thou dost hope when I despair,
And when I hope thou mak'st me hope in vain.   10
Thou say'st thou canst my harms repair,
Yet for redress thou let'st me still complain.

Can Love be rich, and yet I want?
Is Love my judge, and yet am I condemned?
Thou plenty hast, yet me dost scant;   15
Thou made a god, and yet thy power contemned.
That I do live it is thy power;
That I desire, it is thy worth.
If Love doth make men's lives too sour,
Let me not love nor live henceforth.   20
Die shall my hopes, but not my faith,
That you, that of my fall may hearers be,
May hear Despair, which truly saith,
I was more true to Love than Love to me.

V

CAN she excuse my wrongs with Virtue's cloak?
Shall I call her good when she proves unkind?
Are those clear fires which vanish into smoke?
Must I praise the leaves where no fruit I find?
No, no. Where shadows do for bodies stand   5
Thou may'st be abused if thy sight be dim;
Cold love is like to words written on sand,
Or to bubbles which on the water swim.
Wilt thou be thus abused still,
Seeing that she will right thee never?   10
If thou canst not o'ercome her will
Thy love will be thus fruitless ever.

Was I so base that I might not aspire
Unto those high joys which she holds from me?
As they are high, so high is my desire.   15
If she this deny, what can granted be?
If she will yield to that which Reason is,
It is Reason's will that Love should be just.
Dear, make me happy still by granting this,
Or cut off delays if that die I must.   20

Better a thousand times to die
 Than for to live thus still tormented.
Dear, but remember it was I
 Who for thy sake did die contented.

VI

NOW, O now, I needs must part,
 Parting though I absent mourn.
Absence can no joy impart,
 Joy once fled cannot return.
While I live I needs must love;   5
 Love lives not when Hope is gone.
Now at last Despair doth prove
 Love divided loveth none.
  Sad despair doth drive me hence;
   This despair unkindness sends.   10
  If that parting be offence
   It is she which then offends.

Dear, when I from thee am gone,
 Gone are all my joys at once.
I loved thee and thee alone,   15
 In whose love I joyed once.
And although your sight I leave,
 Sight wherein my joys do lie,
Till that death do sense bereave,
 Never shall affection die.   20
  Sad despair doth drive me hence;
   This despair unkindness sends.
  If that parting be offence
   It is she which then offends.

Dear, if I do not return,   25
 Love and I shall die together;
For my absence never mourn,
 Whom you might have joyed ever.
Part we must, though now I die,
 Die I do to part with you.   30
Him despair doth cause to lie,
 Who both lived and dieth true.
  Sad despair doth drive me hence;
   This despair unkindness sends.
  If that parting be offence   35
   It is she which then offends.

VII

DEAR, if you change, I'll never choose again;
   Sweet, if you shrink, I'll never think of love;
Fair, if you fail, I'll judge all beauty vain;
   Wise, if too weak, moe wits I'll never prove.
Dear, Sweet, Fair, Wise, change, shrink, nor be not weak;   5
And, on my faith, my faith shall never break!

Earth with her flowers shall sooner heaven adorn;
   Heaven her bright stars through earth's dim globe shall move;
Fire heat shall lose, and frosts of flames be born;
   Air, made to shine, as black as hell shall prove.   10
Earth, Heaven, Fire, Air, the world transformed shall view,
Ere I prove false to faith, or strange to you.

VIII

BURST forth, my tears, assist my forward grief
   And show what pain imperious Love provokes.
Kind tender lambs, lament Love's scant relief,
   And pine, since pensive Care my freedom yokes.
   O pine to see me pine, my tender flocks!   5

Sad pining Care, that never may have peace,
   At Beauty's gate in hope of pity knocks.
But Mercy sleeps while deep Disdain increase,
   And Beauty Hope in her fair bosom locks.
   O grieve to hear my grief, my tender flocks!   10

Like to the winds my sighs have winged been,
   Yet are my sighs and suits repaid with mocks.
I plead, yet she repineth at my teen.
   O ruthless rigour, harder than the rocks,
   That both the shepherd kills and his poor flocks!   15

IX

GO, crystal tears, like to the morning showers,
   And sweetly weep into thy lady's breast;
And as the dews revive the drooping flowers,
   So let your drops of pity be addressed
To quicken up the thoughts of my desert,   5
Which sleeps too sound whilst I from her depart.

Haste, restless sighs, and let your burning breath
  Dissolve the ice of her indurate heart,
Whose frozen rigour, like forgetful death,
  Feels never any touch of my desert;   10
Yet sighs and tears to her I sacrifice
Both from a spotless heart and patient eyes.

                         X

      THINK'ST thou then by thy feigning
      Sleep, with a proud disdaining,
      Or with thy crafty closing
      Thy cruel eyes reposing,
      To drive me from thy sight,   5
      When sleep yields more delight,
        Such harmless beauty gracing?
      And while sleep feigned is,
      May not I steal a kiss,
        Thy quiet arms embracing?   10

      O that thy sleep dissembled
      Were to a trance resembled,
      Thy cruel eyes deceiving
      Of lively sense bereaving.
      Then should my love requite   15
      Thy love's unkind despite;
        While fury triumphed boldly
      In beauty's sweet disgrace,
      And lived in deep embrace
        Of her that loved so coldly.   20

      Should then my love aspiring,
      Forbidden joys desiring,
      So far exceed the duty
      That virtue owes to beauty?
      No, love, seek not thy bliss   25
      Beyond a simple kiss,
        For such deceits are harmless.
      Yet kiss a thousandfold,
      For kisses may be bold
        When lovely sleep is armless.   30

XI

COME away, come, sweet love,
    The golden morning breaks;
    All the earth, all the air
    Of love and pleasure speaks.
Teach thine arms then to embrace,   5
    And sweet, rosy lips to kiss,
    And mix our souls in mutual bliss.
Eyes were made for beauty's grace,
    Viewing, rueing love-long pain,
    Procured by beauty's rude disdain.   10

    Come away, come, sweet love,
    The golden morning wastes,
    While the sun from his sphere
    His fiery arrows casts,
Making all the shadows fly,   15
    Playing, staying in the grove
    To entertain the stealth of love.
Thither, sweet love, let us hie,
    Flying, dying in desire,
    Winged with sweet hopes and heavenly fire.   20

    Come away, come, sweet love,
    Do not in vain adorn
    Beauty's grace, that should rise
    Like to the naked morn.
Lilies on the river's side,   25
    And fair, Cyprian flowers new-blown,
    Desire no beauties but their own;
Ornament is nurse of pride,
    Pleasure, measure love's delight.
    Haste then, sweet love, our wished flight.   30

XII

REST awhile, you cruel cares,
    Be not more severe than love.
Beauty kills, and beauty spares,
    And sweet smiles sad sighs remove.

Laura, fair queen of my delight, 5
Come grant me love in love's despite,
  And if I ever fail to honour thee,
  Let this heavenly light I see
  Be as dark as hell to me.

If I speak, my words want weight; 10
  Am I mute, my heart doth break;
If I sigh, she fears deceit;
  Sorrow then for me must speak.
    Cruel unkind, with favour view
    The wound that first was made by you; 15
      And if my torments feigned be,
      Let this heavenly light I see
      Be as dark as hell to me.

Never hour of pleasing rest
  Shall revive my dying ghost, 20
Till my soul hath repossessed
  The sweet hope which love hath lost.
    Laura, redeem the soul that dies
    By fury of thy murdering eyes;
      And if it proves unkind to thee, 25
      Let this heavenly light I see
      Be as dark as hell to me.

XIII

SLEEP, wayward thoughts, and rest you with my love.
  Let not my Love be with my love diseased.
Touch not, proud hands, lest you her anger move,
  But pine you with my longings long displeased.
Thus while she sleeps I sorrow for her sake, 5
So sleeps my Love, and yet my love doth wake.

But O the fury of my restless fear;
  The hidden anguish of my flesh desires;
The glories and the beauties, that appear
  Between her brows near Cupid's closed fires. 10
Thus while she sleeps moves sighing for her sake.
So sleeps my Love, and yet my love doth wake.

My love doth rage, and yet my Love doth rest.
   Fear in my love, and yet my Love secure.
Peace in my Love, and yet my love oppressed,   15
   Impatient yet of perfect temperature.
Sleep, dainty Love, while I sigh for thy sake.
So sleeps my Love, and yet my love doth wake.

XIV

ALL ye whom Love or Fortune hath betrayed;
   All ye that dream of bliss, but live in grief;
All ye whose hopes are evermore delayed;
   All ye whose sighs or sickness wants relief;
Lend ears and tears to me, most hapless man,   5
That sings my sorrows like the dying swan.

Care that consumes the heart with inward pain;
   Pain that presents sad care in outward view;
Both, tyrant-like, enforce me to complain,
   But still in vain, for none my plaints will rue.   10
Tears, sighs, and ceaseless cries alone I spend,
My woe wants comfort, and my sorrow end.

XV

WILT thou unkind thus reave me
Of my heart, of my heart, and so leave me?
     Farewell!
     But yet or ere I part, O cruel!
     Kiss me sweet, sweet my jewel.   5

Hope by disdain grows cheerless,
Fear doth love, love doth fear beauty peerless.
     Farewell!
     But yet or ere I part, O cruel!
     Kiss me sweet, sweet my jewel.   10

If no delays can move thee
Life shall die, death shall live still to love thee.
     Farewell!
     But yet or ere I part, O cruel!
     Kiss me sweet, sweet my jewel.   15

Yet be thou mindful ever
Heat from fire, fire from heat none can sever.
Farewell!
But yet or ere I part, O cruel!
Kiss me sweet, sweet my jewel.   20

True love cannot be changed
Though delight from desert be estranged.
Farewell!
But yet or ere I part, O cruel!
Kiss me sweet, sweet my jewel.   25

XVI

WOULD my conceit that first enforced my woe,
    Or else mine eyes which still the same increase,
Might be extinct, to end my sorrows so,
    Which now are such as nothing can release,
Whose life is death, whose sweet each change of sour,   5
And eke whose hell reneweth every hour.

Each hour amidst the deep of hell I fry;
    Each hour I waste and wither where I sit;
But that sweet hour wherein I wish to die
    My hope, alas, may not enjoy it yet,   10
Whose hope is such, bereaved of the bliss
Which unto all save me allotted is.

To all save me is free to live or die;
    To all save me remaineth hap or hope;
But all perforce I must abandon, I,   15
    Sith Fortune still directs my hap a-slope.
Wherefore to neither hap nor hope I trust,
But to my thralls I yield, for so I must.

XVII

COME again! sweet love doth now invite
        Thy graces, that refrain
        To do me due delight,
To see, to hear, to touch, to kiss, to die
With thee again in sweetest sympathy.   5

Come again! that I may cease to mourn
    Through thy unkind disdain.
    For now left and forlorn
I sit, I sigh, I weep, I faint, I die
In deadly pain and endless misery.   10

All the day the sun that lends me shine
    By frowns do cause me pine,
    And feeds me with delay;
Her smiles my springs that makes my joys to grow;
Her frowns the winters of my woe.   15

All the night my sleeps are full of dreams,
    My eyes are full of streams;
    My heart takes no delight
To see the fruits and joys that some do find,
And mark the storms are me assigned.   20

Out alas! my faith is ever true;
    Yet will she never rue,
    Nor yield me any grace.
Her eyes of fire, her heart of flint is made,
Whom tears nor truth may once invade.   25

Gentle Love, draw forth thy wounding dart,
    Thou canst not pierce her heart;
    For I, that do approve,
By sighs and tears more hot than are thy shafts
Did tempt, while she for triumph laughs.   30

XVIII

His golden locks Time hath to silver turned.
    O Time too swift! O swiftness never ceasing!
His youth 'gainst Time and Age hath ever spurned,
    But spurned in vain; youth waneth by increasing.
Beauty, strength, youth are flowers but fading seen;   5
Duty, faith, love are roots and ever green.

His helmet now shall make a hive for bees,
    And lover's sonnets turn to holy psalms.
A man-at-arms must now serve on his knees,
    And feed on prayers which are Age's alms.
But though from Court to cottage he depart,   10
His Saint is sure of his unspotted heart.

And when he saddest sits in homely cell,
    He'll teach his swains this carol for a song:
Blest be the hearts that wish my Sovereign well.   15
    Curst be the soul that think her any wrong.
Goddess, allow this aged man his right
To be your bedesman now that was your knight.

                        [? *Sir Henry Lee*]

XIX

A WAKE, sweet love, thou art returned.
My heart, which long in absence mourned,
    Lives now in perfect joy.
Let love, which never absent dies,
Now live for ever in her eyes,   5
    Whence came my first annoy.

Only herself hath seemed fair,
    She, only, I could love,
She, only, drave me to despair
    When she unkind did prove.   10
Despair did make me wish to die,
    That I my joys might end.
She only, which did make me fly,
    My state may now amend.

If she esteem thee now aught worth,   15
She will not grieve thy love henceforth,
    Which so despair hath proved.
Despair hath proved now in me
That love will not unconstant be,
    Though long in vain I loved.   20

If she at last reward thy love
    And all thy harms repair,
Thy happiness will sweeter prove
    Raised up from deep despair.
And if that now thou welcome be   25
    When thou with her dost meet,
She all this while but played with thee
    To make thy joys more sweet.

                    H h

XX

COME, heavy Sleep, the image of true Death,
   And close up these my weary weeping eyes,
Whose spring of tears doth stop my vital breath,
   And tears my heart with Sorrow's sigh-swoll'n cries.
Come and possess my tired thought-worn soul,   5
That living dies, till thou on me be stole.

Come, shadow of my end, and shape of rest,
   Allied to Death, child to this black-faced Night;
Come thou and charm these rebels in my breast,
   Whose waking fancies doth my mind affright.   10
O come, sweet Sleep, come or I die for ever;
Come ere my last sleep comes, or come never.

XXI

AWAY with these self-loving lads,
Whom Cupid's arrow never glads!
Away, poor souls, that sigh and weep
In love of them that lie and sleep!
For Cupid is a meadow god   5
And forceth none to kiss the rod.

God Cupid's shaft, like destiny,
Doth either good or ill decree.
Desert is born out of his bow,
Reward upon his foot doth go.   10
What fools are they that have not known
That Love likes no laws but his own!

My songs they be of Cynthia's praise;
I wear her rings on holidays,
On every tree I write her name,   15
And every day I read the same.
Where Honour Cupid's rival is
There miracles are seen of his.

If Cynthia crave her ring of me,
I blot her name out of the tree.   20
If doubt do darken things held dear,
Then well fare nothing once a year!
For many run, but one must win;
Fools, only, hedge the cuckoo in.

The worth that worthiness should move   25
Is love, which is the bow of Love.
And love as well the foster can
As can the mighty nobleman.
Sweet saint, 'tis true you worthy be,
Yet without love naught worth to me.   30

[*Fulke Greville, Lord Brooke*]

ༀༀༀༀༀༀༀༀ

The Second Booke of Songs or Ayres, of 2. 4. and 5. parts: With Tableture for
the Lute or Orpherian, with the Violl de Gamba. . . . Also an excelent lesson
for the Lute and Base Viol, called Dowlands adew.   *1600*

I

To the most famous Anthony Holborne

I s A w my lady weep,
And Sorrow proud to be advanced so
In those fair eyes where all perfections keep.
     Her face was full of woe;
But such a woe, believe me, as wins more hearts   5
Than Mirth can do with her enticing parts.

     Sorrow was there made fair,
And Passion wise, tears a delightful thing;
Silence beyond all speech a wisdom rare.
     She made her sighs to sing,   10
And all things with so sweet a sadness move
As made my heart at once both grieve and love.

     O fairer than aught else
The world can show, leave off in time to grieve.
Enough, enough your joyful looks excels;   15
     Tears kills the heart, believe.
     O strive not to be excellent in woe,
Which only breeds your beauty's overthrow.

II

Lachrimae

F L O W, my tears, fall from your springs!
     Exiled for ever let me mourn;
Where night's black bird her sad infamy sings,
     There let me live forlorn.

Down, vain lights, shine you no more!   5
  No nights are dark enough for those
That in despair their lost fortunes deplore.
  Light doth but shame disclose.

Never may my woes be relieved,
  Since pity is fled;   10
And tears and sighs and groans my weary days
  Of all joys have deprived.

From the highest spire of contentment
  My fortune is thrown;
And fear and grief and pain for my deserts   15
  Are my hopes, since hope is gone.

Hark! you shadows that in darkness dwell,
  Learn to contemn light.
Happy, happy they that in hell
  Feel not the world's despite.   20

III

SORROW, stay! lend true repentant tears
  To a woeful wretched wight.
Hence, Despair! with thy tormenting fears
  O do not my poor heart affright.
Pity, help! now or never,   5
  Mark me not to endless pain.
Alas, I am condemned ever,
  No hope, no help there doth remain.
    But down, down, down I fall,
    And arise I never shall.   10

IV

DIE not before thy day, poor man condemned,
  But lift thy low looks from the humble earth.
Kiss not Despair and see sweet Hope contemned,
  The hag hath no delight but moan for mirth.
O fie, poor fondling! fie! be willing   5
To preserve thyself from killing.
Hope, thy keeper, glad to free thee,
Bids thee go and will not see thee.
Hie thee quickly from thy wrong!
So she ends her willing song.   10

V

MOURN! mourn! Day is with darkness fled.
   What heaven then governs earth?
O none but hell in heaven's stead
   Chokes with his mists our mirth.
Mourn! mourn! look now for no more day   5
   Nor night, but that from hell.
Then all must as they may
   In darkness learn to dwell.
But yet this change must needs change our delight,
That thus the sun should harbour with the night.   10

VI–VIII

TIME'S eldest son, Old Age, the heir of Ease,
   Strength's foe, Love's woe, and foster to Devotion,
Bids gallant youths in martial prowess please,
   As for himself he hath no earthly motion,
But thinks sighs, tears, vows, prayers, and sacrifices   5
As good as shows, masks, jousts, or tilt devices.

Then sit thee down and say thy *Nunc dimittis*,
   With *De profundis, Credo,* and *Te Deum,*
Chant *Miserere;* for what now so fit is
   As that, or this: *Paratum est cor meum?*   10
O that thy saint would take in worth thy heart,
Thou canst not please her with a better part.

When others sings *Venite exultemus,*
   Stand by and turn to *Noli aemulare;*
For *Quare fremuerunt* use *Oremus,*   15
   Vivat Eliza for an *Ave Mary;*
And teach those swains that lives about thy cell
To say *Amen* when thou dost pray so well.
                        [attrib. to Sir Henry Lee]

IX

PRAISE blindness, eyes, for seeing is deceit.
   Be dumb, vain tongue, words are but flattering winds.
Break, heart, and bleed, for there is no receipt
   To purge inconstancy from most men's minds.

And if thine ears, false heralds to thy heart,   5
  Convey into thy head hopes to obtain,
Then tell thy hearing thou art deaf by art,
  Now love is art that wonted to be plain;

Now none is bald except they see his brains;
  Affection is not known till one be dead;   10
Reward for love are labours for his pains;
  Love's quiver made of gold, his shafts of lead.

L'envoi

And so I waked amazed and could not move.
I know my dream was true and yet I love.

X

To Master Hugh Holland

O SWEET woods, the delight of solitariness,
O how much do I love your solitariness!
  From Fame's desire, from love's delight retired,
    In these sad groves an hermit's life I led;
  And those false pleasures which I once admired,   5
    With sad remembrance of my fall I dread.
To birds, to trees, to earth impart I this,
For she less secret and as senseless is.

O sweet woods, the delight of solitariness,
O how much do I love your solitariness!   10
  Experience, which repentance only brings,
    Doth bid me now my heart from love estrange.
  Love is disdained when it doth look at kings;
    And love, low-placed, base and apt to change.
  There power doth take from him his liberty;   15
  Her want of worth makes him in cradle die.

O sweet woods, the delight of solitariness,
O how much do I love your solitariness!
  You men that give false worship unto love,
    And seek that which you never shall obtain,   20
  The endless work of Sisyphus you prove,
    Whose end is this: to know you strive in vain.
  Hope and Desire, which now your idols be,
  You needs must lose and feel despair with me.

O sweet woods, the delight of solitariness,   25
O how much do I love your solitariness!
  You woods, in you the fairest nymphs have walked,
    Nymphs at whose sight all hearts did yield to love.
  You woods, in whom dear lovers oft have talked,
    How do you now a place of mourning prove?   30
Wanstead, my mistress saith this is the doom,
Thou art Love's childbed, nursery and tomb.

O sweet woods, the delight of solitariness,
O how much do I love your solitariness!

XI

IF floods of tears could cleanse my follies past,
  And smokes of sighs might sacrifice for sin;
If groaning cries might salve my fault at last,
  Or endless moan for error pardon win,
Then would I cry, weep, sigh, and ever moan,   5
Mine errors, faults, sins, follies, past and gone.

I see my hopes must wither in their bud;
  I see my favours are no lasting flowers;
I see that words will breed no better good
  Than loss of time, and lightening but at hours.   10
Thus when I see, then thus I say therefore
That favours, hopes, and words can blind no more.

XII

FINE knacks for ladies, cheap, choice, brave and new!
  Good pennyworths! but money cannot move.
I keep a fair but for the fair to view;
  A beggar may be liberal of love.
Though all my wares be trash, the heart is true,   5
     The heart is true,
     The heart is true.

Great gifts are guiles and look for gifts again;
  My trifles come as treasures from my mind.
It is a precious jewel to be plain;   10
  Sometimes in shell th' orienst pearls we find.
Of others take a sheaf, of me a grain,
     Of me a grain,
     Of me a grain.

Within this pack pins, points, laces, and gloves,   15
    And divers toys fitting a country fair.
But in my heart, where duty serves and loves,
    Turtles and twins, court's brood, a heavenly pair.
Happy the heart that thinks of no removes,
                Of no removes,   20
                Of no removes.

XIII

NOW cease, my wandering eyes,
    Strange beauties to admire.
In change least comfort lies;
    Long joys yield long desire.
        One faith, one love   5
Makes our frail pleasures eternal, and in sweetness prove.
        New hopes, new joys
Are still with sorrow declining unto deep annoys.

One man hath but one soul
    Which art cannot divide.   10
If all one soul must love
    Two loves must be denied.
        One soul, one love,
By faith and merit united cannot remove.
        Distracted spirits   15
Are ever changing and hapless in their delights.

Nature two eyes hath given
    All beauty to impart
As well in earth as heaven;
    But she hath given one heart;   20
        That, though we see
Ten thousand beauties, yet in us one should be
        One steadfast love,
Because our hearts stand fixed although our eyes do move.

XIV

COME, ye heavy states of night,
Do my father's spirit right.
Soundings baleful let me borrow,
Burthening my song with sorrow.
Come, sorrow, come, her eyes that sings   5
By thee are turned into springs.

Come, you virgins of the night,
That in dirges sad delight,
Choir my anthems. I do borrow
Gold nor pearl, but sounds of sorrow.   10
Come, sorrow, come, her eyes that sings
By thee are turned into springs.

XV

WHITE as lilies was her face.
          When she smiled
          She beguiled,
Quitting faith with foul disgrace.
Virtue, service thus neglected,   5
Heart with sorrows hath infected.

When I swore my heart her own,
          She disdained;
          I complained;
Yet she left me overthrown,   10
Careless of my bitter grieving,
Ruthless, bent to no relieving.

Vows and oaths and faith assured,
          Constant ever,
          Changing never;   15
Yet she could not be procured
To believe my pains exceeding,
From her scant neglect proceeding.

O that love should have the art
          By surmises   20
          And disguises
To destroy a faithful heart;
Or that wanton-looking women
Should reward their friends as foemen.

All in vain is ladies' love,   25
          Quickly choosed,
          Shortly loosed;
For their pride is to remove.
Out alas! their looks first won us,
And their pride hath straight undone us.   30

To thyself, the sweetest fair,
   Thou hast wounded
   And confounded
Changeless faith with foul despair.
And my service hath envied   35
And my succours hath denied.

By thine error thou hast lost
   Heart unfeigned,
   Truth unstained,
And the swain that loved most,   40
More assured in love than many,
More despised in love than any.

For my heart, though set at naught,
   Since you will it,
   Spoil, and kill it,   45
I will never change my thoughts,
But grieve that Beauty ere was born.
[And so I'll live as one forlorn.]

XVI

WOEFUL heart with grief oppressed,
Since my fortunes most distressed
   From my joys hath me removed,
Follow those sweet eyes adored,
Those sweet eyes wherein are stored   5
   All my pleasures best beloved.

Fly my breast, leave me forsaken,
Wherein grief his seat hath taken,
   All his arrows through me darting.
Thou mayest live by her sun-shining,   10
I shall suffer no more pining
   By thy loss than by her parting.

XVII

A SHEPHERD in a shade his plaining made
   Of love and lovers' wrong
Unto the fairest lass that trod on grass,
   And thus began his song:

Restore, restore my heart again,   5
 Which love by thy sweet looks hath slain,
Lest that, enforced by your disdain, I sing:
Fie, fie on love, it is a foolish thing.

Since love and fortune will, I honour still
     Your fair and lovely eye.   10
What conquest will it be, sweet nymph, for thee
     If I for sorrow die?
 Restore, restore my heart again,
 Which love by thy sweet looks hath slain,
Lest that, enforced by your disdain, I sing: 15
Fie, fie on love, it is a foolish thing.

My heart where have you laid? O cruel maid,
     To kill, when you might save!
Why have ye cast it forth as nothing worth,
     Without a tomb or grave?   20
 O let it be entombed and lie
 In your sweet mind and memory,
Lest I resound on every warbling string:
Fie, fie on love, that is a foolish thing.

XVIII

FACTION, that ever dwells
In Court where wits excels,
   Hath set defiance.
Fortune and Love hath sworn
That they were never born   5
   Of one alliance.

Fortune swears weakest hearts
The book of Cupid's arts
   Turn with her wheel.
Senses themselves shall prove,   10
Venture her place in Love;
   Ask them that feel.

This discord it begot
Atheists, that honour not
   Nature, thought good;   15
Fortune should ever dwell
In Court where wits excel,
   Love keep the wood.

So to the wood went I
With Love to live and die,   20
   Fortune's forlorn.
Experience of my youth
Made me think humble Truth
   In desert born.

My saint is dear to me,   25
And Joan herself is she,
   Joan fair and true;
Joan that doth ever move
Passions of love with love.
   Fortune adieu!   30

             [*Fulke Greville, Lord Brooke*]

XIX

SHALL I sue? shall I seek for grace?
   Shall I pray? shall I prove?
Shall I strive to a heavenly joy
   With an earthly love?
Shall I think that a bleeding heart   5
   Or a wounded eye,
Or a sigh can ascend the clouds
   To attain so high?

Silly wretch, forsake these dreams
   Of a vain desire;   10
O bethink what high regard
   Holy hopes do require.
Favour is as fair as things are,
   Treasure is not bought;
Favour is not won with words,   15
   Nor the wish of a thought.

Pity is but a poor defence
   For a dying heart;
Ladies' eyes respect no moan
   In a mean desert.   20
She is too worthy far
   For a worth so base,
Cruel and but just is she
   In my just disgrace.

Justice gives each man his own.   25
    Though my love be just
Yet will not she pity my grief,
    Therefore die I must.
Silly heart, then yield to die,
    Perish in despair.   30
Witness yet how fain I die
    When I die for the fair.

XX

Toss not my soul, O Love, 'twixt hope and fear.
    Show me some ground where I may firmly stand
Or surely fall; I care not which appear,
    So one will close me in a certain band.

Take me, Assurance, to thy blissful hold,   5
    Or thou, Despair, unto thy darkest cell.
Each hath full rest, the one in joys enrolled,
    Th' other, in that he fears no more, is well.

L'envoi

When once of ill the uttermost is known,
The strength of sorrow quite is overthrown.   10

XXI

Clear or cloudy, sweet as April showering,
    Smooth or frowning, so is her face to me.
Pleased or smiling, like mild May all flowering,
    When skies blue silk, and meadows carpets be,
Her speeches, notes of that night bird that singeth, 5
Who thought all sweet, yet jarring notes out-ringeth.

Her grace like June, when earth and trees be trimmed
    In best attire of complete beauty's height.
Her love again like summer's days be-dimmed
    With little clouds of doubtful constant faith.   10
Her trust, her doubt, like rain and heat in skies
Gently thundering, she lightning to mine eyes.

Sweet summer-spring, that breatheth life and growing
    In weeds as into herbs and flowers,
And sees of service divers sorts in sowing,   15
    Some haply seeming, and some being, yours;

Rain on your herbs and flowers that truly serve,
And let your weeds lack dew, and duly starve.

XXII. *A Dialogue.*

[*1st Voice.*]　　HUMOUR, say what mak'st thou here
　　　　　　　　In the presence of a queen?
[*2nd Voice.*]　　Princes hold conceit most dear,
　　　　　　　　All conceit in humour seen.
[*1st Voice.*]　　Thou art a heavy leaden mood.　　　　　5
[*2nd Voice.*]　　Humour is Invention's food.
　　Chorus.　　　　But never humour yet was true,
　　　　　　　　　But that which only pleaseth you.

[*1st Voice.*]　　O I am as heavy as earth,
　　　　　　　　Say then, who is Humour now?　　　　10
[*2nd Voice.*]　　I am now inclined to mirth,
　　　　　　　　Humour I as well as thou.
[*1st Voice.*]　　Why then 'tis I am drowned in woe.
[*2nd Voice.*]　　No, no, Wit is cherished so.
　　Chorus.　　　　But never humour yet was true,　　　15
　　　　　　　　　But that which only pleaseth you.

[*1st Voice.*]　　Mirth then is drowned in sorrow's brim.
　　　　　　　　O in sorrow all things sleep.
[*2nd Voice.*]　　No, no, fool, the light'st things swim.
　　　　　　　　Heavy things sink to the deep.　　　　20
[*1st Voice.*]　　In her presence all things smile.
[*2nd Voice.*]　　Humour frolic then awhile.
　　Chorus.　　　　But never humour yet was true,
　　　　　　　　　But that which only pleaseth you.

*The Third And Last Booke Of Songs Or Aires. Newly composed to sing to the
Lute, Orpharion, or viols, and a dialogue for a base and meane Lute with
fiue voices to sing thereto.* 1603

I

FAREWELL, too fair, too chaste, but too too cruel,
  Discretion never quenched fire with swords.
Why hast thou made my heart thine anger's fuel,
  And now would kill my passions with thy words?
This is proud beauty's true anatomy: 5
If that secure, severe in secrecy.
                              Farewell, farewell.

Farewell, too dear, and too too much desired,
  Unless compassion dwelt more near thy heart.
Love by neglect, though constant, oft is tired   10
  And forced from bliss unwillingly to part.
This is proud beauty's true anatomy:
If that secure, severe in secrecy.
                              Farewell, farewell.

II

TIME stands still with gazing on her face.
Stand still and gaze, for minutes, hours and years to her give place.
  All other things shall change but she remains the same,
Till heavens changed have their course and Time hath lost his name.
Cupid doth hover up and down, blinded with her fair eyes,   5
And Fortune captive at her feet contemned and conquered lies.

  When Fortune, Love, and Time attend on
Her with my fortunes, love, and time I honour will alone.
  If bloodless Envy say Duty hath no desert,
Duty replies that Envy knows herself his faithful heart.   10
My settled vows and spotless faith no fortune can remove,
Courage shall show my inward faith, and faith shall try my love.

III

BEHOLD a wonder here,
  Love hath received his sight,
Which many hundred years
  Hath not beheld the light.

Such beams infused be   5
    By Cynthia in his eyes,
As first have made him see
    And then have made him wise.

Love now no more will weep
    For them that laugh the while;   10
Nor wake for them that sleep,
    Nor sigh for them that smile.

So powerful is the beauty
    That Love doth now behold,
As love is turned to duty   15
    That's neither blind nor bold.

This Beauty shows her might
    To be of double kind,
In giving Love his sight
    And striking Folly blind.   20

IV

DAPHNE was not so chaste as she was changing,
    Soon-begun love with hate estranging.
He that to-day triumphs with favours graced,
    Falls before night with scorns defaced.
Yet is thy beauty feigned, and every one desires   5
    Still the false light of thy traitorous fires.

Beauty can want no grace by true love viewed;
    Fancy by looks is still renewed,
Like to a fruitful tree it ever groweth,
    Or the fresh spring that endless floweth.   10
But if that Beauty were of one consent with Love,
    Love should live free and true pleasure prove.

V

ME, me, and none but me,
    Dart home, O gentle Death,
And quickly, for
    I draw too long this idle breath.
O how I long till I   5
    May fly to heaven above,
Unto my faithful and
    Beloved turtle-dove.

Like to the silver swan
   Before my death I sing,   10
And, yet alive,
   My fatal knell I help to ring.
Still I desire from earth
   And earthly joys to fly.
He never happy lived   15
   That cannot love to die.

VI

WHEN Phoebus first did Daphne love,
And no means might her favour move,
He craved the cause. The cause, quoth she,
Is I have vowed virginity.
Then in a rage he sware and said: 5
Past fifteen none but one should live a maid.

If maidens then shall chance be sped
Ere they can scarcely dress their head,
Yet pardon them, for they be loath
To make good Phoebus break his oath.   10
And better 'twere a child were born
Than that a god should be foresworn.
                    [*attrib. to William, Earl of Pembroke*]

VII

SAY, Love, if ever thou didst find
A woman with a constant mind?
      None but one.
And what should that rare mirror be?
Some goddess or some queen is she?   5
   She, she, she, and only she,
She only Queen of love and beauty.

But could thy fiery poisoned dart
At no time touch her spotless heart,
      Nor come near?   10
She is not subject to Love's bow;
Her eye commands, her heart saith No.
   No, no, no, and only no!
One No another still doth follow.

How might I that fair wonder know   15
That mocks desire with endless no?
      See the moon
That ever in one change doth grow
Yet still the same; and she is so;
      So, so, so, and only so.   20
From heaven her virtues she doth borrow.

To her then yield thy shafts and bow,
That can command affections so.
      Love is free;
So are her thoughts that vanquish thee.   25
There is no Queen of love but she,
      She, she, she, and only she,
She only Queen of love and beauty.

VIII

FLOW not so fast, ye fountains;
   What needeth all this haste?
Swell not above your mountains,
   Nor spend your time in waste.
Gentle springs, freshly your salt tears   5
Must still fall dropping from their spheres.

Weep they apace whom Reason
   Or ling'ring Time can ease.
My sorrow can no Season,
   Nor aught besides, appease.   10
Gentle springs, freshly your salt tears
Must still fall dropping from their spheres.

Time can abate the terror
   Of every common pain;
But common grief is error,   15
   True grief will still remain.
Gentle springs, freshly your salt tears
Must still fall dropping from their spheres.

IX

WHAT if I never speed?
   Shall I straight yield to despair,
And still on sorrow feed
   That can no loss repair?

Or shall I change my love? 5
　For I find power to depart,
And in my reason prove
　I can command my heart.
But if she will pity my desire and my love requite,
　Then ever shall she live my dear delight. 10
Come, come, while I have a heart to desire thee,
Come, for either I will love or admire thee.

　　Oft have I dreamed of joy,
　　　Yet I never felt the sweet;
　　But, tired with annoy, 15
　　　My griefs each other greet.
　　Oft have I left my hope
　　　As a wretch by fate forlorn;
　　But love aims at one scope,
　　　And, lost, will still return. 20
He that once loves with a true desire never can depart,
　For Cupid is the king of every heart.
Come, come, while I have a heart to desire thee,
Come, for either I will love or admire thee.

X

LOVE stood amazed at sweet Beauty's pain.
Love would have said that all was but vain,
　And gods but half divine.
But when Love saw that Beauty would die,
He all aghast to heavens did cry: 5
　O gods, what wrong is mine!

Then his tears, bred in thoughts of salt brine,
Fell from his eyes like rain in sunshine,
　Expelled by rage of fire.
Yet in such wise as anguish affords, 10
He did express in these his last words
　His infinite desire:

Are you fled, fair? where are now those eyes,
Eyes but too fair, envied by the skies?
　You angry gods do know. 15
With guiltless blood your sceptres you stain;
On poor true hearts like tyrants you reign.
　Unjust, why do you so?

Are you false gods? why then do you reign?
Are you just gods? why then have you slain   20
        The life of Love on earth?
Beauty, now thy face lives in the skies.
Beauty, now let me live in thine eyes,
        Where bliss felt never death.

Then from high rock, the rock of despair,   25
He falls, in hope to smother in the air,
        Or else on stones to burst,
Or on cold waves to spend his last breath,
Or his strange life to end by strange death,
        But Fate forbid the worst.   30

With pity moved, the gods then change Love
To Phoenix shape, yet cannot remove
        His wonted property.
He loves the sun because it is fair;
Sleep he neglects, he lives but by air,   35
        And would, but cannot, die.

XI

LEND your ears to my sorrow,
Good people that have any pity;
        For no eyes will I borrow,
Mine own shall grace my doleful ditty.
        Chant then, my voice, though rude like to my rhyming, 5
And tell forth my grief, which here in sad despair
        Can find no ease of tormenting.

Once I lived, once I knew delight,
No grief did shadow then my pleasure;
        Graced with love, cheered with beauty's sight, 10
I joyed alone true heavenly treasure.
        O what a heaven is love firmly embraced!
Such power alone can fix delight
        In fortune's bosom ever placed.

Cold as ice, frozen is that heart   15
Where thought of love could no time enter;
        Such of life reap the poorest part,
Whose weight cleaves to this earthly centre.

Mutual joys in hearts truly united
Do earth to heavenly state convert,   20
Like heaven still in itself delighted.

XII

BY a fountain where I lay,
All blessed be that blessed day!
By the glimmering of the sun,
O never be her shining done!
  When I might see alone   5
  My true love's fairest one,
    Love's dear light,
    Love's clear sight,
No world's eyes can clearer see,
A fairer sight none can be.   10

Fair with garlands all addressed,
Was never nymph more fairly blessed,
Blessed in the highest degree,
So may she ever blessed be!
  Came to this fountain near   15
  With such a smiling cheer,
    Such a face!
    Such a grace!
Happy, happy eyes that see
Such a heavenly sight as she!   20

Then I forthwith took my pipe,
Which I all fair and clean did wipe,
And upon a heavenly ground
All in the grace of beauty found,
  Played this roundelay: 25
  Welcome fair Queen of May!
    Sing, sweet air,
    Welcome fair,
Welcome be the shepherds' Queen,
The glory of all our green.   30

XIII

O WHAT hath overwrought
My all-amazed thought?
Or whereto am I brought,
That thus in vain have sought?

Till time and truth hath taught   5
I labour all for naught.
The day I see is clear,
But I am ne'er the near,
For grief doth still appear
To cross our merry cheer.   10
While I can nothing hear
But Winter all the year.
Cold, hold! the sun will shine warm.
    Therefore now fear no harm.
       O blessed beams   15
       Where beauty streams,
Happy, happy light to love's dreams.

XIV

FAREWELL, unkind, farewell! to me no more a father,
    Since my heart holds my love most dear.
The wealth which thou dost reap, another's hand must gather,
    Though thy heart still lies buried there.
       Then farewell, O farewell!   5
Welcome my love! welcome my joy for ever!

'Tis not the vain desire of human fleeting beauty
    Makes my mind to live, though my means do die.
Nor do I Nature wrong, though I forget my duty.
    Love not in the blood but in the spirit doth lie.   10
       Then farewell, O farewell!
Welcome my love! welcome my joy for ever!

XV

WEEP you no more, sad fountains;
    What need you flow so fast?
Look how the snowy mountains
    Heaven's sun doth gently waste.
       But my sun's heavenly eyes   5
       View not your weeping,
       That now lies sleeping
    Softly, now softly lies
       Sleeping.

Sleep is a reconciling,
    A rest that peace begets.
Doth not the sun rise smiling
    When fair at ev'n he sets?
        Rest you then, rest, sad eyes,
            Melt not in weeping   15
            While she lies sleeping
        Softly, now softly lies
            Sleeping.

XVI

FIE on this feigning!
    Is love without desire,
Heat still remaining,
    And yet no spark of fire?
Thou art untrue, nor wert with fancy moved,   5
For desire hath power on all that ever loved.

    Show some relenting,
        Or grant thou dost now love.
    Two hearts consenting
        Shall they no comforts prove?   10
Yield, or confess that love is without pleasure,
And that women's bounties rob men of their treasure.

    Truth is not placed
        In words and forced smiles,
    Love is not graced   15
        With that which still beguiles.
Love or dislike, yield fire or give no fuel;
So mayest thou prove kind, or at the least less cruel.

XVII

I MUST complain, yet do enjoy my love.
    She is too fair, too rich in beauty's parts.
Thence is my grief; for Nature, while she strove
    With all her graces and divinest arts
To form her too too beautiful of hue,   5
She had no leisure left to make her true.

Should I aggrieved then wish she were less fair?
  That were repugnant to my own desires.
She is admired, new suitors still repair
  That kindles daily love's forgetful fires.   10
Rest, jealous thoughts, and thus resolve at last,
She hath more beauty than becomes the chaste.

                        [*Thomas Campian*]

XVIII

IT was a time when silly bees could speak,
  And in that time I was a silly bee,
Who fed on time until my heart 'gan break,
  Yet never found the time would favour me.
Of all the swarm I only did not thrive,   5
Yet brought I wax and honey to the hive.

Then thus I buzzed when time no sap would give:
  Why should this blessed time to me be dry,
Sith by this time the lazy drone doth live,
  The wasp, the worm, the gnat, the butterfly.   10
Mated with grief I kneeled on my knees,
And thus complained unto the king of bees:

My liege, gods grant thy time may never end,
  And yet vouchsafe to hear my plaint of time,
Which fruitless flies have found to have a friend,   15
  And I cast down when atomies do climb.
The king replied but thus: Peace, peevish bee,
Thou'rt bound to serve the time, the time not thee.

          [*Ascribed to Robert, Earl of Essex*]

XIX

THE lowest trees have tops, the ant her gall,
  The fly her spleen, the little spark his heat.
And slender hairs cast shadows though but small;
  And bees have stings although they be not great.
Seas have their source, and so have shallow springs;   5
And Love is Love in beggars and in kings.

Where waters smoothest run, deep are the fords;
  The dial stirs, yet none perceives it move.
The firmest faith is in the fewest words;
  The turtles cannot sing, and yet they love.   10

True hearts have eyes and ears, no tongues to speak;
They hear and see and sigh, and then they break.
                    [*Ascribed to Sir Edward Dyer*]

XX

WHAT poor astronomers are they
    Take women's eyes for stars;
And set their thoughts in battle ray
    To fight such idle wars.
When in the end they shall approve   5
'Tis but a jest drawn out of love.

And love itself is but a jest
    Devised by idle heads,
To catch young fancies in the nest
    And lay it in fools' beds.   10
That being hatched in beauty's eyes
They may be fledge ere they be wise.

But yet it is a sport to see
    How Wit will run on wheels,
While Will cannot persuaded be   15
    With that which Reason feels:
That women's eyes and stars are odd,
And Love is but a feigned god.

But such as will run mad with Will,
    I cannot clear their sight,   20
But leave them to their study still
    To look where is no light;
Till time too late we make them try
They study false astronomy.

XXI. *Dialogue*

[*1st Voice.*]   COME when I call, or tarry till I come,
                    If you be deaf, I must prove dumb.
[*2nd Voice.*]   Stay awhile, my heavenly joy, I come with wings of love,
                    When envious eyes Time shall remove.
[*1st Voice.*]   If thy desire ever knew the grief of delay   5
                    No danger could stand in thy way.
[*2nd Voice.*]   O do not add this sorrow to my grief,
                    That languish here wanting relief.
[*1st Voice.*]   What need we languish? Can Love quickly fly?
                    Fear ever hurts more than jealousy.   10

Chorus. Then securely envy scorning
    Let us end with joy our mourning.
    Jealousy still defy,
    And love till we die.

A Pilgrimes Solace. Wherein is contained Musical Harmonie of 3. 4. and 5. parts, to be sung and plaid with the Lute and Viols. 1612

I

DISDAIN me still, that I may ever love;
    For who his love enjoys can love no more.
The war once past, with ease men cowards prove,
    And ships returned do rot upon the shore.
And though thou frown I'll say thou art most fair,   5
And still I'll love, though still I must despair.

As heat to life, so is desire to love,
    And these once quenched, both life and love are gone.
Let not my sighs nor tears thy virtue move;
    Like baser metals do not melt too soon.   10
Laugh at my woes, although I ever mourn;
Love surfeits with reward, his nurse is scorn.
        [*Ascribed to William, Earl of Pembroke*]

II

To my worthy friend Mr. William Jewel, of Exeter College in Oxford

SWEET, stay awhile; why will you rise?
The light you see comes from your eyes.
The day breaks not, it is my heart,
To think that you and I must part.
O stay, or else my joys must die   5
And perish in their infancy.

Dear, let me die in this fair breast,
Far sweeter than the Phoenix' nest.
Love raise desire by his sweet charms
Within this circle of thine arms;   10
And let thy blissful kisses cherish
Mine infant joys that else must perish.

III

To ask for all thy love and thy whole heart
        'Twere madness.
       I do not sue
        Nor can admit,
      Fairest, from you   5
        To have all yet.
Who giveth all hath nothing to impart
        But sadness.

He that receiveth all, can have no more
        Than seeing.   10
      My love by length
       Of every hour
     Gathers new strength,
       New growth, new flower.
You must have daily new rewards in store,   15
        Still being.

You cannot every day give me your heart
        For merit.
       Yet, if you will,
        When yours doth go   20
      You shall have still
        One to bestow;
For you shall mine when yours doth part
        Inherit.

Yet if you please I'll find a better way   25
        Than change them;
      For so alone,
       Dearest, we shall
      Be one and one
        Another's all.   30
Let us so join our hearts that nothing may
        Estrange them.

IV

Love, those beams that breed all day long, breed and feed this
    burning,
Love, I quench with floods, floods of tears, nightly tears and
    mourning.
  But, alas, tears cool this fire in vain;
  The more I quench the more there doth remain.

I'll go to the woods, and alone make my moan, O cruel!   5
For I am deceived and bereaved of my life, my jewel.
  O but in the woods, though Love be blind,
  He hath his spies my secret haunts to find.

Love, then I must yield to thy might, might and spite, oppressed,
Since I see my wrongs, woe is me, cannot be redressed.   10
  Come at last, be friendly, Love, to me,
  And let me not endure this misery.

                             V

          SHALL I strive with words to move
              When deeds receive not due regard?
          Shall I speak and neither please
              Nor be freely heard?

          Grief, alas, though all in vain,   5
              Her restless anguish must reveal.
          She alone my wound shall know
              Though she will not heal.

          All woes have end though awhile delayed,
              Our patience proving.   10
          O that Time's strange effects
              Could but make her loving.

          Storms calm at last, and why may not
              She leave off her frowning?
          O sweet Love, help her hands,   15
              My affection crowning.

      I wooed her, I loved her, and none but her admire;
      O come, dear joy, and answer my desire.

                             VI

          WERE every thought an eye,
              And all those eyes could see,
          Her subtle wiles their sights would beguile
              And mock their jealousy.

          Her fires do inward burn,   5
              They make no outward show;
          And her delights amid the dark shades
              Which none discover, grow.

    Desire lives in her heart,
        Diana in her eyes.   10
'Twere vain to wish women true; 'tis well
    If they prove wise.

    The flower's growth is unseen,
        Yet every day it grows;
So where her fancy is set it thrives,   15
    But how, none knows.

Such a love deserves more grace
    Than a truer heart that hath no conceit
To make use both of time and place,
    When a wit hath need of all his sleight.   20

VII

STAY, Time, awhile thy flying,
Stay, and pity me dying;
For fates and friends have left me
And of comfort bereft me.
Come, come, close mine eyes, better to die blessed   5
    Than to live thus distressed.

To whom shall I complain me
When thus friends do disdain me?
'Tis Time that must befriend me,
Drowned in sorrow to end me.   10
Come, come, close mine eyes, better to die blessed
    Than to live thus distressed.

Tears but augment this fuel
I feed by night, O cruel.
Light griefs can speak their pleasure;   15
Mine are dumb, passing measure.
Quick, quick, close mine eyes, better to die blessed
    Than here to live distressed.

VIII

TELL me, True Love, where shall I seek thy being?
    In thoughts or words, in vows or promise-making?
In reasons, looks, or passions never-seeing?
    In men on earth or women's minds partaking?
Thou canst not die; and therefore, living, tell me,   5
Where is thy seat? why doth this age expel thee?

When thoughts are still unseen, and words disguised;
  Vows are not sacred held, nor promise debt;
By passion Reason's glory is surprised;
  In neither sex is True Love firmly set.   10
Thoughts feigned, words false, vows and promise broken
Made True Love fly from earth, this is the token.

Mount then, my thoughts, here is for thee no dwelling,
  Since Truth and Falsehood live like twins together.
Believe not sense, eyes, ears, touch, taste, or smelling;   15
  Both Art and Nature's forced; put trust in neither.
One only she doth True Love captive bind
In fairest breast, but in a fairer mind.

O fairest mind, enriched with Love's residing,
  Retain the best; in hearts let some seed fall;   20
Instead of weeds Love's fruits may have abiding,
  At harvest you shall reap increase of all.
O happy Love! more happy man that finds thee!
Most happy saint, that keeps, restores, unbinds thee!

IX

  Go, nightly Cares, the enemy to rest,
    Forbear awhile to vex my grieved sprite.
  So long your weight hath lain upon my breast
    That, lo, I live of life bereaved quite.
  O give me time to draw my weary breath,   5
  Or let me die, as I desire the death.
  Welcome, sweet Death! O Life no life, a hell!
  Then thus and thus I bid the world farewell.

  False world, farewell! the enemy to rest,
    Now do thy worst, I do not weigh thy spite;   10
  Free from thy cares I live for ever blest,
    Enjoying peace, and heavenly true delight,
  Delight whom woes nor sorrows shall amate;
  Nor fears nor tears disturb her happy state.
  And thus I leave thy hopes, thy joys untrue;   15
  And thus and thus, vain world, again adieu.

X

To my loving countryman Mr. John Forster the younger, merchant of Dublin in Ireland

FROM silent night, true register of moans;
   From saddest soul, consumed with deepest sins;
From heart quite rent with sighs and heavy groans
   My wailing Muse her woeful work begins,
And to the world brings tunes of sad despair,   5
Sounding naught else but sorrow, grief and care.

Sorrow to see my sorrow's cause augmented,
   And yet less sorrowful were my sorrows more;
Grief that my grief with grief is not prevented,
   For grief it is must ease my grieved sore.   10
Thus grief and sorrow cares but how to grieve,
For grief and sorrow must my cares relieve.

If any eye therefore can spare a tear
   To fill the well-spring that must wet my cheeks,
O let that eye to this sad feast draw near,   15
   Refuse me not, my humble soul beseeks.
For all the tears mine eyes have ever wept
Were now too little had they all been kept.

XI

LASSO! vita mia mi fa morire;
   Crudel' amor mio cor consume
Da mille ferite che mi fan morir.
   Ahi mè! Deh! chè non mi fan morire?
Crudel' amor mi fa soffrir mille martire.   5

XII

IN this trembling shadow cast
   From those boughs which thy wings shake,
Far from human troubles placed
   Songs to the Lord would I make.
   Darkness from my mind then take;   5
For thy rites none may begin
Till they feel thy light within.

As I sing, sweet flowers I'll strow
  From the fruitful valleys brought;
Praising Him by whom they grow,   10
    Him that heaven and earth hath wrought,
    Him that all things framed of naught;
Him that all for man did make,
But made Man for his own sake.

Music, all thy sweetness lend   15
  While of His high power I speak,
On whom all powers else depend.
    But my breast is now too weak;
    Trumpets shrill the air should break.
All in vain my sounds I raise;   20
Boundless power asks boundless praise.

XIII

IF that a sinner's sighs be angels' food,
  Or that repentant tears be angels' wine,
Accept, O Lord, in this most pensive mood,
  These hearty sighs and doleful plaints of mine,
That went with Peter forth most sinfully,   5
But not, as Peter, did weep bitterly.

XIV–XVI

THOU mighty God, that rightest every wrong,
Listen to Patience in a dying song.
When Job had lost his children, lands, and goods,
  Patience assuaged his excessive pain;
And when his sorrows came as fast as floods,   5
  Hope kept his heart till Comfort came again.

When David's life by Saul was often sought,
  And worlds of woes did compass him about,
On dire revenge he never had a thought,
  But in his griefs Hope still did help him out.   10

When the poor cripple by the pool did lie
  Full many years in misery and pain,
No sooner he on Christ had set his eye
  But he was well, and comfort came again.
No David, Job, nor cripple in more grief,   15
Christ, give me patience and my hope's relief.

                                   [*Nicholas Breton*]

XVII

WHERE sin, sore-wounding, daily doth oppress me,
There grace abounding freely doth redress me,
So that resounding still I shall confess Thee
    Father of mercy.

Though sin offending daily doth torment me,   5
Yet grace amending, since I do repent me,
At my life's ending will, I hope, present me
    Clear to Thy mercy.

The wound sin gave me was of death assured.
Did not grace save me, whereby it is cured?   10
So Thou wilt have me to Thy love inured,
    Free without merit.

Sin's stripe is healed, and his sting abated;
Death's mouth is sealed, and the grave amated.
Thy love revealed and Thy grace related   15
    Gives me this spirit.

XVIII

MY heart and tongue were twins at once conceived.
  Th'eldest was my heart, born dumb by destiny;
The last, my tongue, of all sweet thoughts bereaved,
  Yet strung and tuned to play heart's harmony.
Both knit in one and yet asunder placed,   5
  What heart would speak, the tongue doth still discover;
What tongue doth speak, is of the heart embraced,
  And both are one to make a new found lover.
New found and only found in gods and kings,
  Whose words are deeds, but words nor deeds regarded. 10
Chaste thoughts do mount and fly with swiftest wings,
  My love with pain, my pain with loss rewarded.

Conclusion

Then this be sure, since it is true perfection,
That neither men nor gods can force affection.

XIX. *Dialogue*

UP, merry mates! To Neptune's praise
  Your voices high advance.
    The wat'ry nymphs shall dance;
And Aeolus shall whistle to your lays.

Steerman, how stands the wind?   5
    Full north-north-east.
        What course?
    Full south-south-west.
        No worse,
    And blow so fair?   10
    Then sink despair!
Come solace to the mind,
Ere night we shall the haven find.
        O happy days!
        Who may contain,   15
    But swell with proud disdain
When seas are smooth, sails full, and all things please?

Stay, merry mates! Proud Neptune lowers!
    Your voices all deplore you;
    The nymphs stand weeping o'er you;   20
And Aeolus and Iris bandy showers.
M[aster].   Boatsman, haul in the boat.
S[teerman].   Hark, hark! the rattlings!
M.   'Tis hail.
S.   Make fast the tacklings.   25
M.   Strike sail.
        Make quick despatches;
        Shut close the hatches;
    Hold stern, cast anchor out,
This night we shall at random float.   30
        O dismal hours!
        Who can forbear
    But sink with sad despair
When seas are rough, sails rent, and each thing lowers?

Conclusion

The golden mean that constant spirit bears   35
In such extremes, that nor presumes nor fears.

XX

WELCOME, black Night, Hymen's fair Day!
Help Hymen Love's due debt to pay.
Love's due debt is chaste delight,
Which if the turtles want to-night
Hymen forfeits his deity,   5
And Night in love her dignity.

Help, help, black Night, Hymen's fair Day,
Help Hymen Love's due debt to pay.
   Chorus.   Hymen, O Hymen! mine
              Of treasures more divine,   10
              What deity is like to thee
              That freest from mortality?

Stay, happy pair, stay but awhile,
Hymen comes not Love to beguile.
These sports are alluring baits,   15
And sauce are to Love's sweetest cates.
Longing hope doth no hurt but this,
It heightens Love's attained bliss.
Then stay, most happy, stay awhile,
Hymen comes not Love to beguile.   20
   Chorus.   Hymen, O Hymen! mine
              Of treasures more divine,
              What deity is like to thee
              That freest from mortality?

XXI

CEASE, cease these false sports, haste away!
Love's made a truant by your stay.
    Good-night! yet virgin-bride!
    But look ere day be spied
    You change that fruitless name,   5
    Lest you your sex defame.
Fear not Hymen's peaceful war,
You'll conquer though you subdued are.
Good night! and ere the day be old,
Rise to the sun a marigold.   10
Chorus.   Hymen, O Hymen, bless this night,
        That Love's dark works may come to light.

ROBERT DOWLAND

A Mvsicall Banqvet. Furnished with varietie of delicious Ayres, Collected out of the best Authors in English, French, Spanish, and Italian. 1610

I. *Anthony Holborne*

MY heavy sprite, oppressed with sorrow's might,
   Of wearied limbs the burthen sore sustains,
   With silent groans and heart's tears still complains,
Yet I breathe still and live in life's despite.
         Have I lost thee? 5
All fortunes I accurse bids thee farewell,
    With thee all joys farewell,
And for thy sake this world becomes my hell.

               George, Earl of Cumberland

II. *Richard Martin*

CHANGE thy mind since she doth change,
   Let not fancy still abuse thee.
Thy untruth cannot seem strange
   When her falsehood doth excuse thee.
Love is dead, and thou art free. 5
She doth live, but dead to thee.

Whilst she loved thee best awhile,
   See how she hath still delayed thee,
Using shows for to beguile
   Those vain hopes that have deceived thee. 10
Now thou seest, although too late,
Love loves truth, which women hate.

Love no more since she is gone;
   She is gone and loves another.
Being once deceived by one, 15
   Leave her love, but love none other.
She was false, bid her adieu.
She was best, but yet untrue.

Love, farewell, more dear to me
   Than my life which thou preservest.   20
Life, all joys are gone from thee,
   Others have what thou deservest.
O my death doth spring from hence,
I must die for her offence.

Die, but yet before thou die,   25
   Make her know what she hath gotten.
She in whom my hopes did lie
   Now is changed, I quite forgotten.
She is changed, but changed base,
Baser in so vilde a place.   30
              Robert, Earl of Essex

III. *Robert Hales*

O EYES, leave off your weeping,
Love hath the thoughts in keeping
   That may content you.
Let not this misconceiving,
Where comforts are receiving,   5
   Causeless torment you.

Clouds threaten but a shower;
Hope hath his happy hour
   Though long in lasting.
Time needs must be attended;   10
Love must not be offended
   With too much hasting.

But O the painful pleasure,
Where love attends the leisure
   Of life's wretchedness;   15
Where hope is but illusion,
And fear is but confusion
   Of love's happiness.

But, happy hope, that seeth
How hope and hap agreeth,   20
   Of life deprive me;
Or let me be assured
When life hath death endured,
   Love will revive me.
           [attrib. to Nicholas Breton]

IV. *D'incerto*

GO, my flock, go get you hence,
　　Seek some other place of feeding,
Where you may have some defence
　　From the storms in my breast breeding,
　　And showers from mine eyes proceeding.　　　5

Leave a wretch in whom all woe
　　Can abide to keep no measure.
Merry flock, such one forgo
　　Unto whom mirth is displeasure,
　　Only rich in mischief's treasure.　　　10

Yet, alas, before you go,
　　Hear your woeful master's story;
Which to stones I else would show.
　　Sorrow only then hath glory
　　When 'tis excellently sorry.　　　15

Stella, fairest shepherdess,
　　Fairest but yet cruellest ever;
Stella, whom the heavens still bless,
　　Though against me she persever,
　　Though I bliss inherit never;　　　20

Stella hath refused me,
　　Stella who more love hath proved
In this caitiff heart to be
　　Than can in good to us be moved
　　Towards lambkins best beloved.　　　25

Stella hath refused me.
　　Astrophel, that so well served,
In this pleasant Spring must see,
　　While in pride flowers be preserved,
　　Himself only winter-starved.　　　30

Why, alas, then doth she swear
　　That she loveth me so dearly,
Seeing me so long to bear
　　Coals of love that burn so clearly,
　　And yet leave me hopeless merely?　　　35

Is that love? Forsooth I trow
  If I saw my good dog grieved,
And a help for him did know,
  My love should not be believed
  But he were by me relieved.   40

No, she hates me, well-away,
  Feigning love somewhat to please me,
Knowing if she should display
  All her hate, death soon would seize me,
  And of hideous torments ease me.   45

Then, my flock, now adieu!
  But alas if in your straying
Heavenly Stella meet with you,
  Tell her in your piteous blaying
  Her poor slave's just decaying.   50

Sir Philip Sidney

v. *D'incerto*

O, DEAR life, when shall it be
That mine eyes thine eyes may see,
  And in them thy mind discover
Whether absence hath had force
Thy remembrance to divorce   5
  From the image of thy lover?

O if I myself find not
By thy absence oft forgot,
  Nor debarred from beauty's treasure,
Let no tongue aspire to tell   10
In what high joys I shall dwell,
  Only thought aims at the pleasure.

Thought, therefore, will I send thee
To take up the place for me,
  Long I will not after tarry.   15
There unseen thou mayest be bold
Those fair wonders to behold,
  Which in them my hopes do carry.

Thought, see thou no place forbear,
Enter bravely everywhere,   20
 Seize on all to her belonging.
But if thou wouldest guarded be,
Fearing her beams, take with thee
 Strength of liking, rage of longing.

O my thoughts, my thoughts, surcease,   25
Your delights my woes increase;
 My life fleets with too much thinking.
Think no more, but die in me
Till thou shalt received be,
 At her lips my nectar drinking.   30
Sir Philip Sidney

VI. *Daniel Batchelar*

To plead my faith, where faith hath no reward;
 To move remorse, where favour is not born;
To heap complaints, where she doth not regard,
 Were fruitless, bootless, vain and yield but scorn.
I loved her whom all the world admired.   5
 I was refused of her that can love none;
And my vain hope, which far too high aspired,
 Is dead and buried and for ever gone.
Forget my name, since you have scorned my love,
 And womanlike do not too late lament;   10
Since for your sake I do all mischief prove,
 I none accuse nor nothing do repent.
I was as fond as ever she was fair
Yet loved I not more than I now despair.
Robert, Earl of Essex

VII. *Tessier*

In a grove most rich of shade
Where birds wanton music made,
May then in his pied weeds showing
New perfumes with flowers fresh growing,

Astrophel with Stella sweet   5
Did for mutual comfort meet;
Both within themselves oppressed,
But either in each other blessed.

Him great harms had taught much care;
Her fair neck a foul yoke bare;   10
But her sight his care did banish;
In his sight her yoke did vanish.

Wept they had, alas, the while,
But now tears themselves did smile,
While their eyes by love directed   15
Interchangeably reflected.

Sighed they had, but now betwixt
Sighs of woe were glad sighs mixed,
With arms crossed yet testifying
Restless rest and living dying.   20

Their ears hungry of each word
Which the dear tongue would afford;
But their tongues restrained from walking
Till their hearts had ended talking.

But when their tongues could not speak,   25
Love itself did silence break.
Love did set his lips asunder
Thus to speak in love and wonder:

Stella, sovereign of my joy,
Fair Triumphress in annoy;   30
Stella, star of heavenly fire,
Stella, lode-star of desire,

Stella, in whose shining eyes
Are the lights of Cupid's skies,
Whose beams when they are once darted   35
Love therewith is straight imparted.

Stella, whose voice when it speaks
Senses all asunder break;
Stella, whose voice when it singeth
Angels to acquaintance bringeth.   40

Stella, in whose body is
Writ the characters of bliss,
Whose sweet face all beauty passeth,
Save the mind which it surpasseth.

Grant, O grant,—but speech alas   45
Fails me, fearing on to pass,
Grant to me,—what am I saying?
But no fault there is in praying.

Grant, O dear, on knees I pray,
(Knees on ground he then did stay)   50
That not I but since I prove you
Time and place from me ne'er move you.

Never season was more fit,
Never room more apt for it;
Smiling air allows my reason;   55
These birds sing, now use the season.

This small wind which so sweet is,
See how it the leaves doth kiss;
Each tree in his best attiring,
Sense of love to love inspiring.   60

Love makes earth the water drink,
Love to earth makes water sink,
And if dumb things be so witty
Shall a heavenly grace want pity?

There his hands in their speech fain   65
Would have made tongue's language plain;
But her hands his hands compelling
Gave repulse, all grace expelling.

Therewithal away she went,
Leaving him with passion rent,   70
With what she had done and spoken,
That therewith my song is broken.

Sir Philip Sidney

VIII. *John Dowland*

FAR from triumphing Court and wonted glory
   He dwelt in shady unfrequented places,
Time's prisoner now, he made his pastime story;
   Gladly forgets Court's erst-afforded graces.
That goddess whom he served to heaven is gone,   5
And he on earth in darkness left to moan.

But lo, a glorious light from his dark rest
   Shone from the place where erst this goddess dwelt;
A light whose beams the world with fruit hath blest;
   Blest was the knight while he that light beheld.   10
Since then a star fixed on his head hath shined,
And a saint's image in his heart is shrined.

Ravished with joy, so graced by such a saint,
   He quite forgat his cell and self denaid;
He thought it shame in thankfulness to faint,   15
   Debts due to princes must be duly paid;
Nothing so hateful to a noble mind
As finding kindness for to prove unkind.

But ah! poor knight, though thus in dream he ranged,
   Hoping to serve this saint in sort most meet,   20
Time with his golden locks to silver changed
   Hath with age-fetters bound him hands and feet.
Ay me! he cries, goddess, my limbs grow faint,
Though I Time's prisoner be, be you my saint.

Sir Henry Lee

IX. *John Dowland*

LADY, if you so spite me,
  Wherefore do you so oft kiss and delight me,
  Sure that my heart oppressed and overcloyed
     May break thus, overjoyed?
     If you seek to spill me,   5
     Come kiss me, sweet, and kill me.
     So shall your heart be eased,
And I shall rest content and die well pleased.

X. *John Dowland*

IN darkness let me dwell, the ground shall sorrow be;
The roof despair to bar all cheerful light from me;
The walls of marble black that moistened still shall weep;
My music hellish jarring sounds to banish friendly sleep.
Thus wedded to my woes, and bedded to my tomb,   5
O let me living, living die, till death do come.

XI. *D'incerto*

Si le parler et le silence
    Nuit à nostre heur esgalement,
Parlons donc, ma chere esperance
    Du cœur et des yeux seulement.
Amour, ce petit dieu volage   5
Nous apprend ce muet langage.

Que le regard vole et revole,
    Messager des nos passions,
Et serve au lieu de la parole
    Pour dire nos intentions.   10
Amour *etc.*

Mais si quelque ame est offencée
    De nous voir discourir des yeux,
Nous parlerons de la pensée
    Comme les anges dans les cieux.   15
Amour *etc.*

Ainsi par un doux artifice
    Nous tromperons les courtisans,
Et nous rirons de la malice
    De mile facheux mesdisans,   20
Qui n'en sçauront pas d'avantage,
Ignorant ce muet langage.

XII. *D'incerto*

Ce penser, qui sans fin tirannise ma vie
    Se montre tellement contre moy conjuré,
Que tant plus je m'efforce à dompter son envie,
    Et tant moins à mon bien je le voy preparé.

J'ai quitté la beauté dont il a pris naissance,   5
    Esperant par l'oubly ses charmes decevoir,
Mai[s] je trouve à la fin que la veue et l'absence
    Sont tous deux differends, et d'un mesme pouvoir.

J'ai maintefois juré du change fair espreuve,
    Pour faire qu'un dessein fust par l'autre deffait;   10
Mais, à toutes les fois, aussi tost je me treuve
    Infidelle en parole, et fidelle en effect.

J'ai des plus fiers dedains la puissance empruntée
  Pour repousser le trait dont j'ay le cœur attaint,
Mais plus je recognois par leur force domptée   15
  Ma douleur veritable et mon remede feint.

Ainsi donc combatant le mal qui me possede
  Sans voir par ces moyens ses tempestes calmer,
Je me vay consommant dans mon propre remede,
  Comme un vaisseau qui brusle au milieu de la mer. 20

Voilà comme en vivant en toute servitude
  Je nourris un penser dont l'impiteux effort
Se monstre en mon endroit si plain d'ingratitude
  Qu'en luy donnant la vie il me donne la mort.

XIII. *D'incerto*

Vous que le bon heur r'appelle
  A un servage ancien,
Mourez aux pieds de la belle
  Qui vous daigne faire sien.

Glorieuse en vostre perte,   5
  Honorez vostre vainqueur,
Qui vous a la porte ouverte
  De la prison de son cœur.

Heureux, venez vous donc rendre
  A celle qui vous a pris,   10
C'est honneur de ce voir prendre
  A qui tient tout à mespris.

Ainsi vostre ame reprise
  Finis toute liberté;
Glorieuse est l'entreprise   15
  Qui guide à l'eternité.

XIV. *Espagnol*

Passava amor su arco desarmado
Los ojos baxos, blando y muy modesto,
Dexávam[e] ya atrás muy descuidado.

¡Quán poco espacio pude gozar esto!
Fortuna, de embidiosa, dixo luego   5
¡Teneos, amor! ¿porqué vays tan presto?

Bolvió de presto a mí el niño ciego,
Muy enojado de verse reprehendido,
Que no ay reprehensión do está su fuego.

¡Ay! prados, bosques, selvas, que criastes   10
Tan libre coraçón como era el mío
¿Porqué tan grave mal no le estorvastes?

[*George de Montemayor*]

XV

STA note mien yava,
Call inferno mescta na my nandava,
Non per ly mei pecate,
Ma per vider chi fanno lyny.

Stando là mi pareva   5
Chi nel medso Plutone ses sedeva
Tra qui Spiriti infernali
Chi donno l'alma tanti stragi mali.

XVI. *Espagnol*

VESTROS ojos tienen d'amor no sé qué
Que me hielan, me roban, me hieren, me matan a fé.
¿Porqué me mirays con tan aflicion
Y a mi coraçon me aprisionays?
Que si vos me mirays yo os acusaré.   5

XVII. *Dominico Maria Megli*

SE di farmi morire,
Con crudeltà pensate,
Certo che v'inganate.
Che da la crudeltà nascono l'ire,
E da l'ire lo sdegno,   5
Che scaccia amor,
Dal suo superbo regno.

XVIII. *Giulio Caccini detto Romano*

DOVRÒ dunque morire?
Pria che di nuovo io miri,
Voi bramata cagion de miei martiri
Mio perduto tesoro non potrò dirvi
Pria ch' io mora 'io moro'?   5
O miseria inaudita,
Non poter dir a voi 'moro mia vita'.

XIX. *Giulio Caccini detto Romano*

AMARILLI mia bella,
Non credi ò del mio cor dolce desio,
D'esser tu l'amor mio?
Credilo pur, e se timor t'assale,
Prendi questo mio strale   5
Aprim' il petto, e vedrai scritto il core:
Amarilli è 'l mio amore.

XX. *Italien*

O BELLA più che la stella Diana
Chi par inansi de la mia patrona.
Mia regina, dolce mi' amore,
Pietà, cor mio, pietà,
Non più dolore   5
Bene mio, caro core.
Mia bella, bella,
Tu se' la mala morte mia,
La fretsa chi mi pass' il core.

ALFONSO FERRABOSCO

Ayres. 1609

I

LIKE hermit poor in place obscure
  I mean to spend my days of endless doubt,
To wail such woes as Time cannot recure,
  Where none but Love shall find me out;
And at my gates Despair shall linger still   5
To let in Death when Love and Fortune will.

II

COME home, my troubled thoughts, stay and retire;
  Call home your erring fellows; make a stand.
Follow not still the colours of Desire;
  False are her wishes, cruel her command.
Come then, obey this summons, come away,   5
For here vain hopes must serve you for your pay.

III

COME away, come away,
We grow jealous of your stay.
If you do not stop your ear
We shall have more cause to fear
Sirens of the land, than they   5
To doubt the Sirens of the sea.

[*Ben Jonson*]

IV

DEAR, when to thee my sad complaint I make,
  And show how oft love doth my death renew;
And how afresh I suffer for thy sake,
  I ever fear this answer to ensue:
Who would bewail the bird that 'scapes the snare,   5
And ever caught, and never can beware.

But my reply is just, that if the eye,
   That sees the danger, yet obeys the heart,
That leads the sense, for his delight to die,
   In that this prey prefers the better part,   10
The gainer should have mercy to forgive.
If beauty be a tyrant, who can live?

V

FAIN I would, but O I dare not,
   Speak my thoughts at full to praise her.
Speak the best, cries Love, and spare not;
   Thy speech can no higher raise her.
Thy speech than thy thoughts are lower,   5
Yet thy thoughts doth not half know her.

VI

COME, my Celia, let us prove,
While we may, the sweets of Love.
Time will not be ours for ever;
He at length our good will sever.
Spend not then his gifts in vain;   5
Suns that set may rise again,
But if we once lose this light,
'Tis with us perpetual night.
Why should we defer our joys?
Fame and Rumour are but toys.   10
Cannot we delude the eyes
Of a few poor household spies?
Or his easier ears beguile
Thus removed by our wile?
'Tis no sin Love's fruits to steal;   15
But the sweet theft to reveal,
To be taken, to be seen,
These have crimes accounted been.

[Ben Jonson]

VII

SO, so, leave off this last lamenting kiss,
   Which sucks two souls, and vapours both away.
Turn, thou ghost, that way; and let me turn this;
   And let ourselves benight our happy day.
We ask none leave to love, nor will we owe   5
Any so cheap a death as saying Go!

Go, go! and if that word have not quite killed thee,
　　Ease me with death by bidding me go too.
O, if it have, let my word work on me,
　　And a just office on a murderer do.　　　　　　　10
Except it be too late to kill me so,
Being double dead, going and bidding go.

　　　　　　　　　　　　　　　　　　[*John Donne*]

VIII

Y OUNG and simple though I am,
I have heard of Cupid's name.
Guess I can what thing it is,
Men desire when they do kiss.
Smoke can never burn, they say;　　　　　　　5
But the flames that follow may.

I am not so foul or fair
To be proud or to despair.
Yet my lips have oft observed
Men that kiss them press them hard,　　　　　　10
As glad lovers use to do
When their new-met loves they woo.

Faith, 'tis but a foolish mind,
Yet methinks a heat I find,
Like thirst-longing that doth bide　　　　　　　15
Ever on my weaker side,
Where they say my heart doth move.
Venus grant it be not Love!

If it be, alas, what then?
Were not women made for men?　　　　　　　20
As good 'tis a thing were past,
That must needs be done at last.
Roses that are overblown
Grow less sweet, then fall alone.

Yet nor churl nor silken gull　　　　　　　　25
Shall my maiden blossom pull.
Who shall not, I soon can tell.
Who shall, would I could as well!
This I know, who e'er he be,
Love he must or flatter me.　　　　　　　　30

　　　　　　　　　　　　　　　[*Thomas Campian*]

IX

DROWN not with tears, my dearest love,
Those eyes which my affections move.
Do not with weeping those lights blind,
Which me in thy subjection bind.
Time, that hath made us two of one,   5
And forced thee now to live alone,
Will once again us reunite
To show how she can Fortune spite.
Then will we our time redeem
And hold our hours in more esteem,   10
Turning all our sweetest nights
Into millions of delights,
And strive with many thousand kisses
To multiply exchange of blisses.

X

I AM a lover, yet was never loved.
  Well have I loved and will, though hated ever.
Troubles I pass, yet never any moved;
  Sighs have I given and yet she heard me never.

I would complain and she would never hear me;   5
And fly from love, but it is ever near me.
Oblivion only blameless doth beset me
For that remembereth never to forget me.
                                    [*Bartholomew Yong*]

XI

WHY stays the bridegroom to invade
Her that would be a matron made?
        Good-night, whilst yet we may
Good-night to you a virgin say.
        To-morrow rise the same   5
Your mother is, and use a nobler name.
        Speed well in Hymen's war,
            That what you are,
        By your perfections we
            And all may see.   10
                                    [*Ben Jonson*]

XII–XIV

SING we then heroic grace,
   So with lovely light adorning
That fair heaven of his face
   As the star that leads the morning;
Body brave for part and whole,   5
Purest seat of purer soul,
Where reposed lodge by nature
Princely strength and comely stature.

Sing the riches of his skill,
   Long by studious toil provided;   10
Wit that never guideth ill,
   Will that never ill is guided;
Judgement that can best discern,
Memory that needs not learn;
Courage where such thoughts assemble   15
Justly may his haters tremble.

Sing the nobless of his race;
   Sing his power, his wealth, his glory,
Breaking all the bounds of place,
   Endless ages' ageless story.   20
Peace that maketh one of two
More than ever war could do;
Terror chased, Justice fixed,
Mercy still with Justice mixed.

XV

WITH what new thoughts should I now entertain
   My mind, if I my sadness should forgo?
What pleasing hopes have I not proved vain?
   Or what false show of joy do I not know?
O partial love, there is no power in thee   5
To make her love, or else to set me free.

XVI

FLY from the world, O fly, thou poor distrest,
   Where thy diseased sense infects thy soul,
And where thy thoughts do multiply unrest,
   Tiring with wishes what they straight control.
O world, O world, betrayer of the mind!   5
O thoughts, O thoughts, that guide us, being blind!

Come therefore, Care, conduct me to my end,
  And steer this shipwracked carcase to the grave.
My sighs a strong and steadfast wind shall lend;
  Tears wet the sails, Repentance from rocks save.   10
Hail Death! hail Death! the land I do descry!
Strike sail! go, soul! rest follows them that die.

XVII

Shall I seek to ease my grief?
  No, my sight is lost with eyeing.
Shall I speak and beg relief?
  No, my voice is hoarse with crying.
  What remains but only dying?   5

Love and I of late did part,
  But the Boy, my peace envying,
Like a Parthian threw his dart
  Backward, and did wound me flying.
  What remains but only dying?   10

She whom then I looked on,
  My remembrance beautifying,
Stays with me though I am gone,
  Gone and at her mercy lying.
  What remains but only dying?   15

Thus my vital breath doth waste,
  And my blood with sorrow drying,
Sighs and tears make life to last,
  For a while his place supplying.
  What remains but only dying?   20

XVIII–XX

If all these Cupids now were blind
  As is their wanton brother;
Or play should put it in their minds
  To shoot at one another;
What pretty battle they would make,   5
If they their objects should mistake,
  And each one wound his mother.

It was no policy of court,
   Although the place be charmed,
To let, in earnest or in sport,   10
   So many Loves in armed.
For say the dames should with their eyes
Upon the hearts here mean surprise,
   Were not the men liked harmed?

Yes, were the Loves or false or straying;   15
Or Beauty not their beauty weighing.
But here no such deceit is mixed;
Their flames are pure, their eyes are fixed;
They do not war with different darts,
But strike a music of like hearts.   20

                                                [*Ben Jonson*]

XXI

So Beauty on the waters stood,
When Love had severed earth from flood.
So when he parted air from fire,
He did with concord all inspire.
And then a motion he them taught   5
That elder than himself was thought;
Which thought was yet the child of earth,
For Love is elder than his birth.

                                                [*Ben Jonson*]

XXII

Had those that dwell in error foul,
And hold that women have no soul,
But seen those move, they would have then
Said women were the souls of men;
So they do move each heart and eye   5
With the world's soul, their harmony.

                                                [*Ben Jonson*]

XXIII

If all the ages of the earth
Were crowned but in this famous birth;
And when that they would boast their store
Of worthy queens they knew no more;

> How happier is that age can give   5
> A Queen in whom they all do live!
>
> [Ben Jonson]

XXIV

UNCONSTANT love, why should I make my moan,
 Or send sad sighs unto thy careless ear,
Since thy affection and thy faith is gone,
 And all those virtues which I once held dear?
Farewell, farewell, most false of all to me   5
That with affection dearly loved thee.

XXV

 O EYES, O mortal stars,
  The authors of my harms,
 That in slumb'ring wage wars
  To kill me with sweet charms;
 If closed you annoy me,   5
 Being open you'd destroy me.

XXVI

A Dialogue between a Shepherd and a Nymph

[*Shepherd.*] FAIR cruel nymph, why thus in grief and anguish
    Mak'st thou him that adores thee pine and languish?
[*Nymph.*] Why, shepherd, dost thou me condemn as cruel,
    Since thine own fancies are thy passions' fuel?
[*Shepherd.*] O but these fancies from thy beauty flow.   5
[*Nymph.*] Then shall relief to thee from bounty grow.
[*Both.*] O how I joy in ⎰ thee ⎱ my happy choice;
        ⎱ this ⎰
    As thou in me, so I in thee rejoice;
    Then let us still together live and love,
    And sing the joys that happy lovers prove.   10

XXVII

A Dialogue

[*1st Voice.*] WHAT shall I wish? What shall I fly?
[*2nd Voice.*] True love I seek.
[*1st Voice.*]   False I defy.
[*2nd Voice.*] Words have their truth.

[*1st Voice.*]   Such ever speak.
[*2nd Voice.*] Deeds have their faith.
[*1st Voice.*]   Such never break.
[*Both.*]   Flattery yields pleasure.
[*1st Voice.*]   Only truth yields weight.   5
[*Both.*]   Happy are they that never knew deceit.

XXVIII

A Dialogue between a Shepherd and a Nymph

[*Shepherd.*] TELL me, O love, when shall it be
                    That thy fair eyes shall shine on me,
                         Whom nothing now reviveth?
[*Nymph.*] I pray thee, shepherd, leave thy fears;
                    Drown not thy heart and eyes with tears;   5
                         Such sighs my sense depriveth.
[*Shepherd.*] Alas, sweet nymph, I cannot choose,
                    Since thou estranged liv'st from me.
[*Nymph.*] O do not me for that accuse,
                    My love, my life doth live in thee.   10
[*Both.*]   Alas, what joy is in such love
[*Shepherd.*]   That ever lives apart,
[*Nymph.*]   And never other comforts prove
                    But cares that kill the heart?
[*Shepherd.*]   O let me die!   15
[*Nymph.*]   And so will I!
[*Both.*]   Yet stay, sweet love, and sing this song with me:
                    Time brings to pass what Love thinks could not be.

THOMAS FORD

Mvsicke Of Svndrie Kindes, Set forth in two Bookes. The First Whereof Are,
Aries for 4. Voices to the Lute, Orphorion, or Basse-Viol, with a Dialogue
for two Voices, and two Basse Viols in parts, tunde the Lute way. The Second
Are Pauens, Galiards, Almaines, Toies, Iigges, Thumpes and such like, for
two Basse-Viols, the Liera way, so made as the greatest number may serue to
play alone, very easie to be performde. 1607

I

NOT full twelve years twice told, a weary breath
I have exchanged for a wished death.
My course was short, the longer is my rest,
God takes them soonest whom he loveth best;
For he that's born to-day and dies to-morrow,   5
Loseth some days of mirth, but months of sorrow.
Why fear we Death that cures our sicknesses,
Author of rest and end of all distresses?
Other misfortunes often come to grieve us;
Death strikes but once, and that stroke doth relieve us.   10
                              [*Henry Morrice*]

II

WHAT then is love, sings Corydon,
    Since Phillida is grown so coy?
A flattering glass to gaze upon;
    A busy jest, a serious toy;
A flower still budding, never blown;   5
    A scanty dearth in fullest store;
Yielding least fruit where most is sown.
        My daily note shall be therefore
        Heigh ho! heigh ho! 'chill love no more.

'Tis like a morning dewy rose   10
    Spread fairly to the sun's arise;
But when his beams he doth disclose
    That which then flourished quickly dies.

It is a self-fed dying hope,
   A promised bliss, a salveless sore,   15
An aimless mark, an erring scope.
     My daily note shall be therefore
     Heigh ho! heigh ho! 'chill love no more.

'Tis like a lamp shining to all
   Whilst in itself it doth decay;   20
It seems to free whom it doth thrall
   And leads our pathless thoughts astray.
It is the Spring of wintered hearts
   Parched by the Summer's heat before.
Faint hope to kindly warmth converts.   25
     My daily note shall be therefore
     Heigh ho! heigh ho! 'chill love no more.

III

UNTO the temple of thy beauty,
   And to the tomb where Pity lies,
I, pilgrim-clad, with zeal and duty
   Do offer up my heart, mine eyes.
My heart, lo, in the quenchless fire   5
   On Love's burning altar lies,
Conducted thither by Desire
   To be Beauty's sacrifice.

But, Pity, on thy sable hearse
   Mine eyes the tears of sorrow shed.   10
What though tears cannot fate reverse,
   Yet are they duties to the dead.
O mistress, in thy sanctuary
   Why would'st thou suffer cold Disdain
To use his frozen cruelty,   15
   And gentle Pity to be slain.

Pity, that to thy Beauty fled,
   And with thy Beauty should have lived,
Ah! in thy heart lies buried
   And never more may be revived.   20
Yet this last favour, dear, extend,
   To accept these vows, these tears I shed,
Duties, which I, thy pilgrim, send
   To Beauty living, Pity dead.

IV

NOW I see thy looks were feigned
Quickly lost and quickly gained.
Soft thy skin like wool of wethers,
Heart unconstant, light as feathers;
Tongue untrusty, subtle sighted;   5
Wanton will with change delighted.
    Siren pleasant, foe to reason,
    Cupid plague thee for thy treason!

Of thine eye I made my mirror,
From thy beauty came my error;   10
All thy words I counted witty,
All thy sighs I deemed pity;
Thy false tears that me aggrieved
First of all my trust deceived.
    Siren pleasant, foe to reason,   15
    Cupid plague thee for thy treason!

Feigned acceptance when I asked,
Lovely words with cunning masked,
Holy vows but heart unholy.
Wretched man! my trust was folly.   20
Lily-white and pretty winking,
Solemn vows but sorry thinking.
    Siren pleasant, foe to reason,
    Cupid plague thee for thy treason!

Now I see, O seemly cruel,   25
Others warm them at my fuel.
Wit shall guide me in this durance
Since in love is no assurance.
Change thy pasture, take thy pleasure,
Beauty is a fading treasure.   30
    Siren pleasant, foe to reason,
    Cupid plague thee for thy treason!

Prime youth lasts not, age will follow
And make white those tresses yellow;
Wrinkled face for looks delightful   35
Shall acquaint the dame despiteful;

And when time shall date thy glory
Then too late thou wilt be sorry.
    Siren pleasant, foe to reason,
    Cupid plague thee for thy treason!   40

                    [*Thomas Lodge*]

V

GO, Passions, to the cruel fair,
    Plead my sorrows never ceasing;
Tell her those smiles are empty air,
    Growing hopes but not increasing,
Hasting, wasting, with swift pace,   5
Date of joy in dull disgrace.

Urge her, but gently, I request,
    With breach of faith and wrack of vows;
Say that my grief and mind's unrest
    Lives in the shadow of her brows,   10
Plying, flying, there to die
In sad woe and misery.

Importune pity at the last,
    (Pity in those eyes should hover);
Recount my sighs and torments past   15
    As annals of a constant lover
Spending, ending, many days
Of blasted hopes and slack delays.

VI

COME, Phyllis, come into these bowers;
Here shelter is from sharpest showers.
Cool gales of wind breathes in these shades,
Danger none this place invades.
Here sit, and note the chirping birds   5
Pleading my love in silent words.

Come, Phyllis, come, bright heaven's eye
Cannot upon thy beauty pry.
Glad Echo, in distinguished voice
Naming thee, will here rejoice.   10
Then come and hear her merry lays,
Crowning thy name with lasting praise.

VII

FAIR, sweet, cruel, why dost thou fly me?
    Go not, O go not from thy dearest.
Though thou dost hasten I am nigh thee,
    When thou seem'st far then am I nearest.
O tarry then and take me with you!   5

Fie, fie, sweetest, here is no danger.
    Fly not, O fly not, Love pursues thee.
I am no foe nor foreign stranger,
    Thy scorns with fresher hope renews me.
O tarry then and take me with you!   10

VIII

SINCE first I saw your face I resolved to honour and renown ye.
If now I be disdained I wish my heart had never known ye.
What, I that loved and you that liked, shall we begin to wrangle?
No, no, no, my heart is fast, and cannot disentangle.

If I admire or praise you too much, that fault you may forgive me;   5
Or if my hands had strayed but a touch then justly might you leave
    me.
I asked you leave, you bade me love, is't now a time to chide me?
No, no, no, I'll love you still, what fortune e'er betide me.

The sun whose beams most glorious are rejecteth no beholder,
And your sweet beauty past compare made my poor eyes the
    bolder.   10
Where Beauty moves and Wit delights and signs of kindness bind me,
There, O there, where'er I go, I'll leave my heart behind me.

IX

THERE is a lady sweet and kind,
Was never face so pleased my mind;
I did but see her passing by,
And yet I love her till I die.

Her gesture, motion and her smiles,   5
Her wit, her voice, my heart beguiles;
Beguiles my heart, I know not why,
And yet I love her till I die.

Her free behaviour, winning looks,
Will make a lawyer burn his books.   10
I touched her not, alas, not I,
And yet I love her till I die.

Had I her fast betwixt mine arms,
Judge you that think such sports were harms,
Wer't any harm? No, no, fie, fie!   15
For I will love her till I die.

Should I remain confined there,
So long as Phoebus in his sphere,
I to request, she to deny,
Yet would I love her till I die.   20

Cupid is winged and doth range,
Her country so my love doth change;
But change she earth, or change she sky,
Yet will I love her till I die.

                              X

How shall I then describe my love,
    When all men's skilful art
Is far inferior to her worth
    To praise th' unworthiest part?
She's chaste in looks, mild in her speech,   5
    In actions all discreet;
Of nature loving, pleasing most,
    In virtue all complete.

And for her voice a Philome;
    Her lip may all lips scorn.   10
No sun more clear than is her eye
    In brightest summer morn.
A mind wherein all virtues rest
    And takes delight to be;
And where all virtues graft themselves   15
    In that most fruitful tree.

A tree that India doth not yield,
    Nor ever yet was seen,
Where buds of virtue always springs,
    And all the year grows green.   20
That country's blest wherein she grows,
    And happy is that rock
From whence she springs; but happiest he
    That grafts in such a stock.

XI

A Dialogue

[*1st Voice.*] FLY not, dear heart, to find me all of snow.
[*2nd Voice.*] Shut not, sweet breast, to see me all of fire.
[*1st Voice.*] And I desire Desire's sweet flames to know.
[*2nd Voice.*] Thy snow inflames these flames of my desire.
          Thy snow nill hurt me.
[*1st Voice.*]   Nor thy fire will harm me.   5
[*2nd Voice.*] This cold will cool me.
[*1st Voice.*]   And this heat will warm me.
[*2nd Voice.*] Take this chaste fire to that pure virgin snow.
[*1st Voice.*] Being now thus warmed I'll never seek other fire.
[*2nd Voice.*] Thou giv'st more bliss than mortal hearts may know.
[*1st Voice.*] More bliss I take than angels can desire.   10
Chorus.   Let one grief harm us,
             And one joy fill us.
           Let one love warm us,
             And one death kill us.

THOMAS GREAVES

Songes of sundrie kindes: First, Aires To Be Svng To the Lute, and Base Violl. Next, Songes of sadnesse, for the Viols and Voyce. Lastly, Madrigalles, for fiue voyces. 1604

I

SHADED with olive trees sat Celestina singing,
Than the warbling birds more sweet harmony ringing.
      With curious cost
      That gold embossed
        Her fingers duly placed;   5
      Whiles voice and hand
      Both at command
        Each other truly graced.
      Thus using time,
      Not losing time,   10
        Right well a-paid,
      She closed her ditty
      With: O 'tis pretty
        To live a maid.

II

FLORA, sweet wanton, be not over-coy.
Nay then, in faith, if you will needs be gone,
Farewell, sweet Flora, sweet Fancy, adieu!
Farewell till Flora her fancy renew.

III

YE bubbling springs that gentle music makes
    To lovers' plaints with heart-sore throbs immixed,
Whenas my dear this way her pleasure takes,
    Tell her with tears how firm my love is fixed.
And Philomel report my timorous fears;   5
And Echo sound my 'heigh-hos' in her ears.
But if she ask if I for love will die,
        Tell her: good faith, not I!

IV

I WILL not force my thoughts to yield to such desire,
    Where light affection only fuelleth the fire.
        Though Cupid's a god,
        I fear not his rod.
        Cupid may hit,   5
        But I do not fear it.
    Cupid's arrow hurts but doth not kill.
        Cupid allures me
        But cannot procure me.
    Cupid hath his might, and I my will.   10

V–VI

I PRAY thee, sweet John, away!
    I cannot tell how to love thee.
    Pish! phew! in faith, all this will not move me.
O me, I dare not before our marriage day.
If this will not move thee, gentle John,   5
Come, quickly kiss me, and let me be gone.

Nay, will ye? Faith, this is more than needs.
    This fooling I cannot abide.
    Leave off, or in faith I must chide.
See now, faith, here are proper deeds.   10
Have done then! I now bewail my hap.
Repentance follows with an afterclap.

Aye me! my joys are murdered with a frown,
And sorrow pulls untimely pleasure down.

VII

WHAT is beauty but a breath,
Fancy's twin at birth and death;
The colour of a damask rose
That fadeth when the north wind blows.
'Tis such that though all sorts do crave it   5
They know not what it is that have it.
A thing that sometimes stoops not to a king,
And yet most open to the common'st thing.
   For she that is most fair
   Is open to the air.   10

VIII–IX

STAY, Laura, stay! do not so soon depart
From him whom thou hast robbed of a heart.
Hear my laments, view but my brinish tears;
One will move pity, the other deaf thine ears.
Fly me not then, I know thou dost but jest   5
And wilt return thy theft with interest.

Inconstant Laura makes me death to crave,
For, wanting her, I must embrace my grave.
A little grave will ease my malady
And set me free from love's fell tyranny.   10
Intomb me then, and show her where I lie,
And say I died through her inconstancy.

X

WHEN I behold my former wandering way,
  And dive into the bottom of my thought;
And think how I have led that soul astray
  Whose safety with so precious blood was bought;
With tears I cry unto the God of Truth: 5
Forgive, O Lord, the errors of my youth.

A blessed Saviour left his heavenly throne
  To seek my straying soul and bring it back,
Himself the way, the way I should have gone;
  The way I left and sought eternal wrack;   10

Which makes me cry in depth of bitter ruth:
Forgive, O Lord, the errors of my youth.

Inestimable gain he did propose
   T' allure my erring fancy to retire;
But idle fancy would have none of those,   15
   Delighting still to wallow in the mire;
Wherefore I cry unto the God of Truth:
Forgive, O Lord, the errors of my youth.

I saw the way, the way itself did clear it;
   I knew the way, the way itself did show it;   20
I marked the way, but fondly did forbear it;
   I left the way because I would not know it.
But now I cry unto the God of Truth:
Forgive, O Lord, the errors of my youth.

Jesu, the only Way, most perfect true!   25
   Jesu, the only Truth of heavenly life!
Jesu, the only Life that doth renew
   My sin-sick soul half slain by Satan's strife,
With tears I beg, teach me the way of truth,
Forgive, O Lord, the errors of my youth.   30

XI

MAN first created was in single life
   To serve his God in fruitful Paradise,
Till heavenly wisdom saw he lacked a wife
   To comfort him and give him good advice;
And from man's side a rib he did remove,   5
And woman made, which woe to man did prove.

With tender flesh the hollow place did fill,
   Near to his heart, which made his heart relenting.
The stubborn rib makes woman full of will,
   Hard bone, soft flesh, she rash, but he repenting.   10
Thus 'gainst poor man his own flesh did rebel,
And woman (woe to man) brought man to hell.

Yet from the flesh which to this bone did cleave,
   A second came from whence a branch did spring,
Not woe to man, but wooing man to leave   15
   An earthly state to serve the heavenly King.
Though woman (woe to man) made man to fall,
This Saviour's blood hath made amends for all.

XII

WHO keeps in compass his desires,
  And calms his mind with sweet content,
Needs not to fear those furious fires
  Whose force will all in smoke be spent,
Whiles proud ambition blows the coals   5
That yields no warmth to humble souls.

XIII–XV

LET dread of pain for sin in after-time,
  Let shame to see thyself ensnared so,
Let grief conceived for foul accursed crime,
  Let hate of sin, the worker of thy woe,
With dread, with shame, with grief, with hate enforce   5
To dew thy cheeks with tears of deep remorse.

So hate of sin shall cause God's love to grow;
  So grief shall harbour hope within thy heart;
So dread shall cause the flood of joy to flow;
  So shame shall send sweet solace to thy smart;   10
So love, so hope, so joy, so solace sweet
Shall make thy soul in heavenly bliss to fleet.

Woe, where such hate doth no such love allure!
  Woe, where such grief doth make no hope proceed!
Woe, where such dread doth no such joy procure!   15
  Woe, where such shame doth no such solace breed!
Woe, where no hate, no grief, no dread, no shame
Doth neither love, hope, joy, or solace frame!

XVI

ENGLAND, receive the rightful king with cheerful heart and hand,
The present joy, the future hope of this his loyal land.
His birth makes challenge to his right, his virtues to our love,
Both are his due, both are our debt, which nothing can remove.
Long have he life, long have he health, long have he happy reign;   5
His seed possess his realms in peace till Christ shall come again.

XVII–XVIII

SWEET nymphs that trip along the English lands,
  Go meet fair Oriana, beauty's queen,
Virtue invites and chastity commands.
   Your golden tresses trim with garlands green,
  For such a sight hath not before been seen.   5
Then sing in honour of her and Diana:
Long live in joy the fair chaste Oriana.

Long have the shepherds sung this song before,
  As prophesying what should come to pass.
The gentle nymphs henceforth lament no more,   10
  The times are changed, it is not as it was.
  Dian shall flower, and Venus fade like grass.
Then sing in honour of her and Diana:
Long live in joy the fair chaste Oriana.

XIX–XX

LADY, the melting crystal of your eye
Like frozen drops upon your cheeks did lie.
Mine eye was dancing on them with delight,
And saw Love's flames within them burning bright,
    Which did mine eye entice   5
    To play with burning ice.
But O my heart thus sporting with desire,
My careless eye did set my heart on fire.

O that a drop from such a sweet fount flying
Should flame like fire, and leave my heart a dying!   10
I burn! I burn! my tears can never drench it,
Till in your eyes I bathe my heart and quench it.
But there, alas, Love with his fire lies sleeping,
And all conspire to burn my heart with weeping.

XXI

COME away, sweet love, and play thee,
Lest grief and care betray thee. Fa la.
Leave off this sad lamenting
And take thy heart's contenting.
The nymphs to sport invite thee,   5
And running in and out delights thee. Fa la.

GEORGE HANDFORD

*Ayres To be sunge to y*e *Lute, and Base Vyole, Newly composed by George Handford.* [1609]

I

COME, come, sweet fire, why stayest thou?
   Alas, come quickly, come;
Consume me all at once, and give me leave to try
If life be sweeter than a lover's martyrdom;
Or dying so to live in love than living die.   5
   Come, come, sweet fire, why stay'st? Nay then I see
That thou wilt yet, alas, in pity cruel be.

Come, come away, O sweet, why do you stay?
   O come away, sweet fire,
And let me prove if rest to love my death can give,   10
Or if my lukewarm ashes have not still desire.
To kindly heat of love wherein I dying live
   Then come, sweet fire, why stay'st? Nay then I see
That thou wilt yet, alas, in pity cruel be.

II

MY mournful thoughts I safely may disclose
Here all alone, if stones can silence keep;
If not, then doth the calm air call me forth,
And bids me to these woods bewray my grief.
   To mourn with me things senseless doth consent,   5
   And stones and trees will help me to lament.

Witness, you trees, how oft I do lament,
And help to number, if you can, how oft
I do let fall a tear, and tear my hair,
And wring my hands under your shady boughs.   10
   O dear woods, and let my Cynthia see
   That Cynthia's name is graven in every tree.

Tell her, if this you tell her feigned be,
A firmer love she shall not live to see.
Echo, say she hates me, and ever ever will,   15
But that unless she leave to hate me still,
Fear of her love at my last obsequy
Already is a present death to me.

III

FLORELLA lay asleeping,
Her Clorus sat by weeping;
    Ay me,
    Quoth he,
Canst thou sleep so secure,   5
While I these pains for want of love endure?
But rest thee still and sleeping lie,
The while I weep, and weeping, die.

With that Florella waked,
And Clorus' weeping slaked;   10
    Ay me,
    Quoth she,
I dreamt I was in love,
But heavens forbid it should in earnest prove;
Which made poor Clorus' heart so bleed   15
He wept afresh, and died indeed.

IV

TWO Cynthias did at once appear,
The one far off, the other near,
One on the earth and very nigh,
The other fixed in the sky.

The heavenly Cynthia blushed to see   5
This one on earth more fair than she,
Then she on earth looked pale for fear
To see bright Cynthia's blushing cheer.

Fear not, fair star, then Cynthia spake,
But let those rays thy wonder make.   10
Though thou on earth, yet sure divine
Thy beauty is that equals mine.

V

GRIEF, press my soul, that I may never find relief,
Since wearied life is still prolonged by uttered grief.
My fruitless tears, distil no more from your sad eye,
But let that passion back return, that I may die.
And as my singing is a mournful swan-like crying,   5
So let my living be a senseless life, a dying.

VI

GO weep, sad soul, and to thy love complain thee,
And beg with tears that she will not disdain thee.
    If still her flinty heart doth grace deny,
        Go weep, sad soul, and sigh, and die.

VII

GROAN, weary soul, too too much oppressed,
Weary of life, yet never death procuring.
    Groan tir'd soul, restless in thine unrest,
Tir'd with grief, yet ever grief enduring.
Groan, groan, my soul, with such a piteous sound   5
As may thine own amazed self confound.

VIII

IF the tongue durst one word speak,
Or the heart dost one thought break,
True Virtue from her seat t' expel,
Tongue and heart be damned in hell.

But tongue now thy thoughts, then hidden,   5
Speak more freely, more forbidden,
And if by no means words can move,
Then speak, eyes, dreams, sighs and love.

Say those sacred eyes and face,
Virtue, doth thy virtue grace;   10
In them the Graces all are found,
And in them sits Virtue crowned.

Cynthia there herself enshrineth,
And in all her glory shineth.
Now then, since they are both divine,   15
I adore both saint and shrine.

IX

Come, sullen night, that in thy silent cover,
Like ruthful birds, my swarming cares may hover.
  Come, sullen night, let cold despair assay
  The restless floodgate of my eyes to stay.
But come what will, alas, noontide or morrow,   5
All seemeth dark in this my night of sorrow.

Yet come, sweet morn, though you my icy fears
Canst not dissolve, or keep truce with my tears,
  Nor that thy pleasure can my pain redeem,
  But that all change of pain doth pleasure seem.   10
Then come what will, alas, noontide or morrow,
All seemeth dark in this my night of sorrow.

X

  Say, ye gods that power have
  Lovers to destroy or save,
What off'rings might your altars please,
A woeful lover to release?
Say where your temples placed are,   5
That to them I may make repair.

  Cupid sweet, shall I divine
  Where thy mother hath her shrine,
If that on earth her temple be?
But, O sweet Venus, pardon me   10
For being so profane to tell
The world where all thy graces dwell.

  Sure my love that temple is,
  Heavenly model of all bliss,
Whose face a sweet consorted choir,   15
Whose eyes the lamplight of love's fire,
Whose lips your altars, where would I,
In offering kisses, live and die.

XI

HIDE not from me those eyes, in whose bright flame
  My heart doth like the salamander burn.
Hide them but now and then, lest by the same,
  My heat o'ercome, thou me to ashes turn.
So shalt thou cherish, not surcharge, desire,   5
And keep me living in a double fire.

O gently gently come, but not too fast,
  And let me feel those kindly burning rays.
Now come away, away, O sweet, make haste,
  Alas, why make you longer longer stay?   10
Make haste, or stay and feed me with desire,
And keep me living in a double fire.

XII

NOW each creature joys the other,
  Passing happy days and hours;
One bird reports unto another
  In the fall of silver showers;
Whilst the earth, our common mother,   5
  Hath her bosom decked with flowers.

Whilst the greatest torch of heaven
  With bright rays warms Flora's lap,
Now making nights and days both even,
  Cheering the plants with fresher sap,   10
My field of flowers, quite bereaven,
  Wants refresh of better hap.

Echo, daughter of the air,
  Babbling guest of rocks and hills,
Doth know the name of my fierce fair,   15
  And sounds the accents of my ills.
Each thing pities my despair,
  Whilst that she her lover kills.

Whilst that she, O cruel maid,
  Doth me and my love despise,   20
My life's flourish is decayed,
  The which depended on her eyes.
But her will must be obeyed,
  And well he ends for love who dies.
                        [*Samuel Daniel*]

XIII

YOU wat'ry issue of a mourning mind,
   Ye tears, true picturers of discontent,
The only help where help is none to find,
   Help me my sad misfortune to lament.
Flow, flow, my tears, no other help I know;   5
No other help but tears, and therefore flow.

XIV

BREATHE out, my sighs, and sigh my lavish breath,
   And like an earthquake shall my panting breast,
That which gives others life shall cause my death,
   Breathing, by too much breathing being suppressed.
And thus my breath my breathless heart shall pine;   5
Her breath did murther me, then why not mine?

XV

FLOW, flow, my tears, as floods and fountains flow,
   Distil my soul out of my wat'ry eyes.
Weep, weep, my eyes, created ev'n for woe,
   Let a full sea of trickling streams arise.
Since she hath turned our sweet to bitter sours,   5
Turn ye your April smiles to April showers.

Flow, flow, my tears, till all my veins ye strain,
   Flow till your conduit pipes be quite drawn dry,
And being dried, gush out afresh again,
   Till overwhelmed in waves of woe I lie,   10
That by too much of tears that flow along,
Mine eyes, washed out, may not behold their wrong.

XVI. *Mall Newberry her Repentance*

COME, tears and sighs, woe's constant woeful mates,
   And cloud the lustre of lascivious eyes,
And tear this yielding heart, that oped the gate
   To sin and shame, to endless misery.
My tears exhaust, and all my sighs be spent;   5
Tears, sighs do fail me when I should lament.

XVII

[Missing from the manuscript]

XVIII

BUT now I rise, and rising live again,
And living love, rich guerdon for my pain.
Her words did raise me up, her smiles gave breath,
Her letters wrote of love, then farewell, death!
Then farewell, death! can kindest Clara love.   5
Then welcome life from my turtledove.

XIX

Pastorella. SEE, O see, sweet Amyntas, with what bashful grace
         Blushing Aurora views the rosy tincture in thy face.
Amyntas. See, Pastorella fair, how Phoebus fears to rise,
         Seeing the heaven-born light darted from both thine eyes.
Pastorella.   O come then, O come dear fire,   5
          Let thy eyes my eyes cover,
          And shade this ardour of desire
              That they have to their lover.
Amyntas.   So shall those starry rays expel
              Life from my heart, light from my eyes.   10
Both.   So shall Aurora cease to blush,
              And fearful Phoebus haste to rise.

XX

Phyllis.   DAPHNE, stay, O stay, and do not still deny me.
Daphne.   No, no, I cannot love.
Phyllis.   Yet do not fly me.
          Sweet, O sweetest Daphne, do but hear.
Daphne.   Mine ears are deaf to love, leave off, my dear.
Thyrsis.   Ay me!   5
Daphne.   Hark!
Phyllis.   Hark!
Thyrsis.   Ay me! hath she bid me adieu?
          Ah, cruel fair!
Phyllis.   O see my Thyrsis true!
Daphne.   Call'st thou him thine, and seek'st to fly him still?   10
Phyllis.   Call thou me thine, and me with kindness kill!

Thyrsis.   Ah, my Phyllis, canst not pity me?
Daphne.   She sues to me, yet cannot pity thee.
Phyllis.   He pleads for thee, yet cannot pity me.
Phyllis & O loving hate, disdainful pity, pity ye powers
   Thyrsis.   divine.   15
              We both for pity plead, and both, alas, for pity pine.
All.   Then let us take hands, dance round and sing;
              Disdain and Pity with Hate and Love all in a ring.

TOBIAS HUME

*The First Part of Ayres, French, Pollish, and others together, some in Tabli-
ture, and some in Pricke-Song: With Pauines, Galliards, and Almaines for
the Viole De Gambo alone, and other Musicall Conceites for two Base Viols,
expressing fiue partes, with pleasant reportes one from the other, and for two
Leero Viols, and also for the Leero Viole with two Treble Viols, or two with
one Treble. Lastly for the Leero Viole to play alone, and some Songes to bee
sung to the Viole, with the Lute, or better with the Viole alone. Also an
Inuention for two to play vpon one Viole. 1605*
[Running title: *Musicall Humors.*]

1. *The Soldier's Song*

I SING the praise of honoured wars,
The glory of well-gotten scars,
The bravery of glittering shields,
Of lusty hearts and famous fields;
For that is music worth the ear of Jove,   5
A sight for kings, and still the soldier's love.

Look! O methinks I see
The grace of chivalry;
The colours are displayed,
The captains bright arrayed.   10
See now the battle's ranged,
Bullets now thick are changed.
Hark! shots and wounds abound,
The drums alarum sound.

The captains cry: za-za!   15
The trumpets sound ta-ra!
O this is music worth the ear of Jove,
A sight for kings, and still the soldier's love.

[II. *A Galliard for the Lute*]

III

TOBACCO, tobacco,
   Sing sweetly for tobacco!
Tobacco is like love, O love it.
   For you see I will prove it.
Love maketh lean the fat men's tumour,   5
   So doth tobacco.
Love still dries up the wanton humour,
   So doth tobacco.
Love makes men sail from shore to shore,
   So doth tobacco.   10
'Tis fond love often makes men poor,
   So doth tobacco.
Love makes men scorn all coward fears,
   So doth tobacco.
Love often sets men by the ears,   15
   So doth tobacco.
   Tobacco, tobacco,
      Sing sweetly for tobacco!
   Tobacco is like love, O love it.
   For you see I have proved it.   20

[IV–CXI *are instrumental pieces*]

CXII

FAIN would I change that note
   To which fond love hath charmed me
Long, long to sing by rote,
   Fancying that that harmed me.
Yet when this thought doth come,   5
Love is the perfect sum
   Of all delight,
I have no other choice
Either for pen or voice
   To sing or write.   10

O love, they wrong thee much
　　That say thy sweet is bitter,
When thy ripe fruit is such
　　As nothing can be sweeter.
Fair house of joy and bliss,　　　　　　　　　　15
Where truest pleasure is,
　　　　I do adore thee.
I know thee what thou art,
I serve thee with my heart
　　　　And fall before thee.　　　　　　　　　20

CXIII

WHAT greater grief than no relief in deepest woe?
Death is no friend that will not end such heart's sorrow.
Help! I do cry; no help is nigh but wind and air,
Which to and fro do toss and blow all to despair.
　　Sith then despair I must, yet may not die,　　　5
　　No man unhappier lives on earth than I.

'Tis I that feel the scornful heel of dismal hate.
My gain is lost, my loss dear cost, repentance late.
So I must moan, bemoaned of none, O bitter gall!
Death, be my friend, with speed to end and quiet all.　　10
　　But if thou linger in despair to leave me,
　　I'll kill despair with hope, and so deceive thee.

CXIV

ALAS, poor men, why strive you to live long
To have more time and space to suffer wrong?
　　Our birth is blind and creeping;
　　Our life all woe and weeping;
　　Our death all pain and terror.　　　　　　5
　　Birth, life, death, what all but error?
Alas, poor men, why strive you to live long
To have more time and space to suffer wrong?

　　O World, Nurse of desires,
　　Fost'ress of vain attires,　　　　　　　　　10
　　What reason canst thou render
　　Why man should hold thee tender?
Alas, poor men, why strive you to live long
To have more time and space to suffer wrong?

Thou pin'st the pale-cheeked Muses,   15
And soldier that refuses
No wounds for country's safety.
He only thrives that's crafty.
Alas, poor men, why strive you to live long
To have more time and space to suffer wrong?   20

On crutches Virtue halts,
Whilst men most great in faults
Suffers best worth distressed,
With empty pride oppressed.
Alas, poor men, why strive you to live long   25
To have more time and space to suffer wrong?

O Virtue, yet at length
Rouse thy diviner strength,
And make no music more.
Out, sad state that's deplore!   30
Then alas, poor men, why strive you to live long
To have more time and space to suffer wrong?

*Captaine Hvmes Poeticall Musicke. Principally made for two Basse-Viols,
yet so contriued, that it may be plaied 8. seuerall waies vpon sundry Instruments with much facilitie. 1. The first way or musicke is for one Bass-Viole
to play alone in parts, which standeth alwaies on the right side of this Booke.
2. The second musicke is for two Basse-Viols to play together. 3. The third
musicke, for three Basse-Viols to play together. 4. The fourth musicke, for
two Tenor Viols and a Basse-Viole. 5. The fift musicke, for two Lutes and a
Basse-Viole. 6. The sixt musicke, for two Orpherions and a Basse-Viole.
7. The seuenth musicke, to vse the voyce to some of these musicks, but especially
to the three Basse-Viols, or to the two Orpherions with one Basse-Viole to play
the ground. 8. The eight and last musicke, is consorting all these Instruments
together with the Virginals, or rather with a winde Instrument and the voice.*
1607

I

*A new music made for the Queen's most Excellent Majesty, and my new-
year's gift to her Highness*

CEASE, leaden slumber, dreaming!
My genius presents
The cause of sweet music's meaning
Now which breeds my soul's content,

And bids my Muse awake   5
To hear sweet music's note,
That cheerfully glads me, so cheerfully.

Methought, as I lay sleeping,
        Dreams did enchant me
With the praise of music and her worth   10
And her eternished fame.
But now I find indeed
My leaden windows open
That cheerfully comforts, full cheerfully.

Night, gloomy veil to the morn,   15
        Dreams affright no more
Where sweet Music is now still appearing.
Leave passions to perplex, for now my soul
Delights in Music's harmony,
Whose heavenly noise   20
Glads souls with tongue and voice;
For now my soul delights in heavenly noise
        Of Music's sweetest joys.

XIV

[*The words are the same as No. cxiii in Hume's 1605 publication*]

XXV

The hunting song, to be sung to the bass viol

(*The call in the morning. . . . The hounds do yawn*)
COME, come, my hearts, a-hunting let us wend,
That echoing cries the hills and heavens may rend
With shouts and sounds of horns and hounds.
(*Blow the 'Uncoupling'*)
Why then, my lads, uncouple Kill-buck, keen Ringwood and Roler,
Chanter and Joler, Trouncer and Drummer, Bowman and Gunner.   5
Actaeon's hounds were ne'er like these I ween.

(*Blow the 'Seek'—the hounds are now a-hunting*)
The stag is now roused, the game is on foot.
(*The hounds hunt still*)
Hark! hark! beauty Dainty prates.
The cry is full. Hark! how they hold the cry.
(*The hounds hunt—the huntsman rates*)

But soft, the huntsman rates! 10
(*The hunt falls*)
Clowder hunts counter, and so doth Mounter, they're all at fault.
Hark! Ringwood spends and makes amends.
(*Play loud, for Joler is in*)
List of Joler! a Joler! a Joler!
(*The cry is full*)
That's he! Ho ho!
(*The hollow—All the standers by must hollow twice—The horns—The[y] hunt still*)
Joler crossed it, else we had lost it. 15
The buck is quite spent since to soil he went.

Why, heavenlier sport than this there cannot be.
(*Hounds do hunt again*)
See, Plowman hath pinched, and Joler ne'er flinched.
Now with full cry they all come, frowling, trowling to the fall.
Wind the morte! 20
(*Wind 'the death of the buck' with horns—the hounds do yawn*)
O well done there, boys! All other sports to these are but toys.

Here endeth the hunting song, which was sung before two kings, to the admiring of all brave huntsmen.

ROBERT JONES

The First Booke of Songes & Ayres Of foure parts with Tableture for the Lute. So made that all the parts together, or either of them seuerally may be song to the Lute, Orpherian or Viol de Gambo. 1600

I

A WOMAN'S looks
Are barbed hooks,
That catch by art
The strongest heart,
When yet they spend no breath. 5
But let them speak,
And sighing break
Forth into tears,
Their words are spears
That wound our souls to death. 10

The rarest wit
Is made forget,
And like a child
Is oft beguiled
With Love's sweet-seeming bait.   15
Love with his rod
So like a god
Commands the mind
We cannot find.
Fair shows hide foul deceit.   20

Time, that all things
In order brings,
Hath taught me now
To be more slow
In giving faith to speech,   25
Since women's words
No truth affords,
And when they kiss
They think by this
Us men to overreach.   30

II

FOND wanton youths make Love a god,
Which after proveth Age's rod.
Their youth, their time, their wit, their art
They spend in seeking of their smart;
And, which of follies is the chief,   5
They woo their woe, they wed their grief.

All find it so who wedded are.
Love's sweets, they find, enfold sour care:
His pleasures pleasing'st in the eye,
Which tasted once with loathing die.   10
They find of follies 'tis the chief
Their woe to woo, to wed their grief.

If for their own content they choose,
Forthwith their kindred's love they lose.
And if their kindred they content,   15
For ever after they repent.
O, 'tis of all our follies chief,
Our woe to woo, to wed our grief.

In bed what strifes are bred by day
Our puling wives do open lay. 20
None friends, none foes we must esteem
But whom they so vouchsafe to deem.
O, 'tis of all our follies chief
Our woe to woo, to wed our grief.

Their smiles we want, if aught they want; 25
And either we their wills must grant,
Or die they will, or are with child.
Their laughings must not be beguiled.
O, 'tis of all our follies the chief
Our woe to woo, to wed our grief. 30

Foul wives are jealous, fair wives false.
Marriage to either binds us thrall.
Wherefore being bound we must obey,
And forced be perforce to say:
Of all our bliss it is the chief 35
Our woe to woo, to wed our grief.

III

SHE whose matchless beauty staineth
What best judgement fair'st maintaineth,
She, O she, my love disdaineth.

Can a creature so excelling
Harbour scorn in beauty's dwelling, 5
All kind pity thence expelling?

Pity beauty much commendeth,
And th' embracer oft befriendeth
When all eye-contentment endeth.

Time proves beauty transitory. 10
Scorn, the stain of beauty's glory,
In time makes the scorner sorry.

None adores the sun declining,
Love all love falls to resigning
When the sun of love leaves shining. 15

So when flower of beauty fails thee,
And age stealing on assails thee,
Then mark what this scorn avails thee.

Then those hearts, which now complaining
Feel the wounds of thy disdaining, 20
Shall contemn thy beauty waning.

Yea, thine own heart, now dear-prized,
Shall, with spite and grief surprised,
Burst to find itself despised.

When like harms have them requited, 25
Who in others' harms delighted,
Pleasingly the wronged are righted.

Such revenge my wrongs attending,
Hope still lives on Time depending,
By thy plagues my torments ending. 30

IV

ONCE did I love, and yet I live
   Though love and troth be now forgotten.
Then did I joy, now do I grieve
   That holy vows must needs be broken.

Hers be the blame that caused it so; 5
   Mine be the grief though it be little.
She shall have shame; I cause to know
   What 'tis to love a dame so fickle.

Love her that list! I am content,
   For that chameleon-like she changeth, 10
Yielding such mists as may prevent
   My sight to view her when she rangeth.

Let him not vaunt that gains my loss,
   For when that he and Time hath proved her,
She may him bring to weeping cross. 15
   I say no more, because I loved her.

V

LED by a strong desire
　　To have a thing unseen,
　Nothing could make me tire
　　To be where as I had been.
I got her sight, which made me think　　　　5
My thirst was gone because I saw my drink.

　Kept by the careful watch
　　Of more than hundred eyes,
　I sought but could not catch
　　The thing she not denies.　　　　　　10
'Tis better to be blind and fast
Than, hungry, see thy love and cannot taste.

　But lovers' eyes do wake
　　When others are at rest;
　And in the night they slake　　　　　15
　　The fire of day's unrest.
Methinks that joy is of most worth
Which painful Time and passed fears brings forth.

　Yet husbands do suppose
　　To keep their wives by art,　　　　20
　And parents will disclose
　　By looks their children's heart.
As if they which have will to do
Had not the wit to blind such keepers too.

　Peace, then, ye aged fools,　　　　　25
　　That know yourselves so wise,
　That from experience' schools
　　Do think wit must arise.
Give young men leave to think and say:
Your senses with your bodies do decay.　　　30

　Love ruleth like a god,
　　Whom earth keeps not in awe,
　Nor fear of smarting rod
　　Denounced by reason's law.
Give grave advice, but rest you there.
Youth hath his course and will; and you youths were.

Think not by prying care
To pick love's secrets out;
If you suspicious are
Yourselves resolve your doubt.   40
Who seeks to know such deed once done
Finds perjury before confession.

VI

LIE down, poor heart, and die awhile for grief.
Think not this world will ever do thee good.
Fortune forewarns thou look to thy relief,
And sorrow sucks upon thy living blood.
Then this is all can help thee of thy hell,   5
Lie down and die, and then thou shalt do well.

Day gives his light but to thy labour's toil;
And night her rest but to thy weary bones.
Thy fairest fortune follows with a foil,
And laughing ends but with their after groans.   10
And this is all can help thee of thy hell,
Lie down and die, and then thou shalt do well.

Patience doth pine, and pity ease no pain;
Time wears the thoughts, but nothing helps the mind,
Dead and alive, alive and dead again,   15
These are the fits that thou art like to find.
And this is all can help thee of thy hell,
Lie down and die, and then thou shalt do well.

VII

WHERE lingering fear doth once possess the heart,
There is the tongue
Forced to prolong
And smother up his suit, while that his smart,
Like fire suppressed, flames more in every part.   5

Who dares not speak deserves not his desire.
The boldest face
Findeth most grace.
Though women love that men should them admire,
They slyly laugh at him dares come no higher.   10

Some think a glance expressed by a sigh,
      Winning the field,
      Maketh them yield;
But while these glancing fools do roll the eye,
They beat the bush, away the bird doth fly.   15

A gentle heart in virtuous breast doth stay.
      Pity doth dwell
      In Beauty's cell.
A woman's heart doth not, though tongue say Nay.
Repentance taught me this the other day.   20

Which had I wist I presently had got
      The pleasing fruit
      Of my long suit;
But Time hath now beguiled me of this lot,
For that by his foretop I took him not.   25

VIII

HERO, care not though they pry,
I will love thee till I die.
Jealousy is but a smart
That torments a jealous heart.
    Crows are black that were white   5
    For betraying love's delight.

They that love to find a fault
May repent what they have sought.
What the fond eye hath not viewed,
Never wretched heart hath rued.   10
    Vulcan then proved a scorn
    When he saw he wore a horn.

Doth it then by might behove
To shut up the gates of love?
Women are not kept by force   15
But by nature's own remorse.
    If they list they will stray;
    Who can hold that will away?

Jove in golden shower obtained
His love in a tower restrained.   20

So perhaps if I could do
I might hold my sweet love too.
  Gold, keep out at the door,
  I have love that conquers more.

Wherefore did they not suspect   25
When it was to some effect?
Every little glimmering spark
Is perceived in the dark.
  This is right; owlets' kind
  See by night, by day be blind.   30

IX

WHEN love on time and measure makes his ground,
  Time that must end, though love can never die,
'Tis love betwixt a shadow and a sound,
  A love not in the heart but in the eye.
A love that ebbs and flows, now up, now down.   5
A morning's favour and an evening's frown.

Sweet looks show love, yet they are but as beams,
  Fair words seem true, yet they are but as wind.
Eyes shed their tears, yet are but outward streams,
  Sighs paint a sadness in the falsest mind.   10
Looks, words, tears, sighs show love when love they leave;
False hearts can weep, sigh, swear, and yet deceive.

                              [*Attributed to John Lilliatt*]

X

SWEET, come away, my darling,
And sweetly let me hear thee sing.
  Come away and bring
My heart thou hast so fast in keeping.

O fie upon this long stay   5
That thus my loving hopes delay!
  Come again and say:
Sweet heart, I'll never more say thee nay.

Dear, be not such a tyrant
Still to rejoice thee in my want.   10
  Come, and do not scant
Me of thy sight so fair and pleasant.

Why hear'st thou not his sighing,
Whose voice all hoarse is with crying?
    Come and do something   15
That may revive thy true love dying.

    This is the pride of women,
    That they make beggars of all men.
We must sigh, we must cry, we must die, and then
Forsooth it may be they will hearken.   20

XI

WEEMEN, what are they? Changing weathercocks
    That smallest puffs of lust have power to turn.
Weemen, what are they? Virtue's stumbling-blocks,
    Whereat weak fools do fall, the wiser spurn.
    We men, what are we? Fools and idle boys   5
    To spend our time in sporting with such toys.

Weemen, what are they? Trees whose outward rind
    Makes show for fair when inward heart is hollow.
Weemen, what are they? Beasts of hyaena's kind,
    That speak those fair'st whom most they mean to swallow. 10
    We men, what are we? Fools and idle boys
    To spend our time in sporting with such toys.

Weemen, what are they? Rocks upon the coast
    Whereon we suffer shipwrack at our landing.
Weemen, what are they? Patient creatures most   15
    That rather yield than strive 'gainst aught withstanding.
    We men, what are we? Fools and idle boys
    To spend our time in sporting with such toys.

XII

FAREWELL, dear love, since thou wilt needs be gone.
Mine eyes do show my life is almost done.
    Nay, I will never die,
    So long as I can spy.
    There be many moe   5
    Though that she do go.
There be many moe, I fear not.
Why then, let her go, I care not.

Farewell, farewell, since this I find is true,
I will not spend more time in wooing you.   10
      But I will seek elsewhere
      If I may find her there.
      Shall I bid her go?
      What and if I do?
    Shall I bid her go, and spare not?   15
    O no, no, no, no, I dare not.

Ten thousand times farewell! Yet stay awhile!
Sweet, kiss me once; sweet kisses time beguile.
      I have no power to move.
      How now, am I in love?   20
      Wilt thou needs be gone?
      Go then, all is one.
    Wilt thou needs be gone? O hie thee!
    Nay, stay, and do no more deny me.

Once more farewell! I see loth to depart   25
Bids oft adieu to her that holds my heart.
      But seeing I must lose
      Thy love which I did choose,
      Go thy ways for me
      Since it may not be.   30
    Go thy ways for me. But whither?
    Go, O but where I may come thither.

What shall I do? My love is now departed.
She is as fair as she is cruel-hearted.
      She would not be entreated   35
      With prayers oft repeated.
      If she come no more
      Shall I die therefore?
    If she come no more, what care I?
    Faith, let her go, or come, or tarry.   40

XIII

O MY poor eyes, the sun whose shine
Late gave you light doth now decline,
    And, set to you, to others riseth.
She who would sooner die than change,
Not fearing death delights to range,   5
    And now, O now my soul despiseth.

Yet, O my heart, thy state is blest
To find out rest in thy unrest,
   Since thou her slave no more remainest.
For she that bound thee sets thee free   10
Then when she first forsaketh thee.
   Such, O such right by wrong thou gainest.

Eyes, gaze no more! heart, learn to hate!
Experience tells you all too late
   Fond woman's love with faith still warreth,   15
While true desert speaks, writes and gives,
Some groom the bargain nearer drives,
   And he, O he, the market marreth.

XIV

IF fathers knew but how to leave
   Their children wit, as they do wealth;
And could constrain them to receive
   That physic which brings perfect health,
The world would not admiring stand   5
A woman's face and woman's hand.

Women confess they must obey;
   We men will needs be servants still.
We kiss their hands, and what they say
   We must commend be 't never so ill.   10
Thus we like fools admiring stand
Her pretty foot and pretty hand.

We blame their pride, which we increase
   By making mountains of a mouse.
We praise because we know we please.   15
   Poor women are too credulous
To think that we admiring stand
Or foot, or face, or foolish hand.

XV

LIFE is a poet's fable,
   And all her days are lies
   Stolen from Death's reckoning table.
For I die, for I die, as I speak
Death times the notes that I do break.   5

Childhood doth die in youth,
  And youth in old age dies.
I thought I lived in truth,
But I die, but I die, now I see,
Each age of Death makes one degree.   10

Farewell the doting score
  Of world's arithmetic.
Life, I'll trust thee no more;
Till I die, till I die, for thy sake
I'll go by Death's new almanack.   15

This instant of my song
  A thousand men lie sick,
A thousand knells are rung;
And I die, and I die as they sing,
They are but dead and I dying.   20

Death is but Life's decay.
Lifetime Time wastes away.
  Then reason bids me say
That I die, that I die, though my breath
Prolongs this space of lingering death.   25

XVI

SWEET Philomel in groves and deserts haunting
Oft glads my heart and ears with her sweet chanting.
    But then her tunes delight me best
    When perched with prick against her breast,
She sings, 'fie, fie', as if she suffered wrong,   5
Till seeming pleased, 'sweet, sweet' concludes her song.

Sweet Jinny sings and talks and sweetly smileth,
And with her wanton mirth my griefs beguileth.
    But then methinks she pleaseth best
    When, while my hands move love's request,   10
She cries, 'fie, fie', and seeming loth gainsays,
Till better pleased, 'sweet, sweet' content bewrays.

XVII

THAT heart, wherein all sorrows doth abound,
  Lies in this breast and cries aloud for death.
O blame not her when I am under ground,
  That scorning wished t' outlive my panting breath.

O do not her despise,   5
But let my death suffice
To make all young men wise.

My loving hopes prolonged my loathed life,
    Till that my life grew loathsome to my loved;
Till Death and I were at no longer strife,   10
    And I was glad my death her wish approved.
        O let not her be shent,
        Yet let my precedent
        Make woman's hearts relent.

XVIII

WHAT if I seek for love of thee?
        Shall I find beauty kind
To desert that still shall dwell in me?
But if I sue and live forlorn,
        Then alas, never was   5
Any wretch to more misfortune born.
Though thy looks have charmed mine eyes,
        I can forbear to love.
        But if ever sweet Desire
        Set my woeful heart on fire,   10
        Then can I never remove.

Frown not on me unless thou hate;
        For thy frown cast me down
To despair of my most hapless state.
Smile not on me unless thou love;   15
        For thy smile will beguile
My desires if thou unsteadfast prove.
If thou needs wilt bend thy brows,
        A while refrain, my dear.
        But if thou wilt smile on me   20
        Let it not delayed be,
        Comfort is never too near.

XIX

MY mistress sings no other song,
But still complains I did her wrong.
Believe her not; it was not so,
I did but kiss her and let her go.

And now she swears I did—But what?   5
Nay, nay, I must not tell you that.
And yet I will, it is so sweet
As 'te-he, ta-ha' when lovers meet.

But women's words they are heedless,
To tell you more it is needless.   10
I ran and caught her by the arm,
And then I kissed her; this was no harm.

But she, alas, is angry still,
Which showeth but a woman's will.
She bites the lip and cries 'fie, fie'.   15
And kissing sweetly away she doth fly.

Yet sure her looks bewrays content,
And cunningly her brawls are meant,
As lovers use to play and sport
When time and leisure is too too short.   20

XX

PERPLEXED sore am I!
Thine eyes, fair love, like Phoebus' brightest beams
    Doth set my heart on fire and daze my sight.
Yet do I live by virtue of those beams,
    For when thy face is hid comes fearful night,   5
        And I am like to die.
Then, since my eyes cannot endure so heavenly spark,
Sweet, grant that I may still feel out my love by dark.

        So shall I joyful be.
Each thing on earth that liveth by the sun   10
    Would die if he in glory still appear.
Then let some clouds of pity over-run
    That glorious face, that I with lively cheer
        May stand up before thee,
Or, since my eyes cannot endure so heavenly spark,   15
Sweet, grant that I may still feel out my love by dark.

XXI

CAN modest plain desire
To the joys of love aspire?
Can worthiness procure
More than hardiness assure?
    No, no, no, where fear of each frown   5
    Takes hope's height down, down, a-down.

Granting is so eschewed,
Lest the grant lie unpursued,
Lest suitors brag they might,
And account the grantors light.   10
    'No, no, no' is a weak defence grown
    Till force bear down, down, a-down.

Yet who would stain love's seat
With a blot of such a feat?
Or for so vile a toy   15
Join repentance with his joy?
    No, no, no, her virtue well known
    Beats vain thoughts down, down, a-down.

ༀༀༀༀༀༀༀༀ

The Second Booke of Songs and Ayres, Set out to the Lute, the base Violl the playne way, or the Base by tableture after the leero fashion. 1601

I

LOVE winged my hopes and taught me how to fly
Far from base earth, but not to mount too high.
    For true pleasure
    Lives in measure,
    Which, if men forsake,   5
Blinded they into folly run, and grief for pleasure take.

But my vain hopes, proud of their new-taught flight,
Enamoured, sought to woo the sun's fair light,
    Whose rich brightness
    Moved their lightness   10
    To aspire so high,
That, all scorched and consumed with fire, now drowned in
  woe they lie.

And none but Love their woeful hap did rue;
For Love did know that their desires were true.
       Though Fate frowned,   15
       And now drowned
    They in sorrow dwell,
It was the purest light of heaven for whose fair love they fell.

II

M Y love bound me with a kiss
   That I should no longer stay.
When I felt so sweet a bliss,
   I had less power to part away.
Alas, that women doth not know   5
Kisses makes men loth to go.

Yes, she knows it but too well,
   For I heard when Venus' dove
In her ear did softly tell
   That kisses were the seals of love.   10
O muse not then though it be so,
Kisses makes men loth to go.

Wherefore did she thus inflame
   My desires, heat my blood,
Instantly to quench the same,   15
   And starve whom she had given food?
Ay, ay, the common sense can show
Kisses makes men loth to go.

Had she bid me go at first,
   It would ne'er have grieved my heart;   20
Hope delayed had been the worst.
   But ah! to kiss and then to part!
How deep it struck, speak, gods, you know.
Kisses makes men loth to go.

III

O H O W my thoughts do beat me,
Which by deep sighs entreat thee.
Hey ho, fie, what a thing is this
Thus to lie still when we might kiss

And play the fool   5
   Here in the cool
Of the stillest, clearest, sweetest evening
Philomel did ever choose for singing.

See how my lips complain them,
Thy lips should thus detain them.   10
Ay me, hark how the nightingales
In the dark each to other calls;
   Whilst thou, O thou
   Dar'st not avow
The enjoying of the truest pleasure   15
Love did ever hoard up in his treasure.

                   IV

DREAMS and imaginations
Are all the recreations
   Absence can gain me.
Dreams when I wake confound me,
Thoughts for her sake doth wound me,   5
   Lest she disdain me.
   Then sinking, let me lie,
   Or thinking, let me die,
   Since love hath slain me.

Dreams are but coward and do   10
Much good they dare not stand to,
   Ashamed of the morrow.
Thought's like a child that winketh,
He's not beguiled that thinketh
   Hath pierced me thorough;   15
   Both filling me with blisses;
   Both killing me with kisses,
   Dying in sorrow.

Dreams with their false pretences
And thoughts confounds my senses   20
   In the conclusion,
Which like a glass did show me
What came to pass and threw me
   Into confusion.
   She made me leave all other,   25
   Yet had she got another;
   This was abusion.

V

METHOUGHT this other night
I saw a pretty sight
    That pleased me much.
A fair and comely maid
Not squeamish nor afraid   5
    To let me touch.
Our lips most sweetly kissing,
Each other never missing,
Her smiling looks did show content,
And that she did but what she meant.   10

And as her lips did move
The echo still was love,
    Love, love me, sweet.
Then with a maiden blush,
Instead of crying pish   15
    Our lips did meet.
With music sweetly sounding,
With pleasures all abounding,
We kept the burden of the song,
Which was that love should take no wrong.   20

And yet, as maidens use,
She seemed to refuse
    The name of love;
Until I did protest
That I did love her best,   25
    And so will prove.
With that as both amazed
Each at the other gazed.
My eyes did see, my hands did feel
Her eyes of fire, her breast of steel.   30

O when I felt her breast
Where love itself did rest,
    My love was such
I could have been content
My best blood to have spent   35
    In that sweet touch.
But now comes that which vexed us,
There was a bar betwixt us,

A bar that barred me from that part,
Where nature did contend with art.   40

   If ever love had power
   To send one happy hour,
      Then show thy might
   And take such bars away,
   Which are the only stay   45
      Of love's delight.
   All this was but a dreaming,
   Although another meaning.
Dreams may prove true, as thoughts are free.
I will love you, you may love me.   50

VI

Whoso is tied must needs be bound,
   And he that's bound cannot be free.
Whoso is lost is hardly found,
   And he that's blind is barred to see.
Whoso is watched with jealous eyes   5
Must sit up late and early rise.

He may well write that cannot come,
   And send his eyes to plead his case.
He may well look that must be dumb,
   Until he find both time and place.   10
He that is tied to hours and times,
Though not himself may send his rhymes.

What hap have they who doth abound
   With all things that the earth doth bear,
And yet for want some time doth sound,   15
   Breathing a life 'twixt hope and fear.
Alas, poor soul, my case is such:
I want my will, yet have too much.

I would, but dare not what I would.
   I dare, but cannot what I dare.   20
I can, but must not if I could.
   I can, I must, I will not spare.
I write no more, but shall I come?
I say no more, but closely mum.

VII

FIE, fie, fie, what a coil is here!
Why strive you so to get a kiss?
Do, do, do what you will,
You shall be ne'er the near.
　　Had I been willing   5
　　So to be billing
You had prevailed long ere this.
Sweet, stand away, let me alone,
Or else in faith I'll get me gone.

Come, come, come, do you not perceive   10
I am not yet disposed to yield?
Stay, stay, stay but awhile,
My love will give you leave.
　　This my denial
　　Is but a trial   15
If faint desire will fly the field.
Whoop! look you now I pray be still.
Nay, then, in faith, do what you will.

VIII

BEAUTY, stand further!
Repine not at my blaming.
　　Is it not murther
To set my heart on flaming?
　　Thus hopeless to take   5
Bare sight of such a glory
　　Doth tempt me to make
My death beget a story.
Then pity me, lest some worse thing ensue it.
My death's true cause will force the guilt to rue it.   10

　　Is it not better
To love thy friend in good sort,
　　Than to be debtor
For kindness name to report?
　　If you had the less   15
For this rich mercy lending,
　　Then should I confess
No thrift were in such spending.
O pity me, the gain shall be thine own all;
I would but live to make thy virtues known all.   20

IX

Now what is Love, I pray thee tell?
It is that fountain and that well
Where pleasures and repentance dwell.
It is perhaps that saucing bell
That tolls all into heaven or hell.   5
And this is Love, as I hear tell.

Now what is Love, I pray thee say?
It is a work on holy day.
It is December matched with May,
When lusty blood in fresh array   10
Hear ten months after of their play.
And this is Love, as I hear say.

Now what is Love, I pray thee fain?
It is a sunshine mixed with rain.
It is a gentle pleasing pain;   15
A flower that dies and springs again.
It is a No that would full fain.
And this is Love, as I hear sayen.

Yet what is Love, I pray thee say?
It is a pretty shady way   20
As well found out by night as day.
It is a thing will soon decay.
Then take the vantage whilst you may.
And this is Love, as I hear say.

Now what is Love, I pray thee show?   25
A thing that creeps, it cannot go;
A prize that passeth to and fro;
A thing for one, a thing for moe;
And he that proves shall find it so.
And this is Love, as I well know.   30

X

Love's god is a boy.
    None but cowherds regard him;
His dart is a toy;
    Great opinion hath marred him.

The fear of the wag   5
Hath made him so brag;
Chide him, he'll fly thee
And not come nigh thee.
Little boy, pretty knave, shoot not at random.
For if you hit me, slave, I'll tell your grand-dam.   10

Fond Love is a child,
    And his compass is narrow.
Young fools are beguiled
    With the fame of his arrow.
He dareth not strike,   15
If his stroke do mislike.
Cupid, do you hear me?
Come not too near me.
Little boy, pretty knave, hence, I beseech you,
For if you hit me, slave, in faith I'll breech you.   20

Th' ape loves to meddle
When he finds a man idle.
Else is he a-flirting
Where his mark is a-courting.
When women grow true,   25
Come teach me to sue.
Then I'll come to thee,
Pray thee and woo thee.
Little boy, pretty knave, make me not stagger,
For if you hit me, slave, I'll call thee beggar.   30

XI

OVER these brooks, trusting to ease mine eyes,
    Mine eyes even great in labour with their tears,
I laid my face, my face wherein there lies
    Clusters of clouds which no sun ever clears.
In wat'ry glass my wat'ry eyes I see;   5
Sorrow's ill-eased, where sorrows painted be.

My thoughts imprisoned in my secret woes
    With flamy breaths do issue oft in sound;
The sound to this strange air no sooner goes
    But that it doth with echo's force rebound,   10
And make me hear the plaints I would refrain;
Thus outward helps my inward griefs maintain.

Now in this sand I would discharge my mind,
  And cast from me part of my burd'nous cares;
But in the sand my tales foretold I find,   15
  And see therein how well the writer fares.
Since streams, air, sand, mine eyes and ears conspire,
What hope to quench, where each thing blows the fire?
                              [*Sir Philip Sidney*]

XII

WHITHER runneth my sweet heart?
  Stay awhile, prithee.
    Not too fast!
    Too much haste
    Maketh waste.   5
But if thou wilt needs be gone
  Take my love with thee.
Thy mind doth bind me to no vile condition;
So doth thy truth prevent me of suspicion.

Go thy ways then where thou please,   10
  So I [am] by thee.
    Day and night
    I delight
    In thy sight.
Never grief on me did seize   15
  When thou wast nigh me.
My strength, at length that scorned thy fair commandings,
Hath not forgot the price of rash withstandings.

Now my thoughts are free from strife,
  Sweet, let me kiss thee.   20
    Now can I
    Willingly
    Wish to die,
For I do but loathe my life
  When I do miss thee.   25
Come prove my love, my heart is not disguised.
Love shown and known ought not to be despised.

XIII

ONCE did I love where now I have no liking.
  Like can I not, for she was never loving.

Once did I prove, but then put by my striking.
  Strike nill I now, though she were ever proving.
To prove or strike it now rests at my will;   5
To make me love or like 'tis past her skill.

Rest in unrest was once my chiefest pleasure;
  Please will I now myself in her disquiet.
Bad for the best I chose at wanton leisure,
  Ease bids me now to brook a better diet.   10
Rich in content I rest to see her plaining
Whose best at best is bad, not worth the gaining.

XIV

FAIR women like fair jewels are,
  Whose worth lies in opinion.
To praise them all must be his care
  That goes about to win one.
And when he hath her once obtained   5
  To her face he must her flatter;
But not to others, lest he move
  Their eyes to level at her.

The way to purchase truth in love,
  If such way there be any,   10
Must be to give her leave to rove
  And hinder one by many.
Believe thou must that she is true
  When poisoned tongues do sting her;
Rich jewels bear the self-same hue   15
  Put upon any finger.

The perfectest of mind and shape
  Must look for defamations.
Live how they will, they cannot 'scape;
  Their persons are temptations.   20
Then let the world condemn my choice,
  As laughing at my folly;
If she be kind the self-same voice
  Is spread of the most holy.

XV

DAINTY darling, kind and free,
Fairest maid I ever see,
Dear, vouchsafe to look on me;
Listen when I sing to thee
    What I will do   5
    With a dildo,
     Sing do with a dildo.

Sweet, now go not yet, I pray;
Let no doubt thy mind dismay.
Here with me thou shalt but stay   10
Only till I can display
    What I will do
    With a dildo,
     Sing do with a dildo.

Quickly, prithee, now be still!   15
Nay, you shall not have your will.
Trow you men will maidens kill?
Tarry but to learn the skill
    What I will do
    With a dildo,   20
     Sing do with a dildo.

Pretty, witty, sit me by,
Fear no cast of any eye;
We will play so privily
None shall see but you and I   25
    What I will do
    With a dildo,
     Sing do with a dildo.

XVI

MY love is neither young nor old,
Not fiery hot, nor frozen cold;
But fresh and fair as springing briar,
Blooming the fruit of love's desire.
Not snowy white nor rosy red,   5
But fair enough for shepherd's bed;
And such a love was never seen
On hill or dale or country green.

XVII

LOVE is a bable;
    No man is able
To say 'tis this or 'tis that.
    'Tis full of passions
    Of sundry fashions;   5
'Tis like I cannot tell what.

    Love's fair i' the cradle,
    Foul in the sable;
'Tis either too cold or too hot;
    An arrant liar,   10
    Fed by desire;
It is; and yet it is not.

    Love is a fellow
    Clad oft in yellow;
The canker-worm of the mind;   15
    A privy mischief;
    And such a sly thief
No man knows which way to find.

    Love is a wonder
    That's here and yonder,   20
As common to one as to moe;
    A monstrous cheater;
    Every man's debtor.
Hang him, and so let him go!

XVIII

ARISE, my thoughts, and mount you with the sun;
    Call all the winds to make you speedy wings;
And to my fairest Maya see you run,
    And weep your last while wantonly she sings.
Then if you cannot move her heart to pity,   5
Let 'O alas! Ay me!' be all your ditty.

Arise, my thoughts, no more, if you return
    Denied of grace, which only you desire;
But let the sun your wings to ashes burn,
    And melt your passions in his quenchless fire.   10
But if you move fair Maya's heart to pity
Let smiles and love and kisses be your ditty.

Arise, my thoughts, beyond the highest star,
  And gently rest you in fair Maya's eye,
For that is fairer than the brightest are.   15
  But if she frown to see you climb so high,
Couch in her lap, and, with a moving ditty
Of smiles and love and kisses, beg for pity.

XIX

  DID ever man thus love as I?
    I think I was made
    For no other trade,
My mind doth it so hard apply,
And all fond courses else doth fly.   5

  Undoing were a petty care,
    Loosing my best hopes
    In their largest scopes.
Two loving when I do compare,
Methinks I could as trifles spare.   10

  All my sad thoughts, though wide begun,
    In her still do meet,
    Who makes thinking sweet;
And then to me again they run
To tell me all that they have done.   15

  Thus do I spend my days and hours
    In a pleasant round
    Where true joys are found;
And there alone my soul devours
All Love's dear food with longing powers.   20

  A heaven on earth is love well met;
    There is more content
    Than can well be spent
When in two fruitful hearts 'tis set,
Which will not be in either's debt.   25

XX

  To sigh and to be sad,
    To weep, and wish to die,
  Is it not to be mad,
    If not hypocrisy?

Men of this sort   5
Are women's sort.
Beauty's alluring looks rob wise men of their reason,
That they speak nought at all, or speak all out of season.

Have all men eyes to see,
And have none wit to know   10
Blossoms commend no tree,
Where never fruit did grow?
Desire doth blind
A lover's mind.
He sees and doth allow that vice in his beloved   15
From which no woman can be free or be removed.

Let every thought of love
Mixed with a world of fears,
At last themselves remove;
O, let consuming tears,   20
Life blood distilled,
No more be spilled,
Since all that 'scape the fall of womanish rejecting
Must yet be subject to the pride of their neglecting.

XXI

COME, sorrow; come, sweet scale,
By the which we ascend to the heavenly place,
Where Virtue sitteth smiling
To see how some look pale
With fear to behold thy ill-favoured face,   5
Vain shows their sense beguiling.
For mirth hath no assurance
Nor warranty of durance.

Hence, pleasures; fly, sweet bait,
On the which they may justly be said to be fools   10
That surfeit by much tasting;
Like thieves you lie in wait,
Most subtly how to prepare silly souls
For sorrows everlasting.
Wise griefs have joyful turnings,   15
Nice pleasures end in mournings.

Vltimvm Vale, with a triplicity of Musicke, Whereof The first part is for the Lute, the Voyce, and the Viole Degambo, The 2. part is for the Lute, the Viole, and foure partes to sing, The third part is for two Trebles, to sing either to the Lute, or the Viole or to both, if any please.   1605

I

Do not, O do not prize thy beauty at too high a rate.
Love to be loved whilst thou art lovely, lest thou love too late.
    Frowns print wrinkles in thy brows,
      At which spiteful age doth smile,
    Women in their froward vows   5
      Glorying to beguile.

Wert thou the only world's-admired, thou canst love but one;
And many have before been loved, thou art not loved alone.
    Couldst thou speak with heavenly grace,
      Sappho might with thee compare.   10
    Blush the roses in thy face,
      Rosamund was as fair.

Pride is the canker that consumeth beauty in her prime.
They that delight in long debating feel the curse of Time.
    All things with the time do change   15
      That will not the time obey.
    Some e'en to themselves seem strange
      Through their own delay.

II

BEAUTY sat bathing by a spring
    Where fairest shades did hide her.
The winds blew calm, the birds did sing,
    The cool streams ran beside her.
My wanton thoughts enticed my eye   5
    To see what was forbidden;
But better memory cried fie.
    So vain delights were chidden.

Into a slumber then I fell.
    But fond imagination   10
Seemed to see, but could not tell
    Her feature or her fashion.

But even as babes in dreams do smile,
   And sometime fall a-weeping,
So I awaked as wise the while   15
   As when I fell a-sleeping.

[Anthony Munday]

III

GO to bed, sweet Muse, take thy rest.
Let not thy soul be so opprest.
     Though she deny thee
     She doth but try thee,
     Whether thy mind   5
     Will ever prove unkind.
O Love is but a bitter-sweet jest.

Muse not upon her smiling looks.
Think that they are but baited hooks.
     Love is a fancy,   10
     Love is a franzy.
     Let not a toy
     Then breed thee such annoy,
But leave to look upon such fond books.

Learn to forget such idle toys,   15
Fitter for youths and youthful boys.
     Let not one sweet smile
     Thy true love beguile.
     Let not a frown
     For ever cast thee down.   20
Then sleep and go to bed in these joys.

IV

SHALL I look to ease my grief?
   No, my sight is lost with eyeing.
Shall I speak and beg relief?
   No, my voice is hoarse with crying.
   What remains but only dying?   5

Love and I of late did part,
   But the boy my peace envying,
Like a Parthian drew his dart
   Backward, and did wound me flying.
   What remains but only dying?   10

She whom then I looked on,
  My remembrance beautifying,
Stays with me though I am gone,
  Gone and at her mercy lying.
  What remains but only dying?   15

Shall I try her thoughts and write?
  No, I have no means of trying.
If I should, yet at first sight
  She would answer with denying.
  What remains but only dying?   20

Thus my vital breath doth waste,
  And my blood with sorrow drying,
Sighs and tears make life to last
  For a while their place supplying.
  What remains but only dying?   25

V

WHAT if I sped where I least expected? What shall I say? Shall I lie?
What if I missed where I most affected? What shall I do? Shall I die?
    No, no, I'll have at all.
    'Tis as my game doth fall.
If I keep my meaning close   5
I may hit, how e'er it goes;
      For Time and I
      Do mean to try
What hope doth lie in youth. Fa la.
      The minds that doubt   10
      Are in and out,
And women flout at truth. Fa la.

She whom above the skies I renowned, she whom I loved, she,
Can she leave all in Lethe drowned? Can she be coy to me?
      Her passions are but cold;   15
She stands and doth behold;
She retains her looks estranged,
As if heaven and earth were changed.
      I speak, she hears,
      I touch, she fears;   20
Herein appears her wit. Fa la.
      I catch, she flies,
      I hold, she cries,
And still denies, and yet! Fa la.

May not a wanton look like a woman? Tell me the reason why.   25
And if a blind man chance of a bird's nest, must he be prattling? Fie!
     What mortal strength can keep
     That's got as in a sleep?
     The felony is his
     That brags of a stolen kiss.   30
        For when we met,
        Both in a net
    That Vulcan set were hid. Fa la.
        And so, God wot,
        We did it not,   35
   Or else forgot we did! Fa la.

VI

    SWEET, if you like and love me still,
    And yield me love for my good-will,
    And do not from your promise start,
    When your fair hand gave me your heart;
      If dear to you I be   5
      As you are dear to me,
    Then yours I am and will be ever;
    No time nor place my love shall sever;
    But faithful still I will persever,
      Like constant marble stone,   10
      Loving but you alone.

    But if you favour moe than one,
    Who loves thee still and none but thee,
    If others do the harvest gain
    That's due to me for all my pain,   15
      Yet that you love to range
      And oft to chop and change;
    Then get you some new-fangled mate;
    My doting love shall turn to hate,
    Esteeming you, though too too late,   20
      Not worth a pebble stone,
      Loving not me alone.
                [*Francis Davison*]

VII

CEASE, troubled thoughts, to sigh, or sigh yourselves to death;
Or kindle not my grief, or cool it with your breath.

Let not that spirit which made me live
Seek thus untimely to deprive
    Me of my life;   5
    Unequal strife!
That breath, which gave me being,
Should hasten me to dying.

Cease, melting tears, to stream; stop your uncessant course,
Which to my sorrow's child are like a fruitful nurse,   10
    From whence Death living comfort draws,
    And I myself appear the cause
        Of all my woe.
        But 'tis not so.
For she whose beauty won me   15
By falsehood hath undone me.

VIII

    CYNTHIA, queen of seas and lands,
    That fortune everywhere commands,
    Sent forth Fortune to the sea
    To try her fortune every way.
    There did I Fortune meet   5
    Which makes me now to sing:
    There is no fishing to the sea,
    Nor service to a king.

    All the nymphs of Thetis' train
    Did Cynthia's Fortune entertain.   10
    Many a jewel, many a gem
    Was to her Fortune brought by them.
    Her Fortune sped so well,
    Which makes me now to sing:
    There is no fishing to the sea,   15
    Nor service to a king.

    Fortune, that it might be seen
    That she did serve a royal queen,
    A frank and royal hand did bear
    And cast her favours everywhere.   20
    Such toys fell to my lot,
    Which makes me now to sing:
    There is no fishing to the sea,
    Nor service to a king.

                  [*Sir John Davies*]

IX

BLAME not my cheeks, though pale with love they be;
   The kindly heat into my heart is flown,
To cherish it that is dismayed by thee,
   Who art so cruel and unsteadfast grown.
For Nature, called for by distressed hearts,   5
Neglects and quite forsakes the outward parts.

But they whose cheeks with careless blood are stained,
   Nurse not one spark of love within their hearts;
And when they woo they speak with passion feigned,
   For their fat love lies in their outward parts;   10
But in their breast, where Love his court should hold,
Poor Cupid sits and blows his nails for cold.

                                [*Thomas Campian*]

X

THERE is a garden in her face
   Where roses and white lilies grow;
A heavenly paradise is that place,
   Wherein these pleasant fruits do flow.
There cherries grow which none can buy,   5
Till 'Cherry-ripe' themselves do cry.

These cherries fairly do enclose
   Of orient pearl a double row,
Which when her lovely laughter shows,
   They look like rose-buds filled with snow;   10
Yet them no peer nor prince may buy,
Till 'Cherry-ripe' themselves do cry.

Her eyes like angels watch them still;
   Her brows like bended bows do stand,
Threatening with piercing shafts to kill   15
   All that presume with eye or hand
Those sacred cherries to come nigh,
Till 'Cherry-ripe' themselves do cry.

                                [*Thomas Campian*]

XI

SWEET love, mine only treasure,
   For service long unfeigned

Wherein I nought have gained,
Vouchsafe this little pleasure:
   To tell me in what part   5
   My lady keeps my heart.

If in her hair so slender
   Like golden nets untwined,
   Which fire and art have fined,
Her thrall my heart I render   10
   For ever to abide
   With locks so dainty tied.

If in her eyes she bind it,
   Wherein that fire was framed
   By which it is inflamed,   15
I dare not look to find it.
   I only wish it sight
   To see that pleasant light.

But if her breast have deigned
   With kindness to receive it,   20
   I am content to leave it
Though death thereby were gained.
   Then, lady, take your own
   That lives for you alone.

XII

THINK'ST thou, Kate, to put me down
With a No or with a frown?
Since Love holds my heart in bands,
I must do as Love commands.

Love commands the hands to dare   5
When the tongue of speech is spare,
Chiefest lesson in Love's school;
Put it in adventure, fool.

Fools are they that fainting flinch
For a squeak, a scratch, a pinch.   10
Women's words have double sense,
Stand away, a simple fence.

If thy mistress swear she'll cry,
Fear her not; she'll swear and lie.
Such sweet oaths no sorrow bring   15
Till the prick of conscience sting.

XIII

WHEN will the fountain of my tears be dry?
   When will my sighs be spent?
When will Desire agree to let me die?
   When will thy heart relent?
It is not for my life I plead,   5
Since death the way to rest doth lead.
      But stay for thy consent
      Lest thou be discontent.

For if myself without thy leave I kill,
   My ghost will never rest,   10
So hath it sworn to work thine only will,
   And holds it ever best.
For since it only lives by thee,
Good reason thou the ruler be.
      Then give me leave to die,   15
      And show thy power thereby.

XIV

FLY from the world, O fly, thou poor distrest,
   Where thy diseased sense infects thy soul,
And where thy thoughts do multiply unrest,
   Troubling with wishes what they straight control.
O world, O world, betrayer of the mind!   5
O thoughts, O thoughts, that guide us, being blind!

Come therefore, Care, conduct me to my end,
   And steer this shipwrack carcase to the grave.
My sighs a strong and steadfast wind will lend,
   Tears wet the sails, Repentance from rocks save.   10
Hail Death! hail Death! the land I do descry!
Strike sail! go, soul! rest follows them that die.

XV

HAPPY he
Who, to sweet home retired,
Shuns glory so admired,
   And to himself lives free.

Whilst he who strives with pride to climb the skies   5
Falls down with foul disgrace before he rise.

        Let who will
      The active life commend,
      And all his travels bend
        Earth with his fame to fill.   10
Such fame so forced at last dies with his death,
Which life maintained by others' idle breath.

        My delights,
      To dearest home confined,
      Shall there make good my mind,   15
        Not awed with Fortune's spites.
High trees heaven blasts, winds shake, and honours fell,
When lowly plants long time in safety dwell.

        All I can
      My worldly strife shall be   20
      They one day say of me:
        He died a good old man.
On his sad soul a heavy burden lies
Who, known to all, unknown to himself dies.

XVI

      DISDAIN that so doth fill me
      Hath surely sworn to kill me,
        And I must die.
      Desire that still doth burn me
      To life again will turn me,   5
        And live must I.
      O kill me then, Disdain,
      That I may live again.

      Thy looks are life unto me,
      And yet thy looks undo me.   10
        O death and life!
      Thy smiles some rest do show me,
      Thy frowns with war o'erthrow me,
        O peace and strife!
      Nor life nor death is either;   15
      Then give me both or neither.

Life only cannot ease me,
    Death only cannot please me,
        Change is delight.
    I live that death may kill me;   20
    I die that life may fill me
        Both day and night.
    If once despair decay,
    Desire will wear away.

XVII

Now let her change and spare not.
Since she proves strange I care not.
Feigned love so bewitched my delight,
That still I doted on her sight.
But she is gone, new desires embracing,   5
    And my deserts disgracing.

When did I err in blindness,
Or vex her with unkindness?
If my heart did attend her alone,
Why is she thus untimely gone?   10
True love abides to the day of dying.
    False love is ever flying.

Thou false, farewell for ever.
Once false proves faithful never.
He that now so triumphs in thy love   15
Shall soon my present fortunes prove.
    Were he as fair as Adonis,
    Faith is not had where none is.
                                        [*Thomas Campian*]

XVIII

Since first disdain began to rise
    And cry revenge for spiteful wrong,
What erst I praised I now despise,
    And think my love was too too long.
I tread in dirt that scornful pride   5
Which in thy looks I have descried.
Thy beauty is a painted skin
For fools to see their faces in.

Thine eyes that some as stars esteem,
   From whence themselves, they say, take light,   10
Like to the foolish fire I deem
   That leads men to their death by night.
Thy words and oaths as light as wind,
And yet far lighter is thy mind;
Thy friendship is a broken reed   15
That fails thy friends in greatest need.

XIX

A T her fair hands how have I grace entreated
   With prayers oft repeated.
     Yet still my love is thwarted.
Heart, let her go, for she'll not be converted.
     Say, shall she go?   5
     O no, no, no, no, no!
She is most fair though she be marble-hearted.

How often have my sighs declared my anguish
   Wherein I daily languish;
     Yet doth she still procure it.   10
Heart, let her go, for I cannot endure it.
     Say, shall she go?
     O no, no, no, no, no!
She gave the wound and she alone must cure it.

The trickling tears that down my cheeks have flowed   15
   My love hath often showed.
     Yet still unkind I prove her.
Heart, let her go, for naught I do can move her.
     Say, shall she go?
     O no, no, no, no, no!   20
Though me she hate, I cannot choose but love her.

But shall I still a true affection bear her,
   Which prayers, sighs, tears do show her?
     And shall she still disdain me?
Heart, let her go, if they no grace can gain me.   25
     Say, shall she go?
     O no, no, no, no, no!
She made me hers, and hers she will retain me.

But if the love that hath and still doth burn me
    No love at length return me,   30
    Out of my thoughts I'll set her.
Heart, let her go; O heart, I pray thee let her!
    Say, shall she go?
    O no, no, no, no, no!
Fixed in the heart how can the heart forget her?   35

But if I weep and sigh and often wail me,
    Till tears, sighs, prayers fail me,
    Shall yet my love persever?
Heart, let her go; if she will right thee never.
    Say, shall she go?   40
    O no, no, no, no, no!
Tears, sighs, prayers fail, but true love lasteth ever.
                   [*Walter Davison*]

XX

OFT have I mused the cause to find
    Why Love in ladies' eyes should dwell.
I thought because himself was blind,
    He looked that they should guide him well.
And sure his hope but seldom fails,   5
For Love by ladies' eyes prevails.

But time at last hath taught me wit,
    Although I bought my wit full dear;
For by her eyes my heart is hit,
    Deep is the wound though none appear.   10
Their glancing beams as darts he throws,
And sure he hath no shafts but those.

I mused to see those eyes so bright,
    And little thought they had been fire.
I gazed upon them with delight,   15
    But that delight hath bred desire.
What better place can Love require
Than that where grow both shafts and fire.

XXI

NOW have I learned with much ado at last
    By true disdain to kill desire.
This was the mark at which I shot, so fast
    Unto this height I did aspire.

Proud Love, now do thy worst and spare not;   5
For thee and all thy shafts I care not.

What hast thou left wherewith to move my mind?
    What life to quicken dead desire?
I count thy words and oaths as light as wind,
    I feel no heat in all thy fire.   10
Go change thy bow and get a stronger;
Go break thy shafts and buy thee longer.

In vain thou bait'st thy hook with beauty's blaze;
    In vain thy wanton eyes allure.
These are but toys for them that love to gaze.   15
    I know what harm thy looks procure.
Some strange conceit must be devised,
Or thou and all thy skill despised.

ༀ

A Mvsicall Dreame. Or The Fovrth Booke Of Ayres, the First part is for the Lute, two Voyces, and the Viole de Gambo; The Second part is for the Lute, the Viole and foure Voices to Sing: The Third part is for one Voyce alone, or to the Lute, the Basse Viole, or to both if you please, Whereof, two are Italian Ayres. 1609

I

THOUGH your strangeness frets my heart,
    Yet must I not complain;
You persuade me 'tis but art
    Which secret love must feign.
If another you affect,   5
'Tis but a toy to avoid suspect.
    Is this fair excusing?
    O no, all is abusing.

When your wished sight I desire,
    Suspicion you pretend;   10
Causeless you yourself retire,
    Whilst I in vain attend.
Thus a lover, as you say,
Still made more eager by delay.
    Is this fair excusing?   15
    O no, all is abusing.

When another holds your hand,
    You'll swear I hold your heart.
Whilst my rival close doth stand,
    And I sit far apart,   20
I am nearer yet than they,
Hid in your bosom, as you say.
      Is this fair excusing?
      O no, all is abusing.

Would a rival then I were,   25
    Some else your secret friend,
So much lesser should I fear,
    And not so much attend.
They enjoy you every one,
Yet must I seem your friend alone.   30
      Is this fair excusing?
      O no, all is abusing.

                           [*Thomas Campian*]

II

      SWEET Kate
        Of late
Ran away and left me plaining.
        Abide!
        I cried,   5
Or I die with thy disdaining.
      Te he he! Quoth she,
      Gladly would I see
Any man to die with loving;
      Never any yet   10
      Died of such a fit;
Neither have I fear of proving.

        Unkind!
        I find
Thy delight is in tormenting.   15
        Abide!
        I cried,
Or I die with thy consenting.
      Te he he! Quoth she,
      Make no fool of me!   20

Men I know have oaths at pleasure;
　　But their hopes attained,
　　They bewray they feigned
And their oaths are kept at leisure.

　　　Her words   25
　　Like swords
Cut my sorry heart in sunder.
　　　Her flouts
　　With doubts
Kept my heart affections under.   30
　　Te he he! Quoth she,
　　What a fool is he,
Stands in awe of once denying!
　　Cause I had enough
　　To become more rough;   35
So I did. O happy trying!

III

ONCE did I serve a cruel heart
　　With faith unfeigned. I still importune
Her piercing looks that wrought my smart.
　　She laughs and smiles at my misfortune;
And says: perhaps you may at last   5
By true desert Love's favour taste.

IV

　　WILL said to his mammy
　　That he would go woo;
Fain would he wed, but he wot not who.
　　Soft awhile, my lammy,
　　Stay and yet abide!   5
He, like a fool as he was, replied:
In faith, 'chill have a wife, a wife, a wife.
　　O what a life do I lead
　　For a wife in my bed
　　I may not tell you.   10
O there to have a wife, a wife, a wife,
　　O 'tis a smart to my heart,
　　'Tis a rack to my back,
　　And to my belly.

Scarcely was he wedded   15
 Full a fortnight's space,
But that he was in a heavy case.
 Largely was he headed,
  And his cheeks looked thin,
And to repent he did thus begin: 20
A fig for such a wife, a wife, a wife!
 O what a life do I lead
 With a wife in my bed
 I may not tell you.
There to have a wife, a wife, a wife,   25
 O 'tis a smart to my heart,
 'Tis a rack to my back,
 And to my belly.

All you that are bachelors,
 Be learned by crying Will,   30
When you are well to remain so still.
 Better for to tarry,
  And alone to lie,
Than like a fool with a fool to cry:
A fig for such a wife, a wife, a wife!   35
 O what a life do I lead
 With a wife in my bed
 I may not tell you.
There to have a wife, a wife, a wife,
 O 'tis a smart to my heart,   40
 'Tis a rack to my back,
 And to my belly.

V

HARK! wot ye what? nay faith, and shall I tell?
I am afraid to die a maid, and then lead apes in hell.
O it makes me sigh and sob with inward grief;
But if I can but get a man, he'll yield me some relief.

O it is strange how Nature works with me;   5
My body is spent, and I lament mine own great folly.
O it makes me sigh, and pour forth floods of tears.
Alas, poor elf, none but thyself would live having such cares.

O now I see that Fortune frowns on me.
By this good light I have been ripe.   10
O it makes me sigh, and sure it will me kill.
When I should sleep I lie and weep, feeding on sorrows still.

I must confess as maids have virtue store,
Live honest still against our wills, more fools we are therefore.
O it makes me sigh, yet hope doth still me good,   15
For if I can but get a man, with him I'll spend my blood.

VI

MY complaining is but feigning,
   All my love is but in jest. Fa la.
And my courting is but sporting
   In most showing meaning least. Fa la.

Outward sadness inward gladness   5
   Representeth in my mind. Fa la.
In most feigning most obtaining
   Such good faith in love I find. Fa la.

Towards ladies this my trade is—
   Two minds in one breast I wear. Fa la.   10
And my measure at my pleasure
   Ice and flame my face doth bear. Fa la.

VII

ON a time in summer season
   Jockie late with Jenny walking,
   Like a lout made love with talking,
When he should be doing. Reason
   Still, he cries, when he should dally: 5
   Jenny, sweet, sweet, shall I, shall I?

Jenny, as most women use it
   Who say Nay when they would have it,
   With a bold face seemed to crave it,
With a faint look did refuse it.   10
   Jockie lost his time to dally,
   Still he cries: Sweet, shall I, shall I?

She who knew that backward dealing
  Was a foe to forward longing,
    To avoid her own heart's wronging,   15
With a sigh love's suit revealing,
    Said: Jockie sweet, when you would dally,
    Do you cry: Sweet, shall I, shall I?

  Jockie knew by her replying
    That a 'no' is 'aye' in wooing,   20
    That an asking without doing
  Is the way to love's denying.
    Now he knows when he would dally
    How to spare: 'Sweet, shall I, shall I?'

VIII

FAREWELL, fond youth, if thou hadst not been blind
Out of my eye thou might'st have read my mind.
But now I plainly see how thou wouldst fain leave me,
    Sure I was accurst
    Not to go at first.   5
  Sure I was accurst. O fie no!
  Sweet, stay, and I will tell thee why no.

Once more farewell, since first I heard thee speak
And had but sung farewell, my heart would break.
But now since I do find thy love is like the wind,   10
    What a fool was I
    To be like to die!
  What a fool was I! I was not.
  Yet say I was a fool, I pass not.

Woe's me, alas! why did I let him go?   15
These be the fruits of idle saying 'no'.
Now that he can disprove me how shall he ever love me?
    Nay, but is he gone?
    Then I am undone!
  Nay but is he gone? O hold him!   20
  Fie! forty things are yet untold him.

IX

How should I show my love unto my Love,
    But hide it from all eyes save my Love's eyes?
The way by pen or tongue I dare not prove,
    Their drifts are oft discovered by the wise.
      Looks are more safe, yet over them are spies.   5
Then what's the way to cosen jealousy
Which martyrs love by marking narrowly?

By all these ways may thy affections walk
    Without suspicion of the jealous guard.
Thy whispering tongue to her closed ear shall talk,   10
    And be importunate till it be heard.
      Papers shall pass, looks shall not be debarred.
To look for love's young infants in her eyes,
Be frank and bold as she is kind and wise.

O who can be so frank as she is kind,   15
    Whose kindness merits more than monarchies?
Boldness with her mild grace Grace cannot find,
    Only her wit over that doth tyrannize.
      Then let her worth and thy love sympathize,
Sith her worth to thy love cannot be known,   20
Nor thy love to her worthiness be shown.

X

O he is gone, and I am here.
    Ay me, why are we thus divided?
My sight in his eyes did appear;
    My soul by his soul's thought was guided.
Then come again, my all, my life, my being,   5
Soul's zeal, heart's joy, ear's guest, eye's only seeing.

Come, sable Care, seize on my heart,
    Take up the rooms that joys once filled.
Nature's sweet bliss is slain by Art;
    Absence' black frost life's spring hath killed.   10
Then come again, my love, my dear, my treasure,
My bliss, my fate, my end, my hope's full measure.

XI

AND is it night? Are they thine eyes that shine?
  Are we alone? and here and here alone
May I come near? May I but touch thy shrine?
  Is jealousy asleep and is he gone?
O gods, no more silence my lips with thine,   5
Lips, kisses, joys, hap, blessings most divine.

O come, my dear, our griefs are turned to night,
  And night to joys; Night blinds pale Envy's eyes;
Silence and sleep prepare us our delight.
  O cease we then our woes, our griefs, our cries.   10
O vanish words! words do but passions move.
O dearest life, joys sweet, O sweetest love!

XII

SHE hath an eye, ah me! ah me!
She hath an eye, an eye to see;
        Ah me! that she hath too
Which makes me sigh as lovers do.
              Heigh ho! heigh ho!   5
  Heigh ho! Ah me, that an eye
Should make her live and me to die.
    Wise men's eyes are in their mind,
    But lovers' eyes are ever blind.

  She hath a lip, ah, ah, alas!   10
Two lips which do themselves surpass.
        Alas, two lips for kisses
Of earthly love the heavenly blisses!
              Heigh ho! heigh ho!
  Alas, O woe, that a heaven   15
Should make us odds that make all even.
    Ladies' kisses are a charm
    That kill us ere they do us harm.

  She hath a heart, ah me! ah me!
A heart she hath which none can see.   20
        Ah me, that I have none!
Which makes me sigh, yea sighing groan,
              Heigh ho! heigh ho!

Heigh ho! ay me! that I part
And live, yet leave with her my heart.   25
Heartless men may live by love.
This she doth know, and this I prove.

XIII

I KNOW not what, yet that I feel is much,
    It came I know not when; it was not ever;
It hurts I know not how, yet is it such
    As I am pleased, though it be cured never.
It is a wound that wasteth still in woe,   5
And yet I would not that it were not so.

Pleased with a thought that endeth with a sigh,
    Sometimes I smile when tears stand in my eyes;
Yet then and there such sweet contentment lieth
    Both when and where my sweet sour torment lies.   10
O out alas, I cannot long endure it,
And yet alas, I care not when I cure it.

But wellaway, methinks I am not she
    That wonted was these fits as foul to scorn;
One and the same even so I seem to be,   15
    As lost I live, yet of myself forlorn.
What may this be that thus my mind doth move?
Alas, I fear, God shield it be not love.

XIV

GRIEF of my best love's absenting,
    Now, O now, wilt thou assail me?
    I had rather life should fail me
Than endure thy slow tormenting.
Life our griefs and us do sever   5
        Once for ever;
Absence, grief, have no relenting.

Well be it foul absence spites me,
    So far off it cannot send her
    As my heart should not attend her.   10
O how this thought's thought delights me!
Absence, do thy worst and spare not;
        Know, I care not;
When thou wrong'st me, my thoughts right me!

O but such thoughts prove illusions,   15
   Shadows of a substance banished,
   Dreams of pleasure too soon vanished;
Reasons maimed of their conclusions.
Then since thoughts and all deceive me,
    O life leave me!   20
End of life ends love's confusions.

XV

IF in this flesh where thou indrenched dost lie,
   Poor soul, thou canst rear up thy limed wings,
Carry my thoughts up to the sacred sky,
   And wash them in those heavenly hallowed springs,
Where joy and Requiem the holy angels sings,   5
Whilst all heaven's vault with blessed echoes rings.

Awaked with this harmony divine,
   O how my soul mounts up her throned head,
And 'gins again with native glory shine.
   Wash with repentance then thy days misled.   10
Then joys with Requiem mayest thou with angels sing,
Whilst all heaven's vault with blessed echoes ring.

XVI

O THREAD of life, when thou art spent how are my sorrows eased!
O veil of flesh, when thou art rent how shall my soul be pleased!
    O earth, why tremblest thou at death,
    That did receive both heat and breath
    By bargain of a second birth,   5
    That done, again to be cold earth?
    Come, Death, dear midwife to my life,
    See Sin and Virtue hold at strife.
       Make haste away,
       Lest thy delay   10
       Be my decay.
     World of inanity,
     School-house of vanity,
      Minion of hell,
      Farewell, farewell!   15

O coward life, whose fear doth tie me in distasting senses,
Infused part, mount up on high, life gets on life offences.
             O fly, immortal, fly away,
             Be not immured in finite clay,
             Where true love doth with self-love fight,   20
             Begetting thoughts that do affright.
             Courage, faint heart! sound trumpet, Death!
             I'll find it wind with all my breath.
                      O case of glass,
                      Confusion's mass,   25
                      A flowering grass!
                 Temple of treachery,
                 Soul yoke to misery,
                      Storehouse of hell,
                      Farewell, farewell!   30

                         XVII

         WHEN I sit reading all alone that secret book,
                 Wherein I sigh to look
                 How many spots there be,
                 I wish I could not see,
                 Or from myself might flee.   5

Mine eyes for refuge then with zeal befix the skies,
                 My tears do cloud those eyes,
                 My sighs do blow them dry;
                 And yet I live to die,
                 Myself I cannot fly.   10

Heavens I implore, that knows my fault, what shall I do?
                 To hell I dare not go.
                 The world first made me rue,
                 Myself my griefs renew;
                 To whom then shall I sue?   15

Alas, my soul doth faint to draw this doubtful breath;
                 Is there no hope in death?
                 O yes, Death ends my woes,
                 Death me from me will loose.
                 Myself am all my foes.   20

XVIII

FAIN would I speak, but fear to give offence
  Makes me retire, and in amazement stand,
Still breathing forth my woes in fruitless silence,
  Whilst my poor heart is slain by her fair hands.
Fair hands indeed, the guiders of the dart   5
That from her eyes were levelled at my heart.

Those eyes, two pointed diamonds, did engrave
  Within my heart the true and lively form
Of that sweet saint whose pity most I crave,
  Whose absence makes me comfortless to mourn,   10
And sighing say: Sweet, would she knew my love!
My plaints perhaps her mind may somewhat move.

But if she knew, what if she did reject?
  Yet better 'twere by her sweet doom to die,
That she might know my dear love's true effect,   15
  Than thus to live in unknown misery.
Yet after death it may be she would say:
His too much love did work his life's decay.

XIX

  IN Sherwood lived stout Robin Hood,
    An archer great, none greater.
  His bow and shafts were sure and good,
    Yet Cupid's were much better.
Robin could shoot at many a hart and miss,   5
Cupid at first could hit a heart of his.
      Hey! jolly Robin,
      Ho! jolly Robin,
      Hey! jolly Robin Hood;
      Love finds out me   10
      As well as thee
    To follow me to the green wood.

  A noble thief was Robin Hood,
    Wise was he could deceive him;
  Yet Marian in his bravest mood   15
    Could of his heart bereave him.

No greater thief lies hidden under skies
Than Beauty closely lodged in women's eyes.
      Hey! jolly Robin,
      Ho! jolly Robin,   20
      Hey! jolly Robin Hood;
        Love finds out me
        As well as thee
      To follow me to the green wood.

An outlaw was this Robin Hood,   25
  His life free and unruly;
Yet to fair Marian bound he stood,
  And love's debt paid her duly.
Whom curb of strictest law could not hold in,
Love with obeyedness and a wink could win.   30
      Hey! jolly Robin,
      Ho! jolly Robin,
      Hey! jolly Robin Hood;
        Love finds out me
        As well as thee   35
      To follow me to the green wood.

Now wend we home, stout Robin Hood,
  Leave we the woods behind us.
Love-passions must not be withstood,
  Love everywhere will find us.   40
I lived in field and town, and so did he;
I got me to the woods; Love followed me!
      Hey! jolly Robin,
      Ho! jolly Robin,
      Hey! jolly Robin Hood;   45
        Love finds out me
        As well as thee
      To follow me to the green wood.

XX

ITE, caldi sospiri, al freddo core,
  Rompete il ghiaccio che pietà contende;
  E se prego mortale al ciel s'intende,
Morte, O mercè, sia fine al mio dolore.
                   [Francesco Petrarch]

XXI

S'AMOR non è, che dunque è quel ch'io sento?
  Ma s'egli è amor, per Dio, che cosa è quale?
  Se buona, ond'è l'affetto aspro e mortale?
Se ria, ond'è si dolce ogni tormento?

S'à mia voglia ardo, ond'è 'l pianto e 'l lamento?   5
  Se mal mio grado, il lamentar che vale?
  O viva morte, O dilettoso male,
Come puoi tanto in me, s'io no 'l consento?
                                        [*Francesco Petrarch*]

ಞಞಞಞಞಞಞಞ

*The Muses Gardin for Delights, Or the fift Booke of Ayres, onely for the
Lute, the Base-vyoll, and the Voyce. 1610*

I

LOVE is a pretty frenzy,
A melancholy fire,
Begot by looks, maintained with hopes,
And heightened by desire.

Love is a pretty tyrant   5
By our affections armed.
Take them away, none lives this day
The coward boy hath harmed.

Love is a pretty idol,
Opinion did devise him.   10
His votaries is sloth and lies,
The robes that do disguise him.

Love is a pretty painter,
And counterfeiteth passion.
His shadowed lies makes fancies rise   15
To set belief in fashion.

Love is a pretty pedlar,
Whose pack is fraught with sorrows,
With doubts, with fears, with sighs, with tears,
Some joys—but those he borrows.   20

Love is a pretty nothing,
Yet what a coil it keeps,
With thousand eyes of jealousies,
Yet no one ever sleeps.

II

SOFT, Cupid, soft! there is no haste,
For all unkindness gone and past;
Since thou wilt needs forsake me so,
Let us part friends before thou go.

Still shalt thou have my heart to use   5
When I cannot otherwise choose.
My life thou may'st command sans doubt,
Command, I say, and go without.

And if that I do ever prove
False and unkind to gentle Love,   10
I'll not desire to live a day,
Nor any longer than I may.

I'll daily bless the little god,
But not without a smarting rod.
Wilt thou still unkindly leave me?   15
Now, I pray God, all ill go with thee!

III

As I the silly fish deceive,
    So Fortune plays with me;
Whose baits my heart of joys bereave,
    And angles taketh me.
I still do fish, yet am I caught,   5
And, taken, am their taking taught.

The river wherein I do swim
    Of streams of hope is made,
Where joys as flowers dress the brim,
    And frowns do make my shade,   10
Whence smiles, as sunshine, gives me heat,
And shadow-frowns from showers beat.

Thus taken like an envious one
   Who glads for others' care,
Since he himself must feel such moan,   15
   Delights all so should fare,
And strive to make them know like smart,
So make I this to bear a part.

IV

THE fountains smoke and yet no flames they show;
   Stars shine all night, though undiscerned by day;
And trees do spring, yet are not seen to grow;
   And shadows move, although they seem to stay.
In Winter's woe is buried Summer's bliss,   5
And Love loves most where Love most secret is.

The stillest streams descries the greatest deep;
   The clearest sky is subject to a shower.
Conceit's most sweet whenas it seems to sleep;
   And fairest days do in the morning lower.   10
The silent groves sweet nymphs they cannot miss,
For Love loves most where Love most secret is.

The rarest jewels hidden virtue yield;
   The sweet of traffic is a secret gain;
The year once old doth show a barren field,   15
   And plants seem dead, and yet they spring again.
Cupid is blind. The reason why is this:
Love loveth most where Love most secret is.

V

WALKING by a river side
   In prime of summer's morning,
Viewing Phoebus in his pride
   The silver streams adorning,
And passing on, myself alone,   5
Methought I heard a woeful groan.

Still I stood as one amazed
   To hear this woeful crying;
Round about me then I gazed
   In every meadow prying,   10
Yet could I not this wight surprise
Although the voice did pierce the skies.

Venus, thou hast killed my heart
    And quite my soul confounded;
Thy son Cupid with his dart   15
    My vital parts hath wounded.
Shoot home, proud boy, and do thy worst,
That she may die that lives accursed.

Draw thy shaft unto the head,
    And strongly it deliver;   20
Draw, that thou may'st strike her dead
    That lives a hopeless lover.
Let come, blind boy, to satisfy
His mind that most desires to die.

VI

I CANNOT choose but give a smile
To see how Love doth all beguile,
Except it be my frozen heart
That yields not to his fiery dart.

Belike I was Achilles like,   5
    Drenched in that fatal hardening flood.
My flesh it fears no push of pike,
    The spear against me doth no good.

Only my heel may Cupid hit
And yet I care not much for it,   10
Because the hurt I cannot feel
Unless my heart were in my heel.

The Answer

I cannot choose but needs must smile
To see how Love doth thee beguile,
Which did of purpose freeze thy heart
To thaw it to thy greater smart.

Suppose thou wert Achilles like,   5
    Drenched in that fatal hardening flood,
That might avail 'gainst push of pike,
    But 'gainst his dart 'twill do no good.

For if thy heel he do but hit,
His venomed shaft will rankle it,   10
The force whereof the heart must feel
Conveyed by arteries from thy heel.

VII

Joy in thy hope, the earnest of thy love,
  For so thou may'st enjoy thy heart's desire.
True hopes things absent do as present prove,
  And keep alive love's still renewing fire.

But of thy hope let silence be the tongue,   5
  And secrecy the heart of loving fire;
For hopes revealed may thy hopes prolong
  Or cut them off in prime-time of desire.

Sweet are those hopes that do themselves enjoy
  As vowed to themselves to live and die;   10
Sweetest those joys and freest from annoy
  That waken not the eye of jealousy.

L'envoi

Thy love is not thy love, if not thine own,
And so it is not if it once be known.

VIII

How many new years have grown old
  Since first your servant old was new.
How many long hours have I told
  Since first my love was vowed to you.
And yet, alas, she doth not know   5
Whether her servant love or no.

How many walls as white as snow,
  And windows clear as any glass,
Have I conjured to tell you so,
  Which faithfully performed was.   10
And yet you'll swear you do not know
Whether your servant love or no.

How often hath my pale lean face
  With true characters of my love
Petitioned to you for grace,   15
  Whom neither sighs nor tears can move.
O cruel, yet do you not know
Whether your servant love or no?

And wanting oft a better token,
  I have been fain to send my heart,   20
Which now your cold disdain hath broken,
  Nor can you heal't by any art.
O look upon't and you shall know
Whether your servant love or no.

IX

THERE was a shepherd that did live
  And held his thoughts as high
As were the mounts whereon his flocks
  Did hourly feed him by.
He from his youth, his tender youth,   5
  Which was unapt to keep
Or hopes or fears or loves or cares
  Or thoughts of but his sheep,

Did with his dog as shepherds do;
  For shepherds wanting wit   10
Devise some sports, though foolish sports,
  Yet sports for shepherds fit.
The boy that yet was but a boy
  And so desires were hid,
Did grow a man, and men must love,   15
  And love this shepherd did.

He loved much, none can too much
  Love one so high divine,
As but herself none but herself
  So fair, so fresh, so fine.   20
He vowed by his shepherd's weed,
  An oath which shepherds keep,
That he would follow Phillida
  Before a flock of sheep.

X

THE sea hath many thousand sands,
   The sun hath motes as many,
The sky is full of stars, and love
   As full of woes as any.
Believe me, that do know the elf,   5
And make no trial by thyself.

It is in truth a pretty toy
   For babes to play withal.
But, O, the honeys of our youth
   Are oft our age's gall.   10
Self proof in time will make thee know
He was a prophet told thee so.

A prophet that Cassandra-like
   Tells truth without belief,
For headstrong youth will run his race   15
   Although his goal be grief.
Love's martyr, when his heat is past,
Proves Care's confessor at the last.

XI

ONCE did my thoughts both ebb and flow,
   As passion did them move.
Once did I hope, straight fear again,
   And then I was in love.

Once did I waking spend the night,   5
   And told how many minutes move,
Once did I wishing waste the day,
   And then I was in love.

Once by my carving true love's knot
   The weeping trees did prove   10
That wounds and tears were both our lots,
   And then I was in love.

Once did I breathe another's breath,
   And in my mistress move;
Once was I not mine own at all,   15
   And then I was in love.

Once wore I bracelets made of hair,
  And collars did approve,
Once were my clothes made out of wax,
  And then I was in love.   20

Once did I sonnet to my saint,
  My soul in number moved,
Once did I tell a thousand lies,
  And then in truth I loved.

Once in my ear did dangling hang   25
  A little turtle-dove,
Once, in a word, I was a fool,
  And then I was in love.

XII

I AM so far from pitying thee
That wear'st a branch of willow tree,
That I do envy thee and all
That once was high, and got a fall.
    O willow, willow, willow tree   5
    I would thou didst belong to me.

Thy wearing willow doth imply
That thou art happier far than I,
For once thou wert where thou wouldst be,
Though now thou wear'st the willow tree.   10
    O willow, willow, sweet willow,
    Let me once lie upon her pillow.

I do defy both bough and root
And all the friends of hell to boot,
One hour of paradised joy   15
Makes purgatory seem a toy.
    O willow, willow, do thy worst;
    Thou canst not make me more accursed.

I have spent all my golden time
In writing many a loving rhyme.   20
I have consumed all my youth
In vowing of my faith and truth.
    O willow, willow, willow tree,
    Yet can I not believed be.

And now, alas, it is too late,   25
Grey hairs, the messenger of fate,
Bids me to set my heart at rest,
For beauty loveth young men best.
 O willow, willow, I must die,
  Thy servant's happier far than I.   30

XIII

As I lay lately in a dream,
 Methought I saw a wondrous thing.
A woman fair transformed was
 Into a fiddle without a string.
A metamorphosis so rare   5
As almost made me wake for fear.
   O this is rare,
   Yea, very rare,
   A wondrous thing,
   So fair a fiddle diddle diddle   10
   Should want a string.

Till honest neighbours dwelling nigh
Said they would all her wants supply;
And said that they have strings in store
For such a fiddle and forty more.   15
For love they bear unto the sport,
They'll make her fit for the consort.
   O this is rare,
   Yea, very rare,
   A wondrous thing,   20
   So fair a fiddle diddle diddle
   Should want a string.

They'll send her first to some that can
Put in the peg, and peg her then.
If that her bridge be broken, so   25
As that the fiddle cannot go,
They'll soon devise some other way
To make her sound the roundelay.
   O this is rare,
   Yea, very rare,   30
   A wondrous thing,
   So fair a fiddle diddle diddle
   Should want a string.

When they have set her in the key,
You must not strain her strings so high   35
For fear the fiddle chance to crack;
Nor let the strings be too too slack.
The diapason is her sound,
The lowest note is most profound.
      O this is rare,   40
      Yea, very rare,
      A wondrous thing,
      So fair a fiddle diddle diddle
      Should want a string.

But note a discord in music,   45
To sound some note without the prick,
And then for keeping of your mood,
Sing three to one, that's passing good.
Of all the notes in gamut scale
The long is that which must not fail.   50
      O this is rare,
      Yea, very rare,
      A wondrous thing,
      So fair a fiddle diddle diddle
      Should want a string.   55

XIV

THERE was a wily lad met with a bonny lass;
Much pretty sport they had, but I wot not what it was.
He wooed her for a kiss, she plainly said him 'no'.
   I pray, quoth he, nay, nay, quoth she,
     I pray you let me go.   5

Full many lovely terms did pass in merry glee;
He coll'd her in his arms, and danced her on his knee.
In fain he would have paid such debts as he did owe.
   I pray, quoth he, nay, nay, quoth she,
     I pray you let me go.   10

Sweet, be you not so nice to gratify a friend;
If kissing be a vice my suit is at an end.
No, no, it is the rule to learn a man to woo.
   I pray, quoth he, nay, nay, quoth she,
     I pray you let me go.   15

For Cupid hath an eye to play a lover's part;
And swift his arrows fly to level at the heart.
Thy beauty was my bane, that brought me to his bow.
  I pray, quoth he, nay, nay, quoth she,
    I pray you let me go.   20

Good sir, alas, you feed your fancy with conceit.
Sweet, sweet, how should we speed if lovers could not speak?
I speak but what I wish, the spirit wills me so.
  I pray, quoth he, nay, nay, quoth she,
    I pray you let me go.   25

With that she swore an oath, and loth she was to break it,
And so, to please them both, he gave, and she did take it.
There was no labour lost true amity to show.
  Adieu, quoth he, nay, stay, quoth she,
    Let's kiss before you go.   30

                          XV

          M Y father fain would have me take
            A man that hath a beard;
          My mother she cries out: Alack!
            And makes me much afraid.
          Forsooth! I am not old enough.   5
          Now surely this is goodly stuff.
          Faith, let my mother marry me,
          Or let some young man bury me.

          For I have lived these fourteen years,
            My mother knows it well.   10
          What need she then to cast such fears,
            Can anybody tell?
          As though young women do not know
          That custom will not let them woo.
          I would be glad if I might choose,   15
          But I were mad if I refuse.

          My mother bids me go to school,
            And learn to do some good.
          'Twere well if she would let the fool
            Come home and suck a dug.   20

As if my father knew not yet
That maidens are for young men fit.
Give me my mind and let me wed,
Or you shall quickly find me dead.

How soon my mother hath forgot   25
   That ever she was young,
And how that she denied not,
   But sung another song.
I must not speak what I do think,
When I am dry, I may not drink,   30
Though her desire be now grown old,
She must have fire when she is cold.

You see the mother loves the son,
   The father loves the maid.
What would she have me be a nun?   35
   I will not be delayed.
I will not live thus idle still;
My mother shall not have her will.
My father speaketh like a man.
I will be married, do what she can.   40

XVI

M Y love hath her true love betrayed.
   Why, 'tis a fault that is too common.
Yet shall it not be ever said
   My faith depended on a woman.
If she did [aught] to prove untrue   5
I shall do worse to change for new.

She hath some virtues, follow them,
   Take not example by her lightness.
Be not amongst the vulgar men.
   Though she be clouded, keep thy brightness.   10
Perhaps herself in time may prove,
What 'tis to wrong a constant love.

The many vows given by my fair
   Were none of hers; the wind did owe them.
Then were they breath, now are they air,   15
   Whence first they came, there she bestows them.
Then marvel not, though women alter,
When all things turn to their first matter.

R r

XVII

ALL my sense thy sweetness gained;
Thy fair hair my heart enchained;
My poor reason thy words moved,
So that thee like heaven I loved.
    Fa la la leri deri dan.   5
While to my mind the outside stood
For messenger of inward good.

Now thy sweetness sour is deemed,
Thy hair not worth a hair esteemed;
While to my mind the outside stood,   10
Finding that but words they proved.
    Fa la la leri deri dan.
For no fair sign can credit win
If that the substance fail within.

No more in thy sweetness glory,   15
For thy knitting hair be sorry.
Use thy words but to bewail thee
That no more thy beams avail thee.
    Fa la la leri deri dan.
Lay not thy colours more to view   20
Without the picture be found true.

Woe to me, alas, she weepeth.
Fool, in me what folly creepeth!
Was I to blasphemy enraged
Where my soul I have engaged?   25
    Fa la la leri deri dan.
And wretched I must yield to this,
The fault I blame her chasteness is.

Sweetness, sweetly pardon folly,
Tie my hair your captive solly.   30
Words, O words of heavenly knowledge,
Know my words their faults acknowledge.
    Fa la la leri deri dan.
And all my life I will confess,
The less I love, I live the less.   35

                    [Sir Philip Sidney]

XVIII

To thee, deaf asp, with dying voice
 Sadly I sing this heavy charm,
That if thy heart do ere rejoice
 And set at nought my grievous harm,
  This verse, writ with a dead man's arm, 5
May haunt thy senseless eyes and ears,
Turn joys to cares and hopes to fears.

By thy Creator's piety,
 By her that brought thee to this light;
By thy dear nurse's love to thee, 10
 By love itself, heavens, day and night,
  By all that can thy sense delight,
When I am cold and wrapt in lead
Remember oft thy servant dead.

So shall my shadow thee attend 15
 Like calmest breath of western wind.
If not with groans it shall ascend
 Like raven, owl, bear, or hellish fiend,
  Rattling the chains which do it bind;
And where thou art by silent night 20
It shall thy guilty soul affright.

Yet seamen tossed with stormy wind,
 Void of all hope, resolved to die,
From powerful heavens oft mercy find;
 And so may I find grace with thee. 25
 No, no, thou canst not pity me.
Asps cannot hear, nor live can I;
Thou hearest not, unheard I die.

XIX

Behold her locks, like wires of beaten gold;
 Her eyes like stars that twinkle in the sky;
Her heavenly face not framed of earthly mould;
 Her voice that sounds the heavens' melody;
The miracles of Time, the worldës story, 5
Fortune's queen, Love's treasure, Nature's glory.

No flattering hopes she likes, blind Fortune's bait;
    Nor shadows of delight, fond Fancy's glass;
Nor charms that do enchant, false Art's deceit;
    Nor fading joys which Time makes swiftly pass,   10
But chaste desires which beateth all these down.
A goddess' look is worth a monarch's crown.

XX

ALTHOUGH the wings of my desires be clipped,
    And my love thoughts from mounting lowly bounded;
Though sly suspect my joys with frost hath nipped,
    So as my hopes with fears are still surrounded;
Yet will I live to love, although through love I die,   5
And cumbers still do grow, and comforts from me fly.
No jealous thoughts shall force me to retire,
But I will hope to enjoy my heart's desire.

Which likes to love and yet the same conceal,
    Remembrance chiefly working my relieving.   10
Though times of joy be short yet will I steal
    Such times, to keep my heart from further grieving.
Force may remove my looks, but not expel my joy,
Though Cupid's shaft give cureless wounds, 'tis no annoy.
Whilst life endures I'll love, though seem to shun   15
That port of rest from whence my comforts come.

XXI

MIGHT I redeem mine errors with mine eyes,
    And shed but for each several sin a tear,
The sum to such a great account should rise
    That I should never make mine audit clear;
The total is too big to pay the score,   5
I am so rich in sin, in tears so poor.

O wretched wealth that doth procure such want;
    Unhappy soul to be so rich in sin,
The store whereof doth make all graces scant,
    And stops thy tears ere they do scarce begin.   10
What once a famous poet sung before
I find too true, my plenty makes me poor.

O might I prove in this a prodigal
   And bate my means by less'ning of my stock,
I should in grace grow great, in sins but small,   15
   If I could every day from forth the shock
But pull one ear. O ten times happy want
When tears increase and sins do grow more scant!

O that my God with such sweet strokes would strike,
   And by his grace so bank-route my estate   20
That growing poor in sin, I, Lazar-like,
   Might daily beg for mercy at his gate,
And crave, though not admittance to his feast,
Some crumbs of grace to feed my soul at least.

GEORGE MASON AND
JOHN EARSDEN

*The Ayres That Were Svng And Played, at Brougham Castle in Westmerland,
in the Kings Entertainment: Giuen by the Right Honourable the Earle of
Cvmberland, and his Right Noble Sonne the Lord Clifford. 1618*

I

A dialogue sung the first night, the King being at supper

[*1st voice.*]   TUNE thy cheerful voice to mine.
         Music helps digesting.
[*2nd voice.*] Music is as good as wine,
         And as fit for feasting.
[*1st voice.*]   Melody now is needful here,   5
         It will help to mend our cheer.
[*Both.*]   Join then, one joy expressing,
[*1st voice.*]   Here is a guest for whose content,
         All excess were sparing.
[*2nd voice.*] All to him present   10
         Hourly new delights preparing.
Chorus.   Joy at thy board, health in thy dish,
         Mirth in thy cup; and in thy bed
         Soft sleep and pleasing rest we wish.

[*1st voice.*]	Earth, and air, and sea consent	15
	In thy entertaining.	
[*2nd voice.*]	All is old which they present,	
	Yet all choice containing.	
[*1st voice.*]	Music alone the soul can feast,	
	It being new and well expressed.	20
[*Both.*]	Join then sweet chords enchaining.	
[*1st voice.*]	Could we to our wished ends aspire,	
	Joy should crown thy dishes.	
[*2nd voice.*]	Proud is our desire,	
	If thou dost accept our wishes:	25
Chorus.	Joy at thy board, health in thy dish,	
	Mirth in thy cup; and in thy bed	
	Soft sleep and pleasing rest we wish.	

II

Another dialogue, to be sung at the same time

[*1st voice.*]	Now is the time, now is the hour	
	When joy first blessed this happy bower.	
[*2nd voice.*]	Here is a sight that sweetens every sour.	
[*1st voice.*]	So shines the moon by night;	
[*2nd voice.*]	So looks the sun by day;	5
[*1st voice.*]	Heavenly is his light,	
[*2nd voice.*]	And never shall decay.	
Chorus.	There is no voice enough can sing	
	The praise of our great king.	

[*1st voice.*]	Fall showers of sweet delight.	10
[*2nd voice.*]	Spring flowers of pleasant mirth.	
[*1st voice.*]	What heaven hath beams that shine more bright?	
[*2nd voice.*]	Here heaven is now, stars shine on earth.	
[*1st voice.*]	In one all honour groweth.	
[*2nd voice.*]	From one all comfort floweth.	15
[*Both.*]	Duty saith that to this one	
	All it hath it oweth.	
Chorus.	Let then that one of all be praised	
	That hath our fortunes raised.	

III
The King's Goodnight

WELCOME, welcome, king of guests
  With thy princely train,
With joyful triumphs and with feasts
  Be welcomed home again.
      Frolic mirth,   5
      The soul of earth
Shall watch for thy delight.
      Knees shall bend
      From friend to friend
While full cups do thee right.   10
And so, great king, goodnight.

Welcome, welcome, as the sun
  When the night is past.
With us the day is now begun,
  May it for ever last!   15
      Such a morn
      Did ne'er adorn
The roses of the east,
      As the north
      Hath now brought forth,   20
The northern morn is best.
And so, best king, good rest!

IV

COME, follow me, my wand'ring mates,
Sons and daughters of the Fates,
Friends of night that oft have done
Homage to the horned moon;
Fairly march and shun not light   5
With such stars as these made bright.
Yet bend you low your curled tops,
Touch the hallowed earth, and then
Rise again with antic hops
      Unused of men.   10
Here no danger is nor fear,
For true honour harbours here,
      Whom grace attends;
Grace can make our foes our friends.

V

A Ballad

DIDO was the Carthage queen
　And loved the Trojan knight,
That, wand'ring, many coasts had seen,
　And many a dreadful sight.
As they on hunting rode, a shower   5
Drave them in a loving hour
　Down to a darksome cave;
Where Æneas with his charms
Locked Queen Dido in his arms,
　And had what he could have.   10

Dido Hymen's rites forgot;
　Her love was winged with haste;
Her honour she considered not,
　But in her breast him placed;
And when her love was new begun,   15
Jove sent down his winged son
　To fright Æneas' sleep,
Bade him by the break of day
From Queen Dido steal away,
　Which made her wail and weep.   20

Dido wept. But what of this?
　The gods would have it so.
Æneas nothing did amiss,
　For he was forced to go.
Learn, lordings, then no faith to keep   25
With your loves, but let them weep;
　'Tis folly to be true.
Let this story serve your turn,
And let twenty Didos burn
　So you get daily new!   30

VI

The Dance

ROBIN is a lovely lad,
No lass a smoother ever had.
Tommy hath a look as bright
As is the rosy morning light.

Tib is dark and brown of hue,   5
But like her colour firm and true.
Jinny hath a lip to kiss
Wherein a spring of nectar is.
Simkin well his mirth can place
And words to win a woman's grace.   10
Sib is all in all to me,
There is no queen of love but she.

All.   Let us in a lover's round
Circle all this hallowed ground.
Softly, softly trip and go,   15
The light foot fairies jet it so.
Forward then and back again,
Here and there and everywhere,
Winding to and winding fro,
Skipping high and louting low.   20

Chorus.   And like lovers hand in hand
March around and make a stand.

VII

A Song

THE shadows dark'ning our intents
  Must fade, and Truth now take her place,
  Who in our right Egyptian race
    A chain of prophecies presents,
    With which the starry sky consents,   5
    And all the under-elements.

Thou that art all divine, give ear
  And grace our humble songs,
  That speak what to thy state belongs
Unmasked now and clear;   10
Which we in several strains divide,
And heaven-born Truth our notes shall guide,
  One by one while we relate
  That which shall tie both Time and Fate.

VIII

TRUTH sprung from heaven shall shine
    With her beams divine
    On all thy land,
And there for ever steadfast stand.

    Lovely peace,   5
    Spring of increase,
Shall like a precious gem
Adorn thy royal diadem.
    Love that binds
    Loyal minds   10
Shall make all hearts agree
To magnify thy state and thee.
    Honour that proceeds
    Out of noble deeds
Shall wait on thee alone,   15
And cast a sacred light about thy throne.

Long shall thy three crowns remain
Blessed in thy long-lived reign.
Thy age shall like fresh youth appear,
And perpetual roses bear.   20
Many on earth thy days shall be;
But endless thy posterity,
And matchless thy posterity.

Chorus.   Truth, peace, love, honour and long life attend
Thee and all those that from thy loins descend!   25
With us the angels in this chorus meet.
So, humbly prostrate at thy sacred feet,
Our nightly sports and prophecies we end.

IX

The Farewell Song

O STAY! Sweet is the least delay
  When parting forceth mourning.
O joy, too soon thy flowers decay,
  From rose to briar returning.
    Bright beams that now shine here,   5
    When you are parted,
All will be dim, all will be dumb,
    And every breast sad-hearted.

Yet more, for true love may presume
  If it exceed not measure.   10
O grief! that blest hours soon consume,
  But joyless pass at leisure.

Since we this light must lose,
Our love expressing,
Far may it shine, long may it live 15
To all a public blessing.

X

The Lords' welcome, sung before the King's goodnight

WELCOME is the word
The best love can afford.
For what can better be?
Welcome, lords, the time draws near
When each one shall embrace his dear, 5
And view the face he longs to see.
Absence makes the hour more sweet
When divided lovers meet.

Welcome once again,
Though too much were in vain, 10
Yet how can love exceed?
Princely guests, we wish there were
Jove's nectar and ambrosia here,
That you might like immortals feed,
Changing shapes, like full-fed Jove, 15
In the sweet pursuit of love.

JOHN MAYNARD

*The XII. Wonders Of The World. Set and composed for the Violl de Gambo,
the Lute, and the Voyce to Sing the Verse, all three ioyntly, and none seuerall:
also Lessons for the Lute and Base Violl to play alone: with some Lessons to
play Lyra-wayes alone, or if you will, to fill vp the parts, with another Violl
set Lute-way.* 1611

I

The Courtier

LONG have I lived in Court, yet learned not all this while
To sell poor suitors smoke, nor where I hate to smile;
Superiors to adore, inferiors to despise;
To fly from such as fall, to follow such as rise;
To cloak a poor desire under a rich array;   5
Nor to aspire by vice, though 'twere the quicker way.

                                           [Sir John Davies]

II

The Divine

MY calling is divine, and I from God am sent;
I will no chop-church be; nor pay my patron rent;
Nor yield to sacrilege. But, like the kind true mother,
Rather will lose all the child than part it with another.
Much wealth I will not seek, nor worldly masters serve,   5
So to grow rich and fat while my poor flock doth starve.

                                           [Sir John Davies]

III

The Soldier

MY occupation is the noble trade of kings,
The trial that decides the highest right of things.
Though Mars my master be, I do not Venus love;
Nor honour Bacchus oft; nor often swear by Jove.
Of speaking of myself I all occasion shun;   5
And rather love to do, than boast what I have done.

                                           [Sir John Davies]

IV

The Lawyer

THE Law my calling is; my robe, my tongue, my pen,
Wealth and opinion gain and make me judge of men.
The known dishonest cause I never did defend;
Nor spun out suits in length, but wished and sought an end.
Nor counsel did bewray, nor of both parties take;   5
Nor ever took I fee for which I never spake.

[*Sir John Davies*]

V

The Physician

I STUDY to uphold the slippery state of man,
Who dies when we have done the best and all we can;
From practice and from books I draw my learned skill,
Not from the known receipt or 'pothecaries' bill.
The earth my faults doth hide, the world my cures doth see; 5
What Youth and Time effects is oft ascribed to me.

[*Sir John Davies*]

VI

The Merchant

MY trade doth everything to every land supply,
Discovers unknown coasts, strange countries doth ally.
I never did forestall, I never did engross,
Nor custom did withdraw though I returned with loss.
I thrive by fair exchange, by selling and by buying,   5
And not by Jewish use, reprisal, fraud, or lying.

[*Sir John Davies*]

VII

The Country Gentleman

THOUGH strange outlandish spirits praise towns, and countries
    scorn,
The country is my home, I dwell where I was born.
There profit and command with pleasure I partake,
Yet do not hawks and dogs my sole companions make.
I rule, but not oppress; end quarrels, not maintain;   5
See towns, but dwell not there, to abridge my charge or train.

[*Sir John Davies*]

VIII

The Bachelor

HOW many things as yet are dear alike to me:
The field, the horse, the dog, love, arms, or liberty.
I have no wife as yet which I may call mine own,
I have no children yet that by my name are known.
Yet if I married were, I would not wish to thrive   5
If that I could not tame the veriest shrew alive.

[*Sir John Davies*]

IX

The Married Man

I ONLY am the man among all married men
That do not wish the priest to be unlinked again;
And though my shoe did wring I would not make my moan,
Nor think my neighbour's chance more happy than mine own.
Yet court I not my wife, but yield observance due,   5
Being neither fond, nor cross, nor jealous, nor untrue.

[*Sir John Davies*]

X

The Wife

THE first of all our sex came from the side of man,
I thither am returned from whence our sex began.
I do not visit oft, nor many when I do.
I tell my mind to few, and that in counsel too.
I seem not sick in health, nor sullen but in sorrow,   5
I care for somewhat else than what to wear to-morrow.

[*Sir John Davies*]

XI

The Widow

MY dying husband knew how much his death would grieve me,
And therefore left me wealth to comfort and relieve me.
Though I no more will have, I must not love disdain,
Penelope herself did suitors entertain;
And yet to draw on such as are of best esteem,   5
Nor younger than I am, nor richer will I seem.

[*Sir John Davies*]

XII

The Maid

I MARRIAGE would foreswear but that I hear men tell
That she that dies a maid must lead an ape in hell.
Therefore if fortune come I will not mock and play,
Nor drive the bargain on till it be driven away.
Titles and lands I like, yet rather fancy can   5
A man that wanteth gold, than gold that wants a man.

[*Sir John Davies*]

THOMAS MORLEY

The First Booke Of Ayres. Or Little Short Songs, To Sing And Play To The Lvte, With The Base Viole. 1600

I

A PAINTED tale by poet's skill devised,
   Where words well placed great store of love profess,
In Love's attire can never masque disguised,
   For looks and sighs true love can best express.
And he whose words his passions right can tell   5
Doth more in words than in true love excel.

II–III

THYRSIS and Milla, arm in arm together,
In merry May to the green garden walked,
Where all the way they wanton riddles talked.
The youthful boy, kissing her cheeks all rosy,
Beseeched her there to gather him a posy.   5

She straight her light green silken coats up-tucked,
And may for Mill and thyme for Thyrsis plucked,
Which when she brought he clasped her by the middle,
And kissed her sweet, but could not read her riddle.
Ah fool! With that the nymph set up a laughter,   10
And blushed and ran away, and he ran after.

IV

WITH my love my life was nestled
  In the sum of happiness;
From my love my life was wrested
  To a world of heaviness.
O let love my life remove   5
Sith I live not where I love.

Where the truth once was and is not
  Shadows are but vanities,
Showing want that help they cannot,
  Signs not slaves of miseries.   10
Painted meat no hunger feeds;
Dying life each death exceeds.

O true love, since thou hast left me
  Mortal life is tedious;
Death it is to live without thee,   15
  Death of all most odious.
Turn again and take me with thee,
Let me die, or live thou in me.

                              [*Robert Southwell*]

V

I SAW my lady weeping,
And Sorrow proud to be advanced so
In those fair eyes, where all perfection kept.
  Her face was full of woe,
But such a woe, believe me, as wins more hearts   5
Than mirth can do with her enticing parts.

VI

IT was a lover and his lass,
  With a hey, with a ho, and a hey nonino,
That o'er the green cornfields did pass
  In spring time, the only pretty ring time,
When birds do sing, hey ding a ding a ding;   5
Sweet lovers love the spring.

Between the acres of the rye,
  With a hey, with a ho, and a hey nonino,
These pretty country fools would lie,
  In spring time, the only pretty ring time,   10
When birds do sing, hey ding a ding a ding;
Sweet lovers love the spring.

This carol they began that hour,
  With a hey, with a ho, and a hey nonino,
How that a life was but a flower,   15
  In spring time, the only pretty ring time,
When birds do sing, hey ding a ding a ding;
Sweet lovers love the spring.

Then pretty lovers, take the time,
  With a hey, with a ho, and a hey nonino,   20
For love is crowned with the prime
  In spring time, the only pretty ring time,
When birds do sing, hey ding a ding a ding;
Sweet lovers love the spring.

VII

WHO is it that this dark night
  Under my window plaineth?
It is one that from thy sight
  Being, ah, exiled, disdaineth
Every other vulgar light.   5

Why, alas, and are you he?
  Be not those fond fancies changed?
Dear, when you find change in me,
  Though from me you be estranged,
Let my change to ruin be.   10

Well, in absence this will die;
  Leave to see, and leave to wonder.
Absence sure will help, if I
  Can learn how myself to sunder
From what in my heart doth lie.   15

But time will these thoughts remove;
  Time doth work what no man knoweth.
Time doth as the subject prove;
  With time still the affection groweth
In the faithful turtle dove.   20

What if you new beauties see?
　Will not they stir new affection?
I will think they pictures be,
　Image-like of saint's perfection,
Poorly counterfeiting thee.　　　　　　25

But the reason's purest light
　Bids you leave such minds to nourish;
Dear, do Reason no such spite;
　Never doth thy beauty flourish
More than in my reason's sight.　　　　30

But the wrongs love bears will make
　Love at length leave undertaking.
No, the more fools it doth shake
　In a ground of so firm making
Deeper still they drive the stake.　　　35

Peace! I think that some give ear,
　Come no more lest I get anger.
Bliss! I will my bliss forbear,
　Fearing, sweet, you to endanger;
But my soul shall harbour there.　　　40

Well, be gone, be gone, I say,
　Lest that Argus' eyes perceive you.
O unjustest Fortune's sway,
　Which can make me thus to leave [you],
And from louts to run away!　　　　　45

　　　　　　　　　　　[*Sir Philip Sidney*]

VIII

MISTRESS mine, well may you fare,
Kind be your thoughts and void of care.
Sweet Saint Venus be your speed,
That you may in love proceed.
　Coll me and clip and kiss me too,　　5
　So so so so so so true love should do.

This fair morning sunny bright,
That gives life to love's delight,
Every heart with heat enflames,
And our cold affection blames.　　　10
　Coll me and clip and kiss me too,
　So so so so so so true love should do.

In these woods are none but birds;
They can speak but silent words;
They are pretty harmless things;   15
They will shade us with their wings.
  Coll me and clip and kiss me too,
  So so so so so so true love should do.

Never strive nor make no noise;
'Tis for foolish girls and boys.   20
Every childish thing can say
Go to! How now? Pray, away!
  Coll me and clip and kiss me too,
  So so so so so so true love should do.

IX

CAN I forget what Reason's force imprinted in my heart?
Can I unthink these restless thoughts when first I felt Love's dart?
Shall tongue recall what Thoughts and Love by Reason once did
  speak?
No, no, all things save death wants force that faithful band to break.

For now I prove no life to love where Fancy breeds Content.   5
True love's reward with wise regard is never to repent;
It yields delight that feeds the sight whilst distance do them part.
Such food fed me when I did see in mine another heart.

Another heart I spied, combined within my breast so fast,
As to a stranger I seemed strange, but Love forced love at last.   10
Yet was I not as then I seemed, but rather wish to see
If in so full a harbour Love might constant lodged be.

So Cupid plays oft nowadays and makes the fool seem fair;
He dims the sight, breeding delight where we seem to despair.
So in our heart he makes them sport and laughs at them that love, 15
Who for their pain gets this again, their love no liking move.

X

  LOVE winged my hopes, and taught them how to fly
 Far from base earth, but not to mount too high.
   For true pleasure
   Lives in measure,
    Which if men forsake,   5
 Blinded they into folly run, and grief for pleasure take.

But my vain hopes, proud of their new-taught flight,
Enamoured sought to woo the Sun's fair light,
    Whose rich brightness
    Moved their lightness   10
  To aspire so high
That all scorched and consumed with fire, now drowned in
    woe they lie.

And none but Love their woeful hap doth rue,
For Love doth know that their desires were true.
    Though Fates frowned,   15
    And now, drowned,
  They in sorrow dwell,
It was the purest light of heaven, for whose fair love they fell.

XI

WHAT if my mistress now will needs unconstant be?
Wilt thou be then so false in love as well as she?
No, no, such falsehood flee, though women faithless be.

My mistress frowns, and swears that now I love her not;
The change she finds is that which my despair begot,   5
Despair, which is my love since she all faith forgot.

She blames my truth and causelessly accuseth me;
I must not let mine eyes report what they do see;
My thoughts restrained must be; and yet she will go free.

If she doth change she must not be in constancy;   10
For why she doth profess to take such liberty;
Herself she will untie, and yet fast bound am I.

If she at once do please to favour more than one,
I agreed in humble sort to make my moan;
I spake not to a stone where sense of love is none.   15

But now let love in time redress all these my wrongs;
And let my love receive the due to her belongs,
Else thus I'll frame my song or change my mistress' longs.

Which if I find, my heart some other where will dwell,
For, loving, not to be beloved it is a hell.   20
Since so my hap befell, I bid my love farewell.

XII

COME, Sorrow, come, sit down and mourn with me;
  Hang down thy head upon thy baleful breast,
That God and man and all the world may see
  Our heavy hearts do live in quiet rest.
Enfold thine arms and wring thy wretched hands   5
To show the state wherein poor Sorrow stands.

Cry not outright, for that were children's guise,
  But let thy tears fall trickling down thy face;
And weep so long until thy blubbered eyes
  May see (in sum) the depth of thy disgrace.   10
O shake thy head, but not a word but mum;
The heart once dead, the tongue is stroken dumb.

And let our fare be dishes of despite
  To break our hearts and not our fasts withal;
Then let us sup with sorrow sops at night   15
  And bitter sauce, all of a broken gall.
Thus let us live till heavens may rue to see
The doleful doom ordained for thee and me.

XIII

FAIR in a morn, O fairest morn, was ever morn so fair?
When as the sun, but not the same that shineth in the air,
But of the earth, no earthly sun, and yet no earthly creature,
There shone a face, was never face that carried such a feature.

And on a hill, O fairest hill, was never hill so blessed,   5
There stood a man, was never man for no man so distressed.
This man had hap, O happy man, no man so happed as he,
For none had hap to see the hap that he had happed to see.

And as he beheld, this man beheld, he saw so fair a face,
The which would daunt the fairest here and stain the bravest
    grace.   10
Pity, he cried, and Pity came, and pitied for his pain,
That dying would not let him die, but gave him life again.

For joy whereof he made such mirth that all the world did ring,
And Pan with all his nymphs came forth to hear the shepherds
    sing,
But such a song sung never was, nor ne'er will be again   15
Of Phillida, the shepherds' Queen, and Corydon, the swain.

                          [*Nicholas Breton*]

XIV

ABSENCE, hear thou my protestation
    Against thy strength,
    Distance and length.
Do what you dare for alteration.
    For hearts of truest metal   5
Absence doth join and Time doth settle.

Who loves a mistress of right quality
    His mind hath found
    Affection's ground
Beyond time, place, and all mortality.   10
    To hearts that cannot vary
Absence is present, time doth not tarry.

My senses want their outward motion,
    Which now within
    Reason doth win,   15
Redoubled by her secret notion;
    Like rich men that take pleasure
In hiding, more than handling, treasure.

By absence this good means I gain
    That I can catch her   20
    Where none can watch her
In some close corner of my brain.
    There I embrace and there kiss her,
    And so enjoy and so miss her.

                       [*attrib. to John Hoskins*]

XVII

WILL you buy a fine dog with a hole in his head?
    With a dildo, dildo, dildo.
Muffs, cuffs, rebatoes and fine sister's thread,
    With a dildo, dildo, dildo.

I stand not on points, pins, periwigs, combs, glasses,   5
Gloves, garters, girdles, busks, for the brisk lasses;
    But I have other dainty tricks,
    Sleek stones and potting sticks.
      With a dildo, diddle diddle dildo.
    And for a need my pretty pods,   10
    Amber, civet, and musk-cods.
      With a dildo, diddle diddle dildo.

XVIII

SLEEP, slumb'ring eyes, give rest unto my cares;
    My cares, the infants of my troubled brain;
My cares surprised, surprised with black despair,
    Doth the ascension of my hopes restrain.
Sleep then, my eyes, O sleep, and take your rest,   5
To banish sorrow from a free-born breast.

My free-born breast, born free to sorrow's smart;
    Brought in subjection by my wandering eye,
Whose trait'rous sight conceived that to my heart
    For which I wail, I sob, I sigh, I die.   10
Sleep then, my eyes, disturbed of quiet rest,
To banish sorrow from my captive breast.

My captive breast, stung by these glist'ring stars;
    These glist'ring stars, the beauty of the sky,
That bright black sky, which doth the sunbeams bar   15
    From her sweet comfort on my heart's sad eye.
Wake then, my eyes, true partners of unrest,
For sorrow still must harbour in my breast.

FRANCIS PILKINGTON

The First Booke Of Songs or Ayres of 4. parts: with Tableture for the Lute or Orpherian, with the Violl de Gamba. 1605

I

N o w peep, bo-peep, thrice happy blest, mine eyes,
  For I have found fair Phyllis where she lies
Upon her bed, with arms unspread, all fast asleep,
Unmasked her face, thrice happy grace. Farewell, my sheep,
    Look to yourselves, new charge I must approve;   5
    Phyllis doth sleep, and I must guard my love.

    Now peep, bo-peep, mine eyes, to see your bliss,
  Phyllis' closed eyes attracts you hers to kiss.
O may I now perform my vow, love's joy t' impart.
Assay the while how to beguile. Farewell, faint heart.   10
    Taken she is, new joys I must approve;
    Phyllis doth sleep, and I will kiss my love.

    Now peep, bo-peep, be not too bold, my hand,
  Wake not thy Phyllis, fear she do withstand.
She stirs, alas, alas, alas! I faint in sprite.   15
She opes her eye, unhappy I! Farewell, delight!
  Awaked she is, new woes I must approve;
    Phyllis awakes, and I must leave my love.

II

M y choice is made, and I desire no change;
  My wandering thoughts in limits now are bound.
The deserts wild wherein my wits did range
  Are now made easy walks and pleasant ground.
Let him that list soothe humours that be vain,   5
    Till vanity all mean exceeds;
Let passions still possess the idle brain,
    And care consume whom folly feeds.
I rest resolved no fancy's fits can me estrange;
My choice is made, and I desire no more to change.   10

Change they their choice to whose delicious sense
  The strangest objects are of most esteem.
Inconstant liking may find excellence
  In things which being not good yet best do seem.
Let gallant bloods still crown their sports with joy,   15
    Whom honour, wealth and pleasure fills,
Let sweet contentment never find annoy
    While Fortune frames things to their wills.
This stirs not me, I am the same I was before;
My choice is made, and I desire to change no more.   20

Be my choice blamed, or be I thought unwise
  To hold my choice by others not approved,
I say that to myself I fall or rise,
  By fear or force I cannot be removed.
Let friends in pity doubt of my success,   25
    Their pity gets no thanks at all;
Let foes be glad to see my hopes grow less,
    I scorn the worst that wish they shall.
Still stand I firm, my heart is set and shall remain,
My choice is made, and never will I change again.   30

III

  CAN she disdain, can I persist to love?
    Can she be cruel, I subjected still?
  Time will my truth, Compassion hers approve,
    Release the thralled, and conquer froward will.
  I love not lust, O therefore let her deign   5
  To equal my desires with like again.

  Am I not pleasing in her prouder eyes?
    O that she knew Love's power as well as I.
  Witty she is, but Love's more witty wise;
    She breathes on earth, he reigns in heaven on high.   10
  I love not lust, O therefore let her deign
  To equal my desires with like again.

  Love scorns the abject earth. His sacred fires
    Unites divided minds, dissevers none.
  Contempt springs out of fleshly base desires,   15
    Setting debate 'twixt love and union.
  I love not lust, O therefore let her deign
  To equal my desires with like again.

IV

ALAS, fair face, why doth that smoothed brow,
  Those speaking eyes, rosed lips and blushing beauty,
All in themselves confirm a scornful vow
  To spoil my hopes of love, my love of duty?
The time hath been when I was better graced,   5
I now the same, and yet that time is past.

Is it because that thou art only fair?
  O no, such graceful looks banish disdain.
How then? to feed my passions with despair?
  Feed on, sweet love, so I be loved again;   10
Well may thy public scorn and outward pride
Inward affections and best likings hide.

Breathe but a gentle air, and I shall live,
  Smile in a cloud, so shall my hopes renew,
One kind regard and second seeing give,   15
  One rising morn, and my black woes subdue.
If not, yet look upon the friendly sun
That by his beams my beams to thine may run.

V

WHITHER so fast? See how the kindly flowers
  Perfumes the air, and all to make thee stay.
The climbing woodbind, clipping all these bowers,
  Clips thee likewise for fear thou pass away.
  Fortune our friend, our foe will not gainsay.   5
Stay but awhile, Phoebe no tell-tale is;
She her Endymion, I'll my Phoebe kiss.

Fear not, the ground seeks but to kiss thy feet.
  Hark, hark, how Philomela sweetly sings;
Whilst water-wanton fishes, as they meet,   10
  Strike crotchet time amidst these crystal springs,
  And Zephyrus 'mongst the leaves sweet murmur rings.
Stay but awhile, Phoebe no tell-tale is;
She her Endymion, I'll my Phoebe kiss.

See how the heliotrope, herb of the sun,   15
  Though he himself long since be gone to bed,
Is not of force thine eyes' bright beams to shun,
  But with their warmth his goldy leaves unspread,
  And on my knee invites thee rest thy head.

Stay but awhile, Phoebe no tell-tale is;   20
She her Endymion, I'll my Phoebe kiss.

VI

REST, sweet nymphs, let golden sleep
    Charm your star-brighter eyes,
Whiles my lute the watch doth keep
    With pleasing sympathies.
    Lulla lullaby, lulla lullaby!   5
Sleep sweetly, sleep sweetly, let nothing affright ye;
    In calm contentments lie.

Dream, fair virgins, of delight
    And blest Elysian groves,
Whiles the wand'ring shades of night   10
    Resemble your true loves.
    Lulla lullaby, lulla lullaby!
Your kisses, your blisses, send them by your wishes,
    Although they be not nigh.

Thus, dear damsels, I do give   15
    Goodnight, and so am gone.
With your hearts' desires long live,
    Still joy and never moan.
    Lulla lullaby, lulla lullaby
Hath pleased you and eased you, and sweet slumber seized
    you.   20
    And now to bed I hie!

VII

AY me, she frowns! my mistress is offended.
O pardon, dear, my miss shall be amended.
My fault from love proceeded, it merits grace the rather,
If I no danger dreaded it was to win your favour.
Then clear those clouds, then smile on me, and let us be good
    friends,   5
Come walk, come talk, come kiss, come see how soon our quarrel ends.

Why lowers my love, and blots so sweet a beauty?
O be appeased with vows, with faith and duty.
Give over to be cruel, sith kindness seems you better,
You have but changed a jewel, and love is not your debtor.   10
Then welcome mirth and banish moan, show pity on your lover.
Come play, come sport. The thing that's gone no sorrow can recover.

Still are you angry, and is there no relenting?
O weigh my woes, be moved with my lamenting.
Alas, my heart is grieved, mine inward soul doth sorrow;   15
Unless I be relieved I die before to-morrow.
The coast is cleared, her count'nance cheered, I am again in grace.
Then farewell, fear, then come, my dear, let's dally and embrace.

VIII

Now let her change and spare not.
Since she proves false I care not!
Feigned love so bewitched my delight,
That still I doated on her sight.
But she is gone, new desires embracing,   5
    And my deserts disgracing.

When did I err in blindness
Or vex her with unkindness?
If my care did attend her alone,
Why is she thus untimely gone?   10
True love abides till the day of dying,
    False love is ever flying.

Then, false, farewell for ever!
Once false prove faithful never.
He that now so triumphs in thy love   15
Shall soon my present fortunes prove.
Were I as fair as divine Adonis,
    Love is not had where none is.

                         [*Thomas Campian*]

IX

Underneath a cypress shade the Queen of love sat mourning,
Casting down the rosy wreaths her heavenly brow adorning,
Quenching fiery sighs with tears, but yet her heart still burning.

For within the shady mourne the cause of her complaining,
Myrrha's son, the leafy bowers did haunt, her love disdaining,   5
Counting all her true desires in his fond thoughts but feigning.

Why is youth with beauty graced, unfeeling judge of kindness,
Spotting love with the foul report of cruelty and blindness,
Forcing to unkind complaints the Queen of all divineness?

Stint thy tears, fair sea-born Queen, and grief in vain lamented;   10
When desire hath burnt his heart that thee hath discontented,
Then too late the scorn of youth by age shall be repented.

X

For his unfortunate friend William Harwood

SOUND, woeful plaints, in hills and woods.
Fly, my cries, to the skies; melt, mine eyes, and heart, languish.
    Not for the want of friends or goods
Make I moan; though alone thus I groan by soul's anguish.
    Time friends, chance goods, might again recover.   5
    Black woes, sad griefs o'er my life do hover,
Since my loss is with despair, no blest star to me shine fair,
    All my mirth turn to mourning.
Heart, lament, for hope is gone; music leave, I'll learn to moan;
    Sorrow's the sad's adorning.   10

    Ay me, my days of bliss are done!
Sorrowing must I sing; nothing can relieve me.
    Eclipsed is my glorious sun.
And mischance doth advance horror's lance, still to grieve me.
    Poor heart, ill hap hath all joy bereft thee;   15
    Gone's the sole good which the Fates had left me.
Whose estate is like to mine? Fortune doth my weal repine,
    Envying my one pleasure.
Patience must me assure, other plaster cannot cure,
    Therefore in this my treasure.   20

XI

    YOU that pine in long desire,
        Help to cry:
Come, love, come, love, quench this burning fire,
    Lest through thy wound I die.

    Hope, that tires with vain delay,   5
        Ever cries:
Come, love, come, love, hours and years decay,
    In time love's treasure lies.

    All the day and all the night
        Still I call: 10
Come, love, come, love.—But my dear delight
    Yields no relief at all.

Her unkindness scorns my moan
　　That still shrikes:
Come, love, come, love, beauty pent alone　　　　15
　　Dies in her own dislikes.

XII

Look, mistress mine, within this hollow breast,
　　See here enclosed a tomb of tender skin.
Within fast locked is framed a phoenix' nest,
　　That, save yourself, there is no passage in.
Witness the wound that through your dart doth bleed.　　5
And craves your cure since you have done the deed.

Wherefore, most rare, and phoenix-rarely fine,
　　Behold once more the harms I do possess;
Regard the heart that through your fault doth pine,
　　Attending rest, yet findeth no redress.　　　　10
For end, wave wings and set your nest on fire,
Or pity me and grant my sweet desire.

XIII

To his loving friend M[r]. Holder, M. of Arts

Climb, O heart, climb to thy rest,
　　Climbing yet take heed of falling.
Climbers oft even at their best
　　Catch love, down fall, th'heart appalling.

Mounting yet, if she do call　　　　　　　　　　5
　　And desire to know thy arrant,
Fear not, stay and tell her all,
　　Falling she will be thy warrant.

Rise, O rise, but rising tell
　　When her beauty bravely wins thee　　　　　10
To soar up where that she doth dwell,
　　Down again thy baseness brings thee.

If she ask what makes thee love her,
　　Say her virtue, not her face;
For though beauty doth approve her,　　　　　　15
　　Mildness gives her greater grace.

Rise then, rise, if she bid rise,
    Rising say thou risest for her.
Fall, if she do thee despise,
    Falling still do thou adore her.   20

If thy plaint do pity gain,
    Love and live to her honour.
If thy service she disdain,
    Dying yet complain not on her.

XIV

THANKS, gentle moon, for thy obscured light;
    My love and I betrayed thou set us free.
    And, Zephyrus, as many unto thee,
Whose blasts concealed the pleasures of the night;
    Resolve to her thou gave, content to me.   5
But be those bowers still filled with serpents' hisses,
That sought by treason to betray our kisses.

And thou, false arbour, with thy bed of rose,
    Wherein, whereon, touched equal with love's fire,
    We reaped of either other love's desire,   10
Wither the twining plants that thee enclose!
O be thy bowers still filled with serpents' hisses,
That sought by treason to betray our kisses.

Torn be the frame, for thou didst thankless hide
    A traitorous spy, her brother and my foe,   15
    Who sought by death our joys to undergo,
And by that death our passions to divide,
    Leaving to our great vows eternal woe.
O be thy bowers still filled with serpents' hisses,
That sought by treason to betray our kisses.   20

XV

I SIGH, as sure to wear the fruit of the willow tree.
I sigh, as sure to lose my suit; for it may not be.
I sigh as one that loves in vain, I sigh as one that lives in pain,
    Very sorry, very weary of my misery.

I hate my thoughts which, like the fly, flutter in the flame.   5
I hate my tears which drop and dry, quench and frid the same.
I hate the heart which frozen burns, I hate the heart which chosen
     turns
To and from me, making of me nothing but a game.

My thoughts are fuel to desire, which my heart doth move;
My tears are oil to feed the fire, smart whereof I prove.   10
She laughs at sighs that come from me, I sigh at laughs in her so free,
Who doth glory in the story of my sorry love.

Her lovely looks and loveless mind do not well agree;
Her quick conceit and judgement blind as ill-suited be.
Her forward wit and froward heart, that like to knit, this glad to
     part,   15
Makes so pretty and so witty not to pity me.

The more I seek the less I find what to trust unto.
The more I hold the less I bind, she doth still undo.
I weave the web of idle love, which endless will and fruitless prove,
If the pleasure for the measure of my treasure go.   20

XVI

DOWN A DOWN: thus Phyllis sung, by fancy once oppressed;
Who so by foolish love are stung are worthily distressed.
     And so sing I, with a down a down a down.

When Love was first begot, and by the mother's will
Did fall to human lot his solace to fulfil,   5
Devoid of all deceit, a chaste and holy fire
Did quicken man's conceit, and woman's breast inspire.
The gods that saw the good that mortals did approve,
With kind and holy mood, began to talk of Love.

Down a down: thus Phyllis sung, by fancy once oppressed;   10
Who so by foolish love are stung are worthily distressed.
     And so sing I, with a down a down a down.

But during this accord, a wonder strange to hear,
Whilst love in deed and word most faithful did appear,
False Semblance came in place, by Jealousy attended,   15
And with a double face both Love and Fancy blended;
Which made the gods forsake, and men from Fancy fly,
And maidens scorn a mate. Forsooth, and so will I.

Down a down: thus Phyllis sung, by fancy once oppressed;
Who so by foolish love are stung are worthily distressed.   20
   And so sing I, with a down a down a down.

[Thomas Lodge]

XVII

DIAPHENIA, like the daffdowndilly,
White as the sun, fair as the lily,
   Heigh ho, how I do love thee!
I do love thee as my lambs
Are beloved of their dams.   5
   How blest were I if thou wouldst prove me.

Diaphenia, like the spreading roses,
That in thy sweets all sweets encloses,
   Fair sweet, how I do love thee!
I do love thee as each flower   10
Loves the sun's life-giving power,
   For, dead, thy breath to life might move me.

Diaphenia, like to all things blessed,
When all thy praises are expressed,
   Dear joy, how I do love thee!   15
As the birds do love the Spring,
Or the bees their careful king.
   Then in requite, sweet virgin, love me.

[Henry Chettle]

XVIII

BEAUTY sat bathing by a spring
   Where fairest shades did hide her.
The winds blew calm, the birds did sing,
   The cool streams ran beside her.
My wanton thoughts enticed mine eye   5
   To see what was forbidden,
But better memory said, fie.
   So vain desire was chidden.
      Hey nonny no, nonny nonny.

Into a slumber then I fell,   10
   When fond imagination
Seemed to see, but could not tell
   Her feature or her fashion.

But even as babes in dreams do smile,
    And sometime fall a-weeping, 15
So I awaked as wise this while
    As when I fell a-sleeping.
        Hey nonny no, nonny nonny.

                      [*Anthony Munday*]

XIX

MUSIC, dear solace to my thoughts neglected,
Music, time sporter to my most respected,
Sound on, sound on, thy golden harmony is such
That whilst she doth vouchsafe her ebon lute to touch,
By descant numbers I do nimbly climb from Love's secluse 5
Unto his courts, where I in fresh attire attire my Muse.

I do compare her fingers swift resounding
Unto the heavens' spherical rebounding.
Hark, hark, she sings! No forced but breathing sound I hear,
And such the concord diapasons she doth rear, 10
As when th' immortal god of nature from his seat above
First formed words all, and fairly it combined, combined by Love.

Divine Apollo, be not thou offended
That by her better skill thy skill's amended.
Scholars do oft more lore than masters theirs attain, 15
Though thine the ground, all parts in one though she contain,
Yet may'st thou triumph that thou hast a scholar only one
That can her lute to thine, and to thy voice her voice attone.

XX

WITH fragrant flowers we strew the way,
And make this our chief holiday.
For though this clime were blest of yore,
Yet was it never proved before.
O gracious king of second Troy, 5
Accept of our unfeigned joy.

Now th' air is sweeter than sweet balm,
And satyrs dance about the palm.
Now earth with verdure newly dight
Gives perfect signs of her delight. 10
O gracious king of second Troy,
Accept of our unfeigned joy.

Now birds record new harmony,
And trees do whistle melody,
Now everything that Nature breeds 15
Doth clad itself in pleasant weeds.
O gracious king of second Troy,
Accept of our unfeigned joy.

[*Thomas Watson*]

XXI

An elegy in remembrance of his worshipful friend Thomas Leighton Esquire

COME, come, all you that draw heaven's purest breath,
    Come, angel-breasted sons of harmony,
    Let us condole in tragic elegy,
Condole with me our dearest Leighton's death.
Leighton, in whose dear loss Death blemisheth 5
    Jove's beauty and the soul of true delight,
Leighton, heaven's favourite and the Muses' jewel,
Muses and heavens only herein too cruel,
    Leighton to heaven hath ta'en too timely flight.

Come then sith seas of tears, sith sighs and groans, 10
    Sith mournful plaints, loud cries and deep laments
    Have all in vain deplored these dreariments,
And Fate inexorable scorns our moans;
Let us in accents grave and saddest tones
    Offer up music's doleful sacrifice. 15
Let these accords which notes distinguished frame
Serve for memorial to sweet Leighton's name,
    In whose sad death Music's delight now dies.

WALTER PORTER

Madrigales And Ayres. Of two, three, foure and fiue Voyces, with the continued Base, with Toccatos, Sinfonias and Rittornellos to them. After the manner of Consort Musique. To be performed with the Harpesechord, Lutes, Theorbos, Base Violl, two Violins, or two Viols. 1632

I

O PRAISE the Lord, for it is a good thing to sing praises unto our God; yea, a joyfull and pleasant thing it is to be thankful. O let your songs be of him and praise him, and let your talking be of all his wondrous works. Remember the marvellous works that he hath done, his wonders and the judgements of his mouth.   5

[*Psalms* cxlvii. 1, cv. 2, 5]

Praise the Lord, O my soul, and forget not all his benefits. Which forgiveth all thy sins and healeth all thy infirmities. And gathereth thee out of the land, from the East and from the West, from the North and from the South. And saveth thy life from destruction and crowneth thee with mercy and loving kindness.   10

[*Psalms* ciii. 2–3, cvii. 3, ciii. 4]

O praise the Lord, ye angels of his, ye that excel in strength, ye that fulfil his commandments and hearken unto the voice of his words. O speak good of the Lord, all ye works of his, in all places of his dominions. Praise thou the Lord, O my soul. Whilst I live will I praise the Lord.   [*Psalms* ciii. 20, 22, cxlvi. 1]   15

II

HITHER we come into this world of woe,
And, feeling to what end we come, we cry.
I' the morning of our age like flowers we blow,
And like God's figures seem too good to die.
But let afflictions touch us, and like clay   5
We fall to what we are, and end the day.

[*attrib. to John Fletcher*]

III

HE that loves a rosy cheek,
    Or a coral lip admires;
Or from star-like eyes doth seek
    Fuel to maintain his fires:
As old Time makes these decay,   5
So his flames must waste away.

But a smooth and steadfast mind,
    Gentle thoughts and calm desires,
Hearts with equal love combined
    Kindles never dying fires.   10
Where these are not, I despise
Lovely cheeks or lips or eyes.

                          [*Thomas Carew*]

IV

SLEEP, all my joys, and only sorrow wake!
    Let mirth to mourning, pleasure yield to plaint;
Whilst I consume in sighing for her sake,
    Whose loss to mind my heavy soul makes faint.
Her love my life, her lack my lingering death,   5
Yea, all my hopes are vanished as her breath.
Although she's dead, yet this from death she said:
I always lived and died a perfect maid.

V

WHO hath a human soul, and music hates,
    Hates his own soul that's made harmoniously.
Then they are devils or right reprobates
    To hate that without which men's spirits should die.
For if the joys of heaven be much in this,   5
Let him to hell to howl, that hates this bliss.

VI

SITTING once, rapt with delight,
In my fairest mistress' sight,
I took pleasure to compare
Her eyes' whiteness to the air.

That which compassed in the ball,   5
I did purest water call;
And the pretty inward round,
I styled earth. But O, I found
While some part I did desire
For to liken unto fire,   10
Ere I knew from whence it came,
I myself grew all aflame.

VII

'TIS but a frown, I prithee let me die,
One bended brow concludes my tragedy.
For all my love I crave but this of thee,
Thou wilt not be too long in killing me.
If that you love not, what avails your smiles?   5
You only warm a ball of snow the whiles,
Which whilst it gathers comfort from your eyes,
With that same comfort melts away and dies.
Thus in the end your smiles, your frowns, are one,
And differs but in execution.   10

VIII

LOOK on me ever, though thine eye
    Murder where it glances.
If by so happy means I die,
    My fortune it advances.
And if by chance a tear you shed   5
    To show my death did move you,
It will revive me being dead,
    And I again shall love you.
Redeem me from so deep despair;
    The power you have, now try it.   10
Think me but fair, and I am fair,
    Although the world deny it.

IX

TELL me, you stars, that our affections move,
Why made you me that cruel one to love?
Why burns my heart, her scorned sacrifice,
Whose breast is hard as crystal, cold as ice?

God of desire, if all thy votaries   5
Thou thus repay, succession will grow wise.
No sighs for incense at thy shrine shall smoke;
Thy rites shall be despised, thy altars broke.
O, or give her my flame to melt that snow,
That yet unthawed does on her bosom grow;   10
Or make me ice, and with her crystal chains
Bind up all love within my frozen veins.

                                        [*Henry King*]

                        X

        OLD poets, that in Cupid's hand
            Put weapons first, did but allow
        One bow, a chain, two shafts, a brand.
    These then were all his arms in all his parts.
    But now he finds in Celia's either brow,   5
        In both her eyes, in all her parts,
    Two bows, ten thousand fetters, flames, and darts.
        Tell me the number of her hairs,
            Count all the glances of her eyes,
        The graces and the careless snares,   10
            That in her looser beauty lies,
        Sweet smiles, and sweeter airs that fly
        Like lightning from her lips; and then
    Tell me how many ways Love murders men.

                        XI

        THUS sung Orpheus to his strings,
            When he was almost slain,
        Whilst the winds, soft murmuring,
            Answered all his woes again:
    'Ah, dear Eurydice', he cried;   5
        'Ah, dear Eurydice'—and so he died.
    'Ah, dear Eurydice' the echoing winds replied.

                        XII

    WHEN first I saw thee, thou didst sweetly play
    The gentle thief, and stol'st my heart away.
    Render 't again, or else send me thine own,
    Two is too much for thee, when I have none;
    Which if thou dost not, I will swear thou art   5
    A sweet-faced creature with a double heart.

Yet pardon, fair one. I did freely give
To thee my heart, and yet without it live.
By powerful flames shot from thy conquering eye
To thee, sweet mansion, let it ever fly;   10
And though I am of my poor heart bereft,
'T may prove a happy union, not a theft.

XIII

END now my life; with daily pains afflicted,
    Since that for all that I have wept and grieved,
        My tears are not requited,
    And trusty faith not any whit believed.
I am in such a hapless state of sorrow   5
    That I could be content, and so relieve me,
Unjust rewards and scorns of her to borrow,
    Only that she would credit and believe me.
                        [*Bartholomew Yong*]

XIV

SINCE all things love, why should not we,
The best of creatures, be as free?
The pearl-eyed fish in every water
Pursues his love, being taught by Nature.
The seely worm, the lamb, and harmless dove,   5
Which knoweth nothing, yet knows how to love.

All senseless things love's passions feel.
The stone attracts th' unyielding steel;
The ivy twines on every tree,
And loves it more than you love me,   10
And in the cold of Winter fresh is seen,
For heat of love is it that keeps it green.

Then learn by seeing what they do,
If they want eyes, hands, tongues, yet woo,
Can you, that have of each the best   15
    Apt for that use, yet use them least?
'Twere sin to think the world did ne'er yet show
So unkind a breast graced with so mild a brow.

The lass that loved the Idean swain
Thought it not base, nor found it vain.   20
Adone was loved, though proud and coy;
Endymion too, that drowsy boy,
Whom for to please such care fair Cynthia took,
That ever since that time she pale doth look.

Then let us love whilst we are in youth,   25
You fraught with beauty, I with truth.
We'll make the world, being in our prime,
Wrinkled with Envy more than Time.
And, when too old to live, the fate draws nigh,
Our loves shall make us too too young to die.   30

XV

FAREWELL, once my delight! Farewell, the nearest
Part of my heart, and of the world the dearest!
I'll plain no more to love, no more to thee;
But cease to mourn where none will pity me.

And though I hate my life since you hate me,   5
I'll cover it to hide your cruelty.
And since my love and me you disavow,
As if to love you were to injure you,

I'll mildly temporize with my unrest,
And fly the face I carry in my breast,   10
Nor farther seek. This only shall suffice me:
My love deserved you, though you did despise me.

Farewell! farewell! and may you ever be
Good as you are, though ne'er so bad to me.
Be you beloved of all, and lastly shine   15
As fair in heaven's eye as you are in mine.

XVI

COME, lovers all, to me, and cease your mourning.
Love has no shafts to shoot, no more brands burning.
He means my pains shall you from pains deliver,
For in my breast he 'as emptied all his quiver.
Had he not been a child he would have known   5
He 'as lost a thousand servants to kill one.

XVII

IN Celia's face a question did arise:
Which were more beautiful, her lips or eyes?
We, said the eyes, send forth those pointed darts
Which pierce the hardest adamantine hearts.
From us, replied the lips, proceed those blisses   5
Which lovers reap by kind words and sweet kisses.
Then wept the eyes and from their springs did pour
Of liquid oriental pearl a shower.
Whereat the lips, moved with delight and pleasure,
Through a sweet smile unlocked their pearly treasure;   10
And bade Love judge whether did add more grace—
Weeping, or smiling pearls,—to Celia's face?

                                 [*Thomas Carew*]

XVIII

TELL me where the beauty lies—
In my mistress? or in my eyes?
Is she fair? I made her so.
Beauty doth from liking grow.
Be she fairer, whiter than   5
Venus' doves or Leda's swan,
What's that Beauty if neglected,
Seen of all, of none respected?
Then tell my mistress that I love her,
Think her fair, 'cause I approve her.   10

XIX

LOVE in thy youth, fair maid. Be wise.
     Old Time will make thee colder.
And though each morning new arise,
     Yet we each day grow older.

Thou as heaven art fair and young,   5
     Thine eyes like twin stars shining.
But ere another day be sprung,
     All these will be declining.

Then Winter comes with all his fears,
     And all thy sweets shall borrow.   10
Too late then wilt thou shower thy tears,
     And I too late shall sorrow.

XX–XXI

HAIL! Cloris, hail! fair goddess of the Spring,
Youth of the year, of thee still will we sing.
Fresh queen of lakes, of lawns and bowers,
Nurse of new loves and of new flowers.
Hail! fairest of Jove's seed. Only of thee   5
That art earth's music, shall our music be.

The birds, the echo, the wandering winds, that throw
Through the air life's sovereign balsam as they blow,
Shall with the lauds and zeal-begetting lays,
Breathed by us hourly in thy praise,   10
Feast the air, and teach the hills, rocks and woods to sing:
Hail! Cloris, hail! fair goddess of the Spring.

XXII

YOUNG Thyrsis lay in Phyllis' lap,
    And gazing on her eye,
'Steemed life too mean for such good hap,
    And fain the boy would die.

When Phyllis, who the force did prove   5
    Of love as well as he,
Cried to him: Stay awhile, my love,
    And I will die with thee!

So did these happy lovers die,
    But with so little pain,   10
That both to life immediately
    Returned to die again.

XXIII

THY face and eyes and all thou hast is fair,
    And for their sakes most men affect thee.
But I perceive in thee something more rare
    Than outward beauty, for which I affect thee.

Thy mind is fairer than thy face or eyes,   5
    And that same beauteous outside which thou hast,
Is but a curious casket, in which lies
    The treasures of a mind virtuous and chaste.

So keep them still, and let not youth deceive thee.
  For when through age thy beauty shall decay,   10
Those that for beauty love thee, then will leave thee;
  But worth will last until thy dying day.

But he that shall for both of these esteem thee,
  And think thee fair, and know thy virtues too,
He cannot choose but ever dearly deem thee,   15
  And much admire thee, as I swear I do.

XXIV

TELL me, Amyntas, Cloris cries,
  As she was sitting by him,
If there be such a thing as Love,
  How hap we cannot spy him?
    Because to see   5
    A boy, quoth he,
  To mortals is forbidden.
    But in thine eyes
    E'en there he lies,
  And in my bosom hidden.   10

XXV

I SAW fair Cloris walk alone,
Whilst feathered rain came softly down,
And Jove descended from his tower
To court her in a silver shower.
The wanton snow flew on her breast   5
Like little birds unto their nest;
But overcome with whiteness there,
For grief it thawed into a tear;
Thence falling on her garments' hem,
To deck her, froze into a gem.   10
                    [*William Strode*]

XXVI

DEATH, there is no need of thee.
Love alone and constancy
Are enough without thy dart,
To tire upon an honest heart.

Yet so hard is not the way   5
To love's fame as many say.
For Love no prize but love regards,
And with itself itself rewards,
And oft, in seeking it, is found
Glory that lives when we are under ground.   10

XXVII

LIKE the rash and giddy fly,
Fluttering about her eyes, I die.
Yet differs this, she burns away
Only by night, I night and day.
She burns only when she brings   5
Near unto the flame her wings.
But my sun burns everywhere
At home, abroad, far off and near.
She knows not that the fire consumes; but I
Foresee my death, and like a desperate die.   10

XXVIII

An Elegy on the Right Honourable Lady, the Lady Arabella Stuart.

WAKE, Sorrow, wake! sith she is fall'n asleep,
    Asleep in death, who was entombed in life.
Eyes weep out sight, or see but still to weep,
    And weep for loss of a most constant wife
Who now is dead. Ay me! ay me! she's dead.   5
Then mind we still her name with hearts of lead.

Arbella, farewell! farewell, dear widow wife!
Farewell in death that faredst so ill in life!
Sole paragon for grace and princely parts,
Thy vault still keeps our thoughts, thy chest our
        hearts.   10

PHILIP ROSSETER

A Booke Of Ayres, Set foorth to be song to the Lute, Orpherian, and Base Violl. 1601

[*Part I: songs composed by Thomas Campian*]

I

MY sweetest Lesbia, let us live and love.
And, though the sager sort our deeds reprove,
Let us not weigh them. Heaven's great lamps do dive
Into their west, and straight again revive.
But soon as once set is our little light,   5
Then must we sleep one ever-during night.

If all would lead their lives in love like me,
Then bloody swords and armour should not be.
No drum nor trumpet peaceful sleeps should move,
Unless alarm came from the camp of Love.   10
But fools do live and waste their little light,
And seek with pain their ever-during night.

When timely death my life and fortune ends,
Let not my hearse be vexed with mourning friends.
But let all lovers, rich in triumph, come   15
And with sweet pastimes grace my happy tomb.
And, Lesbia, close up thou my little light,
And crown with love my ever-during night.

II

THOUGH you are young and I am old,
Though your veins hot and my blood cold,
Though youth is moist and age is dry,
Yet embers live when flames do die.

The tender graft is eas'ly broke,   5
But who shall shake the sturdy oak?
You are more fresh and fair than I,
Yet stubs do live when flowers do die.

Thou, that thy youth dost vainly boast,
Know, buds are soonest nipped with frost.   10
Think that thy fortune still doth cry:
Thou fool, to-morrow thou must die.

III

I CARE not for these ladies
That must be wooed and prayed.
Give me kind Amaryllis,
The wanton country maid.
Nature Art disdaineth,   5
Her beauty is her own.
   Her when we court and kiss,
   She cries: forsooth, let go!
   But when we come where comfort is
   She never will say no.   10

If I love Amaryllis
She gives me fruit and flowers;
But if we love these ladies,
We must give golden showers.
Give them gold that sell love,   15
Give me the nut-brown lass,
   Who when we court and kiss,
   She cries: forsooth, let go!
   But when we come where comfort is
   She never will say no.   20

These ladies must have pillows,
And beds by strangers wrought.
Give me a bower of willows,
Of moss and leaves unbought,
And fresh Amaryllis,   25
With milk and honey fed,
   Who when we court and kiss,
   She cries: forsooth, let go!
   But when we come where comfort is
   She never will say no.   30

IV

FOLLOW thy fair sun, unhappy shadow.
   Though thou be black as night,
   And she made all of light,
Yet follow thy fair sun, unhappy shadow.

Follow her whose light thy light depriveth.   5
    Though here thou liv'st disgraced,
    And she in heaven is placed,
Yet follow her whose light the world reviveth.

Follow those pure beams whose beauty burneth,
    That so have scorched thee,   10
    As thou still black must be
Till her kind beams thy black to brightness turneth.

Follow her while yet her glory shineth.
    There comes a luckless night,
    That will dim all her light;   15
And this the black unhappy shade divineth.

Follow still, since so thy fates ordained.
    The sun must have his shade,
    Till both at once do fade,
The sun still proved, the shadow still disdained.   20

V

MY love hath vowed he will forsake me,
    And I am already sped.
Far other promise he did make me,
    When he had my maidenhead.
If such danger be in playing,   5
    And sport must to earnest turn,
I will go no more a-maying.

Had I foreseen what is ensued,
    And what now with pain I prove,
Unhappy then I had eschewed   10
    This unkind event of love.
Maids foreknow their own undoing,
    But fear nought till all is done,
When a man alone is wooing.

Dissembling wretch, to gain thy pleasure,   15
    What didst thou not vow and swear?
So didst thou rob me of the treasure,
    Which so long I held so dear.
Now thou prov'st to me a stranger,
    Such is the vile guise of men   20
When a woman is in danger.

That heart is nearest to misfortune
  That will trust a feigned tongue.
When flatt'ring men our loves importune,
  They intend us deepest wrong.   25
If this shame of love's betraying
  But this once I cleanly shun,
I will go no more a-maying.

VI

WHEN to her lute Corinna sings,
Her voice revives the leaden strings,
And doth in highest notes appear
As any challenged echo clear.
But when she doth of mourning speak,   5
Ev'n with her sighs the strings do break.

And as her lute doth live or die;
Led by her passion, so must I.
For when of pleasure she doth sing,
My thoughts enjoy a sudden spring;   10
But if she doth of sorrow speak,
Ev'n from my heart the strings do break.

VII

TURN back, you wanton flyer,
And answer my desire
  With mutual greeting.
Yet bend a little nearer,
True beauty still shines clearer   5
  In closer meeting.
Hearts with hearts delighted
Should strive to be united,
Either others' arms with arms enchaining.
Hearts with a thought, rosy lips   10
With a kiss, still entertaining.

What harvest half so sweet is,
As still to reap the kisses
  Grown ripe in sowing:
And straight to be receiver   15
Of that which thou art giver,
  Rich in bestowing?

There's no strict observing
Of times or seasons changing;
There is ever one fresh Spring abiding.   20
Then what we sow, with our lips
Let us reap, love's gains dividing.

VIII

IT fell on a summer day,
While sweet Bessy sleeping lay
In her bower, on her bed,
Light with curtains shadowed,
Jamy came. She him spies,   5
Opening half her heavy eyes.

Jamy stole in through the door.
She lay slumbering as before.
Softly to her he drew near;
She heard him, yet would not hear.   10
Bessy vowed not to speak;
He resolved that dump to break.

First a soft kiss he doth take;
She lay still and would not wake.
Then his hands learned to woo;   15
She dreamt not what he would do,
But still slept, while he smiled
To see love by sleep beguiled.

Jamy then began to play;
Bessy as one buried lay,   20
Gladly still through this sleight,
Deceived in her own deceit.
And since this trance begun,
She sleeps every afternoon.

IX

THE cypress curtain of the night is spread,
And over all a silent dew is cast.
The weaker cares by sleep are conquered.
But I alone with hideous grief aghast,
In spite of Morpheus' charms, a watch do keep   5
Over mine eyes to banish careless sleep.

Yet oft my trembling eyes through faintness close;
　And then the map of hell before me stands,
Which ghosts do see, and I am one of those,
　Ordained to pine in sorrow's endless bands,   10
Since from my wretched soul all hopes are reft,
And now no cause of life to me is left.

Grief, seize my soul, for that will still endure
　When my crazed body is consumed and gone;
Bear it to thy black den, there keep it sure,   15
　Where thou ten thousand souls dost tire upon;
Yet all do not afford such food to thee,
As this poor one, the worser part of me.

X

FOLLOW your Saint, follow with accents sweet;
Haste you, sad notes, fall at her flying feet.
There wrapped in cloud of sorrow, pity move,
And tell the ravisher of my soul I perish for her love.
But if she scorns my never-ceasing pain,   5
Then burst with sighing in her sight, and ne'er return again.

All that I sung still to her praise did tend.
Still she was first, still she my songs did end.
Yet she my love and music both doth fly,
The music that her echo is, and beauty's sympathy.   10
Then let my notes pursue her scornful flight;
It shall suffice that they were breathed, and died for her
　delight.

XI

FAIR, if you expect admiring;
Sweet, if you provoke desiring,
　Grace dear love with kind requiting.
Fond, but if thy sight be blindness;
False, if thou affect unkindness,   5
　Fly both love and love's delighting.
Then when hope is lost, and love is scorned,
I'll bury my desires, and quench the fires that ever
　yet in vain have burned.

Fates, if you rule lovers' fortune;
Stars, if men your powers importune,   10
    Yield relief by your relenting.
Time, if sorrow be not endless,
Hope made vain, and Pity friendless,
    Help to ease my long lamenting.
But if griefs remain still unredressed,   15
I'll fly to her again, and sue for pity to renew my
    hopes distressed.

XII

THOU art not fair, for all thy red and white,
    For all those rosy ornaments in thee.
Thou art not sweet, though made of mere delight,
    Nor fair nor sweet, unless thou pity me.
I will not soothe thy fancies. Thou shalt prove   5
That beauty is no beauty without love.

Yet love not me, nor seek thou to allure
    My thoughts with beauty, were it more divine.
Thy smiles and kisses I cannot endure,
    I'll not be wrapped up in those arms of thine.   10
Now show it, if thou be a woman right,
Embrace and kiss and love me in despite.

XIII

SEE where she flies enraged from me.
    View her when she intends despite.
The wind is not more swift than she.
Her fury moved such terror makes,
    As to a fearful guilty sprite   5
The voice of heaven's huge thunder cracks.
        But when her appeased mind
            Yields to delight,
        All her thoughts are made of joys,
            Millions of delights inventing,   10
        Other pleasures are but toys
            To her beauty's sweet contenting.

My fortune hangs upon her brow,
    For as she smiles or frowns on me,
So must my blown affections bow.   15

And her proud thoughts too well do find
  With what unequal tyranny
Her beauties do command my mind.
    Though, when her sad planet reigns,
        Froward she be,   20
      She alone can pleasure move,
        And displeasing sorrow banish.
    May I but still hold her love,
      Let all other comforts vanish.

XIV

BLAME not my cheeks, though pale with love they be;
  The kindly heat unto my heart is flown,
To cherish it that is dismayed by thee,
  Who are so cruel and unsteadfast grown.
For Nature, called for by distressed hearts,   5
Neglects and quite forsakes the outward parts.

But they whose cheeks with careless blood are stained,
  Nurse not one spark of love within their hearts;
And when they woo they speak with passion feigned,
  For their fat love lies in their outward parts;   10
But in their breasts, where Love his court should hold,
Poor Cupid sits and blows his nails for cold.

XV

    WHEN the god of merry love
      As yet in his cradle lay,
      Thus his withered nurse did say:
    Thou a wanton boy wilt prove,
    To deceive the powers above;   5
      For by thy continual smiling
      I see thy power of beguiling.

    Therewith she the babe did kiss,
      When a sudden fire out came
    From those burning lips of his,   10
      That did her with love enflame.
      But none would regard the same.
    So that to her day of dying
    The old wretch lived ever crying.

XVI

MISTRESS, since you so much desire
To know the place of Cupid's fire,
In your fair shrine that flame doth rest,
Yet never harboured in your breast.
It bides not in your lips so sweet,   5
Nor where the rose and lilies meet,
    But a little higher,
There, there, O there, lies Cupid's fire.

E'en in those starry piercing eyes,
There Cupid's sacred fire lies.   10
Those eyes I strive not to enjoy,
For they have power to destroy.
Nor woo I for a smile or kiss,
So meanly triumphs not my bliss.
    But a little higher   15
I climb to crown my chaste desire.

XVII

YOUR fair looks inflame my desire.
    Quench it again with love.
Stay, O strive not still to retire;
    Do not inhuman prove.
If love may persuade,   5
    Love's pleasures, dear, deny not.
Here is a silent grovy shade,
    O tarry then, and fly not.

Have I seized my heavenly delight
    In this unhaunted grove?   10
Time shall now her fury requite
    With the revenge of love.
Then come, sweetest, come,
    My lips with kisses gracing.
Here let us harbour all alone;   15
    Die, die in sweet embracing.

Will you now so timely depart,
    And not return again?
Your sight lends such life to my heart
    That to depart is pain.   20

Fear yields no delay,
   Secureness helpeth pleasure.
Then till the time gives safer stay,
   O farewell, my life's treasure.

XVIII

THE man of life upright,
   Whose guiltless heart is free
From all dishonest deeds
   Or thought of vanity:

The man whose silent days   5
   In harmless joys are spent,
Whom hopes cannot delude,
   Nor sorrow discontent:

That man needs neither towers
   Nor armour for defence,   10
Nor secret vaults to fly
   From thunder's violence.

He only can behold
   With unaffrighted eyes
The horrors of the deep   15
   And terrors of the skies.

Thus scorning all the cares
   That fate or fortune brings,
He makes the heaven his book,
   His wisdom heavenly things,   20

Good thoughts his only friends,
   His wealth a well-spent age,
The earth his sober inn
   And quiet pilgrimage.

XIX

HARK, all you ladies that do sleep,
   The fairy queen Proserpina
Bids you awake, and pity them that weep.
   You may do in the dark
      What the day doth forbid.   5
   Fear not the dogs that bark;
      Night will have all hid.

But if you let your lovers moan,
    The fairy queen Proserpina
Will send abroad her fairies every one,   10
        That shall pinch black and blue
            Your white hands and fair arms,
        That did not kindly rue
            Your paramours' harms.

In myrtle arbours on the downs,   15
    The fairy queen Proserpina
This night by moonshine, leading merry rounds,
        Holds a watch with sweet Love,
            Down the dale, up the hill,
        No plaints or groans may move   20
            Their holy vigil.

All you that will hold watch with Love,
    The fairy queen Proserpina
Will make you fairer than Dione's dove.
        Roses red, lilies white,   25
            And the clear damask hue,
        Shall on your cheeks alight.
            Love will adorn you.

All you that love or loved before,
    The fairy queen Proserpina   30
Bids you increase that loving humour more.
        They that yet have not fed
            On delights amorous,
        She vows that they shall lead
            Apes in Avernus.   35

XX

WHEN thou must home to shades of underground,
    And there arrived, a new admired guest,
The beauteous spirits do ingirt thee round,
    White Iope, blithe Helen and the rest,
To hear the stories of thy finished love   5
From that smooth tongue, whose music hell can move:

Then wilt thou speak of banqueting delights,
  Of masks and revels which sweet youth did make,
Of tourneys and great challenges of knights,
  And all these triumphs for thy beauty's sake.   10
When thou hast told these honours done to thee,
Then tell, O tell how thou didst murther me.

XXI

COME, let us sound with melody the praises
Of the kings' King, th' Omnipotent Creator,
Author of number, that hath all the world in
      Harmony framed.

Heaven is his throne, perpetually shining.   5
His divine power and glory thence he thunders.
One in all, and all still in one abiding,
      Both Father and Son.

O sacred Sprite, invisible, eternal,
Everywhere, yet unlimited, that all things   10
Canst in one moment penetrate, revive me,
      O holy Spirit.

Rescue, O rescue me from earthly darkness.
Banish hence all these elemental objects.
Guide my soul that thirsts to the lively fountain   15
      Of thy divineness.

Cleanse my soul, O God, thy bespotted image,
Altered with sin so that heavenly pureness
Cannot acknowledge me but in thy mercies,
      O Father of grace.   20

But when once thy beams do remove my darkness,
O then I'll shine forth as an angel of light,
And record with more than an earthly voice thy
      Infinite honours.

ꝏꝏꝏꝏꝏꝏ

[*Part II: songs composed by Philip Rosseter*]

I

SWEET, come again!
Your happy sight so much desired,
Since you from hence are now retired
    I seek in vain.
        Still must I mourn   5
And pine in longing pain,
Till you, my life's delight, again
        Vouchsafe your wished return.

        If true Desire
Or faithful vow of endless love   10
Thy heart inflamed may kindly move
        With equal fire,
        O then my joys,
So long distraught, shall rest
Reposed soft in thy chaste breast,   15
        Exempt from all annoys.

        You had the power
My wandering thoughts first to restrain,
You first did hear my love speak plain.
        A child before,   20
        Now it is grown;
Confirmed do you it keep,
And let it safe in your bosom sleep
        There ever made your own.

        And, till we meet,   25
Teach absence inward art to find,
Both to disturb and please the mind
        Such thoughts are sweet,
        And such remain
In hearts whose flames are true.   30
Then such will I retain till you
        To me return again.

II

AND would you see my mistress' face?
It is a flowery garden place

Where knots of beauties have such grace
That all is work and nowhere space.

It is a sweet delicious morn   5
Where day is breeding, never born.
It is a meadow yet unshorn
Whom thousand flowers do adorn.

It is the heavens' bright reflex,
Weak eyes to dazzle and to vex;   10
It is th' Idaea of her sex,
Envy of whom doth world perplex.

It is a face of death that smiles,
Pleasing though it kills the whiles,
Where death and love in pretty wiles   15
Each other mutually beguiles.

It is fair beauty's freshest youth,
It is the feigned Elysium's truth,
The Spring that wintered hearts renew'th;
And this is that my soul pursu'th.   20

III

No grave for woe, yet earth my watery tears devours;
Sighs want air, and burnt desires kind pity's showers;
Stars hold their fatal course, my joys preventing;
The earth, the sea, the air, the fire, the heavens, vow my tormenting.

Yet still I live and waste my weary days in groans,   5
And with woeful tunes adorn despairing moans;
Night still prepares a more displeasing morrow;
My day is night, my life is death, and all but sense of sorrow.

IV

If I urge my kind desires,
    She unkind doth them reject.
Women's hearts are painted fires
    To deceive them that affect.
I alone love's fires include,   5
She alone doth them delude.

She hath often vowed her love,
   But, alas, no fruit I find.
That her fires are false I prove,
   Yet in her no fault I find.   10
I was thus unhappy born
And ordained to be her scorn.

Yet if human care or pain
   May the heavenly order change,
She will hate her own disdain   15
   And repent she was so strange;
For a truer heart than I
Never lived, or loved to die.

V

WHAT heart's content can he find,
   What happy sleeps can his eyes embrace,
That bears a guilty mind?
   His taste sweet wines will abhor;
No music's sound can appease the thoughts   5
   That wicked deeds deplore.
The passion of a present fear
Still makes his restless motion there,
   And all the day he dreads the night,
And all the night, as one aghast, he fears the morning light.   10

But he that loves to be loved,
   And in his deeds doth adore heaven's power,
And is with pity moved:
   The night gives rest to his heart,
The cheerful beams do awake his soul   15
   Revived in every part.
He lives a comfort to his friends,
And heaven to him such blessing sends
   That fear of hell cannot dismay
His steadfast heart, that is enured the truth still to obey.   20

VI

LET him that will be free and keep his heart from care,
Retired alone remain, where no discomforts are;
For when the eye doth view his grief, or hapless ear his sorrow hears,
Th' impression still in him abides, and ever in one shape appears.

Forget thy griefs betimes, long sorrow breeds long pain,   5
For joy far fled from men will not return again.
O happy is the soul which heaven ordained to live in endless peace,
His life is a pleasing dream, and every hour his joys increase.

You heavy sprites that love in severed shades to dwell,
That nurse despair and dream of unrelenting hell,   10
Come sing this happy song and learn of me the art of true content;
Load not your guilty souls with wrong, and heaven then will soon
    relent.

VII

REPROVE not love; though fondly thou hast lost
        Greater hopes by loving.
Love calms ambitious spirits, from their breasts
        Danger oft removing.
Let lofty humours mount   5
    Up on high, down again like to the wind,
While private thoughts vowed to love
        More peace and pleasure find.

Love and sweet beauty makes the stubborn mild
        And the coward fearless.   10
The wretched miser's care to bounty turns,
        Cheering all things cheerless.
Love chains the earth and heaven,
    Turns the spheres, guides the years in endless peace;
The flowery earth through his power   15
        Receives her due increase.

VIII

AND would you fain the reason know
Why my sad eyes so often flow?
My heart ebbs joy when they do so
And loves the moon by whom they go.

And will you ask why pale I look?   5
'Tis not with poring on my book.
My mistress' cheek my blood hath took,
For her mine own hath me forsook.

Do not demand why I am mute.
Love's silence doth all speech confute.   10
They set the note, then tune the lute;
Hearts frame their thoughts, then tongues their suit.

Do not admire why I admire.
My fever is no other's fire,
Each several heart hath his desire,   15
Else proof is false, and truth a liar.

If why I love you should see cause,
Love should have form like other laws.
But fancy pleads not by the clause,
'Tis as the sea still vexed with flaws.   20

No fault upon my love espy,
For you perceive not with my eye;
My palate to your taste may lie,
Yet please itself deliciously.

Then let my sufferance be mine own,   25
Sufficeth it these reasons shown.
Reason and love are ever known
To fight till both be overthrown.

IX

WHEN Laura smiles, her sight revives both night and day;
The earth and heaven views with delight her wanton play;
And her speech with ever-flowing music doth repair
The cruel wounds of sorrow and untamed despair.

The sprites that remain in fleeting air   5
Affect for pastime to untwine her tressed hair;
And the birds think sweet Aurora, Morning's queen, doth shine
From her bright sphere, when Laura shows her looks divine.

Diana's eyes are not adorned with greater power
Than Laura's, when she lifts awhile for sport to lure.   10
But when she her eyes encloseth, blindness doth appear
The chiefest grace of beauty sweetly seated there.

Love hath no fire but what he steals from her bright eyes.
Time hath no power but that which in her pleasure lies.
For she with her divine beauties all the world subdues,   15
And fills with heavenly spirits my humble Muse.

X

LONG have mine eyes gazed with delight,
   Conveying hopes unto my soul,
In nothing happy but in sight
   Of her that doth my sight control.
But now mine eyes must lose their light.   5

My object now must be the air,
   To write in water words of fire,
And teach sad thoughts how to despair.
   Desert must quarrel with desire.
All were appeased were she not fair.   10

For all my comfort this I prove,
   That Venus on the sea was born.
If seas be calm, then doth she love,
   If storms arise I am forlorn,
My doubtful hopes like wind do move.   15

XI

THOUGH far from joy, my sorrows are as far,
   And I both between.
Not too low, nor yet too high
Above my reach would I be seen.
Happy is he that is so placed,   5
Not to be envied, nor to be disdained or disgraced.

The higher trees the more storms they endure;
   Shrubs be trodden down.
But the mean, the golden mean,
Doth only all our fortunes crown.   10
Like to a stream that sweetly slideth
Through the flowery banks and still in the midst
   his course guideth.

XII

SHALL I come if I swim? Wide are the waves you see.
Shall I come if I fly, my dear love, to thee?
Streams Venus will appease, Cupid gives me wings;
    All the powers assist my desire
Save you alone, that set my woeful heart on fire.   5

You are fair, so was Hero that in Sestos dwelt.
She a priest, yet the heat of love truly felt;
A greater stream than this did her love divide,
    But she was his guide with a light;
So through the streams Leander did enjoy her sight.   10

XIII

AY me, that Love should Nature's works accuse,
Where cruel Laura still her beauty views;
River, or cloudy jet, or crystal bright,
Are all but servants of her self-delight.

Yet her deformed thoughts she cannot see;   5
And that's the cause she is so stern to me.
Virtue and duty can no favour gain,
A grief, O death, to live and love in vain.

XIV

SHALL then a traitorous kiss or a smile
  All my delights unhappily beguile?
Shall the vow of feigned love receive so rich regard,
When true service dies neglected and wants his due reward?

Deeds meritorious soon be forgot,   5
  But one offence no time can ever blot;
Every day it is renewed and every night it bleeds,
And with bloody streams of sorrow drowns all our better deeds.

Beauty is not by desert to be won,
  Fortune hath all that is beneath the sun;   10
Fortune is the guide of Love, and both of them be blind,
All their ways are full of errors which no true feet can find.

XV

IF I hope, I pine; if I fear, I faint and die;
   So between hope and fear I desperate lie,
Looking for joy to heaven whence it should come;
But hope is blind, joy deaf, and I am dumb.

   Yet I speak and cry, but alas with words of woe;   5
      And joy conceives not them that murmur so.
He that the ears of joy will ever pierce
Must sing glad notes or speak in happier verse.

XVI

UNLESS there were consent 'twixt hell and heaven
   That grace and wickedness should be combined,
I cannot make thee and thy beauties even,
   Thy face is heaven, and torture in thy mind.
For more than worldly bliss is in thy eye,   5
And hellish torture in thy mind doth lie.

A thousand cherubins fly in her looks,
   And hearts in legions melt upon their view;
But gorgeous covers wall up filthy books;
   Be it sin to say that so your eyes do you?   10
But sure your mind adheres not with your eyes,
For what they promise, that your heart denies.

But O, lest I religion should misuse,
   Inspire me, thou that ought'st thyself to know,
Since skilless readers reading do abuse,   15
   What inward meaning outward sense doth show.
For by thy eyes and heart chose and contemned,
I waver whether saved or condemned.

XVII

IF she forsake me, I must die;
      Shall I tell her so?
Alas, then straight will she reply:
      No, no, no, no, no.
If I disclose my desperate state,   5
   She will but make sport thereat,
      And more unrelenting grow.

X X

What heart can such long pains abide?
　　Fie upon this love!
I would adventure far and wide　　　　　　10
　　If it would remove.
But love will still my steps pursue,
　　I cannot his ways eschew.
　　　　Thus still helpless hopes I prove.

I do my love in lines commend,　　　　　　15
　　But alas in vain.
The costly gifts that I do send,
　　She returns again.
Thus still is my despair procured,
And her malice more assured.　　　　　　20
　　　　Then come, death, and end my pain.

XVIII

WHAT is a day, what is a year
　　Of vain delight and pleasure?
Like to a dream it endless dies,
　　And from us like a vapour flies.
And this is all the fruit that we find　　　　5
　　Which glory in worldly treasure.

He that will hope for true delight
　　With virtue must be graced.
Sweet folly yields a bitter taste
　　Which ever will appear at last.　　　　10
But if we still in virtue delight
　　Our souls are in heaven placed.

XIX

KIND in unkindness, when will you relent
And cease with faint love true love to torment?
Still entertained, excluded still I stand,
Her glove still hold, but cannot touch the hand.

In her fair hand my hopes and comforts rest.　　5
O might my fortunes with that hand be blest!
No envious breaths then my deserts could shake,
For they are good whom such true love doth make.

O let not beauty so forget her birth,
That it should fruitless home return to earth.   10
Love is the fruit of beauty; then love one
Not your sweet self, for such self-love is none.

Love one that only lives in loving you,
Whose wronged deserts would you with pity view;
This strange distaste which your affections sways   15
Would relish love and you find better days.

Thus till my happy sight your beauty views,
Whose sweet remembrance still my hope renews,
Let these poor lines solicit love for me,
And place my joys where my desires would be.   20

XX

WHAT then is love but mourning?
What desire but a self-burning?
Till she that hates doth love return,
Thus will I mourn, thus will I sing:
Come away, come away, my darling.   5

Beauty is but a blooming,
Youth in his glory entombing.
Time hath a while which none can stay.
Then come away while thus I sing:
Come away, come away, my darling.   10

Summer in winter fadeth;
Gloomy night heavenly light shadeth;
Like to the morn are Venus' flowers,
Such are her hours. Then will I sing:
Come away, come away, my darling.   15

XXI

WHETHER men do laugh or weep,
Whether they do wake or sleep,
Whether they die young or old,
Whether they feel heat or cold,
There is underneath the sun   5
Nothing in true earnest done.

All our pride is but a jest;
None are worst and none are best.
Grief and joy and hope and fear
Play their pageants everywhere;   10
Vain opinion all doth sway,
And the world is but a play.

Powers above in clouds do sit
Mocking our poor apish wit,
That so lamely with such state   15
Their high glory imitate.
No ill can be felt but pain,
And that happy men disdain.

NOTES

THE following information is given at the beginning of the notes on each song-book:

(*a*) The editions through which the song-book passed, if there was more than one.

(*b*) The copy or copies consulted in preparing the text for this volume.

(*c*) The dedicatee(s).

(*d*) Any other information concerning the song-book.

Each song-book the text of which is contained in this book is identified by the surname of the composer or compiler and the date of publication. A roman numeral following this refers to a poem within that song-book.

Example:

Jones 1601, XII = Robert Jones, *The Second Booke of Songs and Ayres*, 1601, No. XII.

John Dowland is referred to by his surname alone, his son Robert Dowland as 'R. Dowland'. Thomas Campian's undated song-books are referred to by their approximate dates of publication, *c.* 1613 and *c.* 1618. In the few instances where a composer or compiler published two books in one year these are distinguished by '*a*' or '*b*' appended to the date. 'Pt. I' or 'Pt. II' in references to Weelkes's *Madrigals* (1600) and Rosseter's *Book Of Ayres* (1601) identify subsections within these books.

Examples:

Morley 1595*a*   = Thomas Morley, *The First Booke Of Canzonets To Two Voyces*, 1595.

Morley 1595*b*   = Thomas Morley, *The First Booke Of Balletts To Five Voyces*, 1595.

Ravenscroft 1609*a* = *Pammelia*

Ravenscroft 1609*b* = *Deuteromelia*

Weelkes 1600, Pt. I = *Madrigals Of 5. and 6. parts*, Part I

Campian *c.* 1613*a* = *First Booke*

Campian *c.* 1613*b* = *Second Booke*

Campian *c.* 1618*a* = *Third Booke*

Campian *c.* 1618*b* = *Fourth Booke*

To facilitate reference the name of the composer or compiler and the date of publication (with appended letter, where necessary) is printed at the top of each left-hand page of the text.

Song-books not contained in this book are referred to either by short title or by the conventional abbreviations 'I a 6', 'II a 5', etc.

Example:

Marenzio II a 5, 1581 = Luca Marenzio, *Il secondo libro de madrigali a cinque voci*, 1581.

Other references

Bullen	*The Complete English Works of Thomas Campion,* edited by A. H. Bullen, London, 1903.
Chappell–Wooldridge	*Old English Popular Music,* by William Chappell, revised by H. Ellis Wooldridge, 2 vols., London, 1893 (reprinted New York, 1961).
Day and Murrie	*English Song-Books 1651–1702,* by Cyrus Lawrence Day and Eleanore Boswell Murrie, London, 1940.
Gardner	*The Elegies and the Songs and Sonnets of John Donne,* edited by Helen Gardner, Oxford, 1965.
Hughey	*The Arundel Harington Manuscript of Tudor Poetry,* edited by Ruth Hughey, 2 vols., Columbus, Ohio, 1960.
Kerman	*The Elizabethan Madrigal: A Comparative Study,* by Joseph Kerman, New York, 1962.
Obertello	*Madrigali italiani in Inghilterra,* by Alfredo Obertello, Milan, 1949.
Ringler	*The Poems of Sir Philip Sidney,* edited by William A. Ringler, Oxford, 1962.
Rollins	*A Gorgeous Gallery of Gallant Inventions,* edited by Hyder E. Rollins, Cambridge, Mass., 1926.
	A Poetical Rhapsody, edited by Hyder E. Rollins, 2 vols., Cambridge, Mass., 1931–2.
	Brittons Bowre of Delights, edited by Hyder E. Rollins, Cambridge, Mass., 1933.
	England's Helicon, edited by Hyder E. Rollins, 2 vols., Cambridge, Mass., 1935.
	The Arbor of Amorous Devices, edited by Hyder E. Rollins, Cambridge, Mass., 1936.
	The Paradise of Dainty Devices, edited by Hyder E. Rollins, Cambridge, Mass., 1927.
	The Phoenix Nest, edited by Hyder E. Rollins, Cambridge, Mass., 1931.
	Tottel's Miscellany, edited by Hyder E. Rollins, 2 vols., Cambridge, Mass., 1928–9.
Vivian	*Campion's Works,* edited by Percival Vivian, Oxford, 1909.

The following abbreviations are used:

A	Altus
B	Bassus
C	Cantus (C^1 = Cantus Primus, C^2 = Cantus Secundus)
Ct	Contratenor
D.N.B.	*Dictionary of National Biography*
M	Medius
O.E.D.	*Oxford English Dictionary*
om.	omitted
Q	Quintus
S	Superius
Sx	Sextus
T	Tenor

PART I · MADRIGALS

ALISON, 1606

Copy: Huntington.   *Dedicatee*: Sir John Scudamore.

The 'late conspiracie' referred to on the title-page was of course the Gunpowder Plot of 1605.

I–II. Poem by Campian, and twice set to music by him. Cf. Campian *c.* 1613*a*, II, and Rosseter 1601, Pt. I, XVIII.

   1 *upright of life*] *of life upright* Campian (both settings).
   8 *sorrows*] B, *sorrow* C¹ C² T Q.

III–VII. *A Gorgeous Gallery of Gallant Inventions,* 1578 (Rollins, p. 50).

IX–X. Also set by East (1604, XVIII–XIX) and Mundy (1594, XVII, stanza 1 only). Poem printed, with a third stanza, in *Reliquiae Wottonianae* (2nd edition, 1654, p. 511) where it is said to have been written by 'Chidi[o]ck Tychborn (being young and then in the Tower) the night before his Execution'. Chidiock Tichborne, a member of the Hampshire family of Tichborne, was executed for his part in Babington's Plot in 1586. The third stanza is as follows:

> I sought my death, and found it in my womb;
>   I looked for life, and saw it was a shade;
> I trod the earth, and knew it was my tomb;
>   And now I die, and now I am but made.
> The glass is full, and now my glass is run,
> And now I live, and now my life is done.

XV–XVI. Two stanzas of a poem by M[aster John]. T[horn]. printed in *The Paradise of Dainty Devices,* 1576 (Rollins, p. 23).

XVII–XVIII. This poem and tune with which it was associated (which Alison paraphrases in his setting) together formed one of the most popular songs of the late 16th and 17th centuries. It was issued as a broadside ballad, and was one of several songs introduced into the Netherlands by English actors; to this day the tune is still sung in Holland to the words of 'Bergen-op-Zoom'. Alexander Gil attributed the authorship to Thomas Campian in his *Logonomia Anglica,* 1619, p. 140, and this is generally accepted. For details of the numerous literary and musical sources see A. E. H. Swaen, *Modern Philology,* iv (1907), p. 397, and v (1908), p. 383; W. H. Rubsamen, *Festschrift Heinrich Besseler* (Leipzig, 1961), p. 259; and David Greer, *Music & Letters,* xliii (1962), p. 304. Day and Murrie 3643.

XIX–XXI. Poem by Campian, and set to music by him (*c.* 1618*b*, VII) and Jones (1605, X).

XXIII and XXIV. These are the two pieces specifically mentioned on the title-page. Both were written in reference to the Gunpowder Plot.

BATESON, 1604

Copy: British Museum.   *Dedicatee*: Sir William Norreys.

o. This unnumbered madrigal was intended as Bateson's contribution to Morley's anthology in honour of Queen Elizabeth I, *The Triumphs of Oriana*, 1601, but arrived too late to be included (for a somewhat similar case see note on Morley 1601, o). It was subsequently printed here with the note 'This song should have been printed in the set of *Orianas*'. The same words were set by Pilkington (1613, XXI).

9–10] This refrain occurs in all the 'Oriana' madrigals; see preliminary note on Morley 1601.

II. Also set by Byrd (1589, XXXIV).
   4 *conceit*] conceits C.

III. Poem by Sidney, *Certain Sonnets*, iv. 1–7, where it is directed to be sung to the tune of 'Non credo già che più infelice amante' (Ringler, p. 137). Also printed in *England's Helicon*, 1600. (Rollins, i, p. 170).
   4 *a thorn her song-book making*] An allusion to the 'pricking', or writing down, of music. Hence 'pricksong', a term long current for any sort of written or printed music.

IV. 3] All parts interpolate *Ay me* at beginning of line.

VI. Set twice by East (1618, VI and XXIV).

VII. Stanza 1 of a three-stanza poem set by Pilkington (1605, V). Stanza 2, with some changes, was also set separately by Pilkington (1613, IV).
   3 *clipping*] embracing.
   5] An allusion to the popular 16th-century song 'Fortune my foe'. See Chappell–Wooldridge, i, p. 76.

XI. Compare Byrd 1589, XV–XVI.
   5 *leese*] set free, unloose. Possibly a scribal error for *lead*, which would meet the requirements of the rhyme.

XII. The same words are used in XXV in this publication.

XIII. Also set by Weelkes (1597, XV), who also composed a setting of the Italian from which these lines are translated (1608, XVII). The source of the Italian is not known.
   3] All parts interpolate *my Phyllis* after *Ay me*.

XVIII. A resetting of the text of Watson 1590, XIII (see note).

XXI. Quoted in *Every Woman in her Humour*, 1609, sig. D3ᵛ.

XXII. 1–2] A reference to the Elizabethan belief in the music of the spheres. Cf. *The Merchant of Venice*, v. i, l.54 f. and Sir John Davies, *Orchestra, or a Poem of Dancing*.
   9–10] Compare the unnumbered madrigal at the beginning of this set, and see note on Morley 1601.

XXIV. 6 *cark*] trouble, distress.

XXVI. A resetting of the text of an anonymous madrigal (XVII) in Morley's *Madrigals . . . selected*, 1598.
   6 *best*] C, om. other parts.

XXVII. 4 *resorting*] resorted 1604.

BATESON, 1618

Copy: British Museum.   *Dedicatee*: Arthur, Lord Chichester.
VII. 7 *lively*] living.

IX–X. 7] Cf. *Hamlet*, III. iv: 'Forth at your eyes your spirits wildly peep.'
    12] A quotation from Marlowe's *Hero and Leander*, sest. i. 176. The same line is quoted in *As You Like It*, III. v, l. 81.

XI. 11 *pains*] *pain* C T.

XII. Stanza 1 of an anonymous two-stanza poem printed at the end of the 'Sonnets of Divers Noblemen and Gentlemen' in Sidney's *Astrophel and Stella*, 1591. See R. B. McKerrow, *The Works of Thomas Nashe* (London, 1905), iii, p. 396. Both stanzas were set by Dowland (1600, XI).

XIII. Also set by Pilkington (1613, XI).

XIV. Compare Morley 1601, XVII.
    3 *groves*] *grove* C T.

XVII. 8 *all*] om. C.

XVIII. Bodleian MS. Rawl. poet. 148, f. 67ᵛ contains a version of this poem consisting of three six-line stanzas. See also Hughey, i, p. 236.

XXV–XXVI. A translation of Anacreon's ode *Ἔρως ποτ' ἐν ῥόδοισι*. A setting of the Greek was sung in *Queen Elizabeth's Entertainment at Mitcham* [1598] (ed. L. Hotson, New Haven, 1953, p. 29). Cf. Spenser, *Amoretti*, 'Upon a day as Love lay sweetly slumb'ring', and Herrick, *The Wounded Cupid*, 'Cupid as he lay among/Roses, by a bee was stung'. See Obertello, pp. 412 and 523.

XXVII. Compare Morley 1595a, XV, 'In nets of golden wires'.
    2 *eyes*] B, *eye* C A T Q Sx.
    4 *nor*] B, *or* C A T Q Sx.

BENNET, 1599

Copy: Huntington.   *Dedicatee*: Ralph Assheton, Esq.

III. A resetting of Yonge 1588, XXV (see note).

V. Compare Morley 1594, XI, 'Come, lovers, follow me, and leave this weeping'.

VI. A resetting of the translation of Ferrabosco's madrigal 'Vorrei lagnarmi a pieno' printed in Morley's *Madrigals . . . selected*, 1598, XV. The original Italian is by Torquato Tasso.

VIII. Also set by East (1618, I).

IX. Also set by Wilbye (1598, VI).
    5] All parts interpolate *alas* after *help*.

X. Also set, with some variants, by East (1618, V).
    2 *and lilies*] *and with lilies* C A.

XI. A resetting of Yonge 1588, XXVI. Compare Vautor 1619, VI.

XII. Also set by Morley as a canzonet for three voices in his *A Plain and Easy Introduction to Practical Music*, 1597, sig. Bb6ᵛ.
    3] All parts interpolate *fond Fancy* after *say*.

XIII. Also set, with slight variants, by Wilbye (1598, IV).

XV and XVI. It is possible that XVI is intended to be the second part of XV, although there is no indication of this in the part-books.

BYRD, 1588

Editions: The researches of H. K. Andrews (see *Music & Letters*, xliv (1963) p. 5) have shown that there are at least four extant editions of Byrd's *Psalms, Sonnets, & Songs*. Three are dated 1588. The fourth is undated, but Andrews's findings point to *c.* 1599 as the date of publication (this is nine or ten years later than the date suggested in most reference books). In the following notes, where variant readings are recorded, the editions are designated 1588–*a*, 1588–*b*, 1588–*c*, and *c.* 1599. We have used 1588–*c* as the basis for our text, but in a few cases we have adopted readings from other editions, where they appear to us to be superior.

Copies: Several surviving sets of part-books are in fact mixed sets, made up of part-books of different editions (see Andrews, op. cit., p. 6). In collating the four editions we have consulted the following part-books:

1588–*a*: British Museum, K.2.f.1 (S M T Ct); Bodleian, E.453–7 (B).
1588–*b*: Folger Shakespeare Library (S M); Royal College of Music, London (T). The Ct and B part-books of this edition are not extant.
1588–*c*: Huntington 79637.
c. 1599: Huntington 14222.

Dedicatee: Sir Christopher Hatton.

I. From John Hopkins's version of Psalm lv in the Sternhold and Hopkins metrical psalter.

IV. 7 *seek*] music text, *search* metrical text.
     20 *mine*] *my c.* 1599.

VIII. 12 *Endure*] *Dure* 1588–*a*, *c.* 1599. In 1588–*a*, however, the error is corrected in the list of errata.

IX. From Thomas Sternhold's version of Psalm vi in the Sternhold and Hopkins metrical psalter.

XI. This poem is very similar in style to Dyer's 'My mind to me a kingdom is' (see No. XIV). It may have been written as part of the same poem.
     2 *force*] regard, care for. Cf. Shakespeare, *Lucrece*, line 1021: 'For me, I force not argument a straw'.

XII. Printed in *England's Helicon*, 1600 (Rollins, i, p. 150), where the words 'Corinna can' in line 4 are omitted.
     4 *cheer*] countenance.
     6 *'chill*] I will. See note on Ford 1607, II.
     8 *wood*] mad, distracted. Cf. Spenser, *The Fairy Queen*, I. v, stanza 20.

XIII. 8 *sort*] group.

XIV. This poem was issued as a broadside ballad, to be sung to the tune of 'In Crete when Dedalus' (see A. Clark, *The Shirburn Ballads*, 1907, p. 113). It is quoted by Ben Jonson in *Every Man Out of His Humour*, I. i. 11–14, and by John Taylor in *The Praise . . . of Beggary*, 1621, sig. B3^v. There is a version with two further stanzas in Bodleian MS. Rawl. poet. 85, f. 19 attributed to Sir Edward Dyer. British Museum MS. Add. 15118, f. 3^v. Day and Murrie 2270. See note on xi.

XV. 31 *since*] *c.* 1599, *fine* 1588–*a*, 1588–*b*, 1588–*c*.

XVI. This poem is the sixth song in Sidney's *Astrophel and Stella* (Ringler, p. 215) with several variants.
     6 *That*] *c.* 1599, *Though* 1588–*a*, 1588–*b*, 1588–*c*.
     15 *case*] *cast* all editions.

XVII. Poem printed in Breton's *Bower of Delights*, 1591 (Rollins, p. 57). In Bodleian MS. Rawl. poet. 85, f. 16 it is attributed to Edward de Vere, Earl of Oxford. See also Bodleian MS. Add. B. 83, f. 28; Bodleian MS. Rawl. poet. 172, f. 6ᵛ; British Museum MS. Harl. 7392, f. 33ᵛ.

2 *beauty*] In the B part-book of 1588–*a*, and the M and T part-books of *c*. 1599, the reading is *beauties*.

9 *haggards*] The term *haggard* was used for a hawk caught after it had become fully grown, and therefore particularly wild and intractable to tame.

11 *buzzards*] The buzzard was an inferior kind of hawk useless for falconry; thus the word came to be used as a term of contempt or reproach.

XIX. Poem printed in *England's Helicon*, 1600 (Rollins, i, p. 139). See also British Museum MS. Harleian 4286, f. 67ᵛ.

18 *dainty*] precious, rare.

XX. Poem printed in *England's Helicon*, 1600 (Rollins, i, p. 153).

3 *beguild*] *beguile* in the M and T part-books of *c*. 1599.

4 *beech*] *tree* in the Ct part-book of *c*. 1599.

11 *despite*] In *England's Helicon* this word is amended to *despair* to rhyme with *fair* in line 9.

XXI. Clearly this is the beginning of a longer poem which for some reason Byrd did not set in its entirety. In this respect compare Byrd 1589, XXXII.

XXII. 2 *glaives*] swords. Derived from the Latin *gladius* through Old French *glaive*.

6 *Golden Fleece*] A reference to the Order of the Golden Fleece.

XXIII. For other songs about Penelope see Byrd 1589, XXVII, and Mundy 1594, XXIX. This poem is a translation of Ovid, *Heroides*, i: 'Hanc tua Penelope lento tibi mittit, Ulixe', and is in quantitative hexameters. It may well be the work of Byrd's friend Thomas Watson. The rhythm of the 'first singing part' in Byrd's setting follows the quantitative metre of the words exactly.

XXIV. These words are from Ariosto's *Orlando furioso*, canto I, stanza 42. Byrd also set to music an English translation of this and the following stanza. See Yonge 1588, XLIV–XLV. Yonge specially mentions them on his title-page, and Henry Peacham refers to them in the *Complete Gentleman*, 1622, p. 100, as evidence of Byrd's excellence in this class of composition.

2 *sulla*] *su la* all editions.

7 *innamorate*] *inamorate* all editions.

XXV. This poem was printed in Thomas Deloney's *The Garland of Goodwill*, 1631 (and later editions), sig. H7ᵛ (F. O. Mann, *Thomas Deloney*, 1912, p. 378), and in *Le Prince d'amour*, 1660, p. 130. It is also contained in British Museum MS. Harl. 7392, f. 37, subscribed 'RA'; British Museum MS. Add. 28635, f. 103ᵛ; Bodleian MS. Rawl. poet. 85, f. 48; Folger Library, Washington, MS. 1.112. A. M. C. Latham accepts it into the canon of Raleigh's poems because of the letters 'RA' in the manuscript mentioned above, and on the grounds of its style (*The Poems of Sir Walter Raleigh*, 1951, pp. 7 and 98–100). See also Hughey, i, p. 274.

XXVI. 15 *wear*] *veare* 1588–*c*.

XXVIII. 7 *be the pirates*] *be pirates c*. 1599.

XXIX. Byrd used this text again, with some variants, in 1589, VIII. A similar poem was set by Lasso and Ferrabosco (Yonge 1588, XIX, XX) and Farnaby (1598, XII). All are based on the Apocrypha story of Susanna.

XXX. Stanza 1 was also set by Dowland (1612, XIII).

19 *means*] *mean* all editions.

24 *paid*] *shed* 1588–*a*, 1588–*c*.

XXXI. Stanza 1 was also set by Pilkington (1624, XIX).
   2 *power] poor* 1588–*c.*
   5 *retchless]* reckless.
   14 *by] thy* 1588–*a* (T and B only) and 1588–*c.*
   20 *thy soul's] the soul's* 1588–*a,* 1588–*b, c.* 1599.

XXXII. 19 *Lo, lo, my] Lo, my c.* 1599.

XXXIII. Stanza 1 is from *A True Report of the Death and Martyrdom of M[aster] Campion, Jesuit and Priest, and M[aster] Sherwin & M[aster] Bryan, Priests, at Tyburn the First of December 1581,* undated, but known to have been published in 1583. Byrd's second and third stanzas, however, are not found among the thirty of the original poem. The poem is traditionally ascribed to Henry Walpole (1558–95), but there is no contemporary authority for this. See Bodleian MS. Rawl. D. 111, f. 93^v; Bodleian MS. Rawl. poet. 148, f. 79^v; Bodleian MS. Eng. poet. b. 5, p. 111; Hughey, *Arundel Harington Manuscript,* i, p. 106.
   14 *renomed]* renowned.

XXXIV. Sidney died in 1586. It may be that Byrd's friend Thomas Watson was the author of this and XXXV. See Watson 1590, XIX, XXIII–XXIV, and XXVII.
   17 *renomed]* renowned.
   18 *oned]* made one.

XXXV. See note on XXXIV.

BYRD, 1589

Editions: Besides the first edition of 1589 two others are extant, both dated 1610. A comparison of all three editions has revealed no significant textual variants.

Copies: 1589, Huntington; 1610*a*, British Museum K.2.f.9; 1610*b*, British Museum K.2.f.10.   *Dedicatee:* Sir Henry Carey.

VIII. See Byrd's other setting of this text, 1588, XXIX. Compare also Farnaby 1598, XII, and Yonge 1588, XIX and XX. All are based on the Apocrypha story of Susanna.

IX. A resetting of Yonge 1588, XXXII and XLIII.

XIV. From Geoffrey Whitney's *A Choice of Emblems,* 1586, p. 191.
   1 *greedy]* eager Whitney.

XV–XVI. Compare Bateson 1604, XI, 'If Love be blind, how hath he then the sight'.

XVII–XVIII. Based on Palestrina's madrigal 'Io son ferito'. See Obertello, p. 83 n.

XIX–XXI. 1 *Cytheron]* A common Elizabethan variant for *Cythera.*
   3 *misers]* wretches.

XXIII. Printed in *England's Helicon,* 1600 (Rollins, i, p. 156).

XXIV and XXV. Byrd included these two choruses, as being set to music for four voices, here among the other compositions of that class. They belong respectively to XXXV and XL (see notes thereon).

XXVI. See Obertello, p. 83 n.

XXVII. Also set by Mundy (1594, XXIX).

XXVIII. From Churchyard's 'Shore's Wife' (lines 127–33) in *A Mirror for Magistrates,* 1563. See also Byrd 1611, I.

1 *unmanned*] A term employed in falconry. To 'man' a hawk was to accustom it to man's presence, and so to tame it.

5 *ne'er the near*] Never any nearer to an aim. A common Elizabethan phrase. *Near* here retains its old comparative sense: Old English *néah*, comparative *néar*.

XXIX and XXXIV. Byrd notes in his edition that XXIX (lines 1–4 of the poem here printed) and XXXIV (lines 5–10) together form the first and second parts of a single work. The words of XXXIV were also set by Bateson (1604, II).

3 *would fain*] *fain would* S M B.

XXX. 8 *the way*] Possibly a misprint for *their way*.

11 *in her danger*] in her power.

XXXI. 5–6] Cf. the ballad of 'Queen Dido' (reprinted in Percy's *Reliques of Ancient English Poetry*, 1765, iii, p. 192), lines 65–66:

> 'Come death' quoth she, 'resolve my smart',
> And with those words she pierced her heart.

XXXII. As set by Byrd this poem is clearly incomplete. In this respect compare Byrd 1588, XXI.

XXXIII. Sidney, *Astrophel and Stella*, 10th song (Ringler, p. 225). Also set as a lute ayre in R. Dowland 1610, V.

8 *Through*] *Though* all parts.

XXXIV. See note on XXIX.

XXXV. The words of this carol by Francis Kindlemarsh were printed in *The Paradise of Dainty Devices*, 1576 (Rollins, p. 12). Byrd printed the chorus ('Rejoice, rejoice, . . .') separately as XXIV.

XXXVI–XXXVII. Petrarch's sonnet XC, 'Erano i capei', has been suggested as the model for this poem. See Kerman, p. 114, and Obertello, p. 83 n.

XL. Byrd printed the chorus ('Cast off . . .') separately as XXV.

XLVI–XLVII. These two Biblical passages form part of the anthem in the Book of Common Prayer to be used in place of the *Venite* on Easter Day.

BYRD, 1611

Copy: British Museum.   *Dedicatee*: Francis, Earl of Cumberland.

I. From Churchyard's 'Shore's Wife' (lines 85–91) in *A Mirror for Magistrates*, 1563. See Byrd 1589, XXVIII.

II. From Geoffrey Whitney's *A Choice of Emblems*, 1586, p. 24. An imitation of Ariosto *Orlando*, VIII. i. See Obertello, p. 84 n.

V. From Geoffrey Whitney's *A Choice of Emblems*, 1586, p. 180.

VIII. From Geoffrey Whitney's *A Choice of Emblems*, 1586, p. 198. An imitation of Ariosto, *Orlando*, XLIV. i. See Obertello, p. 84 n.

4 *woon*] dwell, abide; from the Old English *wunian* or *wonian*.

6 *cotes*] cots, cottages.

IX. Watson 1590 contains two settings by Byrd of this poem, one for six voices (XXVIII) and an inferior version for four voices (VIII). The madrigal printed here is a reprint of the four-voice version. Concerning the poem, which is probably by Watson himself, see note on Watson 1590, VIII.

X. The first two stanzas of an anonymous poem appended to the manuscript of John Redford's interlude *Wit and Science*, *c.* 1540 (British Museum, Add. 15233, f. 39ᵛ). Cf. Day and Murrie 1981.

XIV. Compare Alison 1606, XVII–XVIII.

XVII. 5–6] Compare Jones 1600, XV, 1–3.

XIX. 4 *accents sympathise*] *accents do sympathise* C² T.

XXII. Also set by Pilkington (1624, XV). Poem freely translated from Girolamo Amelonghi's 'Sedendo in su l'arena d'un bel rio' (*Scelta di rime di diversi eccellenti poeti*, 1579, p. 310), set to music by Macque in *Musica Divina*, 1583. Compare Spenser, *Amoretti*, LXXV, 'One day I wrote her name upon the strand', and Sidney, *Certain Sonnets*, XXVIII (a translation of the first song in Book I of Montemayor's *Diana*). See Ringler, p. 157, and Obertello, pp. 411 and 521–2.

XXVII. A translation of the Latin hymn *Hodie Christus natus est.*
    3 *Angels sing*] *Angels do sing* C².

CARLTON, 1601

Copy: British Museum.   *Dedicatee*: Thomas Fermor.

I. The first stanza of an anonymous poem in *A Poetical Rhapsody*, 1602 (Rollins, i, p. 143). In the Folger Shakespeare Library there is a two-leaf folio manuscript which contains a setting of two stanzas of this poem for solo voice and bass accompaniment by Robert Jones. See J. Q. Adams, 'A New Song by Robert Jones', *Modern Language Quarterly*, i (1940), p. 45.

III. 1 *thing*] *things* A T.

IV–V. An imitation of Petrarch's 'Zefiro torna'. Compare Yonge 1588, LII–LIII, and see Obertello, p. 137.

IX–X. From Spenser's *The Fairy Queen*, Bk. V, canto viii, stanzas 1–2.
    18 *captive*] enthrall.

XI–XII. Sir John Shelton was second son of Sir Ralph Shelton of Shelton in Norfolk. He was present at the sacking of Cadiz and was knighted shortly afterwards. His younger brother married a daughter of Sir Robert Jermyn of Rushbrook, the patron of Kirbye the madrigal composer.
    3 *close*] cadence.

XIII. Cf. Bodleian MS. Rawl. poet. 117, f. 196ᵛ.
    5 *Smithfield Fair*] The famous Bartholomew Fair, which was instituted *c.* 1123 by Rahere, formerly the king's jester, and subsequently founder and first Prior of St. Bartholomew's Priory. It was originally a trading fair, but by the beginning of the seventeenth century had lost its business character and was mainly devoted to sports, shows, executions, and feasting. Cf. Ben Jonson's *Bartholomew Fair*. The fair was abolished in 1855.

XIV. From Spenser's *The Fairy Queen*, Bk. V, canto vii, stanza 1.

XV. From Spenser's *The Fairy Queen*, Bk. VI, canto viii, stanza 1.

XVII. This and XVIII would appear to belong to the same poem.
    6 *man*] In the repetitions of the final phrase the word is sometimes *men*.

XVIII. See note on XVII.

XXI. 6 *vade*] An obsolete variant of *fade* (mainly used figuratively—to vanish, pass away) very common *c.* 1530–1630. It is generally found as an intransitive verb: cf. Spenser, *The Ruins of Rome*, line 279: 'Her power dispersed through all the world did vade.'

EAST, 1604

Copies: Folger Shakespeare Library and British Museum.   *Dedicatee*: Sir John Crofts.

II–III. Poem by Nicholas Breton, first printed in *The Honourable Entertainment Given to the Queen's Majesty . . . at Elvetham . . . . 1591.* Three editions of this publication appeared in 1591. In the first edition the poem is entitled 'The Ploughman's Song', which is probably an error. In the third edition the title becomes 'The Three Men's Song, sung the third morning, under her Majesty's Gallery window'. The three men were 'three excellent musicians, who being disguised in ancient country attire, did greet her with a pleasant song of Corydon and Phyllida, made in three parts of purpose.' The progress has been reprinted in J. Nichols's *Progresses and Public Processions of Queen Elizabeth*, 1823, iii, p. 101, and R. W. Bond's *The Complete Works of John Lyly*, 1902, i, p. 431. The poem was also printed in *England's Helicon*, 1600 (Rollins, i, p. 27). Musical settings by John Wilson are contained in two Bodleian Library manuscripts, MS. Don. c. 57, f. 77, and MS. Mus. b. l., f. 135, and also in Henry Playford's *Select Musical Ayres and Dialogues*, 1653, iii, p. 27. Day and Murrie 1776.

    4 *Whenas*] *Whereas* all parts.

IV. Also set by Weelkes (1597, VIII).

VI. 2] In the original edition this line is freely expanded in all three parts by the interpolation of extra words.

XVII. A resetting of Watson 1590, XX (see note).
    2 *besides*] Possibly a misprint for *beside*.

XVIII–XIX. By Chidiock Tichborne. Also set by Mundy (1594, XVII) and Alison (1606, IX–X). See note on Alison's setting.

XXI–XXII. Set also by Cavendish (1598, XIX–XX). See also Vautor 1619, XI, in which lines 7–10 of this lyric occur as lines 3–6, preceded by two lines which are derived from lines 1–4.
    9 *meed*] reward.

XXIII. From Robert Greene's *Menaphon*, 1589. The first of the five stanzas of 'Menaphon's Song in his Bed'.
    3 *Tire on*] feed upon, prey upon.

EAST, 1606

Copy: British Museum.   *Dedicatee*: Sir Thomas Gerard.

VI. 3 *My jewel*] *My sweet jewel* C.

XIII–XIV. Words from Yonge 1588, XXX (see note). Also set by Kirbye (1597, IX–X).

XIX. 2 *stound*] a short space of time.

XX. A resetting of Yonge 1588, XXVII (see note).

XXI. This poem was previously set by East as his contribution to Morley's anthology *The Triumphs of Oriana*, 1601. See the note thereon concerning the attribution of the poem to John Lyly. In this later version much the same musical material is employed, but in somewhat elaborated form.

XXII. For other tobacco songs see Hume 1605, III; Ravenscroft 1614, XII; Weelkes 1608, VI. In the early seventeenth century the craze for tobacco was incredibly extravagant, prompting severe censure from James I in his *A Counterblast to Tobacco*, 1604.

EAST, 1610

Copy: British Museum.   *Dedicatee*: Sir Henry Willoughby.

IV–V. 8 *wert*] C, *was* A T B Q.

VI. 2 *fere*] companion, mate; from Old English *geféra*.

VII–XIV. These eight instrumental fancies are entitled as follows:

VII.	Desperavi.	XI.	Credidi.
VIII.	Peccavi.	XII.	Vixi.
IX.	Vidi.	XIII.	Triumphavi.
X.	Penitet.	XIV.	Amavi.

XVIII. A resetting of the translation of the madrigal by Bicci in Yonge's second *Musica Transalpina* collection, 1597, XXIII.

XIX. Also set by Weelkes (1597, XX).

XX. A resetting (with some variants) of the text of the madrigal by Ferrabosco in Yonge 1588, I (see note). Cf. also the first line of Kirbye 1597, I.

XXI. A resetting of the translation of Vecchi's 'Deh dimmi vita mia' in Morley's *Madrigals . . . selected*, 1598, XI.

XXII. A resetting of Yonge 1588, LI (see note).

EAST, 1618

Editions: One of the sets of part-books consulted was printed in 1618, the other in 1619. A comparison has revealed no differences in the text.

Copies: 1618, Royal College of Music, London; 1619, British Museum.

Dedicatee: Robert, Earl of Essex.

I. Also set by Bennet (1599, VIII).

V. Also set by Bennet (1599, X) with minor variants.

VI. Set again by East as XXIV in this collection, and also by Bateson (1604, VI).

IX. 2 *leasing*] lying, falsehood; from the Old English *léasung*. Cf. Psalm v, verse 6.

XIV. 9–10] Compare Kirbye 1597, XXII–XXIII, 6–10.

XV. These are the opening lines of 'The Humble Suit of a Sinner' by John Marckant, printed in the Sternhold and Hopkins metrical psalter. Also set by Mundy (1594, XIV, with four more lines) and Ravenscroft (1609a, XLV, with eight more lines).

XVII–XVIII. 3 *are a-ringing*] *are now a-ringing* C Q.

xx. Also set by Tomkins (1622, XIX) and Weelkes (British Museum, Add. MSS. 29372–77).

EAST'S FIFTH AND SEVENTH SETS OF BOOKS

The contents of *The Fift Set of Books* (1618) are described by the composer as being 'as apt for viols as voices'. But despite this clear indication that East regarded the compositions as suitable for vocal performance, only a few words are given at the beginning of each composition. Most of these appear to be titles, but some of them may be the opening words of the first line. Nowhere, however, are the texts given in complete form, and with one possible exception (XI) they are not to be found in any other source. This is not the only instance of this peculiar arrangement: East himself repeated it in his *The Seventh Set of Books*, 1638 (see below), and Thomas Whythorne adopted the same procedure in the secular items of his *Duos*, 1590.

The titles or incipits of *The Fift Set of Books* are as follows:

I.	Trip it lightly.	VIII.	Sweet lady stay.	XV.	Come let's be gone.
II.	Turn round about.	IX.	What art thou.	XVI.	I cannot stay.
III.	Fly not away.	X.	No haste but good.	XVII.	Fear not the end.
IV.	Softly for falling.	XI.	White as lilies.	XVIII.	Lively my hearts.
V.	My lovely Phyllis.	XII.	Do what you can.	XIX.	My time is spent.
VI.	And I as well as thou.	XIII.	Mourning I die.	XX.	Smooth and soft.
VII.	Love is a toy.	XIV.	Stay yet awhile.		

The title of XI may refer to 'White as lilies was her face' set by Dowland (1600, XV). See also note on Morley 1600, XV.

East's *The Seventh Set of Books*, 1638, consists of eight 'Duos', nine 'Fancies of 3 Parts', and twelve 'Fancies of 4 Parts'. All have titles, the 'Fancies of 3 Parts' being named after the nine muses. The 'Fancies of 4 Parts' were intended to 'be as well sung as played', but no complete texts are supplied with the music.

EAST, 1624

Copies: British Museum and Royal College of Music.   *Dedicatee*: John, Bishop of Lincoln.

East's *The Sixt Set of Books* consists entirely of church music, but there is also 'added in a vacant page, before these other songs, an air of a canzo, composed in honour of the most illustrious princess, the Lady Elizabeth &c.' The words, by Sir Henry Wotton, are printed in *Reliquiae Wottonianae* (2nd edition, 1654, p. 493) with the heading 'On his Mistress, the Queen of Bohemia'. Day and Murrie 4096.

FARMER, 1599

Copy: Huntington.   *Dedicatee*: Edward de Vere, Earl of Oxford.

I. From Constable's *Diana* sonnets, 1592, Decade v. No. 4, 9–14.

II. From Daniel's *Delia* sonnets, stanza 1 of the final ode. Complete ode set by Handford (1609, XII).

IV–V. A resetting of the translation of Ferrabosco's madrigal 'Donna, l'ardente fiamma' in Yonge's second *Musica Transalpina* volume, 1597, XII–XIII. Also printed in *A Poetical Rhapsody*, 1602 (Rollins, i, p. 217).

VI. From Bartholomew Griffin's *Fidessa* sonnets, 1596, XLVI, 9–14.

IX. From Bartholomew Griffin's *Fidessa* sonnets, 1596, XIII, 1–4 and 13–14.

X. Lines 1–6 of a poem entitled 'The lover deceived writes to his Lady' in Thomas Howell's *Pleasant Sonnets and Pretty Pamphlets* [1568].

XII. 1 *glosses*] Here used figuratively: fair semblances, pretexts.

FARNABY, 1598

Copies: Huntington and British Museum.   *Dedicatee*: Master Ferdinando Heaburn [= Heybourne].

I. A translation of Angelo Grillo's 'Quand'io miro le rose' (*Parte prima delle rime . . . 1589*, p. 75). Compare another translation used twice by Wilbye (1598, X and XXIV): 'Lady, when I behold the roses sprouting'. See also Thomas Lodge, *The Life and Death of William Longbeard* (1593): 'When I admire the rose' (sig. C).

VI. 1 *Pearce . . . Petronel*] Compare VII, line 1.

   6 *Primrose*] Occasionally used in the 16th century with a superlative sense, meaning 'first' or 'best'.

   6 *pricked*] In addition to its sexual connotations, the word is here used in the sense, now obsolete, of 'dressed', 'attired'.

VII. 1 *Pearce . . . Petronella*] Compare VI, line 1.

   2 *La Siamise and La Duncella*] Two dance-tunes so named, and spelt *La shy myze* (sc. *la chemise*) and *La doune cella* (sc. *donnicella*), with a third called *La bounette* (sc. *bonnette*), occur together as Nos. 13, 14, and 15 in Thomas Mulliner's organ book (British Museum, Add. 30513), compiled in the mid-sixteenth century. See Denis Stevens (ed.), *The Mulliner Book* (*Musica Britannica*, i), 1951, pp. 11–12. It may be that Farnaby, who was primarily a composer of instrumental music, knew of this manuscript. Alternatively, these may have been dances that were commonly grouped together.

IX. Compare the sonnet sometimes attributed to Donne, 'Madam, that flea that crept between your breasts' (H. J. C. Grierson, *The Poems of John Donne*, Oxford, 1912, i, p. 459).

XII. A resetting of the text set by both Lassus (XIX) and Ferrabosco (XX) in Yonge 1588 (see notes thereon). Byrd also composed two settings of a similar poem (1588, XXIX, and 1589, VIII).

XV. There is a keyboard transcription of this canzonet in *The FitzWilliam Virginal Book* (ed. J. A. Fuller Maitland and W. Barclay Squire, ii, p. 330).

XVIII. 5 *floted*] skimmed.

XIX. 6 *Danuby*] B, *Daunby* C A T.

XX. 1 *Consture*] construe, interpret, explain.

XXI. 5 *force*] See note on Byrd, 1588, XI. 2.

GIBBONS, 1612

Copy: British Museum.   *Dedicatee*: Sir Christopher Hatton.

I. Day and Murrie 2936.

II. Stanza 5 of a poem entitled *The Passion of a Discontented Mind*, published in 1601. Stanzas 1, 2, and 11 were set by Dowland (1612, X). Concerning the authorship see note on Dowland 1612, X.

    4 *find*] Probably a misprint for *seek*.

III–VI. By Joshua Sylvester (ed. A. B. Grosart, ii, p. 341). Compare Byrd 1588, XI.

    3 *reck*] *reake* 1612.

    10 *sound*] swound, swoon.

IX. A translation of Guarini's 'O come se' gentile' (*Rime*, 1598, f. 83ᵛ). The same translation, with some variants, was set by Vautor (1619, XVIII). Another translation was set by Danyel (1606, II). See Obertello, pp. 408 and 519–20.

X–XI. From Spenser's *The Fairy Queen*, Bk. III, canto i, stanza 49.

XIII. This poem is an imitation of Plato's epigram Ἡ σοβαρὸν γελάσασα καθ' Ἑλλάδος, ἡ νὸν ἐραστῶν (*Greek Anthology*, vi. l). Cf. also Ausonius's translation (Loeb Classical Library, *Ausonius*, ii, p. 194): 'Lais anus Veneri speculum dico: dignum habeat se'.

XIV. This poem is ascribed to Raleigh in several manuscripts, and appears anonymously in numerous others. British Museum MS. Harl. 7332, f. 125 states that he wrote it 'the same morning he was executed', but as it was published in Gibbons's volume six years before his execution that statement is manifestly incorrect. See Agnes M. C. Latham, *The Poems of Sir Walter Raleigh* (London, 1951), pp. 51–52 and 143–5.

XV. Also set by Dowland (1612, II), beginning 'Sweet, stay awhile; why will you rise?' and with a second stanza. It has sometimes been attributed to Donne; see note on Dowland 1612, II.

XVII–XIX. 15 *so*] *thus* C.

XX. Cf. Virgil, *Eclogue II*, lines 17–18:

        O formose puer, nimium ne crede colori:
        alba ligustra cadunt, viccinia nigra leguntur.

    6 *primit*] privet.

HILTON, 1627

    Copy: British Museum.   *Dedicatee*: Dr. William Heather.

HOLBORNE, 1597

Copy: Royal College of Music, London.   *Dedicatee*: Thomas, Lord Burgh.

This little set of compositions by William Holborne was included in his brother Anthony's *The Cittern School*, 1597.

II. 1 *Bonny-boots*] See notes on Morley 1597, XXI, and Morley 1601, VIII.

    4 *bad*] C, *hard* [? = *heard*] A B.

III. Also set, with some variants, by Pilkington (1613, VIII).

V. 3 *O peevish*] *O (most) peevish* C.

JONES, 1607

Copy: British Museum, Cantus and Bassus part-books only. These are the only two part-books now extant, but several of the madrigals have been preserved complete in two manuscripts: a MS. choir-book in the Royal Library, Brussels (VII, VIII, IX, X, XIII, XIV, XXII), and Bodleian Library MSS. Mus. f. 25–28 (XXV–XXVI).

Dedicatee: Robert, Earl of Salisbury.

I. Printed in *A Poetical Rhapsody*, 1602 (Rollins, i, p. 135).

II. Printed in *A Poetical Rhapsody*, 1602 (Rollins, i, p. 140), ending with motto 'Laudo quod lugeo'.

III–IV. 5 *she, like*] *she, most like* C.

V. By Francis Davison. Printed in *A Poetical Rhapsody*, 1602 (Rollins, i, p. 65), with seven more lines. There is also a lute song setting of these words in Bodleian MS. Mus. Sch. F. 575, pp. 4–5. See Obertello, pp. 409 and 520–1.

VI. Also set by Peerson 1620, VII.
     1 *love, then*] *love, my love then* B.

IX. 4] During the repetitions of this line the words are rearranged *Your hens look well you tread* in some parts.

XII. This doggerel verse is simply an expansion of the rubric commonly employed by the madrigalists at the conclusion of each group of compositions written for a certain number of vocal parts, e.g. 'Here endeth the songs of three [four, five, etc.] parts'. There are five compositions for four voices in this volume.

XVI–XVII. Poem by Campian, and set to music by him (Rosseter, 1601, Pt. I, VI). Also printed in *A Poetical Rhapsody*, 1602 (Rollins, i, p. 216).
     5 *But*] *And* B.

XVIII. By Francis Davison. Printed in *A Poetical Rhapsody*, 1602 (Rollins, i, p. 87). Translated from Guarini, *Il pastor fido*, II. ii:

> *Silvio.* Che cosa è questo amore?
> *Dorinda.* S'i' miro il tuo bel viso,
> Amore è un paradiso;
> Ma s'i' miro il mio core,
> È un infernal ardore.

XIX–XX. Poem by Francis Davison. Printed in *A Poetical Rhapsody*, 1602 (Rollins, i, p. 66).
     6 *Chameleon-like my life's maintained*] *Chameleon-like my life maintained* C B. That is, on air instead of food. See Pliny's *Natural History*, XI. 31.

XXI. 1 *haste*] *fly* C.

XXII–XXIV. Poem by Francis Davison. Printed in *A Poetical Rhapsody*, 1602 (Rollins, i, p. 68) with one more stanza.

XXV–XXVI. Poem by Francis Davison. Printed in *A Poetical Rhapsody*, 1602 (Rollins, i, p. 89).

KIRBYE, 1597

Copy: Huntington.   *Dedicatees*: Anne and Francis Jermyn, daughters of Sir Robert Jermyn.

I. 1] Compare first lines of Yonge 1588, 1, and East 1610, XX.

II. Also set by Wilbye (1598, IX).

VI. The same words are set in XXIV.

IX–X. Words from Yonge 1588, XXX (see note). Also set by East (1606, XIII–XIV).

XII–XIII. 5] This line may have been interpolated by the composer.
6 *I be*] *I myself be* 1597.

XVI. 4 *diseased*] lacking ease, troubled.
8 *mends*] reparation.

XX. 1] Compare first line of Wilbye 1609, XIV.

XXII–XXIII. From Spenser's *The Shepherd's Calendar*, November eclogue, lines 53–62
and 173–82.
14 *light*] *height . . . light* C¹.
15 *height*] *light* C¹ T.

LICHFILD, 1613

Copies: British Museum and Royal College of Music, London.   *Dedicatee*: Lady
Cheyney.

II. Stanza 1 of a poem set by Ferrabosco (1609, XVII) and Jones (1605, IV).
1 *seek*] *look* Jones's setting.

III–IV. Daphne figures prominently in Lichfild's madrigals: compare VIII, IX, X, XII,
and XIX.

VII. 2 *glose*] shine, gleam.

VIII. See note on III–IV.

IX. See note on III–IV.

X. See note on III–IV.

XII. See note on III–IV.

XV. 6 *I change my note and say*] Probably interpolated by the composer.

XVI–XVII. Also set by Wilbye (1609, XXVI).

XVIII. Compare Donne's 'Sweetest love, I do not go', lines 17–24 (Gardner, p. 31).
1 *Injurious hours*] Cf. Drayton, *The Legend of Great Cromwell*, line 145, 'Injurious
time'.

XIX. See note on III–IV.

MORLEY, 1593

Editions: There are four extant editions, dated 1593, 1602, 1606, and 1631. A comparison of all editions has revealed no significant variants in the text. However, see
note on XVIII. The last four pieces, XXI–XXIV, do not appear in the edition of 1593.

Copies: 1593, 1606, and 1631, British Museum; 1602, Cambridge University Library
(Bassus part-book only).

Dedicatee: Mary, Countess of Pembroke.

Morley was often extremely free in his handling of the texts of his compositions,
interpolating exclamations and epithets, and frequently rearranging the order of the
words. Nor do the same alterations always appear in all the parts; often, different
alterations occur in each part. The first twenty canzonets in this publication are a
particularly striking example of Morley's freedom in handling his texts, and in many

cases it is extremely difficult to reconstruct from the numerous variant readings anything that could confidently be regarded as a 'basic' text. Indeed, one suspects that in some cases there was never any such thing. For this reason the reconstructions here presented are of an extremely tentative nature, and no attempt has been made to record the numerous variant readings in the notes. It should be stressed that we have frequently adopted a metrically irregular text when, in our opinion, this represents most accurately the text as found in the original editions.

I. Morley included an instrumental arrangement of this canzonet, called 'Join Hands', in his *Consort Lessons*, 1599 (ed. S. Beck, 1959, p. 143).

VI. 9 *sheen*] beautiful.

XIII. 1 *recureless*] incurable.

XVI. See Obertello, p. 105.

XVIII. 6 *yon*] B in 1602 and C in 1606, *you* A B in 1606, *you* C A B in 1593 and 1631.

XX. 3 *yon*] *you* all editions.
  6 *bride-lace*] A piece of gold silk or other lace used to bind up the sprigs of rosemary worn at Elizabethan weddings.
  9 *ye*] *she* C A all editions.
  11 *yon*] *you* all editions.

XXI–XXIV. These four ballets do not appear in 1593.

MORLEY, 1594

Editions: There are two extant editions, dated 1594 and 1600. A comparison has revealed no significant differences in the text (see, however, the note on IV). The last two items, XXI and XXII, occur only in the edition of 1600.

Copies: 1594, Huntington; 1600, British Museum.   *Dedicatee*: none.

I. A translation of Livio Celiano's 'Nel vis'ha un vago Aprile', set as a canzonet by Vecchi (I a 6, 1587, XV). Compare the following lines in Robert Greene's *Perymedes*, 1588:

> Fair is my love for April in her face;
>   Her lovely breasts September claims his part;
> And lordly July in her eyes takes place,
>   But cold December dwelleth in her heart.

Cf. British Museum MS. Add. 15117, f. 9ᵛ.
  2 *July*] Always pronounced *Júly* at this time.

II. Printed in *England's Helicon*, 1600 (Rollins, i, p. 135).
  9 *relying*] Resting upon for support.

IV. A translation of the text of Lassus's madrigal 'Poi che 'l mio largo pianto' (*Musica Divina*, 1583).
  2 *bred*] *breed* A and T in 1594.

V. 2 *stay*] *slay* both editions.

VII. Poem printed in *England's Helicon*, 1600 (Rollins, i, p. 157).

VIII. 1 *fierce*] *false* C in both editions.

XIV. Compare the poem set by Ferretti in Yonge 1588, XXXIII.
  2 *gloses*] flattering words.

XVII. Poem printed in *England's Helicon*, 1600 (Rollins, i, p. 198).

XVIII. 6 *now for our town*] Apparently a catch-phrase shouted by the onlookers to encourage their own representatives in the dance. Compare Weelkes 1597, XII, line 5.

    8 *swelt*] swelter.

XXI and XXII. Added in the 1600 edition.

MORLEY, 1595*a*

Editions: Two are extant, dated 1595 and 1619. A comparison has revealed no significant differences in the text. As Bruce Pattison has pointed out (*Music and Poetry of the English Renaissance*, pp. 97–98), an entry in the Stationers' Register, dated 6 December 1596, records that an Italian version of the first edition was also published: '8. Of Thomas Morley, The First Book of Canzonets to 2 Voices with the same set also in Italian' (E. Arber, *A Transcript of the Registers of the Company of Stationers of London*, iii, p. 76). No copy of this Italian version appears to have survived. Morley's *The First Book of Ballets* (1595) was also published in both English and Italian (see note thereon).

Copies: 1595 and 1619, British Museum.   *Dedicatee*: Lady Peryam.

The texts of all but one of the vocal items in this publication have been identified as translations or imitations of Italian poems. In the following notes the source of the Italian is given. J. E. Uhler, in his facsimile edition (1957) suggests that the poems form a narrative sequence.

The following are for instruments only: IV, VI, IX, XII, XIV, XVI, XVIII, XX, XXI.

I. Anerio I a 4, 1586, I: 'Gitene canzonette'.

II. Anerio I a 4, 1586, XX: 'Quando la vaga Flori.' Anerio's music and the English translation reappear in Morley's *Canzonets . . . selected*, 1597, XVI.

III. Anerio I a 4, 1586, II: 'Su questi fior t'aspetto.'

V. Italian source not known.
    4 *other*] *either* both editions.

VII. Anerio I a 4, 1586, XIII: 'Miracolo d'amore.' Anerio's music and the English translation are also printed in Morley's *Canzonets . . . selected*, 1597, XIV.

VIII. Vecchi III a 4, 1585, XXI: 'Ecco novello Amor.'

X. Obertello (pp. 377 and 507) suggests Vecchi's 'Deh lascia Filli' as the source of this poem.
    2 *tormenting*] *lamenting* C in both editions.

XI. Anerio I a 4, 1586, X: 'Caggia fuoco dal cielo.'

XIII. Anerio I a 4, 1586, III: 'Flori dolce ben mio.' Another translation appears with Anerio's music in Morley's *Canzonets . . . selected*, 1597 ('Flora, fair love, I languish').

XV. Felis IV a 5, 1585, I: 'Di vaghe fila d'oro.' Compare Bateson 1618, XXVII.

XVII. Anerio I a 4, 1586, VII: 'O tu che mi dai pene.'

XIX. Anerio I a 4, 1586, V: 'Io morirei d'affanno.' Morley's *Canzonets . . . selected*, 1597, contains another translation, beginning 'Fain would I die', with music by Viadana.
    1 *recureless*] incurable.

XXI. Entitled 'La Tortorella' in the indexes to both editions.

MORLEY, 1595*b*

Editions: Two English editions are extant, dated 1595 and 1600. A comparison reveals no significant differences in the text; see, however, the note on XII. Like Morley 1595*a* this set of ballets was also issued in 1595 in an Italian edition, copies of which are extant. A German edition was published by Valentin Haussmann at Nuremberg in 1609.

Copies: 1595 and 1600, British Museum.   *Dedicatee*: Sir Robert Cecil.

The sources from which most of the poems in the Italian edition were taken have been identified, and are listed in the following notes. Obertello (pp. 346–72) prints the Italian poems together with the English versions.

I. Gastoldi, *Balletti*, 1591, V: 'Vezzosette ninfe.'

II. Gastoldi, *Balletti*, 1591, III: 'Viver lieto voglio.'

III. Vecchi, *Selva*, 1590: 'So ben mi c'ha bon tempo.' Instrumental version in Philip Rosseter's *Lessons for Consort*, 1609. Day and Murrie 2392.
    12 *barley-break*] An old country game played by three couples holding hands. One couple in the den, which was called 'hell', had to catch the other four players, who were allowed to 'break' and change partners if hard pressed. Cf. Morley 1597, IV; Sidney, *Arcadia*, I, Lamon's song (Ringler, p. 242); and Suckling, *Poems*, 1646, 24, 'Love, Reason, Hate, did once bespeak'.

IV. Gastoldi, *Balletti*, 1591, II: 'A lieta vita.' Cf. *The Knight of the Burning Pestle*, V. I:

> *Merrythought*. It's a brave boy. Can'st thou sing?
> *Boy*. Yes sir, I can sing, but 'tis not so necessary at this time.
> *Mer*. Sing we and chant it
>   Whilst love doth grant it.

V. Stanza 1 only is from Ferretti III a 5, 1570: 'Amore l'altro giorno.'

VI. Gastoldi, *Balletti*, 1591, XV: 'Possa morir chi t'ama'.

VII. Gastoldi, *Balletti*, 1591, XII: 'Questa dolce sirena.'

VIII. Stanza 1 only is from Orologio I a 3, 1593, 'Madonna mia gentile.'

IX. Gastoldi, *Balletti*, 1591, IV: 'Piacer gioia.'

X. Gastoldi, *Balletti*, 1591, VIII: 'Al piacer a la gioia.'

XI. Trofeo I a 6, 1589: 'Al suon d'una sampogna.'

XII. 'La bella ninfa mia'; source not known.
    3 *By*] *My* all parts.
    4 *her*] *my* C (1595), corrected to *her* 1600.

XIII. Gastoldi, *Balletti*, 1591, VII: 'Vaghe ninfe'. Morley's Italian version begins 'Ninfe bella.'

XIV. Marenzio II a 3, 1585: 'A la strada.'

XV. Marenzio I a 3, 1584: 'Le rose frond'è fiori.'

XVI. Marenzio I a 3, 1584: 'Al primo vostro sguardo.'

XVII. 'Inamorato sono, O vita mia'; source not known.

XVIII. Marenzio I a 3, 1584: 'Fuggirò tant' Amore.'

XIX. Ferretti II a 5, 1569: 'Non mi date tormento.'
    2 *it skill not*] it avails not.

XX. Ferretti II a 5, 1569: 'Non dubitar.'

XXI. Croce II a 5, 1592: 'Filli morir vorrei.' This dialogue is set to music by Morley for seven voices, of which the upper three are labelled 'Phyllis's choir', and the lower four 'Amyntas's choir'.

MORLEY, 1597

Copy: British Museum.   *Dedicatee*: Sir George Carey.

Nos. I–XVI were published with a rather makeshift lute part so that they could be sung as solo songs.

I. 2 *Bonny-boots*] See notes on XXI in this publication and on Morley 1601, VIII.
    4 *kindly*] *blindly* C.

II. Cf. Shakespeare, *Venus and Adonis*, lines 55–60.

IV. 2 *barley-break*] See note on Morley 1595*b*, III.

V. Compare Farnaby 1598, V.

VIII. Also set by Pilkington (1624, I).

IX. 1 *Bonny-boots*] See note on Morley 1601, VIII.

XI. 2 *yollow*] *yellow* C.
    6 *humane*] Human, as opposed to *the divinest* of line 3, though perhaps also in the sense of 'kind'. This was the usual spelling at the time.

XIII. This poem seems to refer back to Morley 1595*b*, XVII.
    6 *pang*] This use as a verb meaning 'to afflict with pain' is very rare.

XVII. Also set by Pilkington (1613, II).

XVIII. Also set by Pilkington (1624, IV) with some variants.
    12 *her*] *thee* C, *death* B.

XXI. Henry Noel was a member of a prominent Leicestershire family, being the second son of Andrew Noel, M.P. for Dalby, Leicestershire, by his second wife Elizabeth. According to the Herald's Visitation of Leicestershire of 1619 he was a gentleman pensioner to the Queen. He seems to have possessed all the attributes of the model courtier and to have been a favourite of the Queen (see the accounts of him by Anthony à Wood, *Athenae Oxonienses*, 1691–2, i, coll. 769, and Thomas Fuller, *Worthies*, 1840, ii, pp. 243–4). Morley's elegy implies that he was a singer and lover of music, and Wood asserts that he was 'well skilled in music'. John Dowland composed seven hymns for his funeral in 1597 (ed. E. H. Fellowes, *Tudor Church Music*, Octavo edition, 2nd series, Nos. 79–80), and Thomas Weelkes also composed an elegy in remembrance of him (1600, Pt. II, x). Dowland's *Lacrimae*, 1604, contains a piece entitled 'M[aster]. Henry Noel his Galliard'. It may well be that Noel was the 'Bonny-boots' who figures in a number of madrigals, and whose death is lamented in I and IX in this collection, and in II in Holborne 1597. Bonny-boots, like Noel, seems to have been a popular figure, musical, and a favourite both of musicians and of the Queen. For a complete list of madrigals referring to Bonny-boots see note on Morley 1601, VIII.

MORLEY, 1601

Editions: There are two extant editions, both dated 1601. Variant readings are recorded in the following notes, the most important concerning xx, which has a completely different text in the second edition.

Copies: 1601*a*, British Museum K.3.i.15; 1601*b*, Bodleian Library, Malone 974.

Dedicatee: Charles Howard, Earl of Nottingham.

The Triumphs of Oriana is an anthology of madrigals in honour of Queen Elizabeth I, compiled by Thomas Morley. Its starting-point was a madrigal by Croce, 'Ove tra l'herb' ei fiori', contributed to a similar Italian anthology, *Il Trionfo di Dori*, first published in Venice in 1592. The last two lines of Croce's madrigal are as follows:

> Poi concordi seguir ninfe e pastori:
> Viva la bella Dori.

When Nicholas Yonge included Croce's madrigal in his second *Musica Transalpina* collection, 1597, he translated these lines as

> Then sang the shepherds and nymphs of Diana:
> Long live fair Oriana.

Thus it was that a madrigal in praise of 'La Dori', the bride of a Venetian nobleman, Leonardo Sanudo, was adapted to do honour to Queen Elizabeth ('Oriana'). Four years later Morley adopted this couplet as the characteristic refrain which appears in all the madrigals in *The Triumphs of Oriana*. One of Morley's own contributions to the anthology is in fact a resetting of Yonge's translation of Croce's madrigal, and the music too is a re-working of Croce's.

It may well be that *The Triumphs of Oriana* was compiled for some special occasion. In the preface to his revision of E. H. Fellowes's edition of the music (*The English Madrigalists*, xxxii, 1963) Thurston Dart suggests that the occasion may have been the Maying celebrations which took place at the Highgate home of Sir William Cornwallis, 1601, and which were designed to divert the Queen from her melancholy after the recent execution of the Earl of Essex. Dart further observes that the dedicatee of *The Triumphs* was one of Essex's judges, and suggests that it may have been he who instigated the idea of the anthology. Further observations on the anthology are contained in an article 'Queen Elizabeth I as Oriana', by Roy C. Strong (*Studies in the Renaissance*, vi [1959], p. 251).

0. Michael East's contribution to the anthology arrived too late to be printed and numbered with the rest of the madrigals; it was therefore printed on the back of the title-page with the note: 'This song, being sent too late, and all my other printed, I placed it before the rest rather than leave it out'. East was more fortunate than Bateson, whose contribution arrived too late to be included at all (see note on Bateson 1604, 0). East later published another setting of this poem (see note on East 1606, XXI).

In the first edition the letters 'I.L.' appear under this madrigal in the Cantus, Tenor, and Quintus part-books. These are probably the initials of the author of the lyric, and may well stand for 'John Lyly', the Elizabethan dramatist and poet. The same initials are found under XVIII in all first edition part-books except the Cantus. It would also seem likely that this John Lyly is the same as the John Lisley who composed the music of XXII.

I. In the second edition this poem is also used in xx, instead of 'Bright Phoebus'.

II. It is noteworthy that lines 1–10 are unrhymed.

III. This poem was also set by Hunt (see xvi), who, however, did not use the first line. It would seem, therefore, that Ellis Gibbons added this on his own initiative, thereby beginning his madrigal as it ends, with 'Long live fair Oriana'.

VI. 2 *Lavoltos*] A lavolto was a lively dance for two persons. *-tapstred*] tapestried.

VIII. I *Bonny-boots*] References to this character occur in the following madrigals: Holborne 1597, II; Morley 1597, I and IX; Morley 1601, XXIV. It is noteworthy that according to this madrigal Bonny-boots is still alive, whereas it is evident from the others that he died in 1597 or earlier. The question of Bonny-boots's identity is discussed briefly in the note on Morley 1597, XXI.
   5 *sing requested*] *sing were requested* A T B (both editions).

X. 7 *amaltheias*] cornucopias. According to some traditions Amaltheia was the goat which suckled the infant Zeus, and according to others a nymph who fed Zeus with the milk of a goat. One of the goat's horns later became a symbol of plenty. *twenty*] In line 5 of xv Oriana is described as 'The fairest Queen of twenty'.

XI. Cavendish first published this madrigal in his 1598 publication (XXIV). Thus he was the first composer to adopt the Oriana refrain after it had appeared in Yonge's second *Musica Transalpina* volume, 1597.
   4 *beautiest of beauties*] *beauties of beauties* all parts, both editions. But *beautiest of beauties* in Cavendish 1598, XXIV.

XIII. 9 *roses*] *flowers* T Q (both editions).

XV. 2 *dight*] decked, dressed.
   5] Cf. x, line 7.
   7 *virgin*] *virgins* Q of 1601*a*, and T B Q Sx of 1601*b*.

XVI. The same text is set in III, with an extra line at the beginning.

XVIII. John Milton, the composer of this madrigal, was the father of the poet.

XIX. 6 *to sporting*] *a-sporting* C B (both editions).

XX. These words appear in 1601*a*, but in 1601*b* the words are changed to those used by Norcome (i). The music, however, remains exactly the same. A possible explanation is that by some accident both Norcome and Kirbye set the same text to music, and that for the first edition Morley fitted a new text to Kirbye's music to avoid the duplication, but that for the second edition Kirbye insisted on the original text being restored.

XXII. The question of John Lisley's identity is discussed briefly in the note to the opening, unnumbered, madrigal in this collection.
   I *Minerva sweetly singeth*] Sx, *Minerva singeth* A T B Q, (*sweet*) *Minerva singeth* C. These variants occur in both editions.

   3 *summons*] *summoned* C A B (both editions).

XXIII. This is a resetting of Yonge's translation of Croce's 'Ove tra l'herb' ei fiori', the madrigal which provided the immediate model for *The Triumphs of Oriana* (see introductory notes). The original Italian poem is by G. Belloni.
   8 *mountain*] The Cantus part of 1601*b* has *mountains*.

XXIV. 1 *bird*] With a capital B in original editions. Some commentators have suggested that an allusion to William Byrd is intended.

3 *Bonny-boots*] See notes on VIII and Morley 1597, XXI.

MUNDY, 1594

Copy: Bodleian Library.   *Dedicatee*: Robert, Earl of Essex.

II. This metrical version of Psalm lxix is similar to John Hopkins's version in the Sternhold and Hopkins metrical psalter.

III. From Thomas Norton's version of Psalm cxvii in the Sternhold and Hopkins metrical psalter. Mundy's text differs in some details.

1 *Lord*] *world* Sternhold–Hopkins.

3 *ye*] *the* S T.

IV–V. Sternhold's version of Psalm cxxviii in the Sternhold and Hopkins metrical psalter, with several variants.

VII. Hopkins's version of Psalm xlvii in the Sternhold and Hopkins metrical psalter, with several variants.

8 *thankful*] *skilful* T B.

VIII. Stanza 1 of John Marckant's 'The Lamentation of a Sinner' printed in the Sternhold and Hopkins metrical psalter. The same text, with a second stanza, was set by Ravenscroft (1609*a*, XLVIII).

IX. From John Hopkins's version of Psalm xcv in the Sternhold and Hopkins metrical psalter.

X. 1] Compare the first lines of Ravenscroft 1609*b*, VII, and Bartlet 1606, X, and see Chappell–Wooldridge, i, pp. 141–2.

2 *bear the bell*] take first place; from the custom of hanging a bell round the neck of the leader of a flock of animals. Cf. Weelkes 1608, XXV, line 6.

XII. This poem would seem to refer to Queen Elizabeth I.

XIII. From William Whittingham's version of Psalm cxxx in the Sternhold and Hopkins metrical psalter, with several variants.

XIV. Stanza 1 of John Marckant's 'The Humble Suit of a Sinner' printed in the Sternhold and Hopkins metrical psalter. See the settings of East (1618, XV) and Ravenscroft (1609*a*, XLV).

XV. From Thomas Norton's version of Psalm cxlix in the Sternhold and Hopkins metrical psalter, with several variants.

XVI. From Thomas Sternhold's version of Psalm xxv in the Sternhold and Hopkins metrical psalter.

XVII. Also set by Alison (1606, IX–X) and East (1604, XVIII–XIX). See note on Alison's setting.

XIX. This is a paraphrase of an anonymous poem in Tottel's *Songs and Sonnets*, 1557 ('Tottel's Miscellany'): 'The longer life, the more offence' (Rollins, i, p. 127).

XXII. 1 *'chill*] I will. See note on Byrd 1588, XII.

XXIII. These words appear to be freely adapted from the Bible without any exact reference being possible.

XXVI. This epigram by William Gager is preserved in his own collection of his writings (British Museum MS. Add. 22583, f. 95ᵛ). It has often been wrongly attributed to Edward de Vere, Earl of Oxford. There also exists an 'answer', beginning 'Wert thou a king, yet not command content', which is ascribed to 'Sʳ P. S.' in Chetham College, Manchester, MS. 8012, p. 84. However, Ringler (p. 352) rejects it from the canon of Sidney's works. Gager, together with Stephen Gosson, was one of the prominent protagonists in the War of the Theatres; see E. K. Chambers, *Elizabethan Stage*, chapter on 'Humanism and Puritanism'.

XXVII–XXVIII. Probably written in praise of William Byrd.

XXIX. Also set by Byrd (1589, XXVII).

PEERSON, 1620

Copy: Bodleian Library.   *Dedicatees*: Mary Holder and Sara Hart.

I. 12 *sild-seen*] seldom seen.

II. A conflation of sonnets I and XV in Constable's *Diana*, 1592. Lines 1–4 = lines 1–4 of sonnet I, and lines 5–12 = lines 5–12 of sonnet XV. See Hughey, i, p. 244.

III. 1–4] These four lines form the opening of a twenty-four line poem included in the 1655 edition (and later editions) of Robert Greene's *Pandosto*. In the 1655 edition it is superscribed: 'Dorastus in a love passion, writes these few lines in praise of his loving and best-loved Fawnia'. The poem has only a very general relevance to the plot of *Pandosto*, and it is almost certainly not by Greene.

IV. Poem printed in *A Poetical Rhapsody*, 1602 (Rollins, i, p. 156). Also set by Jones (1605, XVI).
    7 *Disdain*] *Despair* 1620.

V. 6 *the best*] metrical text, *his best* music text.
    8 *and fond*] metrical text, *of fond* music text.

VII. Also set by Jones (1607, VI).
    8 *on the lips*] metrical text, *a the lips* music text.

VIII. Poem printed in *A Poetical Rhapsody*, 1602 (Rollins, i, p. 178), ending with a quotation from Ovid, *Amores*, III. xi. 1: 'Vitiis patientia victa est'. Also set by Jones (1605, XVIII).

IX. Poem by Walter Davison. Printed with four more stanzas in *A Poetical Rhapsody*, 1602 (Rollins, i, p. 110). Also set by Jones (1605, xix).
    11 *Heart*] *Hark* 1620.

X. 10 *drone*] The bass pipe of a bagpipe, which emits only one continuous note. But sometimes used to mean the instrument itself, as is probably the case here. At this time the bagpipe was not exclusively a Scottish or Irish instrument; it was in equally common use in England, and on the Continent.

XII. Stanzas 1–4 of a poem by Richard Verstegan (the pseudonym of Richard Rowlands) printed in his *Odes*, 1601, p. 50. The complete poem is printed in E. Arber's *The Shakespeare Anthology*, 1899, p. 103.

XIII. Sonnet by Sidney, *Arcadia*, Bk. III (Ringler, p. 79). Also set by Vautor (1619, VIII–IX).

XVII. 6] It is possible that this line was interpolated by the composer.

XIX. A dialogue. The bracketed lines are sung simultaneously.

XX–XXI. A dialogue.

XXIII. A dialogue.

XXIV. These lines by Ben Jonson are from *A Private Entertainment of the King and Queen, on May-day in the Morning, at Sir William Cornwallis his House, at Highgate*, 1604. The text of this entertainment was first printed in the 1616 edition of Jonson's works. See C. H. Herford, P. and E. Simpson, *Ben Jonson*, vii, p. 133. It is interesting to note that Peerson did not publish this song until sixteen years after its composition. No doubt the contents of many of the songbooks represent work spread over a number of years.

    6 *as well*] C², om. other parts.
    14 *were*] C² Ct, *was* other parts.

PEERSON, 1630

Copy: Huntington.   *Dedicatee*: Robert, Lord Brooke.

The poems in this collection are drawn entirely from the *Caelica* sonnets of Sir Fulke Greville, first Lord Brooke, with the exception of XXII–XXIII and XXIV–XXV, which are elegies in memory of that poet. Greville died in 1628. In the following notes Peerson's text is collated with the text of the sonnets as printed in 1633.

I–III. *Caelica*, I. Also set by Cavendish (1598, VII).

IV–V. *Caelica*, III.
    1 *of all*] *of that* 1633.
    5 *nymphs*] *Saints* 1633.
    10 *men's*] *man's* 1633.

VI–VII. *Caelica*, IV.
    3 *lies*] *is* A T.
    6 *makes*] *make* 1633.
    8 *Those*] *These* 1633.
    9 *those*] *these* 1633.

VIII–IX. *Caelica*, IX.

X. *Caelica*, XXV.
    6 *hath*] *that* 1630.
    10 *should*] *would* 1633.
    11 *she make*] *she cause* 1633.
    12 *Innocence*] *innocents* 1633.
    13 *bow*] *blow* 1630.

XI. *Caelica*, LXXXV.
    7 *flesh*] *flect* 1630.

XII. *Caelica*, VIII.

XIII. *Caelica*, XXVI.
    1 *so matched*] *so over-matched* 1633.
    5 *child-thoughts of wisdom*] *child-thought of wisdom* 1630, *child-thoughts of mine own* 1633.

XIV. *Caelica*, CIII.
    3] *With whose blear eyes opinion learns to see* 1633
    4 *pity*] *party* 1633.

XV–XVI. *Caelica*, LXXXVIII.
  9 *or*] *and* 1633.
  12 *those*] *these* 1633.
  17] *For goodness only doth God comprehend* 1633.

XVII–XVIII. *Caelica*, V. Also set by Dowland (1597, II), beginning 'Who ever thinks or hopes of love for love'.

XX. *Caelica*, LXXXIV.
  9 *to*] om. 1630.
  11 *The . . . were*] *Thy . . . neere* 1630.

XXI. *Caelica*, LXXXI.
  4 *Church, Princes*] *Princes, Church* 1633.
  6 *Ambition's*] *ambitious* 1633.
  8 *unobserving*] *undeserving* C.

XXIV–XXV. The words are the same as XXI–XXIII except in line 11, where *And virtue* is altered to *Such virtue*.

PILKINGTON, 1613

Copy: British Museum   *Dedicatee*: Sir Thomas Smith.

In the British Museum set of part-books the Cantus and Tenor are dated 1614, the remainder 1613. However, the Dedication in the Cantus and Quintus is dated 'the 25. day of September 1612'. In the other three part-books '25.' and 'September' are omitted, with spaces left for their insertion.

II. Also set by Morley (1597, XVII).

IV. Stanza 2 of a poem set by Pilkington in full in 1605, V. Stanza 1 of this poem was also set by Bateson (1604, VII).
  1 *Stay, nymph*] *Fear not* 1605 version.
  3 *water-wanton*] 1605, *wanton wanton* 1613.

V. 1 *shepherd's*] *shepherd* C.

VIII. Also set by Holborne (1597, III).
  4 *eye's*] *eye* C A.

X. Cf. the 'cuckoo' song sung by *Spring* and *Winter* in *Love's Labours Lost*, V. ii: 'When daisies pied and violets blue.'
  3 *under-spring*] *undergrowth*.
  5 *soote*] *sweet, pleasant*.

XI. Also set by Bateson (1618, XIII).

XIII. 4 *my eyes*] *mine eyes* A B.

XVI. 1 *on*] *o'er* C B.

XXI. Also set by Bateson (1604, the opening, unnumbered, madrigal. See note thereon).
  9–10] This refrain occurs in all the 'Oriana' madrigals. See preliminary note on Morley 1601.

PILKINGTON 1624

Copy: British Museum.   *Dedicatee*: Sir Peter Leigh.

I. Also set by Morley (1597, VIII).

IV. Also set by Morley (1597, XVIII), with two additional lines (7 and 10).

V. Also set by Greaves (1604, III).

VIII–IX. Also set by Danyel (1606, I), who entitles stanza 2 'The Answer'. Cf. also W. Chappell and J. W. Ebsworth, *The Roxburghe Ballads*, ii, p. 530: 'When Daphne from fair Phoebus did fly.' Concerning the tune of this ballad see Chappell–Wooldridge, i, p. 150.

XII. This poem by George Wither is from *Fair-Virtue*, 1622, lines 4273–8 (F. Sidgwick, *The Poetry of George Wither*, 1902, ii, p. 155).

XIV. Lines 5–10 of Dorus's song 'Come shepherd's weeds, become your master's mind' in Book I of Sidney's *Arcadia* (Ringler, p. 13).
   1 *weeds*] clothes.

XV. Also set by Byrd (1611, XXII). See note thereon for further references.

XVI. Thomas Purcell, in whose honour this elegy was composed, belonged apparently to the same family which was later made famous by Henry Purcell. See the article on Purcell in *Grove's Dictionary of Music and Musicians*, 5th edition, 1954.

XVII. 5 *full*] *foul* 1624.

XIX. Also set by Byrd (1588, XXXI) with three more stanzas.
   5 *retchless*] reckless.

XX. Also set by Ferrabosco (1609, IX) with six more lines.
   8 *she*] It is rare to find Time accredited with the feminine gender.

XXI–XXII. 14 *feet*] *foot* T B Q Sx.

XXIV. 5 *hist*] Probably here used in its intransitive sense: 'is silent'. Cf. Milton's use of the word in *Il Penseroso* (line 55), 'And the mute silence hist along'.

XXVII. This instrumental piece is superscribed 'A Pavan made for the Orpharion by the Right Honourable William, Earl of Derby, and by him consented to be in my books placed'. The Stanleys at this time were frequently in residence at Stanley Palace in Chester. Thus they were fellow citizens of Pilkington and Bateson.

RAVENSCROFT, 1609a

Editions: There are two extant editions of *Pammelia*, dated 1609 and 1618. Variants in the text are recorded below.

Copies: 1609, British Museum and Bodleian Library; 1618, British Museum.   *Dedicatee*: none.

All the rounds in Ravenscroft's anthology are anonymous, and according to the preface some were already quite old by 1609. The music has been transcribed and edited by Peter Warlock (London, 1928). In the four rounds with French texts (XLIX–LII) we have preserved the Middle French spelling.

II 2 *maiden*] 1618 *malden* 1609.

III. In *The Maid's Metamorphosis*, 1600, Mopso enters singing the following song (sig. C3):

> Terlitelo, terlitelo, terlitelee, terlo,
> So merrily this shepherd's boy
> His horn that he can blow,

> Early in a morning, late, late, in an evening,
>   And ever sat this little boy
>   So merrily piping.

In *England's Helicon*, 1600, there is a poem of six stanzas attributed to John Wotton, the first stanza of which is as follows (Rollins, i, p. 48):

> Jolly shepherd, shepherd on a hill,
>   On a hill so merrily,
>   On a hill so cheerily.
> Fear not, shepherd, there to pipe thy fill,
> Fill every dale, fill every plain;
>   Both sing and say 'Love feels no pain'.

Cf. also the burden of carol 79A and lines 4–5 of carol 79B in R. L. Greene, *The Early English Carols* (Oxford, 1935), p. 50.

v. For other pedlar's songs see: Ravenscroft 1609*a*, XI; Ravenscroft 1611, VII and XI; Morley 1600, XVII; Dowland 1600, XII.

VII. Day and Murrie 2386.

IX. This item is missing in the 1618 edition, and the numbering goes from VIII to X.

X. Day and Murrie 2396.

XI. See note on v in this collection.
    1 *Walfleet*] *Walefleet* 1609 and 1618. A peninsula between Paglesham and the river Crouch, near Rochford in Essex. Famous for oysters. Cf. W. Rowley, *A New Wonder*, III, 'Oysters, new Walfleet oysters!', and Drayton, *Polyalbion*, XIX, line 126, 'Pure Walefleet, which do still the daintiest palates please'.

XII. 1 *toll*] 1618, *toles* 1609.

XIV. Compare XXXII. Attrib. to Byrd; see *Works*, xvi (1948), p. 104.

XV. *virtutum*] 1618, *virtutem* 1609. Attrib. to Byrd; see *Works*, xvi (1948), p. 105.

XVI. Vulgate, Psalm v. 3–4.
    meae] 1618, *mea* 1609.

XVII. Vulgate, John xvii. 3.

XIX. Psalm xxii. 22.

XX. 4 *stond*] 1609, *ston'd* 1618. A variant of 'stound' (= 'astounded').

XXII. There was a popular song of the 16th and 17th centuries called 'John, come kiss me now'. See Chappell–Wooldridge, i, p. 268.

XXIII. Day and Murrie 2241.

XXIV. 1 *Brainford*] Brentford.

XXVII. Day and Murrie 3219.

XXVIII. In each pair of bracketed lines the first is sung by the guest and the second by the hostess. Day and Murrie 1319.

XXIX. Sung by Bullithrumble, with two more stanzas, in *The . . . Tragical Reign of Selimus*, a play attributed to Robert Greene. The play was first printed in 1594.
    6 *can I*] 1618, *I can* 1609. *tallants*] talons.

XXX. 3–7] A quotation from the song 'The woods so wild', for the text of which see K. Muir, *Sir Thomas Wyatt and His Circle*, 1961, pp. 26–28, and R. H. Robbins, *Secular*

Lyrics of the Fourteenth and Fifteenth Centuries, 1952, No. 20. Concerning the tune of 'The woods so wild', which is also incorporated into this round, see Chappell–Wooldridge, i, p. 119. For further references see J. Stevens, *Music and Poetry at the Early Tudor Court*, 1961, App. B, No. 43, and F. W. Sternfeld, letter in *Times Literary Supplement*, 14 July 1961. Also see note on Dowland 1597, V.

8–11] These lines are sung to a version of the tune 'Dargison'. See Chappell–Wooldridge, i, p. 230.

10 *crag*] neck.

XXXI. 5 *leant unto*] made my way towards.

XXXII. Vulgate, Psalm l. 3. Cf. XIV.
mei] 1618, *meus* 1609. *magnam*] 1618, *magnum* 1609.

XXXIV. Vulgate, Psalm xxx, 2. Day and Murrie 1769.
confundar] *confunder* 1609 and 1618.

XXXV. Cf. Vulgate, Psalm xxxviii. 13.
orationem] 1609, *grationem* 1618.

XXXVI. Day and Murrie 2640.

XXXVII. Cf. Vulgate, John xvi. 23.

XXXVIII. Vulgate, Psalm xcvii. 1.

XXXIX. Cf. Vulgate, Luke xxiv. 29.
Christe] 1618, *Christi* 1609. *inclinata*] *inclinatus* 1609 and 1618.

XL. Cf. Vulgate, Psalm xlii. 3.

XLI. The same text is used in LXXX.
animae vita] 1618, *anima vitae* 1609.

XLII. *descendit*] 1618, *descendet* 1609.

XLIV. Vulgate, Psalm lxxviii. 9.

XLV. From 'The Humble Suit of a Sinner' by John Marckant, printed in the Sternhold and Hopkins metrical psalter. Also set by East (1618, XV) and Mundy (1594, XIV).

XLVI. Stanzas 1–3 of 'The Ten Commandments' by William Whittingham, printed in the Sternhold and Hopkins metrical psalter.
2 *ferly*] strange, wonderful, marvellous.

XLVII. From 'The Lamentation' by John Marckant, printed in the Sternhold and Hopkins metrical psalter.
7 *shent*] punished.

XLVIII. From John Marckant's 'The Lamentation of a Sinner' printed in the Sternhold and Hopkins metrical psalter. Stanza 1 also set by Mundy (1594, VIII).

L. *bontés*] *boutes* 1609 and 1618. By Orlando di Lasso; see *Werke*, xvi, p. 162.

LI. 1 *propose*] *propa se* 1609 and 1618.
2 *veux*] *veni* 1609 and 1618.
3 *D'amer ton*] *damerton* 1609 and 1618.

LII. *Donez*] *Donec* 1609 and 1618.

LV. 5 *bowling*] bowline.
12 *brinks*] to drink, pledge.

LVII. 2 *hounds*] horns 1609 and 1618.

LVIII. Day and Murrie 298.

LX. Day and Murrie 372.

LXII. Cf. Nashe, *Summer's Last Will and Testament* (R. B. McKerrow, *The Works of Thomas Nashe*, iii, pp. 258 and 263):

> Merry, merry, merry, cherry, cherry, cherry,
> Troll the black bowl to me.
> Hey derry derry, with a poupe and a lerry,
> I'll troll it again to thee.

Cf. also *The Knight of the Burning Pestle*, II. viii.
  11 *aflant*] aflaunt: 'in a flaunting state or position' (*O.E.D.*).

LXIII. Numbered LXV in 1618 edition. A snatch of this song is sung by Moros in William Wager's *The Longer Thou Livest The More Fool Thou Art*, performed *c*. 1559. (*c*. 1568 edition, sig. A3).

LXV. Numbered LXIII in 1618 edition.

LXVI. 3 *groan*] 1618, *moan* 1609.

LXVIII. Day and Murrie 1532. Attrib. to Byrd; see *Works*, xvi (1948), p. 114.
  5–10] Cf. *Othello* II. iii:

> And let me the canakin clink, clink,
> And let me the canakin clink.
> A soldier's a man,
> O man's life's but a span,
> Why, then, let a soldier drink.

LXIX. 1–2] These lines form the text of XCVII.
  6 *mine*] 1618, *my* 1609.

LXXI. Throughout this round one voice sings a continuous monotone 'bum bum bum'.

LXXIII. 3 *Fortune my foe*] A popular song of the 16th century. See Chappell–Wooldridge, i, p. 76.

LXXIV. The three dance-songs are arranged so as to form a round, which is sung by the Cantus, Medius, and Tenor, while the Bass supplies a fourth, free part.
  9–13] Concerning the song 'The Cramp' see Chappell–Wooldridge, p. 143.
  14–17] Concerning 'Robin Hood' see Chappell–Wooldridge, p. 273.

LXXVII. Cf. Vulgate, Psalm cxli. 7.

LXXIX. Vulgate, Psalm xxiv. 4.

LXXX. The same text is used in XLI.

LXXXII. Cf. Vulgate, 1 Peter i. 25.

LXXXV. This round is sung by Merrythought and two boys in *The Knight of the Burning Pestle*, IV. v.

LXXXVII. 4 *mome*] dolt, blockhead.

LXXXVIII. 7 *The round and the square*] round- and square-shaped notes.

LXXXIX. 5 *trumpets*] trumpet 1609 and 1618.

XCII. Vulgate, Psalm cxxxiv. 1–2.
  nomen Domini] 1618, *nomen Domine* 1609.

xcv. Stanza 1 of a two-stanza song sung by Dametas in Sidney's *Arcadia* (Ringler, p. 13).

xcvi. Cf. Vulgate, Psalm cxvi. 1.

xcvii. See LXIX, lines 1–2.

xcviii. Vulgate, Psalm xviii. 13.

c. 7–8] These lines are sung by Merrythought in *The Knight of The Burning Pestle*, IV. v, and by Ver in Nashe's *Summer's Last Will and Testament* (R. B. McKerrow, *The Works of Thomas Nashe*, iii, p. 242).

RAVENSCROFT, 1609*b*

Copy: Library of Congress, Washington.   *Dedicatee*: none.

Intended as a sequel to *Pammelia*, as the title-page indicates, this collection contains part-songs and songs for voices and instruments as well as rounds. All the pieces are anonymous. On the title-page 'K. H. Mirth' stands for 'King Henry's Mirth', and 'Freemens Songs' is probably a corrupt form of 'Three-Men's Songs', i.e., songs for three voices.

I. Numerous references to the song of 'John Dory' are given in Chappell–Wooldridge, i, p. 93. Day and Murrie 225.
 19 *mand*] commanded.

II. 28 *galde*] Derived from 'gall', a sore, blister or swelling on a horse.

III. See Chappell–Wooldridge, i, p. 133. Day and Murrie 3577.
 2] The original spelling is 'Pardona moy ie vous an pree'.
 5] This refrain is printed only at the end of stanza 1.
 13 *shot*] A supply or amount of drink.

V. 3 *very*] om. B (the only part which has the words of stanza 1 in this version).

VI. See Chappell–Wooldridge, i, p. 134.

VII. See Chappell–Wooldridge, i, p. 141. Day and Murrie 2562.
 1] Compare first lines of Mundy 1594, X, and Bartlet, 1606, X.
 10–13] Sung by Merrythought in *The Knight of the Burning Pestle*, I. iv. In lines 11 and 13 the lower words in the brackets are sung by the Tenor, the upper ones by the Treble and Bass.

IX. The tune to which these words are sung is variously called 'Browning', 'The Nuts be Brown', 'Browning My Dear', and 'The Leaves be Green'. See Chappell–Wooldridge, i, p. 154. No explanation can be offered as to the meaning of the word 'browning'.

X. This catch is sung by Sir Andrew Aguecheek, Sir Toby Belch, and the Clown in *Twelfth Night*, II. iii, l. 62. Day and Murrie 1386.

XIII. Day and Murrie 3338.

XV. See Chappell–Wooldridge, i, p. 151. Day and Murrie 2165.
 2 *angel*] A gold coin first issued in 1465. It ceased to be minted in the reign of Charles I.

XVI. See Chappell–Wooldridge, i, p. 140. Lines 2, 4, 7, and 8 in each stanza are sung as choruses by all four voices. The rest is sung solo. Day and Murrie 2180.

XVII. This song is sung in *Jack Drum's Entertainment* (first printed in 1601). See H. Harvey Wood, *The Plays of John Marston*, 1939, iii, p. 238.

XVIII. See Chappell–Wooldridge, i, p. 137. Day and Murrie 3910.

XIX. An early sixteenth-century version of the words and music of this song is preserved in British Museum MS. Royal, App. 58, f. 10ᵛ. See also *XX Songs*, 1530, xxii (a publication formerly attributed to Wynkyn de Worde). A fragment of the text is sung by Moros in William Wager's *The Longer Thou Livest The More Fool Thou Art*, performed *c.* 1559 (*c.* 1568 edn., sig A2). For further references see Chappell–Wooldridge, i, p. 46, and J. Stevens, *Music and Poetry at the Early Tudor Court*, p. 435.
    7 and 12 *hey ho*] This is printed only in stanza 1 in the original edition.

XX. Sung to the tune 'Trenchmore', as also is XXI. Concerning 'Trenchmore' see Chappell–Wooldridge, i, p. 224. Lines 2, 4, 8, and 10 in each stanza are sung by all four voices. The rest is solo.
    6 *halloo*] *hallow* 1609.

XXI. Sung to the tune 'Trenchmore', as also is XX. Concerning 'Trenchmore' see Chappell–Wooldridge, i, p. 224. Day and Murrie 3979.
While the Tenor sings the solo section of each stanza the Treble, Medius, and Bassus sing a continuous 'hey trolilo' accompaniment, which has the rubric 'Sing softly'.
    23 and 43 *what-call*] what-do-you-call-it.
    41 *lane*] *laune* 1609.

XXII. See Chappell–Wooldridge, i, p. 136.

XXIII. 5 *pigsny*] A term of endearment.
    15 *bearest the bell*] See note on Mundy 1594, X.

XXVII. Day and Murrie 1509.
    1 *I C U B A K*] I see you be a knave.

XXVIII. 2 *'loath to depart'*] A common term for a song sung or a tune played on taking leave of friends. In addition to the references in Chappell–Wooldridge, i, p. 102, see Jones 1600, XII, line 25. A tune called 'Loath to Depart' is contained in *The Fitzwilliam Virginal Book* (ed. J. A. Fuller Maitland and W. Barclay Squire, ii, p. 317) and Cambridge University Library MS. Dd. ii. 11.

XXIX. 7 *swad*] country bumpkin, clodhopper.
    9 *trull*] wench.

XXXI. These words also appear in Ravenscroft 1609a, LXXXVI, lines 3–9.

RAVENSCROFT, 1611

Copy: Library of Congress, Washington.   *Dedicatees*: Thomas and William Ravenscroft.

Most of the compositions in this collection are consort songs for solo voice, chorus (usually) and instruments. There are also some part-songs and rounds.

I. 5 and 14] *Rise* occurs four times in stanza 2, which is set out metrically, but three times in stanza 1, which is printed with the music.

II. See note on XII concerning a possible dramatic context for this song.
    8] All voices sing this line.

III. See note on XII concerning a possible dramatic context for this song.

IV. The words of the Courtier and Mistress are sung by the Quintus and Medius parts respectively. The other three parts are instrumental.

8 *woo*] *woe* 1611.

V. See note on XII concerning a possible dramatic context for this song.

9–10] All three voices interpolate *down down* etc. during the course of these two lines.

VII. For references to other pedlar's songs see note on Ravenscroft 1609a, V.

1 *pouch-rings*] A ring used for closing a purse or pouch.

5 *cherry ripe*] Campian incorporates this street cry into 'There is a garden in her face' (*c.* 1618b, VII).

5 *Ha'y'any*] *Hay yee any* 1611. Sung to three notes.

IX. Day and Murrie 2273.

6 *she*] *the* 1611.

X. Day and Murrie 1545.

XI. See note on XII concerning a possible dramatic context for this song. For references to other pedlar's songs see note on Ravenscroft 1609a, V.

XII. 3–8] These lines are sung by Audrey in Middleton's *A Trick to Catch the Old One*, IV. v (first printed in 1608). See A. J. Sabol, 'Ravenscroft's "Melismata" and the Children of Paul's', *Renaissance News*, xii (1959), p. 3. In this article Sabol tentatively suggests several dramatic situations that would seem to be appropriate to certain songs in Ravenscroft's *Melismata*. They are here listed:

Anon., *The Maid's Metamorphosis*, I: 'Now flowers your odours breathe' (ii).
Marston, *The Malcontent*, V: 'Haste, haste, post haste' (iii).
Marston, *What You Will*, III: 'Long have we bin perplexed and vexed' (v).
Dekker and Webster, *Westward Ho*, V: 'Where are you, fair maids' (xi).

Many of the songs and catches in Ravenscroft's collections would seem to have belonged to stage productions, though only in a few cases can their dramatic origins be precisely identified.

1 *wittall*] withal.

XIV. 4 *catertray*] i.e., 'cater-trey', the four and the three; dice.

5 *wiseacre*] One who thinks himself, or wishes to be thought, wise.

XV. Day and Murrie 1305.

XX. The refrains (lines 2, 4, and 7 in each stanza) are sung by all four voices, the rest by one voice with instrumental accompaniment.

XXI. See Chappell–Wooldridge, i, p. 142. The refrains (lines 2 and 4 in each stanza) are sung by all four voices, the rest by one voice with instrumental accompaniment.

XXII. See Chappell–Wooldridge, i, p. 138.

23 *him*] *his* 1611.

31 *slop*] This term has been used in connection with such varied types of attire as footwear, breeches, jackets, and coats. Here it would seem to refer to a smock-frock, or some such outer garment.

XXIII. See Chappell–Wooldridge, i, p. 144. Lines 2 and 8 in each stanza are sung by voices, the rest by one voice with instrumental accompaniment. Day and Murrie 2794.

60 *mankind's*] *mankind* 1611.

RAVENSCROFT, 1614

Copy: British Museum.

Dedicatees: the senators and guardians of Gresham College, London (the following names are listed): Sir Stephen Soames, Sir John Garret, Sir Thomas Lowe, and Sir William Craven (Aldermen); Mr. Cornelius Fish (Chamberlain). Of the Mercers Company: Sir Thomas Bennet, Mr. Thomas Bennet (Sheriff) (Aldermen), Sir Baptist Hicks, Mr. William Quarles, Mr. Edward Barnes, Mr. John Gardiner, Mr. William Ferrers, and the two wardens. Sir John Swinerton and Sir Thomas Hayes.

This book was primarily intended as a theoretical treatise, but following the theoretical section there are twenty compositions, mostly consort songs for solo voice, chorus, and instruments. The composer's name is given at the beginning of each piece.

I. See Chappell–Wooldridge, i, p. 86.

III. 6 *truss it*] *O.E.D.* defines this technical term thus: 'Of a bird of prey: To seize or clutch (the prey) in its talons; *spec.* to seize (the quarry) in the air and carry it off.' The term is not to be found in Dame Juliana Bernes's *The Book of Hawking*, 1486.

IV. 7 *seld*] seldom.
8 *truss*] See note on III.
9–12] Different names are sung by each of the four voice parts (Treble, Medius, Tenor, and Bass) simultaneously. In line 9 the Medius also has 'whurr ret Love' after 'Beauty', and the Tenor has 'whurr ret Jew, whurr ret Damsel' after 'Trea'.

V. 1 *Lure*] An apparatus used by falconers to recall their hawks. It consisted of a bunch of feathers to which a long cord was attached. The intransitive verb, as used here, means to call to a hawk while casting the lure.
4 *nyas-hawk*] A corrupted form of *eyas-hawk*, a young hawk.
5 *stiff*] *swift* T.

VI. This song may have been sung in John Lyly's *Endimion*, IV. iii. See G. K. Hunter, *John Lyly*, 1962, p. 372.

VIII. This song is sung in the second act of the anonymous play *The Maid's Metamorphosis*, 1600, sig. C4. See note on IX.

IX. Like VIII, this song is sung in *The Maid's Metamorphosis*, II (sig. D). In the 1600 edition of the play line 8 reads 'For our brave Queen a'. There is also a second stanza.

X. *Of Beer*] Title supplied from table of contents.
11 *be seen in phisnomie*] seemly in appearance, endowed with good looks.

XI. *Of Ale*] Title supplied from table of contents.

XII. For references to other songs about tobacco see note on East 1606, XXII. In the original edition such portions of this poem as are set out metrically are set out in lines of ten or twelve syllables.

XIII. *Three fools*] Title supplied from table of contents.
1 *seek'st*] seekes 1614.

XV. Sung in *Blurt, Master-Constable*, V. ii, an anonymous play performed by the Children of Paul's, *c.* 1600. See A. J. Sabol, *Studies in the Renaissance*, V (1958), p. 145.
13 *so*] see 1614.

XVII–XX. This set of songs in dialect is printed here with the original spelling. In the original edition the use of dialect is carried to extreme lengths in these songs: the tenor part is headed 'Denor', and such terms as 'Zegond bart' are used.

XX. 1 *A borgens a borgen*] A bargain's a bargain.

TOMKINS, 1622

Copy: British Museum.   *Dedicatee*: William, Earl of Pembroke.

In addition to the general dedication to the Earl of Pembroke each of the twenty-eight compositions has a separate dedication. These are included in the following notes.

I. *To my dear father Mr. Thomas Tomkins.*

II. *To Mr. William Walker.*

III. *To Mr. Humfrey Withy.*

IV. *To my brother Mr. Nicholas Tomkins.*
  6 *the sense . . . the brain*] your sense . . . your brain C A.

V. *To Master William Crosse.*
  1 *taste*] find A B.

VI. *To Master Thomas Day.*

VII. *To Doctor Dowland.*

VIII. *To Master John Danyel.*

IX. *To Master John Coprario.*

X. *To my brother Peregrine Tomkins.*
  6 *Not thinking*] And thinks not C T.

XI. *To my brother Robert Tomkins.*

XII. *To my brother Giles Tomkins.*

XIII. *To Mr. Robert Chetwoode.*

XIV. *To my ancient & much reverenced master, William Byrd.*

XV. *To Mr. Nathaniel Giles.*
  7–8] Compare lines 3–4 of XVIII.

XVI. *To Mr. Orlando Gibbons.*

XVII. *To Mr. John Steevens.*

XVIII. *To Mr. Henry Molle.*
  3–4] Compare lines 7–8 of XV.

XIX. *To Mr. Thomas Myriell.* This composition was reprinted in *Musica Deo Sacra*, a collection of Tomkins's church compositions published in 1668, twelve years after his death. The same words were set by East (1618, XX) and Weelkes (British Museum Add. MSS. 29372–7).

XX. *To Mr. Nicholas Carlton.*

XXI. *To Mr. Phineas Fletcher.*

XXII. *To Mr. William White.*

XXIII. *To Mr. Thomas Warwick.*

XXIV. *To Mr. Doctor Heather.*

XXV. *To Mr. John Ward.*

  1] Cf. Daniel, *Delia*, XXXIV, 1: 'Oft do I marvel whether Delia's eyes.' *marle*] Obsolete contraction of *marvel*.

  5 *mell*] mingle. Misprinted *dwell* 1622.

XXVI. *To my brother Mr. John Tomkins.*

XXVII. *To Mr. Doctor Aylmer.* A free paraphrase of Canticles ii. 8.

XXVIII. *To my son Nathaniel Tomkins.*

VAUTOR, 1619

Copy: British Museum.   *Dedicatee*: George Villiers, Marquis of Buckingham.

VI. 1–2] Compare Yonge 1588, XXVI, and Bennet 1599, XI.

  3 *infeoffed*] surrendered.

  10 *thee*] me 1619.

VIII–IX. From Sidney's *Arcadia*, Bk. III, where it is sung by Musidorus to lull Pamela to sleep (Ringler, p. 79). See also Hughey, i, p. 239. Also set to music by Peerson (1620, XIII).

  6] Lacks two syllables because Vautor has omitted *Her sight* from the beginning of the line.

X. A resetting of Watson 1590, II. The poem is translated from Sannazaro, *Arcadia*, seventh eclogue.

XI. 3–8] These lines, with some variants, also occur as lines 7–12 in the poem 'Sly thief, if so you will believe' set by East (1604, XXI–XXII) and Cavendish (1598, XIX–XX).

XIII–XIV. Poem by Campian, and set to music by him (Rosseter 1601, Pt. I, XII).

XV. William Camden in his *Brittania* (1586, p. 142) concludes a paragraph praising the achievements of King Henry II ('hic Alexander noster') with the following words: 'Sed ecce veterem in eius mortem versiculum, qui uno verbo, et haec et omnia, et filii Regis Ricardi primi gloriam plene complectitur:

        Mira cano, Sol occubuit, nox nulla sequuta est.'

XVI. Sir Thomas Beaumont of Stoughton Grange was third son of Sir Nicholas Beaumont of Cole Orton. He owned the Stoughton property in right of his wife Catherine, daughter and heiress of Sir Thomas Farnham. Beaumont died on 27 November 1614.

XVIII. This poem is translated from Guarini's 'O come se' gentile' (see Obertello, p. 408). The same translation, with some minor variants, was set by Gibbons (1612, IX), and a different translation by Danyel (1606, II).

XX–XXI. An elegy in memory of Henry, Prince of Wales, who died in 1612 at the age of eighteen. In spite of his youth the prince had been a great patron of the arts.

XXII. An elegy in memory of Queen Elizabeth I ('Oriana'), constructed on the same lines as the lyrics in *The Triumphs of Oriana* (Morley, 1601).

  10–11] A variant of the characteristic 'Oriana' refrain. See preliminary note on Morley 1601.

WARD, 1613

Copy: British Museum.　　*Dedicatee*: Sir Henry Fanshawe.

I–II. From Sidney's *Arcadia*, Bk. III (Ringler, p. 75).

IV. Poem by Francis Davison. Printed as 'Madrigal II' in *A Poetical Rhapsody*, 1602 (Rollins, i, p. 65). The poem is a translation of Groto's 'Io, madonna, stò bene' (*Rime*, 1587, p. 73).

V. Poem by Francis Davison. Printed as 'Madrigal XII' in *A Poetical Rhapsody*, 1602 (Rollins, i, p. 90). Cf. Daniel, *Delia*, 1592, sonnet 2, and Bartlet 1606, VIII.

VII. Lines 1–4 of sonnet 16 in Sidney's *Certain Sonnets* (Ringler, p. 145). Sidney wrote the sonnet as a reply to Dyer's 'Prometheus when first from heaven high' (see A. B. Grosart, *Sir Edward Dyer*, pp. 37–38).

VIII. The final stanza of the tenth song in Sidney's *Astrophel and Stella* (Ringler, pp. 225–7). The first four and final stanzas also appear in R. Dowland, 1610, v, and the first three stanzas in Byrd, 1589, xxxiii.

IX. By Francis Davison. These lines, with some variants, are lines 9–14 of 'Sonnet V' in *A Poetical Rhapsody*, 1602 (Rollins, i, p. 63).

X. From Bartholomew Yong's translation of Montemayor's *Diana*, 1598, p. 438.

XII. Adapted from lines 38–42 of the dialogue 'As I behind a bush did sit' in Sidney's *Arcadia* (Ringler, p. 58).

XIII–XIV. Thomas Oliphant (*La Musa Madrigalesca*, 1837, p. 286) suggests Michael Drayton as the author of these words. See Kerman, p. 18.
　　9 *bowed*] *bound* 1613.

XV. A resetting of the translation of Ferretti's madrigal 'Una piaga mortal' printed in Morley's *Madrigals . . . selected*, 1598.

XVI. A resetting of the translation of Croce's canzonet 'Mentre la bella Dafne' printed in Morley's *Canzonets . . . selected*, 1597. In Morley's anthology the translation begins 'Daphne the bright'.

XVII. Stanza 2 of Francis Davison's 'Ode III' ('My only star') in *A Poetical Rhapsody*, 1602 (Rollins, i, p. 75).

XVIII. Stanza 1 of a three-stanza poem by Drayton in the second eclogue of his *Poems Lyric and Pastoral*, 1606 (J. W. Hebel, *The Works of Michael Drayton*, II, p. 525). However, the earliest appearance of the poem in print was in *England's Helicon*, 1600 (Rollins, i, p. 167), where it begins 'Near to a bank . . .'.

XXII. Stanzas 1 and 3, with many variants, of a three-stanza poem by Drayton in the second eclogue of *The Shepherds' Garland*, 1593. (J. W. Hebel, *The Works of Michael Drayton*, i, p. 52.)

XXIII–XXIV. Lines 1–6 closely resemble stanza 5 of the ninth eclogue in Drayton's *The Shepherds' Garland*, while lines 9–12 are substantially the same as the first four lines of stanza 11 of the same eclogue. (J. W. Hebel, *The Works of Michael Drayton*, i, pp. 92–93.)
　　2 *rected*] up-lifted.

XXV. 1] Compare the opening line of Dowland, 1600, IV: 'Die not before thy day, poor man condemned.'

XXVI. These words are adapted from a sonnet by Walter Davison printed in *A Poetical Rhapsody*, 1602 (Rollins, i, p. 112). Ward has used lines 1–4, 9, 12–14 of Davison's sonnet, making several alterations to them.

XXVIII. Henry, Prince of Wales, died in 1612 at the age of eighteen. In spite of his youth he had been a great patron of the arts.

6 *Henery*] So spelt in the original part books, and to be sung as three syllables. It may be that Ward has altered the word-order in this line, the original version being *Since death Prince Henery hath slain*, which would provide the rhyme *plain/slain*.

WATSON, 1590

Copies: British Museum and Huntington.   *Dedicatee*: Robert, Earl of Essex.

Thomas Watson's *Italian Madrigals Englished*, 1590, was the second anthology of Italian madrigals to be published in England, the first being Nicholas Yonge's *Musica Transalpina*, 1588. Whereas the fifty-seven madrigals in Yonge's anthology represent the work of at least eighteen composers (the composer of one piece is not known), the twenty-eight in Watson's represent only five composers, with twenty-three pieces being by Marenzio. Watson's approach to the task of translating the texts was also different from that of Yonge. On the whole Yonge's translations are fairly literal, while those in Watson's collection are 'Englished not to the sense of the original ditty [i.e. the words], but after the affection of the note' (title-page). Indeed, many of Watson's 'translations', including the elegies for Sidney and Walsingham (XIX, XXIII–XXIV, and XXVII) are in reality new poems, owing little or nothing to the original Italian. In the following notes references are given to sources from which Watson drew in compiling his anthology. Where known, the author of the original Italian lyric is also given.

I. Marenzio I a 4, 1585: 'Non vide mai.' Italian text by Petrarch, canzona cxxvii, stanza 5.

   2 *Both of Nature*] In *Astrophel both of nature* S Ct.

II. Marenzio I a 4, 1585: 'I lieti amanti.' Italian text by Sannazaro, *Arcadia*, eclogue 7. Also set by Vautor (1619, X).

III. Marenzio I a 4, 1585: 'Veggo dolce mio bene.'

IV. Marenzio I a 4, 1585: 'Zefiro torna'. Italian text by Petrarch, sonnet cccx. For another translation, 'Zephyrus brings the time', see Yonge 1588, LII–LIII, Cavendish 1598, XXII, and Yonge's second *Musica Transalpina* collection, 1597, II.

V. Marenzio I a 4, 1585: 'Madonna sua mercè.' Italian text by Sannazaro, *Arcadia*, eclogue 7.

VI. Marenzio I a 4, 1585: 'Vezzosi augelli.' Italian text by Torquato Tasso, *Gerusalemme*, XVI. 12.

VII. Marenzio I a 4, 1585: 'Ahi dispietata morte.' Italian text by Petrarch, ballata cccxxiv. Also set by Wilbye (1598, XIX).

VIII. According to the title-page Byrd's two settings of this poem were composed at the request of Watson. This one is for four voices, and XXVIII is for six voices. The four voice version also appears in Byrd 1611, IX. It is more than likely that the poem is by Watson himself, since lines 7–8 are virtually the same as the refrain of his 'With fragrant flowers we strew the way', which was set as a lute ayre by Pilkington (1605, XX).

IX. Marenzio I a 5, 1580: 'Lasso ch'io ardo.'

X. Marenzio I a 5, 1580: 'Quando i voṣtri.' Italian text by Sannazaro, *Sonetti e canzoni*, 1530, XVII.

XI. Conversi, 'Sola solette.' Included in the anthology *Musica Divina*, Antwerp, 1583.

XII. Marenzio I a 5, 1580: 'Venuta era madonna.' Italian text by Sannazaro, *Sonetti e canzoni*, 1530, XXIX.
10 *wakes*] *awakes* S T. Both readings occur in M.

XIII. Marenzio I a 5, 1580: 'Ohime dov'e 'l mio ben.' Italian text by B. Tasso, *De le rime di diversi . . . autori*, 1550, p. 63. Also set by Bateson (1604, XVIII).

XIV–XV. Marenzio I a 5, 1580: 'Spuntavan gia.'
3 *among*] *amongst* S M.
11 *satyrs do use*] *satyrs use* S Ct T.
14 *leese*] lose, part with.

XVI. Marenzio I a 5, 1580: 'Madonna mia gentil.'

XVII. Marenzio I a 5, 1580: 'Cantava la più vaga.'
3 *eye it was*] *eye was* S M Ct.

XVIII. Marenzio I a 5, 1580: 'Partirò dunque.'
6 *thy hopes*] *the hopes* S.

XIX. Marenzio I a 5, 1580: 'Questa di verd' herbette.' Watson's English text is an elegy in memory of Sir Philip Sidney (d. 1586). See also XXIII–XXIV, XXVII.
2 *dreary*] *dryry* 1590.

XX. Nanino I a 5, 1579: 'Morir non puo 'l mio core.' Nanino's madrigal was also included in the anthology *Musica Divina*, Antwerp, 1583. Watson's English version was also set by East (1604, XVII).

XXI. Marenzio IV a 6, 1587: 'Talche dovunque.' Italian text by Luigi Tansillo, *Delle rime di diversi eccellenti autori*, 1553, p. 35. Marenzio's madrigal is in fact the *second* part of 'Ne ferò sdegno' (XXII). Watson has not indicated this, and has printed them in the wrong order.

XXII. Marenzio IV a 6, 1587: 'Ne ferò sdegno.' Italian text by Luigi Tansillo, *Delle rime di diversi eccellenti autori*, 1553, p. 35. Marenzio's madrigal is in fact the *first* part of 'Talche dovunque' (XXI). Watson has not indicated this, and has printed them in the wrong order.

XXIII–XXIV. Marenzio IV a 6, 1587: 'Di nettare amoroso.' Italian text by Torquato Tasso, *Scielta delle rime*, 1582, p. 35. Watson's English text is in memory of Sir Francis Walsingham, who is the 'Meliboeus' of this poem. Walsingham died in 1590, the year in which Watson published this anthology of madrigals. Watson also lamented Walsingham's death in *Meliboeus, sive Ecloga in Obitum F. Walsingham*, also published in 1590. The 'Astrophel' of this poem is of course Sir Philip Sidney, who died in 1586, and who was Walsingham's son-in-law. See also XIX and XXVII.

XXV. Marenzio IV a 6, 1587: 'Crudel perchè mi fuggi.' Italian text by Guarini, *Rime*, 1598, f. 61. Also set by Wilbye (1598, XX).

XXVI. Striggio, 'Non rumor di tamburi.' Striggio's madrigal was included in the anthology *Musica Divina*, Antwerp, 1583. Italian text by Ariosto, *Orlando*, XXV, 68.

XXVII. Marenzio IV a 6, 1587: 'Questa ordì il laccio.' Italian text by Giovanbattista Strozzi, *Madrigali*, 1593, p. 62. Watson's English text is in memory of Sir Francis Walsingham ('Meliboeus'). 'Astrophel' is his son-in-law Sir Philip Sidney. See note on XXIII–XXIV.

XXVIII. See note on VIII.

WEELKES, 1597

Copy: British Museum.   *Dedicatee*: Sir George Philpot.

II–IV. Poem printed in *The Passionate Pilgrim*, 1599, and in *England's Helicon*, 1600 (Rollins, i, p. 56).
   13 *One*] *Our* 1597.
   28 *wether's bell*] A bell tied round the neck of the leader of a flock of animals.
   29 *curtall dog*] A dog with a docked tail.

VIII. Also set by East (1604, IV).

XI. 3 *Will for our town*] Compare XII, line 5, and see note on Morley 1594, XVIII.
   5 *ne'er the near*] See note on Byrd 1589, XXVIII.

XII. 5 *For our town*] Compare XI, line 3, and see note on Morley 1594, XVIII.

XV. Also set by Bateson (1604, XIII). Weelkes also set an Italian version of these lines (1608, XVII).

XVI. A translation of 'Donna, il vostro bel viso'. See Weelkes 1608, XXIV.
   3 *by course of kind*] by course of nature.

XX. Also set by East (1610, XIX).

XXI. 1 *spots*] Patches worn on the face. Fashionable in the sixteenth century, as also in the eighteenth.

WEELKES, 1598

Editions: There are two extant editions, dated 1598 and 1608. Except in XVIII there are no significant textual differences.

Copies: 1598, Royal College of Music, London; 1608, British Museum.

Dedicatee: Edward Darcy, Esq.

I. 8 *love*] *loves* 1598 1608.

V. Stanzas 1–2 of Ode 13 in Barnabe Barnes's *Parthenophil and Parthenophe*, 1593 (reprinted by E. Arber in *An English Garner*, v (1882), p. 461).

VII. At the ends of lines 2, 4, 6, and 8 there are refrains sung to 'no no'.

XI. 7–9] Cf. Herrick, 'Corinna's Going a Maying', lines 15–16:

> Rise, and put on your foliage, and be seen
> To come forth, like the spring-time, fresh and green.

XII. 3 *ground*] A musical term; here used in the general sense of 'melody'.

XIV. 5 *Black*] swarthy, weather-beaten. *are our looks*] *is our look* A Q.

XVIII. 1–2] Cf. Sidney, *Arcadia*, Bk. I (Ringler, p. 14):

> [A] We love, and have our loves rewarded.
> [B] We love, and are no whit regarded.

9 *love*] 1608, *heart* 1598.

XXII. 6 *near*] nearer. The word here retains its comparative sense: Old English *néah*, comparative *néar*.

XXIII. 6 *grounds*] A musical term, here used in the general sense of 'melodies'.

XXIV. Thomas, Lord Borough died in Ireland in 1597. An alternative spelling is Lord Burgh; see Holborne, 1597, dedicatee; also B. White, *Index to Chambers' Elizbethan Stage & William Shakespeare*, s.v. 'Borough' and 'Burgh'.
3 *timeless*] untimely. Cf. *Two Gentlemen of Verona*, III. i, ll. 20–21:

> A pack of sorrows which would press you down,
> Being unprevented, to your timeless grave.

WEELKES, 1600

Weelkes's madrigal collection of 1600 was published in two quite distinct parts, each with its own title page, dedication, and numeration. Part I contains madrigals for five voices and Part II madrigals for six voices. But it would seem that they were originally intended to form a single volume, because, while Part II is entitled *Madrigals Of 6. parts*, Part I is entitled *Madrigals Of 5. and 6. parts*, although it only contains five-voice madrigals. Probably Weelkes decided to split the collection into two on the eve of publication but forgot to alter the title page.

Part I

Copy: Huntington.   *Dedicatee*: Henry, Lord Windsor.

I. 2 *brags*] makes a fine display.

IV–V. This madrigal is composed in the form of a ballet, with a 'fa la' after each couplet. But whereas ballets were usually light and cheerful, this is one of Weelkes's most sombre compositions. Here the 'fa las' represent the poet's vain attempt to banish grief.

X. 5 *sane . . . presage*] *save . . . persadge* 1600.

Part II

Copy: Huntington.   *Dedicatee*: George Brooke, Esq.

I. Compare the similar war-like tone of VI and Watson 1590, XXVI.
4 *'tis*] *it's* C.

II. 6 *congés*] bows.

III–IV. 10 *mean lute*] A lute of medium size and compass, as compared with a bass lute or treble lute. *which*] *with* 1600.
12 *ground*] A musical term, here used in the general sense of 'melody'.
13 *consort*] A group or ensemble of instruments.

V. 4 *may*] maid. Cf. Spenser, *The Shepherds' Calender*, November eclogue, line 39: 'The fairest may she was that ever went.'

VI. Stanza 1 of a poem in Robert Greene's *Ciceronis Amor*, 1589, p. 21. Lines 3–4 of the version in *Ciceronis Amor* are as follows:

> On Erecynus mount was Mavors seen,
> And there his ensigns did the god advance.

Compare the similar war-like tone of I and Watson 1590, XXVI.

VII–VIII. 1 *Thule*] Probably Iceland, in the 16th century the northern limit of the known world ('the period of cosmography'). Cf. Milton, *Of Reformation . . . in England*, 1641, p. 88: ' . . . the northern ocean, even to the frozen Thule, was scattered with the proud shipwrecks of the Spanish Armada.'

4 *Trinacrian*] Trinacria, Sicily.

8 *China dishes*] Dishes actually made in, and imported from China. The use of the word to mean 'porcelain' was unknown at this time.

9 *Fogo*] The volcano in Terra del Fuego, then only recently discovered.

X. An elegy in memory of Henry Noel, who died in 1597. See note on Morley 1597, XXI.

WEELKES, 1608

Copy: British Museum.   *Dedicatee*: Edward, Lord Denny.

II. 3 *gull*] booby.

4 *hoody doody*] hoddy doddy; a term having several meanings, including 'simpleton', 'cuckold', and 'hen-pecked husband'. Also 'hoodie-crow', to carry on the allusion to birds.

11 *trampled mortar*] Mortar was mixed by trampling with the feet. Cf. *King Lear*, II. ii: 'I will tread this unbolted villain into mortar'.

18 *smirkly*] smilingly.

V. 11 *sound*] swound, swoon.

VI. For references to other tobacco songs see note on East 1606, XXII.

17 *Trenchmore*] An English dance tune of the sixteenth century. See Chappell–Wooldridge, i, p. 224.

VII. 1 *rampier*] rampart.

VIII. A free rendering of Horace's ode 'Audivere Lyce' (Bk. IV. xiii).

X. These lines appear to be a political or literary skit. The identities of the Ape, Monkey, and Baboon are not known.

2 *Friday Street*] In London, running south from Cheapside to Cannon St., between Old Change and Bread St. Two inns were situated there, the Nag's Head and the White Horse. Presumably it was at one of these that the Ape, Monkey, and Baboon 'broke their fast'.

8 *Paris Garden*] A popular place of amusement at the end of the sixteenth century just as Vauxhall was two centuries later. Bull- and bear-baiting were carried on there. It was situated close to the Globe Theatre, and at this period was owned by Philip Henslowe and Edward Alleyn.

XIV. 5 *confounds*] confound 1608.

XV. 5 *noddy*] fool.

6 *busk-point*] A busk was the strip of whalebone fastened in front of a corset where it was laced up. Cf. Attey 1622, II.

XVII. The source of these Italian lines is not known. Weelkes also set a translation of this text, beginning 'Those sweet delightful lilies' (1597, XV). See also Bateson 1604, XIII.

XVIII. For other songs about morris-dancing see Weelkes 1597, XI and XII, and Morley 1594, XVIII.

13 *napkin*] Morris-dancers had handkerchiefs either held in their hands or tied to their shoulders or wrists. In Kemp's *Nine Days Wonder*, 1600, he tells of a girl at Chelmsford who danced with him and 'would have the old fashion with napkin on her arms' (sig. B2). The woodcut on the title-page shows the equipment of a morris-dancer, with napkins, bells, etc.

14 *dodkin*] A name for the 'doit', a small Dutch coin. Used consequently of any coin of very small value.

XIX. 9 *marmasyte*] marmoset. Used loosely of any kind of small monkey.

XX. 4 *Kemp*] William Kemp, a famous comic actor and dancer of the time, who acted in plays by Shakespeare and Jonson. He played Dogberry in the first production of *Much Ado about Nothing* and his own name was accidentally substituted in both Quarto and Folio texts for that of Dogberry. His remarkable morris-dance from London to Norwich is described by himself in his *Nine Days Wonder*, 1600. He travelled in France and Italy.

XXIV. The source of this Italian text is not known. Weelkes also set a translation of it, beginning 'Lady, your spotless feature' (1597, XVI).

XXV. 3 *quiristers*] *choristers* C. This old form of the word is still in use at Winchester College, where Weelkes was organist.

6 *bears the bell*] See note on Mundy 1594, X.

XXVI. The words of this elegy in memory of Thomas Morley were originally written by John Davies of Hereford as 'a dump upon the death of the most noble Henry, late Earl of Pembroke', and were printed in his *Wit's Pilgrimage* [?1605]. See A. B. Grosart, *John Davies of Hereford*, ii, p. 49.

WILBYE, 1598

Copy: Folger Shakespeare Library.   *Dedicatee*: Sir Charles Cavendish.

IV. Also set by Bennet (1599, XIII).

VI. Also set by Bennet (1599, IX).
5 *help what*] *help alas what* C A.

VII–VIII. Compare Spenser, *Amoretti*, sonnet XV, 'Ye tradeful merchants that with weary toil'. Both Spenser's sonnet and Wilbye's madrigal are imitations of sonnet XXXII in Desportes's *Les Amours de Diane*: 'Marchans, qui recherchez tout le rivage More.'

10 *ambergris*] 'A wax-like substance of marbled ashy colour, found floating in tropical seas, and as a morbid secretion in the intestines of the sperm-whale' (*O.E.D.*). Used in perfumery.

IX. Also set by Kirbye (1597, II).

X. Wilbye used these words again in XXIV in this set. They are translated from Angelo Grillo's 'Quand'io miro le rose' (*Parte prima delle rime* . . . *1589*, p. 75). Compare another translation set by Farnaby (1598, I). See also Thomas Lodge, *The Life and Death of William Longbeard* (1593): 'When I admire the rose' (sig. C).

XI. Translated from Guarini's 'Dice la mia bellissima Licori' (*Rime*, 1598, LXXVIII). Another translation, beginning 'So saith my fair and beautiful Licoris', appears with music by Marenzio in Yonge's second *Musica Transalpina* volume, 1597.

   3] All parts interpolate *Dear* before *Love is*.
   7 *bugs*] bogeys. Possibly from the Welsh *bwg*, a ghost. *amazing*] bewilderment.

XIV–XV. 10 *a-sounding*] a-swooning.

XVIII. The same poem, with many variants, occurs in R. Dowland 1610, IX: 'Lady, if you so spite me.' It is adapted from Yonge 1588, XL: 'Lady, if you so spite me.'
   9 *Leander*] This would appear to be an error for *Maeander*.

XIX. A resetting of Watson 1590, VII. See note thereon.
   7 *refraining*] checking, curbing.

XX. A resetting of Watson 1590, XXV. See note thereon.

XXI. Compare Yonge 1588, LVI.

XXIV. See note on X.

XXVI–XXVII. 9] Cf. Sidney, *Arcadia* (Ringler, p. 57, line 8): 'Long since my voice is hoarse and throat is sore.' *shriking*] shrieking.
   13 *linning*] ceasing.

XXVIII. 3 *attending*] awaiting.
   8 *yoïver*] yours.

XXIX. See Obertello, p. 130.

WILBYE, 1609

Copy: Folger Shakespeare Library.   *Dedicatee*: Lady Arabella Stuart.

I. 12 *wail*] bewail.

III. Adapted from Guarini, *Il pastor fido*, I. ii: 'Cruda Amarilli, che col nome ancora.'

IV. Cf. Shakespeare, *Venus and Adonis*, lines 151–6.

V. 8] Wilbye interpolates a 'fa la' section after *She smiles*.

VII–VIII. Lines 1–7 are in imitation of Petrarch's sonnet CXXXIV, 'Pace non trove'. See Obertello, p. 131.

XI. This poem derives from Luigi Groto's 'Cangiami o ciel pietoso in questo sasso' (*Rime*, 1587, p. 33).

XIII. 1] Compare line 1 of Ward 1613, VI.

XIV. 1] Compare first lines of Kirbye 1597, XX, and Ferrabosco 1609, X.

XVI. 5] For another example of this 'world's a stage' metaphor see Gibbons 1612, XIV.

XVII–XVIII. Adapted from one of the *Basia* (No. 19) of the Dutch poet and statesman Jan Everaerts, also called Joannes Secundus.

XIX. A translation of Boethius, *Philosophiae Consolationis*, III, Met. 7 (Loeb Classical Library, p. 253).

XXI–XXII. 4 *nicely*] coyly.

XXIII. 4 *Flamminia*] Only the Bassus sings this word.

XXIV. 3 *precellent*] surpassing.

XXV. Thomas Oliphant (*La Musa Madrigalesca*, 1837, p. 195) suggested that this madrigal was written in memory of Thomas Morley, who died in 1602. But there is no evidence to support the theory.

XXVI. Also set by Lichfild (1613, XVI–XVII).
2–3 *fond*] foolish.

YONGE, 1588

Copies: British Museum and Huntington.   *Dedicatee*: Gilbert, Lord Talbot.

Yonge's *Musica Transalpina* (1588) was the first and largest of the five Elizabethan anthologies of Italian madrigals, and its publication was crucial in fostering the vogue for madrigal composition in England. As Kerman has pointed out (pp. 48–57), three anthologies published by Pierre Phalèse at Antwerp, *Musica Divina* (1583), *Harmonia Celeste* (1583), and *Symphonia Angelica* (1585), provided the model for Yonge's anthology; in fact, no less than nineteen of the madrigals selected by Yonge had previously been printed in one or other of these Flemish collections. Yonge's translations of the Italian texts are on the whole fairly literal, unlike those of Watson in the second anthology of Italian madrigals to be published in England, *Italian Madrigals Englished*, 1590.

In the following notes reference is given to the earliest publication in which each madrigal appeared, as well as to the Flemish anthologies in the case of the madrigals which were printed therein. Where known, the author of the Italian text is also given.

I. Faignient, *Harmonia Celeste*, 1583: 'Questi ch'inditio.' Italian text by Ariosto, *Orlando*, xxiii. 127. The same text is used in xlvii.
2 *be they*] they be A T.

II. Macque, *Musica Divina*, 1583: 'Non al suo amante' (the incipit is misquoted 'Non più Diana' by Yonge). Italian text by Petrarch, madrigal LII.

III. Palestrina II a 4, 1586: 'Gioia m'abond' al cor.' Italian text by Bembo, *Rime*, 1530.

IV. Palestrina II a 4, 1586: 'Amor ben puoi.'
4 *youth*] years A T.
5] *And time consumed in vain pursuits I languish* A T.
6 *That*] *Which* C.

V. Donato II a 4, 1568: 'Dolor, se 'l mio dolor.' Italian text by Luigi Cassola, *Madrigali*, 1544, p. 33.

VI. Donato II a 4, 1568: 'Come la notte.' Italian text by Ariosto, *Orlando*, xlv. 37.
6 *retires*] *retireth* C A.

VII. de Monte IV a 5, 1571, and *Harmonia Celeste*, 1583: 'Per divina bellezza.' Italian text by Petrarch, sonnet CLIX. 9–14. See also XIII–XIV.

VIII. Palestrina II a 4, 1586: 'Perchè s'annida amore.'

IX. Palestrina II a 4, 1586: 'Amor quando fioriva.' Italian text by Petrarch, ballata CCCXXIV.
7 *here doth*] *doth here* A B.

X. Pordonone I a 4, 1580, and *Harmonia Celeste*, 1583: 'Donna la bella mano.' Same text used in XXXVIII. Compare Vautor 1619, XI.

XI. Wert I a 4, 1564, and *Symphonia Angelica*, 1585: 'Chi salirà per me.' Italian text by Ariosto, *Orlando*, xxxv. 1.

    8 *assotted*] infatuated.

XII. Verdonch, *Symphonia Angelica*, 1585: 'Donna bella e gentile.'

XIII–XIV. de Monte IV a 5, 1571: 'In qual parte del ciel'. Italian text by Petrarch, sonnet clix. Lines 9–14 also used in VII.

    2 *whence Nature hath derived*] *whereby Dame Nature framed* B.

    3 *strived*] *aimed* B.

    12 *he quelleth*] *she quelleth* C.

XV. 'Ogni luogo.' Neither Yonge nor the compiler of *Musica Divina*, 1583, give the name of the composer, but the madrigal is attributed to Palestrina in an anthology entitled *Il secondo libro delle Muse a cinque voci composto da diversi eccellentissimi musici*, published in Venice in 1559.

XVI–XVIII. Marenzio I a 5, 1580, and *Harmonia Celeste*, 1583: 'Tirsi morir volea.' Italian text by Guarini, *Rime*, 1598, f. 132^v–3. Yonge's translation was also printed in *England's Helicon*, 1600 (Rollins, i, p. 178). Compare Porter 1632, XXII: 'Young Thyrsis lay in Phyllis' lap.'

    9] C A T interpolate *yet* after *death*.

    19 *lovers fortunately*] *lovers so fortunately* A B Q.

XIX. Lasso I a 4, 1560, and Thomas Vautrollier's *Recueil du méllange*, London, 1570: 'Susanne un jour.' The same text is used in XX and in Farnaby 1598, XII, and Byrd composed two settings of a similar poem (1588, XXIX, and 1589, VIII). The story is taken from the Apocrypha. See K. J. Levy, ' "Susanne un jour": The History of a 16th Century Chanson', *Annales Musicologiques*, i (1953), p. 375.

XX. 7 *shall refuse*] C, *do refuse* A T B Q.

XXI. Faignient, *Musica Divina*, 1583: 'Chi per voi non sospira.'

XXII. Marenzio II a 5, 1581: 'Io partirò.'

    5 *pains*] *pain* C.

XXIII–XXIV. Ferrabosco, Christ Church, Oxford, MSS. 78–82: 'Vidi pianger madonna.' Italian text by Alessandro Lionardi, *Il secondo libro delle rime*, 1550, p. 15. Compare Dowland 1600, I, and Morley 1600, V.

    8 *storms*] *storming* C A B. Both readings are found in T and Q.

XXV. Ferretti I a 5, 1568, and *Musica Divina*, 1583: 'Sei tanto gratioso.' This translation was also set by Bennet (1599, III).

XXVI. Ferretti I a 5, 1568, and *Musica Divina*, 1583: 'Donna crudel.' This translation was also set by Bennet (1599, XI). Compare Vautor 1619, VI.

XXVII. Marenzio I a 5, 1580, and *Harmonia Celeste*, 1583: 'Che fa hoggi il mio sole.' This translation was also set by East (1606, XX).

XXVIII–XXIX. Felis IV a 5, 1585, and *Harmonia Celeste*, 1583: 'Sonno scendesti.'

XXX. By Palestrina: 'Vestiva i colli.' Music first printed in an anthology entitled *Il desiderio*, 1566, and then in *Musica Divina*, 1583. Italian text by Hippolito Capilupi, *De le rime di diversi . . . autori*, 1550, p. 83. This translation was also set by East (1606, XIII–XIV) and Kirbye (1597, IX–X).

XXXI. Marenzio I a 5, 1580, and *Musica Divina*, 1583: 'Liquide perle.'

XXXII. Lasso I a 4, 1560, and Thomas Vautrollier's *Recueil du méllange*, London, 1570: 'Le rossignol.' The same poem is used in XLIII, and in Byrd 1589, IX.

XXXIII. Ferretti V a 5, 1585: 'In un boschetto.'
  9 *love*] *heart* A T.

XXXIV. Mel I a 5 and 6, 1585: 'Già fu ch'io desiai.'

XXXV. Ferrabosco I a 5, 1587: 'Perle rubine.'

XXXVI. Ferrabosco I a 5, 1587: 'O dolcissimo bacio.'

XXXVII. Ferrabosco I a 5, 1587: 'Già fu mia dolce speme.' Italian text by Torquato Tasso, *Aggiunta alle rime et prose*, 1585, p. 12.

XXXVIII. Bertani I a 5, 1584: 'Donna la bella mano.' Same text used in X (see note).
  2 *That gave*] Pordenone, *Which gave* Bertani.

XXXIX. Conversi I a 5, 1572: 'Alma già dotta.'

XL. Ferrabosco I a 5, 1587: 'Donna se voi m'odiate'. Italian text by C. Rinaldi, *Madrigali*, 1588, p. 14. Yonge's translation is the basis of Wilbye 1598, XVIII. See also R. Dowland 1610, IX.

XLI. Pinello: 'Quand'io voleva' (source unkown).
  5 *still saith*] *so saith* also appears as a variant reading in A T B Q.

XLII. Ferrabosco I a 5, 1587: 'Godea Tirsi gl'amori.' Yonge's translation was also printed in *England's Helicon*, 1600 (Rollins, i, p. 178).
  10 *of mere*] *with mere* C T.

XLIII. The same text is used in XXXII (see note).

XLIV–XLV. Translated from Ariosto, *Orlando*, I, 42. See Byrd 1588, XXIV.

XLVI. Marenzio III a 6, 1585: 'Io morirò d'amore.'

XLVII. Ferrabosco, New York Public Library MS. Drexel 4302: 'Questi ch'inditio.' Italian text by Ariosto, *Orlando*, XXIII. 127. Same text used in I (see note).
  2 *No sighs be they*] *Sighs be they none* Ferrabosco.
  3] *Those have some truce, but these have no relenting* Ferrabosco.

XLVIII–XLIX. Ferrabosco, New York Public Library MS. Drexel 4302: 'Se lungi dal mio sol.' Italian text by Antonio Francesco Rinieri, *Il secondo volume*, p. 547.
  3 *and reposed*] *and still reposed* T B. Both readings occur in Q.

L. 'Ecco ch'io lasso.' Anonymous both in *Musica Transalpina* and *Musica Divina*, 1583. Yonge's translation was also set by East 1610, XX. Cf. also the first line of Kirbye 1597, I.
  4] *To live in her displeasure* Sx.

LI. Marenzio III a 6, 1585: 'Parto da voi.' Also set by East 1610, XXII.

LII–LIII. Conversi I a 6, 1584: 'Zefiro torna.' Italian text by Petrarch, sonnet CCCX. Yonge's translation reappears in his second *Musica Transalpina* volume, 1597, II, and in Cavendish 1598, XXII (lines 1–8 only). For another translation see Watson 1590, IV.

LIV–LV. Ferrabosco, New York Public Library MS. Drexel 4302: 'Fui vicino al cader.'
  8 *by Love*] *with Love* C T Q.

LVI–LVII. Marenzio II a 6, 1584: 'Cantai già lieto.' Compare Wilbye 1598, XXI.
  5 *bonds*] *bondage* C. Both readings occur in T.
  6 *Naked*] *All naked* C T Q Sx.
  8 *nor my*] *nor yet my* C Q S.
  10 *resound*] *do sound* C.

YOULL, 1608

Copy: British Museum.   *Dedicatees*: Nicholas Bacon, Philip Bacon, Nathaniel
Bacon, and Lionel Bacon, sons of Edward Bacon, Esq.

I. Stanza 1 of the fourth hymn in Sir John Davies's *Hymns of Astraea*, 1599. These
hymns were all written in the form of an acrostic, the three stanzas giving *Elisabetha
Regina*. Youll's stanza gives *Elisa* only. See A. B. Grosart, *The Complete Poems of Sir
John Davies*, i, p. 132.

II–IV. See K. Elliott and H. M. Shire, *Music of Scotland 1500–1700* (*Musica Britannica*,
XV, 1957), pp. 182 and 217–18. Day and Murrie 680.
  5 *mavis*] song-thrush.
  16 *barley-break*] See note on Morley 1595*b*, III.

VI. Stanza 1 of the fourth song in Sidney's *Astrophel and Stella* (Ringler, p. 210).
Day and Murrie 2636.

VII. 2 *dight*] made.

VIII. From Ben Jonson's *Cynthia's Revels*, I. ii.
  4 *division*] A musical term meaning a 'florid melodic passage'. The word derives
from the practice of embellishing a melody by dividing its notes into shorter ones.
Hence, 'division' was often used in the 16th and 17th centuries to denote a variation
on a melody.

XXII. Stanza 1 of the first hymn in Sir John Davies's *Hymns of Astraea*, 1599. See note
on I. Youll's stanza gives *Elisa* only. The 'fa la' refrains are of course the composer's
own addition.

PART II · LUTE SONGS

ATTEY, 1622

Copy: British Museum.   *Dedicatees*: Lord and Lady Bridgewater.

The numbering of the songs is incorrect in the original edition. The true consecutive numbering is given here.

I. This poem is translated from a French air, 'Un jour l'amoureuse Silvie', first printed in Pierre Guédron's *2ᵉ Livre d'airs de cour* in 1612. There is a different translation in Edward Filmer's *French Court Airs*, 1629, No. 9. See A. Verchaly, *Airs de cour pour voix et luth*, Paris, 1961, pp. 54 and XLIV.

II. This poem is from Thomas Tomkis's *Lingua*, 1607, sig. D2.

   3 *busk-point*] See note on Weelkes 1608, XV. *peat*] A word of uncertain origin, but in common use *c.* 1570–1640 as a term of endearment.

IV. 7] Compare lines 11–12 of Drayton's 'Fair love rest thee here', printed in *England's Helicon*, 1600 (Rollins, i, p. 103):

> See where little Cupid lies,
> Looking babies in her eyes.

V. This poem by William Browne is from his *Britannia's Pastorals*, Book ii (1616), the second song. See G. Goodwin, *Poems of William Browne*, i, p. 235.

XII. This is a much altered version of a poem by Sir Thomas Wyatt, printed in Tottel's *Song and Sonnets*, 1557 ('Tottel's Miscellany'). Rollins, i, p. 42.

XIII. 3] This line seems to lack two syllables.

XIV. In British Museum MSS. Add. 17786–91 there is an anonymous setting of this poem for voice and a quartet of viols. See P. Warlock (ed.), *The First Book of Elizabethan Songs*, 1926, p. 1.

   2 *Bethelem*] sic.

BARLEY, 1596

Copy: British Museum.   *Dedicatee*: Bridget, Countess of Sussex.

Barley's *A New Book of Tablature* is a treatise on playing the lute, orpharion, and bandora. These seven poems are printed at the beginning and end of the book, and for that reason they may suitably be included among the lutenists' songs. Music for V and VII is printed in the body of the book, but in neither instance is the poem set out in full with the music, nor is the composer's name stated. No music is supplied for the other poems.

I. 8 *life*] Possibly a misprint for *love*.

II. 11] This line seems to be corrupt.

III. This poem by Sir Arthur Gorges is printed in *Britton's Bower of Delights*, 1591 (Rollins, p. 52), *The Phoenix Nest*, 1593 (Rollins, p. 79), *A Poetical Rhapsody*, 1602 (Rollins, i, p. 223), *Wit's Recreation*, 1641, *Wit's Interpreter*, 1655, p. 92, and *Le*

Prince d'Amour, 1660. It is also preserved in several manuscripts. In many of these sources the poem begins 'Her face, her tongue, her wit' and substitutes *her* for *your* throughout. It has often been erroneously attributed to Sir Walter Raleigh. See H. E. Sandison, *The Poems of Sir Arthur Gorges*, 1953, p. 77. It will be noted that the poem is so composed that the groups of two words may be read vertically as well as horizontally; in Barley's book the groups are set out in three columns.

   13 and 20 *mine ear*] *my ear* 1596.
   23 *wit*] *wittes* 1596.

IV. 11 *spine*] *Spaine* 1596. Cf. Fletcher and Shakespeare, *The Two Noble Kinsmen*, I. i, line 1: 'Roses, their sharp spines being gone'. *rosy*] *rorie* 1596.

V. Printed in *The Phoenix Nest*, 1593 (Rollins, p. 76). The poem is a fairly close rendering of Desportes, *Diane*, I, 11.

   2 *crisped*] curly.
   13–14] In the original edition these two lines are placed after line 4. No doubt Barley's intention was to indicate that they should be repeated as a refrain after each quatrain.

VI. Printed in *The Phoenix Nest*, 1593 (Rollins, p. 100). See also Hughey, *Arundel Harington Manuscript*, i, p. 240.

   17 *your*] *you* 1596.

VII. This poem by Thomas, Lord Vaux, was printed in *The Paradise of Dainty Devices*, 1576 (Rollins, p. 72). There is an imitation of it in Peele's *Sir Clyomon and Sir Clamydes*, 1599 (A. H. Bullen, *Peele*, ii, p. 153). See also F. W. Sternfeld, *Music in Shakespearean Tragedy*, 1963, pp. 151, 304.

   4 *with dark clouds over-run*] Compare Dowland 1597, II, line 6: 'With dark clouds of an earth quite over-run.'

BARTLET, 1606

Copy: British Museum.   *Dedicatee*: Sir Edward Seymour, Earl of Hertford.

II. In previous editions of *English Madrigal Verse* it was asserted that this poem was written by Mary, Countess of Pembroke, on the death of her brother Sir Philip Sidney, but there appears to be no evidence to support this statement.

III. Day and Murrie 3736.

IV. Day and Murrie 3908.

V. 11] In this stanza alone the original edition has *Come, let him* for *Let him come*.

VI. 9 *tickle*] difficult.
   14 *worm*] Used in the sense of a harmless or powerless creature.
   18 *parlous*] *perlous* 1606. A syncopated form of *perilous*.

VII. A. B. Grosart included this poem in his edition of the poems of Nicholas Breton (I, t, p. 22).

VIII. 1] Cf. line 1 of sonnet 2 in Daniel's *Delia*: 'Go, wailing verse, the infants of my love.'
   16 *Blazing*] proclaiming.

X. This poem by George Gascoigne was printed in his *Poesies*, 1575 (ed. J. W. Cunliffe, 1907, i, p. 455). As printed in the *Poesies*, the poem consists of nine six-line stanzas. Bartlet's version is made up of stanzas 1–4 and 8, with the final couplet of stanza 7 added to each stanza to form a refrain. For other 'Philip Sparrow' poems see John

Skelton's 'Philip Sparrow' (*Pithy, Pleasant and Profitable Works*, 1568), and Sidney's *Astrophel and Stella*, sonnet 83 (Ringler, p. 208). The sparrow was associated with lechery, but it is unusual to find Philip used as a feminine name, as in this poem.

1] Compare the first lines of Mundy 1594, X, and Ravenscroft 1609*b*, VII.

19 *lays on load*] A phrase in frequent use in the sixteenth century, meaning primarily to 'deal heavy blows', and so, in a figurative sense, to do anything with vehemence and energy.

29 *fend cut*] Phrases similar to this occur in both the Skelton and Sidney poems mentioned above. It means, apparently, to 'act with propriety', 'maintain modest conduct' (see Ringler, p. 482).

30 *peat*] Cf. Attey 1622, II, line 3.

XII. Poem printed in Nicholas Breton's *The Strange Fortunes of Two Excellent Princes*, 1600, sig. G3.

8 *bond*] *band* 1606.

18 *shine*] *shines* 1606.

XIII. 10 *fear*] *fears* 1606.

15 *mourned*] *moude* 1606.

XIV. From George Peele's pastoral *The Hunting of Cupid*, of which only fragments are now extant. See David H. Horne, *The Life and Minor Works of George Peele*, 1952, p. 204.

XVI. 1 *ascribe*] *ascribes* 1606.

XVII–XVIII. 1] This is the same as the first line of Jones 1601, XII, but the two lyrics are otherwise quite different.

5 *ketched*] caught. The verb *ketch* is an obsolete form of *catch*; similarly in line 6, *ketching* for *catching*.

XIX–XXI. In British Museum MSS. Add. 17786–91 there is an anonymous song for voice and a quartet of viols, beginning 'This merry pleasant spring', which incorporates bird-calls in a similar manner and also concludes with the same line as forms the refrain (lines 8, 29, and 37) in this song. See P. Warlock (ed.), *The First Book of Elizabethan Songs*, 1926, p. 5.

14 *stockdove*] wild pigeon. *flatter*] *flat* 1606.

16 *hic-quail*] hickwall, green woodpecker.

24 *cornutos*] cuckolds.

33 *madrigals*] *madrigal* 1606.

CAMPIAN, 1607

Copy: Bodleian Library.   *Dedicatees*: there are separate dedications to King James I, Theophilus Howard (later 2nd Earl of Suffolk) and Lord and Lady Hay.

Campian printed these five songs at the end of his *Description* of the nuptial masque in honour of Lord and Lady Hay, with the following note: 'These songs were used in the masque, whereof the first two ayres were made by M[r]. Campian, the third and last by M[r]. Lupo, the fourth by M[r]. Tho[mas] Giles; and though the last three ayres were devised only for dancing, yet they are here set forth with words that they may be sung to the lute or viol.' Philip Rosseter's *Lessons for Consort*, 1609, contains instrumental versions of Nos. II, III, and V.

I. Campian describes the performance of this song as follows: 'As soon as they came to the descent toward the dancing place, the consort of ten ceased, and the four

Sylvans played the same ayre, to which Zephyrus and the two other Sylvans did sing these words in a bass, tenor and treble voice, and going up and down as they sung, they strowed flowers all about the place.' Only stanza 1 is printed with the music, but both stanzas are printed in the actual *Description*.

II. Campian describes the performance of this song as follows: 'This spoken, the four Sylvans played on their instruments the first strain of this song following, and at the repetition thereof the voices fell in with the instruments which were thus divided: a treble and a bass were placed near his Majesty, and another treble and bass near the grove, that the words of the song might be heard of all, because the trees of gold instantly at the first sound of their voices began to move and dance according to the measure of the time which the musicians kept in singing, and the nature of the words which they delivered.' Only stanza 1 is printed with the music, but both are printed in the actual *Description*. The same music is used in Campian *c.* 1613*b*, XII.

   2 *grove*] thus in the *Description*, *groves* in the musical setting.

III–V. See preliminary note.

CAMPIAN, *c.* 1613*a*

Copy: British Museum.   *Dedicatee:* Francis, Earl of Cumberland.

Campian's first and second books of ayres (here designated *c.* 1613*a* and *c.* 1613*b* respectively) were printed as a single volume, the second book having a separate title-page, dedication, address to the reader, and numeration. The volume is undated, but since the first book contains an elegy in memory of Prince Henry (XXI) and a further passing reference to his death in 1612 (VI), it is possible that the volume appeared the following year, in 1613. It is generally held that Campian was the author of all the poems that he set to music. His prose and poetical works have been edited by Percival Vivian (Oxford, 1909).

II. Another setting by Campian appears in Rosseter 1601, Pt. I, XVIII. The poem was also set by Alison (1606, I–II).

IV. A free paraphrase of Psalm cxxx.

V. 8 *is*] *in c.* 1613*a*.

VI. This poem refers to the Gunpowder Plot of 1605.
   8 *ember*] Used here with the Old English meaning of 'course of time'.

IX. 3 *hath*] *have* C.

XIII. 23 *humbly*] *humble c.* 1613*a*.

XIV. A paraphrase of Psalm cxxxvii.
   16 *ground*] A musical term, here used in the general sense of 'melody'.
   20 *and stone by stone*] *and stone and by stone c.* 1613*a*.

XVIII. Campian used the same music in Rosseter 1601, Pt. I, IV.

XIX. 14 *moorish*] sluggish; used of water found in boggy soil. Cf. Spenser, *The Fairy Queen*, Bk. IV, canto xi, stanza 29: 'The moorish Cole and the soft sliding Breane.'

XX. 19 *tutties*] bouquets, nosegays. A dialect word found in southern England. The phrase 'all of a tutty' was applied to trees in full bloom.
   32 *silly*] simple.

XXI. The subject of this elegy is Henry, Prince of Wales, who died in 1612.
   2 *Hally*] Like 'Hal', a familiar form of 'Henry'.

CAMPIAN, *c.* 1613*b*

Copy: British Museum.   *Dedicatee*: Henry, Lord Clifford.

Concerning Campian's second book of songs see the preliminary note to his first book (*c.* 1613*a*).

III. 7 *traitress . . . tresses*] Note the play on words.

V. 17 *prayers*] *prayes c.* 1613*b*.

VI. 16 *past recure*] *most recure c.* 1613*b*.

VII. 8 *swelling*] *smelling c.* 1613*b*. Bullen and Vivian also made this emendation in their editions of Campian's works.

VIII. 12 *of force*] of necessity.

X. 1–6] These lines also appear as lines 13–18 of 'Turn back, you wanton flyer' (Rosseter 1601, Pt. I, VII). This latter song also uses the same music, with an extra strain inserted into the middle.

XII. The music is the same as that used in Campian 1607, II. British Museum MS. Add. 15117, f. 10, contains a version of this poem set to the music of Morley's 'Now is the month of maying' (Morley 1595*b*, III).
    6 *earthy*] music text, *earthly* metrical text.

XV. This poem was also set by John Wilson: see Bodleian MS. Mus. b. 1, f. 15ᵛ, and *Cheerful Ayres or Ballads*, 1660, p. 134. Day and Murrie 3011.
    24 *roving*] *moving c.* 1613*b*.

XVI. Also set by Jones (1609, I), with several variants.

XVII. 6 *pleasure*] music text, *pleasures* metrical text.

XVIII. 13 *osiers*] willows.

XX. 3 *rubine*] of ruby colour.

CAMPIAN, 1614

Copy: Bodleian Library.   *Dedicatee*: none.

In publishing the *Description* of this masque Campian continued the course he had adopted in his 1607 masque by appending five songs complete with their musical settings. This musical appendix has a separate title-page, worded as follows: *Ayres, made by several authors, and sung in the masque at the marriage of the Right Honourable Robert, Earl of Somerset, and the Right Noble the Lady Frances Howard. Set forth for the lute and bass viol, and may be expressed by a single voice to either of those instruments. 1614.*

I. This song is sung by Eternity. Towards the end of it 'the three Destinies set the Tree of Gold before the Queen'.
    6 *this stock . . . hand*] thus in musical appendix, *the stock . . . hands* in text of masque.

II. ' . . . the Queen pulled a branch from the tree and gave it to a nobleman, who delivered it to one of the Squires.' This song is then sung 'while the Squires descend with the bough toward the scene'.
    5 *Th'uncharmed*] thus in musical appendix, *The uncharm'd* in text of masque.

III. Sung after the masquers' first dance.

IV. 'Straight in the Thames appeared four barges with skippers in them, and withal this song was sung.' The second stanza is sung at the end of the masque 'while the boats pass away'.

14 *these*] thus in text of masque, *those* in musical appendix.

V. The words of this song were first printed in Campian's account of the *Lords Masque*, published in 1613. For comment and a transcription of the music, see F. W. Sternfeld, 'A Song from Campian's Lords Masque', *Journal of the Warbourg and Courtauld Institutes*, xx (1957), p. 373.

CAMPIAN, *c.* 1618*a*

Copy: British Museum.   *Dedicatee*: Sir Thomas Monson.

Like his first and second books of ayres, *c.* 1613, Campian's third and fourth books (here designated *c.* 1618*a* and *c.* 1618*b*) form a double volume, with the fourth book having its own dedication, address to the reader, and numeration of songs (not, however, a separate title-page). The volume is undated, but its approximate date of publication is suggested by the opening lines of the dedicatory address to Sir Thomas Monson,

> Since now those clouds that lately over-cast
> Your fame and fortune are dispersed at last,

which would seem to refer to Monson's pardon following his alleged complicity in the murder of Sir Thomas Overbury. Monson was pardoned in 1617, so the *Third and Fourth Book* must have been published some time between 1617 and Campian's death on 1 March 1619/20. Campian is generally held to be the author of all the lyrics contained in this volume.

II. This poem was also set by Pilkington (1605, VIII) and Jones (1605, XVII). Where Pilkington's and Jones's texts differ from that set by Campian they generally do so in much the same way. There is a parody of the first stanza in Thomas Heywood's *The Rape of Lucrece* (Q1, 1608), second song:

> Let humour change and spare not,
> Since Tarquin's proud, I care not.
> His fair words so bewitch my delight
> That I dote on his sight.
> Now all is gone, new desires embracing,
> And my deserts disgracing.

See Heywood, *Plays* (Mermaid Series), ed. A. W. Verity, p. 347; *Rape of Lucrece*, ed. A. Holaday, lines 553 ff. Concerning the rhyme 'spare not—care not', see also Morley (1594, XII); Yonge (1588, IV); Bodleian Library MS. Mus. f. 17–19 (*Shakespeare Quarterly*, ix, 1958, 112 and 116). See also *Notes and Queries*, new series, xii. 333.

VI. This song was later printed in John Playford's *A Brief Introduction to the Skill of Music*, 1660, p. 50. Day and Murrie 3942.

XI. This song was later printed in John Playford's *A Brief Introduction to the Skill of Music*, 1660, p. 45, and *The Musical Companion*, 1673, p. 119. Day and Murrie 1690.

XIII. 3 and 5] The repetition of *discourses* may be due to an error, but it is difficult to suggest any emendation. Compare XIV, lines 1 and 3.

XIV. 1 and 3] The repetition of *conversing* may be due to an error. Compare XIII, lines 3 and 5.

XVII. British Museum MS. Add. 24665, f. 61ᵛ, contains a version of this song with a fourth stanza (Vivian, p. 366).

   4 *let*] hindrance.

XVIII. British Museum MS. Harl. 6910, f. 150ᵛ, contains a version of this poem with two extra lines, forming a sonnet (Vivian, p. 367). The poem was incorrectly attributed to Joshua Sylvester in the 1633 edition of Sylvester's *Works*.

XX. Playford's *Select Ayres and Dialogues*, 1669, p. 56, contains a setting of this poem by Nicholas Lanier. Day and Murrie 1009.

XXII. 7 *press*] force.

XXVI. 10 *cheer*] countenance. Cf. Byrd 1588, XII, line 4.

CAMPIAN, *c.* 1618*b*

Copy: British Museum.   *Dedicatee*: John Monson, son of Sir Thomas Monson.

Concerning Campian's fourth book of songs see the preliminary note to his third book (*c.* 1618*a*), with which it was published.

V. 9 *served*] *serve c.* 1618*b*. *the Pawn*] A corridor in the Royal Exchange which served as a bazaar, where at this time fashionable ladies made their purchases.

VII. This poem was also set by Jones (1605, X) and Alison (1606, XIX–XXI).

   6 '*cherry-ripe*'] A street cry. See Ravenscroft 1611, VII, line 5.

IX. Also set by Ferrabosco (1609, VIII). There is a version in Nat. Lib. Scotland, Advocates MS. 5.2.14 which has a further stanza (Vivian, p. 369). Day and Murrie 4119.

   9–12] By a printing error these lines in the original songbook are identical with lines 3–6. The correct text has been supplied from Ferrabosco's setting.

X. The music of this song is very similar to that of 'Follow your Saint' (Rosseter 1601, Pt. I, X).

XI. 11] By a printing error this line in the original songbook is identical with line 7. There is no means of ascertaining the correct text of the line. This error is similar to that in song IX.

XII. Compare Corkine 1610, II, which Vivian considers to be by Campian.

XIII. 2 *ungaged*] unbound, by formal promise or otherwise.

XV. 17 *housen*] An interesting example of the old English plural in *en*.

XVII. Also set by Dowland (1603, XVII). There is another setting, with a third stanza, in British Museum MS. Add. 15117, f. 19 (Vivian, pp. 369–70).

XVIII. Also set by Corkine (1610, XI), with a different third stanza and several other variants.

XXII. This is an erotic parody of his 'Mistress, since you so much desire' (Rosseter 1601, Pt. I, XVI).

   7–8] See note on Rosseter 1601, Pt. I, XVI.

XXIII. The first stanza, with several variants, had previously been set by Campian (Rosseter 1601, Pt. I, XVII), but the second and third stanzas are quite new.

XXIV. There is a keyboard transcription by Richard Farnaby of this song in *The Fitzwilliam Virginal Book* (ed. J. A. Fuller Maitland and W. Barclay Squire, II,

p. 263). The tune is also known as 'Quodling's Delight' (*Fitzwilliam Virginal Book*, ii, p. 19), and 'Goddesses (*The English Dancing Master*, 1651, p. 52). It seems likely that the tune was not composed by Campian, but that he set the poem to a popular tune of the time. For further references see Chappell–Wooldridge, i, p. 276. It is noteworthy that Campian has set stanzas 2 and 3 to variations on the melody, maintaining, however, the same bass and harmonic scheme. Day and Murrie 926.

CAVENDISH, 1598

Copy: British Museum.   *Dedicatee*: Lady Arabella Stuart.

This book, like that of Greaves, contains both madrigals and ayres, but it is included here among the lutenists' songbooks because the greater number of the pieces belongs to that class: I–XX are ayres, and XXI–XXVIII are madrigals. The numbering of the pieces is incorrect in the original edition, but the true consecutive numbering is given here. The title-page of the only known exemplar of this work (in the British Museum) is badly damaged, and the principal title remains unknown.

III. 2 *rely*] *relyes* 1598.

IV. 2 *wooed*] music text, *vowed* metrical text.

V. 1 *feat*] graceful, pretty. Cf. Burns, *Hallowe'en*, III, 'The lasses feat an' cleanly neat'.

VI. This poem is based on the sonnet 'No es ciego Amor' from Gaspar Gil Polo's *Diana enamorada*, 1564. In 1598 Bartholomew Yong published a translation of this work, but this poem is not the same as Yong's version. The Spanish and English texts have been edited together by R. L. and M. B. Grismer (Minneapolis, 1959). Cf. British Museum MS. Add. 23229, f. 122ᵛ.
 9 *it*] *yet* 1598.

VII. The words are by Fulke Greville, *Caelica*, sonnet 1. Also set by Peerson (1630, I–III).
 5 *power bereft*] metrical text (printed at the end of the book), *proverb reft* music text.

X. 16 *sons*] songs. This is a very early use of the word in English, although it appears as a Scottish form at an earlier date.

XI. The same words are set in XVII. See Obertello, p. 133.

XIII. The same text is used in XXVII.

XIV. 8 *dyed in grain*] This expression means 'thoroughly dyed' or 'dyed in the fibre'. So here, as applied to flowers, of intense or brilliant colour.

XVII. The same words are set in XI.

XIX–XX. In the original edition there is no indication that XX is Pt. II of XIX, but this is clearly so. The same text was set by East (1604, XXI–XXII). See also Vauter 1619, XI, in which lines 7–10 of this lyric occur as lines 3–6, preceded by two lines which are derived from lines 1–4.
 9 *meed*] reward.

XXI. This poem is Nicholas Yonge's translation of Ferrabosco's madrigal 'Nel più fiorito Aprile' (II a 5, 1587) printed in his second *Musica Transalpina* volume, 1957.

XXII. A resetting of Yonge 1588, LII (see note thereon).

XXIV. This piece later appeared as Cavendish's contribution to *The Triumphs of Oriana* (Morley 1601, XI). Cavendish was the first composer to adopt the 'Oriana' refrain (lines 5–6) following its first appearance in Yonge's second *Musica Transalpina* volume, 1597 (XXIV).

XXV. 2 *loden*] laden.

XXVI. Printed in *A Poetical Rhapsody*, 1602 (Rollins, i, p. 220).
2 *feater*] Cf. V, line 1.

COPRARIO, 1606

Copy: British Museum.   *Dedicatee*: none.

Giovanni Coprario (or Coperario) was the Italianate name adopted by John Cooper, who spent many years of his early life in Italy. In addition to the *Funeral Tears* (1606) and *Songs of Mourning* (1613) he was the composer of songs II, III, and IV in Campian's *Description of a Masque* (1614).

IV. Stanza 1 of this poem was also set by John Dowland (R. Dowland, 1610, X).

COPRARIO, 1613

Copies: Bodleian Library and British Museum.   *Dedicatee*: Frederick V, Count Palatine of the Rhine.

Henry, Prince of Wales, in whose memory this set of songs was written, was the eldest son of James I. He died in 1612 at the age of 18, but he had already shown himself a keen patron of the arts, and particularly of music. Coprario was musical instructor to the children of James I. See the preliminary note to Coprario 1606. Thomas Campian was the author of all the poems in this set (Vivian, pp. 101–10).

IV. 6 *Fate*] *Love* 1613. In the British Museum copy *Love* has been amended to *Fate* in a contemporary hand. Following Bullen and Vivian we have accepted this emendation, which certainly makes more sense of the line.
12 *embraced*] *embarc't* 1613.

V. 1 *How like a golden dream you met and parted*] Vivian (p. 362) points out that the Count Palatine landed at Gravesend on 16 October 1612, and Prince Henry died on 6 November following. Their acquaintance, therefore, did not last a month.

VI. 8 *Than now for one's fate*] music text, *Thou now for one's fall* metrical text.

CORKINE, 1610

Copy: British Museum.   *Dedicatees*: Sir Edward Herbert and Sir William Hardy.

Following the songs in this book are instrumental pieces for the lyra-viol.

I. Compare Corkine 1612, VII.

II. Vivian (p. 369) considers this poem to be by Campian. Compare Campian *c*.1618*b*, XII.
11 *paysed*] *payse* is a variant of the obsolete verb *peise*, meaning to weigh or measure; so, as here, to hold in mutual equilibrium. Cf. the modern English *poise*.

IV. Compare Dowland 1600, XI.

VI. There is a variant version of this poem in British Museum MS. Harl. 6917, f.31ᵛ.

    5 *are*] *am* 1610.

VII. 10 *shale*] A rare use of this obsolete verb in the intransitive sense of seed or grain dropping out of the husk and so being scattered away. Here used figuratively, meaning 'waste away'.

VIII. 5 *things*] *thing* 1610.

IX. This poem by Anthony Munday is printed in *England's Helicon*, 1600 (Rollins, i, p. 28) where it is stated to be by 'Shepherd Tony'. It was taken from the prose romance *Primaleon of Greece*, Book II, chapter 27, translated by Munday and published in 1596. It was also set by Pilkington (1605, XVIII) and Jones (1605, II).

X. For other dialect songs see Ravenscroft 1614, XVII–XX. The original spelling has been reproduced in this instance.

XI. Poem by Campian, and set to music by him (*c.* 1618*b*, XVIII). Corkine's third stanza does not occur in Campian's version, and there are several variants in stanzas 1–2.

CORKINE, 1612

Copy: British Museum.   *Dedicatees*: There are three separate dedications, as follows: at front of book, Sir Edward Dymoke; after song VIII, Sir Robert and Sir Henry Rich; after song XIV, Ursula, daughter of Sir Robert Stapleton, and Elizabeth, daughter of Sir Walter Cope.

Following the songs in this book there are eight instrumental compositions.

II. 11 *guerdonize*] reward.

III. 5 and 9] The repetition of *bewraying* as a rhyme-word may be due to some error.

IV. Poem by John Donne. Corkine's text differs in several details from that printed by Gardner (p. 35). See note on Dowland 1612, II.

VII. Compare Corkine 1610, i.

VIII. See A. B. Grosart, *Sylvester*, ii, p. 341.
    1 *musky*] perfumed with musk.
    3 *glose*] pretence, false show.
    9 *creature*] nature 1612.

IX. From Sidney's *Certain Sonnets*, III, where it is directed to be sung to the tune of 'Non credo già che più infelice amante' (compare Bateson 1604, III). Ringler, p. 136. Sidney later used the poem in the 'new' *Arcadia*, Book III, 15. The poem was also printed without the author's name in Nicholas Breton's *Arbour of Amorous Devices*, 1597, sig. B3ᵛ.
    4 *keepeth*] turneth 1612. The error is here corrected from the version in Sidney's *Certain Sonnets*.

X. 5 *Maugre*] notwithstanding, in spite of.

XI. Compare Campian's 'My sweetest Lesbia' (Rosseter 1601, Pt. I, I).

XIV. 4] The idea that virgins were condemned upon death to lead or dance with apes in hell is alluded to elsewhere. See Rosseter 1601, Pt. I, XIX; Maynard 1611, XII; Jones 1609, V; and Shakespeare, *Much Ado about Nothing*, II. i: 'I will even take sixpence in earnest of the bearward, and lead his apes into hell.' Philip Wayne, the editor of the New Clarendon edition of the play (Oxford, 1954), remarks that he recently discovered a Breton dish inscribed 'Les vieilles filles conduisent les singes en enfer' (p. 132).

XVI. 7 *remised*] released.
   14 *endue*] endow.

XVII. This poem makes elaborate use of terms used in connexion with polyphonic music.
   3] A perfect concord is the harmonic combination of a note and its octave or fifth.
   5 *ground*] The principal melody.
   6 *parts*] The several vocal or instrumental parts which sound simultaneously in polyphonic music. *descant*] A term applied to any melody or melodies performed simultaneously with the principal melody or 'ground'.

XVIII. 5 *baines*] An obsolete form of 'banns'.

DANYEL, 1606

Copy: British Museum.   *Dedicatee*: Anne Green, daughter of Sir William Green. See also XXI.

I. Also set by Pilkington (1624, VIII–IX). See note thereon.
   12 *Green*] an allusion to the dedicatee.

II. A translation of Guarini's 'O come se' gentile' (*Rime*, 1598, f. 83ᵛ). A different translation was set by Gibbons (1612, IX) and Vautor (1619, XVIII). See Obertello, pp. 408 and 519–20.

IV. Sonnet 57 in Samuel Daniel's *Delia* sonnet sequence, where lines 11–12 as printed here occur before lines 9–10. See A. B. Grosart, *Daniel*, i, p. 74. The composer and poet were brothers.
   3 *my Muse according*] metrical text, *my Muse it sounds according* music text.
   10 *Then judge*] metrical text, *Judge then* music text. *gives*] om. music text, which also repeats the word *same*.

V. 2 *For that*] metrical text, *because* music text.

VII. The metrical text is printed here. In the music text there are several interpolations.

VIII. Lines 1–8 are from sonnet 23 in Samuel Daniel's *Delia* (A. B. Grosart, *Daniel*, i, p. 52). Lines 9–16, however, are not to be found among the poet's works.
   6 *help*] metrical text, *aid* music text.

IX–XI. 8 *more*] metrical text, *the* music text.

XII. 2 *envassalled*] *unvassalled* 1606.

XIII–XV. 2 *that*] metrical text, *which* music text.
   3 *ground*] A musical term, here used in a general sense to mean 'melody'.
   7–8] The meaning of these two lines is obscure. Perhaps they could be paraphrased as follows: 'Certain uncertainly-remembered melodies, evoking past thoughts, bring back the grief, and then—though the music dies away again—the grief remains.' *Forecast* here seems to mean *forepast*.

XVI. 3 *dark black*] metrical text, *black dark* music text.

XVIII. In British Museum MS. Add. 30982, f. 36 (middle or late 17th century), this poem is headed 'ii song. Jo: Richards'.
   8 *silency*] silence.

XIX. 11] metrical text, *And they must pine that lovers prove* C¹ C², *Then pine that lovers be* A, *And they must pine that lovers be* B.

XX. 1] Compare line 1 of Petrarch's sonnet 'Or che 'l ciel e la terra e 'l vento tace'.

XXI. This number is a composition for the lute alone, with the title 'Mrs. Anne Green her leaves be green'.

DOWLAND, 1597

Editions: There are five extant editions, dated 1597, 1600, 1603, 1606, and 1613. Textual variants are recorded in the following notes.

Copies: 1597, 1600, 1606, 1613, British Museum; 1603, Manchester Public Library.

Dedicatee: Sir George Cary, Baron Hunsdon.

II. Sonnet 5 in Fulke Greville's *Caelica*, with several variants. This poem was also set by Peerson (1630, XVII–XVIII).

6] Compare Barley 1596, VII, line 4.

III. Poem printed in *England's Helicon*, 1600 (Rollins, i, p. 160). In his manuscript list of the authors represented in *England's Helicon* (British Museum MS. Harl. 280, ff. 99–101) Francis Davison attributes the poem to the Earl of Cumberland. Malone, in his copy of *England's Helicon* (Bodleian Library, Mal. 278), attributes it to 'M[aster]. F[ulke]. G[reville].', and A. B. Grosart included it in his edition of Greville's works (1870, ii, p. 139). R. W. Bond included it in his edition of the works of John Lyly (1902, iii, p. 478), and in recent years Sir Walter Raleigh has been suggested as the author (Walter Oakeshott, *The Queen and the Poet*, London, 1960, p. 157). In earlier editions of *English Madrigal Verse* Dr. Fellowes mentioned a manuscript in which this poem is attributed to 'W. S.' (?William Smith). As Rollins remarks (op. cit., ii, p. 176), the 'author is entirely uncertain'. In Dowland's *Lachrimae, or Seven Tears*, 1604, there is an instrumental version of the music entitled 'Sir John Souch his Galliard'.

IV. British Museum MS. Add. 15117, f. 15ᵛ. In Dowland's *Lachrimae, or Seven Tears*, 1604, there is an instrumental version entitled 'Captain Digorie Piper his Galliard'.

14 *am I*] 1597 1600, *I am* 1603 1606 1613.

V. The music of this song is also known as 'The Earl of Essex's Galliard' (see John Dowland, *Lachrimae*, 1604, and Robert Dowland, *Variety of Lute Lessons*, 1610). It has been speculated that the poem refers to Essex's hopes of Royal forgiveness.

9–10, 21–22] A quotation from a tune called 'The woods so wild' is incorporated into the musical setting of these lines. Concerning the tune see note on Ravenscroft 1609a, XXX.

VI. The music of this song is entitled 'Frog Galliard' in numerous sources (e.g. Thomas Morley, *Consort Lessons*, 1599). See Chappell–Wooldridge, i, p. 274. The first two lines are quoted in Marston's *Eastward Ho*, III. ii (H. Harvey Wood, *The Plays of John Marston*, iii, p. 121). Line 9 quoted in *Every Woman in her Humour*, 1609, sig. B2ᵛ. Day and Murrie 240s.

VIII. Poem printed in *England's Helicon*, 1600 (Rollins, i, p. 158).

9 *locks*] *yokes* all editions. It would seem that *yokes* (from line 4) was accidentally substituted for *locks* when the 1597 edition was being printed, and that the error was carried over into later editions. Compare the similar errors in Campian *c.* 1618*b*, IX and XI.

13 *teen*] sorrow, vexation. Derived from the Old English *téona*, meaning *injury*. Cf. Shakespeare, *Richard III*, IV. i, l. 97, 'And each hour's joy wrecked with a week of teen'.

IX. Compare stanza 2 with Petrarch, sonnet cxx.
   7 *restless*] 1600 1603 1606 1613, *hapless* 1597.
   8 *indurate*] hardened.

X. 3–4] In the 1613 edition the words of these two lines are missing, except for *reposing*.

XI. Printed in *England's Helicon*, 1600 (Rollins, i, p. 158).
   9 *pain*] *pains* all editions.
   25 *river's side*] 1597 1606 1613, *river side* 1600 1603.

XII. 7 *ever*] This word may have been interpolated by the composer; it makes the line longer by two syllables than the corresponding lines in stanzas 2–3.
   25 *proves*] 1597 1600 1603 1606, *prove* 1613.

XIII. See note on Dowland 1600, XI. British Museum MSS. Harl. 3511, f. 1, and Add. 15118, f. 4ᵛ. Day and Murrie 2999. Quoted in *Every Woman in her Humour*, 1609, sig. Bᵛ.
   2 *diseased*] made ill at ease. It may be that this word and *displeased* (line 4) have been accidentally interchanged in the original editions.
   5] Quoted in *Eastward Ho* (H. Harvey Wood, *John Marston*, iii, p. 94).

XV. British Museum MS. Add. 15118, f. 6.
   1 *reave*] bereave.
   4–5] Cf. Beaumont and Fletcher, *The Knight of the Burning Pestle*, I. i (*Works*, ed. A. Waller and A. Glover, vi, p. 177).

XVII. The same stanza form is used by Thomas Lodge in 'Strive no more', printed in *The Phoenix Nest*, 1593 (Rollins, p. 57), and in Jones's song 'Happy he' (1605, XV). There is a rather corrupt version of the music in the Landesbibliothek, Kassel, MS. Mus. 1081, f. 32ᵛ, with Italian words. Day and Murrie 585.
   12 *do*] 1597 1600 1603 1606, *doth* 1613.
   30 *triumph*] 1613, *triumps* 1597 1600, *triumphs* 1603 1606.

XVIII. This poem refers to Sir Henry Lee, the Queen's champion from 1559 to 1590, and it was sung by the royal lutenist Robert Hales on 17 November 1590 at the Tilt Yard on the occasion of Lee's resigning this title in favour of the Earl of Cumberland. This occasion is described by George Peele in his *Polyhymnia* (1590), and by William Segar in *Honour Military and Civil* (1602), pp. 197–200, both of whom print the words of the song (Segar's version is in the first person). Since then the poem has frequently been attributed to Peele in anthologies, but it is almost certainly not by him, and there is some likelihood that it is in fact by Lee himself. In subject-matter and style it is very similar to 'Far from triumphing court and wonted glory' (attributed to Lee in R. Dowland 1610, VIII) and 'Time's eldest son' (printed in Dowland 1600, VI–VIII, and attributed to Lee in Bodleian MS. Rawl. poet. 148, f. 75ᵛ). See D. H. Horne, *The Life and Minor Works of George Peele*, 1952, pp. 165–73 and 231–44; E. K. Chambers, *Sir Henry Lee*, 1936, pp. 142–4; Hughey, i, p. 243, and ii, p. 322. It is not known whether it was Dowland's setting of the poem that Hales performed in 1590. Hales may have composed his own setting for the occasion. One of his songs is printed in *A Musical Banquet* (R. Dowland 1610, III).
   7] Concerning this image of a helmet being used as a beehive see G. K. Hunter, *John Lyly*, 1962, p. 84.
   16 *her*] 1597 1600 1603, *him* 1606 1613. See note on line 17.
   17 *Goddess*] 1597 1600, *Gods* 1603, *Ye Gods* 1606 1613. This alteration, and that in line 16, was made following the death of Queen Elizabeth I and the accession of King James I in 1603.

XIX. There is a version of the music for solo lute in Cambridge University Library Dd. 2. 11, f. 58. Day and Murrie 285.

XX. This poem was also set by Robert Johnson; see Ian Spink (ed.), *Robert Johnson: Ayres, Songs and Dialogues* (*The English Lute-Songs*, 2nd series, XVII), 1961, p. 4.

5 *thought-worn*] *thoughts, worn* all editions.

8 *this*] 1597, *his* 1600 1603 1606 1613.

XXI. No. 51 in Fulke Greville's *Caelica* sonnet sequence. Also printed in *England's Helicon*, 1600 (Rollins, i, p. 159).

10 *foot*] The 1633 edition of *Caelica* reads *wing*.

13 *songs*] 1600 1613, *song* 1597.

DOWLAND, 1600

Copy: British Museum.   *Dedicatee*: Lucy, Countess of Bedford.

When this song-book was published Dowland was serving as court lutenist to King Christian IV of Denmark, and his dedication to the Countess of Bedford is dated 'From Helsingnoure [Elsinore] in Denmark the first of June. 1600'. In his absence the book was published by George Eastland, who supplied another dedication to the same lady, in acrostic verse, and wrote the address to the reader. Litigation arose concerning the song-book, and this has been described by Margaret Dowling in 'The Printing of John Dowland's "Second Booke of Songs or Ayres" ', *The Library*, 4th series, xii (1932), p. 366. Following the songs in this book there is an instrumental piece for the lute entitled 'Dowland's Adieu for Master Oliver Cromwell'.

I. Stanza 1 was also set by Morley (1600, v). See also Yonge 1588, XXIII.

II. *Lachrimae* is the title of the famous tune to which Dowland set these words. In the earliest surviving sources of the music (e.g. Cambridge University Library, Dd. 2. 11, f. 76ᵛ and f. 81, and William Barley's *A New Book of Tablature*, 1596) it is an instrumental pavan, and it would appear that Dowland originally composed it as such, and later added the words. Either as a song or an instrumental composition it was widely known both in this country and on the continent and is preserved in many sources (see O. H. Mies, 'Dowland's Lachrimae Tune', *Musica Disciplina*, iv (1950), p. 59). In 1604 Dowland published a collection of several compositions for consort, entitled *Lachrimae, or Seven Tears* . . . The first of these pieces, headed 'Lacrimae Antiquae', is yet another version of the well-known tune (see P. Warlock's edition, London, 1927). The following are some references to *Lachrimae* by contemporary dramatists: Middleton, *No Wit, No Help Like a Woman*, I. i; Jonson, *Time Vindicated* (ed. Herford and Simpson, vol. vii, p. 662, line 224); Fletcher, *The Bloody Brother*, II. ii; Beaumont and Fletcher, *The Knight of the Burning Pestle*, II. viii; Massinger, *The Maid of Honour*, I. i; Massinger, *The Picture*, v. iii; Webster, *The Devil's Law Case*, IV. Day and Murrie 1016.

7 *lost*] *last* 1600.

III. In British Museum MSS. Add. 17786–90 there is a version of this song for voice and viols with an alternative sacred text.

IV. 1] Compare line 1 of Ward 1613, XXV.

V. 8] Compare line 1 of R. Dowland 1610, X.

VI–VIII. This poem is attributed to Sir Henry Lee in Bodleian MS. Rawl. poet. 148, f. 75ᵛ. In style and subject-matter it has much in common with Dowland 1597, XVIII, and R. Dowland 1610, VIII (which is also attributed to Lee). See note on Dowland 1597, XVIII.

X. Hugh Holland is presumably the poet who is now chiefly remembered as the author of a sonnet prefixed to the first folio (1623) of Shakespeare's plays. He also contributed some commendatory verses to *Parthenia* (1611) and to Farnaby's *Canzonets* (1598). He died in 1633. See *Dictionary of National Biography*, ix, p. 1040, and *Notes & Queries*, New Series, xi (1964), p. 149.

1–2] This couplet, which recurs as a refrain throughout the song, is taken from a poem in Sidney's *Arcadia* (Ringler, p. 68), but the two poems are otherwise quite different. Sidney's poem is in quantitative 'Asclepiadickes' (– – – ∪ ∪ – – ∪ ∪ – ∪ ∪), but Dowland does not follow this scheme in setting the refrain to music.

21 *prove*] *procure* 1600.

31 *Wanstead*] A village on the borders of Epping Forest. The Earl of Leicester had a country house there. In 1578 Sidney's *Lady of the May* was presented before the Queen as she walked in Wanstead Garden. Line 27 may be a direct reference to this occasion.

XI. See note on Bateson 1618, XII. Day and Murrie 1675. In John Forbes's *Songs and Fancies*, Aberdeen, 1666, these words are sung to the tune of Dowland 1597, XIII.

XII. For other pedlars' songs see note on Ravenscroft 1609a, V.

5–7 *the heart is true*] We have followed the original edition in printing the three-fold repetition of this phrase (and the corresponding ones in stanzas 2–3).

11 *th'orienst*] possibly a misprint for *th'orient's*.

XIII. 15 *spirits*] Pronounced *sprites*, thus rhyming with *delights*.

XIV. It may be that this song originally belonged to some dramatic production.

XV. Day and Murrie 3898.

11 *grieving*] *groaning* 1600.

48] This line is missing in the original edition. It is supplied here from a manuscript addition in a contemporary hand in the copy in the library of St. Michael's College, Tenbury, Worcestershire.

XVII. Day and Murrie 2908.

XVIII. No. 28 in Fulke Greville's *Caelica* sonnet sequence. Among other variants, Dowland omits stanza 2 and substitutes the name Joan for Myra in the final stanza. The same substitution occurs in a version of the poem printed on pages 79–80 of the 1591 edition of Sidney's *Astrophel and Stella*, where it is subscribed 'Finis E.O.'

13 *begot*] *beget* 1600.

14 *Atheists*] *Atheist* 1600.

21 *Fortune's*] *Fortune* 1600.

XX. In the original edition the table of contents gives 'finding in fields my Sylvia all alone' as the title of song XX, but the song printed is 'Toss not my soul', and against it there is the note 'for Finding in Fields ye shall find a better ditty'. It is likely that this substitution was made by George Eastland, the publisher, since Dowland himself was in Denmark at the time the book was printed.

9] music text, *When once the uttermost of ill is known* metrical text.

XXII. This would appear to be a song from a masque or entertainment. In British Museum MS. Add. 15117, f. 12, there is a version with a different text beginning 'Say, fond love, what seekest thou here'.

DOWLAND, 1603

Copy: British Museum.   *Dedicatee*: Sir John Souch.

III. Day and Murrie 337.

VI. Ascribed to the Earl of Pembroke in *Poems, Written by the Right Honourable William Earl of Pembroke . . . [and] Benjamin Ruddier*, 1660, p. 115, where there is a third stanza. However, the ascriptions in this book tend to be unreliable. Bodleian MS. Add. B. 97, f. 18 has a fourth stanza.

6 *but one*] This would seem to be an interpolation by Dowland, and to be a reference to Queen Elizabeth I. Compare song VII, line 3.

VII. This poem is perhaps in praise of Queen Elizabeth I.

26] The same line occurs as line 12 in Mason and Earsden 1618, VI.

VIII. Compare song XV in this set.

X. 30 *forbid*] forbade. The old form of the past tense.

XI. 5 *rude like to my rhyming*] The poet illustrates this by avoiding rhyme in the last three lines of this stanza. In stanzas 2–3 the corresponding lines are rhymed.

XII. 16 *cheer*] countenance.

23 *ground*] melody; not necessarily in the highest part.

XIII. 8 *ne'er the near*] See note on Byrd 1589, XXVIII.

XIV. This may be a song from a play. Diana Poulton has pointed out that the situation described in the lyric is similar to that of Jessica leaving Shylock's home with the money she has stolen from him to elope with Lorenzo, in *The Merchant of Venice* (*The Musical Times*, cv (1964), p. 26).

XV. Compare song VIII in this set.

XVII. Poem by Campian, and set to music by him (*c.* 1618*b*, XVII).

XVIII. These stanzas are taken from a poem attributed to the Earl of Essex in numerous manuscripts (including British Museum MS. Add. 5495, f. 28ᵛ and Bodleian MS. Douce 280, ff. 123–4ᵛ) and to Henry Cuffe, his secretary, in a few others (e.g. Bodleian MS. Tanner 76, f. 93). Bodleian MS. Rawl. poet. 148, ff. 87–88, attributes it to John Lyly. The attribution to Essex seems highly likely. William Browne, *Britannia's Pastorals*, i, song 4, ll. 683–96, also associates the poem with Essex. See R. W. Bond, *The Complete Works of John Lyly*, iii, pp. 445–7. British Museum MS. Add. 15117, f. 21. Day and Murrie 3237.

3 *Who fed on time*] There is, of course, a play on the words *time* and *thyme* throughout this song. We have retained a single spelling for both senses of the word, as in the original edition.

16 *atomies*] small insignificant creatures.

XIX. Poem printed in *A Poetical Rhapsody*, 1602 (Rollins, i, p. 186), and there subscribed 'Incerto'. Credited to Sir Edward Dyer in Bodleian MS. Rawl. poet. 148, f. 103, and (rather tentatively) to Raleigh in Bodleian MS. Tanner 169, f. 192ᵛ. See also R. W. Bond, *John Lyly*, iii, p. 482, and Hughey, i, p. 238. Day and Murrie 2136.

XX. 10 *it*] Possibly a misprint for *them*.

12 *fledge*] fledged.

15 *Will*] *Wit* 1603.

XXI. 7 *do*] *die* 1603.

DOWLAND, 1612

Copy: British Museum.   *Dedicatee*: Theophilus, Lord Walden.

I. This poem is ascribed to Lord Pembroke in *Poems, Written by the Right Honourable William, Earl of Pembroke . . . [and] Benjamin Ruddier*, 1660, p. 45. In British Museum MS. Add. 22603, f. 50ᵛ, and Bodleian MS. Rawl. poet. 160, f. 103ᵛ it is ascribed to 'J.D.' The authorship remains uncertain.

II. The name of the dedicatee is spelt 'Juell' in the Oxford University registers (see J. Foster, *Alumni Oxonienses*, Pt. I, p. 835). He matriculated in 1603 at the age of 17, and subsequently became vicar of Rodmersham in Kent. The poem has sometimes been credited to John Donne. It survives in many manuscripts, and in several of these (e.g. British Museum MS. Stowe 961) and the 1669 edition of his poems the first stanza is prefixed to ''Tis true 'tis day' (see Corkine 1612, IV). In Bodleian MS. Ashmole 47, f. 73, it is ascribed to Dr. Corbet. Stanza 1, with several variants, was also set by Gibbons (1612, XV), beginning 'Ah, dear heart, why do you rise'. Although the authorship remains uncertain, it is perhaps of some significance that in this song-book it is followed by another poem associated with Donne. See Gardner, pp. 108 and 245.

III. This poem is an imitation of Donne's 'Lovers' Infiniteness'. See Gardner, pp. 77 and 244.

V. In Dowland's *Lachrimae, or Seven Tears*, 1604, there is an instrumental version of this song entitled M[aster]. Henry Noel his Galliard'. Concerning Noel see note on Morley 1597, XXI.

VI. 16] *But none knows how* 1612. It seems that the words in this line have become transposed. Our amended version preserves the rhyme scheme.

VIII. 8 *debt*] binding.

IX. 3 *lain*] *lyne* 1612.

  13 *amate*] dismay, dishearten. Cf. Keats, *Rem.* I, 12 (1848), 'A half-blown flow'ret which cold blasts amate'.

  14 *nor tears*] *or tears* 1612.

X. Stanzas 1, 2, and 11 of a long poem entitled *The Passion of a Discontented Mind*, printed in 1601 'by V. S. for John Baily'. Stanza 5 was set by Gibbons (1612, II). The authorship is not stated, but Thomas Corser (*Collectanea Anglo-Poetica*, 1867, Pt. III, p. 42) and Jean Robertson (*Poems by Nicholas Breton*, 1952, p. xcii) attribute it to Nicholas Breton. The poem is also contained in British Museum MS. Sloane 1779, f. 208ᵛ, where it is ascribed to the Earl of Essex, and in British Museum MS. Egerton 2403, f. 38. Bodleian MS. Tanner 76, f. 114 contains part of the poem. The question of the authorship is discussed by Edward Doughtie in *Renaissance News*, xvii (1964), p. 1.

XIII. Also set by Byrd (1588, XXX) with four more stanzas.

XIV–XVI. These lines are adapted from a sonnet in Nicholas Breton's *The Soul's Harmony*, 1602, sigs. C3ᵛ–C4. There are several variants in Dowland's text, and as Edward Doughtie has pointed out (*Renaissance News*, xvii (1964), p. 1), lines 1–2 are not by Breton at all. They are derived from stanza 9 of a poem attributed to the Earl of Essex, part of which Dowland set to music in his *Third and Last Book of Songs* (1603, XVIII). The lines in question are as follows:

> Great king of bees, that rightest every wrong,
> Listen to Patience in her dying song.

XVIII. The words of this song were printed in *Speeches delivered to her Majesty this last Progress, at the Right Honourable the Lady Russell's at Bisham, the Right Honourable the Lord Chandos's at Sudeley, at the Right Honourable the Lord Norris's at Rycote*, 1592. The song formed part of the Sudeley entertainment (see R. W. Bond, *John Lyly*, i, p. 479). The poem was also printed in *England's Helicon*, 1600 (Rollins, i, p. 122).

XIX–XXI. These three songs were probably written for the wedding festivities of Theophilus, Lord Walden, to whom this volume of songs is dedicated. Lord Walden married Elizabeth, the second daughter of the Earl of Dunbar, in March 1611/12. Dowland was in his service for a short time before taking up his Court appointment in October 1612.

ROBERT DOWLAND, 1610

Copies: British Museum and Bodleian.   *Dedicatee*: Sir Robert Sidney.

This anthology of English, French, Spanish, and Italian songs compiled by John Dowland's son Robert is unusual in that the authorship of several of the lyrics is stated.

II. Bodleian MS. Rawl. poet. 85, f. 125; Bodleian MS. Rawl. poet. 148, f. 67 (stanzas 1–3); British Museum MS. Add. 15118, f. 2ᵛ.
   30 *vilde*] obsolete form of *vile*.

III. Concerning Robert Hales see Diana Poulton, 'The Favourite Singer of Queen Elizabeth I', *The Consort*, XIV (1957), and note on Dowland 1597, XVIII. A. B. Grosart, in his edition of Breton, i, 'Daffodils and Primroses', refers to a version of this poem among a group of poems known to be by Breton in a manuscript dated 1596. This reference is no doubt to British Museum MS. Add. 34064, f. 7, and the ascription seems probable. This and Bodleian MS. Rawl. poet. 85, f. 45, have an additional stanza.

IV. The ninth song in Sidney's *Astrophel and Stella* (Ringler, p. 221). There are a number of textual differences as compared with the version printed by Ringler, particularly in stanza 4. The poem was also printed in *England's Helicon*, 1600 (Rollins, i, p. 15).
   10 *mischief's*] *measure's* 1610.
   24 *to us*] *ewes* Astrophel and Stella, *by us* England's Helicon.
   28 *must*] (*Muse*) 1610.
   46] *Then adieu, dear flock, adieu* Astrophel and Stella, *Then my dear flock now adieu* England's Helicon.
   49 *blaying*] bleating.

V. Stanzas 1–4 and 8 of the tenth song in Sidney's *Astrophel and Stella* (Ringler, p. 225). Stanzas 1–3 were also set by Byrd (1589, XXXIII), and stanza 8 by Ward (1613, VIII). British Museum MS. Add. 15118, f. 8; Bodleian MS. Rawl. poet. 85, ff. 107ᵛ–108 (subscribed 'Britton'); Hughey, i, p. 116.
   11 *joys*] om. 1610.

VI. Daniel Batchelar seems to have been Sir Philip Sidney's page. See Edward Doughtie, 'Sidney, Tessier, Batchelar, and *A Musicall Banquet*: Two Notes', *Renaissance News*, xviii (1965), p. 123. British Museum MSS. Add. 24665, f. 48ᵛ; Add. 17786–91 (setting by William Wigthorp); Add. 38539 (instrumental version by John Dowland).
   7 *hope*] hopes 1610.

VII. Stanzas 1–17 and 26 of the eighth song in Sidney's *Astrophel and Stella* (Ringler, p. 217). Bodleian MS. Rawl. poet. 85, f. 34ᵛ; British Museum MS. Add. 15232, f. 32; British Museum MS. Harl. 6910, f. 171. Until recently it was thought that the composer was Charles Tessier, whose *Premier livre de chansons et airs de court* was published in London in 1597. But as Edward Doughtie has shown (*Renaissance News*, xviii (1965), pp. 123–6) the composer was in fact Guillaume Tessier, and the music was adapted by Robert Dowland from that composer's four-part setting of Ronsard's 'Le petit enfant Amour', printed in his *Primo libro dell'arie*, Paris, 1582 (sig. C2ᵛ). Tessier's melody has been very slightly altered to fit Sidney's words, and the lower three voices fashioned into a lute accompaniment.

16 *reflected*] *rejected* 1610.
27 *set*] *see* 1610.
58 *the leaves*] *leaves leaves* 1610.

VIII. Concerning Sir Henry Lee (1530–1610) see note on Dowland 1597, XVIII, and *D.N.B.*, xi, p. 797. In this poem he would appear to be referring to himself.

14 *denaid*] *denay* is an obsolete form of *deny*.
21] Compare Dowland 1597, XVIII, line 1.

IX. The words are from Yonge 1588, XL (see note thereon). Also set, with many changes, by Wilbye (1598, XVIII).

X. Also set, with a second stanza, by Coprario (1606, iv).

XI. This air by Pierre Guédron was printed in Gabriel Bataille's *Airs de différents autheurs*, Paris, 1608, p. 47. For a transcription of the music see P. Warlock's *French Ayres from Gabriel Bataille's Airs de différents autheurs (1608–1618)*, London, 1926, p. 34.

XII. This air was printed in Gabriel Bataille's *Airs de différents autheurs*, Paris, 1608, p. 5.

XIII. This air by Pierre Guédron was printed with three more stanzas in Gabriel Bataille's *Airs de différents autheurs*, Paris, 1608, p. 32. For a transcription of the music see P. Warlock's *French Ayres from Gabriel Bataille's Airs de différents autheurs (1608–1618)*, London, 1926, p. 25.

3 *pieds*] *peids* 1610.
15 *l'entreprise*] *l'enterprise* 1610.

XIV. Printed in Gabriel Bataille's *Airs de différents autheurs*, Paris, 1608, p. 38. The words are from Montemayor's *Diana*, III (1574 edition, f. 79ᵛ).

1 *desarmado*] *dessarmado* 1610.
4 *Quán*] *Quam* 1610.
7 *niño*] *nigno* 1610.
8 *de verse*] *enversé* 1610.
9 *do está*] *do sta* 1610.
11 *era*] *ero* 1610.
12 *le*] *te* 1610.

XV. This poem is headed 'Espagnol' in *A Musical Banquet*; it is, of course, in extremely corrupt Italian. For a reconstruction and translation see Diana Poulton, 'Some Corrections to the Three Spanish Songs in "A Musical Banquet"', *The Lute Society Journal*, iii (1961), p. 22.

XVI. Printed in Gabriel Bataille's *Airs . . . second livre*, Paris, 1609.

2 *bielan*] *yelan* 1610.
3 *tan aflicion*] *ta asticion* 1610.
4 *a mi*] *almi* 1610.

XVII. From *Le seconde musiche del Dom. Maria Megli*, 1602, No. 8.

4 *l'ire*] lire 1610.

5 *l'ire*] lire 1610.

XVIII. From Giulio Caccini's *Le nuove musiche*, 1602, p. 16.

XIX. From Giulio Caccini's *Le nuove musiche*, 1602, p. 12.

XX. 1 *più*] pipiu 1610.

3 *Mia*] Mi 1610.

4 *mio*] mia 1610.

7 *Mia*] mio 1610.

8 *mia*] mio 1610.

9 *pass'*] pas 1610.

FERRABOSCO, 1609

Copy: British Museum.   *Dedicatee*: Henry, Prince of Wales.

Alfonso Ferrabosco (*c.* 1575–1628), the composer of these ayres, was the son of Alfonso Ferrabosco the madrigalist, who died in 1588, and some of whose madrigals were printed in *Musica Transalpina* (Yonge 1588).

I. This poem is a translation of Desportes's 'Je me veux rendre hermite et faire penitence' (*Amours de Diane*, II. 8). It was printed in *Breton's Bower of Delights*, 1591 (Rollins, p. 20), *The Phoenix Nest*, 1593 (Rollins, p. 77), *Today a Man, Tomorrow None*, 1644 (where it is credited to Raleigh), and was also set to music by Nicholas Lanier (*Select Musical Ayres and Dialogues*, 1652, Pt. I, p. 1). It is also preserved in several manuscripts, among them British Museum MS. Add. 38823, f. 58^v, British Museum MS. Harl. 6910, f. 139^v, and Bodleian MS. Rawl. poet. 85, f. 25^v. See also Hughey, i, p. 240, A. M. C. Latham, *The Poems of Sir Walter Raleigh*, 1951, p. 11, and R. W. Bond, *John Lyly*, iii, p. 470. Day and Murrie 2048.

II. In the British Museum copy of this song-book a second stanza has been written in an eighteenth-century hand with the rubric 'added from an Anc^t MS':

> Beauty and Love die even as they were born;
>   Time is their foe, the weakest sex their guard.
> Ambitious ends, Death's power or Fortune's scorn
>   Like timeless fruit withers without reward.
> Come then, obey this summons, come away,
>   For here vain hopes must serve you for your pay.

III. This song is from Ben Jonson's *Masque of Blackness* (C. H. Herford, P. and E. Simpson, *Ben Jonson*, vii, p. 178).

V. The opening line is the same as that of a poem attributed to 'W. R[aleigh].' in Bodleian MS. Rawl. poet. 85, f. 43^v, and to '[Sir Edward] Dy[er].' in British Museum MS. Harl. 7392, f. 22. The rest of the poem is otherwise quite different. See A. M. C. Latham, *Raleigh*, 1951, p. 172.

VI. From Jonson's *Volpone*, III. vii (C. H. Herford, P. and E. Simpson, *Ben Jonson*, v, p. 82). For comment see F. W. Sternfeld, 'Song in Jonson's Comedy', *Studies in the English Renaissance Drama*, ed. J. W. Bennett, 1959, p. 150. The same poem occurs in Jonson's *The Forest* (Herford and Simpson, op. cit., viii, p. 102). British Museum MS. Add. 15117, f. 20^v.

VII. Poem by John Donne, entitled *The Expiration* (Gardner, p. 36).

VIII. Poem by Campian, and set to music by him (*c.* 1618*b*, IX). In Ferrabosco's song-book the words are set out in stanzas of three fourteen-syllable lines.
   25 *gull*] booby.

IX. Lines 1–8 were also set by Pilkington (1624, XX).

X. From Montemayor's *Diana*, Bk. I, chap. 2 (sig. A2ᵛ), translated by Bartholomew Yong, 1598. Ferrabosco uses only the first of six stanzas.

XI. Stanza 5 of the Epithalamion in Jonson's *Haddington Masque* (C. H. Herford, P. and E. Simpson, *Ben Jonson*, vii, p. 262).

XII–XIV. This song would seem to be in praise of King James I.

XVI. Also set by Jones (1605, XIV).
   2 *diseased*] ill at ease, troubled. Cf. Dowland 1597, XIII, line 2. *sense*] *soul* 1609.

XVII. Also set by Jones (1605, IV), beginning 'Shall I *look* to ease my grief', and with one more stanza. Stanza 1 only was set by Lichfild (1613, II).

XVIII–XX. From Jonson's *Masque of Beauty* (C. H. Herford, P. and E. Simpson, *Ben Jonson*, vii, pp. 192–3). Cf. songs XXI and XXII.

XXI. From Jonson's *Masque of Beauty* (Herford and Simpson, op. cit., p. 191). Cf. songs XVIII–XX and XXII.

XXII. From Jonson's *Masque of Beauty* (Herford and Simpson, op. cit., p. 193). Cf. songs XVIII–XX and XXI.

XXIII. From Jonson's *Masque of Queens* (Herford and Simpson, op. cit., p. 315). The Queen referred to in the song is Queen Anne, consort of James I.

XXV. St. Michael's College, Tenbury, Worcestershire, MS. 1019, f. 2, contains a version of this song with an Italian translation, beginning 'Occhi stelle mortale', under the English text.

XXVIII. 8 *liv'st*] *lives* 1609.

FORD, 1607

Copy: British Museum.   *Dedicatee*: Sir Richard Weston.

I. In Folger MS. V. a. 345, p. 33, this poem is entitled 'A young mans Epitaph'. In the margin there is the note 'He dyed sep 12, 1604, at the age of 23 yeares'. And below: 'These verses above written, were made by one mr Henry Morrice, sone to mr morrice, Attorney to the Court of awards, who dyed sodenly in milford lane hauing these verses in his pocket.'

II. 9 *'chill*] I will. From the medieval English *ich*, which was still used for *I* in the south in the sixteenth century, especially when conjoined with *have, am, will*, etc., in the forms *'chave, 'cham*, and *'chill*.
   15 *salveless*] that cannot be healed.

IV. This poem is printed between sonnets 39 and 40 in Lodge's *Phyllis*, 1593. Also printed in *The Phoenix Nest*, 1593 (Rollins, p. 62), where it is subscribed 'T. L. Gent.'

VIII. Poem printed in Richard Johnson's *The Golden Garland of Princely Pleasures*, 1620, sig. G4ᵛ, where it is called 'Love's Constancy'. John Cotgrave's *Wits Interpreter*, 2nd edition, 1662, has a version with two extra stanzas and an 'Answer to the third stave'.

IX. Printed in Richard Johnson's *The Golden Garland of Princely Pleasures*, 1620, sig. G7.

XI. 3 *Desire's*] desire 1607.
    5 *nill*] will not.

GREAVES, 1604

Copy: British Museum.   *Dedicatee*: Sir Henry Pierrepont.

Like Cavendish's song-book (1598) this is a somewhat miscellaneous collection, Nos. I–IX being lute ayres, X–XV songs for solo voice accompanied by a consort of viols, and XVI–XXI madrigals for five voices.

III. Also set by Pilkington (1624, V).

X. There is a somewhat similar poem by Lord Vaux in *A Paradise of Dainty Devices* (Rollins, p. 19), beginning 'When I look back, and in myself behold'.

XVI. A song of welcome to King James I.

XVII–XVIII. The 'Oriana' of this madrigal would appear to be Queen Anne, or 'Ori-Anna', wife of James I. Following the death of Queen Elizabeth I the Oriana motif continued to be used both by those who lamented her death and by those who welcomed the new dynasty. It will be noted that the refrain of this madrigal (lines 6–7 and 13–14) is derived from the characteristic refrain of the madrigals in *The Triumphs of Oriana* (Morley 1601).

XXI. 6 *delights*] The use of singular verb-forms with plural nouns was common at this time. This may, however, be a misprint for *delight*, since the latter provides a more satisfactory rhyme.

HANDFORD, 1609

Copy: Trinity College, Cambridge, MS. R.16.29.   *Dedicatee*: Henry, Prince of Wales.

The poems here printed are taken from the manuscript collection of songs by George Handford in the Library of Trinity College, Cambridge (MS. R.16.29). The collection is dedicated to Henry, Prince of Wales, and the dedication is dated 'From Cambridge the 17th of December 1609'. For further details see Edward Doughtie, 'George Handford's *Ayres*: Unpublished Jacobean Song Verse', *Anglia*, lxxxii (1964), p. 474.

IX. 5] *Ah* is interpolated before *alas*.
    7 *icy*] spelt *ysce*.

X. 4 *lover*] loverll 1609.

XI. 4 *heat*] This may be an error for *heart*.
    12 *me*] missing in 1609. Compare line 6.

XII. From Daniel's *Delia* sonnets, final ode. Stanza 1 was set by Farmer (1599, II).
    15 *know*] kowe 1609.

XIV. 2] This line would seem to be corrupt. *an*] *a* 1609.

XV. 3 *ev'n*] even 1609; sung to one note.

XVI. Mall Newberry was a famous prostitute of the time.

1–4] Note the singular-plural rhymes.

3 *And tear*] *antare* 1609.

XVII. This song is missing from the manuscript. It is listed in the table of contents as 'Ah now I fall: yᵉ first part'.

XVIII. This is part II of song XVII, which is missing from the manuscript.

6] This line seems to be corrupt.

XIX. In the manuscript the second voice is headed *Daphne*, but this is an error for *Amyntas*. In the table of contents the song is called 'A Dialogue between Amyntas and Pastorella'.

XX. It is clear from the context and the *he* in line 14 that Daphne is male. Possibly the name should be 'Daphnis'.

10 *seek'st*] *seest* 1609.

18 *all*] Phyllis sings *both*.

HUME, 1605

Copy: British Museum.   *Dedicatee*: William, Earl of Pembroke.

This book is usually known by its running (and punning) title, *Musical Humours*. It consists mainly of instrumental compositions.

I. Hume was a soldier; his life-story is told by Peter Warlock in *The English Ayre*, pp. 82–90. This song contains various types of battle onomatopoeia in the accompaniment.

III. For other tobacco songs see note on East 1606, XXII. *O love it* (ll. 3 and 19) is printed as a separate line in the song-book.

CXII. British Museum MS. Add. 15117, f. 22.

CXIII. This poem was set again by Hume in his *Poetical Music* (1607, XIV).

CXIV. This song is superscribed 'The imitation of Church music, singing to the organs, but here you must use the viol de gambo for the organ, playing the burthen strongly with the bow, singing loud; your praeludiums and verses are to be played with your fingers, singing thereto not over loud, your bow ever in your hand'.

HUME, 1607

Copy: British Museum.   *Dedicatee*: Queen Anne.

Hume's *Poetical Music*, like his *Musical Humours* (1605), consists mainly of instrumental compositions. In the British Museum copy the verso of the title-page contains the following inscription, apparently in Hume's own hand: 'I do in all humility beseech your Majesty that you would be pleased to hear this music by me; having excellent instruments to perform it'.

I. 11 *eternished*] made eternal.

XXV. 10 *rates*] chides, scolds.

JONES, 1600

Copy: British Museum.   *Dedicatee*: Sir Robert Sidney.

II. Poem printed in Richard Johnson's *The Golden Garland of Princely Pleasures*, 3rd edition, 1620, sigs. F7–F8, where it is directed to be sung to the tune 'When Troy

Town' (see Chappell–Wooldridge, pp. 183–6). There is a somewhat similar song in Greene's *Ciceronis Amor*, 1580, sig. D3ᵛ, beginning 'Fond feigning poets make of Love a god'. British Museum MS. Add. 22603, f. 58.

VI. 5 *thy*] *this* 1600.

VIII. 29 *owlets'*] *howlets* 1600.

IX. This poem was formerly in the commonplace book of John Lilliatt (Bodleian MS. Rawl. poet. 148); the first stanza still appears in another hand at the end of the book (f. 112ᵛ) subscribed 'Uni, soli, semper I. L.' The poem may be by Lilliatt himself.
   1 *on*] *and* 1600.

X. The words *Come away* in line 3, *Come again* in line 7, *Come and do* in line 11, and *Come and do* in line 15 are printed thrice in the original edition. In the final stanza only the corresponding line is expanded to an equivalent length by the addition of different words.

XI. Cf. British Museum MS. Harl. 6057, f. 7ᵛ.
   1 *Weemen*] So spelt in the original edition to emphasize the play on words.
   8 *hollow*] *hallow* 1600.

XII. This song is quoted in *Twelfth Night*, II. iii. The tune was popular in its own right both in this country and on the continent. In D. R. Camphuysen's *Stichtelycke rymen*, Amsterdam, 1647, p. 4, it is entitled 'Shall I bid her go' (cf. line 15). Jones parodies both words and music of the song in 'Farewell, fond youth' (1609, VIII). Thomas Percy included the poem in his *Reliques of Ancient English Poetry*, 1765, i, p. 187, with the title 'Corydon's Farewell to Phyllis'.
   5 *moe*] more.

XV. 1–3] Compare lines 5–6 of Byrd 1611, XVII.

XVI. Also set to music by Henry Bowman, *Songs*, 1677, p. 45. Day and Murrie 3124.

XVII. 12 *shent*] punished.

XVIII. British Museum MS. Add. 15117, f. 21ᵛ.

XIX. A fragment of this song is sung by Francheschina in Marston's *The Dutch Courtezan*, II. i (H. Harvey Wood, *John Marston*, ii, p. 88). It is twice quoted in *Every Woman in her Humour*, 1609, sigs. D3ᵛ and Hᵛ. Cf. also J. Starter, *Boertigheden*, sig. Bᵛ (printed at the end of his *Friesche Lust-Hof*, Amsterdam, 1621).

JONES, 1601

Copy: British Museum.   *Dedicatee*: Sir Henry Leonard.

I. Also set by Morley (1600, X).

II. Stanza 1 of this poem was the third of five *Poems and Sonnets of Sundry Other Noblemen and Gentlemen* appended to the 1591 edition of Sidney's *Astrophel and Stella*. Vivian (pp. 350, 376–7) attributes the authorship to Campian.
   10 *seals of love*] Cf. line 6 of the song 'Take O take those lips away' in *Measure for Measure*, IV. i.
   18 and 24 *makes*] make 1601; compare ll. 6 and 12.

III. 12 *each to other calls*] *each to other to calls* 1601.

V. 15 *pish*] Possibly an error for one of the alternative exclamations *push* or *tush*, which would meet the requirements of the rhyme.

VI. 24 *mum*] This obsolete verb used intransitively means to make an inarticulate sound with closed lips indicating inability to speak; hence, to *keep silence*.

VII. 4 *ne'er the near*] See note on Byrd 1589, XXVIII.

IX. Printed in *The Phoenix Nest*, 1593 (Rollins, p. 98), *England's Helicon*, 1600 (Rollins, i, p. 82) and *A Poetical Rhapsody*, 2nd edition, 1608 (Rollins, i, p. 291). In Heywood's *The Rape of Lucrece* (Q1, 1608) stanzas 1 and 5 appear as the third song (ed. A. Holaday, lines 568 ff.; see also Heywood, *Plays*, Mermaid Series, ed. A. W. Verity, p. 347). See also *Cupid's Masterpiece, c.* 1650, sig. A6, *Venus's Looking-Glass, c.* 1670, p. 132, *Westminster Drollery*, 1671, p. 63, British Museum MS. Add. 22601, f. 104, and Rosenbach MS. 186, p. 98. In *England's Helicon*, 1600, it was first credited to 'S[ir]. W[alter]. R[aleigh].', but this was cancelled by a slip of paper, inscribed 'Ignoto', pasted over the initials. Francis Davison's list of authors (British Museum MS. Harl. 280, f. 99) also attributes the poem to Raleigh. A. M. C. Latham (*Raleigh*, 1951, p. 171) regards the attribution as doubtful. It would seem that it was Jones's setting of the poem that was sung in *The Rape of Lucrece*, since the text of the play gives word-repetitions in the last line of each stanza that correspond with those required by Jones's setting.

    4 *sauncing bell*] Another form of *saunce-* or *sanctus-bell*.

    28 *moe*] more.

X. 2 *cowherds*] cowards. Cf. Spenser, *The Fairy Queen*, Bk. VI, canto vi, stanza 26: 'that craven cowherd knight'.

XI. From Sidney's *Arcadia* (Ringler, p. 41).

    2 *their*] *the* 1601.

    8 *flamy*] flame-like.

    16 *writer*] *waters* 1601.

XII. 1] This line is the same as line 1 of Bartlet 1606, XVII–XVIII, but the rest of the poem is quite different.

    11 [*am*]] lacking in 1601.

XIII. 4 *nill*] will not. A contracted form of *ne will*.

    12 *at best is bad*] Possibly an error for *is bad at best*, which would supply an internal rhyme for *rest* in line 11, as in lines 5–6.

XIV. 13 *true*] *fair* 1601. Both sense and rhyme-scheme seem to require this emendation.

XVII. Cf. British Museum MS. Add. 30012, f. 143, and Henry Bold, *Latin Songs*, 1685, p. 42. Day and Murrie 2101.

    12 *It is*] *Is is* 1601.

    21 *moe*] more.

XVIII. 10 *melt*] *meet* 1601.

XX. 6 *sport*] *sports* C.

JONES, 1605

Copy: Royal College of Music.   *Dedicatee*: Henry, Prince of Wales.

Until recently the only known copy of this song-book was the one in the Royal College of Music, which lacks its title-page. Because of this the date of publication was unknown, but all reference books followed one another in assigning it to 1608. The discovery of an undamaged copy in the castle of Schlobitten in East Prussia reveals that the true publication date was 1605 (see O. H. Mies, 'Elizabethan Music Prints in an East-Prussian Castle', *Musica Disciplina*, iii (1949), p. 171).

I. Vivian (p. liv) tentatively suggests Campian as the author of this poem.

II. Poem by Anthony Munday. Also set by Pilkington (1605, XVIII) and Corkine (1610, IX). See note on Corkine's setting.

III. British Museum MS. Add. 15118, f. 8.
   11 *franzy*] frenzy.

IV. This poem was also set by Ferrabosco (1609, XVII), and stanza 1 only by Lichfild (1613, II).

VI. Poem by Francis Davison, and printed in *A Poetical Rhapsody*, 1602 (Rollins, i, p. 81).
   12 *one*] Probably a misprint for *me*.

VIII. This song was sung in a 'lottery' presented before the Queen at Harefield House, near Uxbridge, in July 1602, and printed in the 2nd (1608), 3rd (1611), and 4th (1621) editions of *A Poetical Rhapsody* (Rollins, i, p. 242). It is there assigned to 'I.D.' (Sir John Davies). According to the rubric printed above the song in *A Poetical Rhapsody* 'A mariner with a box under his arm, containing all the several things following, supposed to come from the carrack, came into the presence singing this song'. The carrack here referred to was a vessel captured off the Spanish coast in 1602, carrying a cargo estimated at a million ducats. The text of the lottery has been reprinted by A. B. Grosart, *Sir John Davies*, ii, p. 87. R. W. Bond claims it for John Lyly (*Works*, i, p. 491).
   7–8] An old saying. See Rollins, op. cit., ii, p. 209 for references to other instances of its use.

IX. Poem by Campian, and set to music by him (Rosseter 1601, Pt. I, XIV). It was also printed in *A Poetical Rhapsody*, 1602 (Rollins, i, p. 215).
   3 *it that*] *that which* A T B.

X. Poem by Campian, and set to music by him (*c.* 1618*b*, VII). Also set by Alison (1606, XIX–XXI).

XI. Poem printed in *A Poetical Rhapsody*, 1602 (Rollins, i, p. 130).
   1 *mine*] *my* C.

XIII. Poem printed in *A Poetical Rhapsody*, 1602 (Rollins, i, p. 148).

XIV. Also set by Ferrabosco (1609, XVI).
   5 *betrayer*] *betrayers* 1605.

XV. 24] This line is translated from Seneca, *Thyestes* (Loeb Classical Library, *Seneca's Tragedies*, ii, p. 124):

> qui, notus nimis omnibus,
> ignotus moritur sibi.

XVI. Poem printed in *A Poetical Rhapsody*, 1602 (Rollins, i, p. 156). Also set by Peerson (1620, IV). Cf. British Museum MS. Harl. 6910, f. 154.

XVII. Poem by Campian, and set to music by him (*c.* 1618*a*, ii) and Pilkington (1605, VIII). See note on Campian's setting.
   5 *desires*] *delights—desire* C¹, *desires—desire* C².

XVIII. Poem printed in *A Poetical Rhapsody*, 1602 (Rollins, i, p. 178), ending with a quotation from Ovid, *Amores*, III. xi, 1: 'Vitiis patientia victa est'. Also set by Peerson (1620, VIII).

    1 *first*] *just* C², Peerson, and Poetical Rhapsody.
    4 *too too*] *all too* C².

XIX. Poem by Walter Davison. Printed in *A Poetical Rhapsody*, 1602 (Rollins, i, p. 110). Stanzas 1–2 set by Peerson (1620, IX).

XX. Poem printed in *A Poetical Rhapsody*, 1602 (Rollins, i, p. 137). Samuel Pick published it as his own work in *Festum Voluptatis*, 1639, B3ᵛ–B4.

    13 *those*] *their* 1605.

XXI. Poem printed in *A Poetical Rhapsody*, 1602 (Rollins, i, p. 177) and in the 2nd edition (1614) of *England's Helicon* (Rollins, i, p. 210). In *A Poetical Rhapsody* it is followed by a quotation from Ovid, *Amores*, III. xi, 3: 'Scilicet asservi iam me, fugique catenas'.

    7 *my*] *thy* C².

JONES, 1609

Copy: British Museum.   *Dedicatee*: Sir John Levinthorpe.

I. Poem by Campian, and set to music by him (*c.* 1613*b*, XVI). Day and Murrie 3333.

II. Day and Murrie 3121.

III. 3 *piercing*] *smiling* A.

IV. Day and Murrie 3970.
    7 *'chill*] I will. See note on Ford 1607, II.

V. 2 *apes in hell*] See note on Corkine 1612, XIV.
    10] Some words seem to be missing from this line.

VI. This song is a translation of part of a chanson, beginning 'Ma complainte n'est que fainte', in *Le nouveau recueil des chansons amoureuses*, Paris, 1589, f. 11. For another translation see *The Poems of Sir Arthur Gorges*, ed. H. E. Sandison, Oxford, 1953, p. 41. Day and Murrie 2240.

VII. Cf. Day and Murrie 1870.

VIII. Poetically and musically this is a parody of 'Farewell, dear love' (Jones 1600, XII). See note thereon.

X. 10 *Absence'*] *b* omitted in original edition.

XI. 6 *hap*] *have* C. *blessings*] C alone has the plural.

XIII. 3 *It hurts*] *Yet hurts* C.

XV. 1 *indrenched*] imprisoned (figuratively).
    2 *limed*] Smeared with bird-lime, a sticky substance used for catching small birds.
    6 *echoes*] *echo—echoes* A, *echo* T B.

XIX. 7–12] It may well be that this refrain provides us with the text (which has not survived elsewhere) of the song 'For bonny sweet Robin is all my joy' sung by Ophelia in *Hamlet*, IV. v, l. 183. See F. W. Sternfeld, *Music in Shakespearean Tragedy*, 1963, p. 71.

XX. Lines 1–4 of Petrarch's sonnet cliii.
    1 *al*] *all* 1609.
    2 *contende*] *contente* 1609.

XXI. Lines 1–8 of Petrarch's sonnet cxxxii.
   3 *l'affetto*] *effetto* 1609. *aspro e mortale*] *aspro mortale* 1609.
   5 S'à] Sa' 1609.
   6 *Se*] Sa' 1609.
   7 *dilettoso*] *dilettose* 1609.

JONES, 1610

Copy: British Museum.   *Dedicatee*: Lady Wroth.

III. 4 *angles*] spelt *Angels* in original edition.

IV. 6 *where*] *when* 1610. Compare lines 12 and 18.

V. 24 *desires to die*] *desire to dies* 1610.

VII. 5 *the*] *thy* 1610.

XIV. 7 *coll'd*] embraced.

XV. 4 *afraid*] Possibly an error for *a-feared*, which would satisfy the requirements of the rhyme scheme.

XVI. 5 [*aught*]] lacking in original edition.

XVII. This poem by Sir Philip Sidney is No. 27 in his *Certain Sonnets*, where it is printed with the rubric 'To the tune of a Neapolitan Villanell' (Ringler, p. 156). In Jones's version the refrain in stanzas 2–5 is abbreviated to 'Fa la la dan dan dan'. We have printed it throughout as it appears in stanza 1, which is set out under the music.
   30 *solly*] solely.

XVIII. 18 *raven, owl, bear*] Creatures associated with the hellish or horrific. Cf. the madman's song in Webster's *The Duchess of Malfi*, IV. ii:

> As ravens, screech-owls, bulls, and bears,
> We'll bill and bawl our parts.

XIX. These words were sung in *The Honourable Entertainment given to her Majesty . . . at Cowdray . . . 1591*, which R. W. Bond ascribes to Lyly (*Works*, i, p. 422). The song was sung 'while her Majesty shot at the deer'.

XX. 14 *cureless*] incurable.

XXI. 20 *bank-route*] bankrupt.
   21 *Lazar-like*] Like Lazarus at the gate of Dives.

MASON AND EARSDEN, 1618

Copy: British Museum.   *Dedicatee*: none.

Vivian (pp. li–lii) attributes the authorship of these lyrics to Thomas Campian, but the evidence is not conclusive.

V. This poem was printed in Humphrey Crouch's *Love's Court of Conscience*, 1637, sigs. A7–A7ᵛ (ed. J. P. Collier, *Illustrations of Old English Literature*, vol. ii/6 (1866), p. 10). It was also printed with a different tune in *Wit and Mirth: or Pills to Purge Melancholy*, vi (1720), p. 192. It also occurs in British Museum MS. Add. 27879, f. 220ᵛ (see J. W. Hales and F. J. Furnivall, *Bishop Percy's Folio Manuscript*, 1867–8, iii, p. 260). Day and Murrie 3709.

VI. 12] Cf. Dowland 1603, VII, line 26.

16 *jet*] caper. Cf. Nashe, *Pierce Penniless* (1592, sig. C4ᵛ): 'Mistress Minx . . . jets it as gingerly as if she were dancing the Canaries'.

VIII. Lines 4, 8, 12, 16, 20, and 23 are each sung twice, the first time solo, and then by the chorus.

22–23 *posterity*] The repetition of this word may be due to a misprint. Possibly *prosperity* is the correct reading in line 22.

MAYNARD, 1611

Copy: Bodleian Library.   *Dedicatee*: Lady Joan Thynne.

These twelve poems by Sir John Davies were printed in the 2nd (1608), 3rd (1611), and 4th (1621) editions of *A Poetical Rhapsody* (Rollins, i, p. 239). They are also contained in British Museum MS. Add. 22601, ff. 40–43, and in a manuscript at Downing College, Cambridge, described in the *Third Report of the Royal Commission on Historical Manuscripts*, 1872, p. 325, as 'Verses given to the Lord Treasurer upon New Year's Day, upon a dozen of trenchers, by Mr. Davis'. Sets of trenchers inscribed with these poems are preserved at the Victoria and Albert Museum and the British Museum. In Maynard's volume the twelve songs are followed by a number of lessons for the lute and lyra viol.

II. Bodleian MS. Rawl. poet. 84, f. 44.
   2 *chop-church*] A dealer or trafficker in ecclesiastical benefices.

IV. Bodleian MS. Rawl. poet. 84, f. 44ᵛ–44.

X. Bodleian MS. Rawl. poet. 153, f. 28; Bodleian MS. Eng. poet. d. 152, f. 103ᵛ *Wit's Recreation*, 1640.

XII. Bodleian MS. Rawl. poet. 84, f. 44ᵛ.
   2 *lead an ape in hell*] See note on Corkine 1612, XIV.

MORLEY, 1600

Copy: Folger Library, Washington.   *Dedicatee*: Ralph Bosville, Esq.

The only known exemplar of Morley's *First Book of Ayres* is damaged, and songs XV–XXI and two instrumental compositions, XXII and XXIII, are lacking. Songs XVII and XVIII, however, are preserved in Christ Church, Oxford, MS. 439, and the words have been transcribed from that source.

I. 2 *profess*] *profest* 1600.

IV. These three stanzas are from a seven-stanza poem by Robert Southwell entitled 'Mary Magdalen's Complaint at Christ's Death', printed in *Saint Peter's Complaint*, 1595, sigs. F2–F2ᵛ. Morley has set stanzas 5, 4, and 3 (in that order). See also Christ Church, Oxford, MS. 439, p. 37; Bodleian MS. Don. d. 58, f. 23; J. W. Hales and F. J. Furnivall, *Bishop Percy's Folio Manuscript*, ii, p. 325; Day and Murrie 3999.

V. Also set by Dowland (1600, I) with a second stanza. See also Yonge 1588, XXIII.
   5 *more*] *mennes* 1600.

VI. This song is sung by two pages in *As You Like It*, V. iii.

VII. From Sidney's *Astrophel and Stella*, song 11 (Ringler, p. 233).
   42 *Argus*] *Argues* 1600.
   44 [*you*]] lacking in original edition.

VIII. British Museum MS. Add. 24665, f. 43ᵛ. The refrain is quoted in *Every Woman in her Humour*, 1609, sig D3ᵛ.

   10 *our*] *out* 1600.

IX. 12 *a*] *of* 1600.

X. Also set by Jones (1601, I).

   7 *flight*] *light* 1600.

XII. 10 *sum*] *sunne* 1600.

XIII. Poem by Nicholas Breton, printed in *England's Helicon*, 1600 (Rollins, i, p. 53). It is also to be found in Bodleian MS. Rawl. poet. 85, f. 1ᵛ; British Museum MS. Harl. 6910, f. 140; British Museum MS. Add. 34064, f. 17ᵛ; Folger MS. 2071.7, f. 183ᵛ; and John Cotgrave's *Wits Interpreter*, 1655, sigs. H1–H1ᵛ.

   2 *shineth*] *shined* 1600.

   3–4 and 5–6] These two couplets transposed in original edition.

   4 *shone*] *stood* 1600.

   14 *with*] *for* 1600.

XIV. H. J. C. Grierson (*The Poems of John Donne*, 1912, i, p. 428) lists eight manuscripts containing this poem, one of which (the Hawthornden MS., Library of Society of Antiquaries, Edinburgh) credits it to 'J. H.' Grierson considers that it is probably by John Hoskins. It was also printed in *A Poetical Rhapsody*, 1602 (Rollins, i, p. 225), *Wit Restored*, 1658, p. 108, and *The Grove*, 1721, p. 37. Owing to the fact that the only surviving exemplar of this song-book is damaged, stanzas 2–4 are missing. They are here printed from Grierson's version.

XV. Listed in the table of contents as 'White as lilies'. The words were probably the same as those set by Dowland (1600, XV).

XVI. Listed in the table of contents as 'What lack ye Sir'.

XVII. For references to other pedlars' songs see note on Ravenscroft 1609a, V.

   3 *rebatoes*] Stiff collars worn by both sexes from about 1590 to 1630. *sister's thread*] *Sister* was a variant spelling of *sewster*, a sempstress.

   8 *potting sticks*]=*poking sticks*, for stiffening ruffs. Both terms found elsewhere: *Winter's Tale*, IV. iv. 223; Munday, *Downfall of Robert, Earl of Huntington*, 1601, F4ᵛ.

   11 *musk-cods*] The bag or gland containing musk in various animals, especially the musk-deer.

XIX. Listed in the table of contents as 'Much have I loved'.

XX–XXI. Listed in the table of contents as 'Fantastic love, the first part' and 'Poor soul, the second part'.

PILKINGTON, 1605

Copy: British Museum.   *Dedicatee*: William, Earl of Derby.

III. 10 *She*] *He* 1605.

V. Stanza 1 was set separately by Bateson (1604, VII), and stanza 2 with some changes by Pilkington (1613, IV).

   3 *clipping*] embracing.

   5 *Fortune our friend*] An allusion to the popular sixteenth-century song 'Fortune my foe'. See Chappell–Wooldridge, i, p. 76.

   15 *heliotrope*] *helitrope* 1605.

VIII. Poem by Campian, and set to music by him (*c.* 1618*a*, II) and Jones (1605, XVII). See note on Campian's setting. Cf. British Museum MS. Add. 29291, f. 6ᵛ.

    14 *proves*] *prove* 1605.

IX. In *Wit and Mirth: or Pills to Purge Melancholy* (1720 edition, vi, p. 120) there is another version, beginning 'Underneath the castle wall the Queen of Love sat mourning'. This is followed by a crude parody, beginning 'Underneath the rotten hedge the tinker's wife sat shiting'. The music is quite different from Pilkington's. Day and Murrie 3516.

    4 *mourne*] The meaning of this word, as used here, is obscure, and it is possible that the text is corrupt.

    7 *kindness*] *unkindness* 1605.

XIII. 4 *fall, th'heart*] *fall'th, heart* 1605.

XIV. 6–7] Compare Shakespeare, *Venus and Adonis*, lines 17–18:

> Here come and sit, where never serpent hisses,
> And being set, I'll smother thee with kisses.

    11–12] A line appears to be missing from between these two lines.

XV. 6 *frid*] Possibly a misprint for *frie* (fry).

XVI. This poem from Thomas Lodge's *Rosalynde*, 1590, sigs. N3ᵛ–N4, also appeared in *England's Helicon*, 1600 (Rollins, i, p. 60). There is also an anonymous poem in *England's Helicon* (Rollins, i, p. 121) beginning 'Hey down a down did Dian sing,/ amongst her virgins sitting', which is very similar to it in style and structure.

XVII. This poem was printed in *England's Helicon*, 1600 (Rollins, i, p. 96), subscribed with the initials 'H. C.' It used to be thought that these initials represented Henry Constable, but, as Rollins has shown (*The Times Literary Supplement*, 1st Oct., 1931), they almost certainly belong to Henry Chettle.

XVIII. This poem by Anthony Munday was also set by Corkine (1610, IX) and Jones (1605, II). See note on Corkine's setting. Pilkington alone adds the 'Hey nonny no' refrain.

XIX. 5 *secluse*] A rare use of this word as a substantive meaning *a secluded place*.

    18 *attone*] here used to mean *attune*.

XX. This poem by Thomas Watson is from *The Honourable Entertainment given to the Queen's Majesty . . . at Elvetham . . . 1591* (reprinted by R. W. Bond, *John Lyly*, i, p. 431). It was sung on that occasion by six virgins, three representing the Graces, and three the Hours, who walked before the Queen strewing flowers. The poem was also printed in *England's Helicon*, 1600 (Rollins, i, p. 46). Pilkington has altered Watson's refrain, which is as follows:

> O beauteous Queen of second Troy
> Accept of our unfeigned joy.

This refrain is very similar to the one in Byrd's madrigal 'This sweet and merry month of May' (Watson 1590, VIII and XXVIII, and Byrd 1611, IX).

XXI. Thomas Leighton probably belonged to the Shropshire family of that name, another member of which was Sir William Leighton, the composer and poet, and editor of the volume entitled *The Tears or Lamentations of a Sorrowful Soul*, published in 1614.

PORTER, 1632

Copy: British Museum.   *Dedicatee*: John, Lord Digby.

I. 7 *forgiveth*] *forgivest* C.
   13 *words*] *word* C.

II. This poem is ascribed to John Fletcher in Henry Lawes's *Second Book of Ayres*, 1655, p. 33. See also Bodleian MS. Don. c. 57, f. 32 (Lawes's setting), Bodleian MS. Mus. b. 1, f. 16 (music by John Wilson), and British Museum MS. Egerton 2013, f. 15. Day and Murrie 1379.

III. The first two stanzas of a three-stanza poem by Thomas Carew, printed among his *Poems*, 1640. Also set to music by Henry Lawes: British Museum MS. Add. 11608; New York Public Library MS. Drexel 4257; *Ayres and Dialogues*, 1653, Pt. I, p. 12; John Playford, *Select Ayres and Dialogues*, 1659, p. 23. Day and Murrie 1302. R. Dunlap, *Thomas Carew*, 1949, p. 18.

VI. 4 *whiteness*] spelt *witnesse* and *whitnesse* in the part-books.

VII. Day and Murrie 3372.
   6 *whiles*] *whilst* 1632.

VIII. Bodleian MS. Malone 16, p. 29.
   1 *eye*] *eyes* 1632.

IX. Poem by Henry King, and printed in his *Poems, Elegies, Paradoxes, and Sonnets*, 1657, p. 17. Bodleian MS. Don. c. 57, ff. 61ᵛ–62; Bodleian MS. Eng. poet. e. 30, f. 21ᵛ; Bodleian MS. Malone 22, f. 13; British Museum MS. Sloane 1446, f. 84. Also set to music by John Wilson, Bodleian MS. Mus. b. 1, f. 89ᵛ. Porter was Wilson's kinsman. Cf. M. C. Crum, ed., *Poems of Henry King*, pp. 149 and 225. J. R. Baker, *Poems of Bishop Henry King*, 1960, p. 23.

XI. New York Public Library, Drexel MS. 4175, No. 18. Bodleian MS. Don. c. 57, f. 32ᵛ contains an extra verse.

XII. Cf. the following Bodleian MSS. Rawl. D. 1092, f. 272; Rawl. poet. 116, f. 44; Eng. poet. d. 152, f. 107ᵛ; Eng. poet. f. 25, f. 11ᵛ; Ashmole 38, pp. 134 and 154; Ashmole 47, f. 104ᵛ; CCC. 328, f. 21ᵛ. British Museum MS. Sloane 1446, f. 76ᵛ.

XIII. Lines 1–8 of a twelve-line poem in Bartholomew Yong's translation of Gaspar Gil Polo's *Diana enamorada* (1598). The original Spanish begins 'Tenga fin mi triste vida'. See R. L. and M. B. Grismer, *Gaspar Gil Polo: Diana enamorada*, 1959, pp. 58–59.

XIV. Bodleian MS. Malone 16, p. 19; British Museum MS. Add. 25707, f. 151ᵛ.

XV. 12 *despise*] C, *deny* A T B Q.

XVI. Day and Murrie 683; Bodleian MS. Don. c. 57, f. 92.

XVII. This poem by Thomas Carew was printed in his *Poems*, 1640. It also survives in numerous manuscripts. See R. Dunlap, *The Poems of Thomas Carew*, 1949, p. 6. It was also set to music by Henry Lawes (the 'Cooper Smith' MS. listed by Dunlap).

XVIII. Day and Murrie 3174; Bodleian MS. Don. c. 57, f. 69ᵛ (music by John Wilson); British Museum MS. Add. 25707, f. 58.
   6 *swan*] *swans* 1632.
   9 *tell*] *let* 1632.

XIX. Day and Murrie 2100; Bodleian MS. Ashmole 38, p. 141.

XXII. This poem is derived from Yonge 1588, XVI–XVIII. Day and Murrie 4137.

XXIV. Day and Murrie 3154.

XXV. This poem by William Strode is contained in numerous manuscripts in the British Museum and Bodleian Library. It was also printed in *Parnassus Biceps*, 1656, p. 77. See B. Dobell, *William Strode*, 1907, p. 41. Day and Murrie 1592.

XXVII. Compare Francis Davison's 'Like to the seely fly', printed in *A Poetical Rhapsody*, 1602 (Rollins, i, p. 87).

XXVIII. Lady Arabella Stuart died 17 years before Porter published this volume. Assuming that the elegy was composed at least within a year or so of her death, we here have further evidence that the contents of the song-books sometimes represented the work of many years.

ROSSETER, 1601

Copy: British Museum.   *Dedicatee*: Sir Thomas Monson.

Rosseter's *Book of Ayres* is in two sections, each consisting of twenty-one songs. Those in Part I are by Thomas Campian, and those in Part II by Rosseter himself. Campian is generally regarded as being the author of all the lyrics in Part I, but there is little or no evidence that he also wrote the lyrics in Part II. Both Bullen and Vivian, however, included the lyrics of both Parts I and II in their editions of Campian's poetical works.

Part I

I. This poem is an imitation of Catullus's 'Vivamus mea Lesbia atque amemus'. Compare Corkine 1612, XI, and Ferrabosco 1609, VI.

II. Bodleian MS. Ashmole 36–37, f. 145; Bodleian MS. Douce f. 5, f. 20ᵛ; British Museum MS. Add. 24665, f. 30ᵛ; British Museum MS. Add. 15117, f. 8. Day and Murrie 3330.
    8 *stubs*] tree stumps.

III. British Museum MS. Add. 24665, f. 8ᵛ.

IV. The same music is used in 'Seek the Lord' (Campian *c.* 1613*a*, XVIII).
    20 *proved*] *prou'd* 1601. Here used in the sense of *approved*.

V. British Museum MS. Add. 34608, f. 32ᵛ.

VI. Also set by Jones (1607, XVI–XVII), and printed in *A Poetical Rhapsody*, 1602 (Rollins, i, p. 215).

VII. The music of this song also occurs, somewhat altered, in 'What harvest half so sweet is' (Campian *c.* 1613*b*, X), as do lines 13–18, which there become lines 1–6.
    19 *changing*] Both Bullen and Vivian amend this to *swerving*.

VIII. In British Museum MS. Add. 24665, f. 9ᵛ, there is a song with similar words, beginning 'As on a day Sabina fell asleep'. Possibly alluded to in Allan Ramsay's *Tea Table Miscellany*, 'As afternoon, one summer's day'.

X. The music of this song is very similar to that of 'Love me or not' (Campian *c.* 1618*b*, X).

XII. British Museum MS. Harl. 3991, f. 34ᵛ; British Museum MS. Harl. 6910, f. 150ᵛ (which contains two versions of the lyric in sonnet form. See Vivian, pp. 356–7);

Bodleian MS. Rawl. poet. 153, f. 24; Bodleian MS. Don. c. 57, f. 40ᵛ; Henry Bold, *Latin Songs*, 1685, p. 114; Day and Murrie 3291. Also set by Vautor (1619, XIII–XIV).

XIV. Also set by Jones (1605, IX), and printed in *A Poetical Rhapsody*, 1602 (Rollins, i, p. 215).

XVI. Campian later composed an erotic parody of these words (*c.* 1618*b*, XXII).
    7–8] These lines are quoted in Marston's *Eastward Ho*, III. ii (H. Harvey Wood, *John Marston*, iii, p. 118).

XVII. Stanza 1, with some variants, also forms the first stanza of Campian *c.* 1618*b*, XXIII.

XVIII. Set again by Campian (*c.* 1613*a*, II) and also by Alison (1606, I–II). In addition to the manuscripts listed by Vivian (p. 357) see Bodleian MS. Eng. misc. c. 139, ff. 1 and 21.

XIX. This poem was the first of the *Poems and Sonnets of Sundry Other Noblemen and Gentlemen* appended to the 1591 edition of Sidney's *Astrophel and Stella*.
    35 *Apes in Avernus*] See note on Corkine 1612, XIV.

XX. Cf. Propertius ii. 28:

> Sunt apud infernos tot milia formosarum:
> Pulchra sit in superis, si licet, una locis.
> Vobiscum est Iope, vobiscum candida Tyro,
> Vobiscum Europe, nec proba Pasiphae.

XXI. This poem is one of Campian's experiments in classical quantitative metres. It is in Sapphic metre, and the music to which it is set strictly follows the pattern of long and short syllables, using notes of only two values.

Part II

II. Poem printed in *A Poetical Rhapsody*, 1602 (Rollins, i, p. 214), where it is ascribed to Thomas Campian. Cf. also British Museum MS. Harl. 4286, f. 56ᵛ, and MS. Add. 34608, f. 28ᵛ.

IX. 5] A word of two syllables appears to be missing from this line. Possibly it should begin 'The wanton sprites'.

X. In New York Public Library MS. Drexel 4257 this poem, with two extra stanzas, is set to the tune 'O mistress mine'. See Vincent Duckles, *Renaissance News*, vii (1954), p. 98.

XI. 7] Cf. Horace, *Odes*, II. x. 9: 'saepius ventis agitatur ingens pinus'.

XVIII. British Museum MS. Add. 24665, f. 29ᵛ. Compare Alison 1606, XVII–XVIII.

XX. British Museum MS. Add. 24665, f. 62ᵛ.

XXI. Bodleian MS. Eng. poet. c. 50, f. 34; *Wit Restored*, 1658, p. 107.

ADDENDA TO NOTES

BARTLET, 1606

II. To the note on this poem (p. 727) it should be added that Dr. Fellowes's ascription is a reasonable one, in view of Sidney's fame and the fact that his sister was a poet.

CAMPIAN

In *London Magazine*, new series, vii (1967), pp. 56–65, L. P. Wilkinson draws attention to a number of parallels in Propertius.

Two Books of Airs, c. 1613, title-page (see p. 339). In the copies in the Folger Library and the private collection of A. A. Houghton, jr., this reads, 'The First Booke Of Ayres Containing Diuine and Morall Songs: To be sung to the Lute', etc. The title-page of *The Second Book* is unaltered.

DOWLAND, 1597

v. Dulwich College MS. III. 8, f. 12, contains a version of this poem dated 1596.

DOWLAND, 1600

XII. 18] *Turtles* (= turtle-doves) and *twins* (a reference to Castor and Pollux) are both symbols of affection.

FARMER, 1599

XI. Edmund Keate, the dedicatee, is cited as the composer of a setting of 'Barrow Faustus' Dream' in Rosseter's *Lessons for Consort*, 1609, No. 23.

HUME, 1607

Dr. Edward Doughtie informs us that each of the four extant copies is dedicated to a different person.

JONES, 1609

Title-page (see p. 342). In the copy in the Huntington Library there is a different imprint at the foot of the title-page: 'Imprinted by Iohn Windet, and are to be solde by Simon Waterson, in Powles Church-yeard, at the Signe of the Crowne. 1609.'

RAVENSCROFT

The Melvill Book of Roundels (ed. G. Bantock and H. O. Anderton, London, 1916) and King's College, Cambridge, MS. KC. 1 (see J. Vlasto, *Musical Quarterly*, xl, 1954, p. 222) contain rounds which appear in Ravenscroft's collections. For further information concerning the popular tunes used in the rounds see C. M. Simpson, *The British Broadside Ballad and its Music*, New Brunswick, 1966.

Pammelia, 1609a, I and XVIII. Attributed to William Byrd; see *Collected Works*, xvi (ed. E. H. Fellowes, London, 1948), pp. 120, 104.

A Brief Discourse, 1614, VI, line 5 f. Cf. Shakespeare, *Merry Wives of Windsor*, V. v; Ben Jonson, *The Alchemist*, III. v; Rosseter 1601, Pt. I, XIX.

INDEX OF AUTHORS AND TRANSLATORS
(including uncertain attributions)

Tʜɪs index includes all the identified English authors and translators, as well as the few foreign authors whose work appears in the original language.

(tr.) indicates that the item is a translation.
(?) indicates that the attribution is uncertain.

INDEX OF FIRST LINES

First Line	Source	Page
Never did any more delight to see his enemy	Vautor 1619, VII	263
Never love unless you can	Campian *c.* 1618*a*, XXVII	405
Never weather-beaten sail more willing bent to shore	Campian *c.* 1613*a*, XI	371
New oysters, new oysters new	Ravenscroft 1609*a*, V	201
New oysters, new oysters, new Walfleet oysters	Ravenscroft 1609*a*, XI	203
No grave for woe, yet earth my watery tears devours	Rosseter 1601, Pt. II, III	667
No more I will thy love importune	Tomkins 1622, II	256
No, no, no, it will not be	Pilkington 1613, XX	194
No, no, no, no, Nigella	Morley 1595*b*, VI	149
No, no, thou dost but flout me	Morley 1594, XII	141
No, no! / Though I shrink still	Weelkes 1608, XI	298
Noel, adieu, adieu, thou Court's delight	Weelkes 1600, Pt. II, X	294
Not full twelve years twice told, a weary breath	Ford 1607, I	522
Nought is on earth more sacred or divine	Carlton 1601, XIV	80
Nought under heaven so strongly doth allure	Carlton 1601, IX–X	79
Now cease, my wandering eyes	Dowland 1600, XIII	472
Now Cloris laughs and swears how she affects me	East 1606, XVII–XVIII	90
Now each creature joys the other	Farmer 1599, II	101
Now each creature joys the other	Handford 1609, XII	537
Now each flowery bank of May	Gibbons 1612, XII	112
Now every tree renews his Summer's green	Weelkes 1597, VII	281
Now flowers your odours breathe	Ravenscroft 1611, II	235
Now God be with old Simeon	Ravenscroft 1609*a*, VII	202
Now hath Flora robbed her bowers	Campian 1607, I	363
Now have I learned with much ado at last	Jones 1605, XXI	584
Now I see thou floutest me	Pilkington 1613, XXII	194
Now I see thy looks were feigned	Ford 1607, IV	523
Now is my Cloris fresh as May	Weelkes 1598, XXII	289
Now is the bridals of fair Choralis	Weelkes 1598, XIII	287
Now is the gentle season freshly flowering	Morley 1594, IX–X	141
Now is the month of maying	Morley 1595*b*, III	148
Now is the Summer springing	Hilton 1627, XIX	117
Now is the time, now is the hour	Mason & Earsden 1618, II	614
Now kiss the cup, cousin, with courtesy	Ravenscroft 1609*a*, X	202
Now let her change and spare not	Campian *c.* 1618*a*, II	393
Now let her change and spare not	Jones 1605, XVII	582
Now let her change and spare not	Pilkington 1605, VIII	636
Now let us make a merry greeting	Weelkes 1600, Pt. I, II	290
Now must I die recureless, when faith is thus regarded	Morley 1593, XIII	136
Now must I part, my darling	East 1610, XXII	94
Now must I part, my darling	Yonge 1588, LI	330
Now, O now, I needs must part	Dowland 1597, VI	457
Now peep, bo-peep, thrice happy blest mine eyes	Pilkington 1605, I	632
Now, Robin, laugh and sing	Peerson 1620, X	178
Now, Robin, lend to me thy bow	Ravenscroft 1609*a*, LXIII	211
Now thanked be the great god Pan	Ravenscroft 1609*a*, XCV	218
Now the earth, the skies, the air	Danyel 1606, XX	453
Now what is Love, I pray thee tell	Jones 1601, IX	565
Now winter nights enlarge	Campian *c.* 1618*a*, XII	398
Now would chwore hong'd, zis, but thou most ma wrong	Corkine 1610, X	437
O all ye nations of the Lord	Mundy 1594, III	167
O bella più che la stella Diana	R. Dowland 1610, XX	511
O Care, thou wilt despatch me	Weelkes 1600, Pt. I, IV–V	291
O clap your hands together, all ye people	East 1618, X–XI	97
O come again, my lovely jewel	East 1604, I	82
O come, let us lift up our voice	Mundy 1594, IX	169
O come, shepherds, all together	Lichfild 1613, VIII	130

3 E

PRINTED IN GREAT BRITAIN
AT THE UNIVERSITY PRESS, OXFORD
BY VIVIAN RIDLER
PRINTER TO THE UNIVERSITY